A COMPANION
TO THE
ANCIENT NEAR EAST

BLACKWELL COMPANIONS TO THE ANCIENT WORLD

This series provides sophisticated and authoritative overviews of periods of ancient history, genres of classical literature, and the most important themes in ancient culture. Each volume comprises between twenty-five and forty concise essays written by individual scholars within their area of specialization. The essays are written in a clear, provocative, and lively manner, designed for an international audience of scholars, students, and general readers.

ANCIENT HISTORY

Published

A Companion to the Roman Army
Edited by Paul Erdkamp

A Companion to the Roman Republic
Edited by Nathan Rosenstein and Robert Morstein-Marx

A Companion to the Roman Empire
Edited by David S. Potter

A Companion to the Classical Greek World
Edited by Konrad H. Kinzl

A Companion to the Ancient Near East
Edited by Daniel C. Snell

A Companion to the Hellenistic World
Edited by Andrew Erskine

LITERATURE AND CULTURE

Published

A Companion to Greek and Roman Historiography
Edited by John Marincola

A Companion to Catullus
Edited by Marilyn B. Skinner

A Companion to Roman Religion
Edited by Jörg Rüpke

A Companion to Greek Religion
Edited by Daniel Ogden

A Companion to Classical Tradition
Edited by Craig W. Kallendorf

A Companion to Roman Rhetoric
Edited by William Dominik and Jon Hall

A Companion to Greek Rhetoric
Edited by Ian Worthington

A Companion to Ancient Epic
Edited by John Miles Foley

A Companion to Greek Tragedy
Edited by Justina Gregory

A Companion to Latin Literature
Edited by Stephen Harrison

A COMPANION TO THE ANCIENT NEAR EAST

Edited by

Daniel C. Snell

Blackwell
Publishing

BLACKWELL PUBLISHING
350 Main Street, Malden, MA 02148-5020, USA
9600 Garsington Road, Oxford OX4 2DQ, UK
550 Swanston Street, Carlton, Victoria 3053, Australia

The right of Daniel C. Snell to be identified as the Author of the Editorial Material in this Work has been asserted in accordance with the UK Copyright, Designs, and Patents Act 1988.

First published 2005 by Blackwell Publishing Ltd
First published in paperback 2007 by Blackwell Publishing Ltd

1   2007

Library of Congress Cataloging-in-Publication Data

A companion to the ancient Near East / edited by Daniel C. Snell.
     p. cm. — (Blackwell companions to the ancient world. Ancient history)
Includes bibliographical references and index.
ISBN-13: 978-0-631-23293-3 (hardback : alk. paper)
ISBN-13: 978-1-4051-6001-8 (paperback : alk. paper)
1. Middle East—Civilization—To 622. I. Snell, Daniel C. II. Series.

DS57.C56 2005
939′.4—dc22

                                        2004012928

A catalogue record for this title is available from the British Library.

Set in 10/12.5 pt Galliard
by SPi Publisher Services, Pondicherry, India
Printed and bound in the United Kingdom
by TJ International Ltd, Padstow, Cornwall

Picture research by Kitty Bocking

For further information on
Blackwell Publishing, visit our website:
www.blackwellpublishing.com

Contents

Figures

Maps

Notes on Contributors

Paul-Alain Beaulieu is Associate Professor of Assyriology at Harvard University, where he teaches Akkadian language and literature and the history of ancient Mesopotamia. He is the author of *The Reign of Nabonidus, King of Babylon 556–539 BC* (1989), *Legal and Administrative Texts from the Reign of Nabonidus* (2000), and *The Pantheon of Uruk During the Neo-Babylonian Period* (2003), as well as numerous articles on the history, religion, culture, and intellectual life of Mesopotamia in the first millennium BC. He is currently preparing a series of studies on cuneiform archives from Babylonia dated to the time of the Neo-Babylonian and Achaemenid empires.

Gary Beckman is Professor of Mesopotamian and Hittite Studies and Chair of the Department of Near Eastern Studies at the University of Michigan. He previously taught at Yale University, where he also served as Associate Curator of the Babylonian Collection. He has published widely on the religion of Hatti and on Hittite social organization and diplomacy. In addition he has compiled two catalogues of the Old Babylonian cuneiform tablets held by the Yale Babylonian Collection. He is currently Associate Editor of *The Journal of the American Oriental Society* and of *The Journal of Cuneiform Studies*.

Beckman's recent research has focused on the reception and adaptation of Syro-Mesopotamian culture by the Hittites. He is completing an edition of the tablets of the Epic of Gilgamesh written in various languages recovered from the site of the Hittite capital.

Mark Chavalas is Professor of History at the University of Wisconsin at LaCrosse. He has written and edited *New Horizons in the Study of Ancient Syria* with John L. Hayes (1992), *Emar: Religion and Culture of a Syrian Town in the Late Bronze Age* (1996), and *Mesopotamia and the Bible* (2002).

Carlos E. Cordova is Assistant Professor of Geography at Oklahoma State University, Stillwater. His areas of expertise are geoarchaeology, geomorphology, and palynology. His research focuses on environmental change during the Late Quaternary in the Near East and the Northern Black Sea Region. Recent articles appeared in

Geoarchaeology: An International Journal, The Arab World Geographer, and *Physical Geography.* He is currently writing a book on the millennial transformation of woodlands, steppes, and deserts in Jordan.

Peter T. Daniels is an independent scholar in New York. He has edited *The World's Writing Systems* with William Bright (1996) and *Phonologies of Asia and Africa* with Alan S. Kaye (1997).

Sally Dunham, Ph.D., is an independent scholar and Research Affiliate at Yale University. She has worked on archaeological expeditions in Cyprus, Lebanon, Syria, and Iraq, and has published articles on the art and archaeology of the Ancient Near East in American and European journals. She is currently involved in excavations at the Bronze Age site of Umm el-Marra in Syria.

Marian H. Feldman received her B.A. in Art History from Columbia University and her Ph.D., also in Art History, from Harvard University. She currently teaches Ancient Near Eastern art and archaeology in the Department of Near Eastern Studies at the University of California at Berkeley. Her publications include studies on artistic interconnections between the Ancient Near East, Egypt, and the Aegean, and she has excavated in Turkey and Syria.

Benjamin R. Foster, Professor of Assyriology and Curator of the Yale Babylonian Collection, focuses his research on Akkadian literature and the social and economic history of Mesopotamia. He is the author of *Before the Muses* (1993, 1996, 2004), an anthology of translations from Akkadian literature, abridged as *From Distant Days* (1995), and of the translation *The Epic of Gilgamesh* (2001). His current research includes a history of oriental scholarship in the United States.

Steven J. Garfinkle is Assistant Professor of History at Western Washington University, where he teaches a full range of courses on the Ancient Near East. His current research focuses on the society and economy of Mesopotamia in the late third and early second millennia BCE. He has just completed work on an edition of the Ur III Tablets from the Columbia University Library (with H. Sauren and M. Van De Mieroop), and he is revising a study of entrepreneurs at the end of the third millennium BCE.

Marie-Henriette Gates teaches history and archaeology at Bilkent University, Ankara, Turkey.

Tawny L. Holm is Assistant Professor of Religion in the Indiana University of Pennsylvania and has edited *The Literary Language of the Bible. The Collected Essays of Luis Alonso Schöckel* (2000).

Philip Jones is a researcher with the Pennsylvania Sumerian Dictionary project.

Henri Limet is Professor Emeritus at the University of Liège, Belgium. An authority on Sumerian economic history, his books include *Le Travail des Métaux au pays de Sumer* (1960) and *L'Anthroponymie sumérienne* (1968).

Mario Liverani is full Professor of the History of the Ancient Near East in the University of Rome. Presently he is Director of the Inter-University Research Centre for Saharan Archaeology and of the Archaeological Mission in the Libyan Sahara, editor of the collection "Arid Zone Archaeology."

He has been a member of various archaeological missions in Syria (Ebla, Terqa, Tell Mozan), in Turkey (Arslantepe, Kurban Hüyük), in Yemen (Baraqish), and presently in Libya (Tadrart Acacus).

He is author of 15 books or monographs and about 180 articles in specialized journals. Recent monographs include *Antico Oriente* (1988), *Studies in the Annals of Ashurnasirpal II* (1992), *Uruk: la prima città* (1998), *Le lettere di el-Amarna* (1998–99), *International Relations in the Ancient Near East* (2001), and *Otre la Bibbia*, a history of Ancient Israel (2004). Edited books include *Akkad. The First World Empire* (1993) and *Neo-Assyrian Geography* (1995); *Arid Lands in Roman Times* and *Recent Trends in Reconstructing the History of Ancient Israel* are forthcoming.

Matthew Martin III took his B.A. in History at the University of Oklahoma, Norman, and is a law student at the University of Tulsa, Oklahoma.

Augusta McMahon is University Lecturer in Ancient Near Eastern History and Archaeology and Fellow of Newnham College, University of Cambridge, England. She has participated in fieldwork in Iraq at Nippur and Nineveh, in Turkey at Hacinebi Tepe, and is currently co-director of excavations at Chagar Bazar in northeastern Syria. Her research focuses on the dynamics of small settlements within territorial states and on the continuity of material culture through political and historical change.

Sarah C. Melville is an Assistant Professor of History at Clarkson University, where she teaches courses in ancient medicine, warfare, and culture. Her publications include *The Role of Naqia/Zakutu in Sargonid Politics* (1999) and an article on the social role of royal women in Assyria.

Christopher M. Monroe (Ph.D, M.A., M.I.S.) earned a master's in nautical archaeology at Texas A&M and participated in the Uluburun excavations and several land excavations in the Near East before finishing his doctorate in Ancient Near Eastern studies at the University of Michigan, where he also earned a master's in information science. He is currently an Assistant Curator at the Pierpont Morgan Library in New York City and is publishing his dissertation on the sociology of traders in the Late Bronze Age Eastern Mediterranean.

John F. Robertson, Professor of History at Central Michigan University, Mt. Pleasant, has published several articles on the social and economic role of the temples of ancient Mesopotamia, especially at the city of Nippur, as well as on the role of pastoral nomads in the historiography of ancient southwest Asia. He is also co-author of *Perspectives from the Past: Primary Source Readings in Western Civilization* (1998). He is working on a publication of administrative records from Nippur from the early Old Babylonian period and a survey of Ancient Near Eastern cultures.

Francesca Rochberg, Professor of History at the University of California at Riverside, has focused on Babylonian celestial divination and its cultural context, and has written on various aspects of Babylonian astrology and astronomy. Her publications include *Aspects of Babylonian Celestial Divination: The Lunar Eclipse Tablets of Enuma Anu Enlil* (1988) and *Babylonian Horoscopes* (1998). Her forthcoming book is *The Heavenly Writing: Divination, Horoscopy, and Astronomy in Mesopotamian Culture* (2004).

Ann Macy Roth, Associate Professor of Classics at Howard University, Washington, DC, has published *Phyles in the Old Kingdom* (1991), *A Cemetery of Palace Attendants* (1993), and has translated *Hieroglyphs Without Mystery* (1993). She is the director of the Giza Cemetery Project and editor of the *Journal of the American Research Center in Egypt*. She writes on Egyptian social history, religion, mortuary archaeology, and tomb rituals and equipment.

Gonzalo Rubio is Assistant Professor of Assyriology in the Pennsylvania State University. He works on Sumerian linguistics and literary texts.

JoAnn Scurlock received her Ph.D. in Assyriology from the Oriental Institute of the University of Chicago. She is Adjunct Associate Professor of History and Political Science at Elmhurst College, where she teaches courses in Ancient History, Islamic Civilization and Politics, Western Civilization, History of Witchcraft, and History of Healing Magic. She is the author of *Magico-Medical Means of Treating Ghost Induced Illnesses in Ancient Mesopotamia* (2003). She and medical professor Burton Andersen are currently in the last stages of preparation of a book *Assyrian and Babylonian Medicine: Diagnostics*. The preparation of a further volume, *Assyrian and Babylonian Medicine: Treatments* is being supported by the National Endowment for the Humanities. She is the author of a number of articles on ancient Mesopotamian magic, religion, medicine, and political history.

Jorge Silva Castillo is Professor in the Centro de Estudias de Asia y África in the Colegio de México. He edited *Nomads and Sedentary Peoples* (1981) and translated the Gilgamesh epic into Spanish (1994). He researches nomadism especially in the archives from Mari in Syria.

Daniel C. Snell is L. J. Semrod Presidential Professor of History at the University of Oklahoma, Norman. His books include *Life in the Ancient Near East* (1997), *Flight and Freedom in the Ancient Near East* (2001), and a study of the Biblical Book of Proverbs, *Twice-Told Proverbs and the Composition of the Book of Proverbs* (1993). He is working on an anthology of translations of Ancient Near Eastern texts on slavery.

Anthony J. Spalinger is Associate Professor in the University of Auckland, New Zealand. He has published *Aspects of the Military Documents of the Ancient Egyptians* (1982), *Revolutions in Egyptian Calendrics* (1994), and *The Private Feast Lists of Ancient Egypt* (1996). He is working on a study of the textual transmission of the "poem" about the Battle of Kadesh.

S. David Sperling is Professor of Bible at Hebrew Union College–Jewish Institute of Religion, New York. He was educated at Brooklyn College, Jewish Theological Seminary, and Columbia University. Recent books include *Students of the Covenant: A History of Jewish Biblical Scholarship in North America* and *The Original Torah: The Political Intent of the Bible's Writers*.

Elizabeth C. Stone is Professor of Anthropology at the State University of New York at Stony Brook. Her books include *Nippur Neighborhoods* (1987) and *Adoption in Old Babylonian Nippur* (1992) with David Owen. She has excavated in Syria, at the Iraqi site of Mashkan-shapir, and is now working at Ayanis in eastern Turkey, a site of the Urartian state of the first millennium. She is interested in how urban structures reflect social, political, and economic organization of civilizations.

David A. Warburton, Research Fellow, Aarhus University, Denmark, teaches Ancient Egyptian religion. He works on social, economic, and political systems in early antiquity, stratigraphy, and chronology. Recent books include *Egypt and the Near East: Politics in the Bronze Age* (2001) and *Macroeconomics from the Beginning: The General Theory, Ancient Markets, and the Rate of Interest* (2003). He is currently working on issues of "color" in antiquity and prehistoric religion.

Bruce Wells is Assistant Professor of religion at Gustavus Adolphus College, St. Peter, Minnesota. He is publishing his 2003 Johns Hopkins dissertation as *The Law of Testimony in the Pentateuchal Codes*.

Acknowledgments

I would like to thank Prof. Paul Bell, Dean of Arts and Sciences in the University of Oklahoma, Prof. Robert Cox, Director of the School of International and Area Studies, Prof. Steven Gillon, sometime Dean of the Honors College, and Prof. Robert Griswold, Chair of History, for their support of this project. My graduate student Hava Ben-Yosef and undergraduate Honors student Anna Bostwick gave invaluable help with the initial conference. Anne Petzinger, an Honors student, acted as a research assistant in the final stages of preparation of the manuscript; her care and meticulousness saved me from many errors. The many colleagues in the field, who, if they could not themselves write, helpfully suggested others who could, also deserve thanks, as well as the learned people who actually did accept the assignments proffered. The editor Al Bertrand was ever ready with advice and aid.

DCS

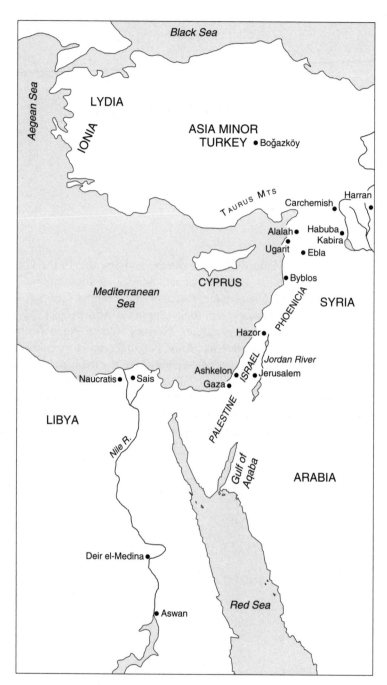

Map 0.1 The Near East

The Near East

Introduction

Daniel C. Snell

These essays stand alone and need no introduction, but it seems wise to clarify issues at the beginning in the form of responses to questions.

What is the Ancient Near East?

The term refers to the ancient area now called the Middle East in the languages of the area and of Europe; we mean the modern countries of Egypt, Israel, Jordan, Syria, Lebanon, Turkey, Iraq, and Iran. The term Near East refers to proximity to Europe and is therefore Eurocentric; Western Asia would be preferable, and some of our essays use that term, but that phrase is not widely understood, and so we have kept to the old terminology.

Is Egypt included?

With the growth of studies of Mesopotamia, ancient Iraq and Syria, we are so specialized that the discipline does not necessarily include Egypt, and there are many fine introductory books on Egypt. Nonetheless we believe that many if not most introductory courses to the Ancient Near East do include Egypt, and that the general public definitely feels Egypt is part of the Ancient Near East. Hence we have included treatment of ancient Egypt where possible. In fact we have slighted it in contrast to the lands further to the east, and most of the experts writing here were trained in Mesopotamian studies, not Egyptian. A longer project would have resulted in a more balanced view, but I felt it was important to acknowledge the very close links between Egypt and the rest of the Ancient Near East, even if full justice could not be done to both sides.

Is the work a companion to a particular textbook?

Not really. It was commissioned by Blackwell, which was in the process of publishing Van De Mieroop's *A History of the Ancient Near East* (2004), but that book was published after several essays had been completed, and the authors here have not necessarily reacted to it in their pieces. While we certainly conceived these essays as an amplification of a political history of the Ancient Near East, we hope that it will be found to be useful by undergraduates and beginning graduate students regardless of what else they may be reading.

What chronology will be used here?

Chronology, the study of the time periods, especially the absolute dates, from the Ancient Near East, is undergoing rethinking now, and we have decided not to impose uniformity in how authors deployed it. Most have resorted to the Middle Chronology, now perhaps in the course of being discredited. But this has been the standard chronology for many years, and if it is wrong by a hundred and more years, it at least affords comparison with other works. When we now pick up historical works on the Ancient Near East from the beginning of the twentieth century, we find ourselves somewhat disoriented by the suggested chronology, and yet one can make sense of what the authors then believed. We beg the indulgence of future readers and can assert that given what we now know, the chronology presented here is a responsible one that will allow the reader to understand at least the relative chronology of events. The chronology used is summarized in J. A. Brinkman's appendix to Oppenheim 1977 for Mesopotamia and Baines and Malek 2000: 36–37 for Egypt.

All the authors have striven, I believe, to present their field in a way that will be accessible to persons without previous exposure to it and in a way that will be useful to scholars fifty years hence. That is a high ambition, and only time will judge whether our efforts really bore the fruit for which we hoped. But I recall with pleasure the response of one of the essayists on seeing the range of topics proposed here; the scholar wrote, "To answer broad and stimulating questions like these is the reason most of us got into the field to begin with." We hope these essays will be as stimulating as the questions that provoked them, and that students and scholars will for a time at least begin here when they seek the ancient and modern meaning of the Ancient Near East.

PART I

The Shape of the Ancient Near East

CHAPTER ONE

Historical Overview

Mario Liverani

Unity and Diversity

The history of the Ancient Near Eastern civilizations is very long: its time-span from the late fourth to the late first millennium BCE is equal to or even longer than the rest of history, from the collapse of the Near Eastern cultures to our own time. It is correct to use the label "the first half of history." We could even say "of our history," because this long trajectory is now considered part and even the very foundation of our own "Western" history – not like other more remote civilizations in India or China or elsewhere.

The reasons for the Western appropriation of the Ancient Near Eastern cultures and history were especially important at the time of their rediscovery. These included the colonialist ideology and practice of the nineteenth century, the interest of the Christian world in Biblical antiquities, coupled with the Islamic disregard for pre-Islamic heritage. In recent decades these motivations have faded, and they are no longer primary to the community of scholars. Yet Biblical connections are still widely of concern to popular audiences, and so the interest in the history of the Ancient Near East is something more serious than curiosity about a remote and alien past.

Our Western civilization acknowledges a privileged role for Greek civilization in generating the foundational values of freedom, democracy, individual personality, economic enterprise, rational thought and science, and the aesthetics of the visual arts and poetry. But our indebtedness to the Ancient Near Eastern civilizations in the material foundations of culture (urban life, political organization, administration, writing) and in the field of religion remains important.

But is the Ancient Near East a unified subject for historical inquiry? The area is characterized by a notable diversity in natural environments (hills and steppe-lands, river valleys and Mediterranean countryside), by different peoples and languages (Semites and Indo-Europeans and others), by various ways of life (urban to nomadic) and modes of production (from agriculture and pastoralism to specialized crafts and complex financial dealings), by different complicated writing systems, by social diversity in access to resources, communication, and decision-making – so that a unitary treatment may seem unjustified. Nevertheless, when compared to other centers of civilization (including the contiguous centers of Egypt, the Indus Valley, the Aegean basin, and Central Asia), and especially when contrasted to the periphery between the centers of the major civilizations, the Ancient Near East seems compact enough to allow for a unified treatment because of intensive cross-fertilization. But such a treatment must not neglect the specific features of the regional sub-units of Lower Mesopotamia, Upper Mesopotamia, the Levant (areas bordering the eastern Mediterranean), Anatolia (modern Turkey), and southwestern Iran.

The history of the region, as far as it can be reconstructed from written and archaeological records, follows a trajectory which is diverse in details but unitary in its major features. The relevance of the environmental factors, the introduction of technological improvements, and socio-economic development, can be followed all over the area with similar patterns.

Environmental constraints, painstaking production of food, the difficult access to basic resources, and the consequent low levels in demographic growth – all these factors contributed to the slow development of the Ancient Near Eastern civilizations. We are accustomed to appreciating the large cities and the monumental temples and palaces, the elegant artistic and literary compositions, and the great polities and "empires" as something obviously resulting from high levels of civilization. We should never forget, however, that such accomplishments were the result of painstaking labor and of forced allocation of the limited resources then available, and that the periodic crises were not an accident but a structural feature in the system.

In fact, the ancient history of the Near East can be summarized as a cyclic sequence of growth and collapse, a sequence that is apparent also in the preservation of the documentary record. The periods of major development – with burgeoning polities, big cities, important monuments, extensive archives, and rich craftsmanship – are separated by "dark ages" of localism and fragmentation. We have to consider that the ups and downs are mostly pertinent to the upper classes, to the political structures, and to the complex urban economy, while the common peasantry in rural villages and pastoral units continued their basic struggle for survival. The ups and downs are the result of a different equilibrium between the two opposed strategies of development and of survival, typically located in the royal palace and in the village, and carried on by the political elite and by the local community. The strategy of development required a leaching of resources from the local communities that was detrimental to the local strategy of survival, and therefore could be carried on only during limited periods, in selected areas, and under specific circumstances allowing the political elites to impose their will, through the exercise of power and through shared ideologies.

Notwithstanding these constraints, we see a long-lasting tendency toward the enlargement in the scale of the political units, the improvement of the technologies of production (and also of destruction), the widening of the geographical horizons, and also the increasing role of individual personalities. The most objective and concrete proxy for expansion, however, namely demographic development, seemed to remain more subject to the recurrent fluctuations than to a positive trend.

The Urban Revolution, about 3500–2800 BCE

The beginning of the historical trajectory is marked by a phenomenon of tremendous relevance, currently assumed to mark the shift from prehistory to history in the proper sense. The phenomenon can be labeled in various ways. We can use the label "urban revolution," if we want to underscore demography and settlement forms, or the "First Urbanization" if we take into account the subsequent cycles of urbanization. We can speak of the origin of the state or the early state, if we prefer to underscore the political aspects. We can also emphasize the beginning of a marked socio-economic stratification, and of specialized crafts, if we want to underscore the mode of production. We can also use the term "origin of complexity," if we try to subsume all the various aspects under a unifying concept. The origin of writing has also been considered to mark the beginning of true and proper history, because of the old-fashioned idea that there is no history before the availability of written sources. But now that such an idea is considered simplistic or wrong, we still can consider writing the most evident and symbolic culmination of the entire process.

The "revolution" took place in Lower Mesopotamia, now southern Iraq, and was the result of particular technological improvements and socio-political strategies. The agricultural production of barley underwent a notable, possibly tenfold, increase thanks to the construction of water reservoirs and irrigation canals, of long fields adjacent to the canals watered by them, and thanks to the use of the plow, of animal power, of carts, of threshing sledges, of clay sickles, and of improved storage facilities. The agricultural revolution could not have taken place without the managerial activity of central agencies, the temples, which were able to overcome the purely local strategy of survival carried on by the rural villages.

The technological improvements alone, however, could generate no "revolution" at all if the food-producers had devoted the entire surplus to their own consumption. The role of the central agency was decisive in diverting most of the surplus to social use: both for financing the common structures (irrigation networks, temple building, defensive walls), and for the maintenance of the specialized craftsmen and the socio-political elite. The "redistributive" economy of the early state, centered on the temples, was not based on the procedure of taxation, that is, the extraction of a part of the product from the producers' families or local communities, but basically on the procedure of forced labor or corvée work imposed on local communities to work the temple lands. In this way the central agency, the owner of the best irrigated lands, could transfer to the local communities most of the social costs, paying just the rations for the workmen but not their families in limited periods of harvest and other seasonally concentrated operations.

The result of the technological improvements was a rate of seed to crop around 1:25 in comparison to 1:5 outside the river valleys. The result of the central management was that only 1/3 of the crop covered the expenditures of seed for the next year, rations for workmen and animals, and 2/3 went to the central agency for the social uses described above. Also the breeding of sheep and goats for the production of wool underwent a tremendous increase under temple management, again thanks to technology (the weaving loom) and social exploitation (slave women and children concentrated in temple factories). The administration of an economy based on unequal transfers of product, rations, and services generated writing. Already available tools (tokens, seals, clay sealings) were coordinated to produce round clay seals we call bullae, then "numerical" tablets, and finally proper clay tablets with numbers and logographic icons for the various items to be recorded. The "archaic texts" from the city of Uruk levels IV–III attest the organization of scribes, schools, and archives.

The transition from the Late Chalcolithic (the Ubaid culture in Mesopotamia) to the early urban economy around 4000 BCE went hand in hand with the sudden increase in the size and structure of the city and of the temples. As for the cities, the transition from the small villages and hamlets of the Ubaid period (under one hectare or 2.47 acres in size) to the walled cities like Uruk (70 hectares or 172.9 acres) is quite impressive. Inside the cities, the small shrines of the Ubaid period, which were devoted to cultic use only, became large buildings including shops and stores besides the sanctuary of the god, along with the apartments of the clergy and the administrative personnel. The social changes were as important: beside the rural communities, based on family structures and communal self-government, a ruling class emerged as the necessary premise, but also the result, of the centralized administration of the economy.

The Uruk culture is so called because of the archaeological discoveries at that site. In Uruk the entire complex of Eanna (with the adjacent Anu temple) has been excavated, while the contemporary levels in other Lower Mesopotamian sites remain hardly touched by digging. The only other important center of the same period in the lowlands is Susa in Iranian Khuzistan. The impression that Uruk could have been the most important center in the period is probably correct, since it is supported by memories preserved in the later mythological and epic literature of Sumer.

The paramount role of the temple in the Uruk period was the obvious result of the strongly unequal relationships that the complex structure of the early state introduced into society. The elite could successfully exploit the rural population only by convincing them that their work was intended to support the god, his house, and his properties. A religious mobilization was necessary in order to keep the unequal relationships effective and enduring. No purely physical constraint could have been effective, but the ideological constraint made the exploitation tolerable. The priestly leadership also had the effect of depriving the kinship groups of their role and thwarted their ambitions for prestige; the priests moved the whole community toward an impersonal management.

Outside the core area, Uruk culture spread in a wide periphery, by means of various types of colonies and outposts. Upper Mesopotamia was colonized both along the Euphrates (at Habuba Kabira and Jebel Aruda) and the Tigris (at Nineveh) and in the Syrian Jazira (at Hamukar and Tell Brak). The most remote colonies were located along access routes to the highlands of Anatolia (at Samsat and Hassek Hoyuk) and on the Iranian plateau (at Godin Tepe). Important local cities were also influenced by the Uruk culture in their autonomous development (Arslan Tepe is the best known site of this type). Trade and access to highland resources (copper and timber in Anatolia, tin and semi-precious stones in Iran) were most probably the main factors for the spread of the Uruk colonies, and the resultant "regional system" brought different ecosystems and cultural traditions into reciprocal relationships. During the same period, the Early Dynastic civilization of Egypt underwent a similar process of state formation and urbanization, but remained separate from Mesopotamian civilization, except for isolated contacts.

The collapse of the entire system came abruptly at the beginning of the third millennium. Most colonies were abandoned in Upper Mesopotamia and in the highlands. The destruction of the Uruk period complex at Arslan Tepe is really impressive, and the burial of a Trans-Caucasian chief on the top of the ruins may hint at the role of the pastoral mountaineers as responsible for the disaster. But the crisis is also visible in Lower Mesopotamia, with no northern intrusion, so that we can doubt whether the nomads were the primary factor in the collapse; they may just have profited from an internal structural crisis. In any case, the unitary horizon of the Uruk period was followed by the emergence of various local cultures: the Jemdet Nasr culture in Lower Mesopotamia, the Proto-Elamite in Susiana, the Ninevite V in Upper Mesopotamia, and others in Eastern Anatolia and in Iran. All of them are characterized by a decline of city life in the river valleys, or even by a total reversion to village life in the periphery. The "first cycle of urbanization" had come to its end.

The "Second Urbanization," about 2800–2000 BCE

The new cycle of urbanization encompassed an enlarged horizon and was based on a deeper rooting in the society. The urban cultures spread again from Lower Mesopotamia in the so-called Early Dynastic period, about 2800–2350 BCE, to include Upper Mesopotamia, the Levant, Anatolia, and Elam. The spread of cuneiform writing in most of these regions, except Anatolia and Palestine, makes the interconnections more visible. The adjacent areas also underwent similar processes of growth and consolidation in Old Kingdom Egypt, in the Early Harappan civilization of the Indus Valley, and in northeastern Iran and Central Asia. All these areas were linked together by trade contacts and cultural cross-fertilization.

The large size of the area involved and the spread of writing made the ethnic diversity much clearer than in the previous period. Lower Mesopotamia hosted two different linguistic groups: the Sumerians prevailed in the south, or Sumer, and the Semites in the north, or Akkad. The two groups, although coexisting in the same polities, differed not only in language and other cultural traits (for example, the style of figurative arts) but also in basic social and political features. The heritage of the temple-city was characteristic of Sumer, while in the Semitic area the influence of the kinship groups and pastoral tribes was more visible. In Upper Mesopotamia the prevailing population was Hurrian, and in Susiana and Anshan, the later Fars, it was Elamite. In Syria an early stage of the later northwest Semitic dialects was represented by Eblaite. For Anatolia we lack direct evidence, but the analysis of later languages and personal names makes us believe that the area was inhabited by Hattians and other non-Indo-European peoples.

The typical polity was the city-state in the densely inhabited regions of the lowlands, and probably some kind of "ethnic" state among the mountaineers and the steppe-dwellers. In the Sumerian south, the city-state was basically a "temple-city" as already described in the Uruk period, although the royal palace acquired a separate political role, leaving to the temples the role of managerial agencies of the economy in addition to their cultic role. The city leader in the south was usually a "priest-king" (e n), or a "city administrator" (e n s i), the ideology leaving the role of the true sovereign to the city god. The temple-city was in theory the property of the god, and was in practice a state centered on the city and dominating a rural landscape of some 10 to 20 km or 6 to 12 miles in radius. The major Sumerian city-states of the period were Ur, whose "Royal Cemetery" provides the most brilliant image of wealth and craftsmanship, Uruk, Eridu, Umma, Lagash, Adab, and Shuruppak. Between the Sumerian south and the Akkadian north, the city of Nippur played a special role as seat of the leading god of the Sumerian pantheon, Enlil – a role of providing political legitimacy to kings who held the city and of providing a symbol of cultural unity for Sumer in the theory that only one king could be paramount at any one time. At an early stage of development, in Early Dynastic II, a "league" of Sumerian cities seems to have played an important political role. More often, competition for agricultural lands could spark wars among neighboring cities, and the long war between Lagash and Umma in Early Dynastic III is well known from the royal inscriptions of Lagash. But the equilibrium between the various city-states seems to have been resistant to imbalance.

In the area of Akkad city-states like Eshnunna or Akshak seem to have shared the southern model. But the most important city, Kish, was formed differently, with a neat prevalence of the palace over the temple, with a larger territory, with a warlike king (l u g a l "big man"), and clear expansionistic intent. It is possible that ethnicity had some influence in generating the two different models, but certainly the eco-logical and economic basis was also a factor. In the north pastoralism was more important, and agriculture was less dependent on irrigation, with local systems of square fields prevailing over the temple-run sets of elongated fields in the south. The modified model also spread to Upper Mesopotamia: along the middle Tigris (at Assur) and the Middle Euphrates (at Mari), in the Jazira (at Tell Brak/Nagar and other centers), and in Syria (at Ebla).

Various administrative archives have been recovered, both in the south (Ur "archaic" in Early Dynastic II, about 2700–2600; Fara in Early Dynastic IIIa, about 2600–2450; and especially Lagash in Early Dynastic IIIb, about 2450–2350), and more recently in the north (Mari, Tell Beydar) and Syria (Ebla, about 2500–2350). The two major archives, Lagash and Ebla, have been correctly contrasted as representing different socio-economic systems. In fact the economy of Lagash was managed through a system of temples, by a class of priestly adminis-trators, and was mostly based on intensive agriculture. Ebla was managed by the palace, with an important role left to the representatives of kin groups and local communities, and it was based on mixed agricultural and pastoral production and on long-distance trade in metals and textiles. The temples at Ebla were devoted to cultic activities and ceremonial redistribution, but nothing comparable to the administrative redistribution of the Sumerian temples.

The competition among the various trade networks was an important factor. Apart from local exchange in city markets and fairs, long-distance trade was especially important in the cities located between the river valleys and their periphery from which most of the raw materials came: Susa trading with the Iranian plateau, Assur with the upper Tigris and Anatolia, Abarsal with the upper Euphrates, Mari and Ebla with Syria. Trade was carried on with caravans of donkeys by merchants dependent on and financed by central agencies. Relationships between merchants and palace or temple were of the "administrative" kind, with fixed prices and a system of yearly accounts, the value of the imported goods being balanced against the value of entrusted goods. But when outside the area of control of the central agency, the merchants were free to negotiate for profit, and could also use their money for loans at interest and loans with personal guarantees.

The competition in trade networks was a factor in the struggles between the most important city-states, especially during the final phase of the Early Dynastic III. In some cases the competition was settled by agreement and delimitation of the respective networks as in the treaty between Ebla and Abarsal, in other cases by recourse to war as between Mari and Ebla. The rise of a new polity in central Mesopotamia, Akkad as heir of Kish, brought about a series of destructive wars. Some of them, under the first ruler of Akkad, Sargon (2335–2279), were intended to conquer the Sumerian south and gave origin to the first regional state that included the entire Lower Meso-potamian river region. After that, more wars were intended to acquire control of the trade network, and were directed against Susa (Iranian network), against Magan (Gulf network), against Mari and Ebla, both of them destroyed by Naram-Sin (2254–2218), the most important king of Akkad. The celebrative inscriptions and monuments of the Akkadian kings were the expression of a new idea of "heroic" kingship and of enlarged territorial control. The deification of Naram-Sin clearly contrasted to the old Sumerian ideology of the city leader as administrative represen-tative of the god. Later legends and epic compositions, while reserving to Sargon the image of the pious and successful king, blamed Naram-Sin for hubris and disaster.

The Akkad dynasty did not survive for long, and the decline started after Naram-Sin. A major factor was the pressure of the outer nomads, both from the mountain-eers (Gutians and Lullubi in the Zagros Mountains) and the steppe tribes (Martu, better known as Amorites). Archaeology also gives a picture of decline of the splendid civilizations of the Early Bronze age, in Anatolia, in the Levant, in Iran, and the Gulf area. We get the impression that the "second urbanization" reached its peak around 2300, and then started a fast decline. The massive intrusions of the Gutians (about 2200) and the Martu (about 2000) in middle and lower Mesopotamia were part of this scenario. In Egypt, the fragmented socio-political order in the first "Intermediate Period" was roughly contemporary. In the Levant, the so-called "Intermediate (Early/Middle Bronze) Period" showed an archaeological picture dominated by pastoralism and decline of urban life. As usual, the periphery was more decisively affected, while the main core of urbanization, in lower Mesopotamia, could better resist the troubles.

The last century of the third millennium, when the crisis was already well advanced in the peripheral areas, was dominated in the river valleys by the third dynasty of

Ur (2112–2004), which represented the most efficient and stable state organization that Mesopotamia ever experienced, in earlier or later times. In a short period, under Ur-Nammu, Shulgi, Amar-Sin, and Shu-Sin, the Ur kings were able to revitalize Sumerian culture and religious ideology, and to extend the model of the temple-city to a wider region in which the former city-states were transformed into provinces. Instead of celebrative monuments, they left temple buildings, including the famous temple-towers or ziggurats, irrigation canals, and defensive walls. They unified prices and measures inside their kingdom, and provided it with a law-code and a land-register. They produced a uniform and efficient bureaucratic record of the economy with the most detailed accounting procedures: crop estimates before harvest, estimates of growth for herds and flocks, balanced accounts for merchants, all based on administrative conventions and fixed rates. Cultic literature and royal hymns flourished during the "Neo-Sumerian renaissance," while cities and countryside in the core of the empire flourished in peace and order.

However, the effect of external troubles could not be avoided forever. In spite of various expeditions carried on in Subartu (Upper Mesopotamia) and on the Zagros piedmont, and in spite of the "Martu-wall" erected from Tigris to Euphrates in order to stop, or at least to check, the infiltration of the West Semitic nomads, the Martu finally succeeded in penetrating in substantial number into Mesopotamia, possibly driven out of their homeland in the Syrian steppe by an unfavorable climatic change. The Martu conquered and ravaged all the provinces, and Ur was left without revenues and protection. The capital city was finally besieged and conquered by the Elamites. The name of the last Ur king, Ibbi-Sin, remained in the handbooks of Babylonian omens as a symbol of disaster.

The "Regional System," about 2000–1200

The cycle of the "Third Urbanization" was quite long (about 2000–1200) and included both the Middle and the Late Bronze periods in archaeological terminology as applied to the Levant and Anatolia; these periods followed each other with no obvious break. The geographic scene was wider than in the previous cycle, but while some areas remained flourishing during the entire period (Egypt from Middle to New Kingdom; the Aegean civilization from the first Minoan palaces to the Mycenean period), others underwent an evident decline toward the mid-second millennium (the Indus Valley and Central Asian civilizations).

This decline – from Middle to Late Bronze – in amount and distribution of settlements (an obvious proxy for demographic estimates) also affected some areas inside the Near East. In Syria and Upper Mesopotamia many large settlements in the semi-arid lands were abandoned, and population concentrated in the areas better provided with water from rainfall or rivers, so that a long-term drier trend can be suspected of being responsible for these general developments.

In contrast to the "second urbanization," which had been clearly centered on Lower Mesopotamia as the area of origin of the basic cultural features and also as the seat of the major political powers, the "third urbanization" was much more multicentric and balanced in technological levels, in socio-political organization, and in military power. The role of Syria and Upper Mesopotamia, and eventually also of a mountain area like Anatolia, became paramount, marking the shift from a mono-centric arrangement with a clear center/periphery contrast to a "regional system" of competing and interacting "peer" polities. The previous periphery became part of the inner system, mountains and steppe were fully integrated into the multi-directional exchange of resources, and peoples formerly considered barbarian became accepted partners.

The entire system, stretching from Egypt and the Aegean in the west to Elam and the Gulf in the east, coalesced into half a dozen regional states. Starting from a marked fragmentation at the very beginning of the period, a process of unification took place during the Middle Bronze period (about 2000–1600), to reach its final shape during the Late Bronze period (about 1600–1200). The regional states (the extent of which ranged from 200,000 to 500,000 km², or 77,220 to 193,050 square miles, roughly from the size of Great Britain to that of France) were: Egypt, the Hittite kingdom in Anatolia, the Hurrian state of Mitanni and later the Middle Assyrian kingdom in Upper Mesopotamia, Kassite Babylonia in Lower Mesopotamia, and Elam on the Iranian plateau.

The minor polities were annexed or integrated into the major powers in two ways, either direct annexation or indirect rule. In some areas, mostly in the river valleys, the former independent kingdoms were annexed as provinces of a conquering kingdom. This process was clear in Lower Mesopotamia and culminated in the annexation by Babylonia under Hammurabi (1792–1750) of the rival kingdoms of Eshnunna and Larsa, which had previously annexed Isin and Uruk, and Mari. Also Assyria developed from a city-state (Assur) to a regional power, structured in a series of provinces and finally (fourteenth–thirteenth centuries) encompassed all of Upper Mesopotamia. In central Anatolia, a series of competing city-states (nineteenth–eighteenth centuries) was unified by the Old Hittite kingdom (seventeenth century). In other areas of Syria, Palestine, southern and western Anatolia, and the mountain lands of Armenia and the Zagros the local polities, be they formal kingdoms in the urbanized area or chiefdoms in the hills, remained autonomous but not independent, becoming vassals of the major powers, namely of Egypt in Palestine and southern Syria, of Mitanni and later Hatti in northern Syria, and of Hatti also in western Anatolia. The extent of the local kingdoms varied from the small city-states in Palestine and on the Lebanese coast (about 2,000 km² or 772 square miles) to the larger ones in Syria and Anatolia (about 6,000 km² or 2,316 square miles).

The leaders of the regional states conceived political relations as based on a hierarchy of "great kings" (the regional powers) and "small kings" (the local city-states), the latter being "servants" of the former, their "masters." In some cases, especially under Mitanni and Hittite rule, formal treaties were required in order to define clearly the duties of the two parties, basically a duty of loyalty from the vassal king toward his master, and of protection from the master toward the vassal. Treaties were also written to regulate specific problems of border, refugees, and compensation. Egypt did not engage in direct military control, only requiring an oath of loyalty from its vassals. Treaties between great kings were rare: treaties between Hatti and

Kizzuwatna in southeastern Anatolia were formally reciprocal but masked an uneven relation. Only the treaty between the Hittite king Hattushili and the Egyptian pharaoh Ramesses II (about 1270) was really conceived in terms of equality.

Diplomatic relations inside and among the regional states were better documented when important archives were preserved. This was especially the case of the "Mari age" (seventeenth century) for Upper Mesopotamia, and of the "Amarna age" (fourteenth century) for the Levant. But the Hittite and Middle-Assyrian archives also provide useful information. The diplomatic language in letters and treaties of the time was Babylonian, and cuneiform writing was also used in most of the area for internal court and administrative records. Interpreters, messengers, and ambassadors carried out diplomatic missions, which were based on the exchange of messages, of gifts, and of women.

Letters had to express "brotherhood," friendly attitudes, wishes of good health for the partner and information about the good health of the sender, and at a formal level the exchange of greetings was the most important message. Letters were normally accompanied by gifts, in order to express generosity and to please the other king. Both to give and to receive gifts increased prestige in the eyes of the kings and of the public. The ideology of gifts based on disinterest and on more valuable return gifts was formally expressed, but actually contradicted by miserable bargains and obvious greed.

Gifts were just the tip of the iceberg when compared to normal trade exchange. It has been calculated that the biggest amount of copper sent as a gift from the king of Cyprus to the pharaoh was just 5 percent of the copper found in a single cargo shipwrecked off the coast of Turkey. And we know from the Old Assyrian trade documents that a 5 percent gift was requested by the Anatolian kings to allow the Assyrian merchants to practice their trade activities in the kingdom. Of course, gifts were personalized and had a social or political aim, while trade was carried on for profit, and in order to get resources not available locally. In both cases, gold came from Egypt, copper from Cyprus, tin and lapis lazuli from faraway Afghanistan, while textiles mostly moved from the urbanized areas to the periphery.

Trade procedures were very well attested in the archives of the Old Assyrian merchants, found at Kültepe, ancient Kanish, in central Anatolia in the nineteenth century. These were the most detailed commercial archives of the entire ancient world – similar for their relevance to our understanding of trade to the documents of the Cairo *genizah* for the Levantine trade of medieval times. The Kanish archives were unique, but the amount and modalities of trade they revealed should have been quite similar in many other cases as well. The Assyrian merchants, organized in family firms, and moving with donkey caravans, exported textiles produced at Assur or Babylonia and tin from Iran and got back silver to be reinvested in more textiles and tin, and their big profits largely covered taxes and risks.

Exchange of women was quite important at the political level. We know of two different systems, one centralized and the other reciprocal. The centralized movement of women was attested in the Mari archives and also in the Hittite kingdom. The great king gave his daughters in marriage to the small vassal kings in order to increase their loyalty and to ensure the local throne to a descendant of the great king.

The Egyptian pharaoh used the centralized system in reverse, by requesting women from the Levantine vassals and from the Asiatic great kings, but never offered his daughters to them, just to increase his own prestige. The reciprocal system was widely practiced by the Asiatic kings, giving and receiving daughters to and from neighboring kings – a system known through the entire period but better documented from the Amarna and Hittite archives. In addition to wives, professionals including artists, scribes, doctors, and magicians also circulated among the royal palaces of the Late Bronze period, increasing cross-fertilization in the cultural sphere.

Inside the various kingdoms, the political ideology and the related socio-economic measures underwent a notable change from the Middle to the Late Bronze period. In the first phase, the most evident feature was paternalism, that is, a view of the king as a "good shepherd" for his people, attentive to the needs of his subjects, and interested in turn in winning the consent of a large free population outside of the limited palace circles. The paternalistic attitude was possibly related to the tribal origin of most royal dynasties in Mesopotamia and Syria, who were the descendants of the Amorite invaders at the turn of the millennium. In any case, the attitude materialized into law codes (the famous code of Hammurabi is just the largest and best preserved in a series) and into royal edicts regulating the remission of debts, and therefore resulting in the liberation of enslaved debtors and in the restitution of land to families.

Toward the middle of the second millennium, the attitude shifted toward a different model of kingship. Also in this case it is possible that the new ideology was linked with the prominence of hill peoples like the Kassites, Hurrians, and Hittites, but even more directly with technological changes. The introduction of the horse and the two-wheeled chariot as the most important war machines changed not only war tactics but also the socio-political relations. The new aristocracy of chariot warriors (the *maryannu*) could condition the behavior of kings, giving rise to a "heroic" attitude whereby the king's prestige was based on his personal merits, rather than on justice and tradition, and this also led to more strained socio-economic relations. The royal edicts of debt remission were no longer proclaimed, debt slavery increased, landed properties concentrated in the hands of creditors, and the basic support for the king was no longer the free population but palace circles and the warrior aristocracy.

Socio-economic relations had already undergone an important change at the beginning of the second millennium, when workers under corvée (forced labor), used widely during the Early Bronze, were replaced by hired workers. Of course, the corvée system was based on the existence of substantial village communities, while hired manpower came from a large dispossessed peasantry. Yet during the Middle Bronze the idea that free families had the right to keep their ancestral lands, and individuals had the right to keep their free status, was still quite strong. The royal edicts reflected this idea. Land could be sold only to relatives, in order to remain in the family; sons had a right to inherit family land which brothers often farmed together. The increased practice of adoption undermined the traditional system, by accepting the alien buyer into the family in order to overcome the time-honored rules and traditions about not selling land outside the family. In the Late Bronze, as an effect of the new ideology, inheritance became something to be earned and won, property could be sold outside of the family, the hierarchy of brothers became ineffective, and the number of dispossessed people increased.

This growing socio-economic harshness, along with the long-term demographic and agricultural decline due to climatic worsening in the semi-arid belt and due to deterioration of the irrigation system in the river valleys, was the precondition for the final crisis of the Bronze Age. This culminated in an external shock, the invasion of the "Sea Peoples" at the beginning of the twelfth century. The invaders of Mediterranean origin destroyed the Aegean, Anatolian, and Levantine coastal cities, and reached the Egyptian Delta about 1180. A few years later the Phrygian invaders in central Anatolia, where the Hittite kingdom collapsed completely, reached the Upper Tigris area. A parallel movement took place on the southern coast of the Mediterranean Sea, where the Libyan tribes moved from the Sahara region to invade the Nile valley. All these movements, probably caused by a sharp climatic drying about 1200 BCE, drastically changed the political and urban system in the area west of the Euphrates. The former regional powers of Hatti and Egypt disappeared, city life and local royal dynasties remained in just a few cases on the Phoenician coast and in some Neo-Hittite kingdoms, and room was left for intruders of pastoral origin, the Arameans and related peoples. The entire socio-political order had to be built anew along different lines. East of the Euphrates, in contrast, the regional powers of Assyria, Babylonia, and Elam were unaffected by the western intruders, although they suffered from Aramean pressure, and were able to continue their life along traditional lines.

The Early Iron Age, about 1200–750 BCE

West of the Euphrates, the serious crisis of the twelfth century had to be surmounted by increasing the basis for productive activities and for political consensus. Various technological improvements were effective to this end. The collapse of the palace-centered scribal schools left freedom for the emergence of the alphabet from the Levantine belt. This writing system was a much more accessible tool that produced a kind of democratization of writing competence. The disruption of international trade in copper and tin made it necessary to have recourse to iron production, for which raw material was more widespread, and making iron was easier than bronze. Agricultural exploitation extended to landscapes that were marginal during the Late Bronze period, into the hills, thanks to wood clearing and terrace building, and in the arid belt, thanks to deeper wells and wadi-bed water capturing systems. Irrigation, previously limited to the large alluvial plains, became a factor also in mountain valleys, because of the Iranian *qanat* (artificial underground water channels), and in the mountain/desert contact areas, because of the huge dams of Southern Arabia. Large desert spaces were opened to more intensive frequentation and use in the breeding of camels in the Iranian plateau and in Central Asia and dromedaries in the Syro-Arabian desert.

Other changes took place in the area of socio-economic and socio-political relations. After the collapse of cities and palaces in the Levant and Anatolia and also in the Aegean area, the difference between small towns and fortified villages became less marked. The increased size of the pastoral tribes generated new political relations based on common descent, language, and religion – as contrasted to the Bronze Age polities based on dependence on a royal palace.

Two kinds of polities characterized the western half of the Near East in the Iron Age: city-states, the direct heirs of the "small kingdoms" of the Late Bronze especially along the coast, and ethnic states especially in the arid belt of Arameans and related peoples and in the hilly areas of the Phrygians in Anatolia, and the Medes and related peoples in Iran. The new royal dynasties reserved a larger political role for collective bodies of elders and assemblies who had previously devoted their time to judicial matters. Royal ideology reverted to a "paternalistic" model stressing justice and protection of the kin-based social structures. Trade and crafts, previously centered on palaces, were left to the free enterprise of private firms or individuals. The independent states of the Levant became centers of a lively artistic and commercial life.

Breeding of camels and dromedaries and parallel improvement in nautical techniques opened enlarged horizons in the Mediterranean Sea, along the caravan roads from Syria to Central and Southern Arabia, and along the caravan roads from the Zagros to Central Asia. Trade routes were centered on the new polities, the city-states of Phoenicia and Greece, the ethnic states of Media and Arabia, and the routes avoided the traditional states of Egypt and Mesopotamia which kept their roles as major areas of demographic concentration and major markets.

The remaining regional states underwent a phase of decline, but were able to reach a new equilibrium. In northern Mesopotamia, Assyria had to suffer from Aramean intrusions and was reduced to its original core in the twelfth and eleventh centuries. But it kept alive the idea that its theoretical borders were those once reached by the Middle Assyrian kings Tukulti-Ninurta I (1243–1207) and Tiglath-pileser I (1114–1076) – that is, from the Zagros Mountains to the Euphrates. The reconquest took up the tenth and ninth centuries, with Assyrian kings leading military campaigns inside Assyrian territory, a process culminating with Assurnasirpal II (883–859), who recovered the entire area to the old borders and celebrated his military success in annals of unprecedented length. Ashurnasirpal was also important as builder of a new capital city, Kalkhu, Calah in the Bible, with a palace decorated with impressive sculptured slabs.

His successor Shalmaneser III (858–824) started a new policy of an "imperial" kind, by invading outer regions in Syria (the Aramean city-states), in southeastern Anatolia (the Neo-Hittite states), in Armenia (the new kingdom of Urartu), and in the Zagros Mountains (the rising ethnic states of Mannea in northwest Iran and Media). For a while it seemed that nobody could stop the growth of Assyria, neither the small city-states in the west, nor the ethnic states in the north, nor the enfeebled Babylonian kingdom in the south. But the growth had been too fast, and competition arose inside Assyria itself. The major governors of the western provinces tried to acquire a position of virtual independence. Half a century of "feudal" fragmentation halted the imperial expansion, and the smaller states west of the Euphrates were able to keep their independence and restore equilibrium in the area.

The case of Babylonia was different. After the end of the Kassite dynasty, and after the brilliant reign of Nebuchadnezzar I (1125–1104), the kingdom suffered from Elamite and Assyrian forays, and from nomadic infiltration of the Arameans along the corridor between the Tigris and the Zagros and later also of the Chaldeans along the lower Euphrates. But the main problem was the disruption of the irrigation system, bringing about a demographic and economic decline. The central power was unable to follow the Assyrian model and recover control of the whole area. Various dynasties of different origin, including Chaldeans, were in control of limited parts of Lower Mesopotamia. The Aramean and Chaldean intruders did not establish independent kingdoms as in Syria, but were not subjugated as in Assyria, and they became components of the political scene. Beyond Babylonia, Elam was strong enough to become a permanent actor in Mesopotamian affairs.

In a sense, the fate of Babylonia was similar to that of Egypt. Egypt was also unable either to reject or to absorb its Libyan invaders, and it fragmented into various dynasties mostly of Libyan origin. It was threatened by Nubia playing the same role as Elam in Babylonia, and it was no longer a factor on the international scene.

Empires, about 750–330 BCE

The situation changed in the mid-eighth century. The state of fragmentation and equilibrium was broken by the sudden expansion of the only major power left, namely Assyria, along the lines already indicated by Shalmaneser III, but on a wider scale and with more stable results. Tiglath-pileser III (744–727) defeated Urartu and its Neo-Hittite allies and conquered most of Syria and northern Palestine. He then penetrated deeply into Media and then finally defeated the Chaldean tribes and proclaimed himself king of Babylon. The empire was organized in small provinces with no possibility for "feudal" fragmentation, and the celebrative apparatus of both texts and images proliferated.

The borders of the empire were extended farther under Shalmaneser V (726–722), Sargon II (721–705), and Sennacherib (704–681), but in different ways in various directions. In the West, the Levant was almost completely annexed except for a few minor and marginal vassal kingdoms like Judah. In Anatolia, the Neo-Hittite kingdoms were also annexed, while Sargon's attempt to conquer the central plateau (Tabal, the later Cappadocia) was short-lived. In the North, Urartu was defeated but remained independent, and Sargon's attempt to extend the provincial system to Media was also brief. Babylonia, which recovered independence under Merodach-baladan, was the scene of important fights between Assyria, Elam, and the Chaldean chiefs, until Sennacherib opted for the final solution of total destruction that brought about serious reaction because of the religious and cultural prestige of the city. The Assyrian capital cities, the ephemeral Dur-Sharrukin, built by Sargon, and Nineveh, finally selected by Sennacherib as metropolis of the empire, were embellished by huge palaces and refined sculptures.

When Esarhaddon (680–669) became king, Assyria apparently had no rival, and the dream of a "universal empire" had become true; the effort of military expansion could end. The only surviving polities belonged to two distinct types. On the one hand three "great kingdoms" were still independent: Egypt, Elam, and Urartu. On the other hand, the tribal polities in the highlands, the Medes, and on the arid steppe, the Arabs, were unified in large confederations. The conquest of the great kingdoms was more prestigious, and they became the major targets for Esarhaddon and for his son Assurbanipal (668–631). Egypt was conquered, but it proved impossible for Assyria – with the logistics of the time – to annex a region so distant, large, and populous. Elam was conquered and its capital city Susa destroyed, but that allowed for the growth of a new power, Persia, in the same area.

As for the Medes and the Arabs, conquering them proved impossible because of logistic problems and because they lacked a political structure suited to being reused as provincial divisions of the empire. The tool of the loyalty oath was therefore applied as a sufficient act of subordination. The "ethnic" periphery of the empire remained basically independent, and was viewed as ideologically irrelevant from the point of view of an empire based on royal palaces, urban centers, formal administration, and an agricultural economy.

The huge royal palaces of Esarhaddon and Assurbanipal in Nineveh, the expensive celebrative programs in architecture, visual arts, and inscriptions, and the enlarged royal court including large numbers of officials and officers, astrologers, and scribes, were supported by an economy that during the conquest phase was partly based on booty and tribute. But during the phase of Assyrian-imposed peace it could only depend on internal production. Wars, destructions, and deportations intended to break local resistance and to provide manpower opened large voids in the productive structure of the empire, and the attempt to colonize marginal lands proved ineffective. Establishment of the empire had been based on the physical and cultural destruction of the annexed areas; the maintenance of the empire proved a very hard task on such a depleted productive basis.

After Assurbanipal, twenty years of wars over succession to the throne were sufficient to bring the empire to its final collapse. The external shock came from two different directions. The Chaldeans of Babylonia and the Medes united their forces to defeat the empire, to destroy the capital cities, and to transform the center of the civilized world into a wasteland. The two conquering powers were quite different and exploited their victory in different ways.

The Medes, the heirs of the pastoral tribes of the Zagros that had been attacked and oppressed for centuries by the Assyrian empire, put all their enraged energy into the destruction of Assur and Nineveh. They themselves later disappeared from the political scene, reverting to a tribal organization and even abandoning the ceremonial centers built during the Assyrian period. They were happy enough to exert their hegemony on the peoples of the highlands.

The Chaldean kings Nabopolassar (625–605) and Nebuchadnezzar II (604–562) inherited the lowlands and the urbanized part of the empire, and basically inherited the Assyrian imperial strategy. They conquered the entire Levant, including Judah, and the sieges of Tyre and Jerusalem remained famous in later historiography. Then they defeated the Egyptians, deported the vanquished populations, and devoted most of their resources to rebuilding the capital city of Babylon as the most populous and splendid metropolis of the time. They also tried to restore lower Mesopotamian agriculture to high levels of productivity.

The mental map of the "universal empire," however, was not so satisfactory in the Chaldean version as it had been in the Assyrian version. Besides Babylonia, the political system included a major state like Egypt (Saite dynasty), a growing state like Persia (heir of Elam), and the Anatolian kingdoms of Lydia, Tabal/Cappadocia, Armenia, and Khilakku/Cilicia. The ethnic confederacies of the Medes and the Northern Arabs were no longer an outer periphery, but they became an integral part of the system. Farther away, the Greek cities and the South Arabian caravan cities were also becoming more and more linked through trade and mercenary military service to the Near Eastern world. The system remained mostly stable during half a century, although the Medes included Armenia and Cappadocia under their hegemony, and the last king of Babylonia (Nabonidus, 555–539) conquered North Arabia at the very end of the period.

The age was significant from a cultural point of view. It is the core of the so-called "Axial Age," with the rise of the monotheistic religions of Judaism and Zoroastrianism, the activity of the major Israelite prophets in the Babylonian exile, and the blooming of the Greek "archaic" civilization with the Ionian philosophers, poets, and artists, and the formative period of democratic ideologies. It is significant that the major innovations took place not in the area of the traditional states of Babylonia and Egypt but rather in the new ethnic states and city-states, and that the most accelerated change took place in the century of disruption between the decline of the Assyrian empire starting about 630 and the consolidation of the Persian empire about 540.

The Persian empire of the Achaemenid dynasty was not the heir of the loose Median confederacy, but rather of the Elamite tradition. Persia was virtually congruent with Elam in its narrow definition, and the Persian administration at Persepolis used the Elamite language and script for its archives. The empire was founded by Cyrus II, called the Great, who defeated the Medes in 550, annexed most of the Iranian plateau, and then conquered Lydia in 547, and Babylonia in 539, while the date of annexation of Bactria and Sogdiana, the "outer Iran" of Central Asia, remains unclear. His successor Cambyses annexed Egypt in 525, approximating again the mental map of the "universal empire" to the inhabited world of his time.

The conquest of Babylonia marked the end of independent Mesopotamian history, at least from the political point of view, since the seat of power shifted to Iran. However, the material basis of civilization remained largely unchanged. No technical innovations mark the new period, and Babylonian irrigation agriculture bloomed spectacularly in the last part of the Chaldean period and the beginning of the Achaemenid period without any breaks. Also the cultural tradition remained unchanged during the Persian period. The Babylonian scribes continued to use their own script and language, and the Babylonian deities were still worshiped in the same temples. Astrologers continued to record the position of the stars and the historical events according to their time-honored tradition, and Akkadian literary texts, omen collections, and lexicographical lists were still copied in the schools as before.

The Persian empire was in a sense a synthesis of different traditions, among which the Babylonian tradition was predominant. The empire inherited from Assyria the very idea of empire, and the basic features of the celebrative apparatus. It inherited from Elam the federal system of governance that had been typical of the Iranian peoples for a long time. And it inherited from Media important features of court life, and probably the Zoroastrian religion. The empire included the Babylonian temple-cities and the Phoenician city-states as different but equally acceptable centers for running the economy. At a symbolic level, it is significant that the celebrative inscription of Darius I (521–486) was written in three different languages, Babylonian, Elamite, and the new Persian script, and that the seat of the court shifted seasonally between the highland cities of Ecbatana, modern Hamadan, and Persepolis and the lowlands cities of Susa and Babylon, as a formal acknowledgment of the role that the four regions of Elam, Babylonia, Media, and Persia played in the building of the empire.

Under Darius I the empire extended farther, to include the Indus Valley in the east, and Ionia in the west, but it left the Arabs and the Scythians alone. The Oriental empire had finally annexed the entire Levantine zone. Oriental despotism had prevailed over the autonomous city-states and the ethnic polities. In the extreme western periphery, in Greece, a few small city-states were still left, however. The expeditions by Darius (490) and Xerxes (480) tried to eliminate that minor anomaly and to absorb the distant and almost irrelevant appendix of the Near Eastern world. But things went differently from what the Persians planned, and the struggle between the universal empire and the last city-states not only ended in the unpredictable rebuff of the Persians, but also generated in Greek, and later European, minds the opposition between East and West, between despotism and democracy, slavery and freedom, magic and rationality, and redistribution and enterprise, which was to mark world history for many millennia to come.

FURTHER READING

The standard historical treatment of the Ancient Near East is Edwards, Gadd, and Hammond 1971–92. A recent synthesis of the subject can be found in Kuhrt 1995. On Mesopotamia proper, the best introduction remains Oppenheim 1977.

For a thematic introduction see Sasson 1995. For more technical discussions see Ebeling et al. 1928–. For historical geography and maps see Röllig 1977–. More synthetic is Roaf 1990. A good collection of sources is Pritchard 1975.

CHAPTER TWO

From Sedentism to States, 10,000–3000 BCE

Augusta McMahon

The first sedentary communities in the Near East appeared about 10,000 BCE, and by 3000 BCE we find urbanized complex societies. The path between these dates is peppered with major innovations – farming and herding, pottery, irrigation, organized religion, public art and architecture. It is temptingly easy to view this span of time as exhibiting progression to civilization. But there are unresolved debates and biases in our approach to this crucial era.

Theory and Bias in Near Eastern Archaeology

The Near East was first explored for its historical archaeology and importance for Biblical and Classical traditions, and there are firmly rooted culture-history and text-based approaches that color study of its prehistory. But problem-driven archaeological research since the 1960s has had a tremendous impact on work in the region, and scholars working in the Near East have led the way on the key questions of agriculture and state origins (Matthews 2003). However, this "big picture" research has a legacy in the lingering assumption of a unilineal trajectory toward agriculture-based complexity, marginalizing alternative economies and political systems in deserts, marshes, and fringes of agricultural communities. Farming-hunting or herding-gathering blended economies and loose tribal groupings were viable long-term possibilities, rather than temporary stages (Zeder 1994), but these alternatives remain under-researched.

Although many archaeologists continue to ask cultural and historical questions, Watkins (1992) and Cauvin (2000) have explored the symbolic revolution in the Near Eastern Neolithic (12,000–6300 BCE), focusing on psychological changes rather than economic, social, and political ones. Beyond fashions in archaeological theory, one of the most difficult problems in reconstructing Near Eastern prehistory is our vision of the region's inhabitants. Are the innovations we see active, brought about by individuals, or reactive, the result of inexorable systemic changes or imbalances? Most importantly, what is the nature of the state when it emerges:

benevolent or tyrannical? Are Western scholars who characterize Ancient Near Eastern states as oppressive and exploitative subliminally affected by their opinions of the modern states of Iraq, Syria, and Turkey?

Labeling Time and Locating Sites

Time blocks and cultural labels are basic vocabulary elements in all archaeological discourse and some generalization is inevitable. But for Near Eastern prehistory, our time units are often over-long; for example the Ubaid period, 5800–4000 BCE, or the Levantine Pre-Pottery Neolithic period, 8200–5600 BCE, are about 2,000 years each. And the material culture used to define these units is often clustered in a few sites or a short time range within longer periods.

Near Eastern prehistory suffers further from the nature of its settlements – small, low sites in a landscape of destruction, which has been exploited for millennia. Identification of sites, even in intensive surveys, favors large multi-period settlements. Low sites are under-recognized in the rolling landscapes of northern Mesopotamia and the Levant, that is, the eastern coast of the Mediterranean, and in southern Mesopotamia sites may be removed by subsequent land use or wind and dune action or covered by river deposits.

Sedentism and its Effects

Sedentism, remaining in one place throughout the year, was first identified as a necessary precursor to agriculture in the 1960s (Binford 1968; Wright 1971; Flannery 1973), and although it is no longer considered a simple equation, the link between sedentism and agriculture in the Near East persists today (Bar-Yosef and Belfer-Cohen 1989). Clearly, sedentism can create "positive feedback." Early semi-sedentary sites already had greater densities of artifacts than did Paleolithic sites (before 18,000 BCE) of mobile peoples, along with more non-portables such as storage facilities, grinding stones, burials, and increasingly substantial architecture (Byrd 1989). Sedentism promoted acquisition, and object ownership meant reluctance to move on and leave things behind. Sedentism had a corollary in increased group size, as female fertility increased and birth spacing and mortality decreased. Larger numbers can also mean disinclination to mobility. Further, increased group size can be linked with more complex social relationships. The mortality rates that were most reduced by sedentism were those of infants and the elderly; not only did group size increase but the nature of the group changed. The larger group contained more old individuals with memories and acquired status, and more young individuals with hopes for the future. And this social environment preceded and provided fertile ground for agriculture.

Sedentary farmers had less free time than nomadic hunter-gatherers (Bender 1975). The schedules and concepts of work differed. Farming involved spikes of intensive labor and troughs of free time, and the free time was differently arranged across the year. This new arrangement opened up vistas for non-subsistence activities. But the effects of sedentism and agriculture were not all positive. Reduction of resource diversity could mean greater risk of catastrophe. A restricted-resource agri- culture-based diet could mean nutritional deficiencies and dental problems (Smith, Bar-Yosef, and Sillen 1984). The tighter arrangement of sedentary villages and their piles of rubbish (and rats) meant higher rates of infectious disease, and closer contact between humans and animals might favor species-jumping diseases, as organisms associated with animals came into contact with new potential hosts. The repetitive manual labor involved in grain processing could cause skeletal stress (Molleson 2000). Apparently, positives did outweigh negatives, but the persistence of hunting well into the historic periods points out the necessity for keeping alternatives open.

Foraging, Cultivation, and Domestication

There is an indivisible continuum from mobile to fully sedentary settlements, mir- rored by a continuum from foraging to farming. Economic stages can be defined: "Foraging" implies opportunistic exploitation of resources; "intensive foraging" indicates strategic decisions to focus on a few species or to exploit a wide range. "Cultivation" means manipulation or taming of individual animals, while "agricul- ture" involves domestication of species, with dependency of plants and animals on humans for reproduction and protection. But in the Near East these economies were neither mutually exclusive nor necessarily linked. A group might rely on both farmed and hunted species. Species might be cultivated but not subsequently domesticated, like the gazelle in the Levant before the Neolithic. And crucially, domestication of plants and animals also "domesticates" human populations, imposing limits on movement and time.

Where Was the Origin of Agriculture?

Experiments by Hillman and Davies (1990) indicate that domestication of grain and consequent changes in the plants may be achieved within 20 to 30 years by specific harvesting techniques but can take 200 years or more. In animals, with lengthier generations, morphological changes are even slower to appear. By the time we see the "first" domestic plant or animal, the decision that brought it about was already generations distant. But this has not prevented many scholars from searching for those elusive "firsts."

Most recent literature reconstructs the center of agriculture in the southern Levant, with subsequent spread to the rest of the Near East and Europe (McCorriston and Hole 1991; Wright 1993; Bar-Yosef and Meadow 1995; Bar-Yosef 2002). But this Levant-centric presentation is clouded by modern political tensions. A smaller amount of archaeological research has been done in the comparable environmental zone of the Zagros foothills along the Iran–Iraq border, and the extant work is mostly pre-1979, creating a knowledge gap there and a bias toward the Levant as the supposed center for agricultural origins. Research in Syria and southeast Turkey has only begun to alter the picture (Willcox 1999).

Many sites have provided archaeological evidence for early "founder crops" with the larger size, restricted dissemination mechanism, and morphological changes that mark them as domesticated. For the Near East the founder crops were emmer and einkorn wheat, barley, lentils, peas, chickpeas, and bitter vetch. Domesticated emmer wheat and barley from southern Levant sites such as Jericho (7500 BCE)[1] and Netiv Hagdud (8260–7800 BCE) were increasingly joined by early domestic grains from sites in other regions: Tell Abu Hureyra on the Euphrates in Syria (einkorn, emmer, and barley 7700 BCE, domestic rye possibly as early as 10,000 BCE), Tell Aswad near Damascus (emmer and barley from 7800–7600 BCE), and in southeast Turkey, Cafer Höyük (einkorn, emmer, and barley 7500 BCE), Çayönü (einkorn, emmer, and barley 7300–7200 BCE), and Nevali Çori (einkorn 7200 BCE).

Archaeologically derived evidence for domestic plants is now supplemented with genetic research. Distribution maps of wild progenitors of domestic species have been updated with this genetic profiling. These studies are complicated by modern agricultural practices and the possibility of relatively recent genetic change within the wild populations (Harlan and Zohary 1966; Heun et al. 1997), but homogeneities found have led to the conclusion that there was a core zone within which grain and legume domestication took place. Accumulation of evidence for einkorn and emmer wheats points toward a southeastern Turkey or northern Syria origin for domestication (Nesbitt and Samuel 1998; Willcox 1999; Lev-Yadun, Gopher, and Abbo 2000; Özkan et al. 2002).

Domestication of animals has also been studied through the bones themselves and through profiles of age and sex at death. Domestic animals are smaller, lighter, and lose defensive mechanisms seen in wild forms. But there are problems with size assessments, as these may relate to climate or topography variations and are complicated by differences between the sexes. Age and gender profiles are more reliable; managed and domesticated animals usually show selective culling of young males and late killing of adult females.

The dog was certainly the first domesticated animal, in the Epipaleolithic in the Levant, about 14,000 years before the present and perhaps much earlier. The dog was unique in that it was domesticated for protection and hunting, a companion and servant rather than a source of meat, milk, hair, or traction, as were the pig, goat, sheep, and cattle that followed. The Zagros foothills have been posited as the core animal domestication zone (Hole 1984). The earliest known domesticated goat bone has been identified from Ganj Dareh, initially on the basis of small size, reconfirmed by gender and age kill patterns (Zeder and Hesse 2000); this is currently radiocarbon dated to about 7960–7660 BCE. Or pigs in southeast Turkey may have been the second animal domestication (Rosenberg 1999).

Food is arguably basic to human concepts of the self and is involved in everything from taboos to feasting, so the species shift, as well as the very fact of domestication, means a major change in self-perception and self-expression. Another issue is that complementary farming-herding practices became common over a wide area during a relatively short time span. Why did this happen?

Agriculture and Herding: Choice or Necessity?

Entwined with arguments over locations are debates over reasons for domestication. Climate change-based hypotheses (Childe 1928) were followed by evolutionary ideas (Braidwood 1960), population pressure theories (Boserup 1965; Binford 1968; Smith and Young 1972; Flannery 1973), systems theory explanations (Redman 1978; Henry 1989), and psychological concepts (Cauvin 2000). Childe named the "Neolithic Revolution," but his vision, that climate drying forced development of agriculture in "oases," is no longer accepted. Nevertheless, the Younger Dryas event, a relatively rapid climatic shift to cooler and drier conditions from about 11,000 before the present, is recognized as impacting human economy, especially in the Levant (Bar-Yosef and Belfer Cohen 1989; Bar-Yosef 1996; Hole 1997; Sherratt 1997; Wright 1993). Some would see the cooling and drying climate as having reduced food supplies and encouraged individuals to reconstruct previously available wild stands of grain and herds in now marginal areas (Moore and Hillman 1992). Others would see climate change encouraging stronger seasonality and the migration of plants to new zones and into contact with semi-sedentary humans (McCorriston and Hole 1991). The impact of this event in Anatolia, modern Turkey, and the Zagros has not been sufficiently researched.

Braidwood noticed that humans and potential domesticates lived together on the "hilly flanks" of the Zagros, Taurus, and Lebanon mountains. There, he postulated, simple proximity and humans' love of experimentation led to cultivation and domestication, although he was later to revise that view (Braidwood et al. 1983). Boserup argued that technological changes responded to human population growth. Her idea was elaborated by identification of optimal zones (Smith and Young 1972) or marginal zones (Binford 1968; Flannery 1973), within which an increasing population might develop agriculture. Systems theory acknowledges positive and negative feedbacks within the relationships among environment, geography, humans, and domesticates, but this reduction of humans to parts of a system may be too impersonal. More recently Watkins (1992) and Cauvin (2000) envision agriculture as embedded within a series of wider changes in symbolic and religious behaviors and in recognition of dichotomies between male and female, natural and artificial, human and "super-human." But there is still no consensus on whether agriculture was chosen or forced.

Sedentism and Definitions of Space

Domestic structures increased in solidity and size during the Epipaleolithic (18,000–8000 BCE) and early Neolithic (8000–6000 BCE). Further, within the Neolithic there was a shift from round to rectilinear houses. It is easier to add to or divide a rectilinear house than a round one, so the shift may point to increasing household size and complexity. Also very different mental concepts are involved in circular and rectilinear architecture. A round house has two units, the continuous wall and a roof. A rectilinear house involves a minimum of five units, four discrete walls and a roof. The investment in a rectilinear house, no matter what size, was higher than in a circular one.

A more permanent definition of private space does not mean that the idea was new, but that visible marking of space had become more important. This may have been due to better definition of edges and internal divisions of communities (Watkins 1992). It might also be linked to notions of land ownership that came with agriculture and household-based production and consumption (Byrd 1994). Or space definition might relate to increases in social distance, as a community increased in size, requiring greater structuring of inhabitants' interactions and communication of taboos and tolerances.

Public buildings, communally constructed if not necessarily community-accessible, also appeared in the early Neolithic and may be seen as indicators of increased attachment to a place. The tower and settlement wall at Neolithic Jericho is an example that has been identified as defensive (Kenyon 1981), or as a means of water management, or a shrine platform (Bar-Yosef 1986). Neolithic Maghzaliyah, in northern Iraq, had a settlement wall, and in southeast Turkey Neolithic sites had special buildings, distinct from houses in plan, construction, and contents (Hauptmann 1993; Özdogan 1999; Schmidt 2000). These buildings may have been exclusive elite advertising, or they may have been communally owned religious structures. But either way, they might have been intended as prominent visual cues of landscape ownership.

Pottery and Structural Bias

Production of pottery was closely coupled with sedentism and farming. Pottery was heavy, breakable, and difficult to transport and was almost exclusively found among sedentary peoples. The lulls in agricultural labor were easily filled by pottery production, and straw generated after harvest made ideal pottery temper. Economy and technology dovetailed perfectly.

But what problem did the invention of pottery solve? Morphologically similar containers existed before pottery, in stone, lime-plaster, basketry, and wood. Ceramic containers were more portable than stone but less so than baskets. Pottery vessels were more secure than pits or bins, so the impact on storage was potentially substantial. However, the earliest pottery vessels were not storage jars, but bowls, small jars, and cooking vessels. The main areas in which pottery had a positive impact were cooking, especially boiling grain, and serving and eating.

As soon as the technical aspects of production were established in the late eighth millennium BCE, the surface of pottery vessels became a canvas for artistic expression in the applied clay blobs and paint dribbles of northern Mesopotamian wares, rocker and punched patterns of Amuq A, and early Zagros "tadpole" ware that may imitate the look of tightly woven baskets. Later, Hassuna period cross-hatching and geometric designs enlivened an otherwise drab fabric (6300–5700 BCE). By the time we reach the Samarran ware (6100–5500 BCE) with its dense geometric or elaborate pictorial decoration, the symbolic coding was rich, potentially signaling wealth and social identity, family or ethnic affiliations, or even archetypal myths. Feasting was the most likely outlet for display of this signaling, but it is unclear whether feasting was competitive or collaborative at this early date.

Ultimately, pottery is implicated in a conceptual bias in our reconstruction of the past. Is pottery production so important that its absence should define a time period (the awkward "Pre-Pottery Neolithic," 8000–6500 BCE)? From the earliest humans through the Pre-Pottery Neolithic, preserved material culture was dominated by stone tools. But from the Pottery Neolithic onward (6500 BCE), the most common artifact was pottery, and pottery becomes our primary instrument for labeling time and society – a shift from tools associated with acquisition to tools associated with consumption. This surely has an effect on our view of society in the later Neolithic and thereafter, consumption seeming to us more civilized and peaceful than the messy and tiring process of acquisition.

Chiefdoms?

A progression from band to tribe to chiefdom to state was first expounded by Service (1975) to replace the progression from savagery to barbarism to civilization popular in nineteenth-century scholarship. Many scholars think chiefdoms preceded states (Wright 1984; Earle 1987), although the possibility remains that chiefdoms were reactions to states or unrelated organizational forms.

The earliest states in the Near East appeared in the later fourth millennium BCE, the Uruk period, in southern Mesopotamia. The argument might be made that a state existed in northern Mesopotamia or Anatolia contemporary with or even prior to that in southern Mesopotamia, since there are urban sites such as Tell Brak in Syria (about 100 hectares or 247 acres) and impressive buildings at Hacinebi and Arslan Tepe in Turkey. The earlier view of these areas as peripheries to a southern core is currently under revision. But despite evidence of complexity, the north has yet to produce a building to rival Uruk's Eanna IV temple complex or artworks like the Warka vase. Nor did northern Mesopotamian material culture expand into other regions as did that of the south. The north was complex and vibrant but still owed much to, and followed the lead of, the south.

If the chiefdom preceded the state, we need to look for it in the Ubaid period of the sixth to fifth millennia (5800–4000 BCE). A chiefdom is structurally kinship-based, with a degree of social complexity and inequality and a single leader, in contrast to the corporate entity implied by a state. The Ubaid does offer many identifiers of chiefdoms: two-tier settlement hierarchies, specialist production of pottery, large well-planned structures at Tell 'Oueili, shrines at Eridu, possible chiefs' houses at Tell Abada, and stamp seals indicating the increased importance of ownership. An unresolved question is whether Ubaid chiefs' power was based on "wealth finance," restricted luxuries, as is traditionally assumed for chiefdoms (D'Altroy and Earle 1985; Earle 1991), or on "staple finance," surplus basic materials such as grain, with control of the land, water, and labor which allowed surpluses (Stein 1994,

1996). Imported luxuries do not appear in quantity in Ubaid sites, while the Tell Abada houses do have space for grain storage and the Tell 'Oueili structures have been interpreted as granaries (Huot 1996). Nevertheless, it seems that the Ubaid power base rested on a combination of basics and luxuries, a strategy that allowed acquisition and advertisement of power at different levels. And later the Uruk state had the same dual foundation.

Origins of the Mesopotamian State

Theoretical approaches to state origins match trends in approaches to agriculture origins, and there are comparable arguments over whether the state was a choice or an inevitability. Explanatory theories have replaced evolutionary assumptions (Childe 1928; Service 1975). Classic explanatory theories developed for other regions, for example the hypothesis that states arose to effect irrigation or to reduce conflict, have proved inadequate for the Mesopotamian situation, but other forces scholars have suggested include population pressure (Smith and Young 1972), climate change, and river shifts (Hole 1994). Systems theory has also been applied, with its identification of the many factors that contribute to social change (Adams 1966, 1981; Redman 1978). But the most enduringly popular explanations for Mesopotamian state origins involve trade and its management (Wright and Johnson 1975; Oates 1993; Algaze 2001a). Scholars have focused on positive aspects of the Mesopotamian river plains – agricultural surplus potential, predictability of rainfall and floods, efficient water transport – but also point out the necessity for local and long-distance trade to acquire and disperse key items and resources, trade which promoted development of a state structure.

But in southern Mesopotamia we have only scattered excavated material of the Ubaid and early Uruk periods.[2] Because of the sparse evidence, we are too willing to place Levantine Neolithic sedentary communities, north Mesopotamian Hassuna farming villages, and Ubaid chiefs' houses in a trajectory leading to urban sites of south Mesopotamia, while these are mere footnotes to the earliest state complexity. This had strictly southern Mesopotamian predecessors, and until excavation in south Iraq is again possible, we have a flimsy framework derived from neighboring regions and limited local material. It may even be the case that the state was seen first and most dramatically at Uruk because of its proximity to the marshes and head of the Arabian Gulf, which offered a unique environmental setting and range of resources. Even Nippur, Umma, and other southern sites may have learned "stateness" from Uruk.

Nature of the State

Most visions of the Mesopotamian state involve centralized control and vertical hierarchy (Adams 1966, 1981; Adams and Nissen 1972; Wright and Johnson 1975; Wright 1977; Nissen 1988). Focus is on the material evidence of elites and of state economic administration – public buildings and art, seals, bullae (clay tags), and tablets which recorded movement of goods, and mass-produced pottery. There is assumed to have been efficient gathering and redistribution of agricultural products, textiles, and other manufactured items, grounded in an urban core and a rural periphery.

Scholars see the Mesopotamian state as urban, typified by Uruk in the Late Uruk period around 3100 BCE, at about 250 hectares or 620 acres and with population estimates of up to 40,000 inhabitants (Nissen 2002). But what do we know of south Mesopotamia beyond Uruk, and what of Uruk beyond its size and the layout of its religious quarter in the final phase?

Urbanization also "ruralizes." Pre-urban and post-urban villages may appear similar, but small villages within a larger system have a new counterpoint in urban sites, and the land between sites takes on a new meaning (Yoffee 1995). The Uruk period with its four-tier hierarchy of site sizes which is visible in survey around Uruk (Adams and Nissen 1972; Nissen 2002) may not exactly match a power hierarchy but does translate into variability in settlement character. Craft production and centers of religion and secular administration may be displaced to urban centers, creating a system of rural dependency. Pottery and flint tool production remained at the village level of production in the Uruk period at Abu Salabikh (Pollock, Pope, and Coursey 1996). But metallurgy seems to have been restricted to urban sites, while centralization of textile production, often assumed, remains unproven. We know a great deal about the vertical inequalities of the Mesopotamian state but need more research into rural sites and into household and private economies. The shift in terminology from "state" to "complex society" in archaeological discourse is welcome, with its emphasis on horizontal variation as well as vertical structures. But it must be applied more comprehensively to the Uruk period situation.

And the vertical inequalities may not necessarily mean exploitation and oppression, as is often supposed. It is notable that images of leaders in the Uruk period generally did not dominate, but rulers were depicted as unifying and protecting. There are a few seal impressions representing a ruler with captives, but the majority of artworks showed him in ritual contexts or symbolic scenes with animals or building projects. Texts interpreted as ration lists for enslaved or disenfranchised workers may equally be lists of payment for part-time work, in an economy where staple goods acted as money.

One recent theory avoids definitions and looks to "effects" of states: "identification, legibility, and spatialization" (Trouillot 2001). Legibility is particularly apt for the early Mesopotamian state, with its new visible language, written and iconographic ruler images, cylinder seals and clay tablets, temple complexes, and the urban sites themselves. It is unclear whether Mesopotamian states brought a new spatialization, with borders and enforced population movements, inside to outside, outside to inside, or displacement within. Population movements were certainly a feature of late Mesopotamian states like the Neo-Assyrian empire. And for fourth millennium BCE Uruk, we see a suddenly larger urban center and depopulation of its immediate surroundings (Adams and Nissen 1972). It is unlikely that this was merely the result of a need for protection or the draw of employment opportunities. But Uruk was an anomaly, and the smaller city-states of Nippur and Adab, mostly built through incremental growth, may be more typical. The identification effect – all individuals within a state identifying as members of it – is related to one of Childe's traits of civilization, which sees membership based on location, rather than kinship. We do not yet have the equipment to assess to what degree early inhabitants of cities and their hinterlands identified themselves as citizens of Uruk or Nippur. But the strength of family relations in Mesopotamia into the first millennium BCE and beyond suggests that identification was negotiated through both physical location and kinship.

Art and Architecture

Natufian carved bone animals and stone human figures from 10,500 to 8200 BCE are the earliest artworks in the Near East. Although their contexts are often unclear, they are surely possessions and expressions of individuals, not of a kin or residence group. And art remained primarily in the realm of individuals into the fourth millennium; the portable figurines of the Pre-Pottery Neolithic through Ubaid periods (8000–4000 BCE) were individually rather than corporately owned. But the Anatolian Neolithic sites of Nevali Çori and Göbekli Tepe present early monumental art: massive stone pillars with relief figures of wild animals or of rough human forms. The effort of transporting and carving the stones was certainly shared across the community, which then owned them corporately. The slightly later wall painting of an onager hunt at Umm Dabaghiyah was also potentially a group effort.

Decoration on pottery was available to all. But art became restricted in access in the Uruk period, even as media and motifs expanded. Figurines representing average humans disappeared and did not reappear in quantity until the later third millennium BCE. Reliefs and statues representing kings, priests, and possibly deities, dominated. Instead of figurines of pregnant women, celebrating fertility, we have cylinder seals showing rows of women at looms, celebrating mass production. Figurines of wild animals were replaced by stylized representations of well-behaved temple flocks. Art was apparently hijacked to the ordered world of the elite as high culture (Baines and Yoffee 1998).

We might view all art produced by an elite as propaganda, to maintain, reinforce, or extend power. But Uruk period art might also have been simply educational. The generic leader figure seen in statues, reliefs, and seals was unlike any prior human representation, just as the leaders themselves were a new category. The rounded hat, schematic beard, and cross-hatched skirt were new ruler identifiers, as was the limited range of contexts in which the ruler was shown: religious, symbolic, occasionally military. Both the easy legibility of this information and its appropriateness meant that much of the visual vocabulary introduced in the Uruk period, like kings killing lions, was still in use in the Neo-Assyrian and Persian periods, 2,700 years later. The division of the world into horizontal registers and conceptual categories, as represented on the Warka vase, similarly presented new concepts and showed comparable persistence.

Monumental architecture can be propaganda; Trigger (1990) points out that monumental architecture in early complex societies was often bigger and more elaborate than was required by function. The building of the Late Uruk temple complexes of Uruk Eanna IV and the Anu ziggurat, followed by unnecessary razing and rebuilding, looks very like an attempt to impress the power of an authority on a subject population. But would a small elite have been able to coerce a large labor pool to build monuments that only served to remind of their oppression? The temples celebrated not the ruling class, but nature-based deities who created and protected "civilized" society. The temple-complexes were not just buildings commissioned by elites, but vibrant places for ritual and houses for the gods. Now unused and depopulated, the buildings appear to us as evidence of tyranny.

Writing

"Prehistory" is as biased as "pre-pottery." Writing's transformation of human life was not entirely for the better. The earliest texts in the Near East, from the end of the Uruk period, about 3100 BCE, were primarily economic; and it is tempting to believe there could be no bias in such basic documentation. But the texts belonged to temple–palace institutions and were instrumental in our vision of the Uruk state as economically centralized. The absence of economic texts from villages does not mean an absence of economic behavior there. The Late Uruk "Professions List" presents us with an indigenous vision of society's vertical and horizontal categories, but this list was written by scribes firmly located near the top (Nissen, Damerow, and Englund 1993: 110–15).

Most scholars believe that numeracy and information storage in the Near East had had a long history (Schmandt-Besserat 1992; Nissen, Damerow, and Englund 1993; Englund 1998). Accounting was present from the Neolithic, in the form of clay and stone tokens, initially loose, then from the late fourth millennium BCE encased in clay bullae, or tags. The idea is that the patterns of the tokens were reduced to impressions and ultimately to incised signs on flat clay tablets, resulting in the earliest writing. This is an elegant theory, linking disparate elements of the archaeological record. Among tokens there were definable size and shape categories, and repetition that implies agreed meanings. But equally there were unique tokens, and we do not know when or how the tokens might have been transferred to two dimensions (Nissen 2002). The archaeological evidence for the relevant period is ambiguous and limited, with tokens in bullae and early numerical and pictographic tablets overlapping in time and a gap in the data existing for the Early Uruk.

And then there is the problem of the transition from numeracy to literacy. Compared to the long life of tokens, writing developed rapidly and surely was a response to the state's need to deal with complex record keeping and transactions (Nissen, Damerow, and Englund 1993; Michalowski 1993b). The complexity of transferal of an aural, oral, and mental code to a visual code does imply that writing was the conscious solution to a problem. And the distance created by such transferal potentially made written communication into something esoteric and restricted. Restricted literacy meant restricted knowledge, and writing itself could be an avenue for bias and deception.

Discussion of the development of writing in Mesopotamia often involves the question of whether writing always signifies or encodes speech. Pictographic writing, such as that of the earliest tablets, can evade connection with speech; a symbol for a ziggurat, for instance, might relate to either a mental image of a temple tower or the spoken word "ziggurat." Neither system of translation, sound to symbol or mental image to symbol, can be called more logical.

Production and Consumption

Archaeologists distinguish craft specializations as "independent" or as "attached," most often with focus on the New World (Brumfiel and Earle 1987; Costin 1991; Inomata 2001). Independent specialization involves production for an assumed, but amorphous, demand for goods from the general population; attached specialization means production of goods for patrons, with implications of complex society and elite control of media and motifs. Attached specialists generally produce valuable goods, while independent specialists produce utilitarian items (Stein 1996).

For the Ubaid period (about 5800–4000 BCE) and Uruk period (about 4000–3100 BCE) in Mesopotamia we have yet to reconstruct the pattern of craft production. Even for the historical periods, with detailed information of who was working for whom and producing what, we often cannot be sure that attached specialists recorded in texts were attached full time or even specialists full time. An Ubaid period potter might create common wares and elaborate painted wares for different clientele, but fire them at the same time in one kiln, blurring the specialization boundaries. Similarly, textile-production might be household-based, although the final products had many destinations.

In the Uruk period, there were surely attached craft specialists who produced cylinder seals, stone vessels, and statues exclusively for the temple or palace and its elite occupants. The "Professions List" points to the existence of potters, weavers, and carpenters who may have been producing for either elite or common demands, or both (Nissen, Damerow, and Englund 1993: 110–15). Were these individuals full-time specialists? And is there any link between value of product and status of producer? Attached specialists may be of low status because of their dependence on patrons. But their esoteric knowledge, artistic skill, and access to restricted media and motifs might be socially valuable. While cylinder seals were clearly valuable because of medium, motifs, artistic skill, and use, what about, for instance, the hundreds of clay cones used for public building decoration? This was clearly an attached specialization, since cones were used exclusively by the temple and palace. But the skill level was low and the medium cheap and ubiquitous. Technically, anyone could have decorated his or her house with cone mosaics. The temple and palace control made clay cones absurdly valuable, but was this status passed on to their producers?

Standardization of pottery was present in shape and style from the Pottery Neolithic (after 6500 BCE). But in the Uruk period, we see probable mass-production. Decoration dropped to a minimum; volumes as well as forms may have been standardized. Many vessels were made on a fast potter's wheel, and it is possible that some pottery production moved from the hands of women to those of men, while women were more often found at the weaving loom. But questions persist about pottery's mode of production.

We cannot agree who was responsible for production of the ubiquitous beveled-rim bowl, nor can we agree on its purpose. Was this a ration bowl, produced under elite management, filled under that management, and distributed by it (Nissen 1970, 2002)? Might it have been produced in less regulated circumstances, within the family or village, but brought to the elite for filling? Or neither? Beveled-rim bowls have also been interpreted as salt containers (Buccellati 1990), bread-molds (Millard 1988; Chazan and Lehner 1990), yoghurt containers (Delougaz 1952), temple-offering bowls (Mallowan 1933; Beale 1978), and vessels used at banquets organized by elites (Forest 1987). The reconstruction of the beveled-rim bowl as ration container is problematic. As any refugee knows, the size of container for receiving rations is irrelevant, a plastic bag or empty tin will do; the sole container for which size is important is that held in the hand issuing rations.

Trade, Interaction, and the Uruk Expansion

In concert with development of the state, about 4000 to 3000 BCE, the Near East witnessed an expansion of population and material culture from southern Meso-potamia into northern Mesopotamia, Anatolia, and the Iranian Zagros Mountains. New sites with purely southern Mesopotamian culture were founded, while at long-occupied sites local traditions were overrun by southern pottery and architecture. These colonies were an essential element of early Mesopotamian complex society, and this phenomenon is one of the most intensively studied aspects of the region. The most popular current model is that these were southern trade colonies, established to ensure continuous and increased access to the resources of the mountainous areas around the lower river plains – timber, stones, and metals. But we are now in the uncomfortable position of knowing far more about the Uruk period at these sites than we do about the contemporary southern Mesopotamian homeland. And the fact that most work on the Mesopotamian state for several decades has necessarily been based in this "Uruk expansion phenomenon" has perhaps meant an overesti-mation of trade's importance for that state. It must be emphasized that the Uruk phenomenon was an intensification of an interaction sphere present in the region for millennia.

Initially these sites were viewed as evidence for the south Mesopotamian core exploiting peripheral areas (Algaze 1993). But it is now generally acknowledged that the north exhibited social complexity before the arrival of southern Uruk people and material culture, and the relationship cannot be considered asymmetrical (Algaze 2001b; Stein 2001). The purpose of the southern expansion is still debated between those who see it as motivated by desire to control resources and those who see it as motivated by desire simply to gain access to resources. There was also great variability within the expansion phenomenon, from genuine southern Mesopotamian settle-ments as at Habuba Kabira in central Syria, through southern outposts embedded within local populations seen at Hacinebi in Turkey, to sites which retained local traditions while borrowing from the south illustrated at Arslan Tepe also in Turkey. Was each colony linked to a different city-state in the south, or did southern cities unite to invest in an array of colonies, or were the colonies' inhabitants economic migrants, no longer associated with the south at all? Questions about the expansion remain, but it is far more important that we return to ask questions in and of south Iraq.

NOTES

1   The date of the Jericho grain has been disputed (Nesbitt and Samuel 1998); the earliest evidence for domesticated grain from this site may date as late as 7200 BCE.
2   For the earlier Uruk period in the south, the Eanna Sounding at Uruk supplies a pottery sequence, but not without problems (Sürenhagen 1986a, 1987; Nissen 2002); a similar stratigraphic sounding at Nippur was also limited in scale (Porada et al. 1992). The Ubaid levels at Eridu (Safar, Mustafa, and Lloyd 1981) and Tell 'Oueili (Huot 1996) offer limited hints of pre-Uruk developments.

FURTHER READING

Useful introductions include Algaze 2001a and 2001b and Stein 1994 and 2001.

CHAPTER THREE

The Age of Empires, 3100–900 BCE

Mark Chavalas

Our goal here is to describe early Ancient Near Eastern empires, the earliest expansive states in human history. First, it seems imperative that we attempt to define and describe the nature of empires in the context of the Ancient Near East, even though the term has been described as a "word not fit for scholars" (Doyle 1986: 11). The term empire has often been taken for granted as if it designated something obvious to everyone. Of course, ethnologists argue that "man is an imperial animal who has an inbuilt need for expansion." Others have said that imperialism and colonialism are as old as the state and they thus define the political process. Of course, if we use these statements, we do not have to give reasons for the expansion of political systems except to say that they are able to expand (Larsen 1979: 98).

Empire comes from Latin *imperium*, with the root denoting order and command. For the Romans, the term described the executive authority possessed by Roman magistrates. By the modern age the term began to denote an expansive polity that incorporated multiple states. An empire, according to Doyle, is a "system of inter-action between two political entities, one of which, the dominant metropole, exerts political control over the internal and external policy – the effective sovereignty – of the other, the subordinate periphery" (1986: 12). Thus, empire is effective control, whether formal or informal, of a subordinated society by an imperial society (Sinopoli 1994: 160).

Empires by definition have an international aspect. They can be achieved by force, by political collaboration, or by economic, social, or cultural dependence (Doyle 1986: 45). Even without consensus or clarity of definition, one should be able to describe the types of empires and how they dealt with subordinate entities. Eisenstadt attempted to distinguish between centralized bureaucratic empires that have well-developed military, political, and financial administrative bureaucracies, which attempt to restructure the political relations with the peripheral areas, and more loosely knit patrimonial states that have limited bureaucracy and little or no restructuring of other polities (Eisenstadt 1963; Sinopoli 1995: 6).

There are some generic aspects of empires: they often exhibit dramatic success at the outset in territorial expansion and consolidation, often beginning because of a period of fragmentation or weakness in their regions. However, many will also experience rapid collapse. They often begin because of the need for protection against external threats, economic goals of security or acquisition of valued resources, ideological factors, or as a result of "natural consequences of power differences between polities." Military conquest is often a last resort and is the most costly, involving the massive disruption of production and lives. Coercive diplomacy with the implied threat of force is often a preferred alternative. Even better is the role of ideology in motivating action, since it provides legitimation and explanations for inequalities in subject populations. Empires often appropriate local beliefs and deities, while imposing new imperial beliefs, gods, rulers, and practices. Wallerstein defines empires as a "mechanism for collecting tribute, while political empires are a primitive means of economic domination" (1974/80, 1990). They are often characterized by massive urban material remains, large-scale monumental art and architecture, road systems, cities, and temples.

Unfortunately, scholars of Ancient Near Eastern studies may very well find it difficult not to have an inferiority complex when it comes to the comparative study of empires, since most general studies altogether ignore the evidence from Mesopotamia, the area of the world that was responsible for creating the first known empires (Eisenstadt 1963; Wittfogel 1957). Moreover, the educated public will no doubt think of the ancient oriental empires of Xerxes, Sennacherib, and Nebuchadnezzar as characterized in Classical and Biblical sources as their datum point for understanding Ancient Near Eastern empires. But most Mesopotamian scholars have rejected old ideas about Mesopotamian states being temple-states or totalitarian states and see the latest empires as outgrowths of earlier states.

Before discussing Ancient Near Eastern empires, one has to come to an understanding of still more basic questions concerning the nature of the ancient state. In other words, we cannot discuss Mesopotamian empires before we understand the concept of the Mesopotamian state. In recent years it has been the anthropologist who has attempted to clarify this problem. Baines and Yoffee define the ancient states in the Near East as "the specialized political system of the larger cultural entities that we denominate 'civilization'" and "the central governing institution and social form in a differentiated, stratified society in which rank and status are only partly determined through kinship" (1998: 199). To complicate matters, some say that, technically speaking, there was no Mesopotamian "state" (Baines and Yoffee 1998: 205). This does not help us in our search for the Mesopotamian "empire," to say the least.

To compound this problem, there has been no consensus concerning the nature of Mesopotamian empires, if in fact they existed. Some have even argued that the concept should be restricted to the late empires of the first millennium BCE (Larsen 1979: 91). However, there has been no substantive attempt to define the term for Mesopotamia. The Mesopotamians, of course, had no term for "empire," but they had no term for "religion" either. Both, however, were realities. All of the ideas of expansion, domination, and exploitation are to be found at one level or another. Larsen concludes, at least for Mesopotamia, that an empire is a supranational system of political control, and such a system may have either a city-state or a territorial state at its center (1979: 91). This is understandably a political definition. Certainly the difference between Old Akkadian and Late Assyrian empires is one of degree.

The Akkadian state certainly contained elements of empire in which there was a methodical and permanent occupation of conquered territory, military garrisons, and a division of the territory into provinces which were accountable to the center.

According to Larsen, the three basic Mesopotamian political structures were city-state, territorial state, and empire, all of which were related and concerned to some extent with territorial expansion (1979: 92). Over the duration of Mesopotamian history there is a clear trend toward more complex organizations after recurrent political breakdowns. Empires also tended over time toward larger units and stronger centralization. Thus, Larsen sees a system of city-states and loosely organized empires in the third millennium BCE, territorial states and "federal" empires in the second, and imperial systems in the first that covered the entire Near East. The periods in between are seen as "dark ages," after which reconstruction begins. However, many of these ideas are not in the mainstream any longer in Mesopotamian studies (Michalowski 1993a: 56). In fact, most empires collapsed after only a few generations.

We will be analyzing a number of "empire" periods in Mesopotamian history, including the so-called "informal empire" of Uruk in the fourth millennium BCE (about 4150–3100) (Wright and Rupley 2001: 85–122), the Kish and Syrian or Ebla traditions of the early to mid-third millennium, and the centralized states of Akkad and Ur III in the late third millennium. We will then briefly look at the Old Assyrian, Old Babylonian, and Syrian kingdoms of the early second millennium BCE, and the states of Hatti, Assyria, Mitanni, and Babylon in the mid-late second millennium BCE, to the break-up of those states (around 1200–900 BCE).

The Uruk "Empire"

Since the 1950s, anthropologists have used an evolutionary model to explain the rise of states, consisting of a stepladder model of bands becoming tribes, chiefdoms, and then states. This, however, has been criticized in the past decade. A chiefdom has been described as an autonomous regional unit under a paramount chief. Another model is world-systems, an attempt to explain the development and function of the European capitalist system on a global scale from the outset of the modern age. This has also been employed as an explanation for archaeological studies of secondary state development, especially when discussing Uruk period Mesopotamia (Wallerstein 1974/80; Algaze 1989, 1993). In a nutshell, world-systems (which do not necessarily encompass the entire globe) develop when various polities start to have high levels of interaction, especially through trade. However, the world-systems theorists argue that by definition there is asymmetry in this relationship, with centralized authorities (that is, the "core") dominating the periphery, the outer edges of the world-system, those polities that are less centralized and weaker than the core. According to Stein, the world-systems theory minimizes the roles of polities in the periphery, and local production and exchange, as well as their complexity (1999: 16). Even if one admits that the world-systems approach works for "world empires," one cannot easily determine the nature of these archaic empires (Stein 1999: 43).

A number of scholars have argued that in the fourth millennium BCE, Uruk in Mesopotamia and nearby areas formed a world-system (Algaze 1989, 1993; Frangiapani and Palmieri 1987). With our present knowledge, it appears that southern Mesopotamia created the earliest known urbanized state society, even though this region lacked the natural resources of metals, lumber, and semi-precious stones that were available in neighboring regions of the northwest in the Taurus Mountains in Turkey and the east in the Zagros Mountains in Iran. In fact, there appear to be efforts to procure these materials as early as the Ubaid period of the fifth millennium in southern Mesopotamia, with the development of chiefdoms (Stein 1999: 85; Oates 1993). But the extent of interaction seems to be the northern adoption of ceramic and architectural styles, as well as religious ideology, showing a commonality of beliefs. There do not appear to be large trade exports, however. And the nature of the Ubaidian state is not clear.

It is, however, clear that in different periods, southern Mesopotamian states obtained raw materials with different strategies, including trade, gift exchanges, raiding or tribute, and conquest. The nature of the interaction changed with the nature of the political organization in Mesopotamia. Large-scale trade networks do not appear to have begun until the Middle and Late Uruk period (about 3800–3100 BCE), which is not only evidenced in southern Mesopotamia at Uruk but in southwest Iran at Susa, northern Mesopotamia, Syria, the Zagros, and southeast Anatolia, modern Turkey. By this period, urbanism, centralized authority, complex settlement hierarchies, social stratification, and administrative bureaucracy were all manifested. The fact that there were a number of urban-centered hierarchies in the south and in Iran suggests to some that there were multiple competing polities, and not a unified state.

Sometime in the early fourth millennium BCE, the Uruk polities economically expanded to outlying areas, creating trading colonies to obtain commodities not accessible in the south. This has been considered the first known colonial system. These "colonial" sites, as they are called, exhibit Uruk-type architecture, ceramics, and material evidence of administrative activity. They were strategically located along major trade routes in the Iranian Zagros, on the northern Tigris, and the Habur River headwaters. This has often been called the Uruk Expansion.

While originally thought to be of short duration, it is now clear that this trading enterprise lasted for over six centuries (Pollock 1992). However, over that period the nature of the expansion varied greatly in both numbers of trading posts and areas. For example, on the Syrian Euphrates, where the population was evidently sparse, the Uruk posts were larger and more numerous. It is apparent that the Uruk ceramic repertoire occurs in the outlying regions, and although it is massive in number, it is limited to beveled-rim bowls and other items. In fact, there are only a few sites that have a full repertoire of Uruk ceramics as well as Uruk-type domestic and public architecture, along with cylinder seals, round stamp seals or bullae, tokens, and clay tablets (Sürenhagen 1986b: 26). These include Godin Tepe in Iran, Tell Brak and Nineveh in northern Mesopotamia, Habuba Kabira and Jebel Aruda on the Syrian Euphrates, and Hassek Hoyuk in Anatolia, among others. They appear to have been strategically placed. Stein has argued for four different types of settlements: 1. sites with Uruk material remains (colonies), 2. Mesopotamian residential quarters inside a Late Chalcolithic settlement (for example, Godin Tepe and Hassek Hoyuk, and Hacinebi), 3. small Late Chalcolithic settlements located near an Uruk enclave, and 4. local sites, which have only minimal interaction with Uruk enclaves (1999: 96).

The political relationship between the colonies and the south is unclear, and once again it is not certain whether this was a singular political enterprise, or a group of competing polities. In fact, Hacinebi appears to receive its Uruk material culture from Susa, and not Uruk proper, suggesting that Susa may have been an independent polity (Stein 2001: 302). The various colonies exhibited a heterogeneous network of interaction with the outlying polities, and the relationships, according to Stein, were exchange, emulation, and the establishment of Uruk settlements in the territories of those outlying polities (1999: 101).

There is no concrete evidence that any of the Uruk settlements actually dominated local polities. In fact, it has only been recently that scholars have spent a lot of time studying these peripheral Chalcolithic period settlements. The highland Anatolian areas were composed of smaller-scale, less complex polities, often described as chiefdoms. These include Arslan Tepe, which showed minimal evidence of Uruk culture, especially in regard to a centralized bureaucracy, which used both Anatolian and Mesopotamian styles of administrative technology. Thus, there appears to have been selective local borrowing of Mesopotamian elite symbolism, but little evidence of Mesopotamian imports.

So, was there an informal empire, as argued by Algaze, meaning an economic hegemony, not simply administrative control (1989, 1993)? Algaze argues that the settlements could only have survived if there was an exchange of manufactured goods from Mesopotamia for unprocessed materials from outlying areas (1993: 61). He states that the relationship took different forms, depending on local conditions. Susa was completely colonized by the Uruk peoples, while more distant areas established colonial enclaves that functioned as gateway communities that regularized the flow of trade. Algaze still accepts the core assumptions of the world-systems theory, that is, that there was asymmetrical exchange, core dominance, and trade as the prime mover of social development (Algaze 2001b).

But excavations in southeastern Anatolia show that there was no such asymmetry in the technological development of the outlying areas and Uruk Mesopotamia, but instead technological parity. In fact, this parity seems to have occurred before the Uruk Expansion, not because of it. Many areas reflect a very advanced copper metallurgy at an early date, and thus highly processed products were probably sent south, not unfinished raw materials. The enclaves could not have survived without local cooperation (Stein 1999: 117). Stein has studied the Anatolian site of Hacinebi in the Euphrates River Valley over 1000 km or 620 miles from the Mesopotamian core and has found evidence for social complexity at the site before pre-contact phases, including evidence for stamp seals and seal impressions (implying a complex social hierarchy), long-distance exchange, a high level of craft production, and complex mortuary and public architecture. When Hacinebi had contact with the Uruk culture about 3700 BCE, it is clear that there was a small Mesopotamian colonial center inside a larger Anatolian regional center, analogous to the Old Assyrian trade with Anatolia of nearly two millennia later. Evidence similar to this can be found at Tell Brak in Syria, where fragments of a casemate fortification encircling the large Chacolithic period site have been found, as well as in surveys at Tell al-Hawa on the Sinjar plains, and Arslan Tepe. This trading relationship may have lasted for as long as one half of a millennium, at least implying a peaceful coexistence.

There is also no evidence that the Mesopotamians were able to monopolize the exchange system. Stein argues for a "distance-parity" model in this case (1999: 163). In fact, the two areas, core and periphery, maintained autonomous economic systems, and there was no dramatic change showing a rapid increase in local complexity after the Uruk presence was manifested. However, there were no apparent Anatolian trade colonies in Mesopotamia, explained in part by the geographic nature of the evidence. Mesopotamia, lacking in raw materials, needed the relationship, possibly more than Anatolia. One could even argue that it may have even been southern Mesopotamia that was dependent upon their resource-rich neighbors, and not vice versa.

What was the nature of the Uruk state? Steinkeller has recently argued that Uruk was a religious capital during this period and the subsequent Jemdet Nasr period, based upon a small number of Jemdet Nasr period tablets that reputedly show different Sumerian cities sending resources to Uruk as ritual offerings to Inanna, one of the primary deities of Uruk (2002a). He argues that this is probably a continuation of a situation that began in the Uruk period, and is analogous to the b a l a distribution system that served Nippur as the religious core during the Ur III period. Of course, if there was such a centralized state at Uruk, it is not mentioned in any later Mesopotamian textual traditions.

The creation of buffer areas between large urban polities implies rival centers, rather than a single entity, and armed conflict was depicted in Uruk iconography (Algaze 2001b: 55). Thus, Algaze has modified his argument to state that southern Mesopotamia in the Uruk period was characterized by a small number of competitive polities, each surrounded by a hinterland that provided both labor and material resources. Uruk itself was certainly the largest and probably most powerful state. In fact the competition between states likely was the catalyst for economic expansion into other areas. Political fragmentation may have fostered conflict and exchange between the centers. Algaze sees this as analogous to the European states and the New World in the early modern era and to the Greek city-states of the eighth century BCE (1993: 113).

At any rate, the Uruk states differed from the later expansionist empires and tribute-demanding states in that it appears that the local elites played a role in creating a significant trading system, apparently beneficial to both parties to some extent. The problem may be one of semantics; was the relationship symmetrical or asymmetrical? Were the Uruk polities creating "trading post empires"? Steinkeller argues that since Sumer did not have such a powerful infrastructure until the late third millennium BCE, it is hard to imagine that it existed at such an early date (1993: 110–11). He argues that it was a commercial enterprise, analogous to the Old Assyrian/Kanish trading mechanism of the Old Babylonian period.

By the late Uruk period there was evidence of a breakdown of the southern economy. City walls were now found at Uruk, as they were at Habuba Kabira and

Godin Tepe, along with settlement pattern changes. Sürenhagen proposed that the outlying areas became hostile and cut off agricultural supplies (1986b). Steinkeller theorizes that since this was a commercial enterprise, movements of new people in the Early Dynastic I period may have ended it, that is, with proto-Akkadians coming in like later Amorites (1993: 116). But this cannot be easily substantiated.

Pre-Sargonic "Empires" in Mesopotamia?

The Jemdet Nasr (around 3100–2900 BCE) and Early Dynastic (about 2900–2300 BCE) periods are no easier to define in terms of political development. The traditional view is that in the Early Dynastic period Sumer consisted of city-states that likely controlled one or more urban centers and a hinterland. The states appear to have been linked to each other in a league that had a religious aspect, but it is not certain that there were any political affiliations. Each state had divinely sanctioned borders that separated the different polities. In a sense, this made expansion or even unification difficult, since each city-state was divinely ordained. The city ruler was the representative of the city god or goddess. There was thus a strong tradition of small states centered on a capital city and its patron, or matron, deity and associated temple (Hallo 1960).

One of the first discussions about the political situation in prehistoric and Early Dynastic Mesopotamia came from Jacobsen, who argued for a large city-state institution that unified all of Sumer into a single political and religious entity, known as the Kengir League, centered around the city of Nippur. Aside from textual evidence from later Mesopotamian traditions, Jacobsen claimed that a group of texts from Uruk III, Early Dynastic Fara, Abu Salabikh, and Old Babylonian Ur, and so-called "city seals" from Early Dynastic Ur contain many depictions of city names which imply a formal arrangement (Jacobsen 1957: 106–9). Thus, the seals, which are dated to the Early Dynastic I period, may show the existence of a league of neighboring cities centered on Nippur in this period, but this is far from clear (Steinkeller 2002a: 257). Matthews has argued that these seals indicate the existence of a "cooperative institutionalized grouping of a number of cities," but is unclear as to their nature, although he argues for a formal military and defensive league (1993: 49). Others have seen the seals as indicating a complex system of storehouses or trade associations. A recently published text from Tell Uqair has the same city seal that appears on the Jemdet Nasr documents studied by Matthews (Green 1986). The implication is that the owner may belong to a supra-city-state institution. If this is correct, it would be the first tangible evidence for a Pan-Babylonian organizational scheme in the Uruk III/Jemdet Nasr periods.

Possibly this organization involved a number of cities that were required to provide ritual offerings for the chief deity or deities of Uruk. The fact that Uruk was so big and played a key role in the development of writing and scribal learning should not be surprising. The propagandistic Sumerian King List spread the doctrine that only one Mesopotamian city-state ruled the whole area at any given period. Even though the document created its own fictional past, the document itself has been said to have its own historical integrity, and it should be called the Mesopotamian city list, where cities were the focal point of political and social struggle in the absence of centralized polities (Yoffee 1993a: 305). The city seals were an acknowledgement of this fact (Yoffee 1993b: 66). They may have had nothing to do with political or economic patterns. Certainly it is true that there was a shared sense of Mesopotamian cultural unity, exhibited by a shared standard literary language, pantheon, and textual tradition, which may be the only thing the seals represent.

During the early third millennium BCE northern Mesopotamia had a substantially different political economy from the south. This region, a dry-farming zone depending on rainfall rather than irrigation, was composed of a series of rival complex chiefdoms that controlled the agricultural surpluses (Schwartz 1994: 153). But these states looked to the more urban south for ideological legitimization. Schwartz argues that agricultural intensification in the north, as well as emulation of southern socio-cultural and political forms may have played a key role in the eventual transformation of the chiefdoms of the Ninevite V period, named after the painted incised pottery recovered in the fifth level of the prehistoric sounding at Nineveh from about 3100–2500 BCE. These states changed into urbanized societies later in the third millennium BCE, between the period of Uruk colonies and the Ebla state around 2600 BCE (1994: 154).

There is evidence of local urbanization and monumental architecture during the Uruk period at Hamukar, Tell el-Hawa, and Tell Brak, and thus the Ninevite V period exhibits a case of an aborted secondary state formation (Schwartz 1994: 164). The new centers were between 40 and 100 hectares or 99–247 acres in size across northern Mesopotamia and Syria, including Tell Chuera, Tell Brak, Tell Mozan/ Urkesh, Tell Leilan, Tell Taya, and Titriş Höyük in southeast Anatolia. This period had little evidence for monumental architecture, writing, and urbanization before the mid-third millennium BCE, with the exception of Mari and possibly Terqa.

Schwartz (1994) argues that during the Ninevite period, polities in the north were more complex than previously imagined and can be described with the chiefdom model proposed by Service (1975). These chiefdoms are described as regional polities that have a relatively modest degree of social and economic organization, hierarchical administration, and elite control of surpluses. This was manifested in the variation of mortuary furnishings and architecture, large-scale storage of staples in granaries, and the frequency of cylinder seals and impressions.

By the mid-third millennium BCE Syria and northern Mesopotamia had become heavily urbanized. Gelb posited a northern Mesopotamian tradition centered around the city of Kish (1981, 1992). He argued for a Semitic power in the north at least two centuries before the Sargonic empire, rivaling the Sumerians in the south. Of course, the discoveries at Mari and Ebla have furthered our understanding of the Kish civilization, causing scholars to recognize that it was geographically far reaching, at least to the coast of the Mediterranean Sea. There was thus a highly developed civilization with its own cities, languages, literary traditions, and polities, somewhat apart from the Sumerian south.

According to the Sumerian King List, the first dynasty of Kish held sway over all of Sumer after the world-destroying primordial flood. Other Kish dynasties were mentioned in the list, while kings and the city itself were also mentioned in scattered references in Sumerian royal inscriptions of the third millennium BCE. There were also other cities with dynasties, including Akshak and Hamazi. The rulers of these dynasties bore Semitic names (Old Akkadian or Eblaite), and a few had Sumerian names. Though the rulers and dating of king lists are disputed, they may reveal a kernel of historical truth about the domination of Kish over the region. From Kish Gelb dates the earliest texts, which were administrative in nature, to the pre-Fara period (before about 2600 BCE). However, they were probably composed by Sumerian scribes.

Ebla and Mari in the north and Kish and Abu Salabikh in the south were linked by scribal contacts. The Early Dynastic Sumerian kings who claimed to have defeated Kish assumed the title King of Kish. These included Mesanepada of Ur (a votive inscription of this king was found at Mari), as well as kings of Lagash and Uruk. Mesalim, described as King of Kish, arbitrated a boundary dispute between Lagash and Umma, possibly around 2500 BCE. In fact, except for Mesalim, all of the rulers who assumed this title had a close relationship with Inanna, but not with Enlil, chief god of Sumer (Maeda 1981). Eannatum is the first known Sumerian to have taken the title of King of Kish. It is not certain whether this title was officially recognized at Nippur, the religious center. In sum, there are very few attestations of rulers who took the title of King of Kish before Sargon. At any rate, the King of Kish was usually described as a mighty ruler able to defeat enemy lands. Sargon's "King of the land" was a broader title, which marked a dramatic step in the developing political ideology of empire (Maeda 1981: 13).

There is no concrete evidence of a Kish empire, however. Kish, as well as Ebla and Mari, appears to have been an autonomous state. But there were cultural similarities, even in certain aspects of systems of weights and measures, year dates, number systems, month names, religion, and Semitic personal names, but not in the area of material culture, law, or art (Gelb 1981: 72). Gelb has argued that the same Semitic language was used in writing at both Mari and Ebla (1992: 124). It does appear that Mari was the catalyst for the Kish civilization that was transmitted to Ebla and northern Syria (Gelb 1992: 201).

Following Gelb, Steinkeller has even argued that there may have been two different political systems in Mesopotamia, both of which endured to the middle of the second millennium BCE (1993). This highly interpretative scenario, however, is very controversial, and has been subject to considerable criticism.

Steinkeller argues that during the Early Dynastic I period, central Mesopotamia was occupied by Semitic proto-Akkadians who created a political and socio-economic system different from that found in the south. For example, there may not have been independent city-states in the north, as in the Sumerian south. It is possible the north at least by Early Dynastic II/III was a single political organism, all the way to Mari, with the focal point at Kish (Steinkeller 1993: 117). There is also a tradition of a war between Uruk and Kish in the literary composition Gilgamesh and Agga, as well as the Sumerian King List, which argues that Kish was the earliest historical dynasty (Steinkeller 1993: 119). Kish was mentioned in Ebla economic texts, while very few other eastern cities were mentioned. Steinkeller argues that this shows a preeminence of Kish. The northerners, according to Steinkeller, also appear to have been more "secular." The King of Kish was a title that even the southerners coveted, implying an autocratic rule, rather than southern control over the north (Steinkeller 1993: 120). The temple domain appears to have been less important in the north, and private ownership of land flourished and may have spread to the south from there.

In this scenario, pre-Sargonic Ebla is similar to the Kish model, not the Sumerian south. Ebla, as well as Mari, also had a stratified society, like Kish, and it has even been argued that there was an "urban oligarchy" in the north, spanning more than a millennium (Steinkeller 1993: 124). Thus the traditions of northern Mesopotamia and Syria appeared to share a common origin. It is possible that contact with the north led the Sumerian south to create more powerful royal institutions, with rulers at Ur and then at Lagash attempting to assume ascendancy over neighboring states. This, of course, is very speculative. By Early Dynastic IIIb, Uruk had claimed rule over Ur, and then a limited rule over the entire south, under Lugalzagessi, who was called "King of the land," implying control of the world outside of Sumer. Lugalzagessi did not create an empire out of the blue, as once thought, but his empire was the product of an evolutionary phenomenon (Charvat 1978). However, it appears that he held primacy within the existing city-state structure. Starting from Umma, he was able to claim rule at Ur and Uruk either by force or dynastic arrangement, and then Lagash, while taking Nippur and its priesthood. He was apparently the first ruler to have unified the whole south, and he claimed rule all the way to the Mediterranean Sea. Because of ideological constraints, he probably never thought of a unified state, although a northerner was to forge such a state soon thereafter. Thus, Steinkeller argues that the Sargonic Empire was not an innovation, since some of the tendencies of Sargon's state (autocratic rule, centralized government, and ideology of conquest) were already in place (1993: 129).

The First World Empire

We can now finally turn to the person who is traditionally viewed as the first empire builder, Sargon of Akkad. Initially, it appears that Sargon began his conquests from Kish in a manner similar to the Early Dynastic expansionists, creating a confederacy of city-states against an enemy. With the defeat of Lugalzagessi, he was able to bring most of the south under his control. He then was able to create his own ideology of domination. He also built a new capital city, Akkad, installed his daughter as high priestess of Ur, and established the principle that only the ruler of the whole area had the prerogative to do this. He also appointed royal officials who served alongside the rulers of the conquered city-states. The royal officials were charged with breaking down administrative barriers and providing material support to the army.

Sargon took the title King of Kish, giving it new meaning, as it now was understood in Akkadian as king of totality, from *kiššatu* "inhabited world, totality." Sargon's grandson, Naram-Sin, added a divinity marker to his name and the title "king of the four quarters" (that is, the earth) (Michalowski 1993a: 88). The emperor was no longer simply a chief, but now had a different essence from other humans, and was called to world dominion. Shar-kali-sharri, a later king, whose name means "king of all kings," went back to being simply the King of Akkad, however. At any rate, Sargon dispensed with previous views, like the king as a shepherd of the people and representative of a city god.

Thus, it is not so easy to defend the idea that the Sargonic Empire was a result of a continuous evolutionary development from village to chiefdom, to city-state, to regional state, to empire. On the other hand, it can be seen that the Akkadian state was not a novelty when compared to Ebla, Uruk, or the early Sumerian states. Many of the charismatic aspects of kingship in the Early Dynastic period were part of a search for an "ideological center," as Michalowski calls it, which created the context for Sargon (1987: 67). Of course, when looking at the contemporary royal inscriptions, monumental art and architecture, and material remains, one can give primacy to Sargon and his successors, although much of our information comes from later traditions, which are suspect at best as historical sources. However, was Sargon's state truly an "empire" that had taken control of a large area of formerly separate city-states?

It is not an easy task to detect Sargon's influence in Iran, Syria, or the Gulf area (Michalowski 1993a: 75–6). Naram-Sin claimed to have conquered Ebla and Armanum, perhaps also in Syria, a feat that he claimed had never before been accomplished. However, Sargon had made the same claim, and the archaeological information is unclear. It is possibly better understood at Tell Brak/Nagar on the Upper Habur. There were at least two Akkadian occupations at the site, one of which built a palace of Naram-Sin. There were traces of a fire, after which there is evidence of Akkadian occupation during the reign of Shar-kali-sharri (Michalowski 1993a: 80). However, most of the material remains at Tell Brak were of local origin, and were not Sargonic. Tell Leilan also has some Akkadian period remains, and there is evidence of population redistribution (that is, Tell Mohammed Diyab, near Tell Leilan, shrank from 50 to 10 hectares or 124 to 25 acres). There is also evidence of a massive city wall at Tell Leilan, intensification of agricultural production, recognizable Akkadian pottery, and agricultural redistribution (Foster 1993b: 59–68). At Tell Mozan/Urkesh Akkadian tablets have been found which show that the Akkadians probably controlled the Habur triangle for a generation or two, but there is no evidence of any longer period of occupation. Certainly there was no war devastation in the area. This was only evidenced with the collapse of the Akkadian state a bit later, when the whole area witnessed a climactic destruction. The Akkadians were also in Assyria, especially at Nineveh and Assur. It is more difficult, however, to see evidence of Akkadian involvement as far away from lower Mesopotamia as Mari on the Euphrates. There was Akkadian evidence at Susa in Iran, where there was a strong administrative presence (Foster 1993b: 61). The fragments of Akkadian evidence in southeastern Anatolia do not prove a permanent presence in the region.

There were signs of instability in the Akkadian state from the outset. The uneasy sharing of power between the royal subordinates and the conquered rulers led to power struggles. The very success of the Akkadians in the north galvanized the conquered peoples to form powerful defensive alliances.

This empire had a great effect on all of Mesopotamian civilization, which was reflected in later historical traditions as shown in chronicles, legends, and omens.

Two figures in particular were represented, Sargon and Naram-Sin. Oddly enough, Sargon was praised, while Naram-Sin, certainly the most successful king in the dynasty, was condemned as unworthy, and was doomed to defeat and destruction because of his sinful pride. Interestingly, although harking back to the remote past of the legendary Uruk kings such as Gilgamesh, Šulgi of the Ur III dynasty implicitly emulated Akkadian tactics, at least in claiming divinity and organizing the state. This approach provided a broader vision of a societal center, which had previously been organized around the city, temple, and city ruler.

The Ur III Centralized State

The next multinational empire in Mesopotamia during the Ur III period (about 2112–2004 BCE) reached its height in two generations, and spectacularly fell within a century. The founder Ur-Nammu claimed hegemony over both Sumer and Akkad, although there is some doubt of his control over northern Babylonia (Steinkeller 1987a: 19). We can call this state an empire by virtue of the fact that it did conquer peripheral regions in the north and east. Sumer was the center of the empire, not just Ur. For the Sargonic kings, the main thrust of expansion appears to have been in Syria. But, because of the strong Amorite presence in Syria, the Ur III kings had a defensive posture toward that area and directed their efforts at expansion toward the mountainous areas east of Mesopotamia. They invoked the remote past of legendary Uruk kings, such as Gilgamesh, who had campaigned in that direction.

Ur-Nammu's son Šulgi, like Naram-Sin, was the true founder of Ur III organizational power. There was an effort to imitate the Akkadian kings, which was not difficult, since they had left monuments that presumably still could be seen by later political elites. During Šulgi's reign Sumer was forged into a highly centralized bureaucratic state. Šulgi was successful in having the king depicted as a god, in reorganizing weights and measures, in making a new calendar, and possibly even in synthesizing the law code once attributed to Ur-Nammu (Steinkeller 1987a: 20–2). He also created a standing army, a taxation system, and a unified administrative system for all of southern Mesopotamia. It has been argued that the Ur III state was the most centralized of any of the early Mesopotamian empires. The former Sumerian city-states were now provinces of the Ur III state.

Second Millennium States

The collapse of the Ur III state was gradual in that governors of outlying provinces began to assert their autonomy from the central administration. By the end, these governors had set up their own dynasties, which denied supplies to the capital. The central state was thus vulnerable to outside attack from Iran, and the Elamites invaded (Jacobsen 1953a).

After 2000 BCE rival states struggled for political power, and many of them were controlled by Amorite dynasties. The next major attempts at empire were about two centuries later, with two ephemeral states founded upon the personality of the kings, Šamši-Adad I (reigned 1814–1781 BCE), an Assyrian king of Amorite descent who was apparently a usurper, and Hammurabi (reigned 1792–1750 BCE), a Babylonian king also of Amorite descent. Šamši-Adad claimed to have conquered all of northern Mesopotamia. He ruled from Shubat-Enlil (most likely Tell Leilan) in Syria. Like his Assyrian successors, he attempted to control the trade routes to both south and north. But the Anatolian colonies were discontinued soon after Šamši-Adad. He had made a conscious attempt at connecting himself with the Akkadian dynasty, claimed descent from Akkadian kings, and rebuilt a temple built by Manishtushu, son of Sargon. However, his empire died with him, as his two sons were unable to keep this large territorial state together.

By Hammurabi's tenth year and his conquest of neighboring Larsa, he was able to unify southern Mesopotamia for the first time since the Ur III dynasty. It is not easy to verify his claims of ruling all of Mesopotamia, including Assur and Nineveh. His system was apparently a loose confederation of states under control of the Babylonian king. Hammurabi's successors continued to rule a smaller state in the south.

There do not appear to be any major centralized states in the Near East until the fifteenth century. Then the international political scene was dominated by Egypt and Mitanni, located in northern Mesopotamia. Although there are no royal Mitanni archives preserved, it is evident from Egyptian, Hittite, and Mesopotamian sources that Mitanni was a political term used to describe a confederation of Hurrian-speaking states and vassals. Each of the vassals had its own king who was bound to Mitanni by a treaty sworn under oath.

It appears that by 1500 BCE Mitanni had expanded into most of Syria under the reigns of Paratarna and Saushtatar, and likely came into conflict with the expansionist policies of Thutmose III of Egypt (reigned 1504–1450 BCE). Later Mitanni kings were known from the Amarna Letters as engaging in diplomatic relations with Egypt, including marriage alliances, probably resulting from the rising powers of Hittites and Assyrians, which threatened the existence of the Mitanni state. Mitanni did become somewhat fragmented during the reign of Tushratta and suffered defeat at the hands of the Hittite king Suppiluliuma. Thus after 1350 BCE the state of Mitanni ceased to play a major role in Ancient Near Eastern politics, although it was a buffer state for nearly two more centuries. The Middle Assyrian empires of Tukulti-Ninurta I (about 1243–1207 BCE) and Tiglath-pileser I (about 1114–1076 BCE) were precursors to the great Assyrian world state of the first millennium, which will be considered in another essay.

Although it is apparent that it is difficult to define the concept of empire, let alone the state, it is true that the norms of thinking about empires were forged in the Tigris–Euphrates valley over five thousand years ago and were perfected to an extent by the Sargonic kings in the third millennium BCE. The early empires were different from the first millennium Ancient Near Eastern and Classical empires in degree but not in kind. Though not as competent, the early empires did contain the elements of empire as we understand it, including permanent occupation of conquered territory, military garrisons, economic exploitation of dominated areas, and an effort to provide ideological justification for their control. Thus any study of the nature of empires must begin with the early states of the Ancient Near East.

FURTHER READING

For empires in general, see Doyle 1986, Eisenstadt 1963, Sinopoli 1994, 1995, and Wallerstein 1974/80. For the Uruk period expansion, see Algaze 1993, Rothman 2001, and Stein 1999. For the pre-Sargonic period and the Akkadian empire, see Liverani 1993a and Steinkeller 2002a. For the Ur III and second millennium BCE empires, see Gibson and Biggs 1987 and Larsen 1979.

CHAPTER 4

World Hegemony, 900–300 BCE

Paul-Alain Beaulieu

Between the ninth and the fourth century BCE the Near East was ruled by a succession of states which fully deserve the label of "empire." The first one was Assyria, which after a period of growth and crisis between about 930 and 745 BCE achieved the true status of centralized empire under Tiglath-pileser III (745–727 BCE), eventually enabling the Sargonid dynasty (721–610 BCE) to exercise its hegemony over the entire region. The second one, Babylonia (610–539 BCE), immediately emerged from the ruins of the Assyrian empire and fell heir to most of its territory. The third one, the Persian or Achaemenid empire (539–331 BCE), replaced the Babylonian empire almost overnight in the autumn of 539 BCE and grew to rule vast territories from Afghanistan in the east to Thracia in Europe and Nubia in northeastern Africa for a period of two centuries. Finally, after his conquest of the Persian empire Alexander the Great laid the foundations for an even larger Greco-Macedonian empire which quickly disintegrated after his death, but by the end of the fourth century the royal house founded by his general Seleucus had firmly established its rule over the core of Alexander's empire.

The first question that arises concerns the very concept of "world hegemony," especially how such hegemony was understood in the native political vocabulary of the Ancient Near East. The second issue is whether we can assert that the period extending between 900 and 300 BCE was characterized by a new phase of world hegemony which differed substantially from what had preceded, both in our view and in the ancient perception. There certainly was a view current in antiquity that during the first millennium BCE the known world had experienced a succession of hegemonies on a scale not seen before, which had succeeded each other without any intervening period of political fragmentation. Such views were circulated at least as early as the Hellenistic period, and they found a literary and spiritual expression in the Book of Daniel, which envisioned in the metaphorical dream and vision of chapters 2 and 7 a succession of four hegemonies: the Babylonians, the Medes, the Persians, and finally the Greco-Macedonians, each kingdom inferior to the preceding, the disintegration of the last one leading to an eschatological climax (Hartman and Di Lella 1978: 29–42).

The geopolitical vision of the period is exemplified by the Babylonian map of the world, in which Babylon stands only slightly away from the center of a roughly circular world, while the text as a whole exhibits a remarkably limited geographic horizon (Horowitz 1998: 20–42). The map can roughly be dated to the eighth or early seventh century, and the vision it presents accommodated both Babylonian and Assyrian pretensions to hegemony, as Mesopotamia and its immediate surroundings were portrayed as coextensive with the civilized world.

Two traits stand out that made the first millennium empires radically different from what preceded. First, there was a departure from the previous imperial models in the level of structural transformation which first millennium empires imposed on both the imperial core and the conquered periphery in the course of their expansion. Second, whereas the previous empires had been rather ephemeral, Assyria in the first millennium eventually grew into something not seen before, not only in scale, but also in a distinctively new imperial structure, its ideological expression, and especially its lasting success.

Like Rome, the history of Assyria was not only the history of the growth of an empire, but also the history of the growth of an imperial idea. Although the Assyrian empire eventually collapsed under the combined assault of the Medes and the rebellious Babylonians, the structure it had created ultimately survived because there was no serious attempt at returning to the previous state of political fragmentation. Assyria's enduring contribution was to create the irreversible fact of empire and to inculcate it so deeply in the political culture of the Near East that no alternative model could successfully challenge it, in fact almost up to the modern era. Therein lies the radical departure from the early forms of Near Eastern imperialism.

The Assyrian Empire

What seems most remarkable about Assyria is its dynamism in the ninth century, at a time when almost every other region of the Near East and the Eastern Mediterranean was still reeling from the economic and demographic depression which had accompanied the transition to the Iron Age around 1000 BCE. The ability of the early Neo-Assyrian kings to levy masses of native troops for their program of conquest, and to launch in addition a program of recolonization of the areas formerly lost to the Aramean invaders, probably means that the country experienced at that time a very strong demographic growth. Assyria's ninth-century revival culminated with Assurnasirpal II (883–859 BCE) and his son Shalmanezer III (858–824 BCE), who transferred the royal residence from Assur to the more northern site of Kalhu (modern Nimrud) and created a provincial system that later became the backbone of the empire and the guarantee of its stability.

Assurnasirpal's foundation of a new capital and royal palace at Kalhu was later emulated by Sargon II at Dur-Sharrukin and Sennacherib at Nineveh, while Tiglath-pileser III, Esarhaddon, and Assurbanipal built palaces in a previously existing administrative center. To build a new capital was a momentous decision for the future of the Assyrian monarchy. It increased the remoteness of the king, shut up in an immense palace and seemingly totally inaccessible to the majority of Assyrians, more and more resembling the cardboard image of the oriental despot dear to the European romantic imagination. Yet at the same time it favored the individualization of the expression of power. Every king with a dominant personality and sufficient resources would now try to put his own imprint on the ideological expression of the monarchy, especially the palace relief decorations, almost exclusively centered on the king as hero and embodiment of the Assyrian state. This focus on the king's heroic and creative person is typically Assyrian and is also observed in the realm of historiography with the elaboration of the genre of annals (Tadmor 1997). These were records, organized chronologically, of the king's conquests and other exploits, narrated in the first person.

The construction of Kalhu is also very significant because it provides the first important example of the systematic restructuring that became a dominant characteristic of the Assyrian state under Tiglath-pileser III and the Sargonids. In this case Assurnasirpal's restructuring efforts focused more on the center than the periphery, which under his reign was still largely a territory to be raided rather than controlled permanently. But the riches amassed thanks to the relentless campaigns to the west enabled him to muster enough resources and manpower to turn Kalhu into an impressive capital, peopled significantly both with old-stock Assyrians and deportees from the newly conquered regions, surely a symptom of a new vision of power and the state.

With Shalmanezer III (858–824 BCE) the policies of Assurnasirpal were largely carried on, with an increased effort to reduce the various Aramean and other states of the Levant to Assyrian clients. Shalmanezer III also consolidated and extended the provincial system in the regions east of the Euphrates, within Assyria's traditional sphere of interest. This provincial system, which probably originated in the creation of a network of forts and supply centers for the annual campaigns of the army, was Assyria's most original contribution to imperial governance. Already the Assyrian state was radically departing from the previous empires created by the Hittites of central Anatolia and the Hurrians of Mitanni in northern Syria, which were little more than feudal assemblages of vassal kingdoms and some directly administered territory under the loose control of the royal household. The new provincial system tended to blend and Assyrianize the conquered lands, and by making the imperial administration more efficient, it paved the way for increased interventionism. Also, in spite of the occasional co-optation of local elites in the Assyrian control system and the fact that provincial capitals were often the former seats of local dynasties, Assyrianization of a region was usually achieved by two different means: at the top by the removal of the former ruling groups and the appointment of Assyrians from the Assyrian heartland to administer the province, and at the bottom by deportation of population and relocation of production centers which destroyed local allegiances and often seriously altered the economic character of a region.

A good example of Assyrianization in the ninth century is Til Barsib (modern Tell Ahmar) on the Euphrates in Syria, the capital of the former Aramean kingdom of Bit-Adini, which was integrated into Assyrian territory by Shalmanezer not too long after his first campaigns in the West and renamed "Port Shalmanezer" (Sader 1987:

47–98). Shalmanezer eventually captured Ahunu, the leader of Bit-Adini, and claimed to have deported 22,000 of his people to Assyria. A large Assyrian palace was built on the acropolis of Til Barsib, and its painted wall decoration depicted scenes typical of Assyrian palaces of the first millennium, with no concessions to local taste and culture. This iconography demonstrated a will to export the Assyrian center and duplicate it in the provinces, a will to transform and to "make Assyrian."

This will to make Assyrian was transmitted in the language of annals and royal inscriptions by a series of expressions which kept a very strong ideological distinction between the "land of Assur" and the outside world, composed first of client states bound to the Assyrian king by various types of agreements and treaties, and then of outlying states not yet reduced to vassal status. Modern historians often make a distinction between Assyria proper and the Assyrian empire, Assyria referring specifically to the small triangular region on the upper Tigris River which formed the original homeland of the Assyrians. Yet in the native political vocabulary no such distinction was made except in a rather allusive manner. When a conquered region, however distant from the center, was turned into a province, it became part of Assyria, the "land of Assur," and the people were made into Assyrian subjects. The deportation of foreign populations, mostly Arameans, to the Assyrian core, and the exportation of Assyrian administrators, architecture, and culture to the provinces, made Assyrianization a reality by gradually eradicating differences between areas of the empire that were previously culturally distinct, to the extent that the northern Syrian city of Harran, well outside Assyria's original area, could become the last Assyrian capital after the fall of Nineveh in 612 BCE. That Syria itself probably owes its name to Assyria vividly testifies to the ancient perception that the two regions eventually fused into one country (Frye 1992). The process was also reciprocal, in that it was accompanied by a gradual aramaicization of the original Assyrian homeland with the influx of deportees from the west.

Assurnasirpal II and Shalmanezer III only initiated the process of homogenization, and Assyria was to undergo a serious crisis before territorial expansion and consolidation would resume. The crisis period, which lasted more than seventy-five years (827–745 BCE), started with a rebellion in the Assyrian heartland which lasted several years and is usually interpreted as a reaction of the old nobility against the expansion of the provincial system which put forward a new class of royal favorites. And indeed, after the suppression of the rebellion, the influence of this new nobility of high officials increased dramatically, especially the influence of the commander-in-chief of the army, whose power often overshadowed the authority of the king. The northern state of Urartu posed a serious challenge to Assyrian hegemony, and together with its North Syrian allies it dominated the trading networks, creating serious economic problems for Assyria. The extent of actual royal authority was at times quite limited, while some provincial governors acted as nearly independent monarchs. If stronger factors of disintegration had been at work, Assyria might have disappeared altogether, or shrunk into complete insignificance as it had at the end of the Middle Assyrian period about 1076 BCE, except that this time it might have happened for good. But once more the country resurrected, and Assyrian expansion started on a new footing.

Historians generally view Tiglath-pileser III (745–727 BCE) as the real founder of the Assyrian empire, although it is obvious that in many respects he only systematized and expanded older administrative practices. One important step he took was to remodel the provincial system, first by splitting the very large provinces, thereby preventing leading high officials from becoming too powerful, and second by expanding the system for the first time west of the Euphrates, where a large number of provinces were created in the wake of the campaigns against the small kingdoms of Syria and the Levant. By abolishing the old border between the land of Assur and the client kingdoms of the west, Tiglath-pileser in fact inaugurated the true imperial phase of Assyria, and after him almost every new conquered land would automatically become a province, pushing the borders of Assyria far beyond the limits reached by any previous Near Eastern empire. Expansion did not focus exclusively on the west, however. Urartu was relentlessly attacked until it was finally neutralized at the end of the eighth century. Tiglath-pileser also invaded Babylonia and ascended the Babylonian throne under the name Pulu, inaugurating the principle of a double Mesopotamian monarchy. This final wave of expansion brought Assyria close to the borders of Egypt and Elam, which also fell prey to Assyrian territorial appetites during the reigns of Esarhaddon and Assurbanipal in the seventh century.

The rapid expansion of the imperial control system from 745 to the fall of Nineveh in 612 posed a number of logistical and ideological challenges which received various answers and attempted solutions. The dominant traits of this new phase were the intensification of the system of deportations and forced resettlements, a planned policy of economic rationalization affecting primarily the provinces, and finally the emergence of an imperial culture celebrating artistic and literary achievements and presenting Assyrian rule in a more grandiose, and sometimes even magnanimous light.

Mass deportations of the population of newly conquered regions were not new in Assyria, and were not even an Assyrian invention. However, the scale on which they were practiced by Tiglath-pileser III and his successors so much surpassed everything in previous recorded history that they must be reckoned as a new phenomenon, almost as a new means of government. The inscriptions of Tiglath-pileser III, Sargon II, and Sennacherib alone mention more than 1,000,000 deportees, which accounts for more than 80 percent of all the people displaced between 745 BCE and the end of the empire (Oded 1979). Even keeping in mind that these numbers must be used with caution, they still convey a certain order of magnitude which reveals the scale of the new policy (De Odorico 1995: 170–6).

Deportations affected everyone, from kings to menial workers. While breaking local resistance and obliterating rival centers of power had been their primary aim before the eighth century, during the imperial period they seem to have also become a tool of economic rationalization. Deportees were resettled where manpower was needed, especially in Assyria proper, which appears to have suffered from a demographic slump in the late eighth and seventh centuries. This of course further increased the cosmopolitan character of the Assyria heartland, especially that of its bloated palatial capitals, and at the same time allowed non-Assyrians, especially Arameans, to gain access to positions of responsibility and eventually to develop some allegiance to the empire (Garelli 1982; Tadmor 1982). Under Tiglath-pileser III the Assyrian army began to include vassal contingents which turned the army from a purely Assyrian one, based on the royal military service, into an imperial one. The influx of foreigners must have created some unease among native Assyrians, whose attitude toward them probably wavered between acceptance and mistrust, but in this respect Assyria was not different from Rome where the process of Romanization of the conquered populations inevitably led to their influx into the center, even at the imperial level, generating similar attitudes of recognition and hostility.

Efforts at economic rationalization were particularly well documented in the Levant, the eastern coast of the Mediterranean Sea. While entire areas like the kingdom of Israel underwent planned depopulation, others expanded demographically and economically because they were targeted by the Assyrian administration to fulfill a specific role in the imperial structure. This was especially true of the Phoenician and Philistine ports which received favorable treatment because of their privileged role in bringing the empire into contact with the larger trading networks of the Mediterranean. A particularly interesting case is the inland Philistine city of Ekron, which vastly increased in size after 700 to become the largest known olive oil production center in antiquity (Gitin 1997). Such industrial concentration can only have happened from Assyrian impetus, and the reason for this concentration may have been to facilitate production and especially distribution of the products, the logistics of transportation favoring one large production center over a myriad of smaller ones. It also appears that some textile production was concentrated at Ekron to make maximal use of the facilities and manpower located there, since the olive oil production season lasted only four months.

At the cultural and ideological level several new traits emerged. One outstanding achievement was the library of cuneiform texts assembled by King Assurbanipal (668–627 BCE) in Nineveh, the largest collection of literary and scholarly texts ever found in Mesopotamia (Leichty 1988a; Potts 2000). In its comprehensiveness and organization it compares, though on a smaller scale, with the other great libraries of the ancient world such as those of Alexandria in Egypt and Pergamon in Turkey in the Hellenistic period. Assurbanipal himself claimed that he had been trained in the scribal art and could read difficult texts, "inscriptions from before the flood," meaning from primordial time, and his personal involvement in the library is evident from the colophons, which contained detailed information on the texts and labeled them as his personal property (Hunger 1968: 97–108). In all respects, but especially in its ambition to gather in one single place the entire knowledge of a civilization, this library must be reckoned as a typical prestige achievement of a self-confident imperial culture at its zenith. A similar impression is gained from the stone reliefs commissioned by Assurbanipal for his palace. In their refinement, thematic breadth, and boldness of treatment they surpass everything produced before in this medium, ranking as one of the superlative artistic achievements of ancient Mesopotamia.

A new concept of space appeared in art and texts. We now find statements that Assyrian kings ruled from the horizon to the heights of heaven, claiming distant conquests located on the edge of the world where people never heard the name of the Assyrian king, or whose existence the Assyrians hardly suspected (Tadmor 1999).

Inscriptions showed an increasing interest in giving distances in miles to convey an idea of the size of the empire and the remoteness of its outlying regions. In art Sennacherib commissioned reliefs abandoning the former flat, one-dimensional, and strip-like display of imagery for a more complex iconography favoring expansive vistas and bird's-eye perspective, a new spatial arrangement no doubt influenced by the widening and deepening horizon of the empire (Russell 1991: 191–222). Science and particularly cosmology were also impacted, with texts now measuring cosmic distances in hundreds of thousands of miles, thereby sharply departing from the tradition which viewed the cosmos as a rather small place, measurable and quantifiable on the same scale as the earth (Horowitz 1998: 177–86).

In religion important changes also took place under Sennacherib (704–681 BCE), who in the wake of his campaigns of destruction in Babylonia imposed a number of religious reforms which aimed primarily at co-opting the Marduk theology created by the Babylonian intellectual elites in the previous centuries into an imperial theology exalting the god Assur (Machinist 1984/85). These reforms also gave primacy to the cities of Assur and Nineveh as cosmic centers, thereby stripping Babylon of that role. The pivotal status of Babylon had been propagated by an array of myths, rituals, and other religious texts which proclaimed its role as center of the universe. This dogma created serious ideological problems for the Assyrians because of their cultural dependence on Babylonian scholarship and literature. The ideological conflict worsened as the rulers of Assyria faced an increasing urge to resolve the contradiction of ruling a world empire from Kalhu, Dur-Sharrukin, or Nineveh, while fostering a literary tradition exalting the centrality of Babylon, a conflict further exacerbated by the staunch opposition of Babylonians to Assyrian rule. Among the various solutions, alternately violent and peaceful, but none satisfactory, Sennacherib's destruction of Babylon was undoubtedly the most radical one.

Another important aspect of Sennacherib's reforms was the identification of the god Assur with the primeval god Anshar, which gave the national god of Assyria a theological primacy and universal character in perfect harmony with the new Assyrian ambitions. Although the new Assur/Anshar theology gained lasting recognition, the anti-Babylonian aspects of his reform ultimately failed. Upon his accession his son Esarhaddon (680–669 BCE) immediately reverted to a more traditional conciliatory attitude which was not basically to change under his successors, even after the suppression of the revolt of Šamaš-šum-ukin in 648 BCE. The official Assyrian attitude toward Babylonia then became very similar to the Roman attitude toward the Greeks after their conquest of Greece and the Hellenized kingdoms, one of deference to cultural superiority mixed with a certain protective attitude stemming from the acknowledged role of the new imperial power as custodian of a shared civilization. However, the simmering ideological conflict found a clear resolution only with the collapse of Assyria and its swift replacement by an empire ruled from Babylon.

At the end of the seventh century it all came to a rather swift end. It has become almost a cliché of Assyriological writing to marvel, sometimes even to express regret at the sudden collapse of Assyria and to try to find some explanation for what is generally regarded as an unnatural event, a historical accident, something that should not have happened. However, a quick survey of world history, especially in the Near

East, will demonstrate that empires generally tend to disintegrate and fall rapidly. This is due to their very nature. Empires often suffer from overextension of resources and from an extreme centralization of decision-making which facilitates the collapse of the entire structure if the core is successfully attacked. Assyria certainly did not fall more swiftly than the succeeding Babylonian or Persian empires, which disappeared from the world scene even faster than they had arisen. Even the Western Roman Empire completely disintegrated in the space of two generations in the fifth century of our era.

Of course, every case is particular, and what were the specific weaknesses of Assyria that made it so vulnerable to attack remains open to speculation. Various factors have been invoked, such as the small size of the Assyrian heartland in relation to the empire, its demographic decline in the seventh century, the fact that richer parts of the Near East lay outside of Assyria while Assyria itself was only a conglomerate of small villages, with the exception of Assur and the large capitals which were largely financed by the spoils of conquest. In the final analysis, perhaps Assyria had been a typical case of a state which massively and successfully invested in one area, the military, and built an empire with the help of that powerful tool and the incentive of an irresistible will to power. One is reminded of Russia under Peter the Great, or Prussia in the eighteenth century, which launched ambitious programs of selective modernization and huge investments in military technology, while structurally they remained massively agrarian and economically backward compared with the emerging capitalist economies of Western Europe.

Assyria proper and its north Syrian extension seem to have lost all dynamism after the fall of Nineveh. The large imperial and provincial capitals where population and resources had been concentrated declined rapidly, leaving the former heart of the empire largely ruralized, a backwater in the political landscape of successor states. It took centuries before Assyria regained some economic and political importance under the Parthians, a fact which may reveal that some structural weakness plagued it during the last phase of the empire. In short, Assyria's collapse was perhaps unavoidable. The powerful allegory of empires found in the Book of Daniel, with its motif of the statue with a head of gold and feet of clay, indicates that in ancient times it was perfectly well understood that empires had an inherent fragility concealed beneath their outward might.

The Babylonian Empire

In Babylonia the old ideology of the Sumerian city-states had never died out in spite of the unification of the country and the creation of a single Babylonian monarchy during the Old Babylonian period (2004–1595 BCE). In contrast to Assyria, Babylonia was a conglomerate of cities with very ancient traditions, built around large and wealthy temples where gods and goddesses reigned like earthly monarchs and owners of the land. This contrast was reflected in the building programs of the two monarchies. Whereas the mammoth architectural undertakings of the Neo-Assyrian period aimed at exalting the king, those of the Neo-Babylonian monarchs were devoted mainly to the care of the gods. True, they built for themselves an impressive palace in Babylon, and, if we are to believe later reports about the famed Hanging Gardens, they spared no expense to provide their residence with delightful surroundings. But we are far from Assyrian palaces which their owners intended as living cosmic centers. In Babylon this role was not filled by the royal residence, but by the city itself.

The emphasis on the cosmic role of Babylon in texts, art, and architecture was the manifestation of a dogma, well illustrated by the inscription of Nabopolassar (625–605 BCE) commemorating the restoration of the inner defensive wall of Babylon. Inserted in the body of the inscription was a hymn to the wall, praising it as "the solid border as ancient as time immemorial," as "the staircase to heaven, the ladder to the netherworld," and with many more epithets extolling its creation in primeval time and status as favorite residence of the gods (Beaulieu 2000b: 307–8). The outer aspect of the city at the time of Nebuchadnezzar II (604–562 BCE), when most of the building works were carried out, must immediately have reminded the onlooker of the city's status as the center of the cosmos, the passageway between heaven, earth, and the netherworld, with the dazzling blue-colored bricks of the ceremonial gates merging into the light brown color of the walls and buildings, like sky and sand dunes meeting at the horizon. The main decorative motif in Nebuchadnezzar's palace was the tall, stylized palm trees of the throne room rising against the walls. Virtually nothing of the artistic display of Assyrian palaces survived into Babylonian imperial iconography, not even the colossal guardians standing at their gates. In Babylon such guardians were depicted in reliefs made of molded bricks, standing in superimposed rows at the city gates. Literally floating in the lapis-blue sky of the glazed bricks, they possessed none of the immediacy and reality of their Assyrian counterparts. They lived in the cosmic realm of the idealized city, not in the concrete world of the royal art of might and power.

Babylon was not the only city in the core of the empire. Sippar, Borsippa, Nippur, Ur, Uruk, Kutha, and several others also laid claim to very ancient traditions, and the Neo-Babylonian kings acknowledged their sanctity by lavishing great riches on their temples. Such largesse allowed them publicly to display their devotion, and thereby to secure their legitimacy. A new official discourse arose which proclaimed the correct performance of religious rituals and duties and the meticulous rebuilding of sanctuaries as the sole reason of the monarchy for being (Talon 1993). This ideology was accordingly reflected in the epithets of the kings, who contented themselves with the titles of "king of Babylon," which reflected the cosmic centrality of Babylon, and "king of Sumer and Akkad," which embodied their duty to provide for the sanctuaries of Babylonia. They generally refrained from using old Mesopotamian titles implying universal dominion, such as "king of the world" and "king of the four quarters," which had formed the mainstay of Assyrian royal titles. Only with Nabonidus (555–539 BCE), who looked back to the Assyrian period and seems to have been more preoccupied than his peers with the political expression of universal dominion, do we find some limited resurrection of imperial titles. From reading the inscriptions of the Neo-Babylonian kings one gains the feeling of a systematic denial of the fact of empire, contrasting with the very obvious exercise of it in practice.

The reasons for this ideological denial are open to speculation. Perhaps the Babylonians, who had never really had an empire, did not exercise universal dominion long enough to be able to create an adequate political vocabulary. Yet there were models to emulate, at least the Assyrian model, the memory of which was still fresh. But several times the official inscriptions of the Babylonian empire commented on the fall of Assyria, and almost always with the same theological explanation, that it was caused by divine retribution for the crimes committed in the past by Assyrian kings, chiefly Sennacherib, against the cult centers of Babylonia. In the inscription of Nabopolassar the theological argument was further developed into a glorification of the contemplative life of the devout king, representing the Babylonian model, contrasted to the brutality of the impious, illegitimate ruler who trusted only in feats of might and power, representing the Assyrian model (Beaulieu 2003a). And history had proven that Babylonian piety had triumphed over Assyrian hubris and savagery. The Babylonian denial of empire may well have originated in this moral condemnation of Assyria by the theologians.

But there was indeed an empire. Yet, how it was administered and how much it co-opted the former provincial system of the Assyrians remain open questions. The evidence from Dur-Katlimmu in northeast Syria seems to suggest that Babylonians just stepped in and reused the former Assyrian administrative structure, but we lack texts to substantiate this (Kühne 1997). Apart from a few documents, no provincial archive from the western part of the empire has been discovered. The texts found in the royal palace in Babylon are still mostly unpublished, and official inscriptions give no information on military conquests. If it were not for the Babylonian Chronicle Series, only partly preserved for that period (Grayson 1975: 87–113), and the Bible, we would know almost nothing about the growth of the empire.

By and large, however, it seems that Babylonian policies were modeled on Assyrian practices, in particular regarding the restructuring of the conquered regions. Mass deportations continued. The case of Jerusalem and Judah is well known from the Bible, yet not unique. Several small towns in Babylonia were named after Levantine cities, suggesting that they had been peopled by deportees from the west. Although some of these settlements may have originated in the Neo-Assyrian period, others were established under Babylonian rule. This is certain for Surru (Tyre), which appears in the cuneiform documentation soon after the capture of its famed Phoenician namesake by Nebuchadnezzar (Joannès 1982). As in imperial Assyria, the influx of foreigners must have increased the diversity of the already composite population of Babylonia. Babylon must have become a real cosmopolitan Babel, if we are only to judge from the few published texts from the palace of Nebuchadnezzar. These record mostly allocations of rations to various deportees and other foreigners stationed in the capital. Among the various people listed we find Philistines from Ashkelon, Phoenicians from Tyre, Byblos, and Arwad, Elamites, Medes, Persians, Egyptians, Greeks (here called Ionians), and Lydians (Weidner 1939).

In some respects Babylonian methods of government surpassed the Assyrians in brutality. The Palestinian policy of Nebuchadnezzar is a case in point. The year 604 saw the annihilation of Ashkelon in the wake of Nebuchadnezzar's campaign to secure the Levant against the ambitions of Egypt (Stager 1996). In the following years Ekron was similarly destroyed. The evidence for planned destruction is massive, and the sites remained deserted until the reign of Cyrus (538–530 BCE), when the Persians allowed activities to resume. Judah and its capital were similarly devastated. It is possible that Babylon did not have the resources to integrate and develop the area in the same manner as the Assyrians had done in the previous century, and therefore a policy of burnt earth may have been instituted in order to prevent the Egyptians from gaining a foothold in the areas. One sector where the Babylonians enjoyed greater success than their predecessors was northern Arabia. The last Babylonian king Nabonidus was able to secure the entire area for the empire down to the modern city of Medina. According to Babylonian sources he built a palace in the oasis of Teima, where he took up residence for about ten years, and destroyed the herds and means of subsistence of the nomadic population, probably with the intention of forcing them to settle in areas under imperial control (Beaulieu 1989: 169–85). In this respect the Babylonian empire again followed the same methods as the Assyrians, in spite of the official tenor of royal inscriptions which recorded only the pious and pacific deeds of the rulers.

Unlike what happened in Assyria, the end of the Babylonian empire did not cause the demise of the Babylonian urban core. Babylonian cities had prospered before the empire and continued to do so under the Persian and Hellenistic monarchies. The empire had brought an influx of riches to Babylon and the old cities of Sumer and Akkad, allowing unprecedented architectural activity to be sponsored by the kings. Yet the spoils of conquest and tribute were certainly not the main source of wealth for imperial Babylonia, if we are only to judge from the fact that under the Persian rulers, well after the loss of political independence, Babylonia contributed the largest amount of precious metal in taxes to the treasury. With such natural riches it is hardly surprising that the Babylonians never looked beyond Babylonia in the elaboration of their ideology of power and of their geographic conception of the world.

The Persian Empire

Since the third millennium various states and nations with their center of gravity east of Mesopotamia, either in the Zagros Mountains, or the plain of Susa, or even further east on the Iranian plateau, had interacted with Mesopotamia. At times harmonious, at others adversarial, these relations had generally tended to stabilize around a point of equilibrium, since Mesopotamian states never succeeded in controlling those regions effectively except for short periods of time and at great military cost, while easterners occasionally raided Mesopotamian territory but never achieved lasting occupation. Why suddenly in the sixth century the balance tipped in favor of the Persians, we simply do not know. It is probable that various economic, demographic, and technological factors worked in their favor, but we lack the kind of information that would make the analysis of those factors possible. The irruption of the Persians onto the world stage and their swift success seem as sudden and unexplainable as that of Islam in the seventh century of our era. In a relatively short span of time the Persians built an empire so territorially extensive that even by modern standards it would seem extremely difficult to administer.

The Persians, led by the ruling family called the Achaemenids, certainly possessed an innate genius for co-opting the administration and structure of the kingdoms they conquered, and this must to some extent explain their success. Egyptian and Babylonian sources reveal that the transition to Persian rule was remarkably smooth. The former Babylonian empire remained whole for a long time, forming the satrapy, or province, of "Babylon and Transeuphratene" which lasted at least until the end of the reign of Darius (521–486 BCE), more than half a century after the conquest of Babylon (Stolper 1989). The superimposition of Achaemenid imperial institutions was therefore slow and cautious. Their function was to ensure the regular flow of taxes to the center for the maintenance of the court and the military. During the entire period of Persian rule one of the most conspicuously attested Achaemenid institutions in Babylonian documents was the regime of military colonies, which was particularly well documented, though indirectly, in the archives of the Murashu family from Nippur (Stolper 1985: 70–103).

Furthermore, the Achaemenid rulers did not try to Persianize their subjects in the same way as the Assyrians and the Romans sought to spread an imperial identity. For the Assyrian kings the world was divided into Assyrians and non-Assyrians, terms which had lost their ethnic connotation very early on to become expressions of the political divide between Assyrian subjects and all the people who had not yet submitted to the yoke of the god Assur. With the Achaemenids, on the other hand, conquered people were fully recognized as distinct and left undisturbed as long as they acknowledged their vassal status within the empire. There is no evidence for the extensive and sometimes brutal restructuring which characterized the previous Mesopotamian empires.

Achaemenid imperial art eloquently reflected the nature of Persian rule. It was a composite art, made up of juxtaposed elements borrowed, almost without alterations, from Mesopotamians, Egyptians, and other subject peoples of the empire. Yet, it also had, in spite of this, a highly distinctive, immediately recognizable style characterized by a cold and distant mood. Achaemenid art created an impression of calm and harmony emerging from the acknowledged diversity of the empire, expressed in its cosmopolitan iconographic repertoire. It also stressed the acceptance of Persian rule, expressed in a unified and subtly refined aesthetic, a far cry from the power art of the Assyrians impudently exalting the heroic and often brutal aspects of the monarchy. Indeed, there were no scenes of war or humiliation of the conquered in Achaemenid art. The procession of subject peoples at Persepolis proclaimed only a voluntary participation of every nation with its own traditions in the celebration of Achaemenid power. Such ideology was not only deduced from the art, but was also made explicit in the foundation charter of Darius I from Susa, which specifically named the nations from all over the empire which provided craftsmen to build the citadel at Susa (Lecoq 1997: 234–7).

It can be objected that such harmony existed only as an ideological claim, yet one suspects that it really tells us something about life in the Persian empire. The relative ease with which Achaemenid rule was installed and maintained almost undisturbed for such a long period, 539 to 331 BCE, contrasts with the enormous difficulties encountered by Assyrian and Babylonian empire builders in the previous three centuries. Assyria especially was surrounded by enemies and powerful rival states, and the empire could be maintained only by costly annual campaigns. Even in the seventh century, when it reached a critical mass, rebellions were always simmering in one or another of its provinces, often encouraged by powerful rivals. More distant countries like Egypt were controlled only briefly, and never fully. The Babylonian empire reached a more harmonious equilibrium with its neighbors, but its hegemonic position was constantly held in check by equally powerful competitors such as Egypt and Persia. With the Persians all these formerly rival powers became finally united into one huge administrative and economic space. One must not forget that the work of imposing the imperial idea and structure had already been accomplished well before the Persians entered the stage. In a sense the Achaemenids gave Mesopotamia the world empire with a vast hinterland which neither Assyria nor Babylonia had ever achieved, although they had taken the initial, most difficult steps in that direction. One important ingredient of Achaemenid success was precisely this absence of competing powers which allowed the ruling elite to exert its hegemony far more efficiently, while using much less force and repression than any previous imperial state.

The fact that the Persian ruling elite was a very small minority in the empire also accounts for the rather tolerant exercise of power. Forced acculturation of conquered people was unthinkable and not even desired. Like the Manchus in China during the Qing period (1644–1911 of our era), the Persians formed a thin aristocratic layer which could survive only by adapting to the nations it conquered as it was co-opting them into a fast-rising imperial structure. The Achaemenids formed an ethnically homogeneous ruling class (Briant 1987). Access to that class was severely restricted because of the fear of being diluted in the mass of subjects, and for the same reasons Persianization was not encouraged by the state, the main purpose of which was to maintain the privileges of that compact and jealously guarded aristocracy. The Achaemenids envisioned no dramatic reshaping or restructuring of their conquests since such policies were not necessary to ensure this basic function of the imperial structure. Indeed, such policies would have been counterproductive and imperiled the very reason of the state for being.

As had happened with Assyria and Babylon, the empire of the Achaemenids seemingly crumbled like a house of cards when faced with the onslaught of Alexander the Great. Should we then conclude that the empire suffered from a structural weakness that made it an easy prey for Alexander's appetites? Such views were indeed propagated by fourth-century Greek writers, who did much to create the myth of Persian decadence and ineffectualness in order to provide a moral justification for the conquest or simply to explain the astonishing ease with which it was accomplished. This view of steady Achaemenid decline, which has survived in modern historiography, has been completely debunked by recent research (Briant 1993). Unlike Assyria on the eve of its destruction, it seems that neither Babylon in the sixth century, nor the Persian empire in the fourth, showed any particularly alarming sign of decline. On the contrary, in both cases the explanation for their demise probably lies in the superior resources and organization of their enemies. In the case of Persia an easy conquest was conceivable, for one could see that once the ethnically homogenous ruling class was successfully attacked and removed, the entire edifice would easily fall into the hands of the aggressors. Yet this does not mean that the empire was a diseased body, for in many respects the Persian state represented the culmination of Ancient Near Eastern empire building, a final synthesis of the oldest civilizations in that part of the world before their irreversible transformation by the ferment of Hellenism.

FURTHER READING

Parpola 1987a discusses the eclipse of Babylonia and Assyria at the end of the Bronze Age. Boardman et al. 1991 offers well-balanced surveys of the political and cultural history of the Assyrian and Babylonian empires. For the growth of the Assyrian empire see Liverani 1988b and Postgate 1991–2, while Parker 2001 offers a more detailed assessment based on its northern frontier. On the rule of conquered territories and the provincial system see Grayson 1995. Reflections of Assyrian ideology and official propaganda in art and texts are treated by Liverani 1979, Tadmor 1981, and Winter 1981. There is no up-to-date comprehensive treatment of the Babylonian empire, but Brinkman 1984 offers a detailed survey of the conditions leading to its rise. For the Persian empire the essential introduction is Wiesehöfer 1996. Briant 2002 is a tour de force of historical writing with in-depth analysis of Greek sources.

PART II

Discourses on Methods

CHAPTER FIVE

Archaeology and the Ancient Near East: Methods and Limits

Marie-Henriette Gates

Archaeology's contributions to Ancient Near Eastern history involve more than supplying the raw data – archives and monumental inscriptions – identifying ancient sites on the ground, and checking chronological outlines, all first steps toward the reconstruction of historical narratives. At the same time, historical documents from the Ancient Near East provide otherwise inaccessible information for many issues pertinent to archaeological analysis of its societies. The two fields of archaeology and history thus complement each other, but by definition examine their subjects by using different sources, and from these orient themselves toward different objectives.

This essay will touch on some aspects of the past and current relationship between archaeology or the archaeological perspective and Ancient Near Eastern history. History is defined here in terms deriving from the *Annales* school of historians in France to cover events and also instances or patterns of social and economic behavior that include mentalities, or culture, and the historian refers to the specialist whose primary sources are written (Bloch 1953; Braudel 1972). The archaeologist, in contrast, relies on the material record rather than the written one, and consults artifacts, building plans, settlement patterns, and other tangible remains of human activity for primary interpretive data. Reconstructing sequences of events and the personalities behind them remains the preserve of the historian, while issues of cultural definition and change, within a specific context and in a broader landscape, concern the archaeologist.

Historian and archaeologist together share the ambition and the need to re-create mentalities and social patterns, Braudel's second tier of historical analysis, and in this respect the two fields would appear to be closely linked. The extent to which they have formed alliances in their mutual program of resurrecting the ancient civilizations of the Near East is presented here from the archaeological side of their association.

Archaeology's Contribution to Historical Accounts
about the Ancient Near East

All general histories of the Ancient Near East refer to sites and objects in their discussions, and often include illustrations, plans, and reconstructions. These have been almost exclusively provided by excavations carried out in the mid-nineteenth to mid-twentieth centuries CE, at Mesopotamian urban sites like Warka, Ur, and Babylon, Assur, and the later Assyrian capitals, and moving west, Mari, Ugarit, and the Hittite capital Hattusha. Although many of these projects are still running, and recent findings from these sites occasionally make their way into new historical accounts, they nonetheless hardly alter, reconfigure, or replace the familiar standards. No excavations begun since the 1950s have enjoyed a similar popularity among historians.

The reasons behind this conservatism are several. The most obvious is that excavations before World War II were carried out on a scale appropriate to recovering historical information. Archaeologists exposed entire cities without being encumbered by sampling techniques, subsistence strategies, micromorphology, post-depositional processes, or the statistical recording of potsherds (for these techniques, see Matthews 2003). Nor did they waste much time on occupational levels later than the period or periods that interested them as historically significant and illustrious, or on levels of occupation within a building or period. The single-minded pursuit of total site recovery for specific levels aimed at, and succeeded in, producing urban plans, placing monumental buildings within their administrative neighborhoods, and uncovering large structures in their entirety (Parrot 1953: 40). We can indeed be grateful for the accomplishments of this stage in the history of archaeological research. It revealed the layouts of cities like Babylon and Assur that are far beyond what the 10×10 meter, or 33-foot, trench – the largest format in current use – can ever hope to expose. By providing a preliminary framework and typology for architecture, urbanism, and art in the Ancient Near East, such projects cleared the way for later generations of excavators to concentrate on a finer-grained recovery of comparable or contrasting sites.

Secondly, a major motive behind the choice of which sites to excavate was to find direct evidence for supplementing and reconstructing history. Urban centers therefore took precedence over towns and villages, as did the excavation of their monumental buildings, the construction of which could more likely be connected to historical episodes and important figures than private houses. Since the mid-nineteenth century, when Botta's and Layard's discoveries at the Assyrian capitals of Khorsabad and Nimrud first showed that palaces could be expected to contain inscriptions on their walls and tablets inside their rooms, and that such contexts might confirm or enrich a historical outline initially drawn from the Old Testament and the Greek historian Herodotus, they became preferred targets because they seemed more informative. Once the deciphered inscriptions and tablets demonstrated the wealth of social and economic detail to be anticipated from such sources, their recovery became a driving force behind archaeological excavation. Excavators were pressed by the need to find cuneiform tablets, as one can read in the prefaces to their reports. By the third day of the first campaign at Mari in 1933, although a statue of Sumerian type had already been found, "we were not satisfied since Paris was urging us to hurry up and discover 'a text'" (Parrot 1974: 15).

Inscribed finds also compensated for stratigraphic complexity, recycling, or imperfect excavating, by generating of themselves the required chronological and contextual information (at Byblos, Dunand 1954: 3–7, 1968: 99–100). That the remarkable series of inscribed statues commissioned by Gudea and his relatives was discovered in a palace built and occupied about 1,800 years after their lifetimes did not affect assigning these early governors of Lagash to their correct historical place (Azarpay 1990: 97; de Genouillac 1936b: 9–10). It seems incidental that the temple in which the dedications originally stood was not recovered, and indeed most likely destroyed, by its excavator (Lloyd 1980: 159–60). The texts inscribed on the statues related, in satisfactory detail, the circumstances surrounding the temple's construction and the name of its patron-god; and a model brick on the lap of Gudea the architect was incised with his divinely inspired temple plan. Sculptures such as these, which prompted museums throughout the world to sponsor projects in the hope of securing display-worthy artwork, also contributed to focusing excavation on royal and urban centers with historic credentials. Thus de Sarzac, the first excavator of Gudea's temple at Telloh/ancient Girsu, could be congratulated for making the Louvre "the chief European treasure-house of early Babylonian (Sumerian) art and history" (de Genouillac 1936a: 1).[1]

Finally, Near Eastern projects carried out before the 1950s were conducted with small teams, large local labor forces, and seasons lasting six months or more, three conditions that favored the emergence of the big picture. The Zimri-Lim palace at Mari, for example, a 2.5 hectare, or 6 acre, complex with over 260 rooms preserved in parts to a height of 5 m, or 16 feet, was dug in only four years (twelve months of fieldwork) by a four-person staff and 230 workmen (Parrot 1953: 28–9, 1974: 19–20). De Morgan, digging at Susa before World War I, considered 1,000 to 1,500 workers an appropriate labor force, although a few decades later Parrot could criticize this as more suitable for a "civil engineering project," with any number above 300 posing a "serious threat to scientific work" (1953: 27). At Mari as elsewhere, supervision of the excavation's progress and the recording of its findings were the responsibility of the single field director and the project head, the two other staff members being assigned to architectural plans and finds illustration, photography, and preliminary conservation.

The results of such broad enterprises suited a narrative publication format whose sweeping conclusions could be readily adapted into historical accounts. Object catalogs and technical discussions for specialists were placed at the end of this narrative, and often set in smaller print. Finds thus illustrated the context, instead of constituting the basis for its interpretation. The recovery of immense quantities of artifacts also favored selecting those few with artistic and historic merit that best served the excavation's immediate aims. One could call this a sampling strategy of sorts, in a research program that made the archaeologist a full partner of the historian. In the words of Parrot, Mari's distinguished excavator, historic sites do not lend themselves to "digging with a microscope" (1974: 19).

From this heroic era of fieldwork emerged a historical and chronological frame-work for the Ancient Near East that today remains unchallenged. The outline has of course been fleshed out and refined, both in its historical and in its archaeological details. In particular, an interest in the dynamic between urban centers and their countryside has introduced into mainstream discussions information collected by later archaeological surveys (Matthews 2003: 182–8), and efforts to understand archival practices and economic systems have encouraged study of the archaeological contexts where individual archives were found (Zettler 1996; Reichel 2001). But such interdisciplinary studies have, on the whole, been initiated by archaeologists who can also read the texts, rather than by specialists in the ancient languages. In fact, the changes that transformed archaeological research after the mid-twentieth century and shaped its many excavation projects do not coincide well with a historical agenda. Current archaeological research might even be thought irrelevant to a historical scheme, given the technical perspective and problem-oriented focus with which most of the recent projects are associated. Hence the tendency has been for historians to sideline new projects in favor of old standards. Even the spectacular (non-epigraphic) finds from Tell Mardikh, ancient Ebla, remain consigned to a few lines only in connection with the conquests of Akkadian kings – hardly more than before the site was excavated, and despite its widely circulated and accessible publications (Matthiae 1977, 1985; Matthiae, Pinnock, and Scandone-Matthiae 1995). Yet Ebla's third millennium BCE urban development says much about Sumerian cultural and economic preeminence over a large geographical area, as other excavations in western Syria can confirm. New historical studies of Early Dynastic Sumer must take these sites into account if they are to explain why the rulers at Ebla and elsewhere turned to the cities of Sumer for models to emulate.

Archaeology and Near Eastern Relative Chronology

The relative chronology used for Mesopotamian archaeology was set up at an international conference in 1929 on the basis of two coordinated schemes: one for prehistory, the other for historic phases. Prehistoric periods were named after the individual sites then thought to characterize best a particular stage of development. These type-sites, standing for distinct cultures, were arranged into a continuous sequence according to the stratigraphic evidence from excavations up to that point. They eventually attributed the earliest Mesopotamian settlement to the site of Hassuna, in northern Iraq, and the latest prehistoric ones to Uruk and Jemdet Nasr in the south. The first occurrence of writing in the Uruk IV and Jemdet Nasr phases prompted, in 1931, the adoption of the label Protoliterate period to describe that stage more vividly, and to highlight a perceived transition into the succeeding chronological scheme (although not without protest: Mallowan 1970: 328–30). The terms Late Uruk-Jemdet Nasr and Protoliterate are still used interchangeably today for the centuries on either side of 3000 BCE.

For archaeological phases following the Protoliterate period, a sequence of prominent historical markers was chosen in preference to the type-site system. The third millennium was divided into three major periods – Early Dynastic, Akkadian, and Ur III or Neo-Sumerian – and coordinated with stratigraphic sequences and artifact typologies mainly from the Chicago Oriental Institute's excavations in the Diyala Valley (Lloyd 1984: 91). This terminology was intended to bind archaeological and historical findings into one harmonious, compatible system. Like the type-site sequence, it assumed that a linear development best reflected ancient Mesopotamian history. It also presumed that historical periods offered a more flexible framework for integrating new archaeological findings than cultural stages could, and that Mesopotamian culture was monolithic, without significant regional variants. It was especially based on the idea that a historical perspective should take precedence over a cultural or archaeological one – a view that was fully endorsed by the excavators themselves (Parrot 1953: 40–1).

This chronological framework has proved a poor fit from both perspectives. Historians have struggled in vain to stretch the Sumerian King List over the three phases of the Early Dynastic period: Early Dynastic I, II, and III (Hallo and Simpson 1971: 34–9; Lloyd 1984: 90–3, Kuhrt 1995: 29–31). In archaeological terms, this system has not proved satisfactory either. The artificial division created by this phasing between Protoliterate and Early Dynastic I has obscured the cultural continuity linking the two periods. The Early Dynastic I archaeological assemblage of pottery types and seals, and households at sites like Abu Salabikh, illustrate the economic decline of southern Mesopotamia after the collapse of Protoliterate state organization, rather than the political structure of the Sumerian city-states that emerged in Early Dynastic II. A more accurate scheme from both the archaeological and the historical perspective would make Early Dynastic I the closing phase of the Protoliterate, followed by a break before the onset of Early Dynastic II–III. Recent general discussions about the Sumerian city-states (Roaf 1990: 79–88; Postgate 1994) have avoided attributing specific developments to all three phases within Early Dynastic, a sign that they are now recognized as coinciding poorly with the current understanding of this period. Akkadian and Neo-Sumerian reflect the next two (brief) cultural and historical stages more comfortably. But for the rest of the second and first millennia BCE, where individual periods last longer and the fit is, in consequence, superficially less awkward, cultural realities in the archaeological record remain concealed or distorted by the need to formulate them in historical parameters applicable to restricted geographical areas only. Shifting population groups and transitional stages before and after the existence of centralized states disappear within this scheme.

Finally, this relative chronology has isolated both Mesopotamian history and archaeology from the greater Near East, which uses the Three Age system: Neolithic, Bronze Age, and Iron Age. Perhaps an initial reason behind choosing the historical sequence was that it was thought a simpler expedient into which archaeological levels could be slotted (Parrot 1953: 40). Implicit to the original scheme, however, was the concept that Mesopotamia, the core civilization, was central to developments elsewhere, and that the burden of cross-dating rested with the peripheries. Efforts to cross-reference the two systems have carried little weight with archaeologists working primarily with Mesopotamian material (Hallo and Simpson 1971). Adopting the

Three Age system would require a complete review of Mesopotamia's diagnostic cultural features to key them in with the sequences in other regions. Because this task can be circumvented by using the two in parallel, however loosely, no radical overhaul has yet been introduced.

The consequences of this relative dating system have hindered rather than clarified issues even pertaining to internal Mesopotamian history, since some of its complexities can be resolved only from outside the core, with reference to the archaeological record. To cite one instance: where, in the larger scheme of things, do the First Dynasty of Babylon and by extension the Old Babylonian period coordinate with specific archaeological phases in the eastern Mediterranean, with which it entertained political relations, but whose sites and levels use the Bronze Age system? This question is only one of many with a direct bearing on absolute chronology, in which archaeology plays the critical role.

Archaeology and Near Eastern Absolute Chronology

Absolute chronology assigns calendar dates to historical events and archaeological periods. It offers an irresistible challenge to historians of the Ancient Near East, where king lists and other documents invite a semblance of chronological precision, second only to Dynastic Egypt. Archaeological research is also keenly interested in absolute dates that allow fixed reference points across different cultural zones. However, it is essential that the absolute dates attributed to historical events conform with the archaeological record, and vice versa. This is the one area of Ancient Near Eastern study that requires the closest collaboration between historians and archaeologists.

The longest chronological debate of this type has involved the regnal years of kings belonging to the First Dynasty of Babylon, the so-called High, Middle, and Low Chronology. It was first formulated in 1928, when the Assyriologist S. Langdon and the astronomer J. K. Fotheringham published a compilation of omens relating observations of the appearance of the planet Venus to specific years for Ammisaduqa, the dynasty's penultimate king. Since this chronology provided a convenient handle on which to hang centuries of historical and archaeological data, it gamely survived all efforts to discredit the reliability of its premises (Neugebauer 1929; Reiner and Pingree 1975), despite eventual disclaimers from some early champions (Smith 1951: 67). The chronological debate was, I believe, conclusively resolved in 1998 only because, for the first time, ceramic typology, stratigraphic analysis, and settlement distribution patterns for mid-second millennium Babylonia were given equal weight with textual data (Gasche et al. 1998). In a second innovative move, the newly proposed chronology was tested against current historical and archaeological dating systems in the rest of the Near East, from Iran to Anatolia, modern Turkey, and Egypt (Tanret 2000).

Since this Babylonian chronology ties in with earlier Mesopotamian history, and affords synchronisms with other parts of the Near East and eastern Mediterranean, its resolution is of momentous significance. Thanks to this, contemporary civilizations where written documentation is spare or inadequate for historical purposes, but which have a high visibility in the archaeological record, can be dated with more accuracy. They include Minoan Crete and Mycenaean Greece, whose export trade in pottery gives a crucial index for cross-dating archaeological deposits in the Levant, the eastern coast of the Mediterranean Sea, and Anatolia. Indeed, the overwhelming outside interest in what might seem a parochial detail of Mesopotamian history underscores the tightly knit fabric of most research questions involving the Ancient Near East (for instance Manning 1999, on the Aegean and eastern Mediterranean).

The issue here is that archaeological deposits rarely provide unequivocal absolute dates with the precision needed to pinpoint historical events, that is, to a specific year rather than a generation or a century. Radiocarbon dates and similar chrono-metric techniques involve margins of error ranging well beyond the duration of most Ancient Near Eastern dynasties, let alone the reign of one king. It is not radiocarbon-dating that will determine, for instance, whether Sargon or his grandson Naram-Sin destroyed Early Bronze III Ebla. In any case, the current radiocarbon sample for Mesopotamia proper is too small and too spotty to provide any conclusive assessment, even when conflated with readings from contemporary sites outside Mesopotamia (Reade 2001: 13–14; Hassan and Robinson 1987: 127–8). The fact that samples processed in the early decades of this technology were several hundred years out of line with traditional chronologies no doubt discouraged systematic collecting on the grounds that it was an imperfect (and costly) pastime (Mallowan 1971: 242–3; Reade 2001: 13). It is also likely that reliance on a historically based Mesopotamian chronology made radiocarbon dating seem irrelevant, and suitable only for prehistoric sites, which have no recourse to written benchmarks.

Dendrochronology, or tree-ring dating, is a far more precise tool, but first one must come by the appropriate sample, and it must have at least fifty to one hundred preserved, countable, and well-patterned rings (Kuniholm 2001). Wood of this caliber was especially used as structural timber, or to span monumental buildings. It can be expected for ordinary housing only in forested regions like central Anatolia. Dendrochronology moreover dates the year when a tree was cut, but this need not be the year when it was incorporated into a building or even less the year when that building fell out of use; in short, it offers a terminus post quem. The timbers from Kültepe-Kanesh and Acemhöyük in central Anatolia provide no more than a series of earliest possible dates (2055, 1832, 1774, and 1761 BCE [Kültepe II and Ib periods/Middle Bronze II A]) for the many generations of Assyrian businessmen who kept records according to the yearly calendar in Assur (Manning et al. 2001). A further cautionary note on how dendrochronology must be evaluated in conjunction with context and associated features is indicated by Acemhöyük. Although its two excavated monumental buildings were used concurrently, their timbers had been felled 152 years apart (Özgüç 1980: 63). Contemporary private housing at Acemhöyük included twenty-four other timbers dendrodated from four to eight centuries earlier (mid-late third millennium BCE!), indicating that informal buildings recycled materials from much older structures (Kuniholm 1996: 331). Still, the ever-expanding database of dendrochronological samples and correlations offers a resource of great promise.

It must also be accepted that archaeological deposits are less discrete than one might wish. Even the well-attested campaigns of Neo-Assyrian kings are difficult to correlate with specific destruction levels at most relevant sites, to say nothing of destructions with weaker credentials, like those attributed to the Biblical patriarchs, or recounted in Near Eastern epics (Forsberg 1995). The factors conspiring to blur the archaeological picture range from human interference (ancient and modern) to the natural processes of erosion, flooding, deposition of soil by rivers, and decomposition. Victorious soldiers stripped buildings of their contents, abandoned houses gradually filled with garbage dumped by their neighbors, moles burrowed through stratified deposits and shifted potsherds, coins, tablets, and similar diagnostic data indiscriminately from one level to another. Identifying these transformations in the field comprises an entire area of archaeological inquiry in itself, and archaeologists have worked out methods to override these confusions (Schiffer 1976). But neither archaeologists nor the archaeological record should be held responsible when their results fall outside the time frames that historians request. An enlightened understanding of each discipline's methods, limitations, and possibilities can achieve conclusive results, as in the case of dating the Old Babylonian dynasty. Chronological problems require the concerted efforts of archaeologists and historians in equal measure, since the system in use for the Ancient Near East inextricably combines the two.

Recent Archaeological Research on the Ancient Near East

Only one aspect of fieldwork remains universal and timeless: financial shortage, a theme common to virtually every excavation report's preface. In other respects, however, archaeological projects initiated in the Middle East during the past fifty years have followed different agendas from those preceding World War II, and have been carried out under more restrictive conditions. Superficial explanations behind these changes involve practical issues. Field seasons, on average, became shorter once academics, who are constrained by university calendars, replaced institute- and museum-sponsored teams as the majority force engaged in excavations. University-based projects also embraced the mission of training students in fieldwork and field-related research. This aim toward instruction speeded up technical improvements, bringing excavating, sampling, and recording practices to much higher standards. Field teams accordingly expanded to include a battery of specialists and site supervisors several times more numerous than the handful recommended by Parrot, at greater expense to transport, house, and feed. The local labor force was reduced as a result of such developments.

These factors shifted the scale of excavation toward smaller trenches and a slower pace. Other types of restrictions also played an important role in modifying the nature of fieldwork. A heightened conscience about preserving sites rather than destroying them led to the argument that soundings and surveys should substitute for excavation,[2] although it is today again recognized that they generate distinct and complementary information (Matthews 2003: 34–5). Industrialization, road work, and hydroelectric dam construction in the Middle East have increased the pressure for salvage projects, which detract from a free choice of site, based on research interests, by focusing efforts instead on short-term and largely random investigations. Much good and unexpected data have emerged from these, but they have also diverted earlier patterns of research.

Underlying these structural changes, however, is a profound shift in perspective within the archaeological discipline itself. I will not even summarize the many theoretical concerns that have rocked the archaeological establishment during these six decades. They belong – in one activist's words – to an internal dialogue that interests only the profession (Trigger 1989: 2, citing Binford). It is enough to say that they query what archaeology does or does not do, particularly in its aims at explanation. One consequence for Near Eastern archaeology has been a preference for prehistoric sites through the Protoliterate period, because they may answer fundamental issues about transformations in the human condition: the invention of farming and animal-breeding, the move from village to urban life, or the development of state systems. For historic periods, a similar turn toward "blue-collar" research led to concentrating on private housing rather than monumental buildings, and on small sites instead of urban centers. To investigate diachronic change and transitions, small, multi-phase soundings replaced broad exposures, so that contrasts from one period to the next could be sampled and highlighted.

Another result of post-World War II fieldwork agendas has been a renewed awareness that archaeological data and historical data produce two distinct classes of information, and therefore require two different styles of research questions in archaeology. The debate is an old one, a sign that its seeds rest at the very core of archaeology as a discipline. It lies behind the American "New Archeology" [sic] movement of the 1960s, spearheaded by L. Binford, and it resurfaced in the 1990s when the collapse of the Soviet Union prompted even its archaeologists to query the premises behind their research design (Klejn 1993). The force of this ideological rift among archaeologists was vividly expressed by the title Renfrew chose for his centenary lecture at the Archaeological Institute of America: "The Great Tradition versus the Great Divide" (1980). Despite the many reasonable arguments urging cooperation and peace between the two factions in the archaeological establishment, they continue to view each other's basic approaches with misgiving.

Whatever their position on this debate, it has led excavators in the Middle East to sheer away from investigating historical problems, since they cannot be formulated – in the present scientific view – as relevant research questions except when set against a much wider backdrop. Woolley's declaration that "a nameless ruin was none other than Ur, so-called Ur of the Chaldees, 'the home of Abraham'" (1930: 14) would not give him either a viable research proposal or funding were his excavations to begin today! It will then hardly come as a surprise that historians of the Ancient Near East find these recent projects less suitable to their purpose, when the archaeologists themselves are questioning whether material culture has anything to do with history.

Still, there is much in current fieldwork that the Ancient Near Eastern historian can apply directly. Projects make increasing use of remote-sensing and aerial techniques to compensate for limited horizontal exposures. They can recover entire and extensive site plans when conditions are favorable: brilliant examples spanning three millennia are Titriş Höyük in southeastern Turkey (Matney and Algaze 1995; Algaze et al. 1996), the Old Babylonian city Mashkan-Shapir (Stone and Zimansky 1992), and the Late Iron Age Median site at Kerkenes Dağ, in north central Turkey (Summers 2000). Judicious selection of which features from the geophysical plan to excavate can also produce results worthy of archaeology's heroic age, but using meticulous technical standards. Thus ten seasons at Kuşakli, the Hittite city of Sarissa, have uncovered several monumental temples and administrative buildings, residential quarters, workshops, the fortification wall and its gates, and an extramural sanctuary – thanks to geoelectrical and geomagnetic surveys that outlined where these buildings lay underneath the ground surface (Müller-Karpe 2002a, 2002b). This ongoing project on the northeastern frontier of the Hittite state has definitively dispelled the established view that only the Hittite capital Hattusha could pretend to urban status. Kuşakli's impact on historical issues concerning the Hittites is as considerable as on archaeological ones.

A second characteristic of recent fieldwork is that it produces clear data on environment, subsistence, and technology, three topics of immediate relevance to ancient economies. Systematic collection and analysis of cereal and faunal remains from well-defined archaeological contexts can provide direct evidence for situations inferred from texts, while relating them to a broader geographical scale. For example, investigations at Early Bronze Tell al-Raqa'i and Tell 'Atij in northeastern Syria concluded – by evaluating architectural and botanical findings in tandem – that these small early-to-mid-third millennium BCE sites served as regional centers for storing cereals (Schwartz and Klucas 1998; Fortin 1998). The social and political administration behind such centers would thus parallel the structure in contemporary Sumer, although no written sources have (as yet) been found to suggest this. Comparable studies on second millennium sites in the region have provided urban centers like Mari with way-stations for agricultural produce (Del Olmo Lete and Montero Fenollós 1998), and documented the shift from Middle Bronze Mari to Late Bronze Terqa for control of the central Euphrates valley's mixed urban, farming, and nomadic economies (Rouault 1998). Since archives tend to be locality-specific and their distribution sporadic, the archaeological record can supply a fuller and more comprehensive picture from which to generalize than the textual one alone.

Questions involving ancient industries can also benefit from the many studies that archaeologists routinely conduct on ceramics, metallurgy, and other materials. Here too, such information fills gaps in the written record, and can redress its biases. At the simplest level, the contents of ordinary households illustrate facets of economic life that lay outside the spheres of official record-keeping, but were nonetheless fully connected to the existing system. The manufacture of pottery on a wheel, which occurred in southern Mesopotamia from the Protoliterate period onward, was a specialized industry in the hands of trained craftsmen. Obvious signs of mass-production are the homogeneity and narrow range of vessel types that characterized Sumerian and Babylonian ceramics over centuries and even millennia (Potts 1997: 150–62). The actual mechanism through which tableware and storage jars were acquired by individuals may be variously imagined, but it certainly involved a supplier – the potter's workshop – and a purchaser. Thus, for the reconstruction of Mesopotamian economic systems after 3400 BCE, any proposal that assumes ordinary families were self-sufficient, even to making their own pottery (for example, Renger 1984: 88), runs in direct contradiction to archaeological realities, and can be considered flawed in its basic premise. In historical contexts where there is no written documentation preserved about economic affairs, the archaeological record provides the only evidence. During the Late Bronze Hittite Empire, for example, ceramics and other products show that highly standardized industries exerted a centralizing control in order to ensure economic stability over the entire territory (Ertem, Summers, and Demirci 1998; Gates 2001).

The historian may find the format in which this class of archaeological data is presented more difficult to approach and adapt than excavation summaries. Nonetheless, it remains essential corroborative evidence for any text-based discussion of economic topics, just as the texts themselves supply details which the archaeologist should consult (Potts 1997: vii).

Prehistory and Parahistory

Prehistory, by definition, belongs to the discipline of archaeology, since it involves reconstructing ancient cultures on the strength of their material remains, without the help of written commentary. But the division between the prehistoric and historic periods in the Near East is – for the archaeologist – a largely artificial boundary. Roots for its early historical developments extend back into prehistoric times. The Late Ubaid phase (4500–3500 BCE) presents many of the characteristics that qualified Protoliterate Sumer for statehood: monumental buildings laid out on a fixed architectural standard, long-distance trade, implantation of South Mesopotamian types (and populations?) in foreign lands, specialized industries, wide cultural distribution patterns, and simple record-keeping devices (Matthews 2003: 102–8). Should the two not be linked into a continuum with several stages, rather than split into separate entities by archaeologists and historians both?

More to the point, however, is the fact that most archaeological contexts, whatever their period, represent ahistoric or parahistoric (almost historic) entities peripheral to, or entirely dissociated from, any relevant framework of events and persons. Regardless of whether a historic or prehistoric setting is concerned, time in the archaeological sense is calculated in units of multiple generations (such as three generations for the average life-span of a house), or in larger blocks of centuries or millennia for cultural phases (Smith 1992). What emerges from the archaeological past, therefore, is a picture of societies within their environment – Braudel's mentalities and patterns – occasionally punctuated by historical detail that gives an additional dimension to the picture.

The analytical techniques used by archaeology are applied in the same way to sites and regions before and after writing appears in the Near East. The only pertinent distinction between the two is whether they speak solely through the words of archaeologists, or whether some members of those ancient societies also manage to express themselves verbally. The example most often cited to illustrate the importance of written testimonials in interpreting an archaeological context is the case of the

Assyrian businessmen who resided in central Anatolia from the nineteenth to seventeenth centuries BCE, and wrote their correspondence and contracts on clay tablets (Veenhof 1995; Matthews 2003: 120). Their presence is attested at Kültepe, where excavations have exposed the largest area of a neighborhood in which they lived, and in smaller communities at Boğazköy and Alişar. They assimilated completely into local culture: house architecture, tableware, even the deities represented on their seals were Anatolian. The only material clues to their presence at these sites are their tablets, their use of cylinder seals instead of stamp seals, and their burials inside houses. Contemporary Acemhöyük and Karahöyük-Konya, although in close communication with Kültepe, produced no tablets and thus no trace of whether foreigners were settled there too. However, the letters of these Assyrian businessmen tell a different (and sadly human) story. Far from acknowledging that they had "gone native" by adopting an Anatolian lifestyle, making a common practice of taking local women as wives, raising their children, and worshiping their gods, they referred to their hosts in strictly pejorative terms and avoided introducing any borrowed words into their written language (Veenhof 1977: 110, 1982: 150–4).[3] If we had only their archives from Assur (which have in fact not been recovered), and did not know the realities of their entrenchment in Anatolian society, our impressions of their activities and interactions would again be incorrect. A balanced perspective drawn from a social setting revealed through archaeology, and from individual commentaries documented in writing, achieves a closer accuracy.

Renewing the Alliance?

I have argued here that Near Eastern archaeologists and historians parted ways half a century ago to follow independent routes, after a healthy partnership that had lasted more than one hundred years. I have also presented cases where the two disciplines continue to run a parallel course, and occasionally intersect with resounding success, such as in resolving Old Babylonian absolute chronology. European scholars especially, thanks to academic training, temperament, and the structure of their institutional settings, still coordinate the two disciplines (Postgate 1994 most brilliantly). But there too, one can envisage eventual separation. An immediate sign is that Near Eastern specialists who divide their scholarly efforts equally between archaeological fieldwork and ancient texts have become increasingly rare. The Ancient Near East is also attracting fewer students in general (Matthews 2003: 189–98).[4]

Paradoxically, one reason for this distancing is that the two approaches have redefined their parameters toward similar expectations and aims, while still claiming territorial independence. Text-based scholars are now likely to define their briefs in broader terms than ancient history. Institutional titles like Ancient Near Eastern Languages and Literatures have been replaced with Ancient Near Eastern Cultures and Civilizations, or Mesopotamian Studies, or Eastern Mediterranean Studies. These are not mere cosmetic changes. As for "cultures" and "civilizations," Near Eastern archaeologists on both sides of the Atlantic had long appropriated them to reflect their concerns more accurately than, for instance, "Mesopotamian Art and

Archaeology." Yet the two perspectives show reluctance to admit that the limitations of one documentation type may well be compensated by the other. One could conclude that the different classes of data they use have directed the two perspectives into increasingly independent rather than connected paths.

Nonetheless, historian and archaeologist should renew their earlier association, this time in the spirit of interdisciplinary research. Archaeological projects involving historical periods should include a historian among their specialists; and historians should consult archaeologists on issues that may be attested in forms other than the written word. A fundamental commitment to a united discipline of Ancient Near Eastern Studies will ensure its future vitality and progress.

NOTES

1   This comment, perhaps made tongue-in-cheek, was written by H. R. Hall, co-author with C. L. Woolley of the excavation report on Tell Al-'Ubaid (Hall and Woolley 1927: 4). De Genouillac misattributes it to Woolley.
2   Replacing excavation with survey and limited soundings was a major tenet of the 1992 European Charter for the Protection and Management of the Archaeological Heritage (Articles 4–5), and reflected a crusade that had gained momentum over the two previous decades. *Antiquity* 67 (1993): 400–45 devoted a special section to this charter, whose ideology has guided and influenced research in the Middle East too.
3   There is evidence for mixed marriages at all social levels, including Assyrian women taking Anatolian husbands, but the recorded instances are few (Veenhof 1982: 152), perhaps because few were formalized. Children raised in these families would surely have been bilingual and bicultural.
4   Matthews, who vigorously endorses combining the efforts of Mesopotamian historians and archaeologists, describes the prospects for training a future generation of Ancient Near East specialists in the UK (and France) as "catastrophic" (2003: 196). The situation is not restricted to European and North American schools. It also applies to Turkey, where archaeology students are attracted in significantly larger numbers to the Classical periods, no doubt because the Greek and Roman worlds are a more familiar aspect of their cultural heritage.

FURTHER READING

Basic introductions in English to the archaeology of the Ancient Near East are Lloyd 1984 and Roaf 1990. For the early historical periods, Postgate 1994 provides a lively survey in which archaeology and ancient texts are superbly interwoven. Potts 1997 is recommended for textual and archaeological documentation on practical aspects of Mesopotamian culture, from agricultural products to kinship structure and burial customs, industry, the survival of temple architecture into the Sassanian era, and much else.

Lloyd 1980 remains the standard history for archaeological research in Iraq through the 1960s. Personal accounts by pioneers in the field (E. Porada, S. Lloyd, T. Jacobsen and

H. G. Güterbock) can be found in Sasson 1995, and make colorful reading. For recent developments, and an impassioned demonstration of Mesopotamian archaeology's current techniques and capabilities, see Matthews 2003. The evolution of archaeological methods and theory is best presented by Trigger 1989. For the promising application of the *Annales* approach to archaeology, see Knapp 1992. Neither Trigger nor Knapp refers specifically to historic Mesopotamia and the greater Near East, however.

CHAPTER SIX

The Languages of the Ancient Near East

Gonzalo Rubio

The Ancient Near East was a constellation of cultures, ethnic groups, civilizations, and languages. A few languages have come to us extremely well documented in vast corpora of texts (Egyptian, Sumerian, Akkadian, Hittite, etc.). Others are represented by a more modest number of texts, but still sufficient for us to be able to understand them for the most part and produce more or less complete translations (e.g., Hurrian, Urartian, and Elamite). A third group consists of languages that have an even smaller corpus and which, in the absence of clearly related languages, can be understood only in a very rudimentary and incomplete fashion (e.g., Hattic and Carian). Another group is formed by languages of which we have no real texts, but simply a few words here and there (perhaps even a word-list in some lexical text) and a handful of personal names (such as Kassite and Amorite and, even more poorly attested, Gutian). Finally, a fifth group is shrouded in the mystery created by the fog of time, the lack of texts, and even words, and includes the languages we know only by name, sometimes exclusively under the shaky inference that an ethnonym may well point to a particular language spoken by that people (e.g., Lullubeans and Subartians).

Sumerian

Birth and death of Sumerian

Sumerian was a language spoken in southern Mesopotamia and is most likely first attested in the archaic texts from Uruk and Jemdet Naṣr (from the end of the fourth millennium to the middle of the third). By the end of the third millennium, Sumerian had died out for the most part as a spoken language. However, it was still used in a wide variety of literary, scholarly, and religious genres, and was preserved in writing until the practical disappearance of the Mesopotamian civilization. Sumerian is an isolate, i.e, it is not related to any other language or language family. Thus, our knowledge of Sumerian grammar and lexicon is mostly based on a large number of bilingual texts (in Sumerian and Akkadian), as well as a stream of scribal and scholastic traditions materialized in a corpus of lexical lists and grammatical texts.[1]

Some scholars believe that Sumerian and its speakers would have not entered southern Mesopotamia until shortly before the Early Dynastic I (around 2900 BCE).[2] In fact, it has been argued that the first textual evidence of the Sumerian language appears in the archaic texts from Ur, but that such evidence is absent in the archaic texts from Uruk (phases Uruk IV and Uruk III). Therefore, some believe that the language of the archaic texts from the Late Uruk period was probably not Sumerian. However, an important factor is that there are some instances of phonetic writing in Late Uruk texts, which point to Sumerian as the language of these texts: phonetic indicators (ŠEG₉+ŠE+BAR = ŠEGBAR = **šeg₉-bar** "fallow deer"); some phonetic spellings, especially in the case of Semitic loanwords, such as MAŠ + GAN₂ (<*maškanu* "threshing floor, empty lot"), etc.[3] Only in Sumerian would those logograms correspond to words with that specific phonetic shape, which would allow the recycling of these signs according exclusively to their phonetic reading.

The murky waters of the early linguistic history of Mesopotamia have elicited diverse theories. Landsberger's (1974=1944) hypothetical pre-Sumerian substratum has been quite influential. This alleged lexical substratum would constitute the only remains of a hypothetical human group that would have inhabited southern Mesopotamia before the speakers of Sumerian. The core of this substratum included designations for occupations and trades (**ašgab** "cobbler, leather worker"; **azlag** "launderer"; **bahar₂** "potter"; etc.). The criteria for the identification of non-Sumerian words were mostly phonotactic (i.e., related to the word structure): they are polysyllabic, while Sumerian seems to prefer monosyllabism; they have similar endings and medial consonantal clusters; and they had no Sumerian etymologies. After a close examination of the lexical items singled out by Landsberger and others, one has to conclude that most of these items happen to be Semitic loanwords, Hurrian, *Arealwörter* (words occurring in many languages within a specific, albeit frequently large, geographical area) or *Wanderwörter* (words that travel with the objects or techniques they name), or properly Sumerian terms (Rubio 1999).

The death of Sumerian as a spoken language has also been debated. Nowadays, it is commonly accepted that Sumerian died out sometime during the Ur III period.[4] Sumerian became then a dead language, although it was probably still spoken in the circles of the **e₂-dub-ba** or "school" (Charpin 1994), as Latin was spoken in many Medieval *scriptoria*. Nonetheless, Sumerian remained in use for another two millennia, as a literary, scholarly, and liturgical language. The vast majority of Sumerian texts date to the long period between the death of Sumerian as a native tongue and the final disappearance of cuneiform writing and the Mesopotamian languages (Sumerian and Akkadian), probably during the first centuries of the Christian era, in the Parthian period (Geller 1997).

Overview of Sumerian

Mesopotamian cuneiform was the logosyllabic script used for Sumerian. Our knowledge of Sumerian phonology is limited by the nature of its writing interface. For instance, it is likely to have had a few "extra phonemes" – which are not explicit in the writing interface – such as the velar nasal /g̃/ or /ŋ/ and /dr/ (probably /ř/). Some final consonants (*Auslaut*) seem to drop (**kala** "mighty" </kalag/), but the same signs have readings with and without *Auslaut*: **kala** = **kalag**; **dug₄** = **du₁₁** "to speak." It was suggested that Sumerian may have had lexical tones (like Chinese), which allegedly would explain the sometimes high number of homophonic terms. However, other factors such as different *Auslaut* consonants and consonantal clusters (not explicit in the writing) can explain this.

As are many other Ancient Near Eastern languages (Hurrian, Elamite, etc.), Sumerian is an agglutinative language, that is, a word consists of a linear sequence of distinct morphemes, and the lexeme to which the morphemes are attached cannot undergo *Ablaut* (English *sing, sang, sung, song*) or infixation. The grammatical gender is based on an opposition between animate and inanimate nouns, but this only surfaces in the concord between pronouns and their antecedents. Grammatical number (plural versus singular) does not need to be marked in writing (**lugal** "king" or "kings"), but can be made explicit through suffixation (**lugal-e-ne**/lugal-ene/ "kings") or reduplication (**lugal-lugal** "kings"). The latter and similar procedures (**lugal gal-gal** KING BIG.BIG "the great kings," etc.) are probably simple orthographic conventions for writing the plural.

In the nominal system there are ten cases, which are marked by attaching suffixes to noun phrases (NPs). Moreover, cases can also be indicated by prefixes in verbal forms. NPs are conventionally called "nominal chains" by Sumerologists, because all the suffixes are heaped at the very end of the last syntagm:

dumu lugal kalam-ma-ka-ke₄-ne-ra	/dumu lugal kalam-ak-ak-ene-ra/
"for the sons of the king of the nation (=Sumer)"	son-king-nation-GENITIVE-GENITIVE-PLURAL-DATIVE

Sumerian is an ergative language, meaning that the subject of an intransitive verb presents the same marker as the object of a transitive verb (the absolutive case), while the subject of a transitive verb presents a marker (the ergative case), that is different from that of the intransitive verb. In English, it would be like saying "**him sleeps" and "**me sleep," but "I saw him" and "he saw me." Sumerian has /-e/ as the ergative suffix, and /-ø/ as the marker of absolutive case: **lugal-e e₂ mu-un-du₃** "the king (**lugal-e**) built the temple"; **lugal i₃-tuš** "the king (**lugal**) sat down"; **nin-e in-tud-en** "the queen (**nin-e**) bore me"; **nin i₃-tuš** "the queen (**nin**) sat down." In fact, Sumerian exhibits split ergativity in its morphology. The ergative alignment is strictly followed only in the nominal system. Independent personal pronouns, imperatives, cohortative verbal forms, and a few non-finite verbal constructions exhibit an accusative alignment (like English). The system of verbal agreement shows a similar split: the *ḫamṭu* forms (perfective) are ergative, whereas the *marû* forms (imperfective) show an accusative pattern.

Verbal stems are usually divided into two major categories: *ḫamṭu* ("quick, sudden" → perfective) and *marû* ("slow, fat" → imperfective). However, these two labels correspond to the understanding of the Sumerian verb by Akkadian-speaking scribes. In an early grammatical text, **lugud** ("short") occurs instead of *ḫamṭu*, and **gid₂** ("long") instead of *marû* (Civil 2002). Thus, the labels refer to the shape of the stems, which would be regarded as long because of reduplication and other possible changes. The problem of the marking of the so-called *marû* stem is still widely discussed. It is likely that all verbs had two stems. Affixation verbs perhaps marked the *marû* stem with an affix /-e/; reduplication verbs (like **gar** "to place") marked it with partial reduplication (**ga₂-ga₂**), as opposed to complete reduplication in *ḫamṭu* forms (**gar-gar**); alternating verbs (such as **e₃** "to go out") with their "expanded form" (/e₃-d/); and suppletive or complementary verbs (such as **dug₄**) with completely different lexemes (**e**) (see Yoshikawa 1993: 1–56, 95–104, 114–26). However, it is also possible that many verbs did not have two different stems, and that the only way to distinguish *ḫamṭu* from *marû* in those verbs was through concord (i.e., through pronominal affixes).

Whereas some modal prefixes indicate always the same mood (**ga-** → cohortative; **nu-** → negative; **ša-** → affirmative), others can mark a different kind of modality, depending on their interaction with the other elements within the TAM (tense, aspect, mood) system. For instance, /ha-/ + *ḫamṭu* marks affirmative constructions (**ha-na-sum** "I have indeed given"), whereas /ha-/ + *marû* marks the precative (**hu-mu-hul₂-le-en** "may you rejoice"). Likewise, /na-/ can mark affirmative (with *ḫamṭu*) and prohibitive (with *marû*), and /bara-/ negation (with *ḫamṭu*) or vetitive (with *marû*). Other prefixes in this slot do not really indicate modality: **u₃-** marks anteriority and /inga-/ is actually a proclitic connective particle.

The number, function, rank, compatibility, and shape of the so-called conjugation prefixes are still a matter of discussion. Probably there were only four morphemes: /ba-/; /imma-/; /i-/; and /mu-/. The prefix /bi-/ would be a combination of the prefix /ba-/ and the locative-terminative infix, and /imma-/ a reduplication of /mu-/ (Karahashi 2000). All verbal forms seem to start with an obligatory conjugation prefix (/mu-/, /ba-/, or /i-/). The choice of prefix seems governed by focus (Vanstiphout 1985): /mu-/ is focused for person but not for locus (place), while /ba-/ is focused for locus but not for person; and /i-/ is not focused. The /i-/ prefix is preferred for supportive, non-substantial material (background), but the foreground of regular narrative discourse is marked by /mu-/ or /ba-/ according to focus. The conjugation prefix /a-/ occurs sometimes in non-agentive passive constructions (**an-na-sum** "it was given to him").

The dimensional infixes mark case functional relations between the verb and NPs that may be explicit or implicit in the sentence. The pronominal prefixes normally agree with the subject of transitive *ḫamṭu* forms (ergative) and the suffixes with the subject of intransitive *ḫamṭu*, as well as the subject of both transitive and intransitive *marû* forms, the latter showing an accusative alignment. Furthermore, the pronominal prefixes can

STRUCTURE OF THE SUMERIAN VERBAL CHAIN

1	2	3	4	5		6	7	8	9	10
Modal prefixes	Connective prefix	"Conjugation" prefixes	Dative	Dimensional infixes		Pronominal prefixes	STEM		Pronominal suffixes	Nominalizer
Ø-		i- (V-)	-a- (1 sg)	-ši- TERMINATIVE	-ni- LOCATIVE	-Ø-/-e- (2 sg)			-en	-en
he₂-		mu- (m-)	-ra- (2 sg)			-n- (3 sg an)			-en	-en
ga-		ba- (b-)	-na- (3 sg)	-da- COMITATIVE		-b- (3 sg in)			-Ø	-e
bara-	inga-	im-ma-	-me- (1 pl)					-ed	-enden	-enden
na-			[-re- (2 pl)]	-ta- ABLAT.-INST.	-e- / -i- LOCAT.-TERM.				-enzen	-enzen
ša-		a-	-ne- (3 pl)						-eš	-ene
u₃-										-a
nu-										
al-										

also specify that a dimensional prefix refers to a second or third person, as well as the gender of any syntactical argument marked with a verbal prefix. The pronominal suffixes are identical for all verbal forms with the exception of the third person singular and plural. A third person in the absolute case shows concord with /-ø/ in the singular and with /-eš/ in the plural. An ergative with a *marû* form shows concord with /-e/ in the singular and /-ene/ in the plural. The absolutive case of a transitive *marû* construction (i.e., the accusative case with *marû*) does not agree with the pronominal suffixes but with the pronominal prefixes (/-b-/ and /-n-/).

	Transitive *ḫamṭu*	Intransitive *ḫamṭu*	Transitive *marû*	Intransitive *marû*
Subject	Prefix (+ suffix in pl.)	Suffix (3rd -Ø/-eš)	Suffix (3rd -e/-ene)	Suffix (3rd -Ø/-eš)
Object	Suffix (3rd -Ø/-eš)		Prefix	

The imperative exhibits a reverse order of verbal constituents: it begins with the stem, which is followed by all the prefixes, as in **sum-ma-ab** /sum-mu-a-b/ "give (singular) it to me"; **sum-ma-ab-ze₂-en** /sum-mu-a-b-enzen/ "give (plural) it to me." This phenomenon is similar to the switch from proclisis to enclisis in the imperative in other languages, e.g., Spanish *me lo das* ("you give it to me") versus *dámelo* ("give it to me").

The suffix /-ed/ can occur in non-finite and finite verbal forms, and can immediately follow the verbal stem and precede the pronominal suffix: **e₂-mu lu₂ i₃-bur₃-de₃** "someone could break (/i-bur-(e)d-e/) into my house"; **e₂ du₃-de₃ igi-zu u₃ dug₃-ga nu-ši-ku₄-ku₄** "in order to build (/du₃-(e)d-e/) the house you will not let sweet sleep enter your eyes." Some consider the /-e-/ in /-ed/ the marker of *marû* (see above). Likewise, the nominalizer suffix /-a/ can be attached to both non-finite and finite verbal forms, and can be followed by case endings and pronouns. When the nominalized verbal form agrees with an explicit (such as **lu₂** "man" → who/that) or implicit noun that has an antecedent in another sentence, it constitutes the equivalent of an English relative clause: **ensi₂ lu₂ e₂-ninnu in-du₃-a e₂-uru-gir₂-su^(ki)-ka-ni mu-na-du₃** "the *ensi*-ruler that built the Eninnu (**lu₂** … **in-du₃-a** ← /i-du₃-a/), built her temple of the city of Girsu." Due to the high number of grammatical functions explicitly marked, there is no obvious syntactical opposition between parataxis (coordination) and hypotaxis (subordination); the latter would correspond entirely to nominalized verbal forms. For instance, the word order tends to be almost always Subject-Object-Verb in all sentences.

The eme-sal dialect: genderlect or genrelect?

Sumerian is called **eme-gir₁₅** (perhaps "native tongue") in native Sumerian sources. In some Mesopotamian scholarly texts, a few lexical items and grammatical forms are identified as **eme-sal** (perhaps "fine language"). It has been argued that **eme-sal** was a women's language (*Frauensprache*) or genderlect, especially because the sign SAL can also be read as **munus** "woman." The fact is that **eme-sal** is attested in compositions of very specific genres: cultic songs performed by the **gala**-priests (Akkadian *kalû*); diverse texts containing Inanna's speech (myths, Inanna-Dumuzi cycle, etc.); some laments over the destruction of cities, usually uttered by goddesses (those of Ur, Eridu, and Nippur); a lullaby supposedly addressed to a son of Shulgi by his mother (Kramer 1971); about thirty proverbs or short sayings from the rhetorical collections of Sumerian proverbs; an unpublished composition, "The song of the millstone" (only 33 lines are preserved); and the "Dialogues between two women" (Alster 1990: 7–8). No text is entirely written in **eme-sal**, and there is no true consistency in its use, so an otherwise "main-dialect" text may present some scattered **eme-sal** words. In origin, **eme-sal** may have stemmed from an actual regional dialect (diatopic variant) or from the particular dialect of a certain group (diastratic variant, genderlect, etc.). However, as we have it attested, in most cases, the occurrence of **eme-sal** forms may be determined mostly by the genre of the text, rather than by the gender of the fictional speaker or even the performer.[5]

Ancient Egyptian

Ancient Egyptian constitutes a branch of the Afroasiatic language family, along with the Semitic, Berber, Cushitic, Omotic, and Chadic branches.[6] Ancient Egyptian is the language of Pharaonic and Ptolemaic Egypt. In three millennia of history, many different dialects are attested in the written record, and they can be subsumed under these general classifications:

- Old Egyptian is attested in texts from the Old Kingdom and the First Intermediate Period (c. 3000–2000 BCE), such as the Pyramid Texts and many so-called "autobiographies."
- Middle Egyptian (or "Classical Egyptian") is attested during the Middle Kingdom and the early part of the New Kingdom, until the end of Dynasty 18 (c. 2000–1300 BCE); it is the language of the Coffin Texts and many secular and religious compositions (instructions, hymns, stories, and so on).
- Late Middle Egyptian (or Neo-Middle Egyptian) is an artificially conservative literary language, attested in religious texts (hymns, rituals, etc.) from the New Kingdom to the end of the Ancient Egyptian civilization. Although its grammar is virtually identical to that of Middle Egyptian, its use of hieroglyphs increasingly departed from that of earlier periods.
- Late Egyptian is a label used in different ways by different scholars (Junge 2001: 17–23); it usually refers to the language of the texts written from the Ramesside to the Saite period (Dynasties 19–26, c. 1300–650 BCE), and it includes some literary compositions (such as love poetry and stories) as well as correspondence, administrative documents, and inscriptions. Many Late Egyptian texts are written in Hieratic, but they are frequently edited in hieroglyphic transcriptions by modern scholars.

- Demotic is both the name of the new script introduced during the seventh century BCE and the specific Egyptian dialect written with it; Demotic texts sprawl from the seventh century BCE until the fifth century CE. The Demotic script was also used to write down some Aramaic texts in Egypt, which are particularly important for shedding light on many aspects of Aramaic phonology as well as for the literary genre of some of them.[7]

It is important to distinguish between names of scripts and those of dialects. Hieroglyphics were written throughout the whole history of Ancient Egypt, especially in monumental inscriptions. Devised quite early (c. 2600 BCE), hieratic was a cursive version of sequences of hieroglyphs with ligatures and diacritics. It was used until well into the Christian era (c. third century CE). Thus, the labels "hieroglyphic" and "hieratic" pertain exclusively to the domain of script. On the other hand, during the reign of Psammetichus I (c. 650 BCE), Demotic, a short-hand and heavily simplified version of hieratic sign groups, was introduced and it was employed to write a specific dialect of Egyptian called Demotic.

Eventually, a version of the Greek alphabet with a few additional Demotic characters was used to write Coptic, the latest member of the Egyptian branch of Afroasiatic languages. The earliest Coptic texts may date perhaps to the second century CE (Quaegebeur 1982; Satzinger 1984). Coptic itself has several dialects: Sahidic, Bohairic, Aḥmimic, Lycopolitan or Subaḥmimic, and Fayyumic. Although after the Islamic expansion Coptic was gradually replaced by Arabic and probably died out as a spoken language sometime after the thirteenth century CE, the Bohairic dialect is still used in the liturgy of the Orthodox (Monophysite or rather Miaphysite) Christians in Egypt.

The phonological structure and inventory of Ancient Egyptian are quite problematic. The scripts (hieroglyphic, its cursive version hieratic, and Demotic) do not write the vowels or mark geminated consonants. Thus, all approaches to Egyptian phonology are necessarily based on a comparison with Coptic and transliterations of Egyptian words in other languages, as well as, to a lesser extent, Egyptian transliterations of foreign words (Akkadian, Hebrew, Greek, etc.).[8] Nonetheless, it seems clear that the traditional transliteration of many Egyptian signs masks the true phonological structure of Egyptian. For instance, in early Egyptian, the segment written with the sign 𓄿 (a vulture), usually regarded as a glottal stop ($ꜣ$=/ʔ/ or /ʕ/), was probably an uvular trill (R), which did eventually become a glottal stop and merged with the sign 𓇋 (a flowering reed). The latter, traditionally transliterated as *i̯*, was originally used for a palatal glide (/j/), which eventually became a glottal stop (ʔ) too. Likewise, the segment corresponding to the sign 𓆓 (a snake), customarily transliterated as *ḏ*, was not a voiced interdental fricative, but a voiced palatal stop (ɟ), or perhaps a voiced palato-alveolar affricate (/ǯ/).

The Egyptian nominal system has two genders (masculine and feminine, the latter marked with -*t*) and three number categories: singular, plural (masculine plural -*w*, feminine plural -*wt*), and dual (masculine dual -*wj*, feminine dual -*j*). Nonetheless, most discussions about Egyptian grammar gravitate around the verbal system. It was through the careful study of and comparison with the Coptic verb that Polotsky and his disciples have shed essential light on these matters (their approach is now labeled the "Standard Theory").[9] The main derivational morphemes marking voice, aspect, and tense in the Egyptian verbal system are the following suffixes:

.*n* → past tense: *sḏm.n=j* "I heard"
.*t* → perfective and prospective: *sḏm.t=f* "he had heard"; *jw.t=f* "he shall come"
.*w* → prospective aspect and passive voice: *jrj.w=f* "it has been done, it shall be done"
.*tw* → passive voice: *sḏm.tw=k* "you are heard"

The finite verbal forms consist of verbal root, an optional morpheme suffixed to the root indicating tense, aspect or voice, and a pronominal suffix. Due to the writing interface, the number of so-called "tenses" is difficult to determine. There is a suffix conjugation, which does not occur in initial position (i.e., it occurs after a particle or a topicalized element); this may include a circumstantial form (indifferent to tense) and a prospective (future), which may have been characterized by different vocalizations. There is another suffix conjugation (so-called "emphatic"), which occurs in initial position and exhibits reduplication of the second radical in verbs whose third radical is a semiconsonant (i.e., III-*j* and III-*w* verbs: *mrr=s wj* "(the-fact-that) she loves me," versus *mrj=s* "she loves, loved, will love"). This pattern is similar to the Akkadian durative *iparras*, although it may not have exhibited gemination, just a /CvCvC/ pattern.

The stative (old perfective or pseudoparticiple) marks the perfective aspect with intransitive verbs, as well as the passive voice with transitive verbs; it was in origin a conjugated verbal adjective (like the Akkadian stative *paris*).

In the suffix conjugation, when a noun fulfilling the function of subject occurs explicitly in the sentence, the verbal suffix is dropped. The verbal system changed substantially through time, and the spelling of some pronominal suffixes fluctuated too. Nonetheless, the following paradigm may give an idea of the structure of the Egyptian verbal system:

	SUFFIX CONJUGATION		STATIVE
1st sg.	*sḏm=j* "I hear, heard"		(*jw=j*) *sḏm.kw* "I was heard"
2nd m.sg.	*sḏm=k* "you hear"		(*jw=k*) *sḏm.tj* "you were heard"
2nd f.sg.	*sḏm=t* "you hear"		(*jw=t*) *sḏm.tj* "you were heard"
3rd m.sg. pron.	*sḏm=f* "he hears"		(*jw=f*) *sḏm.w* "he was heard"
3rd m.sg. nom.	*sḏm rmt* "the man hears"		(*rmt*) *sḏm.w* "the man was heard"
3rd f.sg. pron.	*sḏm=s* "she hears"		(*jw=s*) *sḏm.tj* "she was heard"
3rd f.sg. nom.	*sḏm ḥjm.t* "the woman hears"		(*ḥjm.t*) *sḏm.tj* "the woman was heard"
1st dual	*sḏm=nj* "we (two) hear"		
2nd dual	*sḏm=tnj* "you (two) hear"		
3rd dual	*sḏm=snj* "they (two) hear"	m.	(*jw=snj*/NP) *sḏm.wj* "they (two) were heard"
		f.	(*jw=snj*/NP) *sḏm.tj* "they (two) were heard"
1st pl.	*sḏm=n* "we hear"		(*jw=n*) *sḏm.wjn* "we were heard"
2nd pl.	*sḏm=tn* "you hear"		(*jw=tn*) *sḏm.twjn* "you were heard"
3rd pl. pron.	*sḏm=sn* "they hear"	m.	(*jw=sn*) *sḏm.w* "they were heard"
		f.	(*jw=sn*) *sḏm.tj* "they were heard"
3rd pl. nom.	*sḏm rmt.w* "the men hear"	m.	(*rmt.w*) *sḏm.w* "the men were heard"
		f.	(*ḥjm.wt*) *sḏm.tj* "the women were heard"

The non-finite verbal forms include the infinitive (*sḏm* "to hear"), the negative complement (*sḏm.w* "(not) to hear"), and the participles (masculine singular *sḏm* "hearer/heard"; feminine singular *sḏm.t*; masculine plural *sḏm.w*; feminine plural *sḏm.t*). A very important syntactical phenomenon is the "embedding" of a verbal form in order to mark topicalization (pragmatic topic = theme) or rhematization (emphasized comment = rhema). The so-called "Standard Theory" (stemming from Polotsky) and the traditional approach differ substantially in how they analyze these constructions. For instance, a sentence such as *jrr=ṯ p3 jb ḥr-m* "why are you in this mood?" could be analyzed in two different ways (Loprieno 1995a: 2147–8):

- According to Polotsky's now standard theory, it exhibits a "transposition" of the thema-rhema sequence, generating a "complex adverbial sentence" (literally "that-you-do this mood is on-what"), in which the subject would be the verbal form with its object (*jrr=ṯ p3 jb* "you do this mood"), and the predicate the adverbial phrase (*ḥr-m* "why").
- According to the conventional approach, the verbal form (predicate *jrr* + subject *ṯ*) is followed by an adverbial form marking the pragmatic focus (*ḥr-m* "why"), so the sentence could be literally understood as "why (*ḥr-m*) do you (*ṯ* = nominal subject) do this mood (*jrj p3 jb* = verbal predicate + object)."

Functionally, this kind of construction resembles cleft sentences marking focalization in English (e.g., "it is her smile that I like"), although formally this so-called transposition happens to be surprisingly similar to Celtic cleft sentences (Shisha-Halevy 2000).

Semitic Languages

The boundaries between "language" and "dialect" are particularly murky in the Semitic language family. Nonetheless, one can establish the following language groups within Semitic:

1 East Semitic
   1.1 Akkadian: spoken in Mesopotamia, since c. 2500 to first century CE
   1.2 Eblaite: texts from Ebla (Tell Mardīḫ), Northern Syria, c. 2400–2300 BCE
2 South Semitic
   2.1 Modern South Arabian (MSA): Mehri, Soqoṭri, Jibbāli, Ḥarsūsi, etc.
   2.2 Ethiopian Semitic: Geʿez or Classical Ethiopic, Tigrinya, Tigré, Amharic, etc.
3 Central Semitic[10]
   3.1 Old South Arabian (OSA) or Epigraphic South Arabian (ESA): from the eighth century BCE to the sixth century CE. From north to south: Minean (Maʿin), Sabaean or Sabaic (Sabaʾ), Qatabani (Qaṭabān or Qiṭban), Hadramauti (Ḥaḍramawt).
   3.2 Arabic

- North Arabian pre-Islamic inscriptions from the sixth century BCE to the fourth century CE, in different scripts (Nabatean, Epigraphic South Arabian)
  - Liḥyānite (Liḥyānī) in the oasis of al-ᶜUlā (ancient Dedān)
  - Thamūdic (Θamūdī) corresponding to the tribe of Thamūd (*Tamudi* in the Neo-Assyrian texts); one script with several dialects
  - Ṣafaitic (Ṣafawī/Ṣafaʔī) in the basaltic desert of Ṣafā (southeast of Damascus)
  - Ḥasaean (Ḥāsaʔī) in the great oasis of al-Ḥāṣaʔ (east of Saudi Arabia)
- Pre-classical Arabic: inscriptions from Qaryat al-Fāw (near modern Sulayyil) from the second century BCE to the third century CE; forms quoted by Arabic grammarians
- Classical Arabic (ᶜarabiyya, lisān ᶜarabī): language of the Qurʔān; Modern Literary Arabic (fuṣḥā "pure, clear"); Modern Arabic dialects; Maltese, Uzbeki Arabic

3.3   Northwest Semitic languages
- Amorite: language of the once seminomadic people of the area, attested in personal names (Hammurabi, etc.) from the second millennium BCE
- Ugaritic: language of the texts from Ugarit (Ras Šamra, Syria), second millennium BCE
- Aramaic: Old, Imperial (Achaemenid), and Biblical Aramaic; Palestinian Aramaic; Nabatean; Talmudic Aramaic; Syriac; Classical and Modern Mandaic; Modern Aramaic (Neo-Aramaic) dialects/languages (Maᶜlūla, la, Ṭūrōyo, Modern Mandaic, Northeastern Aramaic)
- "Canaanite": Moabite (ninth century), Ammonite, Edomite, Phoenician and Punic, Hebrew.

There is quite a number of features that characterize the members of the Semitic language family. In the realm of phonology, they exhibit a triadic oppositions of stops: voiced (*d*), voiceless (*t*), and "emphatic" (*ṭ*). The nature of the so-called "emphatics" varies from language to language: from pharyngealized or uvularized consonants (Arabic) to glottalized ejectives (Akkadian, Ethiopic, Modern South Arabian). Moreover, they have a specific set of consonants characteristically pronounced in different areas of the throat:

Laryngeals (glottals): /ʔ/ (=/ʔ/; Arabic ا, Hebrew א) and /h/ (Arabic ه, Hebrew ה)
Pharyngeals: /ᶜ/ (=/ʕ/; Arabic ع, Hebrew ע) and /ḥ/ (=/ħ/; Arabic ح, Hebrew ח)
Uvulars (velar fricatives): /ḫ/ (=/x/; Arabic خ) and /ġ/ (=/ɣ/; Arabic غ)

In their morphology, Semitic languages would seem to exhibit consonantal roots, as if they were consonantal skeletons in which vowels and infixes can be interdigitated, and prefixes and suffixes attached. For instance, from an Akkadian a root √kṣr would generate kaṣārum "to bind"; kuṣur "bind" (imperative); kuṣṣurum "well tied"; makṣarum "bundle," etc. Although this consonantal root is rather an abstraction created by grammarians and linguists, it represents a practical approach to learning Semitic languages (Rubio 2005b). In the nominal system, there are two genders (masculine and feminine, the feminine marker being usually a suffix -*t*) and two number categories, singular and plural. The dual is not very productive and exists only in Arabic, Akkadian, OSA, and Hebrew. There is a specific plural formation known as a "broken plural" (*pluralis fractus*) or internal plural, which is extremely productive in Arabic, Modern South Arabian, and Ethiopic, but of which only traces can be found in other languages (such as Hebrew and Akkadian): Arabic *qalb* "heart" → plural *qulūb*; Mehri (Modern South Arabian) *baḫḫôr* "sailor" → plural *baḥarît*. Arabic, Akkadian, and Ugaritic have three cases in the declension of most nouns: nominative (marking the subject: *-un* or *-um*), accusative (marking the direct object: *-an* or *-am*), and genitive (the adnominal case: *-in* or *-im*). In possessive constructions, a noun occurs in the so-called "construct state" and is followed by a genitive: Akkadian *bītum* "house" → *bīt awīlim* "the man's house." There are alternative constructions in most Semitic languages, such as Akkadian *bītum ša awīlim* "the house of the man."

In the verbal system, the second and third persons of verbal forms can distinguish between masculine and feminine: Arabic *kataba* "he wrote" versus *katabat* "she wrote"; Hebrew *tiktob* "you (masculine) will write" versus *tiktəbī* "you (feminine) will write"; Akkadian *irrubū* "they (masculine) will enter" and *irrubā* "they (feminine) will enter." The number of verbal tenses varies from two (as in Hebrew and Arabic) to three or four (as in Akkadian and Ethiopic). The patterns of the main tenses are as follows:

Non-past (=present/future) *-parrVs*	Prefixed
Past *-prVs* ~ Jussive (imperative-like) *-prVs*	Prefixed
Stative *parVs* -	Suffixed

Semitic languages exhibit a very synthetic capacity to mark voice (and sometimes aspect as well) through specific verbal stems. The most common patterns are these:

-pVrrVs	"Intensive" (plurality of objects/actions)
-pV̄rVs	Conative (cf. applicative in Bantu, IO → DO)
n-prefix	Intransitive (passive or reflexive)
t-prefix/infix	Intransitive (passive or reflexive) or reciprocal
ša-/sa-prefix (or *ha-* and *ʾa-*)	Causative
ista-/asta-prefix (or *išta/ašta*)	Reciprocal, causative, etc.

In terms of syntax, the default word order in Ancient Semitic languages is VSO (Verb-Subject-Object), as in Classical Arabic, Biblical Hebrew, and Classical Ethiopic. Nonetheless, most modern Semitic languages present SVO order. Due to language contact, Akkadian (influenced by Sumerian) and Modern Ethiopian (in contact with Cushitic languages) switched to SOV.

Akkadian

The Semitic language of Ancient Mesopotamia can be divided roughly into the following dialects:

"Old Akkadian"[11] (OAkk)	c. 2500–2000	
Old Assyrian (OAss)	c. 2000–1500	Old Babylonian (OB)
Middle Assyrian (MAss)	c. 1500–1000	Middle Babylonian (MBab)
Neo-Assyrian (NAss)	c. 1000–600	Neo-Babylonian (NBab)
	c. 600 BCE–100 CE	Late Babylonian (LBab)

Most literary texts since the end of the OB period are written in an artificial literary language based on OB, called "Standard Babylonian" (SB). There are a number of peripheral Akkadian "dialects," attested in texts from outside Mesopotamia, such as the diplomatic archive from Amarna (Egypt), the archives from Emar, Ekalte (Tell Munbāqa), and Ugarit (all in Syria), as well as the texts from Alalaḫ (Tell Atchana in Turkey). In actuality, these peripheral texts do not really represent real dialects, but rather the use of Akkadian as a *lingua franca*, as well as a bureaucratic and chancellery language, by scribes whose native language was other (Ugaritic, diverse Northwest Semitic dialects, etc.).[12] Nonetheless, the linguistic importance of these texts lies in the information they provide precisely about the native languages of the scribes (such as the Amarna letters sent by Canaanite rulers).

Akkadian phonology exhibits the almost complete loss of laryngeals (glottals), pharyngeals, and the uvular (velar fricative) /ġ/ (=/ɣ/); only the uvular /ḫ/ (=/ x/) clearly remains: *ʾamārum > amārum "to see"; *halākum > alākum "to go"; *ahlum > ālum "city"; *ḫarāθum > erēšum "to plow"; *ʿazābum > ezēbum "to leave"; *ǵaθayum > ešûm "to confuse." The subsystem of sibilants also exhibits some peculiarities, most likely due to the writing interface. In transliterating Old Akkadian texts, many scholars use a special sign, *ś*, which would correspond to the result of the merger of Semitic *š (to be reconstructed as an original voiceless fricative alveolar, [s]) and *ś (to be reconstructed as an original voiceless fricative lateral, [ɬ]). The merger between *š and *ś eventually converged with the results of *θ. In Old Akkadian (Early Dynastic and Sargonic Akkadian), the result of *θ is written with š-signs, whereas the result of the merger between *š and *ś is written with s-signs (see Rubio 2003a).

Akkadian has three cases in the declension of most nouns: nominative, accusative, and genitive. The declension of *bēlum damqum* ("good lord") and *bēltum damiqtum* ("good lady") is as follows (the dual is mostly limited to natural duals: hands, feet, etc.):

	Masculine	Feminine
Nominative singular	*bēlum damqum*	*bēltum damiqtum*
Accusative singular	*bēlam damqam*	*bēltam damiqtam*
Genitive singular	*bēlim damqim*	*bēltim damiqtim*
Nominative plural	*bēlū damqūtum*	*bēlētum damqātum*
Accusative & genitive plural	*bēlī damqūtim*	*bēlētim damqātim*

Towards the end of the Old Babylonian period, the final nasals (*mimation*) in all morphological endings (cases, pronominal suffixes, etc.) seem to drop. Eventually, in the first millennium most dialects seem to confuse cases easily, probably because the short vowels left after the fall of the nasal were only a conservative orthographic feature and did not reflect any actual segment. Similarly, final short vowels in particles, prepositions, and pronouns can eventually be dropped.[13]

The TAM system (tense, aspect, mood) in Akkadian is more extensive than in the rest of Semitic languages. There are four finite verbal forms:

Durative	Non-past (= present/future) -*parrVs*-	Prefixed & suffixed
Preterite	Past -*prVs*- (cf. imperative *prVs*-)	Prefixed & suffixed
Perfect	Past -*ptarVs*-	Prefixed & suffixed
Stative	Stative **parVs*-	Suffixed only

The number of verbal stems is higher:

G	**-p(V)rVs*-	→Basic stem
D	**-pVrrVs*-	→"Intensive" (plurality of objects/actions)
Š	*ša*-prefix	→Causative
N	*n*-prefix	→"Passive"
t	*t*-infix (with G, D, and Š)	→Intransitive (passive or reflexive)
tn	*tan*-infix (with G, D, Š, and N)	→Iterative (plurality of action)
Št	*šta*-prefix	→Reciprocal, causative, etc.

The *t* and *tan* infixes can occur along with the other stems: Gt, Gtn, Dt, Dtn, Štn, Ntn (*Nt would be an impossible intransitive passive):

G pret.	3rd c.sg.	*i-prus*	3rd m.pl.	*i-prus-ū*
	(3rd f.sg.	*ta-prus*)	3rd f.pl.	*i-prus-ā*
	2nd m.sg.	*ta-prus*	2nd c.pl.	*ta-prus-ā*
	2nd f.sg.	*ta-prus-ī*		
	1st c.sg.	*a-prus*	1st c.pl.	*ni-prus*
Š stative	3rd c.sg.	*šu-prus*	3rd m.pl.	*šu-prus-ū*
	3rd f.sg.	*šu-prus-at*	3rd f.pl.	*šu-prus-ā*
	2nd m.sg.	*šu-prus-āta*	2nd m.pl.	*šu-prus-ātunu*
	2nd f.sg.	*šu-prus-āti*	2nd f.pl.	*šu-prus-ātina*
	1st c.sg.	*šu-prus-āku*	1st c.pl.	*šu-prus-ānu*

Eblaite

The discovery of a large archive at Tell Mardīḫ (ancient Ebla) in the mid 1970s marked a dramatic revolution in our understanding of the early history and culture of Syro-Mesopotamia. Eblaitic grammar cannot be fully described. Many forms in the nominal, pronominal, and verbal systems are not attested, because the texts are written with an abundance of logograms. Even when the words are spelled syllabically, the true phonological nature of the segments is not always clear. For instance, the lateral *l* is not always written, especially when one would expect a *lvC* or a *lv* sign (a phenomenon known as *L-Reduktion*); so A is used for /la/, I for /li/, and U₉ for /lu/: *a-i-núm* (VE 782) → /ʾalīnum/ (cp. Akk. *elēnum* "above"); *i-da-kam₄* (75.G.2420 Rv. × 12) → /ittalkam/ "it has arrived" (G perfect of *alākum*).[14] However, this should be regarded as a mere orthographic conventional phenomenon, lacking any phonological implication. In fact, in pre-consonantal position, several segments are omitted in writing (/l/, /r/, /ʔ/, /ʕ/, /h/, and /ḥ/).

Gelb coined the term "Kish civilization," which would have covered a large area from Ebla in northern Syria (or even further to the west) to Kish, and probably also some areas to the east of Kish (Abū Ṣalābīḫ and the Diyāla region, perhaps up to Assyria). According to Gelb (1992), the "Kishite" cultural continuum exhibited a certain number of common features: (1) a set of scribal conventions; (2) actual scribal schools (and sometimes even the scribes themselves); (3) language; (4) the decimal system (versus the sexagesimal one); (5) the systems of mea-surements; (6) the calendar of twelve months with Semitic names; (7) the year dates at Abū Ṣalābīḫ and Mari; and (8) Semitic anthroponyms, theonyms, and toponyms.

The classification of Eblaite proposed by Gelb seems rather appropriate even if somewhat nebulous. However, the alleged strong similarities between the different East Semitic dialects (Eblaite, Old Akkadian, and the Mari Akkadian of the *šakka-nakku* texts [post-Ur III Mari], all prior to the Old Babylonian period) that were part of the so-called Kishite civilization, are sometimes weak. The phonological inventor-ies in Ebla and in Old Akkadian are substantially different. More mergers took place in Old Akkadian, while Ebla kept specific orthographies corresponding to Semitic *ð, *θ, and *z (š-signs for *ð and *θ and z-signs for *z). Moreover, common scribal practices – probably due to the movement of scribes from one city to another – may be masking further differences (Rubio 2006a). Nevertheless, there are also some important discrepancies in matters of spelling. For instance, the syllabograms *id*, *ug*, *un*, and *su₄* are well attested in Early Dynastic and Sargonic Akkadian, but do not seem to occur in Ebla. On the other hand, the reading *ru₁₂* of EN seems to be exclusive to the Ebla texts during the third millennium. Some syllabograms that are common in Ebla – *ba₄*, *bù*, *buᵧ* (NI), *íb*, *ne*, *zú*, *u₉* – occur (rather scarcely) in Mesopotamian texts from the Early Dynastic and Early Sargonic periods, but they seem attested in later (Sargonic and Ur III) Akkadian texts. All in all, these distribu-tion patterns do point to a close relation between the Eblaitic and the Early Meso-potamian scribal traditions.

In spite of all these nuances, Early Dynastic and Sargonic Akkadian, the Akkadian of the *šakkanakku* texts from Mari, and Eblaite do exhibit the same East Semitic diagnostic isoglosses: verbal forms *iparras*, *iprus*, *paris*, and *iptaras* (the latter being more difficult to identify because it is formally identical to the preterites of *t*-infixed stems); vowel /u/ in the conjugation prefixes of verbs primae *w*; many common lexical items; etc. However, there are some striking (albeit isolated) features occurring only in one or two of these languages or dialects, such as a form *tiprusū/tiparrasū* for the third plural masculine person in the *šakkanakku* texts from Mari and in Ebla (instead of the expected *iprusū/iparrasū*). In sum, Eblaite is not an Akkadian dialect, properly speaking, but a member of the East Semitic group, along with the Akkadian dialects. Thus, it is more accurate to refer to the Early East Semitic continuum as including two major segments: Eblaite and Early Dynastic Akkadian (EDAkk).[15]

Northwest Semitic languages

Amorite is well represented by anthroponyms attested in Mesopotamian cuneiform texts, such as Hammurapi /ᶜammu-rāpiʾ/ "The Paternal Uncle is a healer" and Zimri-Lim /ðimrī-līm/ "The Tribe is my protection." The lexicon and the grammar of these names clearly departs from East Semitic and falls under the general umbrella of Northwest Semitic within the Central Semitic group of Semitic languages.

Ugaritic is the language of the texts found at the Syrian site of Ras Šamra and its vicinity. The vast majority of Ugaritic texts are written with a cuneiform alphabet that does not note the vowels, although there are three *aleph* signs that do indicate vowels. In the absence of explicit vocalization, Ugaritic may look closer to Biblical Hebrew than it actually was. Nevertheless, there is some information on Ugaritic vocalism and phonology in the Ugaritic words syllabically spelled in different genres of Akkadian texts from Ugarit (Huehnergard 1987). The texts as found date to the Late Bronze Age (c. 1400–1200 BCE), but the literary compositions certainly represent an earlier stage of the language than that of the letters and administrative documents. The existence of cases is especially clear in third-weak nouns: nominative *kŝu* /kussiʾu/ "throne"; accusative *kŝa* /kussʾa/; genitive *kŝi* /kussʾi/. Masculine nouns in plural and dual exhibit a final -*m*, and feminine ones -*t* in plural and -*tm* in dual. The verbal system is typical for Northwest Semitic. There are two verbal forms in the indicative mood, a suffix perfective (*qtl*) and a prefix imperfective (*yqtl*). However, the imperfective *yqtl* occurs in poetic texts frequently referring to a past punctual (aorist-like) in narrative sequences; this phenomenon may resemble the construction with *wāw* consecutive in Biblical Hebrew, only that in Ugaritic no conjunction is needed (see below).

Aramaic languages or dialects have been around for almost three millennia already. In the Ancient Near East, one can identify some specific dialects:

- Old Aramaic (until the end of the seventh century BCE)
  - Western Old or Standard Syrian Aramaic: e.g., the stela of Zakkur, king of Hamath; the Sefire stelae
  - Samalian or Yaʾudi: inscriptions from the Neo-Hittite kingdom of Samʾal, modern Zinçirli, in Anatolia
  - The Tell Faḥariya bilingual (Neo-Assyrian-Aramaic), especially important for the history of the Aramaic alphabet
  - Aramaic legal and economic texts, as well as glosses, inscribed on clay tablets in first millennium Mesopotamia.
  - Deir ᶜAllā: a difficult and fragmentary text written on plaster walls and describing a vision of a certain Balaam, son of Beor (the prophet mentioned in Numbers 22–24)
- Imperial Aramaic (from the end of the seventh century to the end of the third century BCE): this is the *lingua franca* used during the last century of the Neo-Babylonian period, the Achaemenid empire, and the beginning of the Hellenistic

period. It is attested throughout the whole Near East (Mesopotamia, Egypt, Anatolia, Ancient Palestine, etc.); this includes the papyri from the Jewish garrison at Elephantine (Egypt) and the letters in the Biblical book of Ezra
- Middle Aramaic (200 BCE–250 CE): inscriptions from Palmyra, Petra (Nabatean Aramaic), Hatra, and other sites in the whole Near East; the Aramaic chapters of the book of Daniel; the Aramaic texts from Qumran, and those in Demotic script from Egypt, etc. (Late and Modern Aramaic is beyond our scope here.)

Old Aramaic exhibits a certain level of polyphony in its script, i.e., the same character actually represents more than one segment. For instance, in Old Aramaic the grapheme ז <z> was frequently used for the sibilant /z/ and the interdental /ð/ (*zhb*/ *ðhb*/ "gold"), instead of ד <d>. This polyphony can be explained because the Northwest Semitic linear alphabet, as used already in the late second millennium in Lebanon and eventually in Ancient Palestine, represented a simplification of the graphemic inventory of the original "Proto-Canaanite" alphabet, as has been pointed out by many (e.g., Puech 1986). This simplification, from perhaps 27 or 28 to only 22 graphemes, was motivated by the fact that Phoenician had undergone, or begun to undergo, the neutralization of several phonological oppositions (ġ/ʿ, ḥ/h, ð/z, ð̣/ṣ) probably already in the Late Bronze period. However, not until much later did these phonological neutralizations take place in other Northwest Semitic languages, which borrowed the Phoenician alphabet, adopted it, and adapted it in the form of the later Hebrew and Aramaic scripts.

In the case of Hebrew phonology, polyphony can be observed in the transliteration of toponyms and anthroponyms in the Septuagint (the Greek translation of the Hebrew Bible), in fragments from other translations (those of Aquila, Symmachus, and Theodotion), and in Origen's *Hexapla*, e.g., Hebrew ʿ*Azzāh* and Greek *Gáza* (Arabic *Ġazza*); Hebrew ʿ*Ămorāh* and Greek *Gomorra* (Blau 1982; Steiner 2005). Although these transliterations are not completely consistent, they do seem to point to a preservation of /ġ/ (written with ע) and /ḥ/ (written with ח). The vacillations and inconsistencies are most likely due to the fact that the distinction between /ġ/ and /ʿ/ and between /ḥ/ and /h/ were probably lost in the spoken language but preserved in the literary/scribal tradition. The opposition between /ġ/ and /ʿ/ was probably neutralized first (as /ʿ/), while that between /ḥ/ and /h/ was marked until a later period.

Aside from phonology and spelling, Biblical Hebrew grammar exhibits a particularly striking phenomenon, somehow reminiscent of one of the functions of *yqtl* in Ugaritic poetry (see above). If a form of the suffix conjugation appears preceded by a proclitic *wāw* (a conjunction meaning "and," "but"), it becomes imperfective: *dibber* "he spoke" → *wĕ-dibber* "and he speaks." Likewise, the prefix conjugation can be turned perfective if preceded by the *wāw* conjunction: *yiqrāʾ* "he calls, will call" → *wa-yyiqrāʾ* "and he called." The use of this *wāw* with a suffix form corresponds to two different constructions, which can be distinguished by accentuation: (1) *wāw-conversive*, *wāw-consecutive*, or *wāw-relative*, when the form with *wāw* depends, in terms of sequence or consequence, on a previous verb; and (2) *wāw-copulative*, when the form with *wāw* rephrases what has been in the preceding sentence. The prefix forms with *wāw* constitute the most common finite verbal forms in Hebrew narrative and it is usually labeled, according to the paradigm verb, simply as *wayyiqtol* ("and he killed"). Along with the Ugaritic use of *wyqtl*, it is important to notice that, in some particularly archaic or early sections of the Hebrew Bible, one can find instances of the prefix form with a perfective value but without *wāw* (e.g., *yāšet* "he made" in Psalm 18:12). Moreover, in the Canaanite letters from Amarna, there are seemingly some traces of the same phenomenon, when the Akkadian stative (*paris* form) preceded by the conjunction *u* is used to mark imperfective.

The other members (besides Hebrew) of the Canaanite group of Northwest Semitic languages (Phoenician and Punic, Moabite, Edomite, and Ammonite) are attested usually in small inscriptions. Phoenician and Punic (the late variety of Phoenician used in Northern Africa and the Western Mediterranean) are better represented, with a decent number of inscriptions. One should notice that the number of Phoenician inscriptions from the core Phoenician areas in Lebanon (Byblos, Tyre, Sidon) is rather small when compared to the corpus of Phoenician and Punic inscriptions from the Aegean and the Western Mediterranean. One of the main differences between Phoenician and Punic lies in the use of *matres lectionis* ("mothers of reading," consonants used to indicate vowels). Although Punic orthography is almost identical to that of Phoenician, Punic does use final *aleph* to indicate *Auslaut* vowels: Punic *qlʾ* /qūlo/ "his voice" versus Phoenician *ql* /qūlo/ "his voice." Moreover, sometimes, Punic uses *aleph* to indicate internal vowels: Punic *mʾš* /mes/ versus Phoenician *mš* "statue."[16] Eventually, Neo-Punic expanded the use of *matres lectionis* (*aleph*, *wāw*, *yod*, and eventually even *hē*, *ḥet*, and *ʿayin*); e.g., *myšql* /misqil/ ("he who/that which makes beautiful"), *rʾps* Rufus. Of the other three Canaanite languages (all from Transjordan), Moabite is particularly close to Hebrew, but it is clearly attested only in two inscriptions (the stela of Mesha, king of Moab, and an inscription from el-Kerak). The Ammonite and Edomite texts are more numerous, but much shorter and frequently fragmentary.

The Arabian peninsula

The Arabian peninsula has yielded inscriptions dating to pre-Islamic times both in Old South Arabian (or Sayhadic) and in different varieties of North Arabian (see above).[17] In the past, Old South Arabian (OSA) used to be regarded as a South Semitic branch (along with Ethiopic and Modern South Arabian); now it is usually placed in the Central Semitic group, mostly because its verbal system seems to have only two forms (-CCvC- and CvCvC-), instead of the three common in South Semitic (-CCvC-, CvCvC-, and -CvCCcC-/-Cv̄CvC-). Since the OSA alphabet does not mark vowels or gemination, the idea that it does not have a form -CvCCcC-/-Cv̄CvC- is based on a contextual analysis. A particularly debatable point of OSA grammar concerns the sibilants. They are transliterated by using conventional signs (s^1, s^2 and s^3), since their actual phonological nature in OSA is not at all clear:

$s^1(s^?)$ ḥ $(<{}^*s^1/{}^*š[s] > $ Arabic/s/س; Hebrew/š/שׁ)
$s^2(š^?)$ ⌐ $(<{}^*s^2/{}^*ś[ł] > $ Arabic/š/ش; Hebrew/ś/>/s/שׂ)
$s^3(ś^?)$ ⌐ $(<{}^*s^3/{}^*s[ʦ] > $ Arabic/s/س; Hebrew/s/ס)

The North Arabian inscriptions (written either in the OSA alphabet or in Nabatean script) are more closely related to Arabic. Following Beeston (1981), one can divide all these dialects or languages into two groups, depending on the shape of their definite article (either *al-* as in Arabic or *ha-/han-* as in Hebrew): (1) *al*-languages, in Arabic names and loanwords in Nabatean and Palmyrean, as well as in early Arabic inscriptions (Namāra, Jabal Ramm, Ḥarrān) and in al-Fāw; and (2) *han*-languages (Thamudic, Liḥyānitic, Ṣafāʾitic, Ḥaṣāʿitic). For our purposes, it is important to notice that even before the first properly Arabic inscription (Namāra, 328 CE), there are vestiges of Arabic words or constructions in Neo-Assyrian (Livingstone 1997) and in some Greek texts (Hämeen-Anttila and Rollinger 2001).

Hurro-Urartian

Hurrian and Urartian constitute a language family. Although Urartian does not stem from Hurrian, one could say that Hurrian was the Hurro-Urartian language attested from the late third to the later second millennium, whereas Urartian is the Hurro-Urartian language attested during the first millennium BCE. There has been some speculation about the possible genetic relation between Hurro-Urartian and other language families – especially the Eastern (or Northeastern) Caucasian family (Diakonoff and Starostin 1986) – but this remains highly hypothetical. Nonetheless, traces of Hurro-Urartian lexicon can be found in Old Armenian (Diakonoff 1985; Greppin and Diakonoff 1991).

Hurrian is attested throughout the Ancient Near East, with its large and generically diverse corpus of texts from Syria, Anatolia, and Egypt: the inscribed lions and cylinder seals from Urkeš (Tell Mozan) dating to the mid or late Sargonic period (Buccellati and Kelly-Buccellati 1995–96); incantations from the Old Babylonian period; diverse texts from Mari; the famous Mitanni Letter, found at Amarna in Egypt (EA 24), from Tušratta, king of Mitanni, to Amenophis III (c. 1370–56); various texts from Ugarit, both in the local cuneiform alphabet and in Mesopotamian cuneiform (including musical, religious, and lexical texts); a wide variety of texts from the Hittite capital, Boğazköy (most of them are rituals, omens, and incantations, and very few are historical or mythological); a few texts from Emar (lexical, medical, and divinatory); and a large number of personal names attested from many archives. The Urartian corpus consists almost entirely of the royal inscriptions of the kings of Urartu (around Lake Van); the earliest texts date to the reign of Ishpuini (i.e., the end of the ninth and the beginning of the eighth century), roughly parallel to the reign of Shamshi-Adad V in Assyria. Although the Urartian inscriptions are in cuneiform, there is a local Urartian script, Urartian hieroglyphs, which appears on ceramic objects and at least one clay tablet.

Hurrian scribes developed an ingenious system to try to write native segments for which there were no signs in Mesopotamian cuneiform (such as /f/ and /ž/). In the consistent orthography of the Mitanni chancellery, there is a distinction between voiced (single spelling) and voiceless (double spelling) consonants (as happens in Hittite orthography). Thus, we know that Hurrian had both a voiceless (/š/) and a voiced (/ž/) alveopalatal fricative, the former written <šš> and the latter <š>. In terms of morphology, Hurrian is an agglutinative language like Sumerian. Its morphosyntax follows the pattern of split ergativity. In the case of Hurrian, split ergativity presents four different syntactical constructions:[18]

1. Intransitive or absolutive: *undu-man inna-me-nin šen-iff-we ašti um-ett-a* (Mit. iii 21) "and now when the wife of my brother comes" (now-and when-3rd sg.-indeed brother-my-of wife-ABS come-will-INTRANS.).

2. Ergative (transitive): *Immuriya-šš-an zalamži tan-ož-a* (Mit. iii 106) "and Immutiya has made a statue" (Immuriya-ERG-and statue-ABS made-PAST-he).

3. Anti-passive (transitive non-ergative): VERB-*i/u*-ABS (-*i*- thematic vowel in anti-passive forms, -*u*- thematic vowel in intransitive verbs): *ḫenni šen-if pašš-ož-i* (Mit. 1 65) "now my brother has sent (an embassy)" (now brother-my sending-PAST-ABS). This construction does not exist in Urartian.

4. Absolutive-essive: the subject is in the absolutive case, whereas the object appears in the essive case (-*a*) and the verbal form is transitive non-ergative: *el(i)-a faḫr-o-ž(e)-a tan-d-i-b... Allani* (KBo 32: 13 i 12 f.) "the goddess Allani threw a great feast" (feast-ESSIVE good-DERIVATION-ADJ.-ESSIVE make-*d*-TRANS.-3[rd]sg. Allani).

There is a very interesting and unusual feature of Hurrian and Urartian morphosyntax, *Suffixaufnahme*, i.e., suffix inclusion, or suffix duplication: "in-the-house in-the-man"="in the man's house"; e.g., *šen(a)-iffu-we-ne-va torub(i)-i-va* (Mit. iii 114): "to my brother's enemy" (brother-1[st]sg.poss.-OF-SINGULAR-TO enemy-3[rd]sg.poss.-TO="to-my-of-brother to-his-enemy").[19] Our knowledge of Hurrian grammar and lexicon has greatly improved in the last two decades, after the publication and study of a long Hurro-Hittite bilingual composition known as "The song of release" or "Epic of emancipation."[20]

Some scholars have stressed the presence of Indo-Iranian (i.e., Indo-European) words in texts from Mitanni. However, apart from the names of some Indo-Iranian deities (four in a list of one hundred theonyms) in the treaty between Shattiwazza of Mitanni and the Hittite king Suppiluliuma I, as well as probably the names of some Mitanni rulers, the bulk of these alleged Indo-Iranian words is properly Hurrian. This is especially important in the case of the term *maryannu* "charioteer," which has been regarded by some as related to Sanskrit *márya-* "young warrior, nobleman," but which is perfectly Hurrian. Moreover, the individuals identified as *maryannu* in Mitannian texts bear completely Hurrian names. Furthermore, the technical vocabulary concerning the taming of horses in a Hittite tractate written by a Hurrian (Kikkuli) may not be Indo-Iranian but pre-Indo-Iranian substrate terms (Diakonoff 1972, 1993).

Anatolian Languages

The early Indo-European languages of Anatolia can be divided as follows:

- Hittite is found in a large number (over 30,000) of cuneiform texts from Hattusa (modern Boğazköy, currently Boğazkale), capital of the Hittite kingdom, to which one can add now the newly discovered tablets from Ortaköy (over 3,000). The language was called "Nesite" by its speaker (*nešili/našili* means "in Hittite"), referring to Neša/Kaneš (modern Kültepe). The corpus of Hittite texts was written down during a period of almost four centuries (c. 1570–1220).
- Palaic, also written with cuneiform, seems slightly more conservative than Hittite and Luwian.
- Luwian can be written with hieroglyphs (Hieroglyphic Luwian) or with cuneiform (Cuneiform Luwian). Luwian seems more innovative than Hittite and it survived the fall of the Hittite empire (1400–700 BCE).

In the first millennium, several Anatolian languages are attested, all written with different alphabets that are very similar to, if not derivative from, the Greek one:

- Lycian (fifth and fourth centuries BCE) is linguistically very close to Luwian.
- Lydian texts date to the same period as Lycian and share many features with Luwian and Lycian.
- Carian inscriptions have been found in Anatolia and Egypt (seventh to third centuries BCE). Although its alphabet is related to that of Greek, it has not been fully deciphered yet. Nonetheless, enough is known to state that Carian is an Indo-European Anatolian language.
- Pisidian is attested in very short funerary inscriptions from Pisidia (southwest Anatolia) dating to the second and third centuries CE.
- Sidetic is attested in six inscriptions from the city of Side, on the coast of Pamphylia, which date to the third century BCE.

All monumental inscriptions at Hattusa are in the Luwian language and hieroglyphic script, dating from Muwattalli II to Suppiluliuma II. There is an inscription (the Ankara silver bowl) mentioning the victory of a Tudhaliya *labarna* (the Hittite royal title), who may not be Tudhaliya IV, but perhaps Tudhaliya I/II, six generations earlier. During the last three generations of the Hattusa dynasty, from Muwattalli II to Suppiluliuma II, Luwian most likely became the main language spoken at Hattusa, while Hittite probably had already died as a spoken language for the most part, surviving mostly as a written language. Perhaps this hieroglyphic script was originally not devised to write Luwian. In fact, older hieroglyphic seals contain Hittite cuneiform. Moreover, in the northeastern outskirts of Hattusa, the rock sanctuary of Yazılıkaya was probably inscribed and decorated during the reign of king Tudhaliya IV (although the shrine itself already existed) with hieroglyphics to write the names of the deities of a Hurrian pantheon (Güterbock 1982, Haas 1994: 632–9).

Cuneiform had been introduced probably already at the end of the third millennium or the beginning of the second. Because of the geographic and chronological proximity, Old Assyrian would seem a good candidate for the source of Hittite cuneiform. Old Assyrian texts come from Kaneš (modern Kül Tepe) in Anatolia. However, the shape of Hittite cuneiform signs resembles quite closely that of Old Babylonian cursive, especially late Old Babylonian cursive from Alalah VII (eighteenth/seventeenth century). Likewise, the Sumerograms and spelling conventions used to write Hittite texts are different from those used in Old Assyrian texts. In general, Hittite spelling conventions belong to a northern tradition shared also by the Hurrian, Alalah (Stratum IV), and Nuzi syllabaries in the second half of the second millennium.[21] Thus, there was a North Syrian link in the process of introduction of Mesopotamian cuneiform into Anatolia. This link was probably a North Syrian version of the Sargonic syllabary. For instance, the use of š-signs in Hittite to write a plain *s* is probably due to the fact that in Old Akkadian the š-signs were employed to write the interdental /θ/, which eventually merged with /š/ in later Akkadian dialects, whereas /s/ was written with z-signs. This would rule out Old Assyrian as the lender: the spelling of sibilants in Old Assyrian points to the merger of *θ, *š, and *ś, which would not explain why Hittite used š-signs for a dental /s/ (Hecker 1968 §§ 40f.).[22]

Hittite is the earliest Indo-European language attested in writing, and it exhibits many features usually labeled as archaic. Of the postulated three Indo-European laryngeals (h_1, h_2, and h_3), Anatolian languages preserved *h_2 and probably *h_3 in *Anlaut*, while *h_1 disappeared.[23] Old Hittite had eight nominal cases distinguishable in the singular, although some became unproductive in later dialects, and two genders (animate and inanimate). The verbal system is particularly puzzling when compared to the rest of Indo-European languages. Hittite verbs fall under one of two conjugations, the *mi*-and the *ḫi*-conjugations; the former corresponds to the Indo-European primary active endings (e.g., Greek *dídōmi* "I give"), but the latter seems to find parallels only in the Indo-European perfect, which was perhaps originally indifferent to tense and marked both present and past stative (Jasanoff 2003). There are two finite verbal forms: a preterite and a present future. The present, past perfect, and future can be expressed with periphrastic constructions (non-finite verbal forms with an auxiliary verb). Some features of Hittite grammar (as with the nominal cases mentioned above) evolved through time, and one can distinguish three periods of Hittite: Old Hittite (c. 1570–1450), Middle Hittite (c. 1450–1380), and Neo-Hittite (c. 1380–1220).

Languages in Ancient Iran: Language Contact and Alloglottography

In the written records from Ancient Iran, at least two autochthonous languages (along with Babylonian and Aramaic as foreign ones) are amply attested: Old Persian and Elamite. The former is an Indo-European language, part of the Indo-Iranian branch; the latter is probably an isolate.[24] Neither the Old Persian language nor, most likely, its script originated in Persepolis, the capital of the Achaemenid empire. Although the basis for the language of the Old Persian inscriptions must lie in the southwestern Iranian spoken in the region of Fārs, the variety attested in the corpus of Achaemenid inscriptions must correspond to a literary and standardized dialect. The language of the Achaemenid inscriptions is fairly close to Avestan, the language of the early Zoroastrian texts preserved in medieval copies. There were other Ancient Iranian languages, but they are unfortunately very poorly attested. Median is the cover term used for the Ancient Iranian linguistic materials attested in Old Persian inscriptions, as well as in texts in other languages (Elamite, Babylonian, Greek, Aramaic, and Egyptian), whose phonology departs from that of Old Persian and mostly resembles that of Avestan. Even less can be said of the language of the Iranian horse warriors known as Scythians (Skúthai) in Greek texts and as *Sakā* in Iranian texts.

The Proto-Elamite texts (c. 3100–2900 BCE) remain, for the most part, undeciphered (Englund 2004). Although they resemble the archaic Mesopotamian texts from Uruk, both scripts (and most likely their languages) are independent. At the beginning of the Old Elamite period, parallel to the late Sargonic period in Mesopotamia, an apparent heir to Proto-Elamite is attested in about twenty inscriptions, Linear Elamite, although neither sign shapes nor semantic reasons clearly prove such a lineage.[25] The Elamite language, written with the cuneiform borrowed from Mesopotamia, can be divided into four dialects, separated by periods of hiatus with no attestations:

1. Old Elamite is attested during the Sargonic period. In the Old Babylonian period, there are a few Elamite incantations (mixed with Sumerian, Akkadian, and Hurrian ones) from Mesopotamia.
2. Middle Elamite appears during the thirteenth and twelfth centuries, mostly in inscriptions and the administrative documents from Tall-i Malyan (in the highland of Anšan).
3. Late Elamite is the language of the texts written during the last century of independence of Elam (c. 717–640 BCE). To the customary inscriptions and administrative texts, this period adds a few letters.[26]
4. Achaemenid Elamite is the language of the texts written during this period.

Elamite is an agglutinative language, but the number of suffixes and clitics is substantially smaller than those of Sumerian and Hurro-Urartian. Little can be said with certainty about its phonological structure. Nouns exhibit classifier endings, based on the gender opposition between animate and inanimate. There are three kinds of inanimate suffixes, productive as derivational morphemes (*-me*, *-t*, and *-n*), but the categories marked with them are frequently unknown. Only the function of *-me* as a derivational suffix seems clear: generating abstracts (*tuppi-me* "writing"; *sunki-me* "kingship"). The verbal system has two finite forms (perfective and imperfective), apparently with an accusative syntactical alignment (like English), and, therefore, two voices (active and passive).

Old Persian nouns can be of three genders (masculine, feminine, and neuter), – compare Hittite, also Indo-European but more archaic, with only two (animate and inanimate). Nouns, adjectives, and pronouns can occur in three numbers (singular, plural, and dual) and six cases. The Old Persian verbal system has three finite forms: present (*kunautiy* "he makes" ← √*kar*); imperfect (with augment, *akunauš* "he made"); and a periphrastic perfect, with the past participle (*karta* "made") and the verb "to be," although the latter is frequently omitted. There are a few forms of an old aorist (past punctual), such as *adaršiy* "I held." This system clearly contrasts with that of Hittite, which is simpler. Old Persian has two voices, active and middle (some verbs have only one). The middle voice is used both for reflexive and passive constructions. Due to the higher level of explicitness of the writing system, and the close relationship between Old Persian and other Iranian languages, Old Persian poses probably fewer linguistic problems to the modern scholar than Hittite does.

The corpus of Achaemenid tablets from Persepolis gives us an idea of the language distribution. Of the 30,000 tablets and fragments found in the fortification wall at the northeast corner of the Persepolis terrace (the so-called Fortification tablets) and the 139 readable tablets found in the southeastern part of the Persepolis Terrace (the so-called Treasury tablets), two tablets are in Babylonian, one in Greek, one in Phrygian, about 700 in Aramaic (still unpublished), and the overwhelming majority in Elamite (Lewis 1994). The fortification tablets date from the thirteenth to twenty-eighth years of Darius I (509–494 BCE), while the Treasury tablets are a bit later, from the thirtieth year of Darius I to the seventh year of Artaxerxes I (492–458 BCE). Some of these tablets – at least 800 of the Elamite ones – include Aramaic epigraphs inscribed on the clay, as happened with many tablets in first-millennium Mesopotamia, whereas some tablets are bilingual (Babylonian and Aramaic) and some still written exclusively in Aramaic (Fales 1986, 2000). Furthermore, 163 Aramaic inscriptions on mortars, pestles, trays, and plates, were found in the Persepolis Treasury building too, dating probably from the seventh year of Xerxes (479/78) to at least the twenty-ninth year of Artaxerxes I (436/35). These Aramaic texts record the manufacture of objects by artisans and the relinquishment of them to treasuries in the satrapy of Arachosia (whose capital was Kandahār, in modern Afghanistan).[27]

The language contact setting in Ancient Iran is quite important as a case study. Moreover, in the history of cuneiform studies it is precisely the trilingual inscription (Babylonian, Old Persian, and Elamite) of Darius in Bīsitūn that opened the door to the decipherment of cuneiform.[28] The Achaemenid language diversity points to the level of ethnic and linguistic complexity of that empire, which conflicted with the conservatism of the Elamite scribal tradition. This surfaces in the clear split between written texts and oral communication. The Old Persian script may not have been used until Darius; the scribes of Cyrus used Babylonian and, to a lesser extent, Elamite. Nonetheless, there is a trilingual inscription (Old Persian, Elamite, and Babylonian) attested five times at palaces built by Cyrus at Pasargadae a generation before Darius (inscription CMa). However, the Old Persian line (the first line of the inscription) was probably added later. There are two other trilingual inscriptions at Pasargadae, one of which occurs three times in Palace P but whose first line (the Old Persian) was destroyed around 1930, after Herzfeld's excavations, and another one preserved only fragmentarily (CMb). Even more complicated problems are posed by the gold tablets bearing inscriptions of Darius' great-grandfather Ariaramnes and of his grandfather Arsames, which may or may not be authentic. In sum, it is difficult to know with certainty whether or not this script was really invented during Darius' reign. Furthermore, as Diakonoff (1970) argued, it may have been devised to write Median rather than Old Persian.

The Elamite version of the Bīsitūn inscription states that this is the first time an inscription is made in "Aryan."[29] This probably refers to the Old Persian script itself, which would have been used seemingly for the first time in the Bīsitūn inscription. Most scholars agree that the Elamite version was the first to be engraved, then the Babylonian, and finally the Old Persian. If the Persian king used Old Persian as his language, one may wonder why Elamite figures so prominently on the rock. Gershevitch (1979) put forward a thought-provoking theory: the Elamite version would be the true original and represent the actual words of Darius, whereas the Old Persian on the inscription would be a retranslation or back-translation (*Rückübersetzung*). This means that the Great King uttered the words in Old Persian, but the scribes wrote them down in Elamite and read them back to him (as the inscription says) in Old Persian. This phenomenon is labeled by Gershevitch as "alloglottography," writing a text in a language different from the language in which it is intended to be read. In spite of the apparent convolutedness of this interaction between utterance and the writing interface, there are some linguistic and philological reasons that would support the existence of alloglottography in Achaemenid Iran. Furthermore, alloglottography clearly existed in some contexts in the Ancient Near East and has sufficient typological parallels across the world.[30]

Poorly Attested and Less Understood Languages

As seen above, there are languages very poorly attested in the Ancient Near East. For instance, Kassite is known by a number of personal and divine names and specific terms (especially concerning horse breeding), as well as an Akkado-Kassite bilingual lexical list (Balkan 1954). Of the language of the Guti or Gutean, we have only a small number of personal names and the like.[31] The evidence concerning the Lullubi or Lullubean (southeast of Lake Urmia) is practically limited to their very name and perhaps a few anthroponyms.[32] This ethnonym is probably related to Hurro-Urartian *lulu/lullu* "foreign(er)," which underwent the same semantic shift Hittite *lulaḫḫi/lulaḫi* (a generic term for "uncivilized" inhabitants of the mountains) underwent when borrowed by Greek as *Léleges* (*Iliad* 11:429; 20:96; 21:86; Herodotus 1.171) to refer to the Carians.[33] Equally nebulous in origin, the label Subartean (or Subir, Subar) was generically used for peoples living to the east of the Tigris and north of the Lullubi, as well as for their languages, without indicating necessarily that they were Hurrian.[34]

Of the less understood languages, the most widely attested is Hattic: over one hundred and fifty tablets and fragments exist, many of them bilingual (with a Hittite translation). As opposed to other Ancient Near Eastern languages that are also understood only in part (Hurrian, Urartian, Elamite), the Hattic corpus does not include inscriptions, administrative documents, or letters, i.e., texts with a specific context, anthroponyms, toponyms, and so forth. The Hattic corpus consists entirely of religious and mythical texts (incantations, rituals, prayers, mythical narratives), which are inherently elliptical and allusive, and frequently elusive. Moreover, the Hittite translations in the Hatto-Hittite bilinguals do not seem to be literal at all. As seen above in regard to Hittite, Hattic was seemingly the language of the original inhabitants of Hattusa. The Hattusa scribes clearly labeled whether texts were written in Hattic (*ḫattili*) or in Hittite (*nešili/našili*). As far as one can tell, Hattic was an agglutinative language. Aside from three or four suffixes, both the nominal and the verbal morphology were dominated by prefixes (including prefixed possessive pronouns), and the verb itself is usually placed at the beginning of the sentence.

NOTES

1 Cavigneaux 1980–3; Civil 1995; Black 1984; Veldhuis 1997.

2 See Englund 1998. But see also Rubio 2005a.

3 On phoneticization and the language of the Archaic texts, see Krispijn 1991–92; M. Krebernik 1994: 383–4; Steinkeller, 1995: 694–5.

4 See Gelb 1960: 270; Kraus 1970: 89–93; Cooper 1973 (*pace* Lieberman 1977: 21 n. 50, and Jacobsen 1988: 123–5).

5 For a discussion of different theories on **eme-sal** and additional references, see Schretter 1990; Diakonoff 1975; Rubio 2001.

6 The terms Semito-Hamitic, Afroasiatic, and Afrasian are synonyms. For an overview of this language family, see Diakonoff 1965, 1988, 1991–92. On Egyptian as a branch of Afroasiatic, see Satzinger 1997; Takács 1999–2001; Loprieno 1995, 1995a.

7 Since the Demotic script can specifically note more segments than the 22 letters of the Aramaic alphabet, these texts provide precious information on the actual shape of early Aramaic phonology; see, for instance, Steiner and Nimms 1983, 1984, 1985; Steiner 1995. The use of an Egyptian script to write down a foreign text was not new, as some Northwest Semitic incantations appear in Hieratic texts from the thirteenth century already; see Steiner 1992.

8 On Egyptian phonology in general, see Peust 1999; Vycichl 1990; Loprieno 1995: 28–50. See also Hoch 1994; Rainey 1998; Muchiki 1999.

9 On the Egyptian verb and its syntax, see Polotsky 1971, 1987–1990; Allen 1984; Doret 1986; Loprieno 1986, 1995, 1995a; Shisha-Halevy 1986; Depuyt 1993.

10 On Central Semitic and the inclusion of OSA, see Voigt 1987 (additional references in Huehnergard's contribution in Kaltner and McKenzie 2002: 3 n. 2).

11 "Old Akkadian" is a cover term that includes three perfectly differentiated varieties of Akkadian: Early Dynastic Akkadian; Sargonic Akkadian; and Ur III Akkadian (the latter attested almost exclusively in personal names and Akkadian words in Sumerian texts). See Hasselbach 2005; Rubio 2006a.

12 Some of these peripheral texts, although written in Akkadian, were probably intended to be read aloud in the native tongue of the scribes. On this phenomenon (alloglottography), see section "Languages of Ancient Iran". See also Civil and Rubio 1999; von Dassow 2003; Rubio 2006.

13 The loss may simply be apparent, both short (e.g., -*š*) and long forms (-*šu* "his; him") may have coexisted in the spoken language of all periods, with geographic and social variations, but without involving any diachronic evolution from long to short; see Rubio 2002, 2006a.

14 VE is a bilingual (Sumerian-Eblaite) lexical list (the Vocabulary from Ebla); see Conti 1990. The tablet 75.G.2420 corresponds to the so-called "Treaty between Ebla and A.BAR.QA" – the latter toponym should be read *A-bar-sal₄*. For the text of this treaty, see Fronzaroli 2003: 43–76.

15 For detailed references on the place of Eblaite within Semitic, see Rubio 2003, 2006a.

16 In Phoenician, *θ, *$\check{s}$, and *$\acute{s}$ merged into /s/. Compare the use of ⁣ᶜ*sr* instead of ᶜ*śr* "ten" (Heb. ᶜ*eśer*, ᶜ*aśar*) in the Eshmūnazor inscription from Sidon. St. Augustine (*Epist. ad Rom. inch. Exp.* 13) makes a pun on Punic *salūs* (*šlš* "three") and Latin *salus* ("salvation"). See Friedrich and Röllig 1999 §§ 43–8; Krahmalkov 2001: 25–6.

17 The term Sayhadic was used by Beeston to cover the four OSA languages, and it is based on the toponym *Ṣayhad*, used by medieval Islamic geographers for the desert now called Ramlat as-Sabᶜatayn. See Kogan and Korotayev 1997: 220.

18 Mit.=Mitanni letter (EA 24). The hyphens in the Hurrian sentences divide roots and morphs and do not correspond to a transliteration. Vocalic length has not been indicated.

19 See Wilhelm's and Wegner's contributions in Plank 1995.

20 Copies of the tablets and fragments were published in KBo 32. For an edition with ample commentary, see Neu 1996. Concerning its importance for Hurrian grammar and lexicography, see, for instance, Neu 1988, 1988a; Catsanicos 1996; Wilhelm 1992, 1993.

21 For a discussion of the issues involved in the borrowing of Mesopotamian cuneiform by the Hittites and further references, see Rubio 2006: 45–8.

22 Typological constraints aside – languages with a single voiceless sibilant have a dental sibilant, not an alveolar one – the Egyptian transliterations of Hittite names use /s/ instead of /š/: *Mrsr*=Muršiliš/Mursilis [mursili-s]; *Htrsr*=Hattušiliš/Hattusilis [hatu-sili-s] (<CC> → voiceless; <C> → voiced); see Kimball 1999: 106. However, the name *Šuppiluliuma* [Suppiluliuma] appears surprisingly as *θpllm* in Ugaritic texts.

23 The laryngeals would have been lost in all the other Indo-European branches (except a few traces in Armenian), but their loss caused different effects, e.g., *$h_1e > e$; *$h_2e > a$;*$h_3e > o$ but *a* in Indo-Iranian, Hittite, and Slavic.

24 A Dravidian-Elamite connection (McAlpin 1981) remains both tantalizing and unsubstantiated.

25 On Linear Elamite, see Hinz 1969: 11–44; Vallat 1986: 339–45; Englund 2004: 104, 143–4.

26 It was argued that a small fragment found at the Urartian fortress of Argištiḫenele (Armavir-blur) contained part of an Elamite translation of the Akkadian Gilgamesh. However, this is most likely either an administrative text (Koch 1993) or an inquiry concerning the marriage between a certain Datukka and his wife, Kušinuya, who is missing (Vallat 1995).

27 The original editor of these Aramaic texts (Bowman 1970) believed that these objects were used in the production of *haoma*, the famous hallucinogenic drink (cp. *soma* in the *Ṛgveda*), and labeled them "Aramaic ritual texts." This hypothesis was largely based on his interpretation of the Aramaic term ᵓ*škr* as related to the Semitic root for "drink," when it is most likely to mean "tribute" or the like. See Naveh and Shaked 1973; Delaunay 1974.

28 It is more accurate to use the actual Modern Persian toponym, Bīsitūn (also Bīsutūn, Bīstūn), rather than "Behistun." The latter form would derive from Modern Persian *Bahistūn/Behestūn* "with good columns," which would correspond to an unattested Middle Iranian *Bahistān* and, thus, lie behind the modern forms (Bīsotūn, Bīsitūn,

etc., meaning "without columns"). This unattested form would actually go back to the unattested old name of the site, OPer *Bagastāna-* "place of the god(s)," which appears as *Bagístanon óros* "Mount Bagistanon" in Ctesias and Diodorus (2.13.1); see Kent 1953:108; Schmitt 1989.

29   DBE iv 2–4: ˡúʰtup-pi-me da-a-e-ik-ki hu-ut-tá har-ri-ia-ma ap-pa šá-iš-šá in-ni šà-ri ku-ut-tá "I made this inscription otherwise in 'Aryan,' which did not exist before" (see Rubio 2006: 38–9).

30   On alloglottography in general, and the Achaemenid case in particular, see Rubio 2006.

31   In spite of the meager linguistic information about the Gutean language, it has been connected to Hurrian (Diakonoff and Starostin 1986: 5–6).

32   See Astour: 1987: 37–8 n. 259.

33   See J. Tischler 1977–2001: vol. 5/6: 70–71. On the Lullubeans in general, see Klengel 1987–1990; Eidem 1992: 50–4.

34   See P. Michałowski 1986, 1999; Gragg 1995: 2162.

FURTHER READING

There is no general reference work that covers all the languages of the Ancient Near East. In Russian, Diakonoff 1967 contains excellent overviews of most Ancient Near Eastern languages (except Egyptian and Anatolian languages), as well as analyzed text samples; and Diakonoff 1979 does the same with only non-Semitic languages. Wider in scope but much shorter in detail, Huehnergard et al. 1992 provides excellent sketches of all languages used in the Ancient Near East. Kaltner and McKenzie 2002 deals only with languages that are pertinent to Biblical studies and focus mostly on historical rather than linguistic matters. Streck 2006 includes grammatical sketches of Sumerian (G. Zólyomi), Akkadian (Streck), Hittite (E. Rieken), Hattic (J. Klinger), Hurro-Urartian (J. Hazenbos), and Elamite (M. Krebernik).

There is no comprehensive reference grammar of Sumerian, but Thomsen 1984 constitutes a very practical and complete (up to the early 1980s) summary of bibliography. The first part of Attinger 1993 contains a detailed discussion of and supplement to Thomsen. A more accessible book on Sumerian is Edzard 2003. For short overviews, see Edzard 1995, Michalowski 2004, and Rubio 2005. Four volumes of the *Pennsylvania Sumerian dictionary* (PSD) have appeared to date, but the project is switching to an on-line format.[35]

There are several grammars of Ancient Egyptian and of all its dialects. Loprieno 1995 is an excellent and sophisticated overview. Regarding Old Egyptian, Edel 1955–64 is still the main reference, and Allen 1984 studies throughly the verb in the Pyramid Texts. For Middle Egyptian, Allen 2000 is a good and readable introduction, as are Hoch 1997, Ockinga 1998, and Englund 1988; Schenkel has published several versions of his detailed grammar of "classical (i.e., middle) Egyptian" (see Schenkel 1997); Malaise and Winand 1999 is a good reference grammar (see Schenkel 2001); Depuydt 1999 is intended as a very detailed teaching grammar; Gardiner 1957 is a beautiful book, both as a reference and as a teaching grammar, but the sections on the verbal system are now mostly obsolete. There are two excellent and complementary grammars of Late Egyptian: Černý 1993 and Junge 2001. For Demotic, Johnson 1986 is a solid teaching grammar, whose third edition is freely available on the web,[36] and her monograph on the Demotic verbal system is an essential reference (Johnson 1976);[37] Simpson 1996 focuses on the Ptolemaic priestly decrees; and Spiegelberg

1925 is still a useful reference. An excellent reference grammar of Sahidic Coptic (the most important dialect in pre-Islamic times) is Layton 2004. Also essential for Coptic and Egyptian syntax are the groundbreaking contributions of Polotsky (1971, 1987–90) and his disciples (Shisha-Halevy 1986 and Depuydt 1993), as is Peust 1999 for phonology. For general dictionaries, the monumental classic is Erman and Grapow 1926–1963. This monumental work may be replaced by a modern reference in the future (see Grunert and Hafemann 1999; Meeks 2002). A helpful one-volume general dictionary is Hannig 1995; as a reversed (German-Egyptian) lexicon, Hannig 2000 is particularly useful. For early Old Egyptian (dynasties 0–3, c. 3150–2600), a dictionary is being published, Kahl 2002, of which three fascicles have been published to date and another three are forthcoming. A general dictionary of Old Egyptian (covering the Old Kingdom and the First Intermediate Period) is Hannig 2003. For Middle Egyptian, Faulkner 1962 is still widely used, and for the Coffin texts one should turn now to van der Molen 2000. For the Late Egyptian lexicon, one can use Lesko and Lesko 2000–2004. For Ptolemaic Egyptian, Wilson 1997 is a mandatory reference. For Demotic, the classic reference is Erichsen 1954, which is being replaced by the *Chicago Demotic Dictionary*, edited by Janet H. Johnson, of which fifteen sections are currently available on the web.[38] The standard Coptic dictionary is Crum 1939; for etymological dictionaries, see Černý 1976, Westendorf 1965–77, and Vycichl 1983 (Takács 1999–2001 is concerned with Afroasiatic macro-comparison, rather than with historically traceable etymologies).

There are some good introductions and overviews of the Semitic language family: Moscati et al. 1964, Bergsträsser 1983, Lipiński 2001, Kienast 2001; Izre'el 2002. Hetzron 1997 includes grammatical sketches of individual languages by different scholars. Huehnergard 1995 provides a short and excellent overview. The two modern comparative dictionaries of Semitic languages are still unfinished: eight fascicles (about 800 pages) of Cohen et al. 1970–99 have appeared to date; Militarev and Kogan 2000 and 2005 cover only anatomical terms and animal names (it is arranged by semantic fields).

The reference grammar of Akkadian is von Soden 1995. Huehnergard 2005 is an excellent and comprehensive teaching grammar of Old Babylonian; a separate key to the exercises may be useful for self-teaching (Huehnergard 2005a). Reiner 1966 and Buccellati 1996 share their structuralistic approach to Akkadian. For other dialects, see Gelb 1961 (OAkk), Hasselbach 2005 (Sargonic Akk), Hilgert 2002 (Ur III OAkk), Hecker 1968 (OAss), Groneberg 1987 (SB), Mayer 1970 (MAss), Stein 2000 (MBab), Hämeen-Anttila 2000 (NAss), and Woodington 1982 (NBab). On NAss, Luukko 2004 is an important reference. There are two dictionaries of Akkadian, one complete already (von Soden 1965–81=*AHw*), and the other near completion, with 23 volumes to date (Gelb et al. 1956-=*CAD*). Black et al. 2000 (=*CDA*) is a useful one-volume dictionary. Regarding peripheral Akkadian, see especially de Meyer 1962 (Susa), Wilhelm 1970 (Nuzi), Adler 1976 (Mitanni), Rainey 1996 and Moran 2003 (Canaanite in the Amarna letters), Seminara 1998 (Emar), Huehnergard 1989 (Ugarit), van Soldt 1991 (Ugarit), and Izre'el 1991 (Amurru Akkadian: Amarna, Boğazköy, and Ugarit). For Mari, one has to still use Finet's excellent but dated work (1956).

An excellent overview of Eblaite can be found in Krebernik 1996. The texts are being edited in two alternative series: "Archivi Reali di Ebla, Testi" (Rome, La Sapienza) and "Materiali Epigrafici di Ebla" (now part of "Materiali per il Vocabolario Sumerico," Rome: La Sapienza). Although there is no comprehensive treatment of Eblaite yet, there is a wealth of information and analyses in the collective volumes edited by Cagni (1981, 1984, 1987) and Fronzaroli (1984, 1988, 1989, 1992, 1997). For further bibliography, see Rubio 2006a.

The main reference for Amorite is Streck 2000. The reference grammar of Ugaritic is Tropper 2000; for an English overview, see Tropper 1999. Segert 1985 is a teaching grammar. The reference dictionary of Ugaritic is del Olmo and Sanmartín 2003 (a work that should be handled with caution due to the dreadful typography employed by the publisher). Huehnergard 1995a is a good and brief overview of Aramaic dialects; Beyer 1986 is slightly longer. The main grammars of Old Aramaic are Degen 1969, Segert 1975, Hug 1993, and Martínez Borobio 2003. On Samalian, see Dion 1974 and Tropper 1993. Lipiński 2000 describes the linguistic situation in Syria at the time of the Old Aramaic texts. For the Deir ᶜAllā texts, see Hoftijzer and van der Kooij 1991. On Aramaic written on clay tablets in first-millennium Mesopotamia, see Fales 1986, 2000, and Lipiński 2002. For Imperial Aramaic, see Folmer 1995, and Muraoka and Porten 1998 (the latter focuses on the texts from Egypt). For Biblical Aramaic, see Rosenthal 1995. The reference grammar of Phoenician and Punic is Friedrich and Röllig 1999. For Phoenician grammars in English, see Segert 1976 and Krahmalkov 2001. The reference dictionary of Northwest Semitic inscriptions (not including Ugaritic) is Hoftijzer et al. 1995. As a Phoenician and Punic dictionary, one can use Krahmalkov 2000. Of the many grammars of Biblical Hebrew, Gesenius and Kautzsch 1910 is still a great reference; for syntactical matters, Waltke and O'Connor 1990 is important. For Hebrew inscriptions, see Renz and Röllig 1995, Gogel 1998, and Schüle 2000. Sáenz-Badillos 1996 is a complete history of the Hebrew language with abundant bibliography. The multi-volume standard dictionary of Biblical Hebrew and Aramaic is now available in two small-size volumes (Koehler et al. 2001). For the other Canaanite languages (Moabite, Ammonite, Edomite), see Parker's contribution in Kaltner and McKenzie 2002 (with references).

On Old South Arabian, see Kogan and Korotayev 1997. Probably the most useful OSA dictionaries (albeit only for Sabaic) are Biella 1982 and Beeston et al. 1982, which now can be complemented with Sima 2000 (for animals, plants, stones, and metals). On the linguistic situation of pre-Islamic Arabia, see MacDonald 2000.

Diakonoff 1971 and Khačikjan 1985 cover both Hurrian and Urartian. Wegner 2000 and Giorgieri 2000 are up-to-date grammars of Hurrian. For a brief overview, see Gragg 1995. Laroche's dictionary (1980) is now rather outdated. Melikišvili 1971 is still useful for Urartian, but should be complemented by the textual notes in Arutiunian's 2001 edition of the corpus and the many articles on Urartian listed in Zimansky 1998: 100–167.

For a general overview of Anatolian languages, see Melchert 1995 (to his bibliography on Carian, add now Kammerzell 1993 and Adiego 2006). The standard grammar of Hittite is still (but not for long) Friedrich 1960–67, although it is now somewhat obsolete. A new massive grammar of Hittite by Hoffner and Melchert (2007), which doubles as a reference and a teaching work, is currently in press. For Luwian, see Melchert 2003 and Payne 2004, as well as the annotations to the corpus in Hawkins and Çambel 1999–2000. For a short introduction, see Werner 1991. Melchert 1994 deals with the phonology of all Anatolian languages, and Kimball 1999 focuses on Hittite. There are two etymological dictionaries of Hittite still unfinished: Tischler 1977–2004 (13 fascicles to date) and Puhvel 1984–2004 (six volumes to date). The *Chicago Hittite Dictionary* (*CHD*) is now in its third volume.[39]

For Old Persian, the standard grammar (including texts and vocabulary) is Kent 1953. P. Oktor Skjærvø's grammar is now available at: http://www.fas.harvard.edu/~iranian/OldPersian/index.html. For Elamite, now the closest thing to a reference grammar is Khačikjan 1998 (cf. Stolper 2001), but one can still profit from Reiner 1969 and Grillot-Susini 1987; for a brief overview, see Gragg 1995. The Elamite dictionary, which includes proper names and toponyms, is Hinz and Koch 1987.

Concerning Hattic, see Girbal 1986, Klinger 1996, and Soysal 2004. On Hattic and other poorly attested and less understood languages, see Gragg 1995. For Kassite, see Balkan 1954.

35 See http://psd.museum.upenn.edu/epsd/index.html
36 http://oi.uchicago.edu/OI/DEPT/PUB/SRC/SAOC/45/SAOC45.html
37 http://oi.uchicago.edu/OI/DEPT/PUB/SRC/SAOC/38/SAOC38.html
38 http://oi.uchicago.edu/OI/DEPT/PUB/SRC/CDD/CDD.html
39 Volume P and two fascicles of S can be downloaded here: http://oi.uchicago.edu/OI/DEPT/PUB/SRC/Elec_Publications.html

CHAPTER SEVEN

The Historian's Task

Daniel C. Snell

Historical methodology is a contested territory in our culture today. Some would say that the connection between historical remains that we can study and the events we wish to study is too distant and problematic to produce widely accepted facts. History then is irredeemably an art. Others maintain that there is a consensus of informed opinion that has a right to a view that is influenced by new data and new arguments in ways governed by reason. So history approaches a science.

Regardless of one's view about these theoretical problems, there is a consensus on practice to be preferred among historians, especially in the Ancient Near East. The practice consists in turning to original documents and attempting to translate them and then placing them in their original contexts. The preference for original texts is common among historians of all periods, but in the Ancient Near East it approaches a fetish (Jordanova 2000). Because the field was created in the last two centuries on the basis of the gradual decipherment of the Ancient Near Eastern languages, attention has focused on reading new texts as they become available. This is not a simple task since our knowledge of the languages is constructed on our philological efforts and is incomplete. There are always corrections and additions to be made. It is hard to make generalizations because new, possibly contradictory, texts will certainly be found. This fact warns us to avoid wide generalizations and limits the interest in any particular text, especially if the language in which the modern scholar presents it is overly modest, as it usually is.

The problem stressed in so-called postmodern theory consists in the discovery in the last century of the problem of perspective. Scholars have come to feel in many disciplines that their own backgrounds and ways of seeing affect what they look for in research as well as how they interpret what they see. For the Ancient Near East Powell in an essay on economic history may have been the first to note that this was the age where we were aware of how our perspective affects our vision (1978).

Historians have tended to view the problem of perspective as the objectivity problem, meaning that an early goal of historians in the 1800s at least was to generate knowledge that would be recognized as valid by any observer, regardless of cultural background. This view was propounded by researchers of middle class background and European culture and was not actually tested by scholars from the Middle East itself or other parts of the world. But the variety of historical questions asked by students from different backgrounds, especially after the end of most colonial occupations after World War II, has caused history theorists, who tend to be philosophers rather than practicing historians, to retreat from claims to objective knowledge. Novick analyzes the North American approach to the objectivity problem (1988). He does not pay much attention to ancient studies, but he does note that James Henry Breasted, the Chicago Egyptologist, opposed entry of the United States into World War I, but when the United States did enter, he presented a rebound German dictionary to his son with the title "Dictionary of the Enemy's Language" on the spine (116). Even ancient historians are swayed by current passion, though Breasted was clearly ironic in his gift and wanted the son to study the enemy's still useful and important language. On the other side, we may note the preface to the Assyriologist Heinrich Zimmern's book on loanwords in Akkadian language, where it is clear that in Zimmern's view the true values of Western culture lay on the German side (Zimmern 1917).

Modern historians acknowledge that others might see problems differently, and yet most historians do assert that the past they study is not wholly fabricated. The modes of discussion of that past may owe a great deal to the conventions our culture expects for storytellers (White 1973). In contrast Gay argued that in spite of style there remain data (1974: 198–217). Some stories did happen and have left evidence which all experts acknowledge. Historical consensuses are established and new theses are advanced, rejected, and modified on the basis of agreements of scholars on what constitutes new knowledge.

Ancient Near Eastern historians assume in general that the methods they use are completely understandable by themselves and thus accessible to any reader. This aspect of Ancient Near Eastern history appears to be a vestige of its origins in breezily self-confident pre-World War I scholarship where pronouncement was sometimes viewed as proof. In most studies scholars launch into the problems and periods they wish to examine without explaining what they themselves have done or why they did so. Among valuable exceptions is Liverani who has a notable introductory chapter on the Ancient Near East as a historical problem (1988a: 5–27). It is true that in the past issues of methods have also been ignored in other sub-fields of history, and reasonable observers may deny that there is any particular thing that may be called historical method. Jordanova, though writing quite a good book on the social contexts in which historians function and what they do, admits there is no method that historians exclusively use and that many other disciplines critically consider the past (2000). And yet, she argues, there is a habit of mind that may be cultivated which seeks to trace conditions back in time. Further, it is clear that when one steeps oneself in a period through broad and deep reading, one can become adept at understanding some of its nuances. More grandiose claims for our abilities to reconstruct the past ring hollow now; yet the researcher, especially the old and canny researcher, does learn the shape and possibilities of the times studied.

Social Contexts of Study

Though there may be no distinct historical method, there definitely are lots of things that historians of the Ancient Near East do that obtain and generate ideas about the past. For Egyptology, Hornung discusses techniques mainly in terms of computer projects and institutions that support research, but he does address the use and meaning of Egyptology (1990: 16–17, 20–1). He notes that one may see many Western institutions and ideas as derived from Egyptian sources. Of special interest too is simply the long period of Egyptian isolation and development, making it an unrivaled laboratory of well-documented human endeavor. Also Egyptian thinkers dealt with questions of abiding concern, but Hornung acknowledges that attempts to derive an esoteric number-based mysticism from the pyramids and other monuments account for some of the interest in Egypt, but by no means all (1990: 16, 139). And the fight against the idea that Egypt has some secret knowledge which has been esoterically passed down to someone or other continues to this day (Hornung 2001).

Another notable scholar who did try to address the question of the modern social role at least of Assyriology, the study of the cuneiform-using languages and cultures, was Oppenheim in his essay "Assyriology – Why and How," in which he nudged the discipline from a humanities outlook more toward a collaborative social scientific approach (Oppenheim 1977: 7–30). He envisioned progress being made in particular in ancient history of science and technology through the interpretation of ancient texts by Assyriologists collaborating with historians of science and technology experts (1977: 28–30). Such approaches generate new understandings, as Oppenheim's work showed, but they are not necessarily applicable to questions about society and economy or religion and literature – questions in which Oppenheim was perhaps not so much interested. Bagnall has made a similar plea for collaborative scholarship in his area of papyrology, the study of written remains in Hellenistic and Roman Egypt (1995: 116–17).

A memorable example of consciousness about models we choose for research is Sasson's paper in which he argues that studies of ancient Israelite state-building have a great deal to do with the preoccupations of the modern researchers involved (1981). He shows that Germans in the nineteenth century were very interested in the coagulation of nations as Prussia and the rest of Germany came together around the king of Prussia, and so they regarded Israelite kingship as the primary focus of research. The pre-monarchic alliance that some of them suggested seems now to echo Germany before unification under the Kaiser. Citizens of the United States, on the other hand, tended to see nations as conglomerations of immigrants from elsewhere. They depicted the formation of Israel as a migration of motley groups from many directions who then formed a consensual confederation, out of which kings later emerged. Sasson admits there were no particularly British or French models for early Israel, though both those countries also had unique paths to national identity and had scholars who considered Israelite origins. What Sasson's observations show is that historians may be influenced in how they see a distant past by their own countries' histories, but also they may not be so influenced, as the British and French cases show. The lesson for practitioners is that one should be as self-aware as possible, but one might still find oneself attracted for good reasons to a received model that might parallel a more recent event and one's own experience.

There have been some studies on the shape of publication within the field, particularly on the relation between general Ancient Near Eastern studies and Biblical studies. Sampling studies in the fields showed that there was relatively little interaction between Ancient Near Eastern and Biblical studies and that Biblical scholars tended to quote from secondary sources about the Ancient Near East instead of going back to translations of original texts. Also Ancient Near Eastern scholars in their citations relied more heavily on serials and less on monographs and commentaries, while Biblicists preferred the reverse. The citation rates for serials in Ancient Near Eastern studies actually resembled the rates in the social studies, with 40–50 percent of all references being to periodicals, while Biblical studies was typical of the humanities, relying on journals for only 20 to 30 percent of citations. Also the Ancient Near Eastern scholars ignored Biblical studies, citing them in less than 9 percent of references (Yitzhaki 1986, 1987).

What this means practically is that the conceptual autonomy of Ancient Near Eastern studies from Biblical studies that has been argued for since the 1920s has apparently been achieved (Landsberger 1976). The reason for the plea for autonomy was that, as the fields of Ancient Near Eastern history were forming and for decades after, the Ancient Near East was seen predominately as the stage for Biblical history, and Ancient Near Eastern scholars came to feel the need to assert that the Mesopotamian world of ancient Iraq was distinct and separate from Biblical concerns because some questions posed of the material did not seem to derive from the material but from Biblical issues. Today, though, this separation comes at a price for Biblicists as they look upon the world surrounding Israel as alien and difficult. It also comes at a price for Ancient Near Eastern scholars as they cut themselves off from audiences interested in Biblical matters through their emphasis on technical issues vetted in journals. Both fields have moved away from ideas that the entire geographical area might have had a unified approach to any particular problem, and the diversity of views and practices is clear in the ancient record, which is now much richer and better understood than it was in the 1920s.

This separation of disciplines seems odd since every small North American college teaches the Bible, and practically many Assyriologists make livings teaching Bible as well as the Ancient Near East. Modern researchers are drawn toward specialization in research but also at the same time toward generalization in teaching. This means that most Ancient Near Eastern scholars are called upon to teach at least some courses on Western Civilization but less often to teach courses in their own specialties. Ancient Egypt's position in modern culture seems anomalous in the extreme. Wilson notes that the autonomy of Egyptology was being established in the first century since the decipherment of Egyptian in 1822, but perhaps at the expense of having jobs (1964: 112; Foster 2002: 45). Even on a popular cultural level there is wide interest in ancient Egypt, but most Egyptologists do not also do Biblical studies, and the number of jobs for Egyptologists is minuscule. I do not understand why popular interest does not translate into academic jobs, but it may have something to do with the lack of intellectual contact with the rest of Ancient Near Eastern, including Biblical, studies, and the isolation of Egyptology as a field. As with Mesopotamian studies, Egyptological training is long and esoteric, and the direct relevance to the humanities as a whole is not always apparent in monographic studies, although the relevance is apparent to any serious student.

Probably the most sustained and direct attack on scholarship in the Ancient Near East was Said's *Orientalism* (1978), which argued that scholars of the Islamic Near East but also earlier periods were working to advance the imperialistic aims of their governments. Said argued that scholars tended to prefer earlier and, for them, more classical forms of texts to the later but more popular renditions, thus depriving more contemporary spokesmen of their voices. He associated noted Orientalists with British and French efforts to control states and events in the Middle East, and more recently scholars from the United States who, he said, advanced the cause of Israel in the region.

Criticism of Said by Orientalists has stressed his error in omitting German scholarship in any portrait of Near Eastern studies; presumably he did so because German imperialist interests were late and unsuccessful, amounting mainly to support of the Ottomans against the allies of World War I. Blanket accusations against whole fields such as Said's do not explain the fields nor do they invalidate the efforts of generations of researchers who actually sought to let the locals speak to the present generation and to link the glorious past of the peoples of the Middle East with the history of all humanity, or at least the West. But they are a useful reminder that the area we study is fraught with modern political tension, and we must be self-conscious in examining our own motives to do particular studies but have enough courage to ask questions that may not be politically palatable to some of our contemporaries.

The literature on epistemological problems and the problem of perspective in history is vast, but it has mostly been ignored by scholars of the Ancient Near East. The reason for ignoring it is the general feeling that progress in understanding actually is being made.

What We Do

People who study the Ancient Near East prefer to find their texts in scientific excavations, but in fact many if not most of the texts have come from the antiquities market. It used to be legal to bring such texts from the Near East as tourist trinkets, and most of the museums in Europe and North America have a collection of Ancient Near Eastern texts. But with the independence of the states of the region came antiquities laws which prohibit the export of historical documents and artifacts. A trade persists in goods that were exported before there were such laws, but it is hard to be sure that small objects like cuneiform tablets were not exported illegally. And by participating in such trade, one is encouraging robbers today to pillage ancient sites in hopes of finding salable objects. In the wake of the 2003 Iraq war especially there was widespread looting of sites, though the objects taken may not yet have reached markets in the West. Clandestinely acquired objects may have important information for historians, but one must consider in using them if one is encouraging the destruction of sites that one day might be scientifically excavated and thus might yield up texts with actual archaeological contexts. The field is not agreed on the proper course of action in this regard, and one can understand that the lure of new texts may overcome qualms about contributing to archaeological destruction. But archaeologists, whose discipline is being deprived of data, uniformly condemn the market in antiquities.

The first goal of Ancient Near Eastern historical investigation is the establishment of archives. By archives we do not mean the modern repositories of manuscripts in which we find texts today. We mean ancient groups of tablets or texts of any sort which were created as a group. The problem for the historian is that the texts were not always preserved together or recovered together by archaeologists or tablet or papyrus robbers who brought them to the antiquities market. The idea is to see what the units of the ancient bureaucracies were and then to investigate the methods of recording, categorizing, and ordering which the clerks used (Gelb 1967; Bagnall 1995: 40–8).

Since few collections of ancient texts have been found in their original situations, historians resort to various devices to identify texts now scattered in different museums and to bring them together intellectually if not physically. The simplest of these devices is prosopography or the effort to constitute group biography. One tries to identify the persons working in or having contact with a particular bureaucracy and then to see if they show up in other texts. This effort involves the use of indices of personal names, and in each period there are more or less serviceable lists, but there are not yet exhaustive lists of names in published texts, and of course few ancient texts that have not yet been published are available in published lists of names (Borger 1975: 141–7). Each of these collections of names is incomplete and antiquated and thus gives only a partial picture of the individuals active in a period. So the effort to establish a list of bureaucrats who served in given capacities is a tentative one, subject to the finding of new texts. And yet good cases can be made that persons appearing in similar texts over time were the same persons and probably served the same institutions.

The criticisms of the method of prosopography that have been important in studies of other periods seem not to be salient in the Ancient Near East. Critics argue that prosopography by its nature groups together only superficial characteristics and does not explore what makes individuals unique (Stone 1971). In particular, ideology, or religious belief, seems to count for little or nothing in group biographies in other periods. The same might be said of studies of Mesopotamian figures; on the other hand, there is almost no information on the interior life and opinions of any Mesopotamian of any age, and we ought not to be surprised if such matters do not impinge on studies of bureaucracies. Still, considerable progress has been made even in unlikely places at reconstructing bureaucracies and how they worked and even something of political developments (Snell 2000). We must not of course simply assume that all the bureaucrats agreed with the party line as put forth in royal hymns and inscriptions, but criticism of that line was rare and muted, though not entirely absent (Snell 1998).

Another way of reconstructing archives and getting at ancient institutions is to look at the forms of the texts. By this we mean the genre, that is, those elements that make up the basic outlines of texts about a particular subject. As with modern genres, strict adherence to form may not be expected, and bureaucrats these days are always tinkering with their forms to make them better at recording different things. Even in the absence of prosopographic links it is sometimes possible to tease out the goals and functions of ancient institutions on the basis of how things were recorded in the texts of the same genre (Snell 1986). Certainly our understanding of kingship derives in large part from close attention to the titles the kings used and to what they considered worthy of representation within the genre of royal inscriptions (Hallo 1957; Von Beckerath 1984).

The very best way to re-create groups of texts is to find them together. In the past this was a rare occurrence since archeological methods were slipshod at best and record-keeping minimal. Nowadays, however, archeologists are obsessive about re-cording every detail, and the location and disposition of ancient texts is a high priority for them. We have found ancient archives in their original situation, though some of the most important groups of texts were not found in that state. One thinks in particular of the important collection of texts from the bureaucracy from the Ur III state in the capital city which were found together but had been reused as fill under a gate (Jacobsen 1953b). In that case the proximity of one text to another might be significant of their bureaucratically created connection, or it might not, given that the texts were transported and re-deposited. The contrast is striking to the finds at Ebla in northern Syria, where careful long-term excavation resulted in the uncovering of a huge ancient archive more or less in the order in which it fell from the burning wooden shelves that once supported it (Matthiae 1981: after 80).

The reconstruction of archives has proven very fruitful in recent Ancient Near Eastern history writing, but we must admit that there is something inherently narrow in the effort. We are learning more about a defined set of texts, all presumably coming from a single site in a limited period of time. But is what we can derive from that archive analogous to other archives even within the same language area and period? We cannot be sure and so are even more timid than we might have been about the scope of our statements. And we wish to ask broad questions not dependent on only one archive (Van De Mieroop 1997b: 302).

The source of ideas for broader studies is varied and dependent on the researcher's interests and reading. One obvious question to ask is how the archive one is studying relates to others either in the same period or in other periods but concerning the same activities, like Snell 1986, where I compared sheep-herding techniques with my Ur III archive's techniques. Another tactic is to look at as many archives as possible from one city in a period, like Van De Mieroop 1992, studying Old Babylonian Ur. Beyond that, scholars draw on analogous disciplines like anthropology to analyze their data and place them in a broader context, like Roth 1987 examining women's age at first marriage through texts about dowries.

Among the shames of the field are the very long delays from initial study to publication. Part of that delay comes from editors' efforts to get peers to read and respond to submissions, but part of the delay is from the breadth of teaching most practitioners are called on to do. This means that one is rarely teaching one's own material, and one finds that the presumed gap between research and teaching, which does not always in fact exist, may get bigger. Another factor in delay of publication is the custom in which museums award the rights to publish to particular researchers, who then may find themselves subject to delay. Because there are so many texts and so few scholars, there is always more to do and more texts to publish, and so everyone who has rights may take an indefinite time to publish even important texts. It may be that journals like *N.A.B.U. Notes assyriologiques brèves et utilitaires* dedicated to quick publication of short notes and other efforts to appear on the Internet may reduce the delays, but the ethic of procrastination is well established, and even technical advances may not frustrate such customs. The great scandal in this regard was the unconscionable delay in publishing all the Dead Sea Scrolls (Shanks 1992: xxi–xxxviii).

The only extended recent treatment of history-writing about the Ancient Near East is Van De Mieroop's 1999 book (Van De Mieroop 1999a). The author is concerned about the illegitimate separation of text from image, two elements that were certainly not divided in the ancient world, but now, because some are trained as text people and some as art historians, this division happens frequently, also in the present volume (Van De Mieroop 1999a: 58). Van De Mieroop attacks the use of "philological history," the putting together of all sorts of data from different periods and times just because they share a name or a word; his well-chosen example is the inclusion in most discussions of Sargon of Akkad who died about 2279 BCE of a text called the Sargon birth legend, which is from at least 1,500 years later. That text resembles the Biblical story of Moses and the bulrushes and may be from a similar time and milieu; Van De Mieroop argues that it tells us almost nothing about the historical Sargon but is much more important for the survival of his myths, that is, Sargon in tradition but not history. But because we have relatively few sources on Sargon, we include this late text even though it is not historically helpful (Van De Mieroop 1999a: 88). This same point was made for Egypt by Björkman about the Instruction for Merikare which is a literary text set in the First Intermediate Period (2125–1975 BCE) but available only in later, Eighteenth Dynasty copies from between 1539 and 1292 BCE and therefore cannot count as a witness to the First Intermediate Period (Björkman 1964). It can of course be seen as a reflection of the traditions about that more distant period and perhaps also of the ideas about how societies collapsed in general. Such texts do have a historical value, but as products of later times and of later ideas and not as images of the times they depicted.

Van De Mieroop attacks what he calls "positivism" in several places. Although he does not define positivism in this book, elsewhere he notes that for him the contrast to positivism is theory-driven scholarship (Van De Mieroop 1997b: 304). An example of the latter may be the three problems addressed in Zettler 2003, where he tries to combine texts and archaeology to study the history of a temple, ideas about radical climate change and societal collapse, and ideas about the crops Mesopotamians grew. What Zettler did was to look at the modern disciplines and questions and to mine the ancient material with these issues in mind.

Positivism includes "The doctrine that the goals and methods of natural science can be transferred to historiography," perhaps including "an anti-speculative conception of history, that stresses empirical research on particular subjects and shuns generalization and the quest for laws ..." (Ritter 1986: 327). Another commentator observes that positivists see "history as a preliminary to a predictive and scientific sociology" (Simon 1973: 538). This so-called "physics envy" is widespread in the social sciences, the very term for which in English expresses this envy. Although ancient historians do not see themselves as conducting experiments and predicting outcomes, what this means in ancient studies is that one sees oneself as building only a small part of an empirical monument through editing original texts and constructing archives. The great synthesis can only come later, in this view. The archival approach described here may be an element of that positivism, but it is hard to see how theory-driven studies can dispense with archives either.

Van De Mieroop raises the very important question of whether social categories translate over time. He writes, "Are we to see a Mesopotamian *wardum* as the equivalent of a Roman slave, whose body belonged to his owner, or as somewhat similar to the medieval European serf, tied to the land he or she worked?"(Van De Mieroop 1999a: 88). The question goes beyond the proper analogy for conditions of servitude to the question of whether social arrangements persisted. There is also the question of whether words in even the same language and culture mean the same thing over time. With slaves we can only answer this question through lots of anecdotes, and not all periods have the properly significant anecdotes. When the good stories are lacking, we have certainly in the past assumed a monolithic continuum especially to social arrangements, and for purposes of argument that sometimes works. But it is not necessarily always the case. For the idea that there was continuity one may note the persistence in the economy of the price of wool of 18 grains of silver for a pound from 2000 BCE into the Neo-Babylonian period before 539 BCE (Snell 1982: 203). But is this a continuity of economic circumstances or of traditional reporting of prices? Certainly it does not mean that economic conditions were entirely similar in two separate periods since other prices did vary over time; indeed the recording of prices indicates that they were expected to change and did.

The assumption of continuity derives from the very old idea, brought forward in the nineteenth century, that the Orient is unchanging. Perhaps the most detailed argument for the assumption is Wittfogel's *Oriental Despotism*, in which he argued that the East has attempted to suppress dissent in general and in politics, arguing that the general good demands uniformity (1957). Wittfogel, an anti-Communist Marxist, saw the origin of this effort in the need to organize irrigation projects in the river valleys. This idea about origins dissolves in confrontation with evidence about the small scale of early irrigation efforts (Adams 1981: 243). But even if Wittfogel has the origins wrong, the argument for a relatively unchanging Orient might still be right. The continuities are plain for all to see – an Egyptian writing system essentially static for 3,000 years, and Mesopotamian concepts of centralized kingship persisting for hundreds of years. And yet there is evidence everywhere for change in technical and state arrangements. It is of course easier for the modern writer to assume a lack of change; then applying the Sargon birth legend text to Sargon's own time makes sense. But historians do not sign up for ease. They seek these days at least to understand change over time.

For the public, part of the attraction of ancient history is its apparent timelessness. For the practitioner, the interesting aspect is change within tradition. As with the Bible, there doubtless was social advantage to keepers of traditional knowledge within the societies to asserting the societies' age and unchanging nature. They seem to assert, "The knowledge we hold is forever applicable and true because it has been unchanging from most ancient times." And yet we can show that even traditions frozen in writing changed over time, as in Gilgamesh and congregational laments (Tigay 1982; Kutscher 1975).

There is too in the assertion of continuity a drift toward the old man's (sic!) view of history: the old days were best, and a return to them is the best we can hope for. Obviously, though, the old men deplore current life and its changes, implying there are changes, but should not be. This may be a basic constituent of human thought, or perhaps just Western thought, where successful revolutions tend to present themselves as conservative returns to earlier and better forms (Berman 1983).

What We Should Do

But we said above that we would be prescriptive and say what ought to happen. One could argue with Van De Mieroop that a more sophisticated approach to data about the past might be a good thing for practitioners of ancient history. But does it necessarily help everyone to have such doubts about epistemology? Perhaps it does, but one is concerned with the sorts of questions that are posed in the future. And that must inevitably be dictated by our own experience and what seems of interest to our culture in the future. Right now it appears that issues of religion will become perhaps more important than in the past. Chronology will continue to be refined, but it will also seem to matter less as we get more firm grips on various periods.

We all face the tension toward specialization in research and breadth in teaching, not only in historical disciplines, and yet I believe we must all think, and publish, as broadly as possible. If we do not exert ourselves in such efforts, we will be more marginalized when hard economic times cause institutions of learning to cut back.

The North African historian Ibn Khaldun, who lived from 1332 to 1406 of our era and originated the study of historical sociology, suggested that the task of the historian was to become an expert in two cultures, one's own and the target culture. As an example, Ibn Khaldun took his contemporaries to task because they assumed that teaching was always an apolitical role. But in early Islam to teach the Quran was in fact to inculcate new members with the values of the elite and was a duty undertaken by the very most politically powerful individuals. Then if we assume that teachers were "rootless and lacking in political power" as they were in Ibn Khaldun's day, not to mention our own, we commit an error (1967: 26–7).

Most students easily grasp the need to study the languages and cultures, including the physical cultures as represented in archaeology, of the Ancient Near East. But the changing institutions and the senses of words are harder to grasp. Harder still perhaps to understand is why one should try to become an expert on one's own culture. This is necessary because it is one's own culture that one is addressing. One may not master all the jargons of all the by-ways of contemporary life, but one writes for people who know these things, or at least may know these things. One can speak to them more clearly and directly if one has some knowledge of how one's culture works. This is particularly true for Ibn Khaldun who thought that a major task of the historian was to draw analogies to contemporary phenomena, guarding always against anachronism. "The past resembles the future more than one drop of water another" (1967: 12), he wrote, but the key is to draw attention to the proper drops of contemporary water and not to become confused by pollution that renders the analogy false.

The task of mastering two cultures is almost impossible for a single lifetime, but luckily we are not limited to a lifetime. Thanks to the ancients' invention of literacy, we may build on the work of many others long dead. Bagnall characterizes history "as the enterprise of a complex community rather than an individual," and the individuals have different strengths and weaknesses (1995: 114–17). If occasionally we do not succeed in understanding the target culture or our own, we end by propagating lies and speaking incomprehensibilities. There is no question that the study of the Ancient Near East has done its share of both, and yet the lure of the remains persists, and it is against the evidence and the consensus of the community of historians interpreting that evidence that we can test our guesses and measure our theories.

If we need to defend concentrating on details of an ancient past, we might remember that to study history is to try on the varieties of being human, and as that variety is increased, so may our sense of humanity increase. Recent observers of the progress of early Egyptology remark on the impact of Napoleon's expedition to Egypt and its publication of the variety of ancient and modern Egyptian phenomena, "Suddenly the world as viewed from western Europe was much larger, older, and stranger than it had been before" (Adkins and Adkins 2000: 17). The historian is always trying to expand the contemporary culture's ideas about humanity, to give depth and nuance to one's fellows' sense of the past and how it might impinge on current problems.

An example still debatable in our culture is the status and roles of women. As Van De Mieroop pointed out (1999a: 138–54), our view of Ancient Near Eastern women is a mixture of the restrictive portrait of the Classical Greek age along with the saga of pre-modern Islamic women's limited social roles. Those who would see a unilinear progression admit that this image does not fit early periods, but that there was then deterioration down to Israel, which then transmitted to the West a limited role for women (Lerner 1986). Subsequent study has indicated that there were ups and downs in women's power and roles throughout Ancient Near Eastern history. The relevance of these findings has not yet been considered in societies of the region now, but it seems clear that ancient precedents for an expanded role for women may have relevance as those societies confront cohorts of women more educated than in the recent past.

There is no nobler intellectual quest than attempting to understand the past, unless it be a more directly altruistic one. The depth of history in its long duration may provide cautionary tales for confident eras, and it may give comfort and hope in darker times. Since we cannot convince ourselves that Gilgamesh is served by our perpetuation of his story, we must hope that our children are served by having a depth of history and knowing that, though not everything has been done before, a very great deal has.

FURTHER READING

On method in general Tosh 2000 by an Africanist is a good survey. On finding and defining research topics and for the minutiae of editing in general Barzun and Graff 1985 is still useful. For cuneiform issues Van De Mieroop 1999a is a good introduction. Hornung 1990 is a broad guide to work in ancient Egypt, as is Bagnall 1995 for Egypt from Alexander to the Arabs. The basic Assyriological bibliography is Borger 1967–75, updated by the annual *Keilschriftbibliographie* appearing in the journal *Orientalia*. For Biblical material the *Elenchus of Biblica* chronicles bibliography, also including much Ancient Near Eastern material. For Egyptology there is the *Annual Egyptian Bibliography*.

PART III

Economy and Society

CHAPTER EIGHT

The Degradation of the Ancient Near Eastern Environment

Carlos E. Cordova

It is not surprising that the Near East, the region with the longest record of agricultural development and urbanization, has received considerable attention from scholars interested in ancient land degradation. While some of the Near Eastern landscapes have sustained large concentrations of population, as is the case of the flood plains, others have hardly been settled, such as the hyper-arid region of the Arabian Peninsula known as the Empty Quarter (Map 8.1a). Despite these differences, all the landscapes of the Near East have been transformed, making it difficult to determine what pre-agricultural landscapes may have looked like.

The designation "land degradation" has a negative connotation since it implies a diminution in landscape quality. Although such a negative implication is undeniable, natural forces often gear mechanisms of landscape change. But who is ultimately to be blamed for the deterioration of the environment? The answer to this question is frequently stalled by the difficulty in distinguishing natural from human-induced impacts on the landscape. Recent advances in the study of climatic phenomena and improved resolution of climatic records provide better pictures of the natural–human causes of land degradation.

Because the main objective of this chapter is human-induced land degradation, the examples discussed here emphasize human influences on landscape change. This, however, is not to downplay the role of climatic change and other natural factors. The different forms of land degradation by region reflect the ecological and cultural differences in space and time (Map 8.1b). For this reason, land degradation should be explained as a cultural phenomenon in the context of an ever-changing physical environment.

The Physical Scene

The backbone mountainous systems in the Near East comprise the Taurus Mountains of southwestern Turkey, the Pontic Mountains in northern Turkey, and the Zagros and Elburz Mountains of Iran. Other minor mountain systems are the Lebanon and

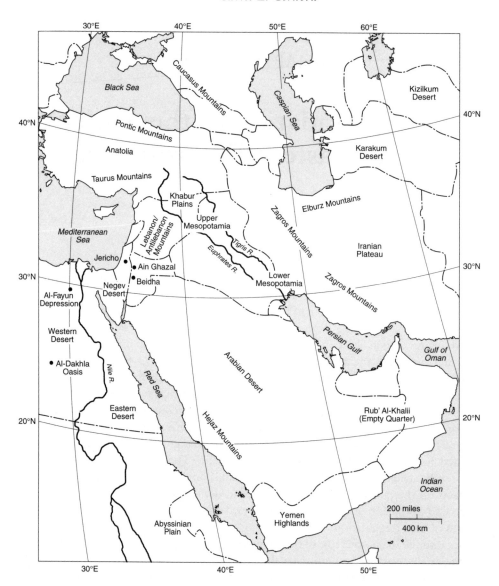

Map 8.1   a) Sites

Anti-Lebanon Mountains in the Levant, and the Hejaz Mountains of the western flank of the Arabian Peninsula. Hilly areas and isolated mountains include the mountains of the Sinai Peninsula, the hills of the Western Desert in Egypt, and numerous smaller, isolated hills in the Syrian and Arabian deserts. The major plateaus include the Anatolian Plateau of Turkey and the Iranian Plateau; smaller plateaus exist in the Sinai Peninsula and the region east of the Jordan Rift Valley.

The lowlands include the flood plains of the main rivers in the region: the Tigris, the Euphrates, and the Nile. Other lowland areas are found in some depressions in

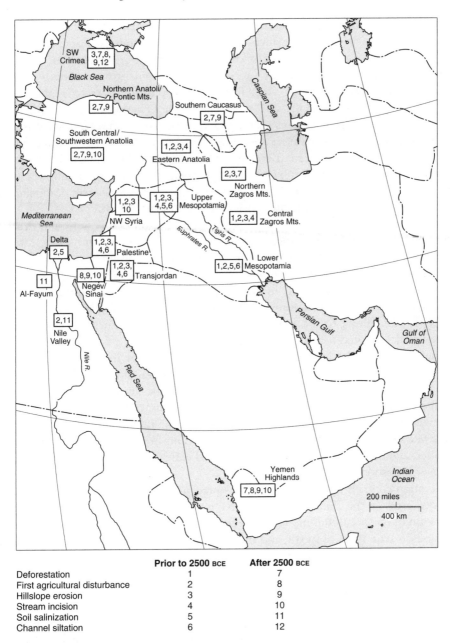

	Prior to 2500 BCE	After 2500 BCE
Deforestation	1	7
First agricultural disturbance	2	8
Hillslope erosion	3	9
Stream incision	4	10
Soil salinization	5	11
Channel siltation	6	12

Map 8.1   b) Prior to 2500, after 2500

the Arabian Peninsula, the Eastern Desert of Egypt, and along the coastal plains of Israel/Palestine and the southern shore of the Persian Gulf. Some interior depressions contain saltpans, which are the relicts of extensive Pleistocene lakes, as is the case in the Syrian, Jordanian, and Arabian deserts, and some areas east of the Iranian Plateau.

Vegetation is another aspect often used to describe the landscapes of the Near East. In general terms, it can be classified into forests, woodlands, steppes, and deserts (Map 8.2a). The northern slopes of the Pontic and Elburz Mountains have the densest forest cover, dominated by various species of mid-latitude trees, both coniferous and deciduous broadleaf. Open forests and woodlands characterize the Taurus and Zagros Mountains, and the smaller systems of the Lebanon and the highlands of Palestine. These are in most cases characterized by the typical evergreen trees around the Mediterranean and deciduous species arranged in altitudinal levels often generalized into Eu-Mediterranean (the lowest) and Oro-Mediterranean (the highest) region. *Maquis* (evergreen shrub lands) and *garrigue* (perennial low scrub) dominate the Eu-Mediterranean region. Pine, Lebanese cedar, and kermes oak dominate the higher elevations, the Oro-Mediterranean region (Zohary 1973).

Steppe landscapes constitute the transition between wooded regions and deserts. The Irano-Turanian Steppe, which consists of a variety of herbs and scrub, extends from the southern foothills of the Zagros and Taurus Mountains to the eastern foothills of the Syrian Anti-Lebanon Mountains (Map 8.2a). The thorny shrubs of the Sudanian province dominate in the lowlands of Egypt's Eastern Desert along the Red Sea, the Sinai Peninsula, Nubia, and the Dead Sea–Jordan depression. The rest of the territories belong to the Saharo-Arabian province, which includes mostly herbaceous plants adapted to extreme aridity.

The climates of the Near East are strongly influenced by its latitudinal location, topographic features, and its location inland. The prevailing westerly winds bring rain into most of the region in the form of cyclonic storms originating in the Mediterranean and Black Seas during the winter. Summers are usually dry and hot throughout most of the region. The exceptions are the mountainous areas facing the Black Sea and the Caspian Sea, where northerly winds bring rainfall in the spring and summer, and the southern third of the Arabian Peninsula, where rain is driven by the summer monsoons of the Indian Ocean.

Elevation controls the amount of annual precipitation and temperature. Thus, the forested areas of the Pontic and Elburz Mountains receive annual amounts of precipitation of up to 1,000 mm, which is enough to maintain a dense forest cover. The lowlands in Iraq, most of Egypt, and the Arabian Peninsula receive amounts less than 50 mm a year. Temperatures drop with elevation at a rate of 1 °C per 100 meters, although at a certain point they decline to 0.6 °C per 100 meters. Temperatures below freezing during the winter months are common in the highest parts of the mountains in Turkey and Iran. Snowstorms are frequent in the highest parts of the mountains, where snow cover may remain for two or three months. The plateaus of the southern Levant (Palestine and Transjordan) are commonly subject to frosts, although snowfall may be common in some years. Temperatures in the lowlands and depression are generally high. Most areas in the Arabian Peninsula and Egypt may experience summer maximum temperatures above 45 °C. However, during the winter months, when northerly winds and scattered rains bring some relief, these areas register pleasant temperatures.

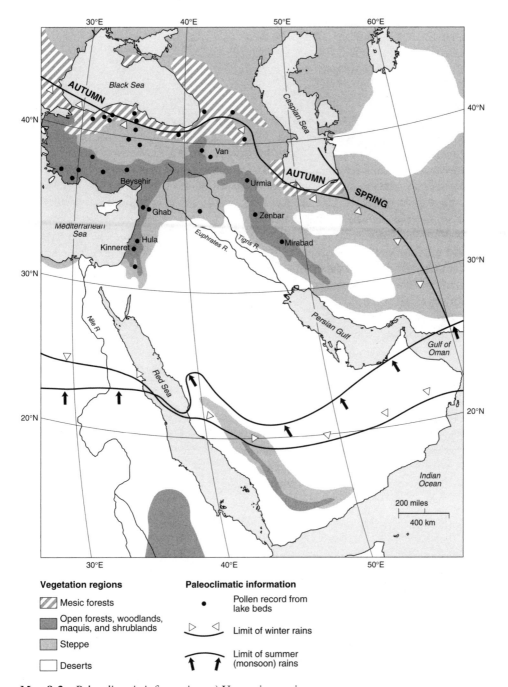

Map 8.2   Paleoclimatic information: a) Vegetation regions

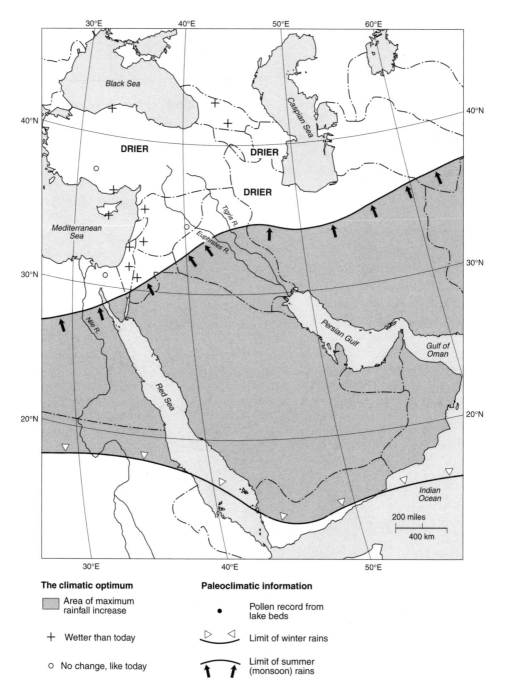

Map 8.2   Paleoclimatic information: b) the climatic optimum

The Climatic and Paleoclimatic Background

Paleoclimatic data for the past 20,000 years in the Near East come from a variety of sources: lake sediment records, marine records, and a series of terrestrial deposits (cave sediments and alluvial deposits). Pollen records are the proxies for the reconstruction of vegetation, which shows a direct and relatively rapid response to climatic change. Pollen-based reconstructions of vegetation and climate have been carried out at a local scale through the study of cores from lake sediments, and at a regional scale through cores from the bottom of the Mediterranean Sea. One problem is that fossil pollen studies are concentrated in areas with lakes, which are mostly the northern part of the region (Map 8.2a).

Among other methods, the study of stable isotopes has provided information on past precipitation patterns. They are studied on cave speleothems,[1] microorganisms in lake and sea bottom deposits, land snails, and teeth (Bar-Matthews et al. 1999; Goodfriend 1999). The signatures obtained through isotopes derive directly from the atmosphere, eliminating the noise of human impact, and that is an advantage over studies of pollen analysis.

The broad picture of paleoclimatic change varies from region to region, due to differences in latitude, altitude, proximity to the seas, and weather patterns. During the coldest phases of the Late Glacial Maximum (about 18,000–16,000 years ago) vegetation in the mountainous regions of Turkey and Iran was characterized by *Artemisia* (wormwood) steppe (Van Zeist and Bottema 1991). Although dry conditions were present in the northern part of the Near East, pollen records from the Ghab Valley in Syria and Lake Hula in Israel show an increase in oak forests. Climatic amelioration in most of the regions of the Near East, attested by the expansion of forests, occurred between 15,000 and 11,000 BP (before the present) as warmer conditions induced more rainfall (Blanchet, Sanlaville, and Traboulsi 1998). A relatively short, dry, and cool period is recorded in some areas of the Near East between 11,000 and 10,000 years BP. This event, usually correlated with the Younger Dryas in Europe, was characterized by the cooling of the atmosphere and the partial return to glacial conditions. Pollen records from the northern areas of the Near East show a reduction of forests (Bottema 1995), and lake records of the same region show low levels (Roberts and Wright 1993). Ironically, it is under the adverse climatic conditions of this dry phase that plant and animal domestication began. Some postulate that dry conditions stimulated plant cultivation among human groups that were already in the process of sedentarization (Henry 1989; Bar-Yosef and Belfer-Cohen 1992). Other scholars disagree with this view and propose an alternative scenario in which dry conditions forced "domesticable" wild plants to migrate to areas where human populations were already manipulating wild plants to increase food production (McCorriston and Hole 1991; Wright 1993).

After 10,000 years BP the picture changed as temperatures rose and rains increased. In particular, the period between 9,000 and 6,000 years BP has been recognized as the Holocene Climatic Optimum (Map 8.2b). During this phase, rains increased considerably in the Eastern Mediterranean region and even in inland areas as far as the

Zagros Mountains (Rossignol-Strick 1999; Van Zeist and Bottema 1991). In addition to the increased winter rains, summer rains occurred in some areas, as suggested by stable isotopes, which in turn point to the enhancement of both cyclonic rains from the Mediterranean in winter and the influence of monsoon rains originated in the Indian Ocean in summer (Blanchet, Sanlaville, and Traboulsi 1998; Bar-Matthews et al. 1999). Pollen diagrams from lakes in the mountains of Iran and Turkey show that woodlands and forests advanced over areas formerly occupied by steppes. However, despite woodland recovery, increased human activities slowed down the recovery of woodlands in some regions (Van Zeist and Bottema 1991). A similar scenario occurred in drylands, where increase of grasslands allowed more possibilities for farming and herding, thus adding more pressure on the environment of the steppes and deserts (Butzer 1995). During this humid stage, lake levels increased, especially the now dry playas of the deserts in the Sahara and the Arabian Peninsula, and the inland seas, the Aral and the Caspian (Butzer 1995). The overall amelioration of the climate during this phase stimulated the establishment of farming villages, and their subsequent growth into urban centers. Gradual desiccation has been observed after about 3500 BCE, a process that eventually gave shape to the modern dry environments of the region.

Deforestation and Alteration of the Vegetation Cover

The considerable reduction of the natural vegetation cover of the Near East was due mainly to the increasing need for wood and the expansion of farming and pastoral activities. Although numerous written records exist for the exploitation of wood in the Ancient Near East, evidence has also been recovered from fossil pollen records, archeobotanical remains, and anthracological (charcoal) analyses. Of these, pollen analysis shows the regional picture of the gradual degradation of vegetation. The evidence of deforestation in pollen diagrams is assessed by the fluctuation of tree pollen, referred to as A.P. (arboreal pollen). The reduction of the A.P. curve in pollen diagrams indicates reduction of trees due either to climatic deterioration or deforestation. The latter is often coupled with the appearance of pollen of cultivated species, especially cereals, and their associated weeds. Several of the pollen diagrams in the Near East confirm that the A.P. reduction correlates with the regional increase of farming villages and in general an increase of population levels, which started in the Neolithic and increased during the Bronze Age. Calibrated dates from lake-bed sediments of the Ghab Valley (Map 8.2a) showed that the depletion of deciduous oaks started between 12,500 and 9,000 years BP due to the beginning of clearing for agricultural activities in the Pre-Pottery Neolithic period (Yasuda, Kitagawa, and Nakagawa 2000).

Intense wood exploitation in areas such as the Lebanese mountains, Mount Hermon, and the Palestinian highlands, led to a reduction in forested areas and tree species. This explains the irony that the Lebanese cedar (*Cedrus libani* L.) is today rare in Lebanon, as compared to the Taurus Mountains and other regions of Turkey (Zohary 1973). Pollen records from the Ghab Valley (Map 8.2a) are probably the best testimony of the depletion of cedar forests in Mt. Ansarie, which is the northern end of the Lebanon Mountain ranges. Pollen records from the Ghab Valley suggest that due to clearance by Early Bronze Age people, Lebanese cedar forests had completely disappeared from the eastern slopes of Mt. Ansarie by 4900 years BP, coinciding with the periods of cedar exploitation reported in Mesopotamian sources (Yasuda, Kitagawa, and Nakagawa 2000).

Oak experienced a trend of depletion similar to cedar. The pollen diagrams of the Ghab Valley show that as oak and cedar decreased, olive (*Olea europaea*) increased. This is explained by the rapid expansion of olive cultivation at the expense of native forests. Pollen records from Lake Hula and Lake Kinneret/Galilee show a similar trend. In particular, the Lake Kinneret pollen record shows that the Early Bronze Age and the Roman–Byzantine periods present the most prominent peaks of olive tree cultivation (Baruch 1990).

The timing of the destruction of the forests seems to be different for each region of the Near East. In Anatolia, modern Turkey, the profound changes in the natural vegetation are not evident until after 4,000 years BP. Such changes were recurrent in almost all the pollen records of lake sediments in Turkey and Greece, and to some degree in Western Iran. Although with regional differences, this phase began about 1500 BCE and ended about 400 CE. Because the best example comes from the deposits of Lake Beyşehir in Turkey, this phase has been named the Beyşehir Occupation Phase (Bottema and Woldring 1990). The high levels of atmospheric moisture during this phase may have encouraged expansion of agricultural activities (Bottema and Woldring 1990). The reasons for the end of this phase are unknown, although possibly they have to do with changes in the agrarian systems toward methods that had different effects on vegetation (Bottema, Woldring, and Aytug 1993).

Accessibility and proximity to the main urban centers were important factors in the destruction of forests in antiquity. The Taurus Mountains, the Zagros Mountains, and the Lebanon and Anti-Lebanon Mountains have been dramatically deforested for timber since the Bronze Age, as opposed to less accessible areas such as the Pontic Mountains and the Euxinian forests of northern Iran, where deforestation did not take place until the Hellenistic and Roman periods (Rowton 1967).

The Impact of Grazing

Overgrazing became one of the most destructive forms of land degradation as nomadic pastoralism appeared on the scene about 9,000 years ago. For millennia, nomadic pastoralism has been a strategy of subsistence in areas with low carrying capacity, requiring seasonal movements of flocks to a variety of ecological zones. For this reason, there is basically no natural region spared from the devastation caused by livestock grazing. The wild ancestors of grazing animals had a minimal impact on vegetation because they occupied specific habitats and predators controlled their population numbers.

In particular, sheep and goats are the most common and destructive grazing livestock in the Near East. These two closely related species developed different ways of grazing. Sheep graze to root level, destroying the herbaceous mat to the ground, while goats graze indiscriminately on trees, shrubs, and herbs. In the end, goats are more destructive, since their devastating effects cover larger areas.

Although pastoralism has a direct impact on the composition of herbaceous vegetation, it also has effects on the arboreal vegetation. Young plants are usually within the reach of livestock, while acorns and seeds are rapidly eaten before they can even germinate. From the ecological point of view, grazing implies the selection of certain species of plants that are preferred by livestock. This means that before the establishment of grazing, the composition of the vegetation in most regions was certainly different from today.

The numerous pollen diagrams in the region show the effects of pastoralism on the natural vegetation in the form of a rapid increase of herbs and scrub associated with grazing. These plants include *Plantago lanceolata*, *Rumex acetosella*, and *Urtica*, which are benefited by nitrates from livestock dung. Livestock also avoids aromatic plants such as those of the mint family (*Labiatae*) and the spiny ones often referred to as *Poterium/Sanguisorba* type in pollen diagrams. In steppe and desert areas, members of the Chenopodiaceae (for example *Anabasis syriaca* and *Noaea mucronata*) and Asteraceae family (for example *Artemisia*) are among the main plants avoided by livestock.

The Human Impact on Fauna

The impact of humans on wildlife can be assessed through the record of extinctions and the reduction of species, for which testimonies exist in the numerous faunal remains in the archaeological record and in representations of animals in rock art. In most cases hunting was the main cause of the reduction of fauna. In other cases the destruction of vegetation, which acts as habitat for fauna, contributed to the elimination of animals.

Despite the amount of data produced by numerous studies of faunal remains, problems exist for the study of some groups of animals. For example, the reconstruction of bird exploitation is limited due to the lack of bone preservation in the harsh environment of the Near East (Gilbert 1995). In addition, most bird species are migratory, making determinations of geographical extent more difficult.

The list of species that went extinct in pre-agricultural times includes the so-called Pleistocene megafauna such as the Asiatic Elephant (*Elephas maximus*), which lived in several regions, and hippopotamus (*Hippopotamus amphibius*), which inhabited the Nile River Valley and the coastal region of the Levant (Gilbert 1995). Among the ungulates commonly exploited by hunters of the Pleistocene–Holocene transition are wild horses (*Equus africanus* and *Equus hemious*), wild boar (*Sus scrofa*), red deer (*Dama mesopotamica*), ibex (*Capra nubiana*), wild goat (*Capra aegragus*), and wild sheep (*Ovis orientalis*), among others (Uerpman 1987).

Those species that survived extinction have been reduced in both numbers and geographic extension. One example is the reduction of the geographical extension of the genus *Gazella* (gazelle) in most regions of the Middle East. Some species, such as the goitered gazelle (*Gazella subgutturosa*) have become extinct (Uerpman 1987). In addition to hunting, the modification of wildlife occurred through domestication, although some domesticated species still have relatives in the wild.

Soil Erosion and Slope Management

Soil erosion and deforestation are perhaps the two most evident forms of land degradation in the Near East. Soil erosion is a natural process that implies the removal of mineral and organic particles from the ground surface by water and wind.

The triggering of soil erosion is linked to the reduction of vegetation, which can occur as a result of both climatic change and human disturbances. The removal of soil particles by soil erosion in upland locations results in rapid accumulation of sediments in valleys and lowlands. Thus, investigating past soil erosion histories starts with the study of sequences of sediments in valleys. This approach allows the reconstruction of events of intense soil erosion in Greece (Van Andel, Zangger and Demitrack 1990), northwestern Syria (Wilkinson 1999), southwestern Turkey (Wilkinson 1999; Rosen 1997b), the Shephelah region of Israel (Rosen 1997a), the Transjordanian Plateau (Cordova 1999, 2000), and Western Iran (Brookes, Levine, and Dennell 1982), among other examples. In addition to evaluating rapid sediment deposition in valleys, geomorphologists often study soils in the uplands, where the thinning of some horizons and an internal structure testify to intense degradation (Van Andel, Zangger, and Demitrack 1990; Cordova 2000).

One of the measures taken by ancient and modern farmers to control soil erosion in the mountainous regions of the Near East has been the construction of hillside terraces, which is still widespread in the mountainous regions around the Mediterranean and the southwestern part of the Arabian Peninsula. But how old is slope terracing in the Near East?

If we consider that olive cultivation has often been associated with terraces, it can be assumed that agricultural terracing was implemented in the Neolithic as olive cultivation increased. However, no clear archaeological evidence exists to support such an assumption. The reuse and rebuilding of terraces, the mixing of datable materials of various ages, and the destruction of diagnostic pottery through continuous plowing make the accurate dating of terraces difficult (Wagstaff 1992). On the slopes of the Judean Hills, around Jerusalem, terraces seem to be associated with Early Bronze Age occupations, but they were continuously repaired in subsequent periods, especially during the Iron Age and the Roman and Byzantine periods (Gibson and Edelstein 1985).

The abandonment of agricultural terraces has proved detrimental to the environment, since the lack of maintenance leads to the breaking of walls and the subsequent removal of soil particles from inside the terraces by torrential overflow. In some cases, depending on conservation practices, terracing itself can have adverse effects. For example, in the mountains of Yemen Wilkinson (1997b) showed that the initial phase of terrace construction implied an increase of erosion, as vegetation was removed and slopes were reshaped. It seems, however, that slope terracing was only a partial solution to the problem of soil erosion.

Irrigation and Soil Salinization

Soil salinization involves the accumulation of salts in the soil, which impedes the development of crops and most plants. Soil salinization is a problem particular, but not exclusive, to arid and semi-arid lands. Although a natural process, soil salinization occurs through human intervention as a result of poor planning in the management of irrigated lands. The problem starts when excess irrigation water produces water-logging, which under conditions of high evaporation rates results in precipitation of salts near the surface of the soil (Artzy and Hillel 1988). For these reasons, the problem of salinization is viewed here in the context of the main irrigation systems in the Near East.

The worst cases of soil salinization in the Ancient Near East occurred in large-scale irrigation systems, especially in the Mesopotamian lowlands, where irrigation was difficult and challenging. One of the major problems was the late spring and early summer floods produced by melting snow and rain in the mountains. Besides creating destruction of fields, these floods brought excess water at the time when it was not needed. On the other hand, the flow of water was relatively low in the late fall and early winter when water was desperately needed. Another problem was that fields lay lower in relation to the main river channels. This situation produced overflowing of water into the fields and made draining the excess water difficult. Consequently, evaporation of the stagnated waters prompted the accumulation of salts in the upper soil horizons. Today, modern technology partially solves the problem through a system of deep drainage to lower and hold down the water table and with the use of chemical amendments to restore soil texture (Artzy and Hillel 1988). However, this technology did not exist in ancient times.

In ancient times, the major breakthrough in partially solving the problem of salinization in Mesopotamia occurred during the Sassanian Period (226–637 CE) when irrigation along the flood plains of the Diyala River, a tributary of the Tigris, was devised (Adams 1981). This system included the Naharawan canal, which was 3,000 km or 1,860 miles long and 50 m or 54 yards wide, and designed to drain the excess water into the Tigris.

In the Nile Basin the situation was far different, for the timing of the floods coincided with the growing of crops. In addition, the fields lay far above the main channel. The adaptation of agriculture to this scheme was much simpler. Floods occurred yearly before the planting season. The flood plain was divided into different basins, which were filled with flood waters, bringing to the fields the nutrients necessary for each agricultural cycle. Once the waters receded to the main channel, the excess water in the fields was drained and the water table lowered. The main problem in the ancient Nile Valley was when floods failed or when they occurred off-season (Butzer 1976). The only areas of Egypt with major salinization problems were the Fayum Depression and the Delta. In the former, the problem lay in the fact that the flow of water diverted from the Nile through the Fayum Canal ended in a closed basin, where excess water had no way to escape (Hamdan 1961). In the lower part of the Delta the water table was often high, especially in areas where the underground was contaminated with salty water from the sea (Hamdan 1961; Stanley and Warne 1993).

Several strategies to cope with the problem of soil salinization have been implemented by farmers on a local scale. One of the common practices in Mesopotamia was to plant the deep-rooted *shoq* (*Prosperina stephanis*) and *agul* (*Alhagi maurorum*) which absorbed capillary water, thus creating deep-lying dry zones that hampered the rise of salinity (Jacobsen and Adams 1958). Among other strategies, selection of well-drained soils for irrigation proved to be useful, but only worked in small-scale irrigation systems. One of these cases is the irrigation around the Dakhla Oasis in the Western Desert of Egypt, where water was lifted using the *saqiya* (animal-powered water wheels) into canals and then into raised plots built on sandy deposits (Brookes 1990). The high porosity of these sandy deposits inhibited salinization by letting the excess water drain freely and minimizing waterlogging, the main factor leading to salinization. This strategy could not have been applied to the Mesopotamian lands, where silts and clays in the soils would impede draining of excess water.

The degradation of soils by salinization means that fertile lands turn into a salty desert, forcing farmers to abandon their fields. Under such circumstances, farmers abandoned their lands to become pastoral nomads; this move meant a more secure procurement of living and probably more flexibility in terms of taxation (Butzer 1995). Under this scenario the supply of food to the city, especially grain, failed, thus having an impact on the entire structure of the state. Salinization has been linked to decline of Mesopotamian civilization (Adams and Nissen 1972), although scholars argue about this issue, especially when dealing with the participation of the state in controlling irrigation systems (Wagstaff 1985).

Soil salinization was not a major problem in the small-scale irrigation systems of the Near East, because it was easier to control and in general was implemented in areas with better drainage. Overall, small-scale irrigation systems were more sustainable and ecologically better suited than the large-scale systems. There are several types of small-scale irrigation systems, of which flood irrigation is the simplest and presumably the earliest (Sherratt 1980). Operation is simple, since the main objective is to build cross-channel dams intended to redirect flood waters produced by sporadic rains and to maintain moisture in the soil. In antiquity, these systems were extensively practiced in the driest parts of the Near East, such as the Negev (Evenari, Shanan, and Tadmor 1982) and the Libyan Valleys (Gilbertson et al. 1994).

There were other small-scale systems that were technologically more complex. They included canal irrigation tapping the waters of smaller permanent streams, usually draining from the mountains into the drier lowlands, as was the case of the *Al-Ghuta* system at Damascus, which to this day taps waters from the Barada River.

Some of the small-scale irrigation systems were known for their technological sophistication, such as the *qanat* system, which consisted of gently sloping tunnels cut through river-laid material and bedrock (usually limestone) to transmit water from beneath the water table to the ground surface. Once on the surface, the water was distributed by canals. The *qanat* system was highly efficient since it reduced loss of water by evaporation and consequently avoided salinization (Beaumont 1971).

Direct and Indirect Alteration of the Fluvial Systems

Through an extensive study of river deposits in streams near archaeological sites, geoarcheologists have linked radical changes in sedimentation and erosion with the appearance and intensification of farming. Mabry (1992) was able to link changes in sedimentation and channel erosion with the growth of early agricultural villages in the Jordan Valley.

The process known to geomorphologists as "channel entrenchment" or "stream downcutting" lies in the destruction of stream beds and fertile flood plains. Rosen linked the abandonment of Early Bronze Age sites in the Shephelah region of Israel with the degradation of streams (Rosen 1997a). A similar scenario has been postulated for the abandonment of the Early Bronze Age site of Khirbet Iskander in Jordan (Long and Cordova 2003).

Silts originated from soil erosion in the upper reaches of the valleys caused numerous problems in the lowland streams of Mesopotamia. Large amounts of silts carried by streams ended up clogging river channels, forcing them to change courses, consequently creating destruction of fields. Irrigation canals collected large amounts of silts, creating the need for enormous cleaning operations every year (Adams 1981). Over the millennia the increase of silts transported by the rivers led to the advance of the Mesopotamian delta into the Persian Gulf and the formation of the marshes in southern Iraq (Sanlaville 1989).

Channel straightening and dike construction along the banks were common practices to maximize irrigation in Mesopotamia. However, in the long run such practices had adverse effects, producing unrelenting flooding and salinization (Adams 1981). A straight channel increases water flow velocity, augmenting the risk of overflow and catastrophic flooding.

Pollution of Air, Water, and Soil

The level of pollution in waters, air, and soil was certainly much lower than today, but little is known about pollution in the ancient environments of the Near East. The burning of wood must have caused contamination of carbon dioxide in the atmosphere, but no figures exist on the extent of such pollution. On the other hand, sedentarization and the expansion of villages are known to have increased pollution in surrounding water bodies (Brothwell 1972), but there are no studies that address the issue directly. Assumptions can be made on indirect data recovered through paleoenvironmental studies of lakes. Increases in nutrients in sediments of Anatolian lakes (Behcet 1994; Eastwood et al. 1999) seem to suggest that lakes were undergoing eutrophication.[2] Large amounts of *Pediastrum* spores in the Neolithic levels of the lake deposits of the Ghab Valley, Syria, are interpreted as a lowering in lake water quality due to accelerated soil erosion and nutrient supply (Yasuda, Kitagawa, and Nakagawa 2000).

Dramatic cases of air pollution similar to those of the industrial era have been documented in the copper mine region in the Araba Valley in southern Israel and

Jordan. Paleoenvironmental data from settlements in the Wadi Faynan region in Jordan showed that their populations were exposed to extremely high levels of contamination produced by copper mining and smelting (Barker 2000). Although initiated in the Chalcolithic period, it was not until the Early Bronze Age that this activity grew to larger proportions (Levy, Adams, and Shafiq 1999). This growth of the smelting industry was the result of the immense social change of this period, and the high demand for copper in the Near Eastern markets (Hauptmann 1992). However, it was not until the Roman and Byzantine periods that heavy metal pollution reached a peak (Barker 2000). Recent geochemical studies have shown that the effects of Roman and Byzantine mining and smelting are still present in the region. The milk, urine, and feces of goats raised by Bedouins in the region have significant levels of heavy metals from grazing on polluted grounds (Barker 2000).

Environmental Crisis at the End of the Third Millennium BCE

A period of apparent environmental and social troubles in the Near East took place toward the end of the third millennium BCE. The Old Kingdom civilization of Egypt, the Akkadian Empire of Mesopotamia, and the Bronze Age civilizations of Syria, Palestine, Greece, and Crete, all of which had achieved their economic peak by 2300 BCE, collapsed by the end of the third millennium. The high complexity of this widespread phenomenon leads to several possible causes of societal collapse. Opinions of scholars working on the subject range from views of worldwide climatic change to ideas about socio-economic crises. Whatever the causes were, this phenomenon is discussed here because land degradation most certainly played a significant role in the collapse.

Weiss (2000) and Weiss and Bradley (2001) support the idea of climatic deterioration, based on examination of paleoclimatic records at local, regional, and global scales. Such records show that the 300–400-year period of low precipitation took place in several regions of the world (Weiss 2000). Evidence exists, for example, of dust deposition at the bottom of the Gulf of Oman, suggesting frequent dust storms (Weiss and Bradley 2001). Those in favor of non-climatic causes provide examples of socio-economic crises that may have occurred regardless of climatic deterioration (Butzer 1997).

This environmental change occurred in a relatively short period so that it was not clearly registered in marine and lake records. Pollen records from lake sediments show evidence of environmental deterioration, but not necessarily due to aridization (Butzer 1997). Deposits by rivers show rapid sediment accumulation followed by channel entrenchment in various streams, especially those areas heavily populated during the Early Bronze Age. It is possible that intense land degradation (forest clearance, grazing, and plowing) crucially impacted the stream courses, which in addition to climatic deterioration prompted the collapse of the socio-economic systems around them.

Wilkinson presents a comprehensive model based on the development and collapse of Early Bronze sites in Upper Mesopotamia (1997a). He bases his argument on the capacity of these settlements to use the natural resources around them while implementing strategies to procure food and other necessities in a highly variable environment. Thus, as population increased, the vulnerability of resource procurement systems became more stressed, pushing the environmental and social systems to the brink of collapse. Wilkinson's model implies that societies contain their growth in order not to cross the threshold of their carrying capacity. However, this threshold dropped as climate deteriorated, thus increasing the probabilities of economic collapse. It is in this part of the argument that land degradation plays an important role. The profound transformation of the Near Eastern environments, initiated with the emergence of agriculture several millennia earlier, reached the highest point in the third millennium BCE, when urbanization reached a peak. Thus, the environmental systems were pushed against their limits, becoming vulnerable to adverse climatic changes and to social and economic crises.

Although Wilkinson's model explains only local and regional collapse in the semi-arid region of Upper Mesopotamia, it does not clarify widespread collapse in the Near East. A wide regional generalization of this model is difficult given the variety of landscapes and economies. Based on historical and paleoenvironmental data from various regions of the Near East and the Eastern Mediterranean, Butzer discusses a possible scenario in which economic crisis in one region was transmitted to neighboring regions in domino fashion (1997). He explains his argument using the collapse of the Old Kingdom in Egypt and its consequences on those polities linked to Egyptian trade. Accordingly, the collapse of the Egyptian state affected the network of Egyptian trade in the Levant and other regions. The crisis was transmitted to neighboring areas dependent on resources and trade with the collapsed regions.

In the lack of substantial, well-dated evidence, it is probably advisable to analyze the role of climatic deterioration and progressive land degradation in the environmental and societal crises of more recent times. The environmental crisis in the 1930s in North America is a modern analog showing a combination of environmental and economic factors in the collapse of agriculture on the Great Plains. The Dust Bowl occurred at the time when drought affected an area experiencing socio-economic collapse in the Great Depression; these two independent factors when occurring together led to detrimental consequences in the socio-economic system of a nation. This alludes to Wilkinson's model, suggesting that the effects of increased land degradation have to be taken into consideration to explain the environmental crisis at the end of the third millennium BCE.

Land Degradation in the Near East: Myths and Realities

The theories of environmental determinism plaguing geographical literature in the early twentieth century impacted the understanding of land degradation in the Near East. These deterministic ideas gave way to the so-called "the desert and the sown" dichotomy, an approach that partitioned the population of the Near East into nomads, as destroyers of the land, versus sedentary peoples, as keepers of the land. Such views were portrayed in the works of Lowdermilk (1944), Tchalenko (1953), and Reifenberg (1955), among others. These authors maintained that the collapse of agriculture during the first centuries of Islamic rule in the Near East could be blamed on a widespread shift to a pastoral economy. Recent works on the problem have shown that such a thing never occurred, and that agriculture actually flourished in some areas, while others went into decline (Kedar 1985). Despite the rejection of its radical views, the "desert and the sown" rationale downplays the role of natural factors in the development of the deteriorated landscapes that we see today in the Near East. The trend followed by scholars in recent years is to look at as many factors as possible, as has been shown in the case of the environmental crisis at the end of the third millennium BCE.

NOTES

1   Cave features formed by slow-moving water containing calcium carbonate. Chemical changes cause calcium carbonate to precipitate, creating various features inside the cave.
2   Depletion of water oxygen supply caused by organic contaminants produced by agriculture activities.

FURTHER READING

For the variety of sources on paleoclimatic reconstruction, see the compilation by Bar-Yosef and Kra 1994. For an integrative study of pollen from lake sediments, see Van Zeist and Bottema 1991; for pollen from sea bottom sediments see Rossignol-Strick 1999.

The best guide to the vegetation of the Near East is Zohary 1973. An overview on fauna can be found in Gilbert 1995. For ungulates (hoofed mammals) in the Near East see Uerpman 1987. Specialized discussions of the deterioration of flora, fauna, soils, and streams in the Eastern Mediterranean region can be found in the compilation by Bottema, Entjes-Nieborg, and Van Zeist 1990.

A comprehensive description of the irrigation systems and their problems with salinization in ancient and modern Mesopotamia can be found in Jacobsen and Adams 1958, Adams 1981, and Artzy and Hillel 1988. For salinization in Egypt see Hamdan 1961, Butzer 1976, and Stanley and Warne 1993.

Multidisciplinary views on the environmental crisis at the end of the third millennium BCE can be found in the compilation by Dalfes, Kukla, and Weiss 1997. Numerous references to the climatic factors involved in this crisis are summarized in Weiss 2000 and Weiss and Bradley 2001.

The works of George P. Marsh (in Lowenthal 2000) are a good example of early deterministic ideas that affected the interpretation of the Near Eastern landscape at the end of the nineteenth century. An alternative view, still with deterministic ideas, was presented by Huntington 1911.

CHAPTER NINE

Nomadism Through the Ages

Jorge Silva Castillo

Contemporary Nomadisms in the Near East

Nomadism takes various forms in different parts of the world, depending on the natural environment, but also depending on the economic, social, and political environment of the human groups that practice it as a response to particular geographic and human circumstances. In the Near East, a region that was the scene of the rise of the first Neolithic cultures and of urban civilization, nomads have herded animals for a long time. There are examples of camel nomadism and of different forms of seminomadism practiced by communities that include both shepherds with sheep and goats as well as farmers.

Camel nomadism

In the greater part of the Arabian Peninsula the average annual of rainfall does not go above 100 mm or four inches. The bedouins, aristocratic warriors and owners of camel herds, dominated the area until World War I. They forced the payment of tribute for protection upon caravans as well as tribes of seminomadic shepherds. The bedouins subordinated tribes composed of artisans, of groups of pariahs, and of slaves in the oases (Coon 1951: 198–210). Thanks to the camels that, since the third millennium BCE, furnished them with milk and meat for their sustenance and served them as mounts and beasts of burden, they defied the adverse conditions of their habitat. Dromedaries can go without drinking water for several days in the summer and several weeks in the winter, which permitted, and still permits, their masters to make long journeys.

But this type of nomadism does not correspond to what is documented in the texts of ancient history. The Arabs appeared late in the history of the Near East at the beginning of the first millennium before our era. However, only many centuries later did their monopolistic control of caravans permit them to get horses and weapons, and thus increase their military power (Bulliet 1990: 87–110). The people present in the region since the dawn of its history and to whom some refer as nomads in fact correspond to what the anthropologists prefer to designate as seminomads.

Forms of seminomadism

In regions that receive 200 mm or eight inches of rain a year dry farming is possible; yet due to the recurring periods of drought, only an average annual rainfall of 300 mm or 12 inches permits truly reliable agricultural productivity (Sanlaville 2000: 8–13). The agropastoral populations knew how to exploit this transition zone between the desert and the zones that had enough rain or which could be artificially irrigated. Herds that pastured in the steppes or the highlands during the rainy season in the winter were led at the end of the spring to the banks of the rivers or to wadis, dry river beds. Sheep and goats fed on the pastures along river banks or on the stubble in the fertile fields, and with their manure they fertilized the fields.

It is difficult to classify the diverse forms of nomadism into categories like seminomadism, semisedentarism, transhumance, and occasional nomadism. The combinations are very varied: the movement of the group can be partial or total; the establishment of the community can be temporary or permanent, in a fixed place, in two places, or more.

Two examples of patterns of movement are illustrative. The tribe of the Ogueidat was established at the beginning of the twentieth century of our era at the confluence of the Habur River with the Euphrates in Syria. The entire community moved on a south–north axis among three levels: a low terrace on the bank of the river, an intermediate, higher terrace, and the hills upriver which enjoyed more than 250 mm or 10 inches of rain and offered good winter pastures. Between May and June the whole group pitched tents in the intermediate terrace; beginning in the middle of June, they moved to the low terrace where the herds fed on the grasses on the river banks, and there the seminomads grew grain and vegetables. In autumn, the community dispersed in various little groups over the neighboring steppes, but if the rain was not sufficient, all the groups moved together to the pastureland of the upper plateau. At the beginning of the 1920s the groups were transformed into agriculturalists, and they created small villages. But as of the 1980s, some of its members who had emigrated to the Arab Emirates returned to the region and once again took up semisedentary pastoralism (D'Hont 1991: 205–6.)

In the second example, the pattern of movement is more complicated. Various groups of the Mawali and of the Haddidini established permanent villages in the district of Salamiyeh, around Hama in Syria, where in years of good rain they grew crops. In winter part of the community dispersed with the herds of small livestock to the steppes to the east. The shepherds returned to the villages at the end of the spring, but in full summer the entire community moved to the west in search of pastures on the banks of the Orontes (Al-Dbiyat 1980: 172–9).

The exchanges of products and services between the groups of shepherds and agriculturalists are fluid because communal management of the natural resources supports group solidarity. But if the shepherds, returning from the steppe, set themselves up on communal lands belonging to another tribe, permission to pasture the flocks and let them eat the stubble must be negotiated. The city dwellers and the rural people integrated into the urban state do not look favorably upon groups of shepherds who establish themselves on the fields around the villages or near crop-lands, although the villagers or the agriculturalists who have sheep use shepherds of nomadic origin (Al-Dbiyat 1980: 180–2).

A social watershed does not exist between nomads and sedentaries in fact, but between those who identify themselves as belonging to a tribe and those who do not assert tribal loyalty. Sedentarization does not necessarily entail detribalization. In Sukhna, a village situated on the eastern tributaries of the Palmyra massif in central Syria, which has been the center of supply for various tribes, some families of seminomadic groups spend a long time in the village, but the members continue to be identified as bedouins of such and such a tribe regardless of whether they are sedentary (Métral 2000: 126–7).

Nomadism is now adapting to technological modernization and the globalization of world markets. There are many factors that have contributed to its decadence: tribal autonomy always has been perceived as a security problem for the state; the political and economic strategy of colonial governments, as well as that of postcolo-nial states, saw in nomadism a relic of an obsolete past and in tribalism an obstacle to the construction of the modern state and to economic development (Fabietti 2000). Traditional customary legal systems have been abolished; the exploitation of oil deposits and industrialization around urban zones have acted as poles of attraction for excess labor among the nomads and seminomads; automobiles have substituted for camels in transport and freight. Some groups of nomads that bred camels have replaced them with sheep, which are more in demand in the urban market. The breeding of sheep, considered despicable by the aristocratic bedouins, has made camel nomadism give way to a new type of pastoralism that prevails among both the bedouins of the desert and the seminomads. Flocks do not need to be led to pastures and water, since forage can be taken to arid places and the water may be transported in tank trucks.

Nevertheless, stationary flocks destroy the natural flora of the area in which they are found because they always use the available vegetation. The alarming degradation of the biomass of the steppes has occasioned a reconsideration of the policies geared to promoting agriculture regardless of the consequences and to fostering the sedentar-ization of seminomads, but to date there are no studies of the results (Bocco 2000: 213–17). One might ask oneself whether the traditional mode of exploitation of arid zones is in the end more rational than the programs developed by governmental experts.

Nomadism in the Ancient Near East

Cuneiform texts, of course, were not written by or for anthropologists; in Sumerian and in Akkadian there are no terms equivalent to concepts like nomadism or semi-nomadism, nor terms that may be translated strictly by clan or tribe. Nonetheless, the historian may deduce that some populations which occupied territories in the dry regions must have practiced some kind of nomadism. Greater consideration will be given here to the Amorites of the early centuries of the second millennium because they are the best documented.

The Amorites: third millennium BCE

In the view of historians of the nineteenth century and the beginning of the twentieth it was customary to assume that Semitic peoples came originally from the Arabian desert, and that all of them were nomads who, in successive waves, had invaded the Near East (Kupper 1957: xiv). There is still a debate about the origin of each population using Semitic languages, but it is accepted that, although they shared the same family of languages, they did not necessarily have a common origin, nor were they all nomads.

It is not impossible that some of them were present in the Syro-Mesopotamian region from very remote times. In the middle of the third millennium Ebla in Syria was a powerful, fully urban, Semitic state. The Akkadians had reached Mesopotamia by the end of the twenty-fourth century. Sargon's achievement was not an invasion but rather the taking of power by a non-Sumerian ethnic group that was already fully established in urbanized Lower Mesopotamia.

In contrast, the Amorites ("the Westerners," M a r t u in Sumerian, *Amurru* in Akkadian), did infiltrate the land of Sumer and Akkad, coming very probably since the end of the third millennium from the northeast of Syria, but not always as invaders. One may deduce that their sociopolitical organization was tribal because the names attributed to them designate political entities based on descent, in other words, what we call clans or tribes: the Yahmadum, the Yamutum, and the Didanum (Buccellati 1966: 242–5).

The Amorites appeared most frequently in the Sumerian texts from the third millennium as groups that pillaged sedentary territory, to such an extent that under the reign of Šu-Sin, monarch of the Third Dynasty of Ur, a "wall of the Amorites which holds back Didnum" was built (Buccellati 1966: 243). It was said contemptuously of them that they lived in the desert, the steppe, or the mountain, dwelled in tents and were considered foreign enemies. It is less clear that it was said that they did not bend the knee and they did not bury their dead (Edzard 1981: 40–1). Nonetheless, some Amorite soldiers and civil servants did live in the cities of Sumer and Akkad, without this implying that they had broken their ethnic links (Edzard 1981: 43). In many texts people called Amorites were not considered Sumerians or Akkadians, but rather a culturally distinct ethnic group (Edzard 1981: 39).

Just after the fall of the Third Dynasty of Ur in the year 2004 BCE the penetration of the Amorites into urban zones of the entire Syro-Mesopotamian region was intensified to such an extent that they constituted the predominant ethnic group. Throughout the first three centuries of the second millennium many of their chiefs took power in many of the old city-states of Lower Mesopotamia and in other cities that had not been important until then, like Babylon.

The Haneans of Mari

Since the first half of the third millennium, the city of Mari, which appeared in the Sumerian King List as the seat of the tenth postdiluvian dynasty, was an important point of control for the river commerce of Lower Mesopotamia on the middle Euphrates (Jacobsen 1939b: 102). In the last quarter of the twenty-fourth century the city was conquered by Sargon of Akkad. The Akkadian governors quickly behaved as independent rulers and founded a dynasty that lasted over more than three centuries. We do not know under what circumstances they lost power. We may only state that toward the end of the nineteenth century the throne of Mari was occupied successively by two dynastic lines of Amorite origin, as was the rest of all the vast region of Syria and Mesopotamia. But there was a fundamental difference: In Lower Mesopotamia, which was densely urbanized and where the economy was based on intensive exploitation of agriculture on the river plains, the Amorite immigrants adopted the way of life of the urban states. Some lived in quarters where they were grouped according to their tribal affiliations; others lived in agricultural areas; among those were some who were shepherds (Postgate 1992: 76, 81–2). But the pastoral groups in Lower Mesopotamia did not constitute autonomous political entities within the states. Only very much later, in the first half of the first millennium BCE, did some ethnic groups of immigrants coming from outside the region, the Chaldeans, manage to constitute autonomous political entities within the territories of urban states. In Mari, in contrast, the Haneans lived in the place of origin of the Amorite ethnic groups, in the steppes in the northeast of Syria, where many of them kept up their tribal ties (Postgate 1992: 86).

Toward the end of the eighteenth century kings and their officials with tribal affiliations adopted forms of government proper to the urban state and tried to subject the tribal groups. But the underlying communities frequently resisted and even rebelled. The tension between the centralizing strategies of the state and the autonomous tendencies of the tribal groups gave rise to a series of compromises and conflicts to which we owe much of our information about these groups.

Haneans, Benjaminites, and Bensimalites

Two great confederations were active in the region of present-day northeastern Syria: the Bensimalites, "The Sons of the North," who originally occupied the region of the triangle of the upper Habur tributaries, and the Benjaminites, "The Sons of the South," who occupied the Syrian steppe along the Euphrates, from the zone around Mari, known as The Banks of the Euphrates, upstream between the Euphrates and the Balih River (Anbar 1985: 24). The Bensimalites at some time came to occupy the Middle Euphrates and were then called Yaradu, "those who descended," and displaced some groups of the Benjaminites, subjecting those who remained. This fact was at the origin of the Benjaminite hostility toward the Bensimalites. The Mari rulers Yahdun-lim and Zimri-lim, of Bensimalite ancestry, thus gave themselves the title King of Mari and of the land of the Haneans with which they tried to reclaim at the same time the sovereignty over the urban state of Mari as well as over all the tribal groups, including Bensimalites and Benjaminites, both of them under a common denomination of Haneans (Charpin and Durand 1985: 337).

Haneans and Akkadians

Haneans came to designate the groups that, regardless of their political tribal loyalties, did not identify themselves culturally with the subjects of the Mari Kingdom. Mari had been conquered by Sargon, became an Akkadianized state, and thereafter its people identified themselves as Akkadians. The opposition between Haneans and Akkadians appears clearly in a very curious text. Horses, still rare in the Near East then, were considered savage animals by Akkadians, who were integrated into the social and economic framework of the urban state. Zimri-lim, a tough and politically insensitive man, at the beginning of his reign apparently used to parade in the city riding on a horse like a tribal chief. A clever high-level official with more political taste took the liberty of giving the king a wise piece of advice:

> If (it is true that) you are the king of the Haneans (it is also true) that you are in second place the king of the Akkadians. (Thus), my Lord should not ride horses but (he has to enter the city) only in a litter or else, (riding) on mules. Might my Lord weigh the dignity of his kingship! (Durand 1998: 2: 484–8 text 732).

The same cultural opposition between Akkadians and tribal populations appears in a ritual funerary banquet of communion with the departed which dated to the period in which Šamši-Adad was sovereign of Mari (Birot 1980: 142). In this document it is indicated that the king ought to offer the banquet to the dead Akkadian kings, Sargon and Naram-Sin, and to Hana, meaning probably the tribal ancestors of the middle Euphrates, and also to Numha, probably meaning the tribal ancestors of the middle Tigris.

Rulers of Mari

Bensimalites	Assyrians
Yahdun-Lim	Šamši-Addu
1815–1799	1812–1780
Sumu-Yaman	Yasmah-Addu
1798	
	1798–1780
Zimri-Lim	
1780–1758	

The political organization of Benjaminite and Bensimalite Haneans

A legal document about the transfer of some communal property registered the names of all the chiefs of extended families who participated, including "five sons of Awin that live in Apan . . . eight sons of Awin of the section of the camp" (Boyer 1958: 8–10, 20–1). This shows the community was divided into two sections, those who lived in a little village and those members of "the section of the camp," the group of shepherds that left with the flocks of sheep to the steppe, where they camped during the rainy season.[1] We are dealing, then, with seminomads, a tribal community that included a group of families that lived in a village and another group specializing in pastoralism.

But not all the tribal groups were seminomads. We read in a letter that the elders of Dabish, of the Yahrurean tribe, in spite of not being part of the Yaradu who had descended to conquer Mari, were willing to join the Bensimalites, and they were disposed to sacrifice a donkey as a sign of their new alliance (Durand 1992: 117). They declared that they did not have a section of the camp nor any pasture field.[2] It is clear they were not seminomads, although they saw themselves as a tribal group, the Yahrureans, part of the Benjaminite confederation. The Bensimalites had no large subgroups, perhaps because they were closely integrated into the Mari state structure. But they had some dozen minor subgroups called *ga'um*, a term also used for big groups of Benjaminites, so it must not be strictly equivalent to either clan or tribe (Talon 1985). The more autonomous Benjaminites included big subgroups, Yahrureans, Yariheans, Amnaneans, Rabbeans (Charpin and Durand 1985: 337), and Ubrabeans, which were subdivisions of a larger confederation. Thus they could be called tribes, while the small groups, which we could call clans, were represented in this text by the elders of the extended families (Bardet 1984: 361).

The government of the village communities: elders, sugagu, and me'ru

In other texts from Mari the elders performed very diverse and important functions. In one of them they went so far as to exercise power when a governor passed away (Durand 1998: 2: 271–3 text 607). The elders' collegial institution appears in numerous documents of other cities and periods, but with fewer responsibilities than in Mari. In contrast, officers of government of the tribal groups and the village communities, called the *sugagu* and the *me'ru*, appear to be unique to Mari. The *sugagu* served as chief of the tribal communities of seminomads and of smaller villages. He was an intermediary between the communities and the state administration (Durand 1998: 2: 494–7). Originally the *sugagu*s were elected by the members of their community. In the case of the *sugagu* of clans living under the kingdom of Mari, the post had to be confirmed by the king himself, after a payment of a tax normally calculated in heads of sheep or the equivalent in silver. One letter explained:

> Earlier Yatarum had exercised the function of *sugagum* of Ya'il, but he died. Today five men from among the principal personages of Ya'il, of the section (of the camp) came to see me. The men of Ya'il said: 'Put one of our relatives as our ruler.' This was what they said. [So] I put Yarkab-Addu as a replacement for Yatarum to fill the office of *sugagum*. He will deliver x minas of silver and x hundreds of sheep and I shall receive from him x minas of silver and x hundreds of sheep as a part payment due from Yatarum (the *sugagu* who had died) (Durand 1997: 1: 209–10 text 81).

When the groups of shepherds left for the steppes, their government required another more specific type of control, the office of the *me'ru*. The *me'ru* was a kind of governor who was named directly by the king himself for the migratory groups. Another letter said:

> The Haneans do not go away from their villages because they were retained by the work of the oxen. When I was at Terqa to see my Lord, I commissioned two men to make the Haneans go out to the camps. I said to them: 'The *me'ru* has already departed; why do you remain?' This same day all the Haneans left! (Durand 1998: 2: 504 text 742)

In this document the tension between the interests of the administration and those of the tribes is revealed very clearly. The *me'ru* had his own plan of work and had to leave for the pastoral zones at a time determined by bureaucratic decisions. The villagers had to combine the work of the croplands and pastoralism. The work in the fields was subject to an unpredictable rhythm. The necessity of plowing the fields, an activity referred to in the texts as the work of the oxen, kept the villagers busy probably because of a delay in the first rains. The *sugagu*s, intermediaries between the village communities and the administration, often found themselves between a rock and a hard place, the rock of the state and the hard place of the people's resistance.

The seminomadic shepherds

In times of peace the administration wanted the shepherds to leave for the high country. But if there were rebellions brewing, the dispersion of the shepherds raised the suspicion that they might join the insurrection. The same person who sent the last letter intended at another time to stop the shepherds from leaving to the high country under the pretext that the rebels could attack the villages; he wrote:

> The men who are in the villages are ready to go away to the highlands. They put their sheep, which are fed in Lasqum, on the way toward the highlands. When one asks them (why), they answer: 'Here there is no pasture and (thus) we are going to the high country.' My police are strong. (If) they surprise one of the Benjaminites, moving from the low country towards the high country, he will be apprehended. (Durand 1998: 2: 423–4 text 680)

The levy of the shepherds

The nomads were required to bolster the ranks of the armies partly because they were considered courageous and partly because they had an excess of manpower. Some documents from Mari provide information about the many ways in which the levy was organized by means of a *tebibtum*, a term which has been translated as "census" (Durand 1998: 2: 332–9). Such documents did not deal with determining the size and the composition of the whole population, but simply with registering the number of men who could be recruited for imminent military campaigns; therefore, it is preferable to translate *tebibtum* as "counting" rather than as "census." Šamši-Addu wrote to his son Yasmah-Addu:

> Go to the heart of the steppe and be accompanied by La'um's employees and the *sugagu*s of the Banks of the Euphrates (= the kingdom of Mari). In the camps there are one thousand men who have not taken the oath. Take care of the center of the steppe. La'um and the *sugagu*s of the Banks of the Euphrates should travel all around the camps and the *sugagu*s of the camps should render the oath by the life of the god. (Durand 1998: 2: 502–3 text 740)

In exchange for their military service, the Haneans received fields from the palace. Šamši-Addu ordered that the fields which had been granted to some Haneans (probably Bensimalites), in the times of the earlier rival dynasty, not be redistributed: "May the Haneans of the camps that had fields earlier on the Banks of the Euphrates keep them" (Durand 1998: 2: 342–4 text 641).

Tribal groups in the economy of the state of Mari

Members of the village communities were also required to provide manpower to harvest the fields of the palace and for the shearing of its flocks, which must have had a large number of animals since at any given moment more than 500 men were needed for this task over several days (Durand 1998: 2: 671–5 texts 852, 853). Tribal communities also contributed to the economy of the realm with the delivery of sheep. Keeping in mind that meat did not constitute the basis of the diet, one can infer that the palace's desire for the sheep can be explained by its need to have provisions of wool for its workshops for making textiles and clothes, an industry that must have been of some importance, as there was a considerable number of administrative texts that refer to this economic activity (Silva Castillo 1981).

Resistance and rebellions

These requirements of the administration were ill received by the tribal groups; some texts speak of their resistance, others of the repression they suffered. In a letter it becomes clear that the governor of the city of Terqa had tried to gather people to harvest the fields within the Benjaminite territory under the pretext of the threat of an enemy attack. But the blackmail did not have the desired effect:

> I sent personnel of Terqa to gather the people of Zurubban, of Hishamta, of Himmaran, and of Hanna. I sent a message to the villages of the Benjaminites and the *sugagu* of Dumtan answered me thus: "Let the enemy come and take our villages." That he responded! Thus, in the harvest of the Benjaminite villages I have not been able to obtain anything. (Durand 1998: 2: 428–9 text 686)

In other documents the resistance of the villagers collided with the strong arm of the state. An official wrote:

For five days in the agreed place I have been waiting for the Haneans and those people have not come. The Haneans (already) came from the camps and are in their villages. Once, twice, I sent messages to the villages. I have summoned them! And they did not gather. And as many as three times! And they did not gather. So then, if it agrees with my Lord, may a criminal be executed at the prison and may his head be cut off and be sent around through the villages from Hutnim to Appan. In this way the people will be afraid and will gather rapidly. (Durand 1998: 2: 176–7 text 559)

The Benjaminites posed major resistance to the state and clearly identified the Bensimalites with the monarchy in power in their two open rebellions against Zimri-lim. They said, "Let us go to the Banks of the Euphrates to attack (the Bensimalite populations)" (Durand 1998: 2: 444–6 text 700).

Cultural unity of the Hanean groups

Other documents seem to offer a panorama in which the feeling of unity prevailed over division. According to a chief of the Ubrabean Benjaminites, if the threat came from a totally foreign enemy, both branches of the Haneans would unite to make a common front against the enemy. The metaphors of the Ubrabean are very eloquent:

May your god Dagan, as patron of the country, break the arms of the Elamites! If they managed to come to the Banks of the Euphrates, would they not differentiate themselves by chance as the ants that are white from one side of the river (while) on the other side they are black? It is true that it is said: "Such a city is Bensimalite and such another is Benjaminite." Regardless, are their clashes not like those of the flood of the river of which the (impetuous) waters upriver clash with the (gentle waters) downriver? (Durand 1998: 2: 488–92 text 733)

The Suteans

Besides the Benjaminites and Bensimalites, the group of the Suteans was a third tribal actor in the history of Mari. The Suteans were a population of Semitic language and culture but, apparently, not of the same branch as the Haneans. The Suteans were active around the steppes of the Syrian Desert and the Jebel Bishri, a mountainous massif between Mari and Palmyra (Kupper 1957: 90).

Some texts of Mari refer to plunder committed by them; some others to the defeats they suffered (Durand 1998: 2: 505–11). The assertion that before the introduction of camels seminomads could only have survived in close relation with farmers does not imply that some of them could not have subsisted by living in tents. The tradition given in the Assyrian King List that the first 17 ancestors "lived in tents" suggests that the ancient editors knew of contemporary groups that lived in such conditions. It is not impossible to think that these populations represented a way of life more precarious than that of the Haneans. The Suteans, who during the Old Babylonian period appeared as secondary actors, were at center stage in the history of the pastoral tribes in the centuries following the collapse of Mari about 1758 BCE.

The Suteans and the Ahlamu in the second half of the second millennium

Mari, occupied by the troops of Hammurabi around 1760 and burned two years later, did not recover its importance. Terqa became the center of an apparently minor Kingdom of Hana. This was very probably a tribal chiefdom, but we do not know. Babylonia, in turn, succumbed to the attack of the Hittites in 1595 BCE which opened the way for the Kassites, mountain people who then became the masters of Mesopotamia. Historical sources were scarce until the fourteenth century, and therefore information ceased about the tribes that had maintained sometimes peaceful, sometimes hostile relations with the rulers of the Old Babylonian period.

In the fifteenth century a document from Alalah, a city on the Orontes River, offers some interesting information. Idrimi, a fugitive king, passed through the land of the Suteans, which must have been the desert of Syria. Once reinstalled on his throne, he stated that he would support the Suteans "who do not have a dwelling-place" (Kupper 1957: 97–8). In the middle of the fourteenth century Suteans were mentioned in the texts from Amarna as having intercepted some messengers between Egypt and Babylonia. Besides a campaign of the Assyrian king Arik-den-ili against the Suteans, the Ahlamu, and the Yauru, some Suteans appeared among the groups that paid tribute to Shalmanesar I of Assyria toward the end of the thirteenth century.

Another tribal group, the Ahlameans, was called Sutean in some texts. Perhaps the Ahlamu were subgroups of the Suteans who were at first of little importance, but then over time they predominated politically to such an extent that they overshadowed other Sutean groups. Or perhaps seminomads had been identified as Suteans in Syria but as Ahlamu in Upper Mesopotamia (Liverani 1988a: 716). It is not impossible that this classification is simply due to a confusion of the bureaucrats and the scribes who edited the documents, since for them the desert tribes had been Sutean for centuries. In the middle of the thirteenth century the Hittite king Hatushili III excused himself for not being able to go to Babylonia because the road was unsafe due to the Ahlamu, although by that time the Assyrian king Shalmanesar I mentioned them among the allies of the Hittites.

The tribal structure of these two big formations is verified by the way in which the groups were identified as the House of X and the individuals as the son of X. We know only a few names of subgroups of the Suteans (Postgate 1981: 53). About their mode of life the documents of the period emanating from urban administrations as well as the literary texts offer us only stereotypical clichés: they lived in the steppe like onagers and gazelles, did not have houses, they lived in tents, their refuge was the mountain, they did not know agriculture, did not recognize agreements, nor human reason, and their speech was that of animals (Malbran-Labat 1981: 74).

The Aramaeans in the first millennium

Like the confusion that occurred between the Suteans and the Ahlamu, the Aramaeans too were called Ahlamu in the first mention of them (Postgate 1981: 49). In the Mediterranean Levant, right after the cyclone of the twelfth century provoked by the invasion of the Peoples of the Sea, some of the Aramaean tribes constituted little states, and the politically dominant population identified itself on the basis of ethnic affinities (Liverani 1988a: 654–60). The Mesopotamian states of Assyria and Babylonia were more solid and thus, at the beginning, the great Aramaean tribal formations within and around Lower Mesopotamia could only fill the spaces of the arid zones between urban and agricultural zones. Many of the Aramaeans in the arid zones initially were devoted to seminomadic pastoralism with goats and sheep. But as a result of their contact with Arab tribes they slowly adopted the breeding of camels as well. While some Aramaean groups continued to practice pastoral seminomadism, others settled down in cultivable areas to the point that they became sedentary agriculturalists and even city dwellers without losing a strong social cohesion and an ethnic cultural identity based on a supposed common origin.

Over the course of the six first centuries of the first millennium BCE the Aramaic language came to prevail among all the tribal and urban populations of the Near East from the Mediterranean to the Persian Gulf. The Chaldeans, an Aramaean subgroup, became the elite that succeeded in making Babylonia the capital of the mighty Neo-Babylonian empire, completing in this way the Aramaicization of the entire Ancient Near East.

The Arabs

In Mesopotamian documents the Arabs, although speaking a Semitic language, were never confused with the West Semitic populations. They appeared at the beginning of the first millennium in Neo-Assyrian texts, from Damascus to Aqaba and from Palmyra to the Euphrates (Fales 1989: 122). The clichés about their way of life were similar to those attributed to other tribes, but the harshness of their habitat was noticed. They were described as "inhabitants of the desert where there are not even savage animals, where the birds of the sky do not build their nest" (Malbran-Labat 1981: 63). They were distinguished from other tribes by their large herds of camels which permitted them greater mobility.

The tribes that lived in Arabia had kings who confronted the Mesopotamian armies or negotiated with them. From the texts about the tribute the Arabs paid to the Assyrians one may deduce that the Arab nomads' economy was then based on breeding livestock, especially camels, and on their participation in the caravan commerce in spices coming from Yemen. Contrary to the traditional image of the aggressive Arabs, the information from some recently published Neo-Assyrian letters paints a more nuanced picture. The Assyrians showed a prudent and at the same time wary tolerance to groups within the territory of their empire. It seems that political relations with the Arabs were just being created, passing from battle to alliance, from pillage to economic relations (Fales 1989: 126–9).

By Way of Conclusion

From what has been written here about tribal groups before and after the Age of Mari, the disproportion of qualitative information that we have becomes evident.

About the Amorites, the Suteans, the Ahlamu, the Aramaeans, and the Arabs, aside from the stereotypical images about their ways of life, what little we know is that they assaulted merchants and messengers, attacked sedentary people, confronted the armies of small and large states, and ended by submitting themselves to them, judging from the fact that they paid tribute or taxes. We have more substantive information about the Aramaeans, but military and political affairs largely predominated here. The texts from Mari also provide that kind of information, but add invaluable anthropological, social, and economic aspects. The haphazard nature of archaeological finds can frequently distort our perspective. If we had more information about Suteans, Ahlamu, and Aramaeans, we would probably find some processes that were at least similar, if not identical, to some of those revealed by the Mari documents.

The view of the Semites as being both nomads and invaders was modified in the first large monograph devoted to Mari. Its author interprets the immigration of the nomads not as a series of tides but as the continuing flow of a river which could be contained by means of dikes if the urban state was strong, but which would overflow if it was weak (Kupper 1957: xiv–xvi and 1959: 124). Further, Kupper presents the nomads as always lying in wait to throw themselves upon the sedentaries, but he also sees them as always in an evolutionary process toward sedentarization themselves (Kupper 1957: xiii). This position was acrimoniously criticized by Luke, who insisted on the social and economic unity of agriculturalists and pastoralists within a village culture (1965: 277–80). The pastoralists for him were not newcomers or hostile invaders but were part of communities which included both agriculturalists and shepherds. Rowton, based on the study of more recent well-documented nomadism, proposed in a series of articles (1965–81) that the case of Mari could be explained as an enclosed nomadism, a kind of seminomadism typical of the regions in which the tribal groups conduct their affairs within the territory under the jurisdiction of an urban state (Rowton 1974) which implies a "close interaction between nomad and sedentary, between tribe and state …" (Rowton 1973a: 201).

Each of those authors has pointed out factors which, if they are not taken as exclusive positions, offer useful elements for approaching the understanding of phenomena revealed by the documents of Mari. The model proposed by Kupper, although probably not thoroughly suitable for the case of Mari since there tribal people were involved, applies quite well to Lower Mesopotamia. One cannot deny that people from arid zones flowed continuously toward urbanized irrigated ones, where they slowly tended to become sedentary, although the movement was not unidirectional or irreversible. The kingdom of Hana affords a good example of this; after the collapse of Mari, Hana became a tribal political entity which lasted several centuries but was probably never a true urban state. The village communities, as presented by Luke, were certainly composed of farmers as well as of seminomadic shepherds whose own interests did not always coincide with those of the state, although sometimes they did. Without going so far as conceiving of an idealistic symbiosis between the seminomads and the state, we can see that their interrelation points to a tribal autonomy in the territories under state jurisdiction, as well as an urban autonomy in a nomadic environment as envisioned by Rowton.

What we glimpse in the documents of Mari is a kind of ambiguous interplay between the state and the tribal groups. In some cases, we find state officials trying to gather villagers for harvesting the fields or shearing the sheep of the palace, but in other cases they tried to have the shepherds depart to the highlands and appointed an official to take charge of them. At still other times the shepherds were prohibited from departing for the highlands in spite of the lack of pasture for their flocks. The shepherds were seen either as eventual recruits or as virtual enemies. Moreover, we find some tribal individuals interested in getting corrupt elders on their side, we find elders planning for their people to adhere to the Bensimalites and to be loyal to the state, and we find other Haneans endowed with fields from the palace. The state needed the contributions provided by the tribal communities, sheep and wool as payment of taxes, recruits for its troops, and the manpower of villagers and shepherds for the exploitation of the rural properties of the palace. The tribal communities, according to the interests of their leaders, expected military protection from the state and the economic advantages derived from the state structure. They collaborated with it when it seemed to be convenient to them, but resisted when it did not. Whenever that happened, the Hanean tribal groups, either Benjaminites or Bensimalites, rebelled, and then the state responded with repression.

All urban states, ancient or modern, act according to a logic of their own. The apparently contradictory attitudes of the Mari officials show how rulers of an urban state, regardless of their tribal origin, subscribed to such logic. If we neglect superficial circumstances and focus on the deep significance of phenomena, would not the attitudes of the administrators of the Mari kingdom remind us of attitudes of today's technocratic experts? The peculiarities of ancient history, of course, differ widely from what happens nowadays among the pastoral tribal communities of the region. However, it is probably not too risky to compare migrations from the steppes to urban zones of the past with migrations from rural to industrialized zones now. They are motivated not by any kind of aggressiveness of the immigrants toward urban people, but by a simple and understandable strategy for survival.

NOTES

1 The term which we here translate as camp referred in southern Mesopotamia to the zone between the cities, but in Mari it was a collective noun which designates the camp including shepherds and flocks.
2 The term *ka-di* we translate "grazing fields," but it is unique to this text. We wish to relate it to *kidu*, meaning "that which is outside, open field."

FURTHER READING

On recent nomadism see Coon 1951, an anthropological description of the nomads' way of life. Mundy and Musallam 2000 has papers written by specialists about the evolution and present situation of pastoralist nomads and seminomads in the Near East.

On tribal pastoralists during the Mari Age the recently published *Documents épistolaires du palais de Mari* by Durand (1997, 1998, 2000) provides the non-specialist reader with an excellent tool to enter the rich documentation of the Mari Age. In English see Heimpel 2003. Matthews 1978 offers a useful synthesis of the history of Mari centered on the issues of nomadism.

On ancient nomadism outside Mari see Buccellati 1966 and 1967, on Aramaeans Lipiński 2000, on Suteans Heltzer and Arbeli-Raveh 1981, on Arabs Ephal 1982, supplemented by Fales 1989. The papers by Edzard on third millennium nomads, by Postgate on second millennium nomads, and by Malbran-Labat on the first millennium still seem valuable syntheses in Silva Castillo 1981.

CHAPTER TEN

Mesopotamian Cities and Countryside

Elizabeth C. Stone

Ancient Mesopotamia was noted for its cities. Urbanism first came into existence in the land between the Tigris and Euphrates rivers sometime in the fourth millennium BCE. Thus at a time when the largest settlements in the rest of the world were no more than small village communities, Mesopotamian cities were so populous that their residents had to craft a way of life that included peaceful coexistence with strangers. In addition, Mesopotamian cities generated textual and archaeological data on urban life which have a level of detail unparalleled elsewhere.

This chapter will attempt to distill these strands of evidence and present a picture of urban and rural life in the time and area that we know the best, southern Mesopotamia in the third and second millennia BCE. I will approach this task from the inside out, beginning with a look at houses and households, moving on to an examination of cities as a whole, and finally placing these cities within their rural contexts. Rather than approaching the data historically, I will instead emphasize continuities, using analogy with modern populations in the area and the denizens of Medieval Islamic cities to allow the artifacts, architecture, and cuneiform documents to provide a picture of a living, breathing society.

Iraqi Landscapes and Mesopotamian Settlement

No understanding of Mesopotamian society is possible without consideration of the extraordinary ecological conditions in southern Iraq both today[1] and in the past. Although capable of generating extraordinary wealth, if mismanaged they could and did result in disaster – the widespread abandonment of permanent settlement accompanied by huge loss of life. In permissive environments, numerous political and agricultural regimes are possible, but in constraining environments, like southern Mesopotamia, that is not the case.

The area south of the city of Samarra represents one of the world's largest deltas, a broad flat expanse of alluvium generated by the accumulating silts of the Tigris and Euphrates rivers that flow through it. The area is so flat that the rivers meander along ridges that rise above plain level, a condition that, without management, results in numerous intertwining branches which are liable to shift with every flood season. Thus the first task of those who established civilization in this area was artificially to raise the levees on either side of the rivers to ensure that a settlement built along one of these channels would not be left high and dry a few years later. Ancient Mesopotamian settlement was built along multiple channels of both the Tigris and the Euphrates with numerous points of connection – a system quite different from that seen today where the Tigris and Euphrates are separate from one another. This multiplicity of interwoven channels greatly limited the ability of political centers to dominate those down-river by threatening to divert water.

These rivers flowed through an area known for its aridity, making irrigation a necessity for agriculture. However, the high river beds made canal irrigation easy – cut a hole in the bank and the water flowed out – and both the archaeological and textual records are replete with evidence for canal construction and use.

All irrigation systems need some management. Canals need to be dug, and if the fields at the end of the system are to continue to receive water, the silt that builds up near the canal mouth as a result of the abrupt drop in water velocity needs to be cleared out on a regular basis. Moreover, in southern Mesopotamia the water table in the area beyond the immediate environs of the rivers is saline and rises close to the surface under conditions of irrigation. This results in progressive salinization of land, rendering it increasingly less arable over time. This process can be delayed by practicing alternate-year fallowing to allow the deep-rooted desert plants to reestablish themselves and drain down the water table, but at least by the late third millennium salinization of land was the inevitable long-term result of irrigation. Such salted-up fields can only recover if they are allowed to revert to desert so that the winds will scour away the salt crust, generating sand dunes.

Irrigated land is and was used in two different ways. Plots close to the main rivers were used as date orchards, with vegetables and other fruit trees grown beneath their canopy. The sweet groundwater in these areas meant that the threat of salinization was averted, making the long-term investment involved in orchard cultivation worth while. By contrast, the areas where the water table was saline were devoted to grain cultivation, mostly wheat in the early days of Mesopotamian civilization, replaced by barley, a more salt-resistant plant, as time went on. Evidence on the economics of agriculture in the 1950s of our era in the irrigated south makes it clear that any system that relies on small, privately owned grain plots lacks the flexibility to be economically viable (Poyck 1962). Then, even as share-croppers gave one-third of their crop to landlords, they gained enough from the benefits of participating in a large managed system to make them significantly better off than small farm owners. The combination of silting and salinization thus means that it is only large systems that can maximize the enormous potential of Mesopotamian grain agriculture.

The areas not irrigated also played an important role in Mesopotamian society. Thickets growing along the rivers could be used for timber and the deserts generated enough shrubs to feed sheep and goats. Desert environments can provide good grazing areas for these animals, and in Mesopotamia where water – the key limiting factor – was never far away, the rearing of sheep was a major activity. Wool was a critical commodity since textiles were Mesopotamia's major export and played a key role in the economy as southern Mesopotamia needed to import stone, metals, and even large timber for construction.

The last resource area is the marshes, places where water pools up in shallow brackish lakes. Most irrigation districts debouched into small marshes, and much larger ones were located in the south and east. These marshes were the sources for materials critical to life in southern Mesopotamia: fish and water birds were hunted, and reeds were woven into mats, built into roofs, twisted into furniture, peeled to make styluses, and even tied together to make houses and boats.

These three different ecological niches should not be thought of as distinct zones but rather were interlocking. The land is so flat that there are few geographical factors that dictate their location. The site of Nippur was in the midst of a marsh when it was first excavated by the University of Pennsylvania in the 1890s, was surrounded by desert in the mid-1970s and is within the cultivated zone today, and this situation is typical for much of Iraq. When fields became no longer productive, they were allowed to lapse back into desert, while new areas were opened up to agriculture, creating new marshes at the ends of the canals. When irrigation systems expanded, they expanded at the expense of both deserts and marshes, covering one with crops and using up the water that was once concentrated in the marshes, and the reverse took place as they contracted.

The result of this ecological mosaic was the presence of three quite different lifestyles – farmer, marsh dweller, and pastoral nomad. But these should not be thought of as permanent ways of life; it is this instability that is reflected in the fluctuations between centralization and chaos that characterized Mesopotamian history. This was part of everyday life, but must have accelerated at moments of crisis as refugees from failed irrigation or political systems sought new ways of survival in the deserts and marshes, and also at moments of centralization when new opportunities lured people into the cities. The written record is full of examples of those with more nomadic backgrounds moving into the cities, but less eloquent on the out-migrations of those who gave up their mud-brick houses for reed huts or tents. Our sources, both written and archaeological, come from those with a stable existence and not from those whose lives were nomadic.

The agricultural system was better adapted for management by large institutions than by individual ownership of plots, but this does not mean that it necessarily led to the widespread exploitation of a large downtrodden peasantry. Such a scenario is not possible without absolute control over the means of production, which in agricultural societies means land. But in southern Iraq land is always temporary and mutable, and changes in lifestyle are always a possibility. Thus it can be argued that as complex society developed in southern Mesopotamia, the key to political power was not so much the ability to control arable land but rather to attract the labor for the creation of arable land through building irrigation canals and exploiting the land (Stone 1997). With time, even when the area of control was extended beyond the cultivated zone, competition for labor between city-states still prevented excessive exploitation.

Sources

What makes the study of ancient Mesopotamia distinctive from that of other early complex societies is the variety and detail of the sources that can be brought to bear on any one problem. The desert environment has preserved details of ancient settlement that are almost unparalleled elsewhere, a circumstance exploited by archaeologists who have conducted broad site surveys in the area. Excavations have also been extensive, but have tended to focus on the large, heavily stratified cities, although some small sites have also been investigated. The use of mud-brick as a construction material at these sites has provided archaeologists with extensive architectural remains, complete with objects and trash deposits. Included in these remains are cuneiform tablets, often found in archives within the buildings where they were used. These include details of administrative activities as well as more private documents like contracts and letters.

The broad survey data provide an overview of the ebb and flow of human settlement in the southern Mesopotamian plain (Adams 1981). The pattern of urban growth and decay is seen as the result of a complex interplay between environmental factors – shifting watercourses, salinization of land – and human factors in the ebb and flow of political relations. However, in the process of documenting changes in individual settlements and settled areas over time, this work also provides a sense of the long duration of Mesopotamian history, an understanding of how the exigencies of life on the southern plain shaped both settlement and society in much the same way over the millennia. The focus of the data collected by these surveys is not on individual houses or even cities, but on the city-states – the networks of settlements of varying sizes, tied together by political and economic ties and a complex irrigation system.

Nevertheless, the survey data are not without flaw. Because of the difficulty of precisely dating a site based only on pottery found on the surface, surveys provide no more than a broad outline of changing patterns of settlement. As a result, for example, two periods which are seen by Assyriologists and archaeologists alike as radically different – the Ur III and Isin-Larsa periods – are grouped together in the survey data (Adams 1981: 163, figure 31).

Excavation has yielded detailed evidence of daily life in both public and private structures. Archaeological excavations have been undertaken in southern Mesopotamia for over a century, and although the focus of many of the early excavators and even some modern ones was on narrow issues of chronology, the question of the nature of urbanism in Mesopotamia was the focus of the most extensive projects conducted in the 1920s and 1930s at Ur and in the Diyala River region. These projects were conducted at a time when huge areas could be cleared through the use of mass labor, providing us with broad expanses of both domestic housing and public architecture. Although in more recent times excavation methods have emphasized in-depth recording and less broad clearance, we do have newer data on site organization.

Textual data provide the details of life on the southern Mesopotamian plain. These data give a picture that is almost antithetical to the results of settlement surveys. All cuneiform texts derive from archaeological contexts, whether they were excavated by archaeologists or looters. They therefore tend to reflect the concerns of the urban population since most excavations have focused on large sites. Also, writing penetrated further into society at some times than in others. By and large the third and early second millennia saw a general increase of those aspects of society that were recorded, moving from archives that reflect the concerns of large institutions to groups of texts which included the interests of private citizens. It would be a mistake, however, to see the pattern as simply one where new types of written documents are consistently added to the corpus. Instead, the use of writing was in some ways reestablished following each period of collapse, so texts were often written in somewhat different ways in each period, following newly developed traditions or genres, sometimes leading those who study them to assume that society itself had changed radically, rather than what was recorded and how it was recorded.

For those interested in Mesopotamian urbanism, the 1970s and 1980s saw a move toward examining private documents organized not by genre but by site – and in some instances relating those documents to the archaeological record. Postgate (1992) and Sasson (1995) have succeeded in replacing the old emphasis on a hierarchical temple-centered society with a more nuanced approach, stressing the flexibility of Mesopotamian social institutions, its entrepreneurial character, and the interplay between hierarchy and social complexity which characterized its political relations.

It is this kind of integration that I hope to achieve in this chapter, one where the textual, artifactual, architectural, and survey data can be brought together to provide a consistent picture of life in ancient Mesopotamia. I will fill in the gaps in our sources by looking at models derived from more recent and better attested societies. A comparison of our information from Mesopotamia with that of more recent Islamic society shows extraordinary similarities in house plans, building materials, agricultural practices, and even patterns of marriage, inheritance, and residence. We can also use ethnographic data from southern Iraq itself to inform us on the ecological constraints within which Mesopotamian society operated, and to fill in the details about rural farmers, nomads, and marsh dwellers whose activities have defied archaeological detection.

Cities – Houses and Households

The most basic unit of organization in Mesopotamian cities was the household. Indeed, Mesopotamians described even the largest institutions, the temple and palace, as large households. Extended patrilineal households were the norm in southern Mesopotamia (Stone 1996). This means that the ideal household would consist of a man, his wife, his unmarried daughters, his sons, their wives, and their children. Such a group would generally continue to reside together until the death of the father, at which time the household would be broken up. It seems likely that girls left the household to be married at a young age – to ensure that they were still virgins – taking with them a dowry consisting largely of household furniture. Men, by contrast, would marry later, when they could afford the bride-price that had to be paid to the father of the bride. Unlike the dowry, which generally stayed the property of the wife even in cases of divorce or widowhood, the bride-price represented a permanent donation to the family of the bride.

Excavations of houses occupied by such families have provided detailed evidence of the lifestyles of average Mesopotamian citizens. Full of the bric-a-brac of daily life, they have often yielded both the graves and written records of their inhabitants. In spite of differences in time and place, there is a remarkable similarity in all of the house areas excavated so far, with one exception. The houses in the northern part of Babylonia tend to be smaller and have larger courtyards than those further south. They also have more substantial staircases than their southern counterparts, suggesting that these may have had second stories (Stone 1996). This would make sense since in the northern part of the river valleys poplar wood is more abundant, making such construction possible. Our evidence suggests that southern houses were roofed with split date-palm logs which would provide a less sturdy platform. The presence of small stairways in many of the houses in the south, however, is an indication that then, as now, the roof served as an important living space.

Studies such as those by Hendrickson (1981, 1982) on the house areas in the Diyala, by Luby on the houses and graves at Ur (1990), and my own work at Nippur (Stone 1981, 1987) all made clear how Mesopotamian residential districts were composed of large well-appointed houses with small, poorly furnished houses nestled between them, and occasional shops. If households were a mixture of extended and nuclear families, then at least some of the differences in size might reflect differences in household size rather than wealth. But an examination of the houses themselves shows that only in the larger houses do we find special-purpose rooms like kitchens, bathrooms, and household shrines, and it is within these houses that the richest of the graves are found.

The range of sizes of these houses is identical to that of modern apartments in European and American cities, between 40 and 500 square meters (400 and 5,000 square feet), with most falling between 60 and 200 square meters. House sizes are generally comparable between excavated areas, whether they are in the same site, between sites, or between sites dating to different periods, although some cities may have been a little more crowded than others, resulting in slightly smaller houses (Stone 1981).

House plans are also similar across both space and time. In most instances the exceptionally large houses had two courtyards but otherwise were similar in organization to smaller houses. Large houses are less common than their smaller counterparts, but they have been found in most large excavation areas in both northern and southern Babylonia, and date to both the third and second millennium (Delougaz, Hill and Lloyd 1967, plate 26, house II; Woolley and Mallowan 1976, plate 124, 13).

The medium-sized houses from all sites and periods, those between around 100 and 200 square meters in size, approximate the typical courtyard house where a central space is surrounded by rooms on all sides (Moorey 1982: 198). It seems likely that this was the ideal since architect's plans of houses found on cuneiform tablets are usually either of this type or have additional rooms added to such a plan (McCown and Haines 1967: plate 52).

There is some complication in distinguishing the smallest houses from the shops that were interspersed in residential neighborhoods. The very smallest structures, consisting of no more than two rooms, may have simply been shops. But more common and more clearly domestic were long, narrow structures with rooms only on two sides of the central court. These are usually found in groups of two or three (Stone 1996: 232–3).

Mesopotamian house areas consist of a mass of architecture, with houses separated from each other by shared walls. Moreover, mud-brick houses are extremely malleable. New walls can be built, doors can be opened in walls or blocked off at will. House sizes represent a mixture of two patterns. One derives from the differences in wealth between households, where some could afford more comfortable housing than others. The second pattern shows the growth of households during the life of the male head of household, from one housing only himself, his wife and perhaps one or two small children, to one which includes the families of his sons. It seems likely that the largest houses represent the amalgamation of more than one courtyard house as families gained in wealth and size, and the smallest mark their breakup into smaller units following the death of the head of household. Indeed, Kepinski-Lecomte (1996) correlates an increase in house size at Haradum with increased household size, whereas texts from one set of houses at Ur indicate that they were occupied by brothers (Stone 1996: 232).

The consistency of these patterns over both space and time suggests significant stability in Mesopotamian social relations, a view which contrasts with the impression of volatility which is how the changes in genre in written documents have often been interpreted. Moreover, the similarity of house sizes to those occupied by modern urban residents, the proximity of houses of the rich and the poor, and the wealth of objects recovered from both large and small houses from cities in northern Babylonia, southern Babylonia, and the Diyala River region, suggest an overall degree of prosperity. This evidence indicates that we can no longer sustain earlier views of Mesopotamian cities where exploitation by religious and political elites was seen to result in the impoverishment of the bulk of the population.

This change in our view of domestic districts in Mesopotamian cities was enhanced by studies that focused on texts from individual cities. Real estate transactions, inheritance documents, and letters allow reconstruction of genealogies and analysis of the economic fortunes and social relations of families. Moreover, in the case of some of the texts from Nippur and Ur, their archaeological contexts were preserved, allowing a direct link to be drawn between the social and economic positions of particular families and the houses in which they lived.

The urban residents whose lives were recorded in these texts owned not only their own homes, but in most cases also date orchards. They might also own grain fields, hold religious offices, or be engaged in professions. The picture is of urban residents who were both independent and connected to the public sector.

Where these family archives can be used to reconstruct genealogies, we find a pattern consistent with high levels of social mobility. Most often these genealogies illustrate the slow decline of families over time. Successive generations can be shown to be increasingly impoverished as family wealth was eroded by a combination of large family size and inheritance customs that gave each heir a share of land (Stone 1987: 41–53). We also see other individuals who suddenly showed up in the textual record, sometimes allying themselves with the older families through adoption, and generally reconstituting what were once large estates through successive purchases of property from various heirs (Stone and Owen 1992). The impression is that these were the sons of wealthy but propertyless individuals. What is striking about these data is how similar they are to the pattern of the rise and fall of both princes and notable families described by Ibn Khaldun for the early Islamic period (1969).

The evidence is overwhelming that differences in wealth and power existed within neighborhoods rather than between them. Even as the archaeological evidence testifies to similarities between the different neighborhoods at Ur in both architecture and the richness of the burials (Luby 1990), clear differences can be seen between the texts from Area EM which was dominated by the clergy and those from AH, which had a more entrepreneurial character (Charpin 1986; Van De Mieroop 1992). In a similar vein, at Nippur, Area TA was occupied by small farm-owners, whereas those living in TB seem to have had stronger ties to a state institution (Stone 1987).

These data, when combined with the results of intramural surveys, suggest an urban landscape made up of numerous small, face-to-face communities. In structure these seem very similar to those documented from Islamic cities. Sauvaget published a plan of an Ottoman neighborhood in Damascus (1934: 452). This was the center of daily activities for its residents and contained all the necessities of life, including a small market, a fountain providing fresh water, a bakery, mosque, and a bath house. Mesopotamian neighborhoods were similar, with small chapels and bakeries found embedded in the urban structure at both Ur and Nippur (Woolley and Mallowan 1976: 30–3; Stone 1987: 55, 86). Like their Mesopotamian predecessors, the Islamic neighborhoods consisted of a mixture of large, medium, and small houses, and the ranges of sizes of these houses seem to be roughly comparable in these cities millennia apart.

Also similar between the two periods is the physical location of the rich and poor. Differences in wealth in Ottoman cities existed more within the neighborhoods than between them, with religion, occupation, or common village origin serving as unifying elements for these residential quarters (Lapidus 1984).

Cities – Temples and Palaces

Data from residential districts within urban centers in Mesopotamia suggest not only that long and unbroken traditions of domestic life persisted, but also that those traditions were characterized by strong neighborhood development and high levels of social mobility. But cities are not just large residential areas; they are defined both by their concentrated populations and, perhaps most importantly, by their institutions.

So far the only real palaces to have been found by archaeologists were of independent rulers of cities, rather than of provincial governors. Thus buildings like the palace at Mari or the Sin-kashid palace at Uruk would not have been features of most cities; instead more modest administrative structures, like the Palace of the Rulers at Tell Asmar and the many other administrative buildings that have been excavated, would have been more common (Frankfort, Lloyd and Jacobsen 1940). Nevertheless, the rich architectural, artifactual, and epigraphic finds from Mari provide a unique window into the lifestyle and the concerns of Mesopotamian royalty and can serve as a model of Mesopotamian ideas of the ideal palace (Parrot 1958, 1959).

The residential apartments for both the royal family and guests were comparable in organization but somewhat larger in size than the largest known private house. These had bathrooms, complete with tubs, of a kind never found in private residences, as well as elaborate kitchens designed to provide food for a large population. But palaces were much more than just royal residences since large-scale storage and administrative quarters filled much of the area of the building. The heart of the palace lay in the audience hall, the place where the ruler fulfilled his role as the arbiter of justice. The large size of such rooms suggests the modern *mudhif,* the tribal guest house. Here the sheikh entertains all who come with tea and coffee, listens to their complaints and requests, and makes decisions in a process that clearly has similarities to the behavior of Mesopotamian monarchs. The important point here is that no sheikh makes a decision in private. All decisions are made in public, making acts of revenge or favoritism very difficult. If the similarity in architecture between ancient throne-rooms and the traditional Islamic places of judgment indicate that the process of decision-making was the same, then there too the public nature of royal decision-making would have ensured fairness to all.

This interpretation is in keeping with more recent assessments of royal power in Mesopotamia. Our written sources tell us that the king was thought to have been chosen by the gods from among the entire (adult male) citizenry of the city. The results of this process may be seen in the numerous, short-lived royal lineages. Postgate has suggested that the city assembly may have been the means by which the gods indicated their choice (Postgate 1992: 269–70). If so, this would reinforce the analogy drawn here between ancient kings and modern sheikhs since the latter are also chosen from among all male tribal members (Fernea 1970: 105–6). Once elected, a Mesopotamian king's areas of responsibility were to maintain the peace, stabilize the economy, satisfy the gods, and protect the weak from the strong. Local governors were appointed by the king, but it seems probable that such appointments must have followed a process similar to that used to choose village or neighborhood leaders, which in both ancient Mesopotamian and Ottoman times involved a combination of election from within and appointment from above.

Kings, governors, and other royal servants were by no means the only institutional forces within Mesopotamian cities. Every city had one or two temples dedicated to the city god or gods and numerous other smaller religious establishments. The latter varied in size from tiny shrines tucked away within the residential matrix to large important temples that may have dominated one sector of the city. The rich textual record from the Inanna Temple at Nippur and the temple at Ischali suggests that kinship relations were critical. The important offices in the Inanna Temple were held by members of a single family who also played key roles in the Temple of Enlil, the most important temple at Nippur. Zettler argues that the family was resident within the Inanna Temple and has identified that residential area (Zettler 1992: 82–6). Residences associated with temples are also known from earlier examples, such as the house attached to the Temple Oval at Khafajah and the residential area within the Šara Temple at Tell Agrab. But while the residence in the important Temple Oval was significantly larger than the largest known domestic structure, that in the Šara Temple was quite small, and the residential apartments in the Inanna Temple at Nippur were comparable in size and organization to the average house.

Temples seem to have been the main landowners in ancient Mesopotamian cities, and they managed these lands through a mixture of land grants to office holders and the provision of "rations." The receivers of rations used to be described as a semi-free component of society, but today the term used, g u r u š, is translated simply as "man," and since the monthly payments of 60 liters or almost two bushels of barley are more than double basic subsistence needs (Clark and Haswell 1967), perhaps the term salary would better accord with their economic position.

Adams pointed out that only communal management of agricultural land is consistent with the needs of the Mesopotamian environment, and data from 1950s Iraq make clear that only large-scale systems were economically viable (Adams 1978; Poyck 1962). Thus the role played by the temples, and to a lesser extent the palaces, in managing agricultural land should be seen not so much as an indication of an exploitative economic system as the most efficient means of promoting economic well-being.

The Urban Landscape

Here we will turn to the intrasite surface surveys in order to answer some of the questions on urban organization that Adams' regional surveys tackled for overall settlement on the Mesopotamian plain. I will focus on our work at Mashkan-shapir, using the data from the other surveys as appropriate, since that project was specifically designed to provide a general view of that Mesopotamian city.

The most striking aspect of this survey was the degree to which Mesopotamian cities were broken up into different sectors, both by canals and by internal walls. Similar canals can be seen in the aerial photographs from Larsa and Ur and have been identified at Uruk (Van Ess, personal communication). Internal walls seen in the aerial photographs taken at Mashkan-shapir separate administrative and cemetery areas from residential districts, and they were found between residential districts in the course of surface scraping on the much earlier West Mound at Abu Salabikh and surrounding the residential district attached to the Temple Oval at Khafajah (Postgate 1983; Delougaz 1940). The internal canals – which resulted in the multi-moundedness characteristic of Mesopotamian urban sites – together with these walls, served to divide the cities into a number of sectors.

Mesopotamian cities were physically dominated by the main temple, raised high on a ziggurat or at least on a high platform. Much as skyscrapers mark modern cities or the spires of cathedrals their medieval counterparts, these features allowed the cities to be seen from a long distance – often from the next city down the river. However, these were generally not located in the center of the city, but on the periphery, perhaps as a way of ensuring the seclusion of the sacred sector. This pattern is seen clearly both at the most sacred city of all, Nippur (Roaf 1990: 81) and at Mashkan-shapir where, as a new foundation, the positioning must be ascribed to deliberation rather than chance. Palaces and major administrative buildings, like the Sin-kashid palace at Uruk, are also found toward the edges of the cities. Here, although it is possible that if these were new constructions, this was the only piece of empty land available, it seems more likely that their position reflects a belief that put the residential sector at the physical heart of the city. It was, after all, that segment of the city which contributed to the assembly, a shadowy institution – because largely unrecorded in the texts – whose importance we should not underestimate.

The broad surveys also allow a test of the impression provided by excavated house areas that these were not segregated by wealth and power but rather reflected different kinship or occupational groups. Objects that can be associated with wealth and power, like the Mesopotamian cylinder seals, which were badges of office, and the key imported items, copper and bronze, are found in all parts of the city and not concentrated in only a few areas. Moreover, the large amount of copper and bronze recovered from the surface of Mashkan-shapir suggests that all citizens had access to metal for tools, jewelry, and weapons. A total of more than 6 kilograms or about 13 pounds of copper alloy was recovered from the surface of the site, compared with only 35 chipped stone tools. Since there is evidence that copper alloys were recycled when broken – something that cannot be done with stone tools – it is clear that differences in wealth were not so extreme as to be reflected in the materials used for practical necessities.

Another feature of the survey data is the light shed on the activity of artisans, who are poorly documented in the written record. Texts suggest that most artisans were private, although they could be contracted by the large institutions, but we have had little archaeological evidence for their activities.

The first pattern identifiable in all intrasite survey data is the concentration of smokestack industries, especially ceramic production. Mashkan-shapir, Abu Salabikh, Larsa, and el-Hiba all have areas where pottery production, and perhaps other pyrotechnic activities, were concentrated, in the case of Mashkan-shapir at least, in the downwind part of the site. But perhaps the most intriguing aspect of the Mashkan-shapir survey is the distribution of small concentrations of copper fragments and copper slag, almost certainly indicators of the presence of small smithies. Although one or two were found elsewhere, these were primarily located along the main east–west street that ran across the center of the site to the large eastern gate. These data, together with the tendency recorded in the texts for artisans in different crafts to be neighbors, might suggest that Mesopotamian cities had an ancient equivalent of a "Main Street" with only the copper workshops leaving identifiable surface indications.

The last question that can be addressed by the survey data is the identification of places for the exchange of goods. Written sources suggest the presence of squares close to city gates as the primary places of trade and exchange (Oppenheim 1969a). We also know that groups of foreign merchants, organized into a guild-like structure, lived in Mesopotamian cities and were associated with the *kārum*, or city quay. The textual references to "the city and the *kārum*" have hinted that the city quay was physically separate from the city, but we should also consider the possibility that it was the social separation between citizens and foreigners which is reflected here.

A number of city gates have been identified at both Mashkan-shapir and Larsa, and perhaps the absence of dense settlement at Mashkan-shapir in the vicinity of the eastern end of the main street may indicate the locus of one of the squares mentioned in the texts. But at both Mashkan-shapir and Ur there are also intramural harbors associated with the canal system, and the aerial photographs of Larsa and Uruk suggest that these cities also had such features (Huot, Rougeulle, and Suire 1989: 22; Van Ess, personal communication). It seems to me likely that these harbors must have played some role in the process of trade and exchange.

The Mesopotamian City

How then can we draw together these data on the Mesopotamian city? The typical Mesopotamian family consisted of a male head of household, his wife, sons, their wives and children, and unmarried daughters. The family was supported by the ownership of a small orchard plot or office-holding or work as an artisan. I suggest that the grown sons, who had no independent economic existence until their father died, might have been those who were listed as receiving rations from the temple or palace. Put a pig in the courtyard and the family should have been able to acquire the pottery, grinding stones, terracotta plaques, and copper and bronze tools which are so ubiquitous a feature of residential districts.

There is only rare evidence for political competition within the family – and that is mostly between brothers following its breakup at the time of the death of the father – but such competition existed at all other levels within the city. The heads of households were engaged in a struggle for dominance in the neighborhood and in the larger urban assemblies, with kinship, clientage, and possibly even scribal education all playing a role. Rivalry also existed between the private sector and the public sector and, in at least some instances, between the temple and the palace. Beyond the urban framework contention between city-states was rampant during the early to mid-third millennium and certainly played a significant role in the intermediate periods between the times when Akkad, Ur, and Babylon dominated the southern plain. But even during times of secure imperial rule, it seems likely that the city-states still competed over the general population, tempting some to change allegiance by building new canals and opening up new land.

I would argue that this competition over people and resources drove the high levels of social mobility seen in our texts. It would have been the ability of people to move between lifestyles and from one city to another that resulted in the lack of evidence for extreme poverty and exploitation in either the textual or archaeological record. Apart from the slaves, who never formed a large sector of the population, people could vote with their feet. The evidence that they did so is seen both in the pattern of shifting settlement documented by Adams in his regional surveys and by changes in urban density and occupation documented for Nippur and Uruk (Gibson 1992; Finkbeiner 1991). When things worked well, this process served to make Mesopotamian cities some of the wealthiest and most successful in the ancient world, but if competition amongst elites resulted in an abandonment of their obligations to their clients and kinsmen, urban flight by the latter was the likely result. It seems probable that a combination of these factors and long-term degradation of arable land led to the periods of turmoil that intervened between the prosperity associated with the Akkadian, Ur III, and Old Babylonian periods.

City and Countryside in Mesopotamia

Mesopotamian cities did not exist in a vacuum; the rural hinterland was replete with settlements varying in size from small towns to hamlets, farmsteads, reed hut settlements, and nomadic tents. Our difficulty is that most of these have remained unexcavated, and some of the smallest settlements – including all where reed huts or tents rather than mud-brick houses dominated – could not be identified in the regional surveys. Nevertheless, two early second millennium village-sized sites, both less than 2 hectares or 5 acres in size, have been largely excavated, providing a model of what such small communities might have looked like. Tell Harmal and Haradum were surrounded by walls, both had administrative buildings, temples, and workshop areas, and both had houses containing tablets indicating both literacy and the same kinds of economic concerns as contemporary urban residents (Baqir 1946, 1959; Kepinski-Lecomte 1992). Their house patterns differed slightly in that they lacked both the rare very large houses and the very small houses found in urban districts. While this might suggest less difference in wealth in these small communities, a comparison of object classes from Haradum and Mashkan-shapir shows that the only types of objects found in the big site and absent in the small one are the inscribed nails and cylinders that testify to royal building projects at Mashkan-shapir. Thus these small mud-brick communities, with populations of fewer than 500 people, nevertheless look more like cities writ small than like a completely different kind of settlement.

This does not mean, of course, that true rural settlements did not exist, but simply that we have yet to find a way to identify them. Steinkeller's (n.d.) analysis of the countryside around Umma references numerous tiny settlements, probably made up of no more than a single family, associated with threshing floors and their silos. These sites were both too small and probably too ephemeral to be identified today. Also present were temples of various sizes, rural estates including palaces, the encampments of nomads, and the reed huts of the marsh dwellers. All of the evidence suggests that it is a mistake to assume that rural Mesopotamia was fundamentally different from the cities. Data from Haradum and Tell Harmal indicate that the inhabitants of these two tiny villages were as wealthy, literate, and sophisticated as their urban counterparts, and the same was probably true of most of those known only from textual records. The mobility characteristic of Mesopotamia, both vertical between the rich and poor and horizontal between ways of life, would not have been possible had there not been a fundamental similarity in social structure.

In sum, just as the population of Mesopotamian cities seems to have been very agrarian, with well over 50 percent of the population making their living through agriculture, so was the rural sector very urban. I close with the suggestion that Mesopotamian households and the neighborhoods or villages that they formed were the real building blocks of society, but it was the ability of the urban centers to provide both a larger political arena and an efficient resource base that led to their popularity. Such a view is significantly different from the temple- and palace-focused approach typical of scholarship half a century ago.

NOTE

1 "Today" may be a misnomer. A combination of dam building in Turkey, Syria, and northern Iraq, which has led to lower river levels with an intensive drainage program in the south, has enormously reduced the area covered by marshes. In the aftermath of the second Gulf War there is some talk of restoring this habitat, but at the time of writing it is not clear whether this way of life, which has existed for at least six millennia, is gone forever.

FURTHER READING

Stone 1995b and Stone in press offer introductions; Van De Mieroop 1992 gives a feel for the cities.

CHAPTER ELEVEN

Money and Trade

Christopher M. Monroe

Introduction: The Lure of the Early Economy

Throughout the Near East, from very early times, trade and money were shaping the material world from which loftier cultural and ideological traits emerged. One of Mesopotamia's enduring tales, Atra-hasis, which includes the flood story, develops out of a mundane labor dispute; a revolt against the higher gods by the gods assigned to work the land was pacified by the creation of human beings, the new working class (Foster 1993a: 158–201). Another myth, Enmerkar and the Lord of Aratta, alludes to the long-distance trade between Uruk and Aratta, a kingdom far to the east and rich in tin and lapis lazuli (Jacobsen 1987: 275–319). A clash between two economic worlds, a newer price-based system and the older, state-run, and tribute-based one, sets the stage for the Egyptian classic, The Report of Wen-Amun (Lichtheim 1976: 224–30). Myth and literature were not merely allegories for everyday matters, but studying trade and money helps us understand how the ancients valued goods, services, and people, and thus adds depth to our view of their daily life.

Methodological Issues

Intriguing contradictions abound on such basic issues as what money was and whether a society was "moneyless" or even "marketless." Each of the following propositions, while arguably false or highly debatable, can be found stated more or less as fact in reputable reference works:

- Money was invented in Anatolia, modern Turkey, in the seventh century BCE.
- Mesopotamia had a bullion system, but no coins and therefore no money.
- Mesopotamia had standardized weights and possibly money, but no markets.
- Ancient Egypt had money but was a moneyless society.
- Ancient Egypt had neither markets nor money.

Recognizing that such statements will remain open to debate is important, though it could be argued that moneyless societies existed neither in Egypt nor the Near East after cities emerged. One can only claim this by adhering to a clear definition of what money is, or better, what it does or what purpose it serves. This would be simple were it not for the complex issues of political economy surrounding it. Gently introducing oneself to this material (as in Snell 1997: 145–58) is recommended, since delving deeper leads one down a twisted path of fascinating but often inconclusive and contentious debate.

Before the third millennium we depend almost solely on archaeology for clues to what various cultures imported and exported to meet human needs and desires. Some facts archaeology demonstrates rather neatly, like that Mesopotamians imported tin, used with copper for making bronze, lapis lazuli and carnelian from the east, wood from the west, copper from the south, and obsidian from the north. Moreover, the clearest evidence for the first interregional economic system in world history, the expansion of the Late Uruk culture of southern Mesopotamia that reached the Upper Euphrates around 3200 BCE, is entirely archaeological, most clearly attested by the distribution of small, utilitarian bowls. Cylinder seals from the Uruk and Jemdet Nasr periods also suggest an organized form of early long-distance trade in southern Mesopotamia and Iran. Egypt's long relationship with the Levant, the coast of the eastern Mediterranean, is hinted at in a few texts, but the main evidence consists of Egyptian scarabs (amulets carved like beetles), statuary, and other inscribed objects found in excavations in Israel, Palestine, Lebanon, and Syria. Similarly, there is a wealth of archaeological finds that point to a Persian Gulf trade stretching as far back as the fifth millennium. But how long-distance exchange was organized, and what standards of value existed, is generally poorly understood before the third millennium, whence come our earliest intelligible archives of cuneiform records.

With records came the explicit identification of goods, individuals, and institutions, either as recipients or distributors of goods, sometimes accompanied by prices or value of the goods exchanged. The more informative third millennium archives come from southern Mesopotamian towns, but we also have tablets from a major Syrian palace at Ebla, to the far northwest. Overall the evidence is still scanty and insufficient when applied to larger questions like who organized trading, who profited by it, was there private enterprise, a free market, or a state-run economy. There are no texts that set out the economic principles of Ancient Near Eastern institutions or towns, describe the experience of traders, chronicle supply and demand forces, or offer analytic descriptions. And if one were to chart the availability of good source materials over time, one would not find a smooth curve rising from relative darkness into later periods of illumination. Rather, after the mid-third millennium we have a generally constant situation of abundant but brief material punctuated by chance archaeo-logical and textual finds of great significance. For example, the Old Assyrian trading colony found at Kültepe, Turkey, provided Assyriologists with unprecedented detail about this family-organized business that connected three disparate regions in profit-making ventures for metals and textiles before 1800 BCE. Analyses of the business correspondence from Kanesh revolutionized the way most scholars conceptualized trade in the Ancient Near East and helped overturn the erroneous view that

Mesopotamia was marketless (Veenhof 1972). Analyses of the inscribed potsherds recovered from a workmen's village at Deir el-Medina in central Egypt between about 1539 and 1075 BCE have similarly reshaped scholarly views on Egyptian money, trade, and markets (Lesko 1994). Most still see Egypt as a redistributive economy, that is, one in which temples and palaces controlled the acquisition and distribution of wealth (Altenmüller 2001). But Egypt is now less easily characterized as a monolithic economy, since we know about black markets and trade that was organized outside the great household institutions.

The interpretation of the Old Assyrian tablets marked a turning point in a century-old intellectual battle known as the formalist–substantivist debate. Understanding this debate is essential to comprehending how the facts are shaped into information and history. Formalists tend to see the capitalistic rationality of modern Western societies represented throughout human history, as if the laws of modern economics (supply and demand, rational choice) were universal. Of course, many of the structures of modern capitalism, like stock exchanges, markets, customs houses, letters of credit, and such, are missing. The substantivists, on the other hand, stress that economies are "embedded," or constructed within parameters of given socio-cultural ideologies. They deny that societies existing before the industrial revolution of the 1700s of our own era and the rise of modern capitalism could exhibit capitalistic traits.

By the 1950s the substantivists, led by Polanyi (1957), were seemingly winning this debate. A steady stream of sociological works analyzing and criticizing the tenets of capitalism was met by another stream of anthropological studies, especially ethnographies, that had been defining the economics of so-called pre-monetary societies, including many in the Pacific Islands. In these settings trade was organized as either barter, redistribution by a ruling institution, or ceremonialized as gift exchanges between elites. Essential was the embeddedness concept, that is, that the economy was determined by a deeper social ideology. Absent, supposedly, were rationality, prices, profit, and other maximizing motives. Many Assyriologists and Egyptologists found tempting parallels in these works, and the notion that early political economies were primitive took firm hold. Despite plentiful evidence for trade, prices, and money in Old Babylonian texts from 2004 to 1595 BCE and Middle Babylonian texts from the Syrian coastal kingdom of Ugarit from 1400 to 1200 BCE, entrepreneurship tended to be dismissed as formalist inference or downplayed as secondary, something merchants did to supplement their income from the palace or temple.

Political philosophy has been a key component of the debate also. Marxist scholars propagated the view of Mesopotamian society as having consisted of two competing sectors, urban dependents of palaces and temples versus free rural peasants (Diakonoff 1982; Zaccagnini 1983a; Liverani 1990). In this two-sector model, trade is considered primarily an arm of the urban ruling apparatus that exploited the rural population. Many other scholars have adopted parts of the German sociologist Max Weber's theory of the patrimonial household, where the kingdom was seen as organized as a pyramid of bureaucrats connected by blood and personal obligations to the king, with all the realm's wealth and information theoretically flowing from the many parties at the bottom to the royal apex (Michalowski 1991). In this model also, trade is primarily an economic component of rulership.

But private ownership of land and movable goods was apparent in the earliest sources, as were traders buying and selling goods for temples, kings, and individuals. If money and trade for profit did not exist in the earliest states of the late fourth millennium, then they appeared soon after. One thing is clear from looking at transactions in the texts themselves: by commodifying the value of objects and services, people at some point began to commodify each other, however indirectly. Because of this inherently anti-social aspect to trade and money, successful merchants have always taken care to appear equitable in their dealings.

Distribution of wealth among different social groups, or political economy, has preoccupied modern scholars and Ancient Near Easterners alike. Customs, laws, and literature show an intention to balance the profit motives of merchants with competing interests of other social groups.

Today scholars appeal to philosophers or sociologists to support their view of how trade was conducted in early states. Marxists tend to stress the corrosive effects of capitalistic trade and its corruption of benevolent despotism; Weberians see all economic action serving the interests of a charismatic ruler who owned everything in his realm; those following Polanyi see most trade as reciprocal in spirit and study how it became depersonalized; and many find Wallerstein's (1974/80) world-system concept useful, suggesting that early states built asymmetrical center–periphery relationships to gain advantages in procuring raw materials. However one justifies one's socio-economic theory, looking back at the origins of money and trade forces one to question not only ancient sources but one's own material conditions and the current systems that facilitate and justify them. This has an effect on the debate, making it less dispassionate and perhaps more exciting.

What Is Money and What Does It Do?

Money and coinage are not the same thing. Practically all coinage is money, but not all money is coinage. The most useful dictionary definitions focus on the functions of money rather than its forms. Indeed, defining the forms eludes us simply because there are so many. In the extreme example, money today becomes increasingly electronic and digital, and one day may have no physical form whatsoever. So it is quite irrelevant to define money as beads, metal bullion, stamped metal as coins, paper, plastic, or invisible 0s and 1s. What money does is much more interesting, and money does minimally the following: it provides a medium of exchange; it stores the value of something perishable in a more stable form; it standardizes value or prices for goods and services; and it facilitates the accumulation and accounting of wealth.

Money is thus not so much a physical good but a technology. Like writing, it is a technology that communicates. And because the information communicated is concerned primarily with prices of things, one might define a given monetary system as a language of value.

Mesopotamian Money and Weights

Based on archaeological finds and texts, money was used in the third millennium. In form it consisted mainly of weights of precious metal, semi-precious metal, and barley. Early examples show a wide variety in heaviness and form of the weights, but reforms attributed to the Old Akkadian period (2334–2194 BCE) imposed a far-reaching and long-lasting standardization. The oldest unit, and the one that remained constant throughout the history of ancient Mesopotamia and beyond, was the talent, or load, of about 30 kilograms or 66 pounds, the conventional amount that could be carried by a single worker. This large weight was divided into 60 minas, each about 500 grams, which in turn was divided into 60 shekels of about 8.3 grams each. The shekel was further divided into "little minas" (a shekel), "little shekels" (1/60 shekel), and "grains" or "barleycorns" (1/180 shekel) for the purpose of weighing small amounts of precious metals that were highly valuable and thus often measured in small quantities.

Though the evidence is not consistently robust after the Old Babylonian period, the Old Akkadian–Old Babylonian system apparently changed little over time, at least in the talent and mina (Powell 1990a). The shekel, on the other hand, was more dynamic, with local systems emerging in different areas. By the Late Bronze Age (1500–1000 BCE), and probably before, three major systems had developed with regionally distinct shekels. Southern Mesopotamia had a mina of 60 shekels; Syro-Palestinians were using slightly larger shekels that counted 50 to a mina; and merchants of the Hittite empire used even larger ones, with only 40 per mina. At Emar around 1300 BCE these three distinct weight systems were in use at one time, an unsurprising fact when one considers Emar's situation in a frontier zone between competing empires. Later the Neo-Assyrians used three different weight standards for silver, the king's, the merchants', and the Carchemish standard, named after a north Syrian city. In Neo-Babylonian times, after 612 BCE and later, the shekel underwent further subdivisions.

Stone weights have been found in many archaeological sites, including some 550 at Ugarit. But the most important single assemblage comes from the Late Bronze Age shipwreck found at Uluburun, Turkey. At least nine different sets of weights, each consisting of stones carved to fit a local weight system, were on board (Pulak 1997). With these weights the ill-fated merchants could have transacted payments in metal or other commodities with Aegeans, Hittites, Syro-Palestinians, Assyrians, or Egyptians. The weights are illustrative of the interpretive complexities in discussing money and trade. Even in the case of royal gift exchange, which is how most would interpret the Uluburun shipwreck, traders needed to be conversant with the major weight systems of the day.

Currency came in many forms, from the everyday and transitory to the exotic and permanent. Grain was probably the earliest standardized indicator of the value of goods, as it signified basic subsistence. Barley was adequate for local trading, since its value as food would not have lessened in transactions conducted over short distances and periods of time. For long-distance trade, however, something more concentrated and durable was required. Shiny metals were highly desired, perhaps because of their malleability and potential for ostentatious display as vessels and other household items. They were also relatively sturdy and low in bulk, making them ideal for long-distance trade. Prices in Mesopotamia and Egypt were sometimes stated in gold or copper, but silver was the most common measure for most of the Bronze and Iron Ages. In Mesopotamia, for most of its history, barley, lead, copper or bronze, tin, silver, and gold (in order of increasing value) functioned as money. These may be divided into monies that were cheap (barley, lead, and copper and its alloys), mid-range (tin), and high-range (silver and gold) monies (Powell 1996). It is interesting that the most utilitarian metals, copper and tin, which when alloyed into bronze constituted the bulk of tools and weaponry, remained less valuable than metals with little utility. The relative value of tin is especially notable considering its rarity in the core areas of civilization. Weighed coils and smaller broken-off pieces of silver, copper, gold, and bronze were used as currency in Ur III to Old Babylonian times (2112–1595 BCE); metal rings may also have been the basis for the Egyptian weight system. In the Late Bronze Age (1500–1200 BCE) gold gained on silver due to an influx of Egyptian gold into the interregional exchange network, but throughout Mesopotamian history value was most commonly stated in weights of silver or barley. During the Neo-Assyrian period (883–627 BCE) there was a shift to copper being the dominant metal money and then back to silver, perhaps as the result of huge amounts of metals imported by conquering armies.

Money and trade met in the figure of the moneyman, an individual with lots of currency who sought to increase it by local trading, foreign trading, or lending silver or barley with interest. We can lump the trader and creditor together in the class of moneymen (which included women) while recognizing that there were various sorts of moneymen who increased their capital through different means. They were all entrepreneurs in the sense that they accumulated wealth not primarily by producing, but by providing access to goods or services generated by others. They were experts in the knowledge of what was available, where, and for how much.

One of the more interesting indicators of merchant success was the suspicion that the consumer and producer sectors of society cast upon the merchant. The Mesopotamian hymn to Šamaš was unusually explicit regarding the conduct of merchants and their weighing practices:

> He who [commits] fra[ud as he holds the ba]lances
> Who switches weights, who lowers the [ ],
> (His) profits are illusory, and he lo[ses the capital].
> The one who is honest in holding the balance, [ ] plenty of [ ],
> Whatever (he weighs) will be given to him in plenty [ ]...
> (Foster 1993a: 540, lines 107–11)
>
> The honest merchant who pays loans by the [ex]tra(?) standard,
> thereby to make extra virtue,
> Is pleasing to Šamaš, he will grant him extra life,
> He will make (his) family numerous, he will acquire wealth,

[His] seed will be perpetual as the waters of a perpetual spring.
(Foster 1993a: 541, lines 118–21)

This can be compared to texts from Egypt, like the Instructions of Amenemope, perhaps from around 1200 BCE in which the student was admonished not "to move the scales nor alter the weights," since Thoth, the god of writing, magic, and wisdom, would know of it in the end (Lichtheim 1976: 156–7). This was a matter for the entire cosmos; the gods were invoked to oversee the weighing process and guarantee the honesty of merchants. Proverbs 11: 1 and Psalm 62: 9–12 (Hebrew: 10–11) in the Bible also suggest that a higher power supervised economic activity.

Mesopotamian Merchants and Money

It is often erroneously claimed that the Lydians of southeastern Turkey invented money, when all they really invented was coinage. Here it is important to note that, even after the introduction of coinage, weights were still used to check the actual worth of coins and conduct business in bullion. Functionally the coin was a quantity of metal weighed and sealed by the state. Since the late seventh century BCE coinage and weighed bullion have coexisted, and in economies where inflation runs high, one can still find weighed amounts of silver or gold metal being used for payment. In even less stable economies, such as wartime Iraq's, less precious metals, such as recycled copper, have become a kind of currency.

It would be difficult to chronicle the prices of goods and services throughout Mesopotamian history, but we may derive a standard wage for the Old Babylonian and Neo-Babylonian periods. In Old Babylonian times a worker could expect to receive 10 liters of barley a day or 300 liters a month. In silver this amounted to 6 grains a day or 1 shekel a month. In Neo-Babylonian times the payment in silver remained the same, but the equivalent payment in barley was considerably less, 6 liters per day or 180 per month (Powell 1990a).

Ratios of value between monies are hard to determine since they varied over time and with different qualities of metal. The gold:silver ratio ranged normally from 2:1 to 10:1 throughout the Bronze Age, and from about 6:1 to 15:1 in the Iron Age after 1000 BCE. Silver was about 180 times more valuable than copper; and silver was 10 to 40 times more valuable than tin (Powell 1990a). The amount of barley one could buy with 1 shekel of silver can also be tracked over this time. Presargonic and Old Akkadian sources may point to an equivalence of about 240 liters of grain per shekel of silver; in Ur III and Old Babylonian times the standard equivalence was 300 liters per shekel, though it was probably less at the end of the period. When sources emerged again under the Kassites, 1 shekel of silver bought only about 150 liters; Neo-Babylonian prices seem to have stabilized at 180 liters of barley per shekel of silver.

We have prices from the middle of Ancient Near Eastern history in the city of Ugarit on the Syrian coast during Late Bronze Age, 1400–1200 BCE (Heltzer 1978). A standard measure of grain (about 150 liters) cost 1 shekel of silver; a jar of olive oil cost about half a shekel; a jar of wine cost about a third of a shekel; an ox cost from 10 to 17 shekels; a sheep, 1 to 1.5 shekels; and donkeys cost from 10 to 30 shekels of silver each. Of course, there are many other prices known for this and other periods. People also were commodified, as is shown by a lively trade in human slaves. Most of these individuals entered into service willingly or were coerced by debt to enter as a means of repayment. Skilled artisans and wives were also exchanged as gifts between royal households.

Prices are also found in legal texts and law collections. While Mesopotamian punishment is popularly understood as "an eye for an eye," the reality was often much more monetary. Law collections often prescribed death for homicide, but they were also full of prices, stated both as guidelines, a sort of price control, and as penalties for various harms done (Roth 1997). Usually the intent was to replace what had been lost by a transgression. This entailed the taking of one life to replace another wrongfully taken, or the replacement of lost persons with slaves from the community of the offender. But for various other crimes the compensation was in silver, and the amounts differed not only by transgression but by social class of the victim. Thus in the Hittite laws, a free person's sight was worth 20 shekels of silver, but a slave's only 10. To prevent cycles of blood-feuding, it was customary for the host community to pay large amounts of silver to the family of the dead if a murderer was not caught. In fact there was no death penalty for homicide in the Hittite laws, only an undefined monetary reimbursement. The penalty for killing merchants was particularly steep at 100 minas (4,000 shekels), perhaps to deter actions potentially harmful to the smooth functioning of the empire.

There is no solid archaeological evidence for a structure corresponding to what Sumerian or Akkadian speakers meant by their terms for "marketplace." This is probably because fixed marketplaces did not exist as we know them, and most trading was done in the merchant's quarter, quay, or dockside. More abstract is the attested extended meaning of "market," in the sense of "current rate of exchange" or "fair market price." The concept of profit, selling for prices higher than what was paid originally, was rarely called a profit in Old Assyrian and Old Babylonian texts, but frequently must be inferred from the price differentials.

The one place where trade and money abounded that has been documented both textually and archaeologically was the *kārum*, an Akkadian term translated as embankment, quay, harbor, harbor district, merchant quarter, or trading colony. All these meanings appear related to early descriptions of places where boats docked, either on rivers or seas. Thus far the only excavated place known to correspond to this term is the Old Assyrian merchant quarter or trade colony at Kanesh in central Turkey around 1800 BCE. Other important harbor towns have been excavated, such as Ur, Minet el-Beida and Ras Ibn Hani (both near Ugarit), and Memphis in Egypt, but none has produced such a wealth of explicit textual information on the *kārum*. We know about institutions and officials connected with the *kārum* from different times and places down to Neo-Assyrian and Neo-Babylonian times, but have no complete understanding of its function in any one situation. The "house of the *kārum*" was the office or building representing the authority of the *kārum* and was probably not so different from the modern customs or exchange house in its functions. It was where one paid import taxes, which were probably divided among the local ruler and the traders in charge of the *kārum*.

The *kārum* was especially important to the merchants themselves since this was where they resided, stored goods, kept money and archives, and formed partnerships with other merchants. Such partnerships were necessary to amass capital and are known from a particular form of "purse-money" contract in the Old Assyrian archives and in references to groups of merchants in Old Babylonian sources. In Old Babylonian texts and Middle Babylonian texts from Ugarit, we learn of an overseer, the *wākil kārim* "the agent of the quay," who was legally responsible for transactions and accidents that occurred in the merchant quarter or harbor. Similar duties may have been the responsibility of a person designated as "man of the *kārum*" a millennium earlier at Ebla in northern Syria. Indeed, the institution of the *kārum* and its personnel appear to be extremely long-lived if one compares the ancient evidence to the duties of the *wākil at-tujjār*, "the agent of the merchants," an official who legally represented foreign merchants in Egypt around 1000 of our era (Curtin 1984: 113–15).

Many traders who were state functionaries no doubt bore the Akkadian title of *tamkārum*, "merchant." So did some traders who were known to the palace as traders but who were not necessarily dependents or functionaries. Unfortunately, most of our material is not as specific as that from Ugarit, where "merchant of the king" and plain "merchant" were apparently distinguished. Moreover, one should be aware that there were many traders or moneymen documented in our texts who bore no title whatsoever, but left just their names and the records of their transactions.

From Ur III through Old Babylonian times this title applied to those working for the great households and to those conducting private enterprise. An unusually illustrative group of Ur III records called "balanced accounts" states allotments, expenses, and debts of merchants working for the palace (Snell 1982). In general they show merchants selling off the surplus foodstuffs produced by the palace, with merchants paying off their debts with a wide variety of goods that included imported luxury items. It is clear from Old Babylonian sources that "merchant" applied to those engaged in local mercantile business as well as long-distance traders. Local merchants made a living redistributing palace goods or buying debts owed to the palace by tenant farmers. Merchants could buy goods with favorable repayment contracts that allowed them to make a substantial profit for themselves. Perhaps more importantly, merchants in the service of kings or temples had access to vast capital, usually silver, which they could translate into many forms and increase in a variety of ways. At Ugarit such merchants were referred to as having royal endowments of silver. The palace benefited by the merchant's assuming responsibilities for transportation and debt collection, as well as keeping perishable commodities circulating in and out of palace storage facilities.

Unlike the generic term "merchant," Early Dynastic records mentioned a profession which seems specifically involved in long-distance or foreign trade. Hittite long-distance traders were known in Late Bronze Age texts from Ugarit, but it is unclear if they were state functionaries or entrepreneurs employed part-time by the Hittite king. The Neo-Assyrian merchant was mainly a royal agent who obtained luxury imports for the court (Radner 1999). Private enterprise in the Neo-Assyrian texts is shown, however, in a group of texts mentioning the "master of the road or venture." Neo-Babylonian temples apparently conducted their long-distance trade by hiring merchants outside the organization, probably foreigners.

It is difficult to say if merchants commonly specialized in local or long-distance trade. It is tempting to conclude they did, since specialized skills were required. Long-distance trade was always more profitable than local, but with greater risks. Overland trade was always threatened by bandits, and some argue that long-distance trade without state protection was unthinkable. More would argue that trade has usually gone before the flag in world history, that is, that trade has tended to precede government intervention. The Old Assyrian *kārum* system was especially lucrative, bringing profits as high as 200 percent to the traders, though this rosy picture does not accurately account for expenses. The prices and profit in this trade were largely a function of distance. Assur was relatively close to the eastern tin supply and could charge two or three times in Kanesh or other Anatolian colonies what the tin cost in Assur. Tin and textiles constituted the bulk of the cargo, all borne by donkey caravans, which was traded for silver and gold in Anatolia. Not all of the profits came back to Assyria. Many traders lived double lives, with a family in Anatolia and one in Assur, while others lived mostly abroad, directing familial matters through correspondence.

The maritime trader seems to have been a specialized job, but one documented spottily in Mesopotamian history. Some of the better sources come from the Old Babylonian cities of Ur and Larsa, which had trading relationships with the Persian Gulf and Indus Valley civilization, called Meluhha. We know precious little about the ships that sailed the Gulf, though texts do allude to a maximum size of about 20 tons. Tablets also mention sailors. Some traders were specifically referred to as "one going to Dilmun," a phrase alluding to the important intermediate trade center that was probably in the island of Bahrain. Oman, ancient Magan, was important to Mesopotamian towns for its production of copper. In Neo-Assyrian and Persian times the Phoenicians carried much of the trade for their overlords and became famous as maritime explorers in the process. Archaeological and textual evidence for ships and seafarers in the eastern Mediterranean include shipwrecks from Turkey, Cyprus, and Israel, excavated harbor towns, and texts from Late Bronze Age Ugarit and later sources (Bass 1995; Wachsmann 1998).

Some traders involved in only domestic trade still had to be experts in river transportation. Much of this business, which involved pilots, towers, loaders, and payments of dues, was organized by *kārums* and groups of merchants. Most of what is known about donkey caravanning, probably the commonest means of overland hauling, is known from the Old Assyrian Kanesh tablets.

Money and Trade in Egypt

Egypt has long been characterized as a socialist or supply state with a redistributive, marketless, or "command" economy. While these conceptions remain useful, one must be mindful that our sources in Egypt are highly biased to represent mostly the funerary and palatial material culture of the ruling class. Traders were seen as palace or temple officials, though there is good evidence for foreign merchants residing in Egypt and participating in, if not conducting, much of its foreign trade. Some scholars view merchants as conducting private business, but only in the New Kingdom, where the pictorial evidence from tomb paintings and recorded confessions of tomb-robbers offered rare and incontrovertible proof of private enterprise.

Janssen (1975, 1994) has compiled the most evidence for prices, debt, and credit and laid the foundations of what we know about Egyptian economics. As in Mesopotamia, Egypt had a system of standardized weights for bullion, which constituted its money, though it was not as fully developed a technology as it was in Mesopotamia. The most common measure for weights of metal was the *dbn*, a word related to words meaning "ring," which was about 13 grams in the Old Kingdom (2575–2150 BCE) and 91 in the New Kingdom (1539–1075 BCE).

Though Egypt was rich in precious metals, especially gold, they never took on the same significance as money as in Mesopotamia. Demand for Egyptian gold was keen in the Near East, and in Egypt it was certainly highly valued; the gold:silver:copper equivalence was about 200:100:1. But gold was not used as a standard, and silver was used in prices only rarely, for example at the workmen's village at Deir el-Medina, where copper was the more common standard.

Whereas barley appears to have been the earliest form of payment in Mesopotamia, in Egypt we have bread and beer being the standard rations given to workers. Ten loaves and a jug or two of beer per day was a common payment. In terms of metal money, 1 copper *dbn* bought a half liter of grain in Ramesside times (1292–1075 BCE), when we have the most evidence for prices.

Although Egypt looked like a supply-state to many observers for much of its history, there are signs of greater economic complexity when Egypt became an empire in the New Kingdom (1539–1075 BCE). The role of the trader in this situation is highly debatable. Some temples employed both merchant ships and traders. Traders appeared only as temple agents, and we do not have evidence of them conducting private enterprise on the side.

There was a lot of movement in grain prices in the Ramesside period. Prolonged grain famine appears to have caused this, and food shortages may also have contributed to a diversifying economy. While there was no word for profit as there was in Mesopotamia, the concept was essentially present in the idea of a good price (Kemp 1989: 252). The vivid paintings from tombs of New Kingdom officials displayed some kind of marketplace, but we have no way of knowing whether the exchanges were barter or price based (Kemp 1989: 254–55). It is apparent from tomb paintings and a few texts that Syrians played a vital role in maritime trade with Egypt's northeastern neighbors. Texts mentioned foreigners living in a harbor community around Memphis during the New Kingdom (Redford 1992: 228).

In contrast to the rich merchants who thrived in Syria and Mesopotamia, it appears the traders had low status in Egypt. They were functionaries or purchasing agents, not free actors, and the foreign traders living in Egypt probably had more wealth than the indigenous traders, if texts from Deir el-Medina are any indication of trader status. According to a school text known as Be a Scribe or the Satire on the Trades from around 1000 BCE, the Egyptian merchant's life was not particularly enviable:

> The merchants travel downstream and upstream. They are as busy as can be, carrying goods from one town to another. They supply him who has wants. But the tax collectors carry off the gold, that most precious of metals. The ships' crews from every house (of commerce), they receive their loads. They depart from Egypt for Syria, and each man's god is with him. (But) not one of them says: We shall see Egypt again! (Lichtheim 1980: 170)

In interpreting this text the student should take care to consider the author's perspective as inherently bureaucratic, not sympathetic to any appeal the trader's life may have held. The text also suggests that Egyptian merchants did indeed travel abroad, an idea supported by the presence of Egyptian names at Ugarit in Syria in the Late Bronze Age (1400–1200 BCE).

Routes and Metals

Many studies of ancient trade are concerned with defining the routes by which prized commodities flowed between regions. The history of the Ancient Near East could be viewed in terms of the constant competition and cooperation to attain resources that were distributed unequally throughout the region. Some of these were natural raw materials, and others were the work of skilled artisans in palaces. Trade routes were like water, following paths of least resistance to their destinations. The main routes went up the Euphrates and Tigris and then through mountain passes, tributary valleys, and wadis running east and west.

Mesopotamia was rich in fish, reeds, bitumen (an all-purpose petroleum product used for gluing, sealing, and coating), various animal products, and mud, but had little of a luxurious or ostentatious quality. With urbanism came increased needs for payments and the need to display one's status prominently in ornate households. From Syria-Palestine one could obtain olive oil, wine, ivory (both hippopotamus and elephant), purple dye, glass, and building woods like cedar, fir, and cypress. Some, probably not all, of the silver came from Anatolia. The gulf trade brought in exotic shells, copper from Oman, and exotic goods from the Indus River valley. From somewhere across the Zagros, perhaps in Afghanistan, came tin, lapis lazuli, and other precious stones. Egypt seems to have had more gold than other regions, and exotic woods and animals came from Africa.

The role of copper in the major trading networks of the Bronze Age seems especially crucial. After the mid-second millennium the gulf trade was usurped by an influx of Cypriot copper. Indeed the geopolitics of the later second millennium and early first millennium hardly makes sense without considering how surrounding empires competed for access to Cypriot copper and Levantine timber. At some point early in the first millennium iron began replacing copper in key weapon and tool industries, causing another major shift in the networks that left Cyprus more on the economic periphery.

Prospects for Studying Trade and Money

Traders and money were closely related and can be viewed together as part of a process that profoundly shaped the development of early and later states. Most approaches to the subject have been materialistic to some degree, following Marx's method of determining how a people creates and distributes its wealth. Because the dominant mode of production in early states was not capitalist (that is, organized to facilitate profit-based trading), many twentieth-century scholars relegated trade to the unimportant dustbin of history. A later group of scholars, influenced by sociology and anthropology, noticed how important demand for luxury goods was in some cases, and started seeing long-distance trade as more pivotal in how societies changed over time.

At this point archaeologists and Assyriologists have made great strides in figuring out how money and trade related to both production and consumption, supply and demand, in the Ancient Near East. We have learned that certain discoveries, like Ugarit, the *kārum* of Kanesh, and the Uluburun shipwreck, can change the field nearly overnight and reveal lives of traders who operated in social and geographic interstices between the great centers. Theirs was a world of particular social relations related to consumption and production, and it had its own dynamics. Technologies such as money, accounting, business correspondence, sailing, caravanning, loading, and weighing were obviously important. Legal protections, endowments by palace and temple, trader partnerships, ethnic and familial bonds, and the suspicion of merchants and their resultant coping strategies – these are all important social relations. These dynamics are beginning to be studied, and there is room for promising discoveries in libraries as well as in archaeological sites. To penetrate this challenging aspect of the Ancient Near East, students will do well to follow the progress of sociology and economic anthropology as well as excavations and text editions.

FURTHER READING

For trade in Mesopotamia see chapters 10 and 11 of Postgate 1992. Hawkins 1977 and Dercksen 1999 contain many individual contributions on various periods. Yoffee 1980 synthesizes much of the research done up to the late 1970s. Larsen 1987b summarizes the key goods and dynamics underlying early interregional trade, and one should consult other articles in that volume also. Veenhof 1972, 1997 provides the first full analysis of the Kanesh tablets and an updated appraisal of the formalist-substantivist debate. On Old Babylonian trade, Leemans 1960 looks at entrepreneurial trade, and Zaccagnini 1983a studies ceremonial gift exchange; on the gulf trade, see Oppenheim 1954. As an introduction to trade and diplomacy in the Late Bronze Age, Liverani 1990 is indispensable though limited to royal concerns. On monetary systems in Mesopotamia, Snell 1995 and Powell 1996 provide considerable detail while remaining intelligible to non-specialists. Mesopotamian law collections, which contain copious amounts of material related to prices and shipping, are in Roth 1997.

For trade and money in Egypt, chapter 6 of Kemp 1989 is highly recommended, as is Redford 1992. Bleiberg's 1995 summary is focused on money and is less biased than Altenmüller 2001, who gives a substantivist perspective. Janssen 1975, 1994 assembles the key materials for monetary systems, pricing, and credit. Evidence from Deir el-Medina is summarized in Lesko 1994. Castle 1992 studies Egyptian shipping and trade for the Ramesside period.

An introduction to political economy in early states is found in the appendix of Snell 1997. One can continue with Diakonoff 1982, Michalowski 1991, Renger 1994, Yoffee 1995, and Van De Mieroop 1997a. Important theoretical and cross-cultural discussions of trade are found in Adams 1974, Curtin 1984, Douglas and Isherwood 1979, Evers and Schrader 1994, and Zagarell 1986. On world-systems see Braudel 1984 and Chase-Dunn and Hall 1997; specific applications to Mesopotamia include Edens 1992, Algaze 1993, and Stein 1999, who critiques world-systems thinking overall.

Bass 1995 explores shipping in the eastern Mediterranean. Pulak 1997 examines the Uluburun shipwreck. Wachsmann 1998 catalogs the archaeological and textual evidence for Bronze Age shipping.

CHAPTER TWELVE

Working

David A. Warburton

The economies of antiquity are characterized as agrarian. The principal elements of both sedentary and pastoral agricultural activity – villages, crops, grazing, and the rest – gradually became the norm for the economies of the Middle East over the course of the millennia from the earliest Neolithic onward. Rural life is viewed as a life of toil. From the start, the sedentary way of life increased the labor burden as house construction and maintenance were supplemented by sowing, harvesting, and herding, at least for those obliged to work in the fields. These activities also increased the scope of production, spurring the manufacture of new tools. Pottery and sedentary life transformed storage, opening up new possibilities for wealth, and above all providing opportunities for a new elite class.

All of this increased the risk of loss since the sedentary villages were concentrations of immovable wealth, which states could either expropriate as taxes or remove as booty, if thieves could be kept at bay. Only the institutions and their representatives in the elite could guarantee or offer protection of property from neighbors or marauders. In return, they assumed a right to expropriate, which in turn led to increased production, and thus made more work. The administration of agricultural production itself became an important new profession. The institutions transformed employment and investment through construction projects and demand for industrial products, while raising wealth.

Rural life became increasingly difficult in the course of the Bronze Age (3500–1200 BCE) as institutions acquired control over land and labor, at once constricting the availability of land and making demands on labor in taxes and other services. The basic rhythms of life did not change: sowing, tilling, harvesting, herding, and weaving remained the same across the Near East. Only the demands increased, on everyone. When the poor had nothing to eat, local officials were held responsible by both those above and below them.

Agricultural production was an elementary aspect of the Ancient Near Eastern economy, but the cities and the peripheral regions were also hubs of industrial activity. Labor was as essential for the production of grain and textiles as it was for the preparation of metal and the erection of major buildings.

Employment

Although the source of all wealth in these ancient societies was agrarian, one should not have any illusions that there was no diversity of employment. Before the end of the Ramesside era in Egypt (about 1200 BCE), a scribe recorded a list of possible subordinates: "craftsmen, manual laborers, office workers, administrative officials, time-servers, stewards, mayors, village headmen, empowered district officers, department heads, scribes of offering tables, commissioners, envoys, administrative messengers, brewers, bakers, butchers, servants, confectioners, cake bakers, wine tasters, project managers, supervisors of carpenters, chief craftsmen, deputies, draftsmen, sculptors, miners, masons, wreckers, stone workers, guardians . . . statue sculptors . . . wood workers, . . . " (Gardiner 1937: 136–7; Caminos 1954: 497–501). The author clearly decided not to make a comprehensive account, and yet it should be evident that the urban world of the Ancient Near East was familiar with more than the essentials. It should be borne in mind that it is not entirely clear that all of the professions listed by the scribe meant that these people were "working," even if they held down jobs. In fact, many of those whose titles are recorded in the documents might not have been working at all but just holding an official position which might or might not involve any effort.

There are several ways of distinguishing employment, for example by sector or employer. One must also distinguish between sources of income and professions as well. There were certainly many who were working. In the agricultural sector were shepherds, cultivators, farmers, gardeners, vintners, and field-workers; other rural occupations included fishermen, foresters, and bitumen collectors. Among the craftsmen were builders, seal-cutters, bow-makers, potters, sculptors, masons, carpenters, basket-makers, and boat-builders. These must be distinguished from the more industrial occupations, such as weavers, textile-workers, and smiths. Among the professional classes were merchants, barmaids, prostitutes, physicians, barbers, priestesses, managers, governors, and scribes. Sailors and soldiers wandered between the various professions, acting at times as merchants and farmers.

In some cases, the occupations were year-round activities, such as bakers and sandal-makers. In others, the occupation and the source of income differed, such as soldiers and foresters who were also farmers, deriving their income from fields, but obliged to perform other services to secure their rights to the fields. In spring and summer, the armies would move across the plains, mowing the crops of the enemy at harvest season, so that soldiers could return to sow and harvest their own crops back home. State-employed artisans and governors benefited in the same way from assigned fields. But while they pursued their administrative tasks, others assured the production of their fields. Others like governors and scribes employed other workers, including soldiers, to work their fields. Some loafers were simply rounded up to work at harvest time. Scribes and bureaucrats were ubiquitous, keeping records and assigning workers but too busy to do any real work, as the Egyptian scribes proclaimed with pleasure (Caminos 1954: 247).

Institutions

Superficially, it would be logical to assume that the importance of the institutional economies cannot be overestimated. Even the millions of liters of grain recorded in the administrative texts pale in comparison with the outlays involved in the pyramids, temples, and palaces. The 2.3 million blocks of stone in the great pyramid at Giza had to be put in place in some 23 years, around 100,000 a year, or 275 a day, or one block every two minutes. This required some 25,000 to 30,000 workers to be on hand at any one time for a score of years (Lehner 1997: 224). Even if they worked in annual and seasonal shifts, the work had to be kept up. And this pyramid was not a mere aberration. Sneferu, the father of Khufu, who was the builder of the great pyramid around 2500 BCE, piled up a cubit meter volume in his two pyramids which almost doubled that of his son, and one of Khufu's successors almost equaled the great pyramid itself (Kemp 1983: 88). If the pyramids before and after this half-century of toil are disappointing by comparison, the temples and private tombs should provide some compensation and made for more work.

Even so, the walls around the pyramid enclosure of Djoser at Saqqara are of a higher quality than those around the contemporary city of Arad in Palestine, and a half-kilometer or 0.31 miles longer. The walls around the New Kingdom temple at Karnak enclose an area larger than most of the contemporaneous cities in the world. Both the walls and the buildings they enclosed had to be constructed, and the workers kept alive.

During the Third Dynasty of Ur (2114–2004 BCE), the grain paid out to the 40,000 state dependents totaled some 30 million liters or 7,736,160 bushels annually (Waetzoldt 1987: 118). Data from Ramesside Egypt imply expenditures of a similar magnitude (Warburton 2000: 69–70, 74 n. 20). One Mari letter from near today's Syrian–Iraqi border records a royal offer to dispatch five million liters of grain on donkey back with a merchant (Durand 2000: 3: 18).

The 2,000 persons employed in the Ur III grain-grinding industry pale into insignificance when placed beside the 15,000 employees in the contemporaneous textile industry in the province of Lagash (Waetzoldt 1987: 119). The production of the Ur III textile industry may have exceeded the requirements of the local market by a factor of 10, implying a dependence upon export markets (Englund 1998: 151 n. 342).

The manufacture and sale of textiles was a very important industry across the entire Near East, from the Aegean to Iraq. In some cases this trade was under the control of central authorities exploiting labor maintained through rations to transform wool into textiles (Dossin 1964). In other cases, women would weave at home and retail their products to state firms (Condon 1984). The economic power of textile distributors affected private economics well beyond southern Mesopotamia, quite aside from the state dependents.

The economic importance of the pyramids seems less when we see that one provincial textile industry was involved in a task of a similar magnitude. The existence of Mesopotamian temple towers, the ziggurats, and the pyramids underscores the capacity of the state to command labor; however, the temples and the related investments are merely the symbolic projection of raw economic power. It was this power that provided the state with a decisive edge in competition.

This image of a wide diversity of professions (masons to silver smiths), concentrations of employees in industrial enterprises, and mind-boggling quantities of grain gives the superficial impression of enormous wealth and concentrated economic power. These concepts lie at the base of the concept of the "palace-economy" system. The institutions played a key role in several different ways. In many cases individuals were assigned land from which they drew income while executing state tasks, such as supervising textile mills or performing temple rituals. The institutions were not only run by the bureaucrats, but utterly dependent upon them. The key to understanding the economy was the capacity of the institutions to determine employment and investment strategies by controlling agricultural production. It was the agricultural production that produced the surplus allowing the institutions to invest in textiles, and it was the institutional agricultural surplus that kept grain prices low, so as to ensure rural poverty among small-holders. It was the scribes who assured that the whole functioned; they formed an essential part of the elite, with vested interest in increasing their own wealth and the strength of the institutions.

The dimensions of the institutional economies must, however, be placed in context. The elite and the immediate dependents of the institutions made up an insignificant proportion of the total population. What gave the institutions economic power was not an overwhelming economic role, but their leverage. The remainder of the population was tied to the land and agricultural production. A small group were professional merchants. The peasants had to pay taxes or rent to the institutions, and the merchants had little hope that the peasants would be interested in exotic items. The institutions and their dependents provided the market for the offerings of the merchants, and their grain surpluses had a decisive effect on the value of grain in the hands of the peasants.

Agriculture was thus the source of wealth in the ancient world. Labor was far more valuable than technology, and the command of labor was decisive.

Institutional Control of Labor and Labor Value: an Example

It is difficult for us to imagine the importance of these various features, so we will jump to a concrete example to understand this: one administrative text from the Third Dynasty of Ur, dated to about 2000 BCE (Englund 1991). In this text a single foreman is responsible for the annual workdays of a group of 40 female laborers. He had to account for 13,419 days. His records indicate that he had a deficit of 7,422 days. The deficit is the difference between what the women were expected to work and what they actually worked. They did not meet the expected quota, and the supervisor could be held responsible for that gap. These days were reckoned as being worth 1 grain of silver for each workday, so 7,422 days would be 41.25 shekels or 343.6 grams of silver. The foreman who could be held responsible for this had an annual income of 20 g u r of barley, usually evaluated at 20 shekels of silver or

166.6 grams. Englund (1991: 279) remarks that this "would have been no easy sum" for an administrator to repay. The deficit would have effectively annulled two full years of administrative remuneration.

There was no way the foreman could eliminate this deficit, since it could only be achieved by increasing the number of laborers for whom he was responsible while failing to file any work-records. This was impossible, and the foreman had to forfeit any hope of resolving the issue of his deficit while avoiding trouble.

We can compare this with labor and market value. It is very rare for the documents to provide an estimate of the individual productivity of a single worker, as we usually have documents which record harvesting or threshing or milling, or combining plow teams and entrepreneurial activity, and thus one can rarely gauge productivity. As it happens, however, there is a relevant ancient Egyptian document dating to about a thousand years after our Ur III text. We may assume a slightly different degree of productivity, but the technology will not have been significantly different. This text records that a governor of the city of Elephantine placed a single laborer with a team of oxen on a piece of land which happened to have been flooded. After the work was over, this one laborer produced 40 sacks of grain (Wente 1990: 130–1). This figure was considered to be disappointing and is thus a minimum. Forty sacks of grain are roughly 3,000 liters. In Ramesside Egypt, this grain would have been valued at about 110 grams of silver, so that an amount of 4,000 liters of grain, which would be more satisfactory to the administrators, would be worth about 145 grams of silver, or a bit less than the Ur III foreman's salary.

The annual wages of a single skilled craftsman in the Egyptian village at Deir el-Medina consisted of around 66 sacks of grain, or about 5,000 liters (Janssen 1975: 460–73). This grain was collected from the peasants through a taxation system and assigned to the workers as compensation for their work. The grain received exceeded the calorie requirements of ten individuals (Warburton 1997). The annual income of a middle class family could thus be produced by two workmen, who also fed themselves.

At these rates, some 20 percent of the population would be able to produce sufficient grain to feed 100 percent of the population. These were agricultural economies and thus alternative employment possibilities did not exist. Increasing production on family plots could achieve nothing except to drive the price down at harvest time. Those 20 percent of the population who grew the crops were exploited and paid minimum rations or left to fend for themselves from the surpluses of their plots, while a small elite of no more than 5 percent of the population shared responsibility for assuring that the work was carried out. The other 75 percent tried to eke out a living between the lowest levels of society and the elite, performing odd jobs such as those listed by our Ramesside scribe above. Most of the population could only hope to avoid joining the unluckiest souls at the base of society, from which there was no escape.

Record-Keeping

We may, therefore, be able to restrain any excessive sympathy we might feel for a poor administrator controlling the work of some 40 people. He had it pretty good himself.

And we should be able to understand just why there are over 90,000 texts preserved from the Ur III period. The institutions had to contend with the inducements to corruption, and requiring written records was one way of restraining corruption. All across the Near East, each administrator's accounts required considerable scrutiny. Even the transport of the records was scrutinized, and itself recorded (Veldhuis 2001: 90).

Land, Labor, Technology, Administration, and Markets

Much of our modern understanding of development in antiquity has been strongly influenced by interpretations of modern Western economic history, emphasizing "private property" and "technological innovation," assuming that these are universal principles of economic development. As far as we can tell, "private property" played a very different role in early antiquity and "technological innovation" played practically no role in economic change, since there was virtually no change in the technological means of production between the Chalcolithic and the Industrial Revolution (4000 BCE to 1750 CE). It is, therefore, extremely significant that economic change did take place, and we can best grasp this in terms of the market.

Production was based on labor, but the relationship between production and economics differed from that commonly assumed in our own day because of the comparatively low value of labor and the overwhelmingly agricultural character of the economies. Given the economic constraints on production, technological innovation played a very different role in antiquity. One was the familiar development of new techniques and new sources related to raw materials, quarrying and working lapis lazuli or smelting copper, for example. The other form of technological innovation was the work of the palaces and temples where philosophers studied the cosmos. Once conceived, this philosophical speculation was transformed into major public works, which likewise required labor. This had an enormous economic impact. On the one hand, worship of the gods required temples, which absorbed labor. On the other, these temples then became economic centers in their own right.

The discussion of labor in antiquity is restricted by the source material. Production that came within the purview of the officials had a greater chance of preservation in the record than other activity. But this bias should not mislead students about the overwhelming role of the market in spurring production and dictating palace investments. The wealth of the centers of the ancient world lay in their capacity to purchase the exports of the periphery. This was acquired through the sale of agricultural products for silver, and also through the transformation of an agricultural surplus into textiles which were sold for profit.

The fundamental transformation which changed the economies of the Neolithic into those of the Bronze Age was the creation of the state. The first written texts reveal that the states exploited labor. This was done in several different ways, through (a) the direct control of labor, (b) taxation, and (c) the gradual acquisition of land. As the institutions purchased more land, the former owners were reduced to poverty or debt, forcing them onto the labor market, or transforming their former tax payments into rent. As the institutions secured more grain income, this further eroded the value of labor and land.

In the Old Akkadian period, the value of 300 *qú* (250 liters) of grain was 1 shekel (8 gr.) of silver; by the end of the Old Babylonian period this had fallen to 150 *qû* (125 liters) (Zaccagnini 1997: 367). During this time, the standard wage in Meso-potamia remained at about 3,000 liters annually; wage-rates in silver rose, but remained steady in terms of barley (Farber 1978: 33–8). Some earned less, and some more, but similar rates also prevailed in Egypt by the end of the second millennium, with the family of a well-off workman receiving about 5,000 liters a year, more than enough for a nuclear family (Janssen 1975: 460–71).

The adjustments in the value of silver and grain meant that the value of labor stabilized at a higher value – in terms of silver – over the course of the second millennium. Institutional income was measured in grain, and wages remained steady in grain. The increase in the silver value of the wage-rate by the end of the Old Babylonian period does not reflect an increase in the standard of living, but rather an increase in the economic power of the institutions, expressed in market terms. Even where the institutional control of labor was loose, and the value of labor subject to increases in terms of silver, the value of the product of labor remained largely an institutional prerogative.

Barley had not acquired a universal convertible value by the Ur III period (Veldhuis 2001: 100). Only after barley prices rose in terms of silver – in the middle of the second millennium – did a universal system allow direct conversions between silver, copper, oil, labor, and barley, by simple mathematical equivalencies. Before that period, the value of labor performed a role in transforming value which was not measured in either grain or silver. Once the mid-second millennium BCE system was established, the value of a week's labor would remain the same in terms of grain for the next 2,000 years (Warburton 2003: 293–5). Although the market evened out the issue of value, the fundamental social and economic structures did not change.

Unable to participate in the exchange economy, an agricultural laborer could only toil without hope or flee, as is frequently documented from the beginning of the second millennium BCE. This led to an increase in urban employment with manual laborers and specialized craftsmen (Hayes 1972). Given their grain income, the institutions employed these urban craftsmen as well, either as independent entrepreneurs or as institutional dependents. During the fourth and third millennia, the direct control of labor was the chosen means, as evidenced by the earliest records through the archives of Ur III (Englund 1991, 1998). By the Persian period, awards of land plots allowed entrepreneurs to manage land for the aristocracy, and thus the entrepreneurs were responsible for arranging the labor (Stolper 1985).

The second millennium documentation includes economic refugees (Hayes 1972), and notes about the difficulties of finding labor at harvest season (Birot 1993: 11–13). Lack of labor was a typical second millennium problem, reflecting the role and means by which the institutions exploited labor. During the fourth and third millennia, the states controlled labor due to a lack of alternatives. The territories beyond the state were chaotic and unenticing to fugitives from the urban and rural economy of the states. The role of the institutions and the private economies changed, and the world of the second millennium transformed, becoming increasingly commercial. During the third millennium, craftsmen may have been closely linked to the institutions. In the second, craftsmen were free to sell their labor, but as private entrepreneurs, independent of the palace, and so they became suspect to its administrators.

The laws of Hammurabi (paragraphs 253–8; 274) specify the remuneration of artisans and casual labor in terms of grain or silver and time, but not the value of the products of labor, which were subject to the vagaries of the market (paragraphs 66, 104), particularly grain where the law specifies "as agreed" (paragraph 59) rather than a specified amount.

The importance of prices in determining agricultural behavior can only be understood in terms of the market. By the mid-second millennium BCE, labor, land, and grain had prices defined in terms of silver. This meant that any other commodity could be valued in the same fashion, anywhere from the Aegean to the Indus. During the Ur III period, barley could not be converted into oil (Veldhuis 2001: 100). The same applies to labor, where rations could be linked to individuals, but the value of the labor in silver was not linked to its cost in barley. Second millennium conversions linked wages, rations, and costs. However, even by the end of the first millennium BCE, linking the value of the harvest to the cost inputs, including labor, was impossible.

The costs remained constant, but the value of the harvest depended upon the price of grain, regardless of the costs. Increased labor would lead to a bountiful harvest and a plunge in the price of grain. Initially, state taxes in grain mopped up the surplus. However, from the early second millennium – at the latest – the state sold this surplus on the market (Stol 1982; Charpin 1987). The utility value of grain lay in its nutritional value; its monetary value depended upon the supply of grain in the market, but also that of silver, since grain was valued in silver.

During the third millennium the importance of the institutions and the aristocracy reflected the concentration of wealth and the lack of alternative forms of employment. The giant stone pyramids of third millennium Egypt did give way to the diminutive mud-brick pyramids of the early second millennium. The relative decline in the royal pyramids was already visible in the growth of the size of the tombs of the officials in third millennium Egypt, as individual members of the elite participated. Many tombs of Old Kingdom Egypt were built at the expense of tomb-owners who compensated workmen for their labor (Müller-Wollermann 1985: 142–4). The growth of private demand thus antedated the collapse of centralized political power, and the earlier concentration reflected not only the power of the courts, but also the poverty of alternative sources of employment.

Until the Ur III period, labor was the single most important source of value. The silver to grain value of labor diminished the value of silver and increased that of grain, and the link between grain and labor remained, with everyone conscious of the conversion rates, and the value of metals. The documentation of the palace at Mari reveals the strained relationship among the rulers and the craftsmen about grain, metals, and labor at the beginning of the second millennium (Durand 1997: 1: 221–317). Šamši-Adad and Zimri-Lim were both concerned about accounting for silver and gold, and expected the craftsmen and the officials to use the specified quantities of metal. The very same administrators could find themselves worrying about silver and grain, and arguing with craftsmen and rulers (Rouault 1977). While it is highly probable that a great deal of pilferage nevertheless took place, all this arguing kept everyone busy. The contrast between the millennia in the documentation clearly reflects a growing market and increased opportunities during the second millennium.

Movement of Goods and People

There were effectively four different systems organizing the output of work in antiquity. (1) "Free market" production lay beyond the control of political actors in the core regions; prices dictated the production and acquisition of silver, copper, and tin. Within the regions controlled by the institutions three systems prevailed. One (2) involved the collection of levies on those who produced various goods from grain to pots. This system of taxation or "rent" was based on the provider voluntarily relinquishing part of the yield of harvests of fish or grain from normal activity, without a corresponding payment made in return. Another (3) involved state control of labor, with the workers controlled by remuneration or coercion as in grain rations for textile workers. In return for subsistence support, the state appropriated the products of the labor. Another (4) system involved the sale of articles acquired through taxation or the use of corvée labor. This system formed part of the local market whereby the institutions and members of the elite could purchase articles from the population of their own community.

The international market determined the flow of silver into Mesopotamia, Syria, and Egypt, and silver determined value. Those employed by the institutions were only a small part of the population, and while participating in the markets, the institutions were responding to the markets. The result was that ultimately the markets determined all economic activity. Price differentials and political coercion were thus the alternative means of encouraging people to abstain from leisure. Direct coercion was impossible beyond the range of one's political authority. However, as major social units, the institutions were able to influence behavior beyond their realm of immediate political control by taking advantage of price competition, and also by influencing production within their realm of control through political measures.

Those who were under the control of the institutions could be shipped around the world. Egyptian physicians would be sent to the Hittites, or Syrian builders sent from one city to the next. Rationed laborers could remain in the same region, but be assigned very different tasks from day to day (Englund 1991). Even specialists – carpenters and weavers – could be assigned agricultural tasks when the need arose (Zaccagnini 1983b).

Individual specialists moved from region to region in search of work. The case of a Greek bronze sculptor who worked in Yemen during the Roman era is but one example of a widespread phenomenon which can be pursued back to the dawn of history (Weidemann 1983: 18). The craftsman who made the Jebel Arak knife handle in fourth millennium Egypt skillfully combined exotic Elamite art with an Egyptian form, revealing the mobility of specialized labor.[1] These individual independent craftsmen moved beyond the borders of their own political systems in search of work or rather gain. They thus reflected the trend opposed to that of the workers who converged at the royal cities of the Persian Empire, or those sent by their ruling institutions to serve at foreign courts.

There were also those who remained in place and served a market niche, such as lapis lazuli workers at Shahr-i Sokhta in Iran, or amulet-makers at Thebes in Egypt. The former were stay-at-homes who served the international market for lapis lazuli. The latter were stay-at-homes who served the local market. The workers at Shahr-i Sokhta relied upon the close proximity of the material and the scale of the market across the Near East. The lapis lazuli came from the mines to the craftsmen, who prepared it for re-export (Casanova in press). The workers at Thebes relied upon the local passion for funerary and prestige goods. They acquired the materials through trade and resold them. In both cases, the customers were from the elites, and thus a member of the Egyptian elite could purchase an article of lapis lazuli which had been imported from Central Asia and then transformed into an Egyptian article (a scarab, a beetle-shaped amulet) by local craftsmen.

Quite aside from market niches, there were distinct differences between Egypt and its neighbors in the Middle East. As a major territorial nation state, legal guarantees and commercial activity in Egypt differed substantially from city-states such as Ugarit, but also even from empires in Babylonia. Whereas the Egyptian state took income in grain, and remunerated its servants in grain (Warburton 2000: 68–89), the palace at Ugarit even paid its agricultural employees in silver (Heltzer 1982: 39).

In the core areas of Egypt and Mesopotamia virtually every member of society was incorporated into the system and supervised. Šamši-Adad of Assyria was obliged to assure that his son, a viceroy, understood how, when, and from whom to expect grain, silver, oil, and wine (Durand 1997: 1: 122–4), while he himself led his armies. Zimri-Lim of Mari held his own officials responsible if the harvest failed and people starved (Birot 1993: 75). Kings supervised the distribution of metals and the plucking of sheep. Much of the "working life" of early antiquity can be reconstructed from the documents. Most of this reflected the view of the official world, but allowed a glimpse at the social organization of labor.

Rural Life

In the agricultural world of the Ancient Near East, grain was available to everyone, if only because those without access starved to death. The means of acquiring the grain differed from case to case, for institutions and individuals. The peasants would deliver it to landowners as taxes or rent, or as part of an employment arrangement. The peasants would generally keep part of their harvest, if free laborers, but might never touch any of it if they were rationed dependents or slaves.

The institutions merely had to assure that the people had sickles to harvest grain, millstones to grind it, and facilities to store it. Mercifully, Mesopotamia had enough clay for the necessary storage buildings and vessels, but virtually everything else had to be imported – including probably even much of the wood for building the ships to move the stuff around. Some of the grain could be produced locally, but the copper for the sickles and stones for the grinders had to be imported. This placed Mesopotamia in the unenviable position of concentrating on the production of manufactures and agricultural products for export, to acquire the silver to pay for the imports. The economy was thus oriented heavily towards trade and production for export.

Markets assured that imbalances were eliminated, at the cost of the poor, and to the benefit of the institutions. The international markets assured the delivery of imports, and the local markets determined the distribution of grain. The institutions would sell the grain to acquire silver. A good harvest would drive down the cost of grain, and thus punish overproduction. A bad harvest would drive the price up, and thus offer the institutions a stranglehold. Locusts and bad harvests could ruin one region, impoverishing the residents. The institutions with access to reserves or other regions could thus corner the market. One official from Mari was assigned to a district which suffered from bad harvests, locusts, and crickets in succession (Birot 1993: 73–87). The poor official was held responsible, but the palace could view such catastrophes with equanimity; at one point, a neighboring king offered to send five million liters of grain to another. The offer was proudly declined (Durand 2000: 3: 18). The institutions could cope with grain shortages. This flexibility – due to enormous reserves acquired through taxes and rents – gave them decisive leverage.

Wood-Gathering

The work of the foresters in the forests of the Levant, the east coast of the Mediterranean, has gone largely unrecorded, as has that of most of the wood-gatherers elsewhere in the Ancient Near East who must have provided important lumber for the cities and fuel for the furnaces and kilns. Steinkeller notes that the Ur III period marked a time of the systematic exploitation of resources (1987b: 101); yet, in reality, the system of quotas represented the systematic exploitation of labor. The deliveries of wood to the community of workmen at Deir el-Medina in New Kingdom Egypt were also recorded, but it is unclear if the entire "forest sector" was organized.

The Umma foresters were usually members of the same nuclear family organized into working groups by forest. They were classified according to the rations they received. They were required to work for several months during a period from the sixth month through the thirteenth month. This matches the period between sowing and harvesting, and also the best time for gathering grass and wild plants. However, since the "foresters" were also soldiers, they were free to campaign during the summer and gather wood during the winter, and thus it is more probable that this determined their annual schedule than the weather or the agricultural cycle. Tamarisk, willow, and poplar grew along the banks of the Euphrates, among reeds and grasses. The foresters not only delivered logs and beams, but also levers, pegs, stakes, plow shares, and other prepared forms of wood. The deliveries were made directly to the authorities of the state.

During this period, the foresters were provided barley and wool. Their 60-liter-a-month rations were thus for subsistence and supplemented their other income as beneficiaries of land grants. They also owned sheep and cattle. The supervisors may also have acquired income through the sale of grasses.

Possibly in a similar way, fishermen in Egypt were obliged to pay an in-kind tax on their revenues, resulting in the state receiving tons of fish, some of which was passed on to state dependents. Some fishermen were employed by the state in Mesopotamia; their produce delivered to the state authorities was sold on the market.

Transportation

The movement of articles around the world was an important part of labor. A large part of this was entrepreneurial. Institutional authorities could sell articles to entrepreneurs who would transport them and sell them in turn. Merchants could be entrusted by the state to convey state products to an assigned destination on donkey-back. Institutions could also rent boats and pay sailors to move state products. Vessels belonging to the institutions and the elites could also employ entrepreneurs to trade in grain, textiles, and honey.

Crafts

It was noted above that the institutional economies were obliged to produce piles of documentation. The private firms operated under very different circumstances. The family was encouraged to maintain its resources, and thus the records would have a practical value. At the same time, they sought to avoid the attention of rapacious authorities with an incentive to tax, coerce, and otherwise despoil them. Some of these private activities were visible in the documents, when palaces made purchases or arranged contracts. In other cases, the activity was visible in the archaeological record. In the core areas of the Ancient Near East, many of the craftsmen were employed by the state or institutions. Some of these were free craftsmen who sold their labor, or the products of their labor. In Egypt, potters were obliged to deliver part of their production to the state as an obligatory payment (Warburton 1997: 237–60).

Institutional craftsmen were given raw materials and specific instructions to manufacture a given product (Sallaberger and Westenholz 1999: 277). The records preserved the entire sequence of the operation. Ivory from India was imported by state organs, from markets in the Persian Gulf (Leemans 1960: 25–6). The palace at Mari purchased lapis lazuli when available on the open market in Syria (Durand 2000: 3: 15–18). The raw materials were acquired by purchase at near and distant markets by merchants responsible for palace acquisitions. These were weighed in the palace and then delivered to the craftsmen with instructions (Sallaberger and Westenholz 1999: 282–3). At the palace at Mari, the craftsmen would be issued materials for fashioning, for example, a chariot (Limet 1986: 21). Pieces of furniture and other articles would be produced in the same fashion, with a record of the item, and the official responsible (Limet 1986: 37, 54). In other cases, the material would be specified in bulk, and the desired products enumerated as issued to a particular specialist; 1.5 kg of ivory was transferred to an ivory cutter who transformed the raw material into figurines (Sallaberger and Westenholz 1999: 277–8). The finished products were collected and weighed and the workers compensated with rations. In many cases, the finished products were designated in advance as intended for use in temples or palaces, or as diplomatic gifts.

The artisan was merely compensated for the labor and the actual value of the raw materials; the value of finished products was resolved by the authorities. Lack of access to raw materials limited the freedom of the craftsmen, and thus their choice of both clients and employment. Again, the institutional wealth enabled the acquisition of precious materials and provided leverage.

Deir el-Medina

The activities of the craft workers in the community at Deir el-Medina in Egypt are among the best documented in the ancient world (Janssen 1975; Valbelle 1985). Not only are wage lists preserved, but so are the tombs they were paid to excavate and decorate, as well as the inherited state housing in which they lived. The documentation is abundant for the Ramesside period at the end of the Bronze Age. Various institutions were responsible for providing their income, with regular wages of almost 5,000 liters or 142 bushels of grain annually supplemented with cakes, firewood, dried fish, pottery, and other oddities (Janssen 1975: 455–93). During an economic downturn at the end of the reign of Ramesses III, the workers even went on strike.

Otherwise, they worked regular hours. They crossed the ridge over to the Valley of the Kings to work. The masons cut the tomb out of the rock and the draftsmen decorated the walls. The state provided and kept track of tools. Although their duties may have been onerous while excavating and decorating a royal tomb during a short reign, many found time to excavate, decorate, and equip their own tombs as well. They used leisure to manufacture funerary goods for the upper classes, and they sold the goods to supplement their state income. Like everyone in the Bronze Age, they were expected to account for their official time. The record-keeping was precise (Janssen 1980). Illness was a major excuse for absence from work, but workmen could get a day off for a daughter's birthday, or because their wives were having their periods. "Carrying stones for the scribe" is among the explanations for absence from work recorded at Deir el-Medina, and it might have been harsh duty in comparison with celebrating a birthday at home, but these workers were hardly the worst off in the Ancient Near East.

NOTE

1 The exact case is problematic. Boehmer (1991) believes the craftsman was an Elamite in Egypt; Pittmann (1996) assumes an Egyptian in Egypt familiar with Elamite forms. The current writer prefers the concept of a West Asian in Egypt, but would argue that were an

Egyptian capable of such close conformity to Elamite forms, he would have to have been familiar with Elamite craftsmen, demonstrating the mobility of craftsmen in any case.

FURTHER READING

Englund 1991 is enlightening on details. For surveys of practices, see Powell 1987, Postgate 1992, Snell 1997, Snell 2001, and the articles on economy in Sasson 1995. For Egyptian views see Valbelle 1985, Warburton 1997. This chapter has emphasized the basic features of activity, without distinguishing between "slaves" and "free" since "slaves" were effectively to be found in virtually all of the occupations, working alongside and occasionally employing the free (Dandamaev 1984).

CHAPTER THIRTEEN

Law and Practice

Bruce Wells

The societies of the Ancient Near East provide us with the oldest written legal records in the world. When considering these societies from a legal point of view, scholars find that a number of questions arise. How can one gain access to their law and discover what it was? What did these societies view as their sources of legal authority? In describing the practice of law in the Ancient Near East, what types of issues must we consider? What is the relationship between this – the oldest law known to us – and other legal systems, both in antiquity and in more modern times? Although this essay cannot cover all issues related to these matters, these are the basic questions that it seeks to address.

The essay will focus on three general areas. The first has to do with the quest to discover Ancient Near Eastern law. How does one go about this task and what are the key questions to be faced? The second looks at particular issues that arise in any attempt to describe the law that was actually practiced in Ancient Near Eastern societies. Finally, in the third section, the essay considers a few of the connections between Ancient Near Eastern law and the later systems of early Greek and Roman law. It should be noted that this essay restricts itself to what might be called societal law and does not delve into issues related to ritual or strictly religious law.

Looking for Law in the Ancient Near East

Efforts to identify the law that was in effect in Ancient Near Eastern societies must invariably come to grips with the issue of sources. This is a two-pronged problem that requires a distinction in how the term source is used. First, the term can be used with a view to the past to refer to those items that functioned as sources of law for the societies of the Ancient Near East. That is, it can refer to the entities that contained the law, just as constitutions and legislative statutes do for many modern societies today. Second, the term can refer to those items that have been preserved from the Ancient Near East and that are, in the present, sources for historians in their effort to discover Ancient Near Eastern law. Regrettably, we have limited access to the former type of source. At times it is apparent that certain royal decrees contained authorita-tive law, but for the majority of the rules that seem to have governed these societies, there is virtually no mention in the surviving documents regarding their source. Many scholars believe it was simply custom that functioned as the principal source of law for the inhabitants of the Ancient Near East.

First, the possible sources at the disposal of modern scholarship for doing legal-historical study of the Ancient Near East must be considered. The items that could potentially serve as sources for the legal historian are vast – so much so, in fact, that the research to date has yet to encompass them all, much less to analyze them sufficiently and synthesize their data. There are tens of thousands of extant docu-ments (mostly clay tablets from Mesopotamia with cuneiform inscriptions) from the Ancient Near East that could be characterized as legal. The difficulty comes in deciding which material yields clear insight into the law of Ancient Near Eastern societies and which only appears to do so. Some material offers evidence that could easily lead to a distorted picture of Ancient Near Eastern law. It is problematic to accept the provisions of contracts, the stipulations of law codes, or even the verdicts of trial courts at face value and to assume they are untarnished sources for the historian.

Law Codes

This can best be demonstrated with an issue that has received a great deal of scholarly attention, namely, the nature of the so-called law codes or, more accurately, law collections. Nine such documents have survived – seven in the form of cuneiform on clay and two from the Hebrew Bible. They are: the Laws of Ur-Namma (LU), the Laws of Lipit-Ishtar (LL), the Laws of Eshnunna (LE), the Laws of Hammurabi (LH), the Hittite Laws (HL), the Middle Assyrian Laws (MAL), the Neo-Babylonian Laws (NBL), the Covenant Code in Exodus 21–3, and the Deuteronomic Code in Deuteronomy 12–6.[1] These codes or collections have been the primary focus of much of the legal-historical study of the Ancient Near East.

The most famous of these is LH, and its suitability as a source for studying Ancient Near Eastern law has been under scrutiny for some time (Kraus 1960; Westbrook 1985; Bottéro 1992a; Fitzpatrick-McKinley 1999; Roth 2000). It contains approxi-mately 280 law-like stipulations. A cursory glance at the code's epilogue would seem to show that these stipulations formed the law of the land. There, King Hammurabi of Babylon states:

> In order that the mighty not wrong the weak, to provide just ways for the waif and the widow, I have inscribed my precious pronouncements upon my stela . . . Let any wronged man who has a lawsuit come before the statute of me, the king of justice, and let him have my inscribed stela read aloud to him, thus may he hear my precious pronounce-ments and let my stela reveal the lawsuit for him . . . May any king who will appear in the land in the future, at any time, observe the pronouncements of justice that I inscribed upon my stela. May he not alter the judgments that I rendered and the verdicts that I gave . . . (Roth 1997: 134)

A close analysis of the actual stipulations in the code reveals, however, that the code, in and of itself, would not have made for very effective law. First, the collection of rules in the code is far from comprehensive, omitting a number of important issues, including murder.[2] Second, many of the provisions in LH assume a certain amount of legal savvy on the part of the reader. This suggests that there was a substantial body of law apart from LH, and the authors of LH believed their readers would have knowledge of it. Third, quite a few of the laws treat situations that were unlikely to occur; they appear to be essentially hypothetical.[3] In addition to all of this, it is not at all clear that LH was treated as law by the ancient Babylonians themselves. Perhaps the most telling sign is that LH was never cited in any of the hundreds of trial records stemming from the same general time as LH as the legal basis for a trial court's verdict. Other documents of practice – legal texts such as contracts and letters – also omit mention of the code (for two possible but uncertain references to LH, see Roth 2000: 22–9). This is in contrast to the frequent reference in such documents to royal decrees and edicts, about which more will be said below.

The purpose of Hammurabi's publication of these laws, then, must have been for some other reason than to enact legal statutes for the governing of his land. After much study of the collection, along with its prologue and epilogue, most scholars now agree that the code was created to justify and legitimize Hammurabi's reign. Simply put, LH is political propaganda. Its target audience was the gods and the ruling elite, and its provisions were meant to show the wisdom, fairness, and equity of the king. The prologue to LH virtually says as much. Hammurabi himself probably had little to do with composing the individual provisions in LH and most likely assigned the task to a group of his officials and scribes.

The other law collections are subject to the same basic critique. Based on their own prologues, LU and LL also appear to be propagandistic tools in the hands of their respective kings. The biblical codes are used in the service of a religious agenda. LE and NBL come to us on scribal exercise tablets. They may well have been copied from larger monumental inscriptions and, thus, may be interpreted in the same manner as LH, though it is conceivable that they were really nothing more than scribal exercises. Both HL and MAL come from royal archives and may have had some applicability within the confines of the palace personnel, but there is no indication that either was intended as binding legislation. Thus, it is likely that the primary purpose of each of the codes had little or nothing to do with establishing societal law. To be sure, they yield important insights into the various Ancient Near Eastern societies from which they come – insights into royal ideology, politics, scribal training, and religion. But do they tell us anything about law?

This question is still one of sources, but it takes us one level deeper. We must now ask what were the sources for the provisions in these law collections. This is where scholarship diverges and disagreements are keen. The starting point is usually the idea that the codes are the product of the same pseudo-scientific efforts that gave us other collections or lists: god lists, astronomical lists, omen lists, mathematical lists, and medical lists (Bottéro 1992a). All of these lists appear to be products of scribal schools; thus, it seems reasonable to conclude that the law codes – or law lists – are as well. But whence did the scribes obtain the individual stipulations contained in the codes? Did they simply make them up? For some of the provisions, particularly the ones that seem more hypothetical, this may in fact be what happened. Some have argued, though, that virtually all of the provisions in the law codes derive entirely from scribal intellectual activity and constitute scribal wisdom or, as one scholar dubs it, scribal advice (Fitzpatrick-McKinley 1999). According to this view, there is very little connection, if any, between the provisions in the codes and the law that was in effect in Ancient Near Eastern societies. Conversely, other scholars believe that the codes are an excellent source for the historian to learn about Ancient Near Eastern law (Westbrook 1989; Greengus 1995). They argue that the scribes drew heavily upon the law that was being practiced in their societies as they formed the codes or law lists. From this perspective, then, the stipulations of the codes are descriptive, rather than prescriptive, and they are an important point of access into the law of that time.

There is data to support both points of view. Several studies have highlighted points of correspondence between contemporary practice and certain provisions in the law collections (Petschow 1984; Ries 1984; Oelsner 1997). It is true that documents demonstrating such correspondence are not abundant, but they do raise the possibility that the codes contain descriptions of operative law. On the other hand, there are studies that have shown that some provisions in the codes were not followed in practice – that there are, in fact, contradictions between what was done in real life and what was called for by the codes (Jackson 1973: 10; Fried 2001: 74–5). There is not, however, an abundance of this material either. Ultimately, it seems that the law collections represent the practiced law of their societies accurately to some degree and inaccurately to some degree. But in either case, we do not know to what degree. Further research may help to clarify the situation.

Documents of Practice

Documents that chronicle legal transactions are often one of the most fruitful sources for legal historians of the Ancient Near East. These are texts that record property sales, marriage agreements, wills, loan arrangements, rental contracts, trial records, letters, and the like. Reading these documents uncritically, however, can also run the risk of a distorted view of Ancient Near Eastern law. Such documents do not carry legislative force; rather, they operate within the bounds of existing law. As Westbrook states, "A contract is not direct evidence of legal norms, but of the reactions of the parties to those norms ... The norms of positive law remain a shadowy presence behind the terms of the individual transaction, still to be reconstructed by the historian" (2003: section 1.1.2.6).

Let us take marriage agreements as an example. Several records of marriage agreements from the Old Babylonian period state what should be done to the wife if she divorces, or attempts to divorce, her husband. They specify rather severe punishments. The following text, *BAP* 90 (Meissner 1893), is typical:

> Rimum, the son of Shamhatum, married Bashtum, the daughter of Belisunu, the priestess of Šamaš and the daughter of Usi-bitum. Belisunu has received [?] shekels of

silver as the bride-price of Bashtum. Her heart is satisfied. If Bashtum says to Rimum her husband, "You are not my husband," Bashtum will be thrown into the river (to drown). If Rimum says to Bashtum his wife, "You are not my wife," he will give her 10 shekels of silver as her divorce payment.

Documents like this one might lead to the conclusion that wives were forbidden by law to divorce their husbands during this period. After all, if the woman who was part of this marriage tried to divorce her husband, she would have suffered the ultimate punishment, death. But, because contracts do not constitute statutory law, this conclusion is unwarranted. The very fact that divorce by the wife was treated as it was in this document points to the opposite conclusion: that divorce by a wife was legal. The woman above was not prevented from divorcing her husband by law but by contract. If divorce by a wife were already treated in this manner by societal law, the contract would have been silent on the issue. Contractual stipulations, therefore, should not automatically be equated with law.

Trial records are another important source of law for the legal historian, but they, too, must be handled with care. Owing to the fact that extenuating circumstances often influenced court decisions, not every verdict in a trial can be assumed to reflect precisely the law governing the issue at trial. To compound the situation, large numbers of extant trial records contain no verdict, leaving scholars at a loss to know how the ancient courts ruled on many of the matters brought before them.

Even when it comes to trial law and procedure, trial records can be perplexing. The one site from which more trial records come than any other is that of ancient Nuzi in central Iraq. In a number of instances at Nuzi, one of the parties at trial brought one or more supporting witnesses, and it was the testimony of those witnesses that won the case for that party. Some important details, however, were not made clear. To begin with, there are no recorded cases in which both parties brought witnesses to court (Liebesny 1941: 132–3). It seems hardly possible that this situation never occurred, but we simply do not know how judges acted when confronted by witnesses from both sides. In other trials, a party brought witnesses, the witnesses testified in favor of that party, but the judges were not satisfied. Instead they required that one of the parties or their witnesses go through a particular ritual, the lifting up of the gods (Frymer-Kensky 1981). It was by means of this ritual that the winner was determined. The document *JEN* 347 (Chiera 1934) provides an example:

Tehiptilla entered into a dispute, concerning a stolen sheep, with Arsimika before the judges. The witnesses of Tehiptilla gave testimony before the judges that Arsimika was in the process of stealing the sheep of Tehiptilla from the midst of the [pen?], and the witnesses caught him in the act. The judges spoke to Arsimika and said, "Lift up the gods before the witnesses." Arsimika lifted the gods before the witnesses. Tehiptilla won the case. And the judges imposed upon Arsimika a fine of 12 sheep to be paid to Tehiptilla.

It is not clear why the judges at Nuzi would issue an immediate verdict after hearing the testimony of some witnesses and why they would call for the lifting-of-the-gods ritual in other instances when they have heard witness testimony. Trial records are often drafted tersely, and the procedural law they reveal is sometimes rather obscure.

Royal Edicts

Documents known as royal edicts or decrees are another important source for law in the Ancient Near East. Into this category fall extant documents recording decisions made by kings in several Ancient Near Eastern societies, including the Hittite kingdom and Egypt. They seem to have been occasional, ad hoc rulings covering a variety of matters including administrative instructions, the fixing of prices and tariffs, and the release of debts. Such decrees were frequently referred to in documents of practice, but the actual text of only a few decrees is preserved. One of the most well preserved is the Edict of Ammisaduqa, a king from the Old Babylonian period. It is one of the so-called debt-release decrees.

The purpose of a debt-release decree was essentially the same as a modern-day economic stimulus package. The economies of ancient city-states and small kingdoms often fell on hard times. This could be due to war or drought or any number of factors. Signs of a serious economic downturn usually included large numbers of people who were so deeply in debt that they were losing property and selling their family members or even themselves into slavery to stave off starvation. Debt-release decrees would be enacted in order to rejuvenate the economy and give people a fresh start. Many debts owed to the government and private citizens would be canceled, and property or persons that had served as collateral and had gone into the possession of creditors were allowed to return to their original owners and families. It was traditional for rulers who issued these decrees to characterize themselves as establishing justice throughout their lands and doing great favors for the economically disadvantaged. The following excerpt from the Edict of Ammisaduqa outlines that decree's overall intent:

> Whoever has given barley or silver to an Akkadian or an Amorite either [as a loan at in]terest or as a demand-loan [. . .] and has had a (legal) document drawn up (about it) – because the king has established equity for the land, his tablet will be voided; he may not collect barley or silver according to the wording of the tablet. (Hallo and Younger 2000: 362)

These decrees sound like legislation. The chief difference, however, is that Ancient Near Eastern debt-release decrees sought to regulate actions that had taken place in the past, while modern legislation typically seeks to regulate future behavior. Moreover, the decrees pertained only to a specific period, canceling debts and other obligations that had taken effect during that time. Scholars generally assume that the provisions of the decree functioned as binding law but that they applied to very specific situations and were only temporary.

Gaps in the Law

Law codes, records of trials and legal transactions, royal edicts, as well as other types of documents such as lexical lists and letters, provide the legal historian of the Ancient

Near East with an untold wealth of data. These sources require careful treatment, since they reflect Ancient Near Eastern law imperfectly, each in their own way. For the historian studying one particular society within the Ancient Near East another type of problem arises. The sources that relate specifically to one society fail to provide a complete picture. Inevitably, there will be significant gaps in the reconstruction of that society's law. In light of this, is it methodologically legitimate to look to the data from other Ancient Near Eastern societies in order to fill in those gaps?

This question speaks to the issue of continuity versus discontinuity. Some have argued that the societies of the Ancient Near East operated on a shared set of legal customs and procedures, that is, there was a great deal of continuity from one legal system to another (Westbrook 1985). There certainly were differences in the details. Nevertheless, the commonalities were so great that one may speak of a common legal culture that spanned the Ancient Near East chronologically and geographically. According to this view, it is legitimate, even desirable at times, to look to one society to fill in the gaps in the law of another.

There are also strong advocates for a view of discontinuity, though they often differ on how to understand the nature of the discontinuity and will allow for varying degrees of continuity (Finkelstein 1981: 17–20; a number of the essays in Levinson 1994 that respond directly to the work of Westbrook; Yaron 2000). Some Ancient Near Eastern societies were separated from each other by a great swath of distance, time, and language. Why should the law of one be presumed to reflect the law of another? Furthermore, it is difficult for the proponents of discontinuity to conceive how a common legal culture would have spread across the Ancient Near East. It may be understandable that certain legal traditions were spread by the scribal schools that were prevalent in Mesopotamia. But would this transmission of legal customs and concepts have made its way into western Syria and Palestine?

Both points of view – continuity and discontinuity – face difficult questions. The continuity school has no clear evidence to show the dissemination of law from one culture to another. It draws inferences from the legal commonalities among various Ancient Near Eastern societies, but it lacks a clear mechanism for explaining how those commonalities came to be. It is these very shared features, however, that pose a problem for the discontinuity school. Is their existence due simply to coincidence or to the characteristics that agrarian societies from that region of the world should be expected to share? A number of studies have drawn attention to points of connection between the legal systems of different Ancient Near Eastern societies, far removed from each other in terms of both time and space. This phenomenon deserves an explanation, but a truly satisfying one remains elusive.

Tradition and Custom

To return to the first part of the source question, it would appear that we can be no more precise, as of yet, than to say that tradition and custom were indeed the sources of the rules that possessed legal authority for Ancient Near Eastern societies. Certainly, there is no Ancient Near Eastern society for which it can be said that a particular document or collection of documents contained that society's law. Bits and pieces, or even large portions, of that society's law may appear in some texts, such as the law collections, but those texts themselves were not the repositories of the law, merely the reflections of it. Instead, the repositories were most likely bodies of knowledge that were transmitted orally from one generation to another. When the first legal records appeared in the mid-third millennium, much of this knowledge seems already to have been in place and to have had the authority of law. Moreover, many of the legal tenets that were in force early on remained unchanged for much of Ancient Near Eastern history. Practices that were in use in the third millennium regularly reappear throughout the second and even well into the first. Many components of the societies and cultures of the Ancient Near East changed very slowly over the course of time, and law appears to have been one of the most conservative.

Describing the Law of the Ancient Near East

Despite the problematic nature of many of the historian's sources, scholarship has been able to ascertain many components of the legal rules that governed Ancient Near Eastern societies (Westbrook 2003). Detailed studies have been done on a range of topics, including contract law (Greengus 1969), litigation (Falkenstein 1956–7; Dombradi 1996), marriage law (Roth 1989), and lending practices (Westbrook and Jasnow 2001). Any attempt to describe the law that was actually practiced, however, faces issues that stem from the nature of the Ancient Near Eastern societies themselves. Here we shall highlight three of those issues. The first has to do with the concept of status and the function of slavery. The second issue comes from the role that gender played within Ancient Near Eastern societies and how it affected the issue of inheritance. The third relates to the modern distinction between civil and criminal law – a distinction that appears to be missing in Ancient Near Eastern legal systems.

Status and slavery

An important distinguishing factor that Ancient Near Eastern law used in its treatment of individuals had to do with status. The most basic distinction lay between freedom and slavery. If a person was a free citizen, one set of rules applied; if a slave, then another set took effect. Other types of status were also important. If a person was a pledge who had been set aside as security for a debt, yet another set of rules often applied. Adult children still living with their parents were frequently treated as having their own particular status.

The status of slavery presents further complications. As far as can be determined, there were three basic types of slaves in the Ancient Near East: the chattel-slave, the debt-slave, and the famine-slave (Westbrook 1995). A chattel-slave was owned virtually in the same manner as any other piece of property; certain rules, however, regulated owners' actions (for example, owners could be punished for killing a slave, Exodus 21: 20–1). People became chattel-slaves most often when captured in war or when born to a female chattel-slave.

Debt-slaves, on the other hand, were sold into slavery. It was the sale transaction that transferred them from the status of free citizen to the status of slave. This typically occurred when the due date to repay a loan arrived and the debtor was unable to pay. The latter would sell himself or herself or a family member to the creditor as a slave. As opposed to chattel-slaves, it appears that debt-slaves could not then be sold to a different owner. They were usually in the possession of their first owner (the creditor) until they could be redeemed. Redemption occurred when the debt and any necessary interest were paid. Debt-slaves could also be released at the issuance of a debt-release decree, and some legal systems placed limits on the amount of time a person could remain in debt-slavery (LH 117 three years; Exodus 21: 2–6 six years).

It was not uncommon for parents, during times of war or economic distress when there was too little to eat, to sell their children as famine-slaves so that the buyer would feed the children and the money from the sale would buy food for themselves. The text below, *Emar* 217 (Arnaud 1986) from central Syria in the 1300s BCE, is a poignant example:

> Zadamma and Ku'e, his wife, have sold their two sons and their two daughters – Baal-abia, Adad-belu, Ishma-Dagan, and Baal-ummi, a daughter at the breast – into slavery for 60 shekels of silver, the entire price, to Ba'al-malik, the diviner. If anyone sues to reclaim the four children of Zadamma, they must give ten other persons as compensation to Ba'al-malik. And now Zadamma, their father, and Ku'e, their mother, have pressed their feet into clay.

It was also possible for famine-slaves to enter slavery for no sale price whatsoever. They would put themselves into slavery simply in order to survive. While famine-slaves who were sold into slavery could usually be redeemed when the purchase money was repaid, another group of famine-slaves often had stipulations inserted into their contracts describing the conditions under which they could go free. The most common provision was that a substitute slave be provided to take the place of the famine-slave.

One of the most perplexing issues that the status of slavery raises comes from situations where a person appears to be a slave in one context and a free citizen in another. The situation of a Jewish woman in Egypt during the fifth century is a case in point. The woman, Tamet, is mentioned in several Aramaic papyri from Elephantine. In the document *TAD* B3.3 (Porten and Yardeni 1986), she marries Ananiah, who appears to be a perfectly ordinary free person. Twenty-two years later, in *TAD* B3.6 (Porten and Yardeni 1986), a man named Meshullam manumits her and her daughter from slavery. In the meantime, however, she has been playing the role of a free person, taking possession of a piece of property in *TAD* B3.5 (Porten and Yardeni 1986) and acting as a seller of property, along with her husband Ananiah, in *TAD* B3.12 (in Porten and Yardeni 1986). It seems as if Tamet, during the first twenty-two years of her marriage to Ananiah, functioned as a free spouse with respect to Ananiah, but as a slave with respect to Meshullam. Other Ancient Near Eastern documents, particularly from the Old Babylonian period, reveal similar situations. In the Ancient Near East, apparently, it was possible for a person, man or woman, to possess the status of slave with respect to one person, but the status of free citizen with respect to another (Westbrook 1998). While this seems to be the most reasonable conclusion based on the extant evidence, the full nature of these situations has yet to be explicated.

Gender and inheritance

Related to the issue of status is that of gender. Throughout Ancient Near Eastern history, women appear to have had nearly as much legal capacity as men. They could sue in court, testify, own property, sell property, and function as parties to contracts. This view must be tempered, however, by the consideration that many, if not most, of the women who acted on their own in these roles were very likely widows. While still married, they probably would have been expected to act in conjunction with their husbands. Thus, even though Ancient Near Eastern women may have enjoyed greater legal privileges than many of their counterparts in more recent centuries, notions of equality cannot be seriously entertained.

This is especially true when it comes to gender and inheritance. In many parts of the Ancient Near East, daughters were not legally entitled to any share of their father's estate, the exception being Egypt, where daughters had inheritance rights the same as sons. Daughters received some compensation for this in the form of a dowry, but even that often disappeared into the assets of their husbands upon marriage (Ben-Barak 1996). If a man had no sons, however, it was possible for his daughters to become his heirs, though certain conditions often applied. In ancient Israel, for example, daughters who inherited from their father were required to marry into their father's extended family (Numbers 36: 7–9). This ensured that their father's property would remain in his clan and would not be transferred to another clan when the daughters married. Texts from the Late Bronze Age sites of Nuzi and Emar reveal a different approach. If a man had only daughters for potential heirs, he would adopt them as sons, as in this document (Lacheman 1976: 133–4, text 2):

> This is the tablet of the testament of Unaptae to his daughter, Shilwaturi. He drew up a will for her. This is what Unaptae said: "I have established my daughter Shilwaturi as a son.[4] All of my fields, my buildings ... all of my property ... its entirety ... I have given to Shilwaturi, my daughter, whom I have established as a son." Unaptae also said: "I have established my wife, Shakutu, as a father for my daughter, Shilwaturi. As long as Shakutu is living, Shilwaturi shall care for her. When Shakutu dies, Shilwaturi shall mourn her, and she shall bury [her]."

Apparently, the legal fiction of converting a daughter into a son satisfied the law and made inheritance by the daughter permissible. This stands out as an imaginative strategy for circumventing the obstacle of gender and complying with the letter of the law.

Civil and criminal law

As opposed to most modern systems, the legal systems of the Ancient Near East do not appear to have had a distinction between civil law and criminal law (Renger 1977; Westbrook 1992). Misdeeds such as murder and theft were considered wrongs against an individual victim in the same manner as adultery, fraud, failure to make a required payment, and flight from slavery. In all of these situations, victims could take their case to the courts to seek redress. In the case of murder (about which there are very few texts), the victim's closest relatives would be the ones to initiate the quest for justice. Moreover, it was typically the wronged party who had the right to decide, within the bounds of the law, what type of redress to seek and to whom any compensation was paid. LH paragraph 129 contains a provision along these lines with respect to adultery:

> If a man's wife should be seized lying with another male, they shall bind them and cast them into the water; if the wife's master allows his wife to live, then the king shall allow his subject (the other male) to live. (Roth 1997: 105)

The fate of the adulterous wife was ultimately in the hands of her husband. As the wronged party, he could decide if the death sentence should be carried out or if the penalty should be mitigated. Similar rules seem to have applied to theft and even murder. If the family members of a murder victim could be convinced to accept monetary compensation in lieu of executing the murderer, then they had the right to choose that option. One of the responsibilities of the law courts was to ensure that victims did not exact a penalty which outweighed the severity of the wrong itself. In the case of assault and physical injury, for example, the penalty could take the form of the same injury being inflicted on the perpetrator, but any greater penalty was disallowed. Again, the right to choose either the fullest extent of the law or a less harsh penalty rested with the victim.

Connections with Later Legal Systems

The long-acknowledged ancestor of the two great modern legal systems – the common law and the civil law systems – is ancient Roman law. Early Greek law, too, played an important role. It is becoming increasingly apparent, however, that the Greco-Roman systems have their ancestors to some degree in the Ancient Near East. This points to the Ancient Near East as the source of at least some of the legal ideas and customs that have accompanied human civilizations throughout much of history. Although scholars can now trace many of the legal connections between the societies of the Ancient Near East and those of the Greco-Roman only in outline, identifying these connections is a crucial step toward understanding the historical development of law in general.

Both early Greek and Roman law seem to have been the beneficiary of what was the primary method of legal reasoning in the Ancient Near East. This mode of reasoning is perhaps best characterized as the case law method. Most of the individual provisions in the Ancient Near Eastern law collections are formulated as conditional clauses beginning with a term equivalent to "if." A scenario is presented in the protasis (an "if" clause); the resolution to that scenario comes in the apodosis or conclusion. This type of formulation prevails in the Greek Code of Gortyn from Crete (Willetts 1967) and in many works recording early Roman law, including the Twelve Tables (Crawford 1996: 578–83; Wolff 1951: 98–9).

More specific connections between the legal systems of the Ancient Near East and Roman law include issues related to flood damage to agricultural fields (see LH paragraphs 53–6 and the Roman legal texts cited in Watson 2001: 138–47), penalties for assaulting free citizens and slaves (see HL paragraphs 1–4, 7–8, 11–16; LH paragraphs 196–205; and the Twelve Tables I 14, Crawford 1996), and the distinction between theft at night, theft in the daytime, and the different levels of liability of one who defends against such theft (see LE paragraphs 12–13; Exodus 22: 1–2; and the Twelve Tables I 17–18, Crawford 1996).

Another possible point of connection between Ancient Near Eastern and early Greek law has to do with oaths in court. There is no question that the judicial oath originated in the Ancient Near East, the earliest evidence stemming from Mesopotamia in the late third millennium. Throughout much of Ancient Near Eastern history, trial courts frequently required one of the parties at trial to take an oath in the name of one or more gods. By taking the oath, parties would swear to the veracity of their claims and thereby subject themselves to divine punishment if in fact they were lying (Lafont 1997). If the party required to swear went through with the oath, that party automatically won the case.

A notable development occurred, however, in Mesopotamia during the mid-first millennium, the Neo-Babylonian period. The number of instances when a court required someone to take an oath dropped dramatically. Instead, courts much more frequently demanded further evidence from parties, primarily in the form of witness statements. The jurisprudential scene became one in which the courts demonstrated a preference for testimonial evidence over oath-taking as a means of deciding a trial. This is similar to an attitude reflected in the Greek Code of Gortyn, which dates to the mid-fifth century. There, reference is made to several different types of disputes about which the text instructs judges to make their decisions based on witness testimony. Only if there are no witnesses, or if there are conflicting witness statements, might the judge, according to the code, decide the case by taking an oath himself and then rendering a verdict.[5] Thus, a tendency to prefer witness statements over the use of an oath appears in early Greek law as well. Whether a connection in fact exists and what the nature of that connection might be are issues that warrant further investigation.

Similarities between Ancient Near Eastern and early Greek law occur in other areas as well, primarily in family law. Issues related to inheritance (LL paragraph 2; Numbers 27:8, 36:8; Gortyn VII 15–24), divorce (LH paragraphs 138–41; Gortyn II 45–55), the handling of a wife's dowry (LH paragraph 163; Gortyn III 30–5), and adoption (LH paragraph 191; Gortyn XI 9–17), reveal a number of striking resemblances between the two.

All in all, there can be little doubt that the Ancient Near East was home not only to the world's earliest legal records but also to principles and practices which spread to other civilizations. The few connections outlined above between the legal systems of the Ancient Near East and the Greco-Roman world mark the beginning of a long period of transmission. While the current debates within legal scholarship of the Ancient Near East will continue, some of the most important work in the future may relate to the task of describing the role that Ancient Near Eastern law played in the overall development of law and in the formation of modern legal systems.

NOTES

1   The cuneiform codes are listed in chronological order. For a discussion of their probable dating, see Westbrook 1985. Scholars are divided in their opinions on how to date the biblical codes. The priestly or levitical codes from the Hebrew Bible are omitted from discussion in keeping with this essay's goals.
2   It is possible to infer from LH paragraph 1 about false testimony that the penalty for murder was death. Still, there is no provision in LH directly dealing with homicide.
3   For instance, LH and several other codes treat the issue of a pregnant woman who was caused to abort her fetus due to being physically struck – accidentally or intentionally – by another. This situation is not mentioned in any other extant documents from the Ancient Near East. The goring ox laws that occur in three of the codes are another case in point. See Finkelstein 1981: 17–20.
4   This is the exact same language as that used when males from another family were adopted as sons; see, for example, *CT* 51 1 (Walker 1972) and *JEN* 788 (Lacheman and Maidman 1989).
5   This use of the oath in Greek judicial practice differed from Mesopotamian use where a party to the dispute took an oath (Willetts 1967: 32–34).

FURTHER READING

The most up-to-date and comprehensive analysis and description of Ancient Near Eastern law and practice is Westbrook 2003, a massive work that involved the collaboration of more than twenty scholars. For a much more concise treatment, though at times over-simplified, see Versteeg 2002. Roth 1997 provides a superb and convenient set of translations for all of the law codes. The essays by Roth, Westbrook, Lafont, Yaron, and Otto in *La codification des lois dans l'antiquité* (Lévy 2000) contain excellent discussions of the issues surrounding the nature of the law codes. For studies of the royal edicts, see Kraus 1984 and Veenhof 1997–2000. Joannès 2000 contains a very nice collection and analysis of trial records. For biblical law one of the best starting points is still Patrick 1985.

CHAPTER FOURTEEN

Social Tensions in the Ancient Near East

John F. Robertson

Outside utopian fantasies, there has never been a human society without tensions and conflict. If we had an Ancient Near Eastern counterpart of the *New York Times* or *Guardian*, we would readily recognize the social forces at work: the poor and weak being dominated by the wealthy and powerful, country folk envious and skeptical of sophisticated, privileged city dwellers who mocked them as rural bumpkins, natives disdainful and suspicious of immigrant outsiders.

In reconstructing tensions within Ancient Near Eastern societies we are stymied by the paucity and the partiality of our sources. With the exception of the Hebrew Bible, all written sources for the history of Ancient Near Eastern societies are hard won – or clandestinely acquired – fruits of archaeological excavation or of the study of often badly weathered, fragmented monuments. Although thousands of documents are available to us, they do not provide a continuous or comprehensive record in time or space. Compounding these inadequacies, most of these documents were recovered from the large mounds that are the remains of ancient cities and especially of the powerful city-based institutions of temples and palaces, and thus may not be representative of most of the people, who lived in the country.

Also, literacy in the Ancient Near East generally was the prized possession of a tiny part of the population. The scholars and bureaucrats who produced most of the documents were city-dwelling men conscious of their special status as wielders of the tools of reading and writing – a status that they owed to the powerful palace and temple institutions they served. The records and works that they produced reflected those institutions' interests and perspectives. We can tease from the evidence, however, echoes of the Ancient Near Eastern "street." Scholars have used evidence about traditional societies in the contemporary Middle East to develop complex reconstructions of ancient societies that incorporate non-urban components, thus offsetting the urban prejudice of the ancient scribes.

Survival and Identity

This essay focuses on two factors, (1) the imperative to ensure survival of the individual and the group by promoting access to the essential necessities of existence, and (2) the construction and demarcation of identity, recognizing that an individual might belong to different social groups and thus possess overlapping, complementary, or competing identities. Historically, such identities have been based on various criteria:

a) blood or kinship ties,
b) differences in ways of life, principally defined by a group's traditional mode of subsistence,
c) conflict between interests of rulers and interests of those whom they ruled, including the conflict between conquering or transplanted newcomers and conquered or indigenous inhabitants that developed with the formation of an empire,
d) differences based on ethnic identity or on a sense of others as "foreign" or "outsiders," and
e) differences created by conflicts of religious beliefs.

Survival, Environmental Instability, Societal Tension, and Change

In northern Mesopotamia, Iran, Anatolia, Syria, and Palestine, food production was based on agriculture dependent on rainfall. Even a small reduction in the normal amount of precipitation could significantly diminish the harvest; periods of drought would result in famine, leading to undernourishment, disease, and death. But along the lower Tigris and Euphrates rivers and the Nile, where rainfall was insufficient to sustain agriculture, great civilizations were based on irrigation through trapping the rivers' waters. The rivers of Mesopotamia were notorious, however, for disastrous spring floods that wiped out a portion of the harvest. Sometimes one of the rivers left its banks and carved a new course, leaving settlements high and dry. On some occasions, a ruler upstream from a rival city diverted the river's flow in order to harm that rival. In Egypt, on the other hand, the Nile was famous for the regularity and beneficence of its annual summer flood, whose life-giving water and silt sustained Egyptian civilization. A flood too high or too low could spell disaster, however, reducing the area that could be cultivated, diminishing the harvest, and threatening the population's survival.

Except for mythological tales of great floods, ancient sources reflected little awareness that even short-term environmental change could cause major societal conflict. But modern scientists have reconstructed climatic shifts and changes in rivers' courses that might have caused the famines and population movements reflected in the textual and archaeological record. For example, the period 2200 to 2000 BCE witnessed a shift to a drier climate. These more arid conditions contributed to the decline and fall of the empire established by the Akkadian king Sargon and his grandson Naram-Sin, and to a decline in urban settlement and population. In Palestine especially, most of the major urban communities of this time seem to have been abandoned, and their former inhabitants turned to seminomadic pastoral herding supplemented with small-scale farming. The social instability involved must have been severe.

This period of increased aridity coincided in Egypt with the transition from the highly organized Old Kingdom to the decentralized, chaotic conditions of the First Intermediate Period. Increased aridity and consequently diminished rainfall in central Africa probably produced a series of low Nile floods. The Egyptian state's survival was linked to the efficacy of those floods. The literary composition known as the Admonitions of Ipuwer provided eloquent, if hyperbolic, testimony to the chaos of this calamitous time:

> ... A man looks upon his son as his enemy...
> The virtuous man goes in mourning because of what has happened in the land...
> Foreigners have become Egyptians everywhere...
> The land is full of gangs, a man goes to plough with his shield...
> Indeed, the ways are blocked, the roads are watched,
> Men sit in the bushes, until the night traveler comes, in order to plunder his load.
> What is upon him is taken away; he is thrashed with blows of a stick and criminally slain...
> Indeed, the scribes of the land-register – their writings are destroyed, the grain of Egypt is common property.
> Indeed, the laws of the council-chamber are thrown out,
> Men walk on them in public places,
> Beggars break them up in the streets...
> Beggars come and go in the Great Houses [law courts].
> Indeed, the children of princes are cast out in the streets...
> The king has been disposed of by beggars. (Hallo and Younger 1997: 94–6)

This description might have been exaggerated for didactic effect or to add legitimacy to the ascension of a later new ruler. Nonetheless, it vividly recounts the chaos caused when society broke down and people's survival was threatened.

Tensions among Farming Villagers, Pastoral Nomads, and City Dwellers

Scholars recognize three social categories based on way of life: peasant village farmers, beginning at least as early as the eighth millennium BCE, nomadic pastoral herders, who developed in response to the establishment of agricultural villages, probably by the sixth millennium BCE, and the inhabitants of urban settlements, starting with the first cities of Sumer, already well founded by the mid-fourth millennium. The boundaries between these categories, however, were permeable.

Village peasant farmers

Ethnographic studies of traditional Arab societies reveal that social values in villages are egalitarian, and dominated by kinship ties and strong attachment to the land. Ancient texts from Mesopotamia, Syria, and Israel reflect the importance of village elders in regulating disputes both within and between villages and in representing their villages before state authority. For example, from around 1800 BCE the letters from the city of Mari, now on the Syrian–Iraqi border, show that Amorite farming villages were managed by headmen who were appointed by the palace administration. Women's informal social networks at both the intra- and inter-village levels likely promoted mutual support among village households as women worked together. They also enhanced inter-village cooperation, since women from other villages were sought as marriage partners; the resulting kinship webs helped to "maintain peace among contiguous settlements and increase the likelihood that related families would come to each other's assistance in times of economic or personal troubles" (Meyers 2003: 190–2).

Nowadays conflict can erupt when the attachment to the land, water rights, or basic social values such as motherhood, marriage and children, respect for parents and the elderly, and cooperation are threatened (Barakat 1993: 55–6). Disputes tend to be resolved through mediation and reconciliation within the community itself, on the basis of custom and precedent, without resort to outside legal authority.

Social tensions in ancient villages were rarely mentioned in the records produced by the city-based scribes. Evidence of such tensions can be inferred, however, from the records of the administration of rural lands controlled by temple and royal authorities, and lands from which local villagers were required to deliver a cut of the harvest. In regions of rainfall agriculture villages tend to be more isolated and dispersed, and so less susceptible to control by a central authority; they also manage their water resources locally and are more autonomous. But the early historical development of the state depended on its ability to dominate the countryside by controlling farmland and enforcing the delivery of crops by rural villagers. Villagers not only had to produce enough to feed themselves but also had to turn over part of their harvest in taxation, and perform required labor service as well. The palace records from Ebla in western Syria around 2350 BCE reveal the extension of palace control into the countryside, as the king, members of the royal family, and high officials were assigned lands in outlying villages. One such official, for example, was assigned more than 30,000 units of land that included fields in 21 different locales. Personnel connected with the Ebla palace administration were regularly dispatched to collect the villagers' crops, and cultivation was an obligation fulfilled by forced laborers. These villagers also had to contribute livestock to the Ebla palace (Archi 1990: 17–19).

Some of our best evidence of the extension of city-based interests into rural villages comes from the town of Nuzi, east of the Tigris in northern Mesopotamia, in a region along the interface of rainfall-based and irrigation-based cultivation. The more than 6,500 cuneiform tablets recovered from Nuzi dating from 1500 to 1350 BCE document the activities of the royal elite, but also of a class of major landowners who had suburban residences at Nuzi but also owned land in villages outside the town. We also see a class of smaller landholders living at a subsistence level. Especially striking in these records is how they reveal "progressive economic polarization" and "general pauperization within the private economy" as small landholders, perhaps because of poor harvests or growing indebtedness, were bought out and reduced to tenant farmers or even debt slaves (Maidman 1995: 943–4). This contravened a basic value of peasant village society, kin-based attachment to the land, and associated feelings against alienating that land outside the family. At Nuzi, this fundamental social value was circumvented by the "adoption" of the wealthy buyer into the family of the seller, after which the seller might give the buyer his "inheritance" reciprocated by a "gift" that equaled the purchase price of the land. The seller and his family might continue to work the land and support themselves as tenants of the new owner, but their status had changed from independence to dependence. We see in the Hebrew Bible the importance of the family retaining its ancestral lands. For example, in Numbers 36: 5–9, Moses ordered that the daughters of Zelophehad marry a man from a clan of their father's tribe on the principle that "No inheritance shall be transferred from one tribe to another."

Kinship ties and attachment to the land were similarly important social values in the irrigation-based farming villages of the Tigris–Euphrates floodplain and the Nile. However, because in Lower Mesopotamia cultivation was linked to the irrigation water from the rivers and canal systems, villages tended to be clustered near waterways and were less dispersed. This made them more susceptible to control by city-based managers and landlords, especially during periods of strong political authority such as the Akkad, Ur III, and Old Babylonian dynasties (2334–1595 BCE). These kings' inscriptions celebrated their construction and maintenance of extensive canal systems that provided water for the cultivating of thousands of acres and facilitated the transport of the harvest to temple and royal granaries. Study of earliest Mesopotamian civilization has often focused on the roles of "Great Institutions," the temple and the palace. While the evidence shows an important component of private land ownership in the Old Babylonian period (2000–1595 BCE) alongside lands controlled by the palace, the records of the mid- and late third millennium BCE are most informative about the temple- and palace-based administration of huge cultivated acreages. Records from the Sumerian city of Girsu dating to the mid-third millennium BCE reveal highly organized central planning by city-based bureaucrats who organized planting and harvesting, as well as year-round water management that was carried out by residents of the countryside, from whom the urban authority required labor service. After the harvest, the city-based managers extracted from individuals a grain tax that was then transported to city granaries (Powell 1990b). The records of Girsu's scribes showed no concern for the personal interests of the villagers and workers whose lives they were organizing.

In Egypt most of the administrative records were written on perishable and thus long-disappeared materials, or they lie buried in ancient towns whose remains lie beneath their modern successors. Our reconstruction of Egyptian rural village life must therefore be based on monumental or official texts often designed to extol the virtues of the pharaoh's rule or on literary compositions that were intended more to edify other Egyptians then than to inform us now.

What emerges is an image of a seemingly tranquil countryside, where city-based elites set themselves up in villas to escape squalid urban existence. The villages come off as peaceful but crowded, their inhabitants contented with life within their immediate families but also respectful of their obligations within the larger community. Tomb paintings commissioned to portray an idyllic situation depicted people working together in the epitome of communal harmony and solidarity.

The reality was quite different. The image perpetuated by royal documents, of an all-powerful king with monolithic control over the country's resources, has not stood up well to scholarly analysis. The management of irrigation, in fact, seems largely to have been left in local hands. Nonetheless, especially during periods of effectively centralized authority (the Old, Middle, and New Kingdoms), the royal administration strove to ensure constant revenues to support itself and its monumental construction projects, "collecting, storing, and disbursing revenue in grains, animals and animal products, raw materials, and finished items" (O'Connor 1995: 320–1).

The official version of all this effort promoted an image of stability and contentment, but the intrusion of government agents empowered to help organize cultivation, ensure the collection of grain taxes, and compel men to leave their families and villages for months at forced labor caused stress within village societies, fostering a sense of shared identity among villagers who felt hard pressed by the state's demands. Abuse of a peasant by a state official was the theme of the Middle Kingdom composition The Eloquent Peasant, in which a simple farmer was robbed and beaten by the subordinate of a high steward. The Satire of the Trades similarly suggested that peasant farmers were subject to ridicule and abuse by the elite servants of the state, although we cannot be certain if this text simply employed exaggeration for the purpose of satire. The farmer

> wails more than the guinea fowl, his voice is louder than a raven's; his fingers are swollen and stink to excess. He is weary…A peasant is not called a man, beware of it…See, there's no profession without a boss, except for the scribe; he is the boss. Hence if you know writing, it will do better for you than those professions I've set before you, each more wretched than the other. (Hallo and Younger 1997: 122–5)

The literary composition known as the Instruction of Amenemope from around 1000 BCE enjoined the royal "overseer of grains" to be fair in his dealings, and listed several reprehensible acts the scribe should not commit – thereby suggesting how rural farmers were all too often victimized:

> Do not cheat a man through pen on scroll, the god abhors it;…do not assess a man who has nothing, and thus falsify your pen. If you find a large debt against a poor man, make it into three parts; forgive two, let one stand…Beware of disguising the measure, so as to falsify its fractions…Measure according to its true size…Do not accept a farmer's dues and then assess him so as to injure him. (Hallo and Younger 1997: 119–20)

Pastoral nomads

Modern studies of traditional nomadic groups indicate that fundamental to their social values and organization is the framework of blood and kinship ties, within which are embedded values of tribal solidarity, egalitarianism, communal ownership, and consensus-based decision-making. Nomadic groups tend to resist control by city authority, and during periods of weak central power they assert their autonomy in the countryside. Nomads tend to disdain village farmers as weak and submissive and their attachment to the land as humiliating; they similarly regard city dwellers as corrupted, soft, and cowardly. In return, farm villagers see the nomads as parasites, "irresponsible, uprooted vagabonds bent on raids and thievery" (Barakat 1993: 54–5).

We must also bear in mind that, for most of early antiquity, we are not dealing with camel-herding Bedouin, who do not appear on the Middle Eastern social landscape until after 900 BCE, but with sheep and goat nomads. Because their flocks as well as the donkeys upon which these groups moved needed regular access to water and pasturage, these nomads did not venture as far into the desert. Their lifestyle was more tied to the peasant villagers, and sometimes they farmed part-time to supplement their food supply.

New archaeological techniques to detect the remains of nomad camps promise to further our understanding of ancient nomadic societies. Otherwise, our knowledge of the social organization, values, and tensions within Ancient Near Eastern nomadic groups is meager. Their tribal organization was evident in the Mari letters, with their many references to Amorite pastoralists and villagers who were grouped under a number of tribal divisions and subdivisions (Fleming 2004). The Mari texts also revealed that the government's relations with Amorite groups were volatile, but could include cooperation or co-optation, as exemplified in the use of Amorite leaders to assemble tribesmen for labor and military service. Farther east, the ruler of the city of Eshnunna married the daughter of a local Amorite chieftain in the hope of managing tensions with local tribesmen (Whiting 1987: 48–9). A less carnal symbiosis was celebrated in the Sumerian composition The Herdsman and the Farmer, which highlighted the complementary activities and products of the two disputants (Averbeck 2003: 52).

What looms large is the nomads' propensity to prey upon villages, and thereby undercut the central political authority. The nomads' aggression against villages and cities might have stemmed from periodically heightened need for agricultural commodities, perhaps after an environmentally caused breakdown of village farming societies, response to military harassment, or simply the allure of wealth and opportunity (Schwartz 1995: 254–5). The Akkad dynasty's fall was traditionally ascribed to the Gutians, non-sedentary mountaineers from the Zagros region. The history of late third and early second millennium BCE Mesopotamia was dominated by the encroachment of Amorite tribes and their gradual assumption of political control. The towns of the Hittite kingdom in Anatolia, even its great capital city Hattusha, were under constant threat of raids by the non-sedentary peoples known as the Kashka, who inhabited the region along the southern Black Sea coast.

Ancient sources reflected the scorn and apprehension with which the city-based intelligentsia regarded nomads. Mesopotamian literature often ridiculed Amorite manners and customs. Egyptian literature projected a similarly dim view of pastoral nomads, the "Asiatic" desert dwellers who infiltrated the eastern Nile Delta to weather the summer months. The Middle Kingdom Prophecies of Neferti reflected wariness of them: "The land is burdened with misfortune because of those looking for food, Asiatics roaming the land" (Hallo and Younger 1997: 108). Finally, a New Kingdom letter described them as thieves who hid in the bushes, who stood more than seven feet tall and had wild faces, and whose "thoughts are not pretty" (Hallo and Younger 2002: 13).

City dwellers

Cities were the pre-eminent centers of political authority and hubs for the economic activities and administration of the villages around them, and this is also why they are our chief source of documentation concerning societal values, organization, and conflict in general. Their populations were large, dense, diverse, and internally differentiated into socioeconomic classes. They were places where internal social tensions festered. Cities and their inhabitants were resented from the outside, by villagers and nomads alike, as intruders who demanded the products of their labors or tried to control their movements. At the same time, though, the wealth and opportunities that cities represented had a strong attraction for people of the countryside.

Old, traditional urban centers of the modern Middle East comprise a mosaic of quarters and sub-quarters differentiated by ethnic, religious, or socioeconomic characteristics and relatively self-sufficient, even insular. We ought not simply to conclude that similar conditions typified ancient cities of the region. The internal structure of ancient Egyptian cities is extremely poorly known because those cities long ago disappeared under later occupation. A similar dearth of physical evidence holds true for most of the rest of the Near East, although the evidence from some regions is more substantial, such as the residential areas at Ur and Eshnunna, and at the site of Mashkan-shapir. The waterways within these cities determined internal geography, along with streets that paralleled or ran into them. At both Eshnunna and Mashkan-shapir, the blocks demarcated by these streets encompassed about 1 hectare (about 2.5 acres), which, as it so happens, is "both the average size of small Mesopotamian village sites and the size of residential neighborhoods – the face-to-face communities that served as the building blocks of those pre-industrial cities outside Mesopotamia that have been studied" (Stone 1995a: 240). Rich and poor lived next to each other, at close quarters, in houses along intricate networks of narrow, winding lanes, similar to what one finds today in the older quarters of Middle Eastern cities.

Mesopotamian sources suggest that one's residence in a local neighborhood or quarter was an important determinant of social and legal identity, and that one's more immediate family ties mattered more to city dwellers than did tribal or clan allegiance. Local quarters were monitored by officials empowered to issue warnings or convene hearings about matters of public concern, such as houses in dangerous disrepair or domestic animals that might cause harm. Local residents could also "be called upon...to investigate the conduct and chastity of a woman who repudiated her husband" or be enjoined to watch out for strangers (Greengus 1995: 469).

Some prayers to the sun god suggest that, for the Mesopotamian city dweller, peril was almost omnipresent, and inescapable without divine assistance. One prayer beseeched the god "because of the evil of unfavorable signs and portents which are present in my house, which have stymied me...On account of the evil omen of a snake which I saw come right into my house for its prey, I am afraid, anxious, frightened...On account of this dog that has urinated on me, I am afraid, anxious, frightened..." (Foster 1996: 633–4). Another prayer asked for deliverance from anything "unlucky for mankind," "whether, as I walked through a street, an accursed man touched me, or, when I crossed a square, I stepped in a puddle of wash water, or, I walked over nail pairings, shavings from an armpit, a worn-out shoe, a broken belt, a leather sack (holding things) for black magic, a leper's scales..." (Foster 1996: 653).

Nor did life in Egyptian towns seem any less frightening, in view of the many magical devices their residents employed to ward off dangers. Expressive evidence of this was discovered at Deir el-Medina, a New Kingdom settlement for the craftsmen who built and decorated tombs in the Valley of the Kings. Hence it cannot be regarded as entirely typical of larger Egyptian towns. The stone doorways of houses bore inscriptions pleading for divine protection, and the houses themselves often contained altars and niches for statuettes. Bed footboards and wooden headrests sometimes bore carvings of protective deities. Throughout Egypt, people wore amulets to ward off dangers, real and imagined; some of them listed as life's main hazards "fevers, childbirth, snake and scorpion bites, accidents on pilgrimages, journeys by water, and the collapse of houses" (Pinch 1995: 364–5). A modern observer might consign much of this to the realm of magic and superstition, but surely it testifies to an underlying tension and strongly felt need for protection against the perils of daily living.

Deir el-Medina is famous for its many inscribed potsherds upon which the tomb workers and their overseers, living for days at a time in huts near their actual work site, dispatched messages back to the settlement. Vividly human, they dealt with a wide range of concerns, from making sure laundry was done to letting a colleague know that his wife was cheating on him, to workers arranging to have items prepared for their own tombs. The buffeting and strains of personal relationships in a tightly knit, interdependent community emerge starkly. In one example, a worker vented his frustration with his overseer:

> What's the meaning of your getting into such a bad mood as you are in that nobody's speech can enter your ears as a consequence of your inflated ego? You are not a man since you are unable to make your wives pregnant like your fellowmen...You abound in being exceedingly stingy. You give no one anything. (Wente 1990: 149)

Such tensions could erupt into conflict, even violence. To resolve grievances internally, and avoid subjecting them to royal interference, the community resorted to peer pressure and to the convening of a local tribunal. These methods likely served to reinforce communal solidarity and responsibility (Lorton 1995: 359).

Evidence from Deir el-Medina as well as from larger ancient towns and cities all across the Near East documented a more polar relationship of power and status: that between master and slave. Slavery in the Ancient Near East was never as extensive or as fundamental to basic economic systems as it was in the Roman Empire or the American South before the Civil War. Nonetheless, slaves appeared in very early documents, frequently as captives of military expeditions (mostly female at first; males were apparently maimed or slain). Slaves often provided the urban temples and palaces important menial labor; often they were set to weaving. One's slave status might be marked by a haircut, branding, tattooing, or even mutilation. Some slaves worked as craftsmen and might accumulate personal wealth and purchase their freedom, although this was seldom feasible. We also find evidence of debt slavery. A debtor who was unable to repay a loan with interest rates on loans of barley as high as 33 or even 50 percent placed his family and even himself into servitude to a creditor.

Whether resulting from indebtedness or captivity, enslavement fueled resentment and class consciousness. Letters, legal texts including the Laws of Hammurabi as well as the Hittite Laws, and treaties referred to the capture and return of runaway slaves, whose flight seems to have been a persistent and serious problem. Disdain for slaves as untrustworthy, as well as whiny, complaining, and lazy was clear in proverbs, as in "The dirt was not apparent to the slave girl. To her lady it kept increasing." And the lustful slave owner was warned of future problems as the proverb advised, "Do not have sexual intercourse with your slave girl, she will call you 'Traitor!'" and another noted, "Your slave girl who has been brought down from the mountains, she brings pleasure, but she also brings danger." The proverbs knew too that the slave resented the status (Snell 2003: 16).

Tensions between Ruler and Ruled

We can contrast officially propagated images of ideal rulership and exercise of authority with evidence of how rulers successfully regulated these tensions or exacerbated them. The sources predictably glorified the virtues and beneficent intentions of the rulers, and omitted mention of problems or protest. An Akkadian proverb succinctly asserted the centrality of kingship in Mesopotamian society: "People without a king are (like) sheep without a shepherd" (Foster 1996: 338). In his elaborate "code" of laws, Hammurabi of Babylon called himself the shepherd whom the gods established "to make justice prevail in the land, to abolish the wicked and the evil, to prevent the weak from oppressing the strong, to rise like the sun god Šamaš over all humankind, to illuminate the land" (Roth 1997: 76–7). Instructions given to officials dispatched by the Hittite court expressed similar sentiments about dealing fairly with subjects. For instance, in the Instructions for Commanders of Border Garrisons, frontier governors were enjoined to judge fairly the cases brought before them:

Let no one take a bribe. He is not to make the stronger case the weaker, or the weaker the stronger one. Do what is just...Judge a case for anyone who has one and make things right. If a man's slave, or a man's female slave or a widow has a case, judge it for them and make things right. (Hallo and Younger 1997: 224–5)

Mesopotamian and Hittite legal documents, as well as the Hebrew Bible, show that royal officials might participate with town or city elders in adjudicating local griev-ances, and were especially relied upon in cases involving treason or homicide. Literary compositions of Middle and New Kingdom Egypt exhorted royal officials to be fair-minded and generous in their dealings with commoners. Even more eloquent, though suspiciously overblown, testimony to what one authority has termed the "justice, charity, understanding and kindliness which formed the guiding ethic of Egyptian public life" is found in the biography written on the wall of the tomb of the Eighteenth Dynasty royal vizier Rekhmire in the 1400s BCE:

I judged both [the insignificant] and the influential; I rescued the weak man from the strong man; I deflected the fury of the evil man and subdued the greedy man in his hour...I succored the widow who has no husband; I established the son and heir on the seat of his father. I gave [bread to the hungry], water to the thirsty, and meat, oil and clothes to him who had nothing...I was not at all deaf to the indigent. Indeed I never took a bribe from anyone. (James 1984: 57)

To promote a sense of solidarity between rulers and their subjects, and perhaps to buffer themselves against a potentially restive population, ruling authorities some-times transcended the good intentions of such "official versions" and effected more specific measures to provide economic relief, or even psychological release, for their subjects. For instance, Old Babylonian kings periodically issued edicts that canceled taxes owed to the palace and provided relief to those who sold property or even members of their family to pay off their debts. We find a parallel to this in the Hebrew Bible's Book of Jeremiah chapter 34, where King Zedekiah freed debt slaves and canceled debts. Such actions surely were welcomed by most of the populace, though resisted by wealthier citizens deprived of repayment. Hittites in economic distress could petition the king for relief from tax burdens or forced labor, and in one Hittite–Hurrian bilingual text the Hittite ruler was advised to issue a proclamation releasing citizens from debt slavery (Hoffner 1995: 562–3).

The alleviation of societal tensions was not limited to cancellation of debts, how-ever. The Egyptian year was replete with religious festivals sponsored by the many temples. A feature of these festivals was the colorful procession of the god's statue from the temple through the local community, where it delivered oracles intended to resolve questions and disputes, but also intended, from the point of view of temple and royal authorities, "to reinforce devotion to god and pharaoh" (O'Connor 1995: 322). These festivals also featured the distribution of food and beer to the surround-ing communities, as well as a ribald carnival atmosphere complete with acrobats, dancers, and musicians. The resulting merrymaking and general inebriation at official expense strengthened the psychological bond between the ruler and the masses.

But those ruled did suffer at the hands of their rulers, whose foremost motivation was to perpetuate their own power and prestige and ensure their revenue flow. In sharp contrast to the benevolence and fair-mindedness implied in Hammurabi's laws and his successors' economic-relief edicts, Neo-Babylonian literary texts from the middle of the first millennium BCE alluded to abuses and suggested that they were not always rectified by royal intervention. The composition "King of Justice" told of how the "strong would oppress the weak, while they had insufficient means to go to court for redress. The rich would take the belongings of the lowly. Neither governor nor prince would appear before the judge on behalf of the widow or orphan . . . a judge would accept a bribe or present and would not consider (the case)," or would throw away the tablet recording a legal decision, thereby leaving a plaintiff with no legal redress. Another text advised the ruler to regard "due process" and maintain the traditional privileges of the old cities of Babylonia, taking care not to impose fines or imprison their citizens, or force them to labor or abuse their fields or flocks – all of which surely implied that past rulers had indeed infringed upon old privileges (Foster 1996: 745, 748).

Some of the most eloquent testimony to the abuse of subjects by their rulers is to be found in the Hebrew Bible. Its compilations of laws and wisdom literature abound in evidence concerning the social values and organization of early Israel. Implicit in these sources were standards and expectations of just kingship – among them, the protection of the poor and weak – to which Israel's kings were to be accountable. Though we must remember that the books of the prophets were compiled by learned men with their own political and social agendas, it is clear in the prophetic books that Israelite kings all too often were guilty of abusing their subjects. The prophet Amos, for instance, dwelt on the many sins of Israel's ruling elite: " . . . you trample on the poor and take from them levies of grain . . . for I know how many are your transgressions, and how great are your sins – you who afflict the righteous, who take a bribe, and push aside the needy in the gate" (Amos 5: 11–12). Similarly, Isaiah condemned the rulers of Israel "who make iniquitous decrees, who write oppressive statutes, to turn aside the needy from justice and to rob the poor of my people of their right, that widows may be your spoil, and that you make the orphans your prey!" and predicted their demise at the hands of mighty Assyria (10: 1–2).

The rise of Assyria was the harbinger of a sequence of imperial systems that introduced new elements into the dynamic of ruler versus ruled. The looting, destruction, killing, rape, mutilation, and enslavement that typically accompanied military conquest had been grim facts of ancient life from earliest recorded times. The imperial systems of the first millennium BCE, however, employed still other means of ensuring political domination and crushingly systematic economic exploitation. Most famously under the Assyrians, wealth and resources were coercively extracted and transported to the imperial capitals; local economies in the empire – and with them the livelihoods and prosperity of much of the population – likely were devastated.

From the standpoint of local communities, especially destructive was the mass deportation and relocation of conquered people to regions far from their homelands. Although such practices were employed at least as early as the Bronze Age Hittite conquests, their effects are best known and depicted graphically in the wake of the Assyrian destruction of the Israelite kingdom of Samaria in 722 BCE and the later Babylonian conquest of Jerusalem in 587 BCE. The Display Inscription of the Assyrian king Sargon II records that 22,290 people were deported from Samaria, and in that process families were broken up, and the deportees were forced to subsist on meager rations (Younger 2003). Upon reaching their destinations, either Assyria itself or the region of Media in Iran, they were compelled to toil as agricultural or construction laborers, often living (or not) on too small rations which rendered them more susceptible to disease, or they were settled in regions where farming was only marginally possible. The resulting psychological trauma and deprivation of identity were vividly expressed in the Book of Lamentations with its heart-rending recollection of the devastation and abject humiliation felt by the people of Jerusalem upon their expulsion by the armies of Nebuchadnezzar:

> Our inheritance has been turned over to strangers, our homes to aliens. We have become orphans, fatherless; our mothers are like widows. We must pay for the water we drink; the wood we get must be bought. With a yoke on our necks we are hard driven; we are weary, we are given no rest ... We get our bread at the peril of our lives ... Our skin is as black as an oven from the scorching heat of famine. Women are raped in Zion, virgins in the towns of Judah. Princes are hung up by their hands; no respect is shown to the elders. Young men are compelled to grind, and boys stagger under loads of wood. (Lamentations 5: 2–13)

Because of fear or resentment of political authority, or perhaps as refugees from social or economic calamity, people might simply opt out of being ruled and become stateless persons, moving out beyond the reach of authority. This is one possible interpretation for the term *habiru*, an imprecisely understood social designation that appeared as early as the late third millennium and throughout most of the second millennium BCE. In the Mari letters *habiru* were brigands; several centuries later they were similarly (though not exclusively) referred to as outlaws who based themselves in the mountainous areas of Palestine and Syria, beyond the reach of local rulers and Egyptian imperial authorities (Morrison 1992: 1157; Lemche 1992: 6–7). Neither exclusively nomadic nor settled, nor identifiable with a specific ethnic group, the *habiru* represented yet another significant aspect of the complex relationship of ruler versus ruled in the Ancient Near East.

Societal Tensions Produced by Ethnic Differences or Alienness

Tensions ascribable to ethnic differences were seldom detected in our sources; a tendency toward coexistence and assimilation more often emerged. For example, there is little evidence of ethnic tension between the Sumerians and Akkadians in early Mesopotamia. Likewise, Amorites appear to have settled peacefully among Sumerians and Akkadians as early as the late third millennium BCE, and the Kassites who ruled Babylonia after the fall of Hammurabi's dynasty became so thoroughly assimilated that we still have little knowledge of their language. Nuzi's population around 1500 BCE included several possibly ethnic groups with no evidence of friction among them. In New Kingdom Egypt, Asiatics who had arrived as nomads or slaves were assimilated, individuals bearing Asiatic names entered the ranks of officialdom, and Asiatic deities were absorbed into the Egyptian pantheon. Nubians and Libyans also were incorporated into the ranks of the Egyptian military. By and large, then, being of different ethnicity did not necessarily entail social disadvantage.

Complicating this assessment, though, is an Akkadian proverb: "Flesh is flesh, blood is blood, alien is alien, foreigner is foreigner" (Foster 1996: 346). Being a foreigner could indeed make a person "other" if a foreigner did not adopt local norms and customs. Thus, in Mesopotamia, to the extent that they remained beyond the pale of civilized behavior, Gutians and Amorites were seen as barbarians. Until they actually began to reside in Egypt, surrounding peoples were similarly regarded as despicable and uncivilized. The Hebrew Bible also revealed that resident aliens might be subject to exclusion, or be forbidden to own land (Avalos 1995: 623–4). Especially notable is the stigma that was imposed on foreigners from Syria and southern Babylonia whom the Assyrians brought to Samaria to replenish its population after deporting the Israelites. Centuries later, the Jews regarded their descendants, the Samaritans, as pariahs who were not allowed membership in the Jewish community (Lemche 1995: 1213).

Tensions Produced by Religious Differences

The mention of ostensibly religion-based antagonism between the later Samaritans and the Jews leads to a more general observation: except for the conflicts stemming from differences in religious belief that figured in the Hebrew Bible, Ancient Near Eastern societies seem conspicuous in the almost complete absence of such tensions. Indeed, the sources reflect a general toleration and inclusiveness with regard to the gods and cults of foreigners or newly arrived people. Noteworthy is the syncretism in Ancient Near Eastern religions, that is, the process where attributes and beliefs associated with one deity were transferred and melded with those of another. A distinctive feature of Egyptian religion during the New Kingdom was the acceptance of Asiatic deities. In a similar vein, the Mittanian king Tushrata told Amunhotep III (1390–1353 BCE) that he was sending to the Egyptian court the statue of the goddess Shaushka of Nineveh, "mistress of all lands," and said, "May Shaushka, the mistress of heaven, protect us, my brother and me, 100,000 years, and may our mistress grant both of us great joy... Is Shaushka for me alone my god(dess), and for my brother not his god(dess)?" (Moran 1992: 61–2).

At least two episodes, both of them in Egypt, may have either engendered or been the result of tensions stemming from religious differences. Most famous was the religious reformation attempted by the pharaoh Akhenaten (1353–1336 BCE), who temporarily proscribed the cults of the many gods of Egypt in favor of his favored deity, the sun disk called the *Aten*. Although later Egyptians reversed his heresy and reviled Akhenaten for this attempt to upset the established order, we know little of the broader social impact of his policy. To the extent that local religious festivals, with their customary distributions of food and drink to the populace, might have been affected, the impact could have been significant, but there is no evidence of religiously motivated persecution of common people in Egypt during this era.

The other episode occurred many centuries later, during the time of Persian domination. By this time a Jewish garrison had been established in southern Egypt, on the island of Elephantine. Aramaic texts from there indicate that this group's relations with the indigenous community were marred during the late fifth century BCE when conflict with the priests of the local Egyptian god resulted in the burning down of the Jewish shrine to their god, Yahweh, as well as the death of some of the Egyptians at the hands of the Jews. We can speculate that differences in religious belief or custom may have been a contributing factor.

Whatever the reasons for these events, the emergence of monotheism centered on the Israelite god Yahweh injected into societal relationships in parts of the Ancient Near East a new and divisive element: the fervent acknowledgment of only one supreme deity, coupled with rejection and intolerance of other, "false" gods and beliefs. Detailing the complexity of that phenomenon, and its consequences, lies beyond the scope of this essay, but its continuing elaboration within the framework of Jewish, Christian, and Muslim history was destined to cause profound societal changes, both uplifting and destructive, in the history of the Middle East.

FURTHER READING

There are very few works that treat Ancient Near Eastern social tensions both as broadly and as analytically as has been attempted here. An excellent place to start is Freedman 1992 and especially Sasson 1995, both of which provide many authoritative articles on social, economic, and legal aspects of various Ancient Near Eastern civilizations. Among the more useful monographs are James 1984 and Brewer and Teeter 1999 for Egypt, Snell 1997 for the Ancient Near East, and Bryce 2002 for the Hittites. Insights derived from ethnographic and more recent historical study are to be found in Barakat 1993 and Eickelman 2002. An ambitious recent study analyzing social structures in the Bronze Age Near East is Schloen 2001.

CHAPTER FIFTEEN

Gender Roles in Ancient Egypt

Ann Macy Roth

As in most agricultural societies, the traditional roles played by men and women in ancient Egypt were clearly differentiated. Men were responsible for food production, crafts, administration of the institutions of state and temple, defense of the state, and most other duties outside the domestic sphere. Women's activities, in contrast, were largely restricted to the home: bearing and rearing children, producing clothing, cooking food, and caring for the sick. There was a tendency, when women did work outside of the domestic sphere, for them to take on tasks mimicking their household roles: weaving, serving as wet-nurses, preparing and serving food and drink, maid-service, and, probably, prostitution.

Gender and Cosmology

In Egyptian culture, however, this separation of gender roles was not merely a social custom, but had a theological and cosmological basis. As Erik Hornung has pointed out, the Egyptians believed that before the creation of their world, the universe was a single uniform substance that filled all space, with no internal distinctions or separate parts (1982b: 172–85). Four basic characteristics of this single substance were personified by eight gods, four male–female pairs in which both sexes served the same function. Clearly there were no gender distinctions in this substance; it was wholly androgynous, since even its characteristics were both male and female. More-over, religious statements about the nature of things before creation included the explicit statement that the creator god had no mother and no father.

The initial creation was asexual. At the moment of creation, the creator god, who was an indistinguishable part of this undifferentiated substance, brought into exist-ence two gods, one male and one female. Sometimes this was said to have been done through spitting or sneezing, but perhaps most often it is described as having been done through masturbation. Since the creator god himself was part of the undiffer-entiated nonexistence, he was sexually androgynous. He recounted that he "acted as husband with my fist, I copulated with my hand" (Allen 1988: 28). Since the word "hand" is feminine in Egyptian, this was essentially a sexual union with himself, emphasizing the androgynous character of the nonexistence of which he was an indistinguishable part.

The gods created by this act were distinguished from each other in other ways (as dry air and moisture, or as light and heat) in different versions of the story, just as the creator god who was credited with their creation varied, but the separation of their sexes was essential to the definition of existence itself. Existence was defined by such contrasts rather than by mere physical presence; nothing could exist unless it could be contrasted with something else. For men to have existed, women must have been in existence from the very same moment; the two sexes were therefore regarded as of equal antiquity and equally essential to the existence and functioning of the created universe. The maintenance of the boundaries between the two sexes and their contrasting expression in the gender roles of the population were thus essential to the existence of any people at all. It is significant that the Egyptian word for people, sometimes mistranslated as "men," normally has both male and female determinatives (Fischer 2000: 46).

For this reason, any blurring of the boundaries between the gender roles that represented this sexual differentiation was seen as endangering existence. Maintaining the opposition of gender roles prevented the world from reverting to the uniform substance of pre-creation chaos – what was seen as nonexistence. This maintenance of opposing dualities was expressed in many aspects of ancient Egyptian life, the divisions between east and west, Upper Egypt and Lower Egypt, the valley and the desert, active historical kingship and ancestral kingship, or cyclical and linear time. But the division of the male from the female was a fundamental contrast.

In art, this contrast was expressed by contrasting skin colors. Women were conventionally represented with yellow or gold skin, while men were represented with skin of dark red or red-brown. This coloration may originally have been an exaggeration of the skin color difference created by men's outdoor work and women's work inside the house; in some cases peasant women could be represented with darker skin, while sedentary older men were shown in yellow. But as a general rule, the difference denoted a difference in gender.

In addition to their skin color, women, particularly elite women, were often shown in a passive pose, standing with their feet close together, and their hands embracing their husbands, or at their sides, or on their opposite shoulder, or holding lotuses to their noses. Men's poses were more active and outgoing. One foot was conventionally shown striding forward, and one hand reached out to hold a staff or an offering, while the other held an emblem of official power. This association of physical stance with gender was particularly clear in the rare cases in which a man's tomb chapel had been converted for a woman's use: the pose had to be altered along with the shape of the body to indicate the gender difference (Roth 2002).

A final difference in the representations of men and women is that of scale. When a husband and wife were shown together, the wife was often, though not always, depicted at a smaller scale. Since this hierarchy of scale was also used to differentiate between kings and officials and between landlords and peasants, it is clear that women, despite their equal status mythologically, were viewed as socially inferior to men.

Ancient Egyptian Sexuality and Fertility

This distinction between male and female was, of course, sexual as well as social. The male role in sexual reproduction was seen as the actual creation of new life, which was then implanted in the female. Fundamentally, children were viewed as extensions of their father's life force; the mother's role in determining their nature was decidedly secondary. Instead, women seem to have had a dual role: they aroused the man and stimulated his creative act with their beauty and sexual attractiveness, and then they nourished the life that his creative power produced. The fact that the female was not credited with the creative side of fertility, which is commonly attributed to women in most other ancient cultures, may perhaps be due to the unusual geography of Egypt. Rather than a female earth, fertilized by rain from a male sky, Egypt's agricultural fertility came from the annual flooding of the Nile River. The earth, therefore, was seen as masculine, its fertility perhaps stimulated by the nude, star-spangled figure of the sky goddess above it. This reversal of the more common view of the earth as female and the sky as male may have had profound effects on the ancient Egyptians' views about gender (Roth 2000).

Sexual acts were not often represented in formal Egyptian art, although depictions of sexually aroused men were comparatively common. Gestures of affection were quite frequently shown in couples. In some cases these were mutual, but more often it was the woman who was shown embracing, supporting, or affectionately touching the man. Simpson has shown, however, that this is a general pattern, which seems to reflect power relations more than gender; kings were shown to be similarly affectionate with relation to gods (1977). In this, as in other ways, the man was seen to be superior in status to the woman, despite the equal importance and complementarity of their roles.

Subtle depictions of sexual congress occurred in the "divine conception" scenes in temples and later in birth houses attached to Graeco-Roman temples. There the couple was depicted seated on a bed, while the male extended the life hieroglyph to the nose of the female, and she often supported his elbow. Over time, these figures tended to be separated by increasing amounts of space, and in later birth houses, the life sign could become extremely long.

One hieroglyphic sign depicting the sexual act was preserved in the tomb of Khety at Beni Hassan, and showed the man, with red-brown skin, lying atop a woman, whose skin was light gold, facing him, on an ebony bed. This sign was quite clear on the wall, although it was depicted in the late nineteenth-century publication as a break (Newberry 1893: pl. 14). Since this sign appears to be a generic hieroglyphic ideogram, the form the intercourse took was presumably the norm. Other depictions of sexual intercourse, in much less conventional positions, occur on the Turin Erotic Papyrus and assorted inscribed potsherds from the New Kingdom. There, men with sexual organs as long as their arms approached or penetrated scantily clad and uncomfortably positioned women. Even more generously endowed men were represented in sculptures of the late period, some of which were possibly of religious significance or to be used as amulets.

It has been suggested that the Turin papyrus served as a manual or a bill of fare at a house of prostitution (Manniche 1987: 107), but in fact the institution of female prostitution was not well attested until the later periods of Egyptian history, when it occurred in the Greek-influenced story of Setne-Khaemwas and possibly other texts. During the pharaonic period, the two characters in literary works who offered to pay for sex were in both cases women. In the story of the unfaithful wife in papyrus Westcar, the wife of the high priest sent a box of clothing to a man of the town to engage his attention (Simpson 1973: 16), while in the Tale of Two Brothers, the wife of Anubis offered to make her brother-in-law fine clothes if he would sleep with her (Simpson 1973: 95). Interestingly, when she repeated the proposition to her husband, as coming from his brother, no remuneration was mentioned. Given that cloth may have served as a kind of informal currency, and that it was a product produced by women, mention of it in these contexts suggests a stereotype.

Male homosexual interest and sexual relations, though not well attested, were mentioned in several literary works. Such a violation of gender roles, in view of the cosmological importance of gender distinctions, was clearly seen as violating the norms. In the myth recounting the contest of the gods Horus and Seth for the throne of Egypt, Seth claimed to have taken the active role in homosexual intercourse with Horus, and this was apparently felt to disqualify Horus for the kingship; he was spat upon by the other gods (Parkinson 1991: 120–1; Simpson 1973: 120–1). No disgrace seems to have attached to Seth for his part of this activity, however, presumably because he claimed to have taken the male role, and therefore did not violate societal expectations. Horus's (alleged) transgression was in taking the female role, not merely in participating in homosexual intercourse. Nevertheless, in at least some contexts, homosexual activity was seen more as a subject for humor than as a shocking violation of societal norms. A Middle Kingdom story about a king of the Old Kingdom, the long-reigning Pepi II, recounted his scandalous behavior with a general "in whose entire house was no woman." The story seems to represent the attempts of outraged citizens to discover and discourage such activities as laughable, and in one case, thwarted by court musicians (Parkinson 1991: 54–6).

There were no textual allusions in the ancient Egyptian corpus to female homosexuality outside of dream books and protestations of innocence put in the mouths of the dead (Manniche 1987: 22). This may be due to the fact that most literature was produced by men. Nor is transvestitism attested, perhaps because the clothing and hairstyles of men and women were in many periods too similar to serve as a marker of gender. In one interesting statue, however, Sobeknofru (1760–1755 BCE), a reigning queen at the end of the Twelfth Dynasty, was shown wearing a man's kilt over the traditional close-fitting woman's dress (Callender 2000: 170–1).

Law and Social Custom about Women

Despite the sharp distinction between the sexes, ancient Egyptian society seems to have been somewhat less patriarchal than most of its neighbors. Women had, in theory, the same legal status and rights as men, although social custom and community pressure seem to have prevented them from exercising them very often (McDowell 1999: 40–1). Women could own property, including agricultural land, and could sell or bequeath it as they desired. They inherited shares that were equal to the shares of their brothers from their parents' property. In a pre-industrial society, this control over land, the most productive type of capital investment, presumably implied considerable economic power. In the Graeco-Roman and Coptic periods (332 BCE–641 CE), women flourished as money-lenders, a similar type of capital investment (Pomeroy 1990; Wilfong 2002). And throughout the pharaonic period (3100–332 BCE), women produced cloth in their homes, a durable commodity which served as a unit of economic exchange, particularly in the early periods. In the Old Kingdom tomb of Akhethetep, men were shown examining strips of cloth and putting them in boxes, while other men distributed jewelry to women, who departed wearing it, suggesting that any excess in this private production could be sold and that the profits were their own (Ziegler 1993: 116–18; Fischer 2000: 65 n. 104).

In addition to holding economic power, some women were also politically important. Kings' mothers seem to have been highly respected, and in the case of minor kings, often served as regent for their sons. Several other queens, notably Sobeknofru (1760–1755 BCE) in the Twelfth Dynasty, Hatshepsut (1473–1458 BCE) in the Eighteenth Dynasty, and Tawosret (1198–1190 BCE) in the Nineteenth Dynasty, became pharaohs and ruled in their own right. The monuments of both Hatshepsut and Tawosret were intentionally defaced and usurped after their deaths, but it is unclear what this persecution truly represented. Some have argued for a general resentment of female rule (Wente 1984). However, the persecution of reigning queens may also be attributed to the fact that such queens tended to rule as the last members of a dynastic line, and subsequent rulers may have attacked their legitimacy as a means of emphasizing their own. Kings' mothers who reigned during the minority of their sons were honored by them, in at least one case for their political effectiveness. Queen Ahhotep (1590–1530 BCE) of the early Eighteenth Dynasty was praised by her son for having cared for the army and recovered fugitives and deserters from it, and for having expelled rebels (Vandersleyen 1971: 129–96).

In twentieth-century histories of Egypt, the role of male advisors who were prominent during these reigns was heavily emphasized: "It is not to be imagined, however, that even a woman of the most virile character could have attained such a pinnacle of power without masculine support" (Gardiner 1961: 184). It is often implied that these men behind the throne had sexual relationships with the queens they served, although there is no evidence for such assertions. To judge from the example of a later female pharaoh, Cleopatra VII (51–30 BCE), however, it is at least not impossible that these earlier women in fact ruled Egypt during their reigns.

Another office held by women was that of "God's Wife of Amun." This position was held in the Eighteenth Dynasty by royal wives and other women of the royal family and was presumably largely ceremonial in its duties, though perhaps quite generous in its remuneration. In the Third Intermediate Period (1075–715 BCE), it was revived in a different form as a kind of high priesthood of Amun and king's deputy in southern Egypt. These later God's Wives were depicted on the walls of their monuments performing the king's role in traditional rituals before the gods, and they seem to have held political as well as religious power. Again the question has arisen of the extent to which they were simply figureheads, with their male stewards holding the true power. It has been remarked that the tombs of the stewards and other officials serving the God's Wives were extremely large and elaborate, many times the size of the small tombs of the women themselves. Nonetheless, the location of these smaller tombs in a temple complex may have signified their greater importance, despite their smaller size. The women who held this office in its later form were royal daughters who did not pass the office on to their own daughters, but to daughters of the next king, whom they adopted. Because their successors were adopted and because no husbands of these women were attested, they are usually presumed to have been celibate, although this was clearly not true of earlier holders of the office. They were sometimes also called "Divine Votaress," "Divine Adoratrice," or "God's Hand," the last title being a reference to the role of the hand of the creator god in the story of creation.

Non-royal women could also serve in temples. In the Old Kingdom and Middle Kingdom periods, elite women could serve as prophets in the cults of goddesses (most commonly Hathor and Neith), and kings' daughters of the early Old Kingdom served in the mortuary cults of their fathers. Later, women's roles in temples seem to have been more limited and specialized; they served as "chantresses," providing music at rituals of both male and female divinities, a role also attested in earlier periods.

The most common career for women, however, seems to have been marriage and family. Marriage was a strictly social institution. It apparently had no religious implications, and it was not marked by any religious ceremony. Nor was it normally seen as a concern of the Egyptian state. It was sometimes constrained by a contract between the parties, usually when property or children from previous unions were involved. The constraints imposed by social customs and expectations were presumably considerably more restrictive. While both parties seem to have had equal rights within the marriage legally, literary sources suggested a double standard: adultery in women was often punishable by death, while in men it did not seem to have been seen as meriting punishment, though the adulterous man was sometimes made to look ridiculous. Wisdom texts advised men against seducing women, but essentially because of the danger of alienating their male relatives for so trivial a reason.

Changes in Gender Roles over Time

Galvin pointed out a marked decrease in the importance of women's roles in the Hathor priesthood between the Old Kingdom and the Middle Kingdom (1984), and Fischer has shown that this change was a more general phenomenon (2000: 45). One Old Kingdom woman was accorded the title of "overseer of (female) doctors," implying that other female doctors existed to be overseen. In the tomb of Princess Watetkhethor of the early Sixth Dynasty, women were depicted who held the titles "steward" (literally "overseer of the house"), "overseer of equipment," "overseer of cloth," and "overseer of ornaments." Elsewhere, women had the titles "overseer of singers," "overseer of a dance troupe," and "overseer of the house of weavers" (Fischer 2000: 18–20). Interestingly, the feminine form of the title "overseer" itself is only attested for the Old Kingdom and the early Middle Kingdom (Ward 1986: 3–4). These positions indicate supervision only of other women, and are usually attested in the households of other women. Similarly, female doctors probably also served only women. These titles may thus be the result of a degree of sexual segregation of upper class women rather than evidence for a high degree of professional specializations among women. Nonetheless, the fact that these women were depicted with their professional titles showed that public decorum allowed such women a greater degree of visibility than was possible in later periods.

Religious institutions also showed a decrease in professional female staff over time. The title "prophet" was attested for women primarily in the cults of goddesses in the Old and Middle Kingdom; women could hold a lower title, "*wab*-priest," in the cults of male gods in the Middle Kingdom. Later, women serving in the cults of both gods and goddesses were limited to the musical roles that had always been the principal type of temple service for women.

The literacy of women has long been a question. There is no explicit evidence for female literacy in the Old Kingdom, although one would think it was probably necessary to perform such offices as steward. A female form of the title "scribe" is attested in the Middle Kingdom, though some have argued that it should be translated "cosmetician." Women in the New Kingdom period were sometimes shown with scribal equipment, and a scribal palette bearing the name of a king's daughter was found in the tomb of Tutankhamun. A clear example of a female scribe existed in the Twenty-Sixth Dynasty (664–525 BCE); she served in the household of the God's Wife of Amun (Piacentini 2001: 193). Given the Twenty-Sixth Dynasty enthusiasm for reviving older forms, her role may have been inspired by the women who served as administrators in the households of Old Kingdom royal women.

Summary

The ancient Egyptian view of the world stressed the creation of women and men at the same time and their essential equality, as well as their contrasting and complementary roles. Their equality was reflected in Egyptian laws, but was limited and modified by social pressures and traditions. It is clear that men were viewed as having higher status socially than women. This was shown when a married couple was represented and the woman was depicted at a markedly smaller scale and by the fact that affectionate gestures so often were directed by women toward men.

One of the main controversies in Egyptological scholarship about gender relations has been between those who would emphasize the independence and autonomy of Egyptian women as an (admirable) anomaly in the ancient world and those who prefer to stress the evidence that, despite the fact that a few women seem to have held economic and political power, most of the female population were occupied with domestic duties and were economically dependent upon their male relatives. Much of the evidence on this question is a matter of interpretation. Were female rulers and

God's Wives truly exercising authority by themselves, or were they merely figure-heads? Are letters that seem to have been written by women truly evidence that at least some women were literate, or were they simply dictated to scribes? Despite such questions, it is clear that Egyptian women, particularly those of the upper class, had considerably greater legal rights and social autonomy than was found in many ancient civilizations and could sometimes exercise real political and economic power.

FURTHER READING

There is an extensive recent literature about women in ancient Egypt, although less has been written on gender and sexuality. For a very full bibliography, occasionally updated on line, see Wilfong 1992. Among the general semi-popular books in English, Robins 1993 is the most comprehensive, offering a clear presentation of most of the evidence. Other useful general works on the topic are those of Tyldesley 1994, Nur el-Din 1995, Hawass 2000, and the more popular Watterson 1992. Two exhibitions dealing with women have catalogs focusing on expressions of gender in material culture and containing useful essays, Capel and Markoe 1996 and Wilfong 1997.

More specific studies have dealt with particular communities, where the roles of women were especially well attested, for example the community of Deir el-Medina (Pinch 1983, Sweeney 1992, McDowell 1999) and the much later Coptic town of Djeme (Wilfong 2002). Troy 1986 deals with the royal women of Egypt and their particular sexual and symbolic roles.

Shorter periods of Egyptian history have also been subjected to more detailed study of gender. For the comparatively greater autonomy of women in the Old Kingdom, see Galvin 1984 and Fischer 2000. For the often neglected Middle Kingdom period, see Ward 1986, 1989, and Lustig 1997. The New Kingdom period tends to be the main focus of the more general works, but is specifically addressed in Robins 1989. Considerable work has been done specifically on the roles of women in the Graeco-Roman period; see Pomeroy 1990. For gender questions more generally in the same period, see Montserrat 1996.

For sexuality in the pharaonic period, Manniche 1987 offers a useful collection of the sources. One area of sexuality where much has been written is its role in mortuary beliefs. The necessity for sexual union to re-conceive the dead in the afterlife was first suggested by Desroches-Noblecourt 1953 and Westendorf 1967; no synthetic study of this phenomenon has yet appeared in English, although several aspects of it are discussed in Roth 2000.

CHAPTER SIXTEEN

Royal Women and the Exercise of Power in the Ancient Near East

Sarah C. Melville

All of the diverse societies that made up the long continuum of Mesopotamian history were ruled by kings, and those kings were men. Only one woman was ever acknowledged as a ruler in her own right. According to the Sumerian King List, Ku-Baba, a tavern woman, ruled Kish as king (not queen) for a hundred years during the third millennium. Ku-Baba, about whom we know little else, remained an anomaly, however (Jacobsen 1939b: 104–5).

Although women could not be rulers and were, like everyone else, subordinate to them, those women who were closest to the king – his wife or wives, mother, sisters, and daughters – did take part in political, administrative, and religious life. Women who exercised power did so on behalf of their husbands or sons, rather than independently, and the power they wielded derived from typical female activities such as marriage, childbirth, or household management. The women of the royal household could be extremely valuable to the king or his heirs, and these women were often active, dynamic contributors to their family's interests. Ideally, members of the royal family, including the king, acted to further the interests of what was essentially a corporate body, that is, the family, tribe, or dynasty. Royal women did not exist in marginalized isolation, but played vital roles that were developed to fulfill both political needs and social requirements.

We cannot expect that women of all periods or in all places experienced life in the same way. The evidence concerning royal women is incomplete and difficult to interpret: sometimes plentiful and varied, sometimes scarce or overly specific. The different types of evidence we encounter range from economic documents, letters, and monumental inscriptions to artistic representations, jewelry, and other personal items, but rarely, if ever, do we have anything like a complete array of evidence for any one woman let alone a single time or place. In spite of the often frustrating lack of data, there is still too much to consider thoroughly here. Therefore, I have chosen examples from different periods and areas of Mesopotamia that illustrate particular points especially well.

Royal Women and the Royal Household

Although it has often been assumed that the women of the kings' palaces lived cloistered, cut off from public interaction, architectural remains do not support such a conjecture (Westenholtz 1990: 513–16), nor, with the possible exception of the Middle Assyrian period, is there evidence that women were required to be veiled in public (Stol 1995: 124). It is important, therefore, that we should not confuse the women of the Ancient Near East with the exotic harem courtesans evoked in modern romance. Numerous women of varying status lived and worked in the palace; the mother of the king or the king's primary wife was usually of the highest rank. It is not always possible to determine how many women were attached to a palace, but texts such as ration lists indicate that the female population could be substantial. For instance, at Ebla toward the end of the third millennium, distribution records show that the number of royal wives increased from twenty or thirty to fifty over a short period (Archi 2002: 3). A thousand years later in Assyria, wine lists suggest that perhaps as many as three hundred women of different ranks lived at the palace (Kinnier-Wilson 1972: 44). Of the many women associated with the palace, only the most elite – the queen mother, royal spouse, king's daughters and occasionally sisters – have left much evidence of their active involvement in affairs of state; hence it is to these women that we limit our investigation.

There is almost no information concerning the education royal women received, although the accomplishments evinced by some of them prove that they were capable of creative self-expression. Enheduanna, the daughter of Sargon, founder of the Empire of Akkad around 2334 BCE, is the world's earliest identified author. She was responsible for composing a cycle of hymns dedicated to the goddess Inanna (Hallo and Van Dijk 1968). Some of the royal women of the Ur III period (2112–2004 BCE) have been credited with authoring poems such as a lament for the death of the king Ur-nammu, a lullaby for a crown prince, and a love lyric for the king Šu-Sin (Hallo 1978: 32). It is unknown whether any of these women could actually write, but in light of the fact that only two kings in Mesopotamian history claimed that ability, Šulgi and Assurbanipal, it seems likely that the women relied on scribes to record their compositions.

The fact that women received particular titles indicates that rank was as important for women as it was for men. In most cases, women's titles can be consistently translated as in queen mother or king's daughter, but the title designating the king's spouse varied a great deal and did not always mean queen. For this reason, we use the neutral term wife except in specific cases where queen is appropriate.

Royal women were rarely depicted on public monuments or mentioned in inscriptions, but when occasionally they did appear, they were subordinate only to the king or divinities. Thus, Enheduanna appeared on a sculptured disc worshiping Inanna (Winter 1987; Bahrani 2001: 113–17), and on a bronze relief, Naqia, the mother of Esarhaddon (680–669 BCE), was portrayed in a ritual pose behind her son (Melville 1999: 25–6; Ornan 2002: 461–77).

Grave goods also attest to the fact that the king's primary wife and mother were particularly revered. The Early Dynastic III graves at Ur in the late third millennium contained a seal bearing the inscription of Puabi, the queen. The rich finds associated with the grave and the practice of retainer burial – killing and burying subjects with the ruler and his wife – reveal that Puabi's status was comparable to that of the king (Pollock 1991: 372–9). The high regard accorded royal burials is evident throughout Mesopotamian history. Recent excavation of the tombs of two Neo-Assyrian consorts at Nimrud produced extraordinary examples of gold jewelry, crowns, and personal objects (Harak 1990; George 1990).

Men could gain status through their relationships with elite women, but at the same time, a man's honor was intimately tied to "his" women. At Ebla in the mid-third millennium the brothers of the queen mother received goods and rank as a direct result of their relationship to her (Archi 2002: 6). Sometimes men became legitimate rulers only through marriage into the royal family, and certainly a king's virile image was enhanced by having more women, and therefore more children, in his household. If, on the other hand, a man lost control of the women of his household, he lost status. The capture of royal families became a topos in Assyrian royal inscriptions, symbolizing the utter defeat and humiliation of the enemy. For instance, when Tiglath-pileser I (1114–1076 BCE) defeated Kili-Teshub, the king of Kutmuhi on the upper Tigris River, and took "his wives, his sons, the offspring of his loins, (and) his household" (Luckenbill 1926: 75), he not only dealt a terrible blow to the enemy tribe; he cuckolded its leader. By taking over the household of an enemy, a king assumed all the power and authority that had belonged to his adversary. This gesture was widely recognized in the Ancient Near East and appears in the Bible (2 Samuel 12: 11, 16: 21–2) and accounts of Alexander the Great (Brown 1981: 2; Hoff 2002: 243). Royal women were highly regarded and symbolically important, but their official roles are much more difficult to determine. They varied according to whether the context was administrative, political, or religious.

Royal Women and State Administration

Where there is evidence of royal administration of land, trade, and the economy, there is evidence that royal women were active as well, often holding positions of responsibility on behalf of the king or taking part in private transactions of their own. Excavations of the Early Dynastic levels at Lagash, for example, uncovered large numbers of tablets which proved to be the archive of an agricultural institution called the "household of the wife" administered by the ruler's wife. These women managed the cultivation of over ten thousand acres, or 4,048 hectares, of land and were responsible for a huge and complex administration which employed a large number of men, women, and children to labor in the fields, tend livestock, and produce textiles in return for food rations. Institutions like that of Lagash existed in several cities and functioned throughout the early periods of Mesopotamian history (Van De Mieroop 1989: 54). The royal women of the Sargonic period similarly administered large estates in their own right and traveled freely between them (Foster 1987b: 53; Sallaberger and Westenholz 1999: 70–2). The significant contributions made by royal wives of the Ur III state (2112–2004 BCE) to the administration of the state economy are well attested in several cities of the empire (Kang 1971: 2–7; Sallaberger and Westenholz 1999: 182–5).

Royal women often held positions of great responsibility and were sometimes second only to the king. At Ebla in the mid-third millennium the king's mother and the queen were among the most dominant people at court (Biga 1987: 41–7; Archi 2002: 1). From Mari, a city now near the Iraqi–Syrian border, around 1800 BCE there is copious evidence for the administrative activity of royal women. A large archive of letters to and from Shibtu, the wife of the ruler Zimri-Lim, demonstrates that when the king was away on campaign, she acted as his representative. He sent her directions and information, and she in turn carried out his orders and reported back to him. From her letters it is apparent that the king delegated authority and tasks to Shibtu, yet there seems not to have been any one specific area or institution over which she exercised sole control. Although Shibtu was subordinate to the king, her administrative role mirrored his; she participated in virtually all areas of administration, and her sphere of influence extended beyond the bounds of Mari itself (Artzi and Malamat 1971: 83–6; Batto 1974: 15). Letters show that she was usually carrying out her husband's instructions, so it is best to exercise caution in ascribing to her real political power. Shibtu's power seems to have derived from her personal talents, the king's trust, and the privileges of her office.

But not all rulers' wives were as autonomous or active as Shibtu. A few years earlier a letter from Šamši-Adad to his son complained that the son did not treat his primary wife with the respect due her position and as a result she had little input either in palace administration or over her own fate (Batto 1974: 20–1). This suggests that the extent to which royal wives participated in administration depended on their own abilities and above all on their relationship with their husbands.

During the Neo-Assyrian period (934–610 BCE) elite women took part in economic affairs, owned and administered estates, and fulfilled tax obligations. The king's primary wife was wealthy in her own right; she received a share of tribute and audience gifts which other women did not, and she could even own her own palace. The consort and the queen mother employed a large number of men and women and ran households that were in many respects mirror images of the king's or the crown prince's (Melville in press). Some of the king's secondary wives probably came to court through diplomatic marriage, bringing with them suitable attendants and personal assets, over which they maintained some control. Evidence for the economic activity of secondary wives and concubines is scanty, but it is likely that they were free to carry out business transactions using their personal wealth. Neo-Assyrian royal women could act individually, dispose of their own property as they wished, and administer large domains, but it is likely that whatever wealth they acquired reverted to the king when they died, and therefore their independence was something of a fiction.

Privileged women of all periods, especially the ruler's wife or his mother, played important administrative roles. It is not always possible to determine when they were acting in an official capacity and when they were dealing as private persons. Nor is it clear whether and in what way their activities may have been curtailed by gender constraints. Nonetheless, the highest ranking women enjoyed economic freedoms and administrative responsibilities which were on a par with, or exceeded, those of many men.

Women and Politics

Although royal women could be important in civil administration, in the political arena their roles tended to be symbolic rather than active. A strong royal wife might be her spouse's true partner; the king's mother might help him gain the throne, and his daughters could, when married to vassals or other kings, be important political tools. These women never acted on their own behalf, but always as representatives of men. Thus, the role of the king's wife in diplomacy tended to be gender specific; she dealt primarily with other women as in the case of an Early Dynastic consort, Baranamtara of Lagash, who exchanged gifts with Ninizkimti, the wife of the ruler of Adab before 2400 BCE (Hallo 1978: 28). Such exchanges demonstrated to both sides that the rulers were the heads of proper families of equal status who knew and followed the rules of diplomacy.

Toward the end of the second millennium, the Hittite queen Pudu-hepa corresponded with both the Egyptian pharaoh, Ramesses II, and his wife, Nefertari, but this correspondence was restricted to perfunctory formal greetings and some negotiation about the marriage of a Hittite princess to the Egyptian king (Otten 1975: 26). Undoubtedly Pudu-hepa's letters were meant to show that the Hittite royal couple were equal to the Egyptian ruler and his wife, but they also reflected a practice peculiar to the Hittites, that the queen, rather than the king, chose which royal daughter would marry.

The mothers of kings could sometimes enter the political fray, though they always did so on behalf of their sons. Some of the most powerful women in Mesopotamian history acquired their authority by helping their sons gain or keep the throne (Ben-Barak 1987: 34–40). The Neo-Babylonian king Nabonidus (555–539 BCE), who was not of royal birth, was introduced at court by his mother, Adad-guppi, who was instrumental in his rise to power and later provided him with a convenient rationale for claiming legitimacy; her pious deeds brought him to the attention of the gods, who then put him on the throne (Beaulieu 1989: 78–9). Adad-guppi lived to the ripe old age of a hundred and four and was a great help to her son, symbolically if not actually.

The Neo-Assyrian queen mothers, Shammu-ramat (Semiramis of legend) and Naqia, both played important roles during their sons' reigns. Naqia corresponded with officials in cities throughout the empire, made donations to temples, built a palace, and administered her estates. Naqia was a prominent and respected figure at court, but there is no evidence that she actually took part in politics except on one occasion when, after her son's sudden death, she fulfilled his wishes and imposed a loyalty oath on the Assyrian populace on behalf of her grandson, the new king, Assurbanipal (668–627 BCE) (Melville 1999: 79–90). These women were undoubtedly exceptional, but they did not directly wield political power. They always acted on behalf of their sons or grandsons for the benefit of their families and dynasties.

There were three basic types of political marriage in the Ancient Near East: dynastic marriage, diplomatic marriage between equal states, and marriage to tie a vassal to the lord. Around 2150 BCE it was the custom at Lagash for the ruler to gain the throne by marrying a daughter of the previous ruler or, if there was none, a daughter of the ruling family. In this way Gudea became ruler of Lagash by marrying Ninalla, the daughter of Urbaba (Röllig 1974: 12–13). Marriage continued to be used as one of the chief ways for a man to legitimize his claim to the throne. By marrying Shibtu, the daughter of the ruler of the powerful state of Yamhad, Zimri-Lim acquired sufficient military backing to reclaim the throne of Mari and implement his lifelong but ultimately unsuccessful effort to extend his territories. The complex political marriages of the Neo-Babylonian period (626–539 BCE) offer another example of this type of union: Neriglissar, the son of an official, married into the royal family and then murdered his brother-in-law, the king Amel-Marduk. Neriglissar then claimed the throne on the strength of his link to the dynasty through Amel-Marduk's sister (Weisberg 1974: 448).

During the Sargonic period (2334–2193 BCE) one of the daughters of the king of Marhashi in northwest Iran joined the royal family of Akkad by marrying either the king or his son. Less than a century later, Ur-Nammu, the first king of the Ur III dynasty (2112–2004 BCE), arranged a marriage between his son and the daughter of the king of Mari, thus establishing a friendly relationship between the two city-states. Sometimes marriage alliances failed to achieve the desired political objective, however. In his thirty-first year, Šulgi, the third king of the Ur III dynasty, married his daughter to the king of Anshan on the Iranian plateau. The marriage was a diplomatic failure, for Šulgi destroyed Anshan shortly afterwards. The daughter of Šu-Sin was married to the king of Shimanum in the mountains north of Iraq, but the couple was subsequently deposed, and Šu-Sin had to go to war to restore them to power (Hallo 1978: 31).

Not only did the Mari king Zimri-Lim use his daughters to set up alliances and secure vassals, but once they were installed in their new homes, these women gathered intelligence for their father and many of their letters contained reports on the political maneuvers of their husbands (Lafont 1987). When the marriage and the alliance were successful, the daughters led rewarding lives, but if the political circumstances deteriorated or the marriage itself failed, then the situation of the daughter could become intolerable, prompting her to write to her father begging him to call her home. Zimri-Lim was sensitive to the plight of his daughters. Once Zimri-Lim responded to an urgent request to return to Mari by telling his daughter to "Go ahead and gather your household. If that is not possible, (just) cover your head and depart" (Sasson 1973: 65). However uncertain their situations sometimes were, the daughters of Zimri-Lim actively and enthusiastically corresponded with their father, whom they expected seriously to consider their reports and counsel. In one case, a princess even went so far as to remind her father of the negative consequences of not heeding her advice (Sasson 1973: 68). Because Zimri-Lim and his daughters operated in a limited geographical area among a homogeneous ethnic group, the royal women of Mari were able to take part in political exchanges to an unprecedented degree. When the political stage grew to include a wide area and many different cultures, however, the significance of diplomatic marriage changed and with it the role of the women involved.

During the Late Bronze Age (1500–1100 BCE), diplomatic marriage was carried out not only between kings and their vassals, but on a grand scale at an international level as the Great Kings of the Hittites, Mitanni, Assyrians, Kassites, and Egyptians schemed to make alliances and outwit their enemies. The diplomatic correspondence recovered from Amarna in Egypt contains a number of revealing letters about arranged royal marriages. But the diverse cultures involved had different concepts of the political relationships created by marriage ties. The pharaoh did not permit Egyptian royal women to marry foreign kings, but he did allow foreign women to join his household. Thus the Egyptians saw marriage alliances as acknowledging their own superiority, while the Near Eastern kings considered that they gained the upper hand by becoming the fathers-in-law of the pharaoh (Meier 2000: 170–1). No matter how the different kings presented such marriages to their own subjects, the fact is that they helped secure parity between the great powers rather than creating vassal relationships.

Marriage agreements between equal powers were accomplished only after lengthy negotiations (Artzi 1987: 23–6). To prove her worth and thus the worth of her father, a royal bride-to-be was sent to her new home accompanied by a large number of attendants and a huge dowry, and the groom paid a sizeable bride-price for his new wife. Anything less would have been demeaning. The Kassite king Burnaburiash wrote indignantly to the pharaoh asking, "Who is going to take her to you? With Haya (the Egyptian messenger) there are five chariots. Are they going to take her to you in (only) five chariots? Should I in these circumstances allow her to be brought to you from my house, my neighboring kings would say, 'They have transported the daughter of the Great King to Egypt in five chariots'" (Moran 1992: text 11).

Kings were always anxious to safeguard their daughter's status because it reflected their own. When the Hittite king Suppiluliuma (1344–1322 BCE) negotiated a marriage contract between the king of Mitanni and his own daughter, he insisted that "You shall not bring my daughter into the position of second wife. In Mitanni she shall rule as queen" (Schulman 1979: 178 n. 3). Even though the kings maintained lively communication via messengers and embassies, once a woman married a foreign king, she was not able to remain in close contact with her original family. In fact, the Kassite king Kadashman-Enlil (1374?–1360 BCE) felt compelled to complain to the pharaoh, "Here you are asking for my daughter in marriage, but my sister whom my father gave you was (already) there with you, and no one has seen her (so as to know) if now she is alive or if she is dead" (Moran 1992: text 1).

Since so many diplomatic marriages took place during this period, kinship ties between the different royal houses became complicated, sometimes with serious political consequences. For example, Mubalitat-Sherua, the daughter of the Assyrian king Assur-uballit I, married the Babylonian king Burnaburiash II and bore a son. When that son was subsequently murdered in a rebellion in 1333 BCE, Assur-uballit, as the murdered king's grandfather, retaliated by invading Babylonia, putting down the revolt, and choosing the next Babylonian king.

It is clear that the treatment of foreign-born royal wives fluctuated with changing political situations. After the Hittite king Suppiluliuma died in 1322 BCE, his Babylonian-born wife was accused of using witchcraft to kill the wife of the new king, Murshili II. Although Murshili got permission from the gods to execute his stepmother, he decided instead to remove her from priestly office, thus substantially reducing her power (Murphy 2002: 441). The accusation was undoubtedly politically motivated, probably in part by the desire to oust a foreigner from an influential position. Under the successive large empires of the first millennium, the Assyrian, Babylonian, and finally Persian, diplomatic marriages usually took place between the prevailing king and his vassals, rather than between kings of equal status as in the Late Bronze Age (Röllig 1974: 21–3; Dalley 1998b).

In all periods ultimate authority resided with the king, and every king struggled to gain, maintain, and expand his authority. He mustered the help of everyone he could, particularly family members. Thus, kings called upon the women most closely associated with them – their wives, mothers, and daughters – to carry out civic, political, or religious duties.

Women and Religion

There is no word for religion in Akkadian or Sumerian. But religion was of elemental importance to the cultures of the Near East whose peoples worshiped numerous deities and whose cities each boasted one or more great temples. The king was the link between the mundane world and the divine one, and as such usually took a leading role in the worship of the most important god or gods. Custom also required that the king's close relatives, both male and female, participate in worship, but there was a political element to their involvement as well. Particularly important temples could be rich and influential, and the king had always to check their acquisition of power and look after his own interests by taking an active role in the performance of religious duties, by appointing those closest to him to key priestly positions, or by encouraging family members to patronize temples which he supported. Although not all cultic activity was politically inspired, and certainly not all priests or priestesses were members of the royal family, royal participation in cult practice, if it was particularly visible or overtly generous, had a political payoff. The royal family, including female members, carried out cultic duties and ran temple administrations during all periods of Mesopotamian history. Royal women participated in religious activities on three levels: as private individuals, as occasional celebrants, or as official priestesses whose lives were dedicated to the service of the gods.

Royal women made offerings to deities on behalf of themselves, the king, or their sons. Dedications took various forms including small statues, plaques, jewelry, or temple accouterments. Thus, Watartum, the wife of the Ur III king Ur-Nammu, dedicated an agate plaque to the goddess Inanna for the life of their son, Šulgi (2094–2047 BCE) (Sollberger 1967: 69; Steinkeller 1981: 77). Over fifteen hundred years later Naqia, the mother of Esarhaddon (680–669 BCE), made a similar dedication on an inscribed pectoral, or breast ornament, petitioning "the Lady" of a temple for "the life of Esarhaddon and for herself, her own life, the length of her days, the stability of her reign and her well-being" (Melville 1999: 43). If the king's wife or mother was particularly concerned about something, such as the welfare of the king while on campaign, she might consult oracles or diviners. Aside from making personal contributions or seeking reassurance, royal women might be expected to provide animals and fresh produce for daily temple offerings, and also contributed gold or other material toward temple construction, the fashioning of a divine statue or temple furniture (Melville 1999: 112). The contributions made by royal women to temples were comparable to those made by high officials or male members of the royal family other than the king.

Some religious ceremonies required the involvement of the king and his wife. The worship of certain deities, not just female ones, called for female suppliants, and the celebration of particular festivals needed both high-ranking women and men. In addition, a great deal of ritual was dedicated to promoting the welfare of the king and his family, who were the main performers in such ceremonies. The wives of the rulers of Lagash during the Early Dynastic period carried out cultic duties at temples in cities throughout the state (Asher-Greve 1985: 146–55). The royal princesses of Ebla, who were married to foreign kings, returned to their home city to perform rites on special occasions such as royal births or marriages (Archi 2002: 4). Likewise, the royal daughters of Mari had cultic duties which they continued to perform even after they were married and had moved to another city (Sasson 1973: 77). In Assyria, royal women participated in both occasional rites and ones that were a regular part of the cultic calendar. When Esarhaddon's wife died, her daughter, daughter-in-law, the king's secondary wives, and perhaps concubines all took part in the funeral (Melville in press). The king's closest family members, both male and female, participated in the annual celebration of the marriage of the gods Nabu and Tashmetum (Cole and Machinist 1998: 56).

When the king named a sister or a daughter to a priestly position, there were sometimes far-reaching political implications. Sargon appointed his daughter Enheduanna about 2300 BCE to be high priestess of the moon god Nanna at Ur, and perhaps high priestess of An at Uruk. The move was apparently calculated to help consolidate Sargon's rule of the city states. By giving his daughter a Sumerian name and appointing her to a prestigious Sumerian post, Sargon aimed to unify the Sumerian south and tie it to the Akkadian north. Sargon must have successfully achieved his political objectives through the appointment because for the next five hundred years kings continued to assign their daughters to the post of high priestess at Ur. Through much of the second millennium this office was one of the major symbols of legitimate rule in Babylonia, and only the ruling dynasty could place a member of its household in the position. The office of high priestess was held for life, and a replacement could only be made after the death of the incumbent (Hallo 1978: 29–30).

Much later the Neo-Babylonian king Nabonidus revived the tradition by making his daughter high priestess of the moon god. By promoting the moon god, he probably hoped to counteract the political machinations of the powerful priesthood of the god Marduk in Babylon (Weisberg 1974: 449–50; Beaulieu 1989: 71).

Further, by restoring an ancient tradition, he could claim to ally himself with the ancient kings who began it and, in effect, to borrow legitimacy and status from them.

Conclusions

The roles of elite women were complex, various, and subject to a high degree of fluctuation due to changing political circumstances. In administration and religion royal women acted both officially as administrators or priestesses, and privately, by carrying out economic transactions of their own or making personal dedications to temples. In politics, however, women's official roles were symbolic. Although we may imagine that powerful women took part in personal politics at least on the level of court intrigue, there is little direct evidence for that.

Women did wield power right alongside men, but they had different roles, different means of exercising influence, and different avenues of authority from men. According to deeply ingrained cultural principles, the head of a dynasty, tribe, or state had to be male; therefore even the most exalted woman was always second to at least one man. For the same reasons, when royal women took part in administration or politics, they always did so to further the interests of the royal family as a whole. Women were critically important to the highest ranking men; a woman's beauty, brains, and ability to bear children were not only practical assets, but augmented her husband's reputation. The royal women of ancient Mesopotamia fulfilled their societal roles with competence, verve, and occasional panache.

FURTHER READING

For surveys on women in Mesopotamia see Bottéro 1965, Harris 1992, Nemet-Nejat 1999, and Stol 1995. Collections of studies on women and gender in the Ancient Near East include Durand 1987, Lesko 1989, and Parpola and Whiting 2002. Excellent discussions of theoretical, especially feminist, approaches to the study of women in the Ancient Near East appear in Westenholz 1990, Asher-Greve 1997b, and Bahrani 2001. For women in the third millennium, see Hallo 1978, Asher-Greve 1985, Foster 1987b, Van De Mieroop 1989, and Pollock 1991. Batto 1974 provides a good study of women at Mari. On the role of diplomatic marriage see Röllig 1974, Artzi 1987, and Meier 2000. For the first millennium see Melville 1999, Melville in press, Weisberg 1974, and Brosius 1996.

CHAPTER SEVENTEEN

Warfare in Ancient Egypt

Anthony J. Spalinger

War is one way cultures express their hostilities and individuals further their ambitions. It probably is as old as human groups, and disruption of such groups is a legacy of its practice. War presents humans at their worst, but frequently in the past some have seen it as a noble endeavor devoted to the protection of particular groups.

Our study of the wars of the ancients tends to stress their achievements in logistics, in organizing and supplying armies especially in lands far from home. Ancient sources underline such triumphs and tend to ignore refugees and even casualties on our side, though the many killed and captured among the enemy may be noted, to our glory.

We think war was central to the organizing of some if not all ancient states, by which we mean large political organizations that proceeded more on the basis of the continuity of the institution rather than the personality of an individual leader. Without military coercion the famous states might not have arisen or might have had a very different shape from what they actually had.

This process may be most clearly seen in Egypt where sources early and late stress war's power to shape and reshape Egypt's organization. The other state with a long military history is Assyria, but its prowess is not attested over so long a period, only about 1400 to 612 BCE, while Egypt's stretches from 3100 BCE through to Cleopatra, who died in 30 BCE, and beyond. And the Assyrian sources have not been so fully exploited as for Egypt (Saggs 1984; Fales 2001).

Thus we will concentrate here on Egypt, but Egypt was not isolated in the development of military organization or of equipment. Here we shall try to give a sense of developments from earliest times to the end of the New Kingdom in the 1000s BCE, though of course the story continues after that.

Egyptian weaponry was not highly developed in Pre-dynastic times (Dreyer 1998). There appear to be no differences between north (Lower Egypt) and south (Upper Egypt), since differences do not show up in writing of key military terms in ancient Egyptian (Loprieno 1995a).

The sources stress the naval profession in the Old Kingdom (Third to Sixth Dynasties about 2650–2175 BCE), and the extensive maritime trade with the Levant, the east coast of the Mediterranean Sea, provides additional clues of the importance of the navy (Eichler 1993). Late Old Kingdom scenes from private tombs also show the beginning of siege warfare with infantry. The military system and equipment seem primitive (Shaw 1996: 242–3, 259). The development of warfare may have been arrested early in Egypt around 3100 BCE, when kings united the Nile valley, secured internal stability, eliminated opposition, and so required no more innovation. The Egyptian state wanted increasingly to protect its trade routes in the northeast, south, and west and to establish a series of border posts (Ziermann 1993). The Old Kingdom sent garrisons to Nubia for diorite mine development and occupied the oases in the Sixth Dynasty (2325–2175 BCE) (O'Connor 1991: 145–65).

From its etymology we can see that the word "army" originally referred to a host which went forward or proceeded. The word was not limited to a group of armed individuals. Hunters as well as teams of quarrymen were called by this term, and the official in charge was an "overseer" (Posener-Kriéger 1992: 44–8; Berlev 1971).

The military men were called "troops," and they performed such activities as patrolling the frontiers, heading quarrying expeditions, and they were even found instructing royal children (Posener-Kriéger 1992: 44–8). Perhaps this word for troops in the Old Kingdom meant young men, but the early Middle Kingdom (1975–1640 BCE) indicated soldiers under a more general designation of "young men" (Berlev 1967a: 11–14). Yet we also read of "men" among such troops. Both age groups composed the "troops."

But there appears to have been no need for a permanent army in the Old Kingdom. In this period temple decrees frequently described hired male Nubian servants as guards, equivalent to security police (Goedicke 1967: 62–3). Texts from Aswan in the south of Egypt show that in the Sixth Dynasty (2325–2175 BCE) the import trade in luxury goods from the interior of Africa had been put in jeopardy (Lichtheim 1973: 23–7). And small independent city-states had sprung up in southern Palestine.

The foreign situation was fraught with trouble because the state of military preparedness and development was poor. There was no metal armor. Horses and chariots did not exist. There were no sharp and light swords (Shaw 1991: 31–9).

Texts from the First Intermediate Period (Ninth to Eleventh Dynasties 2175–1975 BCE) as well as the archaeological data still indicated a rudimentary military system. Furthermore, the danger to the state of young men in arms was recognized in biographical texts of local leaders and in the Instruction for Merikare (Seidlmeyer 2000: 127–37; Lichtheim 1997: 25–6).

The leaders of this uncertain time, whether pretender pharaohs or local "big men," developed a new politics in which the head of state was at the same time the head of an army. In their propaganda the "good shepherd" motif was introduced, balanced by the "astute leader" (Gnirs 1999: 78–9).

We find Nubian archers in Upper Egypt where they hired out their services to the local war leaders and then to the young Theban state. They also held large plots of land (Fischer 1960).

There were two main divisions in the military. The first consisted of naval troops who provided the most rapid means of transportation. The second group, the foot soldiers, was divided into archers and axe men who fought as a solid mass. They stood a distance from the enemy, often behind firmly planted shields or a protective wooden wall (Shaw 1991). With this arrangement the Egyptians employed their archers more to impede the advance of enemies than to kill them. The main burden remained on those foot soldiers who directly faced the enemy and pushed their way up against them. Near the end of the Eleventh Dynasty (1940 BCE) we have wooden statues of soldiers that enable us to re-create what the soldier looked like (Winlock 1945); their weapons and protection still seem very simple.

The southern Theban Kingdom pushed downstream as well as upstream, and the Mentuhotep II Ballas Inscription lays emphasis upon the "comradeship" between pharaoh and troops around 1948 BCE (Franke 1997). Now it was necessary to claim the beneficent aspects of royal leadership along with the martial ones.

As the Middle Kingdom began, the importance of the navy in the use of the Nile waterway for quick and dependable service in war grew (Berlev 1967b, 1972). The pharaohs of the newly reunified Egypt were able to found a true empire to the south with a time-consuming project of fortress construction, especially at the Second Cataract (Shaw 1991: 18–23; Kemp 1986, 1989: 172–9).

Stasis and Revolution

The pharaohs spent great amounts of resources and time moving southward for a purely economic reason: the acquisition of gold. In the Twelfth Dynasty (1938–1755 BCE) we read for the first time the phrase "Gold of Kush," and in order to secure this lucrative item a foreign policy was forged (Vercoutter 1959; Berlev 1987). With the development of ships it became possible to supply a series of defensive garrisons in the vulnerable cataract regions (Trigger 1976; O'Connor 1993). Complex fortifications, with granaries, slips for boats, thick crenellated walls with eye-sights for the use of archers, and defensive mounding all bear witness to an increased technology of defense.

With this building activity came a long series of wars. Many pharaohs personally led their troops into the heartland of modern Sudan. They burned tents and destroyed fields of grain. Now the king had his own troops, men who were personally dependent upon him for a career (Berlev 1971). This group of soldiers formed the nucleus of the army and was the precursor of the later Egyptian standing army.

The Twelfth Dynasty records prove that an army did exist within Egypt, and that the term "standing" might apply (Berlev 1967b). The elite group consisted of the soldiers in the fleet. In fact, all of the lower state officials in lists from the king's palace at Thebes were directly associated with the military sector (Quirke 1990: 81–3). They were also employed for labor service; army men were used in building projects. Soldiers were chosen when young.

One navy veteran recorded that he went north as far as Avaris in the Northeast Delta and as far south as Kush (Gardiner 1916: 100; Berlev 1967b). He must have been led by a "commander of the ships," the leader who stood over the normal "troops of the naval team." The first deputy of the pharaoh, the vizier, communicated directly with the commanders of the ships. Indeed the vizier may be considered the actual commander of the fleet (Van Den Boorn 1988). The organization of the army at this time allowed only the colonization of that part of Nubia that was close to the river, the control of Kush farther south in Africa, and just possibly the indirect control of several Levantine ports.

Egyptian military activity in Asia was seaborne during the Middle Kingdom. In the Twelfth Dynasty the king's troops served beside other troops who owed loyalty to other powerful magnates of the land. Only with the attrition of the Middle Egyptian governors or nomarchs did the military system become a real branch of the central government (Franke 1991).

Our information on the army in the Twelfth and Thirteenth Dynasties (1938–1630 BCE) comes from private inscriptions. From them we can infer a fixed military hierarchy that was recruited from middle-level families.

Throughout Egypt and Nubia as well most transportation was by ship on the Nile. Hence we find the infantryman usually being transported by boat (Bourriau 2000). Recent archaeological discoveries at the site of Avaris in the northeast make it evident that the horse was brought into Egypt during the early to middle Thirteenth Dynasty (1755–1630 BCE) (Rommelaere 1991; Von Den Driesch and Peters 2001).

The army of the Middle Kingdom had many troops that performed the role of garrison soldiers. In the Nubian fortresses the archers hid on top of the walls while their comrades still on foot engaged the foe close to the forts. An increased population contributed the troops to mount invasions in a field where the sheer numbers were a major determinant of success. The gradual introduction of bronze allowed even greater success.

Bronze is composed of tin and copper. Since Egypt had no tin supplies, it was necessary to import this metal. From Europe and Anatolia, today's Turkey, it was shipped south to Syria or by sea to Ugarit and Byblos on the Syro-Lebanese coast, and then on to Egypt. The military technological level of the Egyptians was superior to Nubia, but was only on a par with Asia.

Egypt, a large and cohesive state, faced small, unattached city-states in Asia. None of the latter could muster soldiers to equal an Egyptian host. They resisted conquest because they lived in fortified cities that could only be taken by siege (Berlev 1967b).

In the south the Egyptians stopped at the Second Cataract, but sometimes troops penetrated further up the Nile. There was a powerful chiefdom called Kerma situated around the Third Cataract that blocked any Egyptian advance. Here, many troops were needed to continue the wars; the enemy was numerous and could easily retreat in case of loss. In order to hold the land additional troops and support were needed, and the area of Kerma was not the best in which to establish large garrisons because it was open to side attacks, both from the east and west.

The technique of bronze manufacture most certainly aided the Egyptians in fighting in the south. The rapid movement of soldiers by water enabled the kings of the Twelfth and Thirteenth Dynasties to maintain control over Lower Nubia, but on land their speed was the same as the enemy's.

Loss of the North in the Second Intermediate Period (1630–1520 BCE)

The standard interpretation attributes the success of the Hyksos, the foreign invaders from Asia who brought the Middle Kingdom to an end, to their new weapons of war.

But the slow expansion of the Fourteenth Dynasty in the northeast already had helped to weaken the native Egyptian state of the Thirteenth Dynasty (1755–1630 BCE). The Hyksos had military superiority and solidarity among themselves. The new military system is reflected in the Egyptian nomenclature for the newly arrived chariot and horse; the terms are West Semitic.

The Hyksos were successful immediately. First they overwhelmed the northeast Delta. Memphis then fell and most of Middle Egypt was lost to the Hyksos. Their move south into Egypt was facilitated by their chariot warfare, but they also employed ships for rapid movement. As before, the fast movement of troops in Egypt still proceeded by river. The next Theban state of the Seventeenth Dynasty (1630–1540 BCE) copied many of its aspects from earlier times. But there was a strong consciousness of being on the defensive (Franke 1990).

Bronze weapons were effective on the southern front, but the inability of the Egyptian kings of the Thirteenth Dynasty (1755–1630 BCE) to resist the Hyksos invaders proves that bronze metallurgy was not the key to a successful defense. A key to Hyksos victory was that Hyksos society included a permanent warrior elite.

The military reorganization during the Second Intermediate Period (Thirteenth to Seventeenth Dynasties) forced other major social and economic changes within Egypt. The Theban government had acquired horses, which were expensive and required a great deal of food. The investment in chariots required a constant, dependable supply of flexible yet hard wood, a commodity that was rare in the Nile Valley (Giumliá-Mair and Quirke 1997).

The northern-based Hyksos had immediate access to the two metals necessary for the forging of bronze; the southerners did not. So how could the Thebans of the Seventeenth Dynasty (1630–1540 BCE) overrun the Hyksos in only two generations of warfare? Toward the end of the Second Intermediate Period, the Egyptians mobilized on the river. This is most evident in the war record of the naval officer Kamose (Habachi 1972; Smith and Smith 1976). His quick dashes downstream – first to the Cusae region in Middle Egypt and then up to Avaris – are remarkable. Memphis does not appear to have been a major obstacle.

The king Kamose (1545–1539 BCE) was able to strike the north so quickly because the king's fleet descended upon the Hyksos capital of Avaris and besieged it. Egyptian cities were not prepared for internecine warfare, and they surrendered quickly to Kamose. But in the Delta problems arose. The waterways were not as regular or reliable as the single conduit of the Nile south of Memphis. Moreover, the land was damper and less suitable for chariots. The mounds upon which the Delta cities rose were ideally positioned to withstand a siege. The Hyksos capital had major defensive fortifications, unlike those of Nile Valley towns. For these reasons the naval profession continued to be an important one in the late Seventeenth Dynasty (1540 BCE), only declining when Egypt moved vigorously on land into southern Palestine. By the reign of Thutmose I (1493–?BCE) the amphibian army came to an end, and a new land-based army, the core of which consisted of the chariot force, took over (Berlev 1967b: 19–20).

Meanwhile the Egyptian counterattack in the south retook Lower Nubia with remarkable speed, attributable both to the Theban fleet and to the superiority of

Egyptian arms. Now on the offensive, Kamose sent troops upstream to Buhen at the Second Cataract to take that key fortress-city. Rapid deployment over water positioned the Egyptian soldiers to use their superior weapons and their horses and chariots against the Nubians. Still, Kamose's stela never mentions chariots in battle. He was afraid of being caught in the rear by Hyksos troops. Thus he might have been thinking that the enemy might try to send one segment of their army southward, through the Western Desert, in order to outflank the local populace. This account mentions horses, and so we know that the Thebans used them too. But Kamose's fleet could bypass a fortified city on the way to conquering a more important center, thereby neutralizing the detoured area.

The warfare between the Thebans and the Hyksos, though involving new armaments, followed the earlier military practices of the Egyptians. The fragmentary battle scenes of Ahmose from Abydos depicted river encounters, most probably in the Delta (Bourriau 2000: 210–15).

Dynasty Eighteen: First Half

Ahmose of Dynasty Eighteen (1539–1514 BCE), after uniting the entire country again, still depicted his army following the Middle Kingdom type. But during the opening century of the Eighteenth Dynasty the military organization of Egypt appears to have undergone a major transformation (Gnirs 1996; Kemp 1978; Yoyotte and López 1969; Schulman 1964). This is most noticeable in the gradual development of the importance of the chariotry as well as the use of the word for "general." The army still depended upon the conventional approach, one based on the navy as well as upon garrisons. The swift invasion of Lower Nubia was consolidated by the administration of a garrison commander at Buhen, an office common in the warlike Theban state (Kemp 1978). The venerable title "king's son" represented the economic dependence of a high-ranking soldier upon the ruler (Schmitz 1976). It reflected the archaic paternalistic outlook of the early state where the highest military officials were called "sons." (Spalinger (2004) covers the entire New Kingdom military system.)

Fast-moving armies of large size were not necessary for the opening push of the Egyptian state southward (Gnirs 1999: 83–7; Shaw 1991: 39–49; Spalinger 2002a). As late as Amunhotep I (1514–1493 BCE) and Thutmose I (1490s BCE) there were commemorations of naval battles at specific water channels. The pharaohs did not perceive the warhorse to be a key element of the Egyptian military in the south. In contrast, there were no large rivers in Palestine; feet and chariots transported men and material.

The focus on Asia, then, was the determining factor in the rise of a professional chariot corps. The Egyptians occupied strategic locations. In Palestine, Gaza was one of them. Inland, the Egyptians sought to control the key political and geographical centers of Palestine. Megiddo's rebellion during the last months of Hatshepsut's reign (1458 BCE) occurred when the pharaoh's army withdrew and the small number of garrison troops could not cope with the major revolt. Freedom of the roads was necessary to Egypt, for both commercial and military reasons. Unlike Nubia, there was no viceroy administering the Egyptian-held lands in Palestine.

Latent problems with this policy can be identified as soon as the pharaohs extended their area of influence further north into Syria. It was necessary to cross and protect the major rivers there, the Euphrates and the Nahr el Kelb near Beirut. There was also a major state in the interior of north Syria, Mitanni, also called Naharain. This kingdom, often described as a loose confederation of smaller states, was experienced in chariot warfare and horsemanship. For many years it had successfully resisted Hittite control from Anatolia. Mitanni, like the Hyksos, had an established warrior caste specializing in chariotry.

The war records of Thutmose III (1479–1425 BCE) show again that the Egyptians sent their well-organized navy into action (Säve-Söderbergh 1946). Key ports in Lebanon were quickly brought under permanent control. A garrison was established at Kamid el-Loz in southern Syria, and Kadesh on the Orontes River was forced to surrender. Egyptian garrisons remained small. The pharaoh raided down the Euphrates with his chariotry in tow, but a regular system of taxation is nowhere evident (Liverani 1990).

Around the end of the reign of Thutmose III and on into that of Amunhotep II (1426–1400 BCE), army titles referring to horses and chariots reflected the increasingly more distinct career paths for professional military men (Gnirs 1996). At the beginning of the Eighteenth Dynasty (1539 BCE) the generals appear to have come from bureaucratic careers. By the close of the reign of Amunhotep III (1353 BCE) the members of the officer class owed their promotions to their length of service within the army and not in the bureaucracy as before. A split between the civilian and the military officialdom had come to pass (Gnirs 1999: 84–5; Shaw 1996: 154-5; Spalinger in press).

The Military Age of the New Kingdom

From the Seventeenth Dynasty (1630 BCE) onward the pharaoh always led his army. The phraseology and iconography of the day reflected this martial spirit (Spalinger 1982; Lundh 2002). The king was forever a young hero, advancing at the front of his able-bodied men, smiting the enemy. Ahmose's stroke of public relations genius was to commission war reliefs for his temple at Abydos. By the reign of Thutmose II (?–1479 BCE) land battles were depicted, and the figure of the king in his chariot became a cliché (Spalinger 2002a).

By the reign of Thutmose III (1479–1425 BCE) a standard system of military organization had been created. Systematization replaced serendipity of promotion, with soldiers recruited as boys, as before, and those from important families remaining in the service until retirement. Chariot warriors became the elite unit within the army. (Redford (2003) now provides a detailed and up-to-date study of the Asiatic campaigns of Thutmose III.)

During Amunhotep II's reign (1426–1400 BCE) we can recognize many outside influences. Asiatic gods entered Egypt, some additional foreign words became part of the Egyptian vocabulary, and even literary elements from Asia penetrated Egyptian culture. Biographies show that the number of private individuals who were connected to Asia significantly increased in the middle of the Eighteenth Dynasty. The Empire was creating opportunities abroad, and this was slowly transforming society at home.

A good example of foreign influence is the story of Astarte and the Sea, which combined Asiatic mythological elements with a military outlook, dated to the reign of Amunhotep II (1426–1400 BCE) (Collombert and Coulon 2000). Egypt's main enemy, Mitanni, became the place Egyptians thought of as exotic, but it was also seen as a hostile land (Kitchen 1969).

There was an increasing specialization of army careers and chariot technology in the Eighteenth Dynasty (Gnirs 1996). Perhaps this occurred because the wars with Mitanni had come to an end when it was dismembered by the Hittites and the Assyrians, and the Egyptian state had less need of campaigns in Asia. Now there was time for the development of a regular professional system.

As the Eighteenth Dynasty disintegrated around 1292 BCE, the Hittite threat reemerged in North Syria. When Egypt suffered a series of defeats, the king reorganized the military arm of the state in order to mend northeastern defenses. At the beginning of the Nineteenth Dynasty the capital was moved from Memphis to Avaris in the Delta, signaling the political importance of Asia. Horemheb, a military man who became the last pharaoh of the Eighteenth Dynasty (1319–1292 BCE), sent forays northward that were repeated under Seti I and Ramesses II (1290–1213 BCE) (Darnell 1991). The pharaohs marched through Palestine and Syria many times before the fateful Battle of Kadesh under Ramesses II around 1274 BCE (Von Der Way 1984; Goedicke 1985).

A massive production center was established in Avaris (Bietak 1996). The flotilla was strengthened in response to pirates and other Sea Peoples who threatened Egypt from the reign of Ramesses II onward. The Delta location of the capital was crucial for the ground defenses of the state as well. A large contingent of troops was quartered there. Also fortresses were built in the west to restrain the Libyans, who had become more dangerous (Kitchen 1990).

Technological development in the Nile Valley had finally placed Egypt on a par with the major powers of the Ancient Near East. In the Nineteenth Dynasty (1292–1190 BCE) the state supplied the weapons for its solders (Sauneron 1954). Warhorses remained a state or royal monopoly. Middle- and high-ranking soldiers had plots of land to cultivate, and they were economically secure.

Mercenaries had to be recruited. The Sherden pirates, for example, who were part of the Sea Peoples movement, had a contingent within the Egyptian army. By the Nineteenth Dynasty these hired soldiers resided in Egypt and worked year-round. For the first time within Egypt a permanent standing group of troops was established whose entire life was devoted to war. Normally, the Egyptian soldiers would go home after a campaign, but not the mercenaries. In the Nineteenth Dynasty special "shock troops" of Asiatic auxiliaries appeared.

In the Nineteenth Dynasty scribes of the state began to express antipathy toward military career men (Spalinger in press). The bureaucrats separated the soldiers into two ranks: simple foot soldiers and charioteers. These anti-military tracts indicate the military had become a caste rivaling scribal officialdom for prestige. They had also become an integral and necessary part of Egyptian society.

From economic records of the Ramesside Period (Nineteenth to Twentieth Dynasties 1292–1075 BCE) we can see a number of social changes that were connected to the military. A series of stories was composed about the places of Asia through which Egyptian soldiers had traveled (Spalinger 2002b). Generals and even kings appeared as the protagonists in these stories. Also in the account of the Battle of Kadesh Ramesses II's charioteer is an important figure. The accompanying reliefs allow one soldier to speak. In the war reliefs of Seti I (1290–1279 BCE) a certain Mehy appeared, who was not from the royal family (Murnane 1995). The life of a high-ranking soldier was considered worthy of commemoration and even emulation.

Military men were found in key positions at the court. All the king's sons were expected to become military men (Fisher 2001). At an early age they went with the army on campaign. They were trained to be warriors and not merely future administrative leaders. All the sons who could not expect to become the next pharaoh had career security in the military.

The record of the Battle of Kadesh also provided data about the Hittites as well as the Egyptian army. The Hittite chariots played a major role in the action. For example, the Hittite king Muwatallis employed his three-men-to-a-chariot arm in order to break through the marching Egyptian army. Clearly, the two-men-to-a-chariot system of the Egyptians was at a disadvantage. The Egyptians could not use their chariots as a continual moving platform for archers. Also the Hittite chariotry was more tactically proficient. The Egyptians now faced a rapidly advancing foe. These elite chariot soldiers were the deciding factor in the military encounter, although the Battle of Kadesh actually ended in a draw.

Defensive Measures

The war machine of Egypt became essential for the preservation of the kingdom. In the reign of Seti I, at the beginning of the Nineteenth Dynasty, the Egyptians had to face armed enemies from Libya. Later, under his son Ramesses II (1279–1213 BCE), foes in the Mediterranean threatened the coast of Egypt. The Delta capital was also exposed (Dothan and Dothan 1992). Ramesses II campaigned against both foes and built a series of western fortresses.

Both of these enemies became a major threat under pharaohs Merenptah (1213–1204 BCE) and Ramesses III (1187–1156 BCE). At least four separate defensive wars were fought, and the attacks undermined the Egyptian state. But the reasons for their success are hard to identify. We must presume that the enemy had more men at arms in proportion to the total population than the Egyptians did.

For the Sea Peoples piracy or trade was their profession, depending upon the relative strength of their potential enemy. The Sea Peoples found it expedient to join with other marauding groups, among which were the Libyans. Owing to overpopulation or to the increasing arid climate of their homelands, the Libyans were intent upon invasion and conquest if they were not allowed to migrate eastward. (See the series of important articles in Oren (2000) concerning the Sea Peoples.)

The Egyptian army was mainly geared to the defense of an empire and small raids, but it was not organized for massive invasions. The war activities of Seti I, Ramesses II, and Merenptah in Palestine eventually necessitated some large actions, but it was impossible to carry on a systematic war against a foe that was not urbanized. Rather, the Egyptians preferred to send small contingents of troops after such opponents, and only infrequently was there a major campaign (Yurko 1986, 1997).

Against the Libyans, fortresses and defensive measures proved ineffective. The Libyans may have been intent upon forging a major state of their own at the expense of the Egyptians (O'Connor 1990). The fact that Ramesses III had to defeat the Libyans on two separate occasions within six years revealed how dangerous the enemy was. The Sea Peoples compounded the Libyan threat by supplying men and arms to the enemy and by waging their own war. Thus the Egyptians were forced to fight on two borders. The eventual successes of Merenptah and Ramesses III depended upon their use of mercenaries. (Manassa (2003) presents a very important study of the war records of Merenptah against the Libyans.)

The estimations of the total population of Egypt are helpful in determining the total number of men-at-arms that Egypt could provide. An approximate figure of 3.2 million is now the accepted total population of Ramesside Egypt (Grandet 1994: 128 n. 8). Archaeological and historical research has tended to lower the earlier estimates. The success of the Libyans in the later Third Intermediate Period (1075–715 BCE) tended to indicate that Egypt was not at all highly populated, simply because the Libyans continued to settle in the Nile Valley and soon became farmers, administrators, and eventually leaders.

Ramesses II said that at the battle of Kadesh in 1274 BCE the enemy mustered 3,500 chariots (that is, 10,500 men), not counting foot soldiers. The Egyptians would have had roughly the same number. Allowing for an equal number of men and women in Egypt, and setting the population at three million, this would imply that one out of 150 Egyptian males participated in this encounter. The ratio is much too high since the peasant population was large, permanently settled, and engaged in agricultural activity that was essential for the war effort. Kemp, for example, posited six people per household, purposely excluding servants from his calculations (Kemp 1989: 308–13; O'Connor 1972: 690–5).

There is a land survey document that covered a geographical area of about 150 kilometers, about 90 miles, in Middle Egypt. It revealed that the categories of persons who rented fields from temples included the following:

Stable masters 22%	Small farmers 12%
Soldiers 17%	Herdsmen 11%
Ladies 14.5%	Sherden mercenaries 7.5%
Priests 12.4%	Scribes 3 1/3%

This remarkable analysis reveals that the main cultivators of the northern areas of Middle Egypt were, in fact, connected to the army. Moreover, less than one-quarter were what we would call professional: the small farmers and herdsmen. Kemp argued that this might have been a local peculiarity of the region, although it reflected the practice of settling army veterans on the land (Kemp 1989: 308–13). But the presence of the stable masters calls to mind one significant Late Egyptian Miscellany which points out that the future charioteer gets his horses from the state, i.e., from the stalls where the stable masters must have worked (see also Katary 1983). No wonder that the stable masters formed such a large and imposing percentage of the total number of cultivators in Middle Egypt.

In this text even the Sherden, related to the Sea Peoples, formed a large group, more than double that of the scribal bureaucracy. Within the military we can derive the following percentages: Sherden mercenaries, 16.2 percent; soldiers, 36.5 percent; and stable-masters, 47.3 percent. The land in this survey was owned by the temples and the state. The document did not take into consideration other plots that were privately owned. Recent attempts to make a more exact statistical survey conclude that the account dealt with only one-fifth of the total arable land in Middle Egypt. Still, the percentage of the renters of this temple-owned land who were in the army was high, and a possible solution for this surprising concentration might be to interpret the stable masters as non-combatant troops, who were to maintain the horses for the chariotry.

The Military Society (Dynasty Twenty 1190–1075 BCE)

Egyptian society changed more noticeably in the Twentieth Dynasty than in the Nineteenth. The military pervaded politics and other aspects of life. By this time the Sherden mercenaries had become permanent residents and "citizens" of the country. They owned parcels of land, they had inheritance rights, and they formed part of the elite divisions of the army. They participated in all of the subsequently recorded wars. But the Egyptian state was caught in an ever-increasing defensive pattern of behavior. Two Libyan invasions, an attack on Egypt's shores by the Sea Peoples, and an earlier move into Palestine under Merenptah strained the resources of the state (Widmer 1976). As there were no breakthroughs in the technology of warfare, the Egyptian government got deeper in debt by paying elite mercenaries, giving them land, and stationing them at military settlements in the Delta, and probably also in Middle Egypt (Kemp 1989: 308–13; O'Connor 1972: 690–5).

If foreigners, and not only Sherden, became officials of the state, we can ask just how serious were the attempts to ward off the outside threat. By the death of Ramesses III in 1156 BCE, Libyans and Sea Peoples had managed to move into some of the higher posts of the land. In fact, throughout the rest of the Twentieth Dynasty peaceful Libyan immigration became as much a fact of life as incursions.

Under Ramesses III one Sea Peoples invasion moved up the Delta channels of the Nile while a second traveled overland along the coast of Palestine. Libyans, as well, were a threat in the West Delta, and, in the reign of Merenptah, as far south as Heliopolis and Memphis.

In the south, the High Priests of Amun at Thebes saw themselves as the controllers, not only as defenders, of the region. Having established a principle of hereditary succession, they felt that the next step was the amalgamation of army and temple

(Jansen-Winkeln 1987, 1992, 1994). This fusion was welcome because of the troubles that Egypt was encountering with the viceroys of Nubia. By late Twentieth Dynasty (1190–1075 BCE), the highest state official in Nubia saw himself as geographically very far removed from the king and the capital, and even more philosophically removed from the northern political orientation of the state. The major invasions of the Delta by Libyans and Sea Peoples had not directly affected him. Hence, the viceroy and his troops became a military institution more and more independent from the crown, and this disaffection grew during the reigns of Ramesses IX to XI (1126–1075 BCE).

The Nile Valley began to separate into three segments. The pharaohs of the Twentieth Dynasty held Avaris, and their political, military, and economic orientation was to Asia and the Mediterranean. It was not too difficult for them to hold parts of Middle Egypt. But the south reverted to its center at Thebes, now run by the high priests of Amun. They were forced into military disputes with the viceroy of Nubia, who had the advantage of possessing an established war machine of his own.

Thus the close of the Twentieth Dynasty around 1075 BCE saw warfare in the south between the high priests, nominally under the control of the pharaoh, and the Nubian viceroy. This situation eventually paved the way for the loss of all Egyptian control in Nubia. In the south the high priests set up a quasi-independent regime of their own. The continual internal disputes led to the dependence of each potentate upon his army.

The Twenty-First Dynasty (1075–945 BCE) resembled the preceding phase in that the war machine played a key role in the political and economic affairs of the state. The Libyans, as warriors and clans, continued to move into the northwest and settle there, thus further militarizing the country, while at the same time weakening the central power. Egypt of the beginning of the Third Intermediate Period (Twenty-First to Twenty-Fourth Dynasties 1075–715 BCE) was socially very similar to the last half-century of the New Kingdom. Virtually all of the large temples, with the exception of Theban Karnak and the Amun complex, lost power, and the local leaders, often of military heritage, took over control of the lands.

By the reign of Ramesses IX (1126–1108 BCE) soldiers were organized according to their specific location within the Nile Valley. The army had become geographically fragmented. The ordinary soldier was rooted to land, which he rented. Such men cared about their city, their county, which we call a nome, using a later Greek term, and they had a limited geographic horizon. They no longer did duty abroad. As a result, the soldiers owed their loyalty more to their local military superior than to the pharaoh. And now powerful army leaders began to rise, some of whom were of Libyan descent.

The end of the Twentieth Dynasty around 1075 BCE did not usher in a new age. This time it was not equipment or inventions that paved the way for modifications in the Egyptian army. Rather, the increasing particularization of Egyptian society affected the military too.

The later history of the Near East shows that the relatively large population of Egypt occasionally allowed its rulers to exert their military power in Asia and in Africa. But the ancient period of consistent Egyptian dominance was over. The

Egyptian logistic and organizational achievements were considerable, but under Assyrian and Persian rule they became more commonplace and did not confer power on the Egyptians. Spalinger (2004) covers the New Kingdom war machine from a socio-historical point of view.

FURTHER READING

Yadin 1963 studies war in all of Western Asia but is dated and not accurate about Egypt.

Gnirs 1999 emphasizes modern literary analysis. Shaw 1991 is worthwhile for beginners, supplemented by Shaw 1996. Partridge 2002 has excellent photographs. See also Redford (2003) and Manassa (2003).

The importance of the horse for Egyptian society is well analyzed by Rommelaere 1991. On chariots see Herold 1999. Heinz 2001 is a study of battle reliefs. A more general survey is Gaballa 1975. The crucial analysis of Berlev 1967b on the Middle Kingdom military remains unsurpassed.

The military history of the rest of the Ancient Near East has not received the attention it deserves. Malbran-Labat 1982 and Mayer 1995 study the Neo-Assyrian Empire. The older work of Sasson 1969 is very useful for the early second millennium BCE in Syria. Unfortunately, Mesopotamia in the Bronze Age has yet to receive a proper treatment. The Hittites, however, are well represented by Beal 1992.

PART IV

Culture

CHAPTER EIGHTEEN

Transmission of Knowledge

Benjamin R. Foster

A courtesy of Mesopotamian letter writing style demanded that the correspondent of inferior social position communicated information to his superior as if his superior already knew it. So too, a polite disclaimer among experts of equal rank was that what one did not know, the other did, while whatever the one knew the other knew as well. Presumption of superior knowledge in proportion to social status implied a theory that useful knowledge was transmitted vertically, from above to below; for example, from the powerful to the weak, the erudite to the unlettered, the elderly to the young. Evidence for such a Mesopotamian theory of the transmission of knowledge abounds, but consideration of knowledge must begin with writing itself and the specialized knowledge that the literate arts entailed.

The invention of writing in southern Mesopotamia, toward the end of the fourth millennium BCE, shows that human beings were by then contending with the problem of how to communicate over space and time (Glassner 2003). The near simultaneous appearance with writing of representational and monumental art shows that rulers and elites were, in the same process, learning how to mold and control subjects' belief and action, using imagery, just as communication theorists were refining techniques to represent language in symbols (Michalowski 1990). The creation of a set of codes or symbols at once differentiated those who manipulated and understood them from those who did not. Small wonder, then, that one Mesopotamian theory of knowledge saw it as transmitted from centers of management and authority, redistributed, so to speak, in controlled doses to a passive audience. Yet by the early second millennium, knowledge of writing had spread from administrators to private possession, making possible new patterns of acquisition and dissemination of literate culture, using a reduced number of simplified symbols and expression closer to the spoken vernacular. By the second half of the first millennium, though, this process may have been reversed so that writing beyond basic literacy and scholarship was once more dominated by a small ruling elite and a few extended families (Larsen 1987a). Thus the relationship among literacy, knowledge, and authority fluctuated through the three millennia of Mesopotamian written tradition beyond the capacity of a brief essay to describe it authentically, but Mesopotamian written tradition, to which modern knowledge of Mesopotamian intellectual endeavor is largely owed, always placed literacy first as the gateway to knowledge.

Highest knowledge, according to Mesopotamian literate tradition, was transmitted by the gods. In exceptional cases, gods might choose favored human beings to communicate directly with, through speech, dreams, or visions. Tradition told of certain sages, such as Adapa or the flood hero Atrahasis (also called Ut-napishtim), who enjoyed sublime wisdom through direct divine favor, and their sublime wisdom might in some cases be claimed by scholars as the basis for their profession (Gammie and Perdue 1990; Michalowski 1980). Certain rulers or dynasties show a predilection for supernatural communication: Gudea, ruler of Lagash in the late third millennium BCE, tells of a motivating dream from his city god: "Gudea saw the lord, divine Ningirsu, in a vision of the night, He ordered him to build his house" (Edzard 1997: 69). Assyrian kings of the late eighth and early seventh centuries BCE often referred to supernatural events as sources of understanding, and a millennium and a half after Gudea the Babylonian ruler Nabonidus (sixth century BCE) also claimed privileged access to the gods through dreams: "At the outset of my perduring reign, the gods Marduk and Sin (= the moon) caused me to have a dream: Marduk, the great lord, and Sin, luminary of heaven and of the world below, stood side by side. Marduk said to me, 'Nabonidus, king of Babylon, bring bricks on your own steed, build the temple Ehulhul and set up the abode of Sin, the great lord, within it'" (Beaulieu 1989: 108; Oppenheim 1966). Those who do not admire rulers may impugn such revelations, as might critics of Constantine, Luther, or Joseph Smith, but Mesopotamian society accepted divine communication as normative, so no clear instance of expressed cynicism about the veracity of such communications survives (Pongratz-Leisten 1999a). On the other hand, prophecy, which seems to be at home outside of Mesopotamia proper, though a well-attested feature of the Amorite culture of the early second millennium BCE, could involve kings taking seriously ecstatic utterances even from the riffraff of society (Charpin 2001). The revelations so communicated were not large, systematic bodies of doctrine or policy, however, but brief, colorful comments and warnings on royal projects and well-being.

From the perspective of Mesopotamian higher learning, divine knowledge was transmitted indirectly through an infinite range of events and phenomena, observed or elicited, in the heavens and on earth, at home and abroad, decodable through divination, Mesopotamia's premier science after the turn of the second millennium (Bottéro 1974). The origins and development of the Mesopotamian mantic world-view are obscure; the modern reader knows it best through late prodigious Mesopotamian scholarly reference compendia of observations and consequences, as well as formal queries and reports of observations, passages in narratives referring to its principles and practice, and even diviners' prayers for professional competence in their metier. In theory, the diviner's sourcebook was the entire visible universe.

Terrestrial phenomena apprehendable to a casual observer, sights, sounds, events in the home, workplace, street, community, or countryside, perhaps a bit of rubbish in the street, birds flying overhead, or ants on the wall, portended something for the observer: "If water is spilled in the doorway of a man's house and it has the shape of a man with an arm outstretched, (this portends) that the man will himself stretch out his arm (to beg) in the street of his city" (Freedman 1998: 233). Cosmic events, such as eclipses, portended good or ill for the nation or its leadership, as did the birth of monstrous animals.

A guild of professionals stood ready to interpret portentous phenomena and to suggest often complicated means of avoiding a negative outcome, presumably for a fee, and the costs of materials used in divination were sometimes high: "With respect to the ritual that goes with the spell 'You are a Monstrous Evil,' about which the king my lord wrote to me, it is performed to drive away an evil demon or a disease. As soon as something has afflicted someone, the exorcist comes and hangs a mouse and a stalk from a thorn bush above the person's door. The exorcist gets dressed up in red clothing and puts on over it a red cloak. He holds a raven in his right hand, a falcon in his left hand ... (finally) he makes a second exorcist walk around the sufferer's bed with a censer and torch, reciting the spell 'Evil Demon, Go Away!', then up to the door, and next conjures the door. He does this every morning and evening until the affliction goes away. With respect to the moon and sun appearing in opposition on the thirteenth instant, there is a ritual to be performed against (the portent of) that ..." (Parpola 1993b no. 238). Experts naturally sought to justify their intellectual interests and skills to the ruling establishment in return for support and patronage and for the opportunity to consult on political, diplomatic, and military undertakings (Oppenheim 1975).

Higher knowledge was therefore a kind of sublime uncanny power open to the elite, as much as a body of human skills to be acquired and expanded. Hence there was no teacher in the divine pantheon nor school in heaven. Nor did anyone, when bragging of his proficiencies, refer to his teachers. Special knowledge came neither from study nor even mentoring but from revelation or unique experience. According to the Epic of Gilgamesh, the alpha and omega of knowledge was understanding what transpired before the flood, which was seen as the beginning of empirical time, and what happens to a person after he dies, obviously the end of it. The epic hero Gilgamesh brings an account of both of these to the human race, one from the narrative of the flood hero, whose abode Gilgamesh reaches in his valor, and the other through a vision of his dying friend Enkidu, reworked from a Sumerian poem in which Enkidu rashly goes to the Netherworld to retrieve Gilgamesh's athletic equipment, consigned there by divine action (Foster 2001).

For most educated people, however, a body of knowledge was given to them at school, and scarcely came from the gods. This knowledge was both practical and theoretical and had the sanction of long tradition behind it. Their objective was to master a body of lore that set the educated apart from the uneducated. From the early second millennium, various narratives tell about school and its subjects and how they were acquired, with the usual rhetoric about rigors of school life (Civil 1985):

"This is the roster of days I spent at school:
"I had three days off a month,
"There were three holidays a month,
"That makes twenty-four days a month
"That I spent at school, oh no, that wasn't so long!"

Much is known about the second millennium school curriculum and how writing, reading, and arithmetic were taught (Sjöberg 1976). The student began with simple signs and numerals, progressed to short sayings, excerpts, and calculation exercises, then moved on eventually to full-scale literary works and more involved problems. He was supposed to master Sumerian, which was only a learned cultural language by the time the school days narratives were composed, hence of the same status as Latin or Greek in European education of the nineteenth century (Vanstiphout 1979). To this end, long lists of signs and traditional equivalences were learned, a surprising amount of no practical value: "I can give 600 (= numerous) lines beginning with the LÚ-sign," a young scholar brags (Civil 1985; Glassner 1999). Accounting, reckoning, and the standard form for every type of contract, learned by heart, filled his days. In addition to daily recitations, there was homework. For would-be historians, epigraphic training required deciphering old tablets picked up in ruins (Visicato and Westenholz 2000: 1123) or copying historic inscriptions in temples (Kraus 1963). For advanced scholarship, such as divination and astronomy, there was presumably some form of apprenticeship to a master (McEwan 1981: 17–21); some learned professions were transmitted through successive generations of one family, where the father taught the son his lore and the son copied his father's scholarly works (Cohen 1988: 1: 24–5).

Education was sometimes carried on in private academies set up in the homes of literate men who sought to increase their income by taking on students (Charpin 1986). The successful student could hope for a post in government or at a large establishment, such as a temple; the less successful could sit near the city gate waiting to draw up contracts for a fee or to make records of court cases. Some scholars became the confidants of kings and were entrusted with the task of writing out royal correspondence and drawing up historical narratives of the king's deeds (Parpola 1987b: 257). As one would-be court scribe expressed this, "I can draw up in good form my lord's commands, I can remind my lord of what he has forgotten" (Durand 1997: 1: 103–10). Thus a person with a good control of traditional and practical knowledge enjoyed high expectations, whereas unemployed and underpaid scholars painted their lot in the gloomiest terms (Parpola 1987b; Foster 1993c, 1996: 884–5): "I cannot afford a pair of sandals or the cost of a tailor, I have no change of clothes and carry a debt of six minas of silver plus interest ..." (Parpola 1993b no. 294); "I shiver with cold in an out-of-the-way place, I go my way empty-handed, a scholarly squint afflicts me" (Durand 1997: 1: 103–10).

Beyond mastery of the formal content of a discipline, Mesopotamian literate scholarship esteemed skill in bipolar thought: appreciation of pairs and correspondences, matching and contrasting phenomena, balancing multiplicity of interpretations derived from manipulating signs and symbols. The more potential one saw, the richer one's store of knowledge, in preference to a single response or "right" answer. Only shadowy outlines of this aspect of Mesopotamian thought are discernible today in the scattered ruins of its scholarly achievement, and little seems compatible with contemporary reasoning strategies (Jeyes 1980; Cavigneaux 1987; Glassner 1995; Pearce 1998; Seminara 2001: 420–4).

To the literate, then, knowledge, be its source in revelation, observation, or reasoning, was to be found in written records. Recourse to the past was common parlance (Charpin 1998). So it was that the obligation to leave written records for the future became a literary device, and in a literary autobiography purportedly carved on a stela, a chastened monarch blames a remote predecessor for not warning him of what to expect (Foster 1996: 264):

> (King Enmerkar) did not write upon a stela,
> nor leave it for me,
> Nor did he publish his name, so I did not bless him.

But was writing enough? Some see a pivotal role for "masters" whose teaching, now lost to us, had a decisive effect on certain bodies of written tradition. Their putative teaching relied on the spoken word and perhaps compilation of authoritative text editions, both referred to by the Babylonian expression "that of the mouth of ...," or, "according to the wording of ..." The form and content of such teaching could be referred to centuries later (Lambert 1959). Explanations of passages, words, and concepts, presumably derived from such teaching, seem to the modern reader esoteric or even freely associative in character, but only a beginning has been made in understanding the fragments that survive (Livingstone 1986: 219): "The shoe which they take (in the ceremony) to the temple of the Lady of Babylon – this is a token, the god sends it because they will not release him nor can he come out." Some purportedly esoteric knowledge was transmitted with injunctions of secrecy, enjoining that only the initiate be shown the material (Westenholz 1998): "Let one who understands disclose this to one who understands, the one who does not understand must not see it!" The motivations for keeping such lore secret are not further explained. Esoteric lore may have been associated with religious knowledge.

Physical preservation of knowledge took the form of accumulations of tablets in homes and institutions, which could be treasured like fine books in modern personal or institutional collections. Scattered information concerning study and preservation of manuscripts, retrieval of documents, and collecting and consulting written materials shows that the written word enjoyed high prestige, just as in Mesopotamian law a written record was an essential component of a contractual relationship or the conclusion of a court case. The very act of writing a tablet could be a religiously meritorious deed (Pearce 1993).

Transmission of knowledge outside of formal education relied on the spoken word: references to public speeches, use of heralds, reading aloud, exchange of messengers, and systematic interrogation abound (Oppenheim 1960). From this process came "understanding," the basic metaphors for the acquisition of which in Akkadian derived from hearing and tasting. The understanding person had "heard widely," or "had the taste of" (*tēmu*) something, in his ear and mouth respectively (Glassner 1995). Through these two portals, the Mesopotamians believed, knowledge was absorbed by the human mind. Knowledge was "deep" or "profound." There was no independent concept of "well read," so this idea was probably implied in having "heard widely," as "reading" was expressed by using a verb to speak aloud.

For many branches of knowledge, such as midwifery or military tactics, no written tradition existed; hence they had no resonance or prestige in surviving Mesopotamian scholarship, despite their importance in everyday life. Crafts, for example, were learned by apprenticeship. Contracts of apprenticeship are best known from the Neo-Babylonian and Achaemenid periods, in which free workers undertook to educate apprentices, especially slaves, in such tasks as weaving, bleaching, cooking, seal engraving, leather work, even rat-catching, for a fixed period, often several years. The master promised to teach the entire art of his profession, for a fee and the services of the apprentice during the years of apprenticeship, the slave owner providing basic clothing and sustenance (Bongenaar and Jursa 1993).

Sometimes, on the other hand, scribes wrote out what purport to be procedures for manufacturing certain products, such as aromatics or pyrotechnic goods like faience and glass (Oppenheim et al. 1970), not to mention what resemble recipes for *haute cuisine* (Bottéro 1995). Efforts to reproduce these commodities according to the instructions have not been successful because incomplete information was given, so such manuals apparently had at best only mnemonic value. Perhaps some of these were drawn up in the spirit of encyclopedists, so scribes could boast that they knew the technical vocabulary of every profession. Some may have seen knowing the vocabulary as mastery of the essence of the profession, but a Babylonian spoof in which a "learned" man lectures a cleaner in scientific, detailed technical terminology on how to clean his garment, and is told by the cleaner to wash it himself, warns against taking such a view too seriously (Foster 1996: 92–3).

The largest part of the Mesopotamian learning process took place, then, beyond the narrow horizon of literacy, and so must be deduced from chance references. Fathers were supposed to instruct their sons not to loiter in the streets, to avoid conflicts and congregating places of lowlifes, such as taverns and brothels, and to offer them other good advice of the same ilk. Mothers' advice to daughters is inaudible to us, behind the closed doors where proper young ladies were supposed to reside. Special knowledge of women is sometimes alluded to in passing: child bearing and rearing and the interpretation of dream symbolism, for example (Foster 1996: 756; Asher-Greve 1987; Harris 2000).

A comprehensive Mesopotamian theory of knowledge is developed in the Epic of Gilgamesh (Foster 1987a). This implies that the first step in adult knowledge was sexual self-awareness. This was followed by knowledge of another human being on an equal basis, by exploring another mind and spirit, accepting and offering personal sacrifices to the needs and desires of another. Beyond this came knowledge of one's own self, transcending gratification, roles assigned by society, and unexamined assumptions. The more one defined one's self, paradoxically, the less distinct from the rest of the human race one became. Finally, according to the poem, the highest form of knowledge was recognition that the only significant knowledge was that transmitted to the future in written form – only this could transcend the self, which was doomed to die and disappear. The obvious bias of this scheme is that it privileges the very Epic as a source of highest knowledge. Even if most people probably did not believe this or had not even heard of it, the poet's thesis stands as a well thought out Mesopotamian perspective on the transmission of knowledge.

Although some rulers, such as the Sumerian king Šulgi and the Assyrian king Assurbanipal (Foster 1996: 714), boasted of their superior knowledge, they were exceptional, as most rulers did not. Šulgi claimed to be, among other achievements, an expert diviner, a superb musician on both string and wind instruments in theory and performance, as well as a composer, an architect, jurist, diplomat, linguist, athlete, scribe, administrator, and author (Castellino 1972). These extravagant pretensions can hardly be read as a meaningful survey of useful knowledge, for, as one would expect, they seem for the most part to be courtly accomplishments.

Praise for gods and rulers usually focused on their power and authority, and with these the ability to punish or forgive. Ignorance was occasionally ridiculed, as when scholars chortled over the efforts of the Babylonian king Nabonidus to participate in a technical discussion of omens (Machinist and Tadmor 1993), or when a physician did not know even elementary Sumerian (Foster 1996: 819–20), but, outside of school, learning and intelligence were in general esteemed less highly than skill and strength. Perhaps it was because of this that the later Gilgamesh Epic reinvented Gilgamesh as a man of knowledge rather than a man of strength. In this instance learned men sought to place knowledge ahead of strength as something permanent, taking revenge on the powerful, whose favor they needed to survive, for they knew that time was on their side.

Yet emphasis on passive reception of knowledge should not obscure that Mesopotamians had as well a doctrine of revelation or breakthrough, when new and important knowledge suddenly flashed into a person's consciousness (Foster 1991). A flowery but light-hearted description of such a moment, when a seemingly wonderful idea forms in the mind, is found in a Sumerian epic poem of the late third millennium BCE. Here the Sumerian king, Enmerkar, king of Uruk, has been presented with a trial in the form of a riddle by his rival, the lord of Aratta: he is to bring him grain in net sacks and no other form of container. Enmerkar makes elaborate preparations for the usual sacrifices made to obtain divine assistance, when, in the midst of it, a brilliant idea comes to his mind, thanks to the goddess of grain, who, not coincidentally, is also the goddess of scholarly attainment, the tablet her "field," the stylus like a stalk of grain standing in it (S. Cohen 1973: lines 318–324, freely rendered):

> Enmerkar, son of Utu, was proceeding apace.
> At that moment, she who is the ready writing field of a tablet,
> the standing stylus about to inscribe,
> That golden image sprung to life at the right moment,
> Beautiful Inspiration, maturing like the grain goddess herself
> in tareless yield,
> Divine Nisaba of the grain field, mistress of garnered wisdom,
> Opened to him her treasure house of insight!
> He, ushered in to that heavenly temple, listened to her words.

Enmerkar lets old grain sprout, making it easy to carry in the net sacks. "Brilliant idea" was a "golden image" sprouting in the mind; potentiality realized was portrayed as the pregnant moment a stylus was about to plunge into the ready clay. Thus a Mesopotamian poet expressed the joy of adding new knowledge to the accumulated store.

FURTHER READING

See on writing Glassner 1995, 2003, on divination Larsen 1987a, on the link to art Michalowski 1990, on the roles of intellectuals Oppenheim 1975, and on secret knowledge
Westenholz 1998.

CHAPTER NINETEEN

Ancient Near Eastern Literature: Genres and Forms

Tawny L. Holm

Introduction

In the Ugaritic epic of Aqhat, the hero Aqhat is tempted by the goddess Anat's offer to give him eternal life in return for his hunting bow. He responds, "Do not lie, Maiden, for to a hero your lies are rubbish! What does a mortal get as his fate? What does a mortal get as his end? Glaze will be poured on my head, lime on top of my skull... the death of all I will die. I too will certainly die!" (KTU 1.17:VI.34–8). His defiant response to the powerful goddess echoes the fatalism of another hero in Ancient Near Eastern epic, that of Gilgamesh, famous king of Uruk in Mesopotamia, who loses the plant of rejuvenation to a serpent and finally resigns himself to his mortal destiny; he too will die, he is not a god, and must give up his quest to live forever. The Ugaritic epic from Syria and the Akkadian-Sumerian cycle of Gilgamesh, both from among some of the oldest literatures in the world, demonstrate the timeless concern with fate and the human condition.

Somber reflection about death, however, does not alone characterize the flavor of the Ancient Near East's contributions to world literature. Humor abounds in jokes and stories; animal fables appear, as do erotic love poetry, instructional texts of both the serious and the tongue-in-cheek variety, autobiographies of the ancient rich and famous, prayers and hymns to the gods, or even the purported words of the gods themselves set down as oracles and prophecies, and the stories of the deeds of the gods in mythological texts. The genres of ancient Syria-Palestine, Egypt, and Mesopotamia are diverse, yet appealing still today in their choice of religious and secular subjects.

A survey of the kinds and nature of literature in the Ancient Near East must necessarily be selective. One first notes that while writing for accounting and administrative purposes begins with Sumer in southern Mesopotamia toward the end of the fourth millennium BCE, literary compositions in Sumerian do not emerge until around 2600–2500 BCE at Fara (ancient Shuruppak) and Abu Salabikh. The first literary compositions in Akkadian – or rather East Semitic in general, including the language of Ebla (modern Tell Mardikh in Syria) – date to around 2450–2400 BCE. In Egypt, which developed its own independent writing system also before 3000 BCE, our oldest literary pieces date to about 2400 BCE on private tomb inscriptions. As for Syria-Palestine, whose Canaanite alphabetic script goes back to the early second millennium BCE, pride of place in the literary impetus goes to the Ugaritic texts from Ras Shamra on the coast of Syria which date to around 1400–1200 BCE. The writings of the Hebrew Bible or Old Testament, which represent the most extensive corpus of literature from Syro-Palestine before the Hellenistic period, by comparison probably date mostly to 586–165 BCE. The study of the biblical writings constitutes a discipline on its own, and thus the Bible will be mentioned only sporadically.

In formal terms, one may define literary texts as connotative, that is, admitting different levels of ambiguity and evoking a variety of secondary associations of a diverse nature (e.g., intellectual, sensory, cultural).[1] This is in contrast to non-literary texts such as those that are administrative, legal, or scientific, which are instead denotative or more strictly referential. Unfortunately, while scholars can agree to some extent on what is "literary" in the Ancient Near Eastern texts (Gronenberg 1996: 60), other aspects such as genre, authorship, readership, and purpose, remain difficult. Not only is there no outline of native poetics or literary precepts in the sense that the West has it in the Aristotelian Poetics, but it is difficult to analyze ancient aesthetics when one is far removed in time and language from the original context (Black 1998: 24–8; Parkinson 1997: 12; Rubio 2004). Drawing on stylistic devices and other kinds of signals from within the texts and utilizing Fowler's typology of features shared by texts of the same genre (1982: 54–74), this discussion will be organized around the following categories of Ancient Near Eastern literary texts:

1. Mythological narratives;
2. Epics, tales, and legends;
3. Laments and prayers;
4. Wisdom or didactic literature (including instructions, satire, dialogues, fables, and proverbs);
5. Autobiographies; and
6. Love poetry.

The list is not intended to be exhaustive, and some categories necessarily overlap with each other.

Not discussed here are legal, juridical, or administrative texts, omens, incantations or rituals, word-lists, or finally, scientific texts of varying kinds (medical, astronomical, mathematical, magical, divinatory, etc.), even if some of these are also found beside literary texts on scribal exercises, or even if they also have occasional connotative characteristics (such as is the case with metaphors and puns in omens). Also not included are texts that are to be discussed in other chapters of this volume, such as historiographical or historical texts, religious texts, and royal inscriptions. Not only are these covered elsewhere, but they may also be said to be more documentary or more referential than perhaps literary; although such a judgment admits its difficulties.

Native Terms and Genres

The genres and titles assigned to Ancient Near Eastern literary compositions by scholars are primarily modern. Native terms in titles, headers, colophons, or repeated sections across different texts, are helpful but not always conclusive for deciding whether or not certain texts belong together (Black 1998: 25; Michalowski 1999a).[2] For example, the label "balbale" ("dialogue" or "duet") is attached to Sumerian compositions that do not seem to share a unifying set of characteristics. Likewise, the term "song" in many languages (*ḥs* in Egyptian, *šir* in Hebrew, SÌR as a Sumerogram adopted especially by Hittite for some incipits, *zamāru* in Akkadian, etc.), is used for a very wide variety of compositions from love poems, hymns, epics, to mythological narratives, and cannot be confined to one genre. The same is true for terms in headers and incipits that indicate a composition should be sung with particular instruments, usually drums, tambourines, harps, or other stringed instruments (although the Sumerian laments with such labels as "eršemma" or "balag," are rather more reliable). In Egyptian, one of the most consistently used terms for an "instruction" or "teaching" (*sb3yt*), is assigned to compositions that are not necessarily works of didacticism. Moreover, one of the most common native terms for a narrative in Egyptian is *sḏdt*, "that which is told," and it was used for nearly any kind of story, historically based or not, although it was not generally used of myths or narratives about religious knowledge (van Dijk 1995: 1698; compare this to Greek *mythos*, which also referred to something that was told). On the other hand, the term *mdt nfrt* "good words," in Egyptian, might just indicate a term for *belles lettres* in general (Kaplony 1977).

Poetic Devices

With regard to dividing Ancient Near Eastern literatures into the broad genres of "poetry" versus "prose," one might be better served by looking at the texts individually, since certain stylistic devices occur in all kinds of literary texts. Literary texts often utilize poetic devices such as rhythm, different kinds of repetition on all levels of language (sounds, words, whole phrases or lines), stereotypical idioms or epithets, or rhetorical figures and wordplay. Short lines are organized into larger units of two, three, four, or more lines by parallelism to create stanzas. While meter or rhythm, and perhaps rhyme too, often elude us (especially in certain Ancient Near Eastern writing systems that do not indicate vowels, such as Northwest Semitic languages, Egyptian, etc.), the most common characteristic shared by Ancient Near Eastern literatures is the concept of parallelism (*parallelismus membrorum*). Parallelism refers to the repetition of one poetic line (or half-line) in the next line (or half-line); that is, the "repeated formulation of the same message such that subsequent encodings of it restate, expand, complete, contrast, render more specific, complement, or carry further the first message" (Foster 2005: 14).

Parallelism may occur in both poetry and prose, however, prose will often have longer passages of narrative without it. The following is an example from the Akkadian Epic of Atrahasis (Atrahasis I, 70–3, Lambert and Millard 1969: 47):

mišil maṣṣarti mūšum ibašši	It was night, half-way through the watch,
bītum lawi ilu ul īdi	The temple was surrounded, but the god did not know.
mišil maṣṣarti mūšum ibašši	It was night, half-way through the watch,
Ekur lawi Enlil ul īdi	Ekur was surrounded, but Enlil did not know.

The repetition of the two bicola (lines 1–2 versus lines 3–4) is semantically significant in that the second line of the second bicola (line 4) expands the message; it progresses from the vague to the precise: "Ekur" is the temple that is surrounded, the god who did not know is "Enlil."[3] Moreover, the alliteration of nasals and sibilants in lines 1 and 3 may convey a sensorial evocation of nocturnal silence.

Ancient authors found many ways to play with the possibilities of semantic, syntactic, or other kinds of parallelism. Another example, from Ugaritic, shows parallelism with synonyms as well as with ellipsis, that is, the absence in the second line of one element from the previous line[4]:

dm rgm / iṯ ly w argmk /	For I have a matter that I will tell you,
hwt w aṯnyk	A word, that I will recount to you (KTU[2] 1.3.III.20–2)

Of course whole passages are repeated as well, and even minor changes in word choice or order are meant to resonate poetically. Since repetition, and specifically parallelism, is a characteristic of traditional or oral poetry, there has been much discussion about the relationship of written compositions to orality in the Ancient Near East.[5] Regardless of the textual prehistory and genesis of these compositions, probably the transmission of Ancient Near Eastern literary texts had both a written and an oral component, which may have differed in details from region to region.

Authors

We do not often know the names of the authors of Ancient Near Eastern texts. This may well be due to the fact that the names were simply lost (not transmitted with subsequent copying of a text), or more likely, that the scribe was not concerned with indicating an author, i.e., either authorship was not particularly relevant, or some compositions ultimately stemmed from common lore. When authors are named, the reason has probably little to do with pride in creativity in the modern sense (Foster 1991). With regard to Mesopotamia, the Standard Babylonian version of the Epic of Gilgamesh demonstrates the difficulties of understanding concepts of authorship. We know from a Neo-Assyrian catalog from the first millennium that the Mesopotamians believed one Sin-leqi-unninni was responsible for the epic. In fact, there is more than one person with that name in several periods, so it is not certain in which period the Sin-leqi-unninni associated with the Babylonian Gilgamesh actually lived (George 1999: 28–9). For instance, an individual with that name is attested in a couple of documents from the city of Ur dating to the Middle Babylonian period (the second half of the second millennium). However, an Old Babylonian version of the Babylonian Gilgamesh is attested in at least two textual witnesses from the first half of the second millennium (the Pennsylvania and the Yale tablets of Gilgamesh). He might be, in fact, only responsible for a particular recension of the epic. In addition, throughout the Ancient Near East, the names of authors may be given only to lend prestige to the work; historical or pseudo-historical characters, or even deities might be designated. In the case of Akkadian texts, the stress is on the inspiration or divine authority behind the text, even if a human author is named. Sometimes the text is said to be "revealed" and approved by a god, and the text itself is a sign or blessing from the god for all people, and its naming of the deity and recitation may have an apotropaic function (Foster 2005: 20–1). In the poem of Erra, for example, attributed by the composition itself to a certain Kabti-ilani-Marduk, those who "honor" the poem will escape pestilence and other evils.

In Sumerian literature anonymity seems to be the rule. One famous exception, however, was Enheduana, daughter of Sargon, king of Akkad (c. 2334–2279 BCE), who was high priestess of the Moon God at Ur, and the legendary author of several Sumerian compositions (on the nature of her "authorship," see Michalowski 1995: 2279–80). Whether or not she herself actually composed any of them, she can nevertheless be said to be the first attributed author in history.

Egyptian wisdom texts and autobiographies almost always have a pseudepigraphical attribution of authorship (Lichtheim 1973: 6); by claiming that an ancient sage was the author, the work achieved a certain authority. In addition, Egyptians may have thought all literature was ultimately of divine authorship, from the god of writing (Derchain 1996).

In Ugaritic literature the most famous author of literary texts is Ilimilku (or Ilimalku), who produced at least the Baal Cycle, the Kirta epic, and probably Aqhat. On the colophon of the last tablet of the Baal Cycle, he states that he is the student of one Attenu, chief of the priests under King Niqmaddu (probably Niqmaddu III). Ilimilku was thus likely a "theologian" using his artistry with mythic or epic themes to legitimate the royal house (Korpel 1998; Wyatt 1996).

Overview of Literary Texts

Mythological Narratives

In anthropological definitions, "myth" is defined mostly in terms of its function of ordering or explaining the present physical, political, and social world for the society which produced it (Kirk 1970). In the mythic narratives of the Ancient Near East, this often means a traditional tale about a deity or deities and their deeds, with the purpose of explaining the origin of certain features of the natural or social world

(George 1999: xxxiii; Baines 1996: 361; Smith 2001: 22–3). As with any genre, myth is not a closed category with the same characteristics in all cultures (Kirk 1970: 28), and it may even overlap with folktales or legends. Generally, however, folktales or legends take place in the simple human sphere and deal with human subjects. When deities appear in folktales or legends, they are not the focus, and anything fantastic is merely for adventure and not for reflection.

Mesopotamian myths of origins and theogonies include stories of the flood and creation. A catastrophic deluge is known in several versions from Mesopotamia (Sumerian, Babylonian, Assyrian, and derivative traditions), and the hero saved by his god who tells him to build a boat is variously named Utanapishtim (in the Epic of Gilgamesh), Atrahasis (in the Epic of Atrahasis), or Ziusudra/Xisuthros (in the Eridu Genesis and Berossus' Babylonaica). The Epic of Atrahasis from the first half of the second millennium BCE contains a long version of the flood, as opposed to the shorter version in Tablet XI of the Epic of Gilgamesh, the latter preserved in two versions, one from the second millennium and the other from the first, and in a copy from Ugarit in the thirteenth century (see Schmidt 1995). The shorter version gives no explanation for the flood or why Enlil grants immortality to the survivors, whereas the longer version probably did (although that section is now lost), and also shows the flood as the solution to a long series of espisodes after the creation of humans. As slaves of the gods, in the longer version humans are too noisy and Enlil tries to reduce the number of humans so he can sleep, but the god Enki/Ea thwarts him at every turn. When Enlil seeks to annihilate humans in totality, Enki chooses to save one human, Utanapishtim, out of the lot. A future flood is avoided by choosing other means to solve overpopulation; a certain number of women will be sterile or will otherwise not be able to succesfully bear children. In the Eridu Genesis from c. 1600, the survivor/hero here too is given immortality in that he is sent to Dilmun to be like a god. The biblical flood of Noah in the book of Genesis chapters 6–9 (first millennium BCE), shares continuity and numerous plot details with other Ancient Near Eastern flood stories. The biblical narrative may not be directly dependent on any of the others but simply draws from the same common tradition.

Enuma elish ("When on High") is a Babylonian creation narrative that explores the ascendancy of Babylonian Marduk over the other gods via his defeat of the primordial salt water goddess, Tiamat. After his victory, Marduk creates the cosmos by splitting Tiamat's body, and creates humans from the blood of her consort Qingu, whom he also slays. This first millennium BCE myth in the Akkadian language demonstrates an intersection of the political worlds of both humans and deities. The justification for Babylon's supremacy over other cities is that Babylon's city-god Marduk defeated all other gods. Still, Enuma elish was not thought to be the sole word on creation; competing stories such as the Akkadian Theogony of Dunnu, a fragmentary and complicated mythological piece about the incest, matricide, and patricide of the deities of the city of Dunnu, illustrate that there was no single tradition about creation, and perhaps each city had its own (Dalley 1989: 278). Ancient Mediterranean theogonies all bear a strong resemblance to each other, in that they involve successive generations of deities with the younger generations attacking and overthrowing the older ones; for example, the Hurrian theogony in the Hittite composition The Heavenly Kingship (Alalu, Anu, Kumarbi, and Tessub); Hesiod's Theogony (Uranos, Kronos, Zeus); and later on Philo of Byblos in the second century CE (Elyon, Uranos, El-Baal Hadad). In Mesopotamia, an account of the creation of humans is also found in the Epic of Atrahasis, in which humans were created by the goddess Mami with the help of Ea out of clay and the blood of a slain god (compare this to the use of Qingu's blood in Enuma elish).

Other common themes in Mesopotamian mythological literature are *anabasis* and *katabasis*, that is, the journey up to heaven or down to the Netherworld. In the Sumerian and Akkadian Descent of Inanna/Ishtar (Inanna in Sumerian and Ishtar in the later Akkadian version), the goddess of carnal love and war goes to visit the Netherworld. As she descends, she is forced to give up one item of clothing or jewelry at each of the seven gates. When she reaches the core of the Netherworld she is naked and powerless, and the world above loses its fertility as a result of her disappearance. She is revived by a being (in the Akkadian version) or several beings (in the Sumerian version) sent by the god Enki/Ea. In the Akkadian version, the god Dumuzi, her lover, is made to take her place in the Netherworld. In the longer Sumerian version, moreover, Dumuzi's sister Geshtinanna agrees to replace him for half the year so that his presence on earth during that time will once again promote fertility and growth (see Reiner 1985: 29–49 for analysis). There are variant versions of the story in other Sumerian compositions, in which, for instance, Dumuzi has to be captured to take Inanna's place (e.g., Dumuzi's Dream).

Nergal and Ereshkigal is a mythic narrative in Akkadian that belongs to the subgenre of *katabasis*. In it, Nergal insults the vizier of the Netherworld goddess Ereshkigal and is sent down to the Netherworld for his punishment; however, he ends up marrying the goddess. In its Middle Babylonian version (from Amarna in Egypt, fifteenth or fourteenth century), Nergal takes the throne by force, but in the Neo-Assyrian and Late-Babylonian versions (seventh century and later) the narrative turns into a romance in which Ereshikigal longs for Nergal when he abandons her for the world above (Reiner 1985: 50–60). His return and claiming of the throne is welcomed by the goddess.

The Akkadian Story of Adapa, on the other hand, is a narrative about *anabasis*, a journey to heaven. It shares with the Epic of Gilgamesh the theme of a human losing an opportunity for immortality, and with Nergal and Ereshkigal the motif of the contaminating food and drink of an other-worldly place. In Adapa, the sage called Adapa breaks the wing of the south wind and is brought to heaven for an audience with Anu. The god Ea counsels him to dress in mourning garb to please the guards at heaven's gate, but also counsels him not to eat or drink of anything he is offered, because it will be "bread of death" and "water of death." However, after he follows Ea's counsel, he finds out later that the bread and water would have instead granted him eternal life (Izre'el 2001). Etana, a narrative whose ending is not preserved, may also be an example of *anabasis*. It is about a childless man who saves an eagle from a pit and rides on its back toward heaven in order to obtain the plant of birth.

Other Mesopotamian mythological narratives report more deeds of the gods: *Anzu*, *Erra*, *Lugal-e* ("The exploits of Ninurta"), and Enki and the World

Order. There are also etiological narratives, such as the Sumerian How Grain Came to Sumer.

Hittite literature was syncretistic and seems to have absorbed the myths of the surrounding cultures (Hoffner 1998: 9). In the Old Hittite period, the Hittites took on myths from the Hattians – the original population of the Hattusa area – in which the myths relate a ritual to be performed. The most productive kinds of myths were the myths of the vanishing or disappearing gods; in these, the gods are incapacitated or kidnapped, or they walk off in anger. The Disappearance of Telipinu (the son of the great Storm god) is the most important of these, but there are also versions in which other gods disappear. For instance, in Telipinu and the Daughter of the Sea God, the Sea kidnaps the Sun god and Telipinu has to retrieve him. When the Storm God Thunders Frightfully is about the Moon god falling from the sky, but to his chagrin, no one notices. Two versions of the Illuyanka tale of seemingly Hattic origin exist. In it, a serpent conquers the Storm god, who then finds an ally to help him trick and kill the serpent.

The Hurrian myths translated by the Hittites were less tied to ritual. The most important of the Hurro-Hittite myths are the six "songs" in the Kumarbi cycle, which recount the competition for kingship over the gods between Kumarbi, a Netherworld deity, and Tessub, a celestial deity (Hoffner 1998: 40–65). Another important myth is the Song of Release or the Epic of Emancipation (Neu 1996). It is a Hurro-Hittite bilingual in five tablets in which the city of Ikinkal (between Uršu and the Taurus) and someone called Purra ask for release from the city of Ebla which has enslaved them. Their request is supported by the god Tessub of Kummi. The text is fragmentary but perhaps one scene depicts a feast in the palace of Allani, goddess of the underworld, attended by Tessub in a celebration of Ikinkal's emancipation from the Syrian city of Ebla. Finally, Hittite myth even includes bits of a narrative probably of Canaanite influence about interactions between Elkunirsa (that is, the "Creator of the Earth," *El-qônēh-ʾereṣ*, a name for the West Semitic god El), his wife Ashertu, and Baal.

In comparison to the rest of the Near East, Egypt had few mythological narratives. Myths were instead transmitted orally or in other ways (perhaps by an elite group such as priests of the state cult), since there are many allusions to them in several kinds of texts from the earliest periods (van Dijk 1995: 1697). One of the best examples of this is the myth of Osiris and Isis, which, although its origins have to have been far in the past (the Pyramid texts of the Old Kingdom allude to it), is not fully reported in continuous narrative form until the second century CE by Plutarch in Greek (*De Iside et Osiride*, Griffiths 1960 and 1970). Both Osiris and Isis and The Contendings of Horus and Seth from the New Kingdom (on a Twentieth Dynasty papyrus), relate accounts of the struggles for supremacy between Osiris, god of order, and Seth, his brother, the god of disorder. In the first, Osiris is murdered by Seth and his body reclaimed by his sister and wife Isis, after which his son Horus is posthumously conceived to triumph later over Seth. Plutarch's version of the Osiris myth differs in details with the Egyptian sources (the most complete Egyptian version is in an Eighteenth Dynasty hymn to Osiris). However, the result of the myth is that Osiris becomes the god of the Netherworld, and that Horus his son is seen as Osiris' living reincarnation embodied in the human pharaoh; the king of Egypt was thus viewed as Horus, and thought to be the representative of the gods among humankind. The Contendings of Horus and Seth (Nineteenth Dynasty) consists of a series of episodes in which Horus and Seth struggle for the office of Osiris in contests judged by the Ennead (the nine deities of the Heliopolitan theogony). Horus is ruled the victor in each case, sometimes through physical combat, and often with the help of Isis, his mother. In one famous episode Horus and Seth attempt to sexually penetrate and impregnate each other; of course it is again Horus who wins this contest through a trick.

Egyptian accounts of creation stem from the cosmogonies developed in the four religious centers at Heliopolis, Memphis, Hermopolis, and Thebes. In actuality, the four schools did not produce competitive theologies, rather the Heliopolitan school should be viewed as the basis of the other three, although all four impacted each other's development (van Dijk 1995: 1699; Allen 1988). On the other hand, the sources for our knowledge of these cosmogonies are many and incomplete: the Pyramid texts, a rare "treatise" here or there (Lichtheim 1973: 51), incantations, rituals, and iconography.

There is no flood account in Egyptian, but there is a narrative of human destruction from The Book of the Cow of Heaven, found on the walls of several New Kingdom royal tombs (Hornung 1991). The relevant section of the Book describes how the sun god Re sent his Eye - the goddess Hathor - to destroy humankind because of a plot to rebel against him. To keep her from slaying too many humans, Re pours across the fields 7,000 jars of beer dyed the color of blood, which Hathor drinks to satiation. The narrative provides several etiological explanations, including why the first waters of the Nile's life-giving inundation in the summer are red (Redford 1995: 2230-1).

Another Egyptian myth, Astarte and the Sea, is obviously of Canaanite influence or origin reflecting the battle between Baal and Yamm (Sea). It recounts a tale of the Sea's threat to cover the heaven, earth, and sky if he does not receive tribute. Once Astarte goes to him to deliver the tribute, he demands that she be given him in marriage. The tale breaks up after mentioning Seth, and since Seth is elsewhere the Egyptian counterpart of Canaanite Baal, one assumes Seth battles and defeats the sea.

Among the Ugaritic texts from coastal Syria, discovered in 1929, the Baal Cycle seems to be the longest work of a mythological nature. It appears on six large tablets and some fragments (KTU 1.1–1.6), and only about half of its lines are preserved. The cycle used to be thought to date to 1400–1350 BCE, but is probably from a century later, during the reign of Niqmaddu III (Singer 1999: 689). This story treats at least three topics: the struggle of Baal with the god Yamm (Sea) over who should be king of the gods, the building of a palace for Baal once he is king, and the struggle of Baal with the god Mot (Death). As Mot's captive in the final episode Baal descends to the Netherworld, but his sister Anat finds his body and slays Mot. Baal is resurrected and fertility returns to the world. The two gods Baal and Mot, also somehow resurrected, live to fight again. The fact that neither one is decisively defeated by the other suggests an ongoing seasonal cycle in the fixed order of the universe that involves both death and life at the proper times. Other mythological texts from Ugarit include some amusing stories about El, the otiose and ineffectual father god, such as The Birth of the Gracious Gods and El's Divine Feast (Parker 1997).

Later narratives seem to know variants of the Baal myth: for example, the Phoenician History of Philo of Byblos as found in the *Praeparatio evangelica* of Eusebius and in Porphyry (see Attridge and Oden 1981). Some of the same deities at Ugarit also appear in the Hebrew Bible (Athirah/Asherah, Baal, El, Astarte, Mot [Death], Yamm [Sea], etc.), and now, since the discovery of the Ugaritic texts in 1929, we understand their place in the early Israelite cosmos better. In addition, there are several biblical passages in which Ugaritic mythic imagery is used in connection with Israel's god Yhwh (Smith 1995: 2035–40; Smith 2001: 18–24). For example, Yhwh is described as a chariot-riding storm god in much the same terms used for Baal (Psalm 77:19; Psalm 18:10; or Psalm 29, Job 38); as a warrior-king with the same imagery as Baal and Anat (Psalms 50, 97, 98; Judges 4–5); and as a god who is enemies with the old Ugaritic gods or monsters: Leviathan, Tannin, Yamm, and Mot (Psalm 93:3–4; Isaiah 25:8, 27:1, 28:15 and 18, Psalm 74:13–14). Yhwh's holy mountain in the Bible is also called Ṣaphon ("north"), just like Baal's mountain in the Ugaritic texts.

Epics, Tales, and Legends

The focus of an epic is on heroes and heroic events that are foundational to a culture's understanding of its past. Egypt lacks epics, just as it nearly lacks mythological narratives, but has an abundance of entertaining tales.

In Mesopotamia, we have the compositions about Enmerkar, Lugalbanda, and Gilgamesh whose themes involve the actions of the rulers of the early city-states, their interrelationships with each other and their deities, and their competitions of skill and cunning. These Sumerian compositions focused on early and mostly legendary rulers do not really deal with the foundation of the city-states, or even with the expected heroic deeds that characterize most epic struggles. Thus, the Enmerkar and Lugalbanda cycles may be regarded rather as simple tales (Edzard 1994). As for the Epic of Gilgamesh, while it has sometimes been understood as a myth, it is better viewed as "a document of ancient humanism" in generic terms (Moran 1991: 15–22; 1995: 2327–36). According to Andrew George, "even for the ancients, the story of Gilgamesh was more about what it is to be a man than what it is to serve the gods" (1999: xxxiii).

The matter of Aratta includes the cycle of Enmerkar and the cycle of Lugalbanda, and deals with relations between Enmerkar, the ruler of Uruk (modern Warka), and the lord of Aratta, a city in what is now Iran (Alster 1995; Vanstiphout 2003). In the two stories of the Enmerkar cycle, Enmerkar and the Lord of Aratta and Enmerkar and Ensuhgirana (or Enmerkar and Ensuhkeshdanna), the lords challenge each other in various contests of wit, but each time it is Enmerkar who defeats the lord of Aratta. In the first, the contest includes a dare by the lord of Aratta to Enmerkar to perform three insurmountable tasks (to transport barley in mesh nets; to make a scepter not of wood, metal, or stone; and finally, to make a cloth of no specific color). In Enmerkar and Ensuhgirana a magician is enlisted to help Ensuhgirana, and a fishing contest occurs.

The Lugalbanda epics (Lugalbanda I and II) involve a leader of Enmerkar's army called Lugalbanda. In the first epic, the youngest of eight brothers (Lugalbanda) becomes ill on the way to fight beside Enmerkar in a battle against Aratta. He is left in a cave, and upon waking is able to survive by making the gods favor him. In the second, Lugalbanda again demonstrates his superior abilities by convincing the Anzu bird to give him gifts, including the ability to run fast. This is advantageous later when he rejoins his army and volunteers to run for a message from the goddess Inanna in Uruk in order to help defeat the city of Aratta.

The many stones of Gilgamesh are all concerned with the exploits of the hero and his friend Enkidu, and their quest for glory and fame as they battle deities and monsters. The Babylonian versions of the Epic of Gilgamesh in the Akkadian language were preceded by five independent Sumerian stories about the semi-divine hero Gilgamesh from the Old Babylonian period: Gilgamesh and Huwawa (versions A and B); Gilgamesh and the Bull of Heaven; Gilgamesh, Enkidu and the Netherworld; Gilgamesh and Agga; and The Death of Gilgamesh.[6] Some of the early stories in Sumerian were incorporated into Babylonian Gilgamesh, such as the story of the monster Huwawa (Humbaba in Akkadian) in the Cedar Forest, the sending of the Bull of Heaven against Gilgamesh upon Inanna/Ishtar's request, and some aspects of the dreams of Gilgamesh, but others were not (the fight with Agga, the descent of Enkidu to the Netherworld to retrieve Gilgamesh's lost game equipment).

In native catalogs, the Old Babylonian version of Gilgamesh is referred to by its incipit, "Surpassing all other kings," and the Standard Babylonian version appears listed as "He who saw the deep." The great popularity of the epic is demonstrated by the fact that the Standard Babylonian version is preserved in seventy-three manuscripts, thirty-five alone from the libraries of Assurbanipal at Nineveh in the seventh century BCE (George 2003: 379).[7] The Standard version may have originally consisted of up to 3,000 lines in eleven tablets, of which 2,400 are attested in varying degrees of preservation, leaving us with a readable text of about two-thirds of what once was there (George 2003: 418).[8] The Old Babylonian version, which predates the Standard Babylonian version, by contrast probably had a little more than 1,000 lines (Tigay 1982: 39–54). The Old Babylonian version pulls together some of the Sumerian traditions of Gilgamesh to give a greater role and background story to his companion Enkidu and to accent the themes of Gilgamesh's fear of death and search for immortality. It also adds Gilgamesh's journey to the end of the world to hear Utanapishtim's story about how he survived the great Flood.

The Standard version of Gilgamesh adds to the Old Babylonian prologue twenty-six lines, in order to bring a polished sense of completion to the epic as a whole. Anticipating the adventures and deeds that will be told in the upcoming narrative, the prologue presents Gilgamesh as having come back from a long journey, weary but at peace. It portrays him as having found at last some contentment in his role as king of his city, and no longer preoccupied with other kinds of fame or immortality.

Other interesting Mesopotamian epics include the unpublished Epic of Zimri-Lim from Old Babylonian Mari, the Epic of Tukulti-Ninurta I, and the various legends on the third-millennium Akkadian kings Sargon and Naram-Sin (Goodnick Westenholz 1997; Lewis 1980).

There are several Hittite epics involving deities and mortals (see Hoffner 1998: 81–9), including A Tale of Two Cities: Kanesh and Zalpa, a tale that might even have been a truly Hittite (instead of a borrowed) tale. In this last, the queen gives birth to thirty sons which she exposes, and thirty daughters which she keeps. The Song of Release, mentioned above, also has epic elements in that it is concerned with the oppression of the city of Ikinkal by the city of Ebla.

While Egypt has no epics or legends (in the sense of heroic narratives about historical or semi-historical founders, etc.), its variety of other tales is great. The richest period for narratives is the Middle Kingdom, but there are also many tales from the New Kingdom and in Demotic; many of the latter are still unpublished. There are tales of wonder in the Papyrus Westcar (sixteenth or seventeenth century) and The Tale of Apophis and Seqenenre (early Nineteenth Dynasty); and folktales such as that of The Shipwrecked Sailor who is stranded on an island inhabited by a giant talking snake, The Prince and his Fate (or The Doomed Prince, early Nineteenth Dynasty), and The Tale of Two Brothers (Nineteenth Dynasty). The Story of Sinuhe is an adventure tale, as is The Taking of Joppa. The Report of Wenamun from the twenty-first dynasty (eleventh century) may or may not have a historical core in its tale of a trip to Byblos in Lebanon for lumber. The allegory of Truth and Falsehood is probably related to the myths about Seth and Osiris. In Demotic literature there are fables (such as those in the The Myth of the Sun's Eye), further tales of magicians, priests, and prophets (such as Setna I and II), a long story collection with up to seventy embedded stories (The Stories of Petese), and warrior epics such as the stories in the Cycle of Inaros.

At Ugarit, the Epic of Aqhat and the Epic of Kirta include folkloric elements, such as the concern of a childless king or patriarch to bear a son, the attempt of a son to usurp his father, the appeasement of an insulted goddess, and the revenge of a sister for a brother (Wyatt 1999). In the Epic of Aqhat, Aqhat's death is caused by the goddess Anat when he refuses to let her have his well-crafted hunting bow. Kirta, on the other hand, is a wifeless, childless king who is finally blessed with both wife and progeny, although one son later seeks his father's throne. Other Northwest Semitic stories include courtier tales such as Aḥiqar in Aramaic (but see below "Didactic and Wisdom texts"), the fragmentary Hor-son-of-Pawenesh text from Elephantine, and the biblical stories of Daniel, Esther, and Joseph.

Laments and Prayers

Poems of lament over the destruction of a temple or city, the death of an individual or king, or for the god Dumuzi, were a common genre in Mesopotamia. On the other hand, in Egypt the lament was not a productive genre. One example, however, is a Ptolemaic period text called The Lamentations of Isis and Nephthys, which consists of laments for Osiris by the goddesses Isis and Nephthys. Appended to the text are instructions for its use in the cult which include its recitation in a secluded place by two women "with beautiful bodies." The text was perhaps adapted for private funerary services as well (Lichtheim 1980: 116–21). The Hebrew Bible has only a few examples of the lament: the book of Lamentations devoted to lamenting the destruction of Jerusalem by the Babylonians, as well as some congregational laments in Psalms 44, 74, 79, 80, and 83. The book of Lamentations shares with the Mesopotamian city laments its basic theme: a city is allowed by its patron deity to be destroyed by enemies. On the other hand, Lamentations, unlike, for instance, the Nippur Lament, does not include a reversal of fortunes in which the deity favors the city again.

The most important Mesopotamian laments can be divided into liturgical or cultic laments, and city laments. The genre of cultic laments had a performative and ritual function and includes different kinds of subgenres, especially the *balag* compositions (laments for a harp or drum, Cohen 1988) and the *eršemma* hymns ("wail of the *šem*-drum," Cohen 1981), both attested throughout the second and first millennia BCE. The city laments, however, were literary works copied only during a short period of time, and there is no unequivocal evidence that they were ever performed. If they were performed at all, they were done so only on very specific occasions, as opposed to the customary ritual role of the *balag* and *eršemma* compositions (Tinney 1996: 47–53). The main Sumerian examples of city laments are the Destruction of Ur, the Lamentation over the Destruction of Sumer and Ur, the Nippur Lament, the Eridu Lament, and the Uruk Lament. The Destruction of Ur and the Nippur Lament exhibit features of the Emesal dialect of Sumerian (Tinney 1996). The Curse of Agade (written during the Ur III period) laments the fall of the Sargonic dynasty to the Gutians and depicts Naram-Sin as the victim of his own hubris (Cooper 1983).

The laments written in the Emesal dialect were sung by women, goddesses, or gala singers. The "šuilla" or "hand-lifting" prayers were compositions in this dialect seeking appeasement of a deity for the community, while the Akkadian prayers of the same name were for the distress of the individual.

Other Mesopotamia laments include those over the dying and resurrecting god Dumuzi, as well as laments for kings such as The Death of Ur-Nammu. Individual laments include the two elegies attributed to Ludingira ("man of god," also mentioned in Ludingira's Message to his Mother) and The Assyrian Elegy, a poignant composition for the death of a woman in childbirth. Individual laments are also found in both private and royal letter-prayers, in both Sumerian and Akkadian or in bilinguals, as well as in the *eršahunga* prayers ("wail for the appeasing of the heart," Maul 1988), a subgenre of a very personal nature quite popular during the first millennium BCE, in which sins are confessed to a deity (Hallo 1995).

Hittite prayers often occur in other kinds of texts such as rituals and oracles, but some have been preserved independently, such as the prayers of Mursili II and Muwattalli II, and Hattusili III and Puduhepa, a royal couple. There are three types of prayers in Hittite, with native names: *arkuwar* (prayer of defense), *mugawar* (invocation of a deity to approach), and *walliyatar* (hymn); see de Roos 1995.

Wisdom or Didactic Literature

Instructional or so-called "wisdom" literature in the Ancient Near East is usually concerned with themes of right conduct, cosmic order, and the search for well-being, and is often cloaked as the teachings of elders, parents, or sages from the royal court.[9] Proverbs, popular sayings, instructions, and even fables serve to reinforce conceptions of an ordered world in which piety toward a deity or deities results in a guarantee of prosperity (Lambert 1960: 15). On the other hand, wisdom literature also includes writings that, if we understand them correctly, question such a straightforward view of cosmic relations. These compositions are skeptical about "traditional" understandings of reality, seeing the world instead as a place where inequities and oppression abound and even the righteous suffer. Thus, in addition to proverbs and instructions, wisdom literature includes invectives, satires, theodicies, and parodies as well.

The genre of "instruction" (*sb3yt*) abounds in Egyptian literature, and functioned at the royal court. The instructions are always attributed to a worthy author, although probably merely as a pseudonym (Lichtheim 1996: 244). The earliest instruction bears the name of Prince Hardedef of the Fourth Dynasty but it probably dates to the Fifth (Lichtheim 1973: 7); other popular instructions from that time on to the Ptolemaic period are connected to sages such as Ptahhotep, Merikare, Amenemhet, Ani, Amenemope, Onchsheshonqy, and others whose names are not preserved. Proverbs 22:17–24:22 in the Hebrew Bible has been shown to be dependent on the Egyptian Instructions of Amenemope (Bryce 1979), and shares with all the Egyptian instructions the themes of living in accordance with truth or order (*m3ᶜt* or *maat* in Egyptian, or the slightly related term *ḥokmāh* "wisdom" in Hebrew), proper speech, responsibility, correct relationships with officials and one's family, obedience, humility, and self-control. The Demotic instruction of Papyrus Insinger counterposes the "wise man" with the "fool," but is unique in the Egyptian instructions in that it closes each of its chapters with paradoxical statements in which God arbitrarily allows fate and fortune to bring evil and not good (Lichthcim 1980: 138–50).

The Satire of the Trades or the Instruction of Dua-Khety is overtly an instruction of a father to his son about the preference for being a scribe in contrast to other professions. The descriptions of the other professions are satirical: the brick-layer has sore kidneys, the fisherman has to deal with crocodiles, etc., while the scribe inhabits the best office of all. The text became very popular and was often copied in the scribal schools (Lichtheim 1996: 253). Other Egyptian wisdom texts are theodicies. The Dialogue of a Man with his Ba is a conversation between a sufferer and his *ba* ("soul" or "divine power"), in which the sufferer longs for death and his *ba* encourages him to enjoy life or it will leave (Lichtheim 1973: 163; for an alternative interpretation, see Simpson 2003: 178ff.). Without his *ba* the sufferer would not have a resurrection after death, and eventually, the *ba* decides to stay. Harper's Song of Antef has a pessimistic or agnostic attitude about the afterlife, and stresses that one should enjoy life rather than prepare for death and the beyond. In fact, it shows awareness of the proverbs from the instructions of the famous sages Imhotep and Hardedef, but asks about those worthies: "What of their places? / Their walls are in ruins, / And their places are no more, / As if they had never existed" (Simpson 2003: 332). The Eloquent Peasant is the story of a poor man who has been robbed and pleads for justice before the king's steward, who becomes enthralled with the poor man's eloquence. The poor man exhausts himself in fine speech before the king finally rewards him.

Some prophecies could be considered wisdom literature. The Prophecy of Neferti and the Admonitions of Ipuwer from the Middle Kingdom are political-propagandistic works set in the mouths of ancient sages as prophecy after the fact (*ex eventu*). The Prophecy of Neferti was probably composed in the reign of Amenemhet I (Twelfth Dynasty) to legitimate his reign by placing a prophecy back in the days of Snefru, a pharaoh of the Fourth Dynasty. When Snefru asks for entertaining words about the future, the magician Neferti "forecasts" for him a period of catastrophe which is to be ended by the coming of a king from the south named Ameny (Amenemhet). The Admonitions of Ipuwer is a work that also relates various calamities of a period long past, and imparts instruction as it depicts the paradoxes of chaos and order. The Demotic Chronicle and the Oracle of the Lamb are two examples of this genre from the Ptolemaic period in Demotic; their propaganda is directed against the Greeks.

Mesopotamian "wisdom" includes Sumerian proverbs in several collections (Alster 1997), as well as teachings and instructions such as the Instructions of Šuruppak, and the Akkadian Counsels of Wisdom (Lambert 1960; Alster 2005). The Akkadian *Ludlul bēl nēmeqi* ("I shall praise the lord of wisdom"), the Sumerian Dialogue of a Man with his God, the Babylonian Theodicy, and the Dialogue of Pessimism are theodicies, struggling with the problem of evil in much the same fashion as the biblical Job. *Ludlul bēl nēmeqi* is a monologue by an individual who is forsaken by his gods and fellow humans, afflicted with every kind of disease, and who is finally restored to prosperity and health by the god Marduk (Lambert 1960: 21–62). The Babylonian Theodicy (Lambert 1960: 63–91; Foster 2005: 914–22), the Dialogue of a Man with his God, and the Dialogue of Pessimism (Foster 2005: 923–6) are dialogues: the first between a sufferer and his friend; the second between a man and his god; and the third between a master and slave. The Babylonian Theodicy as an acrostic poem of twenty-seven stanzas with lively stylistic devices including rhythm, is a "technical tour-de-force" (Foster 2005: 914). The sufferer debates with his friend the inequities of life and finally persuades him that inequities exist because the gods allow it. The Dialogue of Pessimism takes the argument even further, and at the end when the master despairingly asks his servant what is good in the face of the paradoxes of life, the servant suggests suicide!

Further humor and satire are found in other Akkadian compositions (B. Foster 1974; D'Agostino 2000). The Poor Man of Nippur is a folktale about a fellow who wreaks revenge upon a mayor for an injustice he has done him (Cooper 1975). Another humorous composition contains a dialogue between a launderer and his client who gives him absurd instructions for cleaning a garment, after which the launderer suggests the client clean it himself (Foster 2005: 151–2). The Jester seems to be the routine of a buffoon who jokes about his abilities, satirizes the profession of exorcist, and describes a disgusting monthly diet that includes, among other things, dog feces (Foster 2005: 939–41).

Israel's sapiential literature is represented in the three books of Proverbs, Job, and Ecclesiastes in the Massoretic canon of the Bible, and in the books of Ben Sira (Ecclesiasticus) and the Wisdom of Solomon in the Alexandrian canon or Septuagint. Psalms 1, 19, 33, 39, 49, and 127, and other books of the Bible have also been discussed in this connection. While Proverbs illustrates traditional Israelite wisdom, Job and Ecclesiastes are of the more skeptical variety of wisdom; Job explores the question of suffering and death, whereas Ecclesiastes turns to a more distanced musing on the paradoxes of life. Elsewhere in Syro-Palestinian literature we have the story and proverbs of Aḥiqar, an apparently very popular composition in that we have texts in several languages and periods, starting with an Aramaic copy from fifth-century Egypt to later versions from the Christian era in Syriac, Arabic, Armenian, and other languages (Lindenberger 1985: 480–1). Although the text was probably originally in Aramaic, it has an Assyrian setting, and perhaps the story originated there. In the story, Aḥiqar, a wise courtier of Sennacherib and Esarhaddon's courts, is unjustly denounced by his nephew Nadin and only saved from death by an appeal to an official whose life he had once saved. The proverbs and narrative are in slightly different Aramaic dialects, and the appended proverbs used to rebuke the ungrateful nephew may well originate from Syria (Lindenberger 1983: 290).

Autobiographies

There is no true autobiography in the ancient world, if we mean "the retrospective interpretation of the author's own life" (Greenstein 1995: 2421). But there are texts that seem autobiographical in the sense that there is a first person narrator who purports to tell a narrative of his or her own life. On the other hand, nearly all autobiographies were written by a scribe commissioned by the subject, and not by the subject himself or herself, who is usually but not always a public figure. Such autobiographies do not necessarily reflect a historical account of that life; the goal is usually to project a positive self-image for the public or the gods.

The autobiography is the oldest genre in Egypt, and was an exceptionally consistent genre from the Old Kingdom to the Late Period (Lichtheim 1988). Autobiographies are found in four places: in necropolises or cemeteries, in temples, on roadsides, and on sarcophagi. They contain two kinds of material: self-portraits full of epithets, and narrative passages about the owner's life (Perdu 1995: 2243–7). The narrative is in the first-person singular, is of variable length depending on space and the subject's importance, and is addressed to "all you who pass by." The autobiographies in the necropolis or temple, usually on stelae or statues, always include a request to passers-by for an offering of food or libations to the funerary cult. It was important to list the rank and epithets of the deceased in order to make the deceased important or interesting enough to be thought a sufficient intercessor once the gifts were given. Autobiographies along desert routes or in quarries, on the other hand, were the equivalent of a non-royal person's triumphal stela, and represented only the event of the owner having passed by the place. On sarcophagi the purpose of the praise of the owner was to "act as advocate for the deceased before the god of the dead" (Perdu 1995: 2246). Important autobiographies include those of Weni and Nekhebu of the Sixth Dynasty, those of Amenemhet and Khnumhotep II at Beni Hasan during the Middle Kingdom, New Kingdom autobiographies such as that of Ahmose, and the Ptolemaic Period inscription of Taimhotep, the wife of the high priest of Ptah at Memphis. Weni's inscription is very long and recounts a career that spanned three pharaohs and includes his expeditions against the Sand Dwellers. The tomb at Elkab of Ahmose, a ship's captain, speaks of battles against the Hyksos at Avaris. Such autobiographies may be considered a genre somewhere between literary and historiographical (Gnirs 1996: 191).

Autobiographical compositions in Mesopotamia are written in the first-person under the pseudonym of a royal personage, and claim that they were originally written on a stone monument (a *narû*). They also often carry a didactic or moral message (just as many of the Egyptian autobiographies).[10] The most important examples include the Sargon Birth Legend, the Cuthean Legend of Naram-Sin, and various autobiographies attributed to Assurbanipal, Sennacherib, and others, including perhaps Hammurabi's prologue to his code of laws, and the inscription on the stela of Adad-guppi (the mother of Nabonidus) in Harran. Some Akkadian "prophecies" have been discussed in connection to this genre: the Marduk Prophecy, the Šulgi Prophecy, the Uruk Prophecy, the Dynastic Prophecy, and Text A from Assur (Longman 1991).

In Syria we have the Akkadian inscription of Idrimi, king of Alalakh, on his statue, and the inscriptions of Azatiwada, regional governor or regent of Awariku, king of the Danunians, from the city named after him. These last were written on the gates and orthostats in five places, twice in Luwian hieroglyphic and three times in West Semitic alphabetic characters. The only fully preserved inscription is in Phoenician (Greenstein 1995).

Love Poetry

Perhaps the most famous love poem from the Ancient Near East is the Song of Songs in the Hebrew Bible. Its joyfully erotic expressions of romantic and sexual love between humans are echoed in similar poems in Egyptian from the New Kingdom, fifty-five of which are still extant.[11] The Egyptian poems and Song of Songs each focus on the physical and psychic sufferings and joys of unnamed young lovers of no particular social status. "Rather than presenting a grand, symbolic, typical, archetypal, abstract or universal love, the love poets seek to capture and convey nuances of ordinary human emotion and desire" (Fox 1985: 296). In addition, the poems are unconcerned with the social or religious aspects of love such as procreation or marriage. The Egyptian poems are called "sweet sayings," "songs of delight," or the like, and were surely often meant to be sung (Lichtheim 1976: 181). The Song of Songs, the sole Israelite example of a love poem, is as titled, literally "The song of songs" in Hebrew (*šîr haššîrîm*), and is attributed to King Solomon, who is said to have loved many women (1 Kings 11).

Mesopotamian love lyrics, however, differ significantly from the Syro-Palestinian and Egyptian, in that they extend human emotions and actions into the divine sphere. Thus, what is perhaps mostly secular entertainment in Egypt and Israel is more properly religious and might have also had a cultic setting in Mesopotamia (Goodnick Westenholz 1995: 2472–8). The most common kind of love poem in Mesopotamia is that depicting the courtship, wedding preparations, and the wedding itself of the divine pair Inanna/Ishtar, the goddess of love, with Dumuzi, her shepherd husband (Sefati 1998). Other divine lovers are occasionally the subject of poems too, including Nabu and Tashmetu in a Neo-Assyrian poem (Foster 2005: 944–6), and Nanaya and Muati from first-millennium Babylonia (Foster 2005: 160–1), among others. The Inanna-Dumuzi compositions have been connected to the so-called "sacred mar-riage" ritual, in which the roles of Dumuzi and Inanna were perhaps played by the king and a high priestess, who had, or pretended to have, sexual intercourse; thus symbolically renewing the fertility of the land. However, evidence for the actual practice of such a ritual proves elusive (Cooper 1993, Rubio 2001).

While Song of Songs and the Sumerian and Akkadian love lyrics often take the form of both dialogues and monologues (note that the Sumerian term "balbale" often used for love lyrics denotes a dialogue or duet), Egyptian love poems do not utilize true dialogues since the speakers do not respond to each other's words. They instead use monologues and double monologues that juxtapose speeches of the lovers with only minimal reference to each other (Fox 1985: 259–65; Guglielmi 1996: 343). A remarkable feature of all Ancient Near Eastern love lyrics is that love is portrayed as an egalitarian emotion, with the female speaker portrayed sometimes as even more sexually aggressive than the male. In Song of Songs, the female voice is never absent, while the male lover is often off-scene or passively waiting for her. She is portrayed as actively seeking him out, as well as freely expressing her wishes for their reunion.

Common to all Ancient Near Eastern love lyrics in varying details are metaphors involving the natural world and utilizing all five senses: gardens, orchards, fruits, and spices are everywhere, animal metaphors abound; even jewels and architectural elem-ents are seen as erotic. The female lover in Song of Songs is described by the male as having eyes like doves, hair like a flock of goats cascading down a hill, breasts like twin gazelles, a neck like a royal tower, and so forth (ch. 4). She describes him in similar terms. The lovers see their world as lush and fruitful, and their descriptions of each other are fanciful and hyperbolic, viewed from an unrealistic romantic perspective (Sasson 1987: 737).

The Egyptian love poems seem less sexually explicit perhaps than the Israelite or Mesopotamian. Certainly the Mesopotamian poems directly speak of specific actions in love-making, and incorporate rather direct euphemisms as in the use of "wool" or other terms to denote pubic hair, and the use of "apple tree" and "pillar of alabaster" to refer to the phallus. The Egyptian and Israelite poems on the other hand avoid direct mention of intercourse, but use other suggestive imagery: "Until the day breathes and the shadows flee, I will hasten to the mountain of myrrh and the hill of frankincense" (Song of Songs 4:6).

In the Ugaritic compositions of Kirta and The Betrothal of the Moon and Nikkal, there are sections that use jewel and agricultural imagery in their descriptions of a beloved. Also, two ritual texts, RS 24.255 and 24.291, may or may not reflect sacred marriages (Pardee 2002: 90–3, 96–9). In Aramaic written in Demotic Egyptian script, there is a poem featuring the goddess Nanay as a divine lover (Papyrus Amherst 63, col. xvii; see Steiner 1997, in *COS* vol. 1, 322). The monologue of a male lover requesting Nanay's kisses, describing her bed, and beseeching that she be brought into her chamber, is reminiscent of the Mesopotamian divine love poems.

In sum, the diverse Ancient Near Eastern literatures offer us a rich repertoire of genres and compositions, which open a window on to their ancient civilizations, as well as provide us with the same intellectual and aesthetic pleasure we find in all literatures. In spite of the geographical and temporal distance, the literary fabric – from metaphors and alliteration, to the fear of death and the love of life – has remained the same throughout the centuries.

NOTES

1 See Empson 1930 on ambiguity; see García Berrio 1989: 51–107, in defence of a formalist view of literariness.
2 For extensive studies of rubrics, titles, or subscriptions in ancient texts see, for example, Wilcke 1976 for Sumerian, and Schott 1990 for Egyptian.
3 On Akkadian stylistics in general, see Reiner 1985, Hecker 1999 and 1974; and for Sumerian, see Black 1998, and Veldhuis 2004: 39–80.
4 On Ugaritic stylistics, see Watson 1999, Dijkstra 1999, and Zurro 1987, among others. For Hebrew stylistics, see O'Connor 1997. The poetry of Hebrew, also a Northwest Semitic language and similar in some respects to Ugaritic, has less parallelism, fewer formulas and forms, and the length of cola are more varied.
5 Against the idea that there were a high number of features marking a literary composition as having oral origins, see for Sumerian, Vogelzang and Vanstiphout 1992, 1996.
6 Some scholars believe that the name of the hero in the Sumerian versions is perhaps to be read as "Bilgames" or "Bilgamesh" (George 1999: 141).
7 The latest manuscript is from Babylon, c. 130 BCE.
8 Tablet XII of the Standard version seems to be independent of Tablets I–XI, in that it is a translation of the Sumerian Gilgamesh, Enkidu and the Netherworld, which as an episode in the epic would be entirely out of place since Enkidu dies in Tablet VII and is buried in Tablet VIII.
9 "Wisdom literature," as an imported term from biblical studies, is perhaps not so appropriate for Mesopotamian or Egyptian literature (Lambert 1960: 1–2). For example, in the Akkadian composition *Ludlul bēl nēmeqi*, "I shall praise the lord of Wisdom," it is the god Marduk who is the lord of Wisdom, and his particular "wisdom" is really a skill in exorcism. However, there is enough similarity in content and themes otherwise to justify the continued use of the term to designate a variety of Ancient Near Eastern compositions.
10 See Goodnick Westenholz 1997: 16–24 for a discussion of the various terms used by Assyriologists to describe these compositions.
11 The main collections are: Papyrus Harris 500, Turin Museum Papryus 1966, Papyrus Chester Beatty I, and some hieratic ostraca in the Cairo museum. They are in Late Egyptian and date from the thirteenth to the eleventh centuries BCE. Hermann's numbering of the poems is usually followed (Hermann 1959; see also Mathieu 1996).

FURTHER READING

Important general anthologies of translations of numerous Ancient Near Eastern texts are found in: Pritchard 3rd edn 1969 (abbreviated as *ANET*); Kaiser, Borger, et al. 1983– (abbreviated as *TUAT*, in German); and Hallo and Younger 1997 (abbreviated as *COS*).

On Egyptian literature, anthologies of translations may be found in: Bresciani 1999 (Italian); Brunner-Traut 1989 (8th edn, German); Erman 1923 (German, but English translation 1927, reprint with new introduction 1966); J. L. Foster 1992, Lefebvre 1949 (French); Kaster 1968; Kitchen 1999; Lichtheim 1973–80; Maspero 1915 (reprint 1967); Parkinson 1997; and Simpson 2003. Hymns and prayers: Assmann 1975; Barucq and Daumas 1980; Bresciani 2001 (Italian). Love poetry: J. L. Foster 1974; Fox 1985; Hermann 1959. Autobiography see: Lichtheim 1988. Wisdom: Brunner 1988; Lichtheim 1983. Important discussions: DePauw 1997; Loprieno 1996.

On Mesopotamian literature, anthologies of Sumerian literature: Jacobsen 1987; and electronic texts in Black et al. 1998– (online at http://www-etcsl.orient.ox.ac.uk/), 2004. Anthologies of Akkadian literature: Dalley 1989; B. Foster 1995, 1996, 2005. The most recent translations of Gilgamesh: B. Foster 2001, George 1999, 2003. Autobiography: Longman 1991. Wisdom: Lambert 1960. Love poetry: Cooper 1971; Goodnick Westenholz 1995; Sefati 1998. Important discussions: Reiner 1985; Black 1998; B. Foster 1991; Veldhuis 2004.

On Syro-Palestinian literature, anthologies may be found in: Coogan 1978; Driver 1956; Gibson 1978; del Olmo Lete 1981, Parker 1997. Philo of Byblos: Attridge and Oden 1981. Aqhat: Aitken 1990; Landy 1981; Margalit 1989. Baal Cycle: Smith 1994–. Ahiqar: Contini and Grottanelli 2005 (Italian); Kottsieper 1990 (German); Lindenberger 1983, 1985; Porten and Yardeni 1993; Religious texts: de Moor 1987. Myths: Gibson 1999.

Ugaritic cuneiform texts are found in KTU^2 (also cited as *CAT*): M. Dietrich, O. Loretz, J. Sanmartín, *The Cuneiform Alphabetic Texts from Ugarit, Ras Ibn Hani and Other Places* (ALASP 8, Münster: Ugarit-Verlag, 1995), the second edition of *Die keilalphabetischen Texte aus Ugarit* (AOAT 24/1, Neukirchen-Vluyn: Neukirchener Verlag; Kevelaer: Verlag Butzon and Bercker 1976).

On Hittite literature, anthologies: Hoffner 2nd edn, 1998; García Trabazo 2002 (Spanish); Pecchioli Daddi and Polvani 1990 (Italian). See also Haas 2006.

CHAPTER TWENTY

Ancient Near Eastern Architecture

Sally Dunham

The architecture of the Ancient Near East is a vast subject.[1] Over the past century and a half excavations have uncovered architecture in many of the capitals and major cities of the Bronze and Iron Ages in all parts of the Near East. New capitals have been discovered,[2] smaller city and village sites have been investigated, and the beginnings of architecture have been discovered to be much older than previously thought. Semi-permanent settlements first appear in the Near East around 14,000 BCE (Aurenche 1981: 293), while the development of urbanism happened in the fourth millennium BCE.

Although the corpus of Ancient Near Eastern architecture is large and very rich, buildings and other structures are always found incomplete to some degree.[3] Sometimes preservation is quite spectacular, due to sudden destruction of the buildings, as in the case of the Old Babylonian palace at Mari on the Euphrates in Syria (Parrot 1958; Margueron 1982) or the Iron Age buildings at Hasanlu in north western Iran (Dyson 1989). More often archaeologists only find the ground plan – the lower parts of the walls, the floors and the foundations, if any. Even in the best of cases, second stories and roofs are not preserved in their original locations, but are deduced from such evidence as thickness of walls, remains of staircases, fallen roof material or the stratigraphy of the artifacts and collapsed walls that fill the buildings (Margueron 1982; Dyson 1989: 119–20). Nevertheless, from the ground plan, building materials and methods, and contents of a building, archaeologists can often gain convincing ideas about its relation to other structures contemporary with it at the same site or other sites, its probable function, and the possibilities for what its original appearance might have been. In addition, a building may have had several phases, which are traceable archaeologically and can, hence, show its development. Also, at multi-period sites, earlier and later levels may reveal the predecessors and successors of a building, and so give a diachronic view of its place in the architecture of a site. While comparison with other excavated structures is the prime method for evaluation and interpretation of architectural remains, it can be supplemented by three other resources: (1) ancient artistic representations, (2) ancient texts (in literate periods and places), and (3) comparisons to village architecture in the Near East in recent times.

The first of these, ancient artistic representations, can depict parts of buildings which are usually not preserved, such as domed roofs or battlements and parapets on city walls. An example is Porada's 1967 study of battlements and their symbolic meaning in different periods. Another is Heinrich's 1957 study of architectural depictions in southern Mesopotamian art of the fourth and third millennia. One thing he analyzes is ancient depictions of reed buildings, which were not found preserved in excavations, but which probably were very much like the reed houses of the Iraqi Marsh Arabs of recent times (Heinrich 1957: 11–20). A special class of objects, which has been recently studied by Bretschneider (1991), is that of the so-called "architectural models." These are objects, usually for some cultic or ceremonial purpose – ossuaries, altars, offering stands, small shrines – which appear to be in the shape of a building and to show architectural details such as windows, doors, and battlements. While interpretation of these in relation to real-life architecture is difficult, they can be understood as depicting what were some of the important symbolic parts of architectural structures for the ancients.

Indeed, the symbolic role of architecture in defining and reinforcing the order of a society's world should not be underestimated. It is certainly expressed in the second resource mentioned above, the ancient texts available from the literate places and periods of the Ancient Near East. For instance, in the prologue to the Epic of Gilgamesh the narrator exhorts the listener to

> Go up, pace the walls of Uruk,
> Study the foundation terrace and examine the brickwork.
> Is not its masonry of kiln-fired brick?
> And did not seven masters lay its foundations?
> One square mile of city, one square mile of gardens,
> One square mile of clay pits, a half square mile of Ishtar's dwelling
> Three and a half square miles is the measure of Uruk! (Foster 2001, 3)

City walls were military defensive works, designed for protection from attacking enemies. Archaeologists rightly interpret them as evidence of conflict among competing kingdoms. Here, however, the military aspect is not mentioned. Instead the focus is on the excellent brickwork, the expert building, and the different parts of the city enclosed within the wall. The city wall is here a symbol of a prosperous and powerful Uruk.[4]

Besides revealing the ancients' attitudes toward their architecture, however, ancient texts in the form of building inscriptions stamped on bricks, carved in door sockets, or written on tablets in foundation deposits can also identify a building's purpose and builder (Sauvage 1998: 38–40). Furthermore, there are many archival texts – business and legal documents of private individuals or public institutions (temples, palaces) – that have been found in houses and other buildings of various cities. Detailed study of these in conjunction with their archaeological and historical contexts can reveal some of the social and political dynamics of urban life and how this may be reflected in the architecture. Such is convincingly presented in Stone's study of two areas of houses in Nippur in the Isin-Larsa and Old Babylonian periods (Stone

1987). In her study, Stone observes that the texts found in the houses of these two areas, TA and TB, show that the residents in TA were mostly small property owners who gained their livelihood through management of privately held real estate and temple offices, while those of TB were landless officials tied to the temple bureaucracy. These differences in occupation are reflected in the houses of each area. The houses in TA were variable in size, shape, organization, and quality of construction, as might be expected where the buildings were constructed by their owners. In TB, however, where the houses were built by the dominant institution, they were generally uniform in plan and well constructed (Stone 1987: 126).

The third resource mentioned above, comparisons with village architecture of the Near East in recent times, is one that has been used ever since systematic archaeology began in the Near East (Krafeld-Daugherty 1994: 3). Archaeologists realized that the architecture of the villages in the areas around their excavations was built with the same materials and technology and in the same environment as the ancient structures whose remains the excavations uncovered. They also noticed that the processes of abandonment, decay, and rebuilding were similar to those observed in archaeological excavations (Frankfort 1934: 5–6). Thus, they realized that by observing contemporary village architecture they could better understand the structural qualities and possibilities of the ancient building remains they found (Heinrich 1934; Pfälzner 2001: 12).

The study of contemporary villages with the goal of gathering data that will aid in the understanding of archaeological remains has developed over the past several decades into an approach called ethnoarchaeology. In relation to the study of Ancient Near Eastern architecture, this has meant that contemporary villages are studied with the goal of determining how the present customs and ways of life of the inhabitants might be traceable in an archaeological deposit (Watson 1979a, 1979b; Kramer 1979, 1982).[5] This is felt to be a valid source for comparison to the archaeological record because many aspects of rural life in the Middle East are seen to have cultural continuity with ancient times (Kramer 1982: 259; Aurenche 1984: 12, Watson 1979a: 3, 7; Pfälzner 2001: 71). Such studies have been carried out in Iran, Turkey, Syria, and Iraq.[6] Examples of this use of ethnographic data in specifically architectural studies include Aurenche 1981, Krafeld-Daugherty 1994, and Pfälzner 2001. Aurenche traces the development of domestic architecture from its beginnings up to the mid-fourth millennium BCE. Krafeld-Daugherty analyzes the evidence for different activity areas (sleeping, work, living, storage, cooking) by comparing the ethnographic data with the archaeological evidence in Mesopotamia from the middle of the fourth millennium to the end of the Old Babylonian period. In his study of house types in north Mesopotamia in the third millennium BCE, Pfälzner studies how different types might reflect the different socioeconomic situations of the inhabitants (nomads, semi-sedentary herders and farmers, fully sedentary farmers).

Building Materials and Methods

In the Ancient Near East the main building materials were mud and mud bricks, stone and wood.[7] The way these were used varied somewhat in different periods and regions according to availability, climate, and socio-cultural factors. Although these materials were usually used in conjunction with each another in any one structure, here each will be discussed separately, beginning with mud and bricks.

While mud may not have been used in the earliest dwellings found in the Near East (Aurenche 1981: 185; Wright 1985: 282 figure 202), pressed mud (called in Arabic *tauf*) already appears in the Natufian period (about 10,000–8300 BCE) at Mallaha, Israel, as plaster and walling, and at Beidha, Jordan, for a wall (Aurenche, 1981: 56). Pressed mud walls are built by mixing soil, water, and a temper such as straw to a plastic state and then forming each course of the wall either by hand modeling or by pressing it into a vertical frame with wooden sides (Aurenche 1977: 58 and figure 135, 1981: 58 figure 9). In this method each course of the wall must be allowed to dry for a day or two before the next course is made.[8] Pressed mud walls continued to be used from the tenth millennium onwards, but when mud brick was developed, it became the dominant material of Ancient Near Eastern architecture. Aurenche (1981: 60) suggests that mud-brick walls became preferred because with prefabricated building units (bricks), one could build faster, while Moorey (1994: 304) notes that *tauf* (also called *chineh*) walls are weaker than mud-brick walls.[9]

Mud-brick walls are made from the same type of mud mixture as *tauf* walls, but the individual bricks are made before building the wall. These bricks are produced by modeling by hand or by pressing mud into a mold.[10] The bricks are then dried for a period of time which can be from several days to several months, before being laid in the wall with mud mortar (Aurenche 1981: 66; Sauvage 1998: 20–3; Oates 1990: 388). The earliest bricks appear in the Near East around 8000 BCE in widely separated areas: Jericho in Palestine, Ramad in Syria, and Nemrik 9 and Mlefaat in northern Iraq. These bricks are hand modeled, plano-convex in form, and often (but not always) have finger impressions on the convex side. At some sites, especially the eastern ones, the bricks can be very long – over fifty centimeters or 20 inches. Aurenche (1993: 71) and Sauvage (1998: 90) suggest that the invention of the brick represents a stage of technological development that happened in several places and was linked to sociological changes with the development of permanent settled villages. In the same levels as these earliest bricks *tauf* walls and the older type of semi-sunken round houses were still used, and contemporaneous sites did not always use mud bricks at all (as at Mureybit in Syria or Qermez Dere in Iraq, Aurenche 1993: 71). Thus, these earliest bricks are only a first step in a long process which would see the development of standardized mold-made bricks of various types and complex rectilinear architecture over the next four millennia, a process that was part of the developing social complexity that led to the rise of urbanism and literate civilization (Aurenche 1981: 60–70; Sauvage 1998: 87–109).

The probable reason that mud brick became the most prevalent building material of Ancient Near Eastern architecture is that it is both versatile and economical. For local, private use the materials were abundantly available and the technology was simple (Oates 1990: 389). Though water can seriously damage mud brick, in the Near East the summer is arid, so there is time to repair damage and the necessary materials are right at hand (Dunham 1980: 24). Older houses' walls can be cut down and used as foundations for a new house built over them (Dunham 1980: 289); or older building ruins can be quarried for material to make mud bricks. Yet for public purposes mud brick was also suitable to build massive city walls, impressive tall temples with elaborately niched and buttressed facades, or giant stepped platforms – the famous ziggurats, or temple-towers, of Mesopotamia.

Indeed, Mesopotamia was the region where building in mud brick was the most highly developed for such public projects. For instance, with the development of urbanism in the late fourth millennium BCE in southern Mesopotamia, monumental public works demanded more efficient and faster building methods. Sauvage notes that this is probably the reason for the appearance of a new type of brick, the *Riemchen* (= "little strip") brick. *Riemchen* bricks are mold-made, rectangular bricks with an equal width and height. In a wall these bricks were all laid as headers with a row of stretchers along a face of the wall every two or three courses. Sauvage observes that since the *Riemchen* bricks had equal width and height, a mason could lay them faster in a wall because there was no difference whether they were on edge or flat; and the thicker the wall, the more the saving in time (Sauvage 1998: 112–13, plate 12b). Baked bricks were also developed at this time in southern Mesopotamia, and they were used mostly for pavements or for installations exposed to water, where they were set in bitumen. Another innovation at this time was the decoration of mud-brick walls with colored mosaics made of baked clay cones inserted into the wall plaster to form geometric patterns. The best-preserved examples were found at Warka (ancient Uruk) in southern Iraq (Moorey 1994: 309–10; Strommenger and Hirmer 1964: 380 and plate 13). In the third millennium during the Early Dynastic period the distinctive mold-made plano-convex bricks were used. These were rectangular, but with a convex top. They developed from *Riemchen* bricks, but with the added shortcut of not smoothing off the brick top in the mold, so they could be made faster (Tunça 1984: 120–30; Sauvage 1998: 115–24). In a wall they could be laid flat, or diagonally on edge so that one row over another formed a herringbone pattern, a technique that helped the mason increase the height of the wall faster.

Columns (free standing and engaged), and arches and vaults (corbeled, radial, flat, and pitched brick) were all built by the ancient Mesopotamians with mud bricks, sometimes specially shaped (molded or cut) ones (Sauvage 1998: 35–6; Oates 1990: 399–405; Besenval 1984). In the early second millennium BCE mud bricks were used to produce engaged columns in the shape of spirals or date palm trunks as monumental decoration of temples (Oates 1990; Weiss 1985). These were found both in southern Mesopotamia (Ur, Larsa) and in the north (Tell Rimah, Tell Leilan). At Tell Rimah they involved an intricate sequence of courses of specially shaped bricks so that not only would the desired pattern be achieved, but also the engaged column would be firmly bonded into the wall (Oates 1990: 392–6, figure 4). In the Late Bronze Age the Kassite kings used molded bricks to make anthropomorphic relief decoration. A great quantity of fallen bricks found at Warka near the ruins of a temple were able to be reconstructed to show a relief of mountain gods alternating with river goddesses set in niches (Strommenger and Hirmer 1964: 424 and plate 170). This technique was also used in Iran at Susa where part of an anthropomorphic relief of baked bricks from a temple built by a twelfth century BCE Elamite king was able to be reconstructed (Harper, Aruz, and Tallon 1992: 141–4). In the late second and in the first

millennium glazed bricks were also used, sometimes flat, sometimes in relief. At Susa
were found some modeled glazed bricks dated to the twelfth century BCE, unfortunately out of context (Harper, Aruz, and Tallon 1992: 141). Inscriptions of the
Middle Assyrian kings speak of using glazed bricks, but the earliest archaeological
attestation in Assyria is a glazed, flat brick orthostat of Tukulti-Ninurta II (890–884
BCE) from Assur (Moorey 1994: 315; Andrae 1925: plate 7). Orthostats are usually
hewn stone slabs of varying thickness stood on edge as a facing to the lower part of a
wall, which is sometimes of mud brick, but can be of packed rubble stone and mud in
which case the orthostats (usually thicker in this case) function as a load-bearing
element. Often they are on a low stone plinth. There is ample evidence after this for
the Neo-Assyrian kings' use of glazed flat bricks in their palaces and temples, but
modeled or shaped glazed bricks are very rare (Moorey 1994: 317). From the Neo-
Babylonian period, however, come some of the most famous examples: the glazed
brick reliefs of striding lions and the bulls and dragons of the processional way and the
Ishtar Gate at Babylon (Strommenger and Hirmer 1964: 457–62 plates XLIII–XLIV,
277). The tradition of glazed brick relief was to continue in the Achaemenid period as
examples from Susa show (Harper, Aruz, and Tallon 1992: 223–40).

The main kinds of stone used in Ancient Near Eastern architecture were limestone
of various hardnesses and colors, basalt, sandstone and gypsum, especially in its
crystalline form, alabaster (Aurenche 1981: 11–15; Wright 1985: 338–40; Naumann
1971: 33–4; Reich 1992: 1–5; Moorey 1994: 335–6). Stone for building was
obtained either by gathering loose surface stones ("fieldstones") or by quarrying
blocks of various shapes from bedrock outcrops. Not much is known about the
quarries used in the Near East in the period under consideration, although some
examples have been found (Wright 1985: 342–3; Shiloh and Horowitz 1975; Naumann 1971: 34–43; Mazzoni 1986–7; Moorey 1994: 336; Hult 1983: 21). Wright
notes a process called insolation in which extremes of diurnal temperatures act on the
diverse mineral constituents of certain rocks to break up the surface into a network of
cracks and make the rock break off in flat layers. Where such beds of rock are exposed
it is relatively easy to break away flat angular stones of more or less parallelepiped[11]
form, to create rather tightly bonded, neat-looking rubble stone walls, as in the Early
Bronze Age temple at the site of Ai in Israel (Wright 1985: 340–1; Reich 1992: 4).
This also may be the process responsible for the flat rectangular mud stones used in
walls at the neolithic site of Beidha (Aurenche 1981: 13, 110–11 figures 65–6, 72).

Stone as a building material was used for both free-standing and retaining walls,
platforms, and architectural details such as columns, column bases and capitals, stairs,
door sills, and door sockets.[12] Most often stone only formed the foundation and
lower part of a wall, which continued up in mud bricks. When stone was used in free-
standing walls, usually the two faces of the wall would have larger stones arranged to
form straight lines, while the interior of the wall would be filled with smaller irregular
stones, often packed with mud. The masonry of the wall faces deserves some comment. Fieldstones could be used in their natural shape, piled on top of one another
(often with the largest at the bottom) and the spaces between them would be filled
with small stones or chips to make a tight-fitting bond. This is called rubble masonry,
or fieldstone masonry (Reich 1992: 4; Shiloh 1979: 50). It was used as early as the

Pre-Pottery Neolithic B period (7600–6600 BCE) at Jericho to build a massive town wall (Kenyon 1981: 79 and plates 65, 222), and it continued to be used in the Bronze and Iron ages alongside other types of masonry. Fieldstones can also be arranged in a tighter bond with their edges fitting close to one another so that as few small stones as possible are needed to fill the interstices (Reich 1992: 3 figure 5). This is called polygonal bonding and examples can be seen at Boğazköy in Anatolia, modern Turkey, in the Late Bronze Age (Naumann 1971: 67 figure 44).

Finally, the stones can be hewn into blocks, square (cube) or rectangular, and set in the wall in horizontal courses. This is called ashlar masonry and the blocks are called ashlars or ashlar blocks (Dinsmoor 1975: 388). This technique was used since the beginning of the third millennium in Egypt and to a lesser extent in the Near East from the middle of that millennium, but the ashlar blocks were not always perfectly rectangular nor the courses always of equal height nor the vertical joints always perpendicular (Hult 1983: 1, 91). Furthermore, fieldstone and polygonal masonry continued to be used and were often used in the same building, or even the same wall, as ashlar masonry. In Egypt narrow walls would be made of ashlars in their full thickness with alternate rows of headers and stretchers, while thick walls were made with rubble behind well-dressed ashlar faces (Hult 1983: 61, 70). In the Near East, isolated occurrences of ashlar masonry attest to knowledge of the technique in the third millennium (Early Bronze Age) (Hult 1983: 38–40; Matthiae 1977: 68), but the first extensive attestations are in the early second millennium (Middle Bronze Age) when it is used for ashlar orthostats in North Syria and Palestine (Hult 1983: 38–40). Use of orthostats continued in the Late Bronze Age, when they were sometimes carved with reliefs (in Hittite Anatolia at Boğazköy, Alaça Hüyük, and Malatya). This tradition continued in the Iron Age in Anatolia, North Syria (Orthmann 1971), and Achaemenid Iran. Perhaps the most famous orthostat reliefs are those of the Neo-Assyrian kings, who are considered to have gotten the idea from North Syria (Moorey 1994: 343).

A few examples of ashlar blocks laid in courses in walls have been found in Middle Bronze Age contexts in Syria at Alalakh, Byblos, and Ras Shamra (Hult 1983: 71), but in the Late Bronze Age coursed ashlar masonry is extensively used for important buildings at Ras Shamra and nearby Ras Ibn Hani. At Ras Shamra the walls are usually ashlar-faced rubble walls, but sometimes the ashlars are laid as both headers and stretchers. The visible surface of blocks could be worked to a smooth face, or it could be marginally drafted with only a border near the edges flattened, leaving a protruding boss in the middle. This is done on the side of the block that shows on the wall face. Such blocks were used both where they would and would not be seen (as in foundation courses). At Ras Ibn Hani the excavators found part of a wall made completely of marginally drafted ashlar blocks laid as headers and stretchers (Bounni et al. 1979 figure 13), thus prefiguring the use of ashlars in Israelite masonry in the tenth and ninth centuries BCE (Hult 1983: 71, 82). Some examples of coursed ashlar masonry of the Late Bronze Age are also found in Palestine, but without marginal drafting and of a poorer quality than found at Ras Shamra (Hult 1983: 71). In Anatolia the Hittites developed an ashlar masonry late in this period, which consisted of huge, pillow-shaped blocks and was often used with polygonal masonry in the same wall (Naumann 1971: 72 figure 56; Hult 1983: 72). Sometimes the Hittites used marginal drafting, the best example being the sanctuary at Eflâtun Pinar (Naumann 1971: 73 figure 57). The Iron Age heirs to the Hittite masonry tradition seem to be the Urartians, because at the site of Ayanis the south fortification wall has a facing of rectilinear, dark andesite blocks carefully worked at the margins to form very close joints, while the central part is a softly protruding bulge (Çiligiroglu 2001: 26–7 figures 5–9).

Israelite masonry of the tenth to ninth centuries BCE made much use of marginally drafted blocks for foundation courses, while for visible walls the faces were worked to a smooth surface. Ashlars were still used in conjunction with fieldstone masonry, sometimes as piers in a fieldstone wall (Shiloh 1979: plate 25.1). However, completely ashlar-built walls were also made, and as Wright notes, the finest examples are excellent ashlar masonry in their dressing of blocks and their setting with joints of only a few millimeters (Wright 1985: 402). Nevertheless, such prime examples occur only in limited stretches and in many instances blocks were finely dressed for close jointing only at the face margins, while at the rear the block was roughed away and the jointing made up with chips and mortar (Wright 1985: 405).[13] As suggested above, Israelite ashlar masonry was an heir to Late Bronze Age masonry traditions, especially as found at Ras Shamra and Ras Ibn Hani. It is often considered to belong to a larger "Phoenician" masonry tradition, because a similar masonry style survived on the Levantine coast at Phoenician sites in the Achaemenid, Hellenistic, and Roman periods (Wright 1985: 406; Mallowan 1978: 158; Dunand 1966). Mallowan has discussed it in relation to Assyria (1978: 158–9), while Wright notes that it is more aligned with Classical Greek masonry than Egyptian Pharaonic masonry, because of its uncompromising use of horizontal bedding and vertical rising joints and its association with the proto-Aeolic capital (Wright 1985: 406–7; Betancourt 1977; Shiloh 1979). However, the refinements that will distinguish later Greek masonry – precisely formed blocks with carefully drafted margins and central bosses and fine jointing achieved by *anathyrosis*[14] – were first seen in the Ancient Near East in early Achaemenid times at Pasargadae, where there is strong evidence to show that it was the work of Lydian and Ionian masons (Nylander 1970; Stronach 1978: 8–23).

Wooden parts of Ancient Near Eastern buildings are usually not preserved, but their former presence is sometimes detected by the discovery of post holes, stone bases for columns, or gaps in mud brick or stone walls where wooden beams had been placed. If a building had been destroyed by fire, sometimes pieces of fallen roofing will have burned wood beams in them, or burned door panels may be partly preserved as charcoal. From this evidence wood appears to have been used in antiquity much the same way as in village architecture of recent times. Wood was used in the earliest houses, as for instance at Mureybit (8300–7600 BCE) where impressions of wooden posts in the mud walling of one house showed that the wall had been propped up by a palisade of upright poles, themselves plastered over with mud (Aurenche 1981: 85). In the Early Dynastic Temple Oval (third millennium BCE) at Khafaje a fire had preserved substantial chunks of collapsed roof in House D, which were made of a timber framework covered by mud plastered reeds or reed mats (Delougaz 1940: 49–65, 133–6 figures 121–3). In areas where earthquakes are frequent and wood plentiful, timber beams were inserted in the stone or brick masonry to improve the elasticity of the wall. An example is the Middle Bronze Age palace at Beycesultan, Anatolia, where timber beams were set longitudinally and crosswise at intervals both in the stone foundations and the upper brickwork of the walls (Lloyd and Mellaart 1965: 8 and figure A.5). The corpus of scientifically identified samples of wooden architectural parts is too small to make generalizations, but the types include cedar of Lebanon (Nuzi, Khorsabad), oak (Mureybit, Brak, Nimrud), palm (Larsa), pine (Brak, Nimrud, Ur), poplar (Brak, Tell ed-Der, Larsa, Mureybit) and tamarisk (Abu Salabikh) (Moorey 1994: 360; Moorey and Postgate 1992: 197–9).

Buildings

The architecture of the Ancient Near East, covering a period of over nine thousand years – from about 10,000 BCE (or before) down to the conquest of Alexander the Great in the fourth century BCE – includes a large variety of styles in different periods and places. Sometimes this long period allows one to see the survival and development of an architectural motif or practice from deep in prehistoric times to the end of Ancient Near Eastern civilization. Such is the case in Mesopotamia with the articulation of mud-brick walls by buttresses and niches, which first appear in a practical function in the sixth millennium BCE, but become important symbols for public and sacred architecture in the succeeding millennia (Sievertsen 1999). As examples of buildings, I will discuss an example of a house, a palace, and a temple because these three types of buildings are the architectural expressions of the main sectors of the Ancient Near Eastern economy – private citizenry, palace, and temple (Diakonoff 1995: 91).

At Ur in southern Mesopotamia two areas of well-preserved private houses were found. In one of these, the "AH Site," private archives of tablets which were found in some of the houses showed that the inhabitants of this neighborhood were successful businessmen who engaged in activities such as money lending, financing trade expeditions, and collecting rents and taxes (Van De Mieroop 1992: 163–4). Such prosperity was reflected in the house architecture, since much baked brick was used, sometimes up to eighteen courses on exterior façades, an ostentatious use of an expensive material, as Woolley notes.[15] As an example, one can consider the house "Number 1, Old Street," which may have been the house of Ea-nasir, a merchant involved in trade with Dilmun, since some of his business documents were found in the ruins.[16] This house (Figure 20.1), the rooms of which all had baked brick pavements (except Room 7, which was a cooking area), had a central courtyard (2), entered through a vestibule and surrounded on all sides by rooms.[17] On the southwest side a long, narrow room (3) contained a staircase which led up over a lavatory (4), either to a second story or just to the roof.[18] The most important and largest rooms, (5) and (6), lay on the northwest side of the courtyard where a central door led through the thickest wall in the house to Room 5 with walls of twelve courses of baked bricks above floor level. Both Rooms 5 and 6 had vaulted tombs (not excavated) under their pavements and both had, at their south ends, mud-brick "altars"

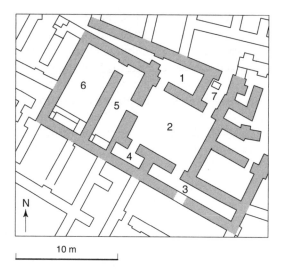

Figure 20.1   Ur. House of the Old Babylonian Period. "Number 1 Old Street."
Source: Woolley and Mallowan 1976, plate 124. Courtesy the University of Pennsylvania
Museum of Anthropology and the British Museum Company Limited

and mud-brick "tables" with a recessed panel decoration and infant burials flush with
the pavement in front of them.[19] Woolley plausibly suggests that the installations in
Room 5 were not original to the room, but added later, because only Room 6 has a
niche for a "chimney" in the wall behind the altar, as happens in other houses. This
pair of rooms occurs in other large houses in the neighborhood, and Woolley
interprets them as a reception room for visitors (the front room, here 5) and a private
domestic chapel (6). Even if one does not agree with all the details of Woolley's
interpretations,[20] one can see that this set of rooms, with their thick front wall and
their use of baked brick and built-in installations, were meant to express the prestige
and prosperity of the house owner.

The palace of the Neo-Assyrian king Assurnasirpal II (883–859 BCE) at Nimrud is a
good example of the large scale and ostentation of royal building (Figure 20.2).
Assurnasirpal II says in one of his inscriptions that he removed the older ruin mound,
dug down to ground water and built up a terrace on which he built his palace which
he decorated with exotic woods, glazed bricks, and bronze (Grayson 1976: 173–4).
While these decorations are not preserved in this palace, the extant remains of his
work are very impressive. Along the bank of the Tigris, above which the palace was
situated, a retaining wall of large limestone blocks about ten meters high (33 feet) and
six and a half meters (21 feet) wide was built against the bedrock which had been cut
to receive it. Above this rose a thick mud-brick wall preserved up to six and a half
meters in some places (Mallowan 1966: 78–81). Today the remains of the palace still
cover 2.4 hectares (about 6 acres) (Mallowan 1966: 94) and include a large outer
court on the north for administration, south of which was an official part, all of whose
walls were sumptuously decorated with reliefs and sculptures. A recent study of these

reliefs and sculptures suggests they were meant to express a fourfold Assyrian ideology of military success, service to the gods, divine protection, and Assyrian prosperity, while the subject and placement of the decoration of each suite of rooms was influenced by the function of that suite (Russell 1998: 712). For instance, the façade and inner walls of the large throne room B were decorated with large reliefs and sculptures of protective guardians and scenes of Assyria's victorious might aimed at convincing the visitor of the king's invincible power.

The extensive use of sculptural decoration in a different cultural context, that of a temple, is well illustrated by the Late Bronze–Early Iron Age temple of 'Ain Dara in North Syria. In its final phase (900–740 BCE) this temple consisted of a recessed porch with two columns, a wide ante-cella, a square cella (16.7 × 16.8 m. or 55 × 55 feet) with its back half filled by a podium, and a surrounding corridor (termed an ambulatory) built around the outside of the temple (Assaf 1990: figures 14, 18 = here Figure 20.3). On the outside, the lowest parts of the ambulatory walls were decorated with orthostats carved with lions or sphinxes. Wide basalt steps with a guilloche pattern carved on their risers led up to the porch. Orthostats with lions on them stood at each side of the porch, and of the doorways to the ante-cella and cella. Foreparts (termed protomes) of lions (or sphinxes), some probably two meters (6½ feet) tall,[21] were carved on separate blocks and lined up next to the sculptures at the entrances to the porch, ante-cella, and cella, so that each doorway was guarded by several lions or sphinxes on each side. Other sculptural decoration included orthostats carved with a "false window" panel in the ante-cella, figural decoration on some orthostats in this room, as well as on pillar-like steles in the ambulatory that helped support the roof,[22] a low basalt socle with a relief of mountain gods, bull men and griffons on it that was found on the podium in the cella, and two rows of guilloches carved on the basalt socles at the bases of the walls of the porch, ante-cella, and cella. The most striking details to modern eyes, however, are the giant foot prints (97 × 35 cm. or 38 × 14 inches) carved into the large limestone thresholds of the doorways to the ante-cella and the cella, as if a supernatural being was walking into the temple.

The ambulatory with its outside orthostats was an addition to the temple, which had two earlier phases without it. The first of these the excavators date to 1300–1000 BCE, as the relief of the mountain gods on the socle has close stylistic parallels in the Late Bronze Age (Assaf 1990: 39). This dating is also supported by the discovery of two fragments of Hittite steles in the vicinity of the temple, although in secondary contexts (Assaf 1994). The original plan of the temple (without the ambulatory) had a long ancestry reaching back to the third millennium in Syria (Assaf 1990: 23, 1994; Werner 1994). Assaf suggests tentatively that the addition of the ambulatory might be Phoenician influence, since later Phoenician temples sometimes have such an ambulatory (Assaf 1990: 24). Monson (2000: 34), however, suggests that such side chambers might have been more common than hitherto realized. He feels the 'Ain Dara temple has some striking parallels to Solomon's temple as described in the Bible. Perhaps not the least is the powerful image that each must have been for the community of people to whose god it was dedicated.

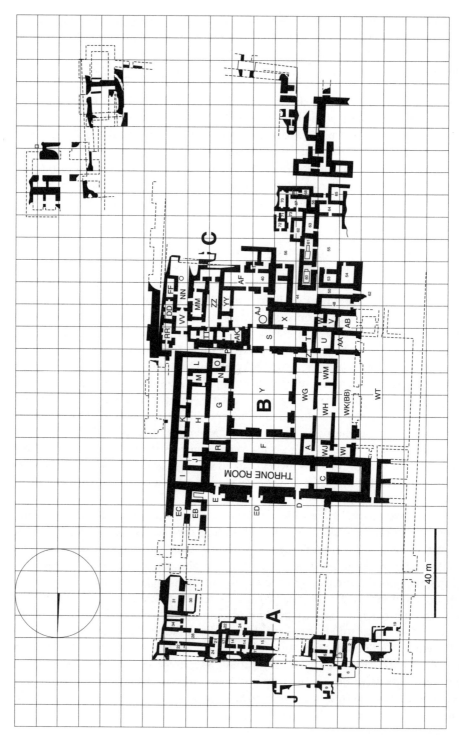

Figure 20.2 Nimrud. Palace of Assurnasirpal II. A=Administration, B=Official part, C=Private part. Source: Overall plan drawn by R. P. Sobolewski. Courtesy S. Paley and R. P. Sobolewski.

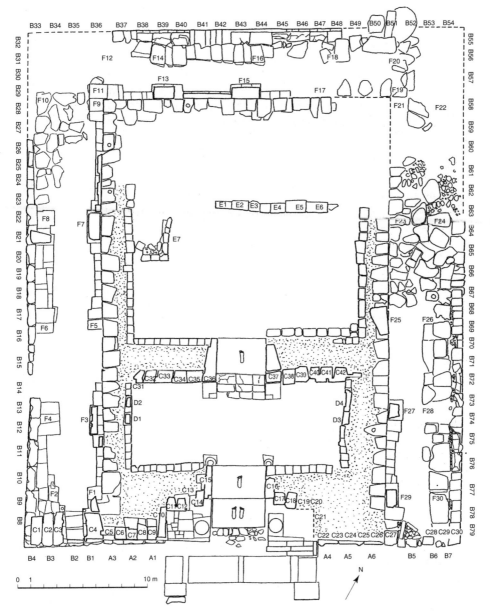

Figure 20.3 Tell 'Ain Dara. Temple. A1–A6: Orthostats of lions and sphinxes; B1–B79: Orthostats of lions and sphinxes; C1–C42: Protomes of lions and sphinxes; D1–D4: Reliefs of the ante-cells; E1–E7: Socle reliefs on the podium; F1–F30: Steles of the ambulatory. Source: 'Assaf 1990, figure 18. Courtesy Dr. Abu Ali 'Assaf

NOTES

1 This essay will not discuss Egyptian architecture.

2 Two examples are Ugarit, the capital of a Late Bronze Age kingdom on the Mediterranean coast in Syria, which was discovered in 1929 (Yon 1997) and Ebla, the capital of a third millennium kingdom in Syria, which was discovered in 1975 (Matthiae 1977).

3 With the exception of tombs, which have sometimes been found complete (as at Ugarit, Saadé 1979: 141, figure 46). Sometimes details of buildings, such as doorways or windows, have been found complete, and walls have been preserved up to the start of the ceiling (as at Halawa, Meyer 1989: 41.).

4 Trigger 1990 discusses one aspect of the symbolic power of monumental architecture – the use of "conspicuous consumption" to express oppressive power.

5 Ethnoarchaeology is an anthropological approach that, of course, has a much wider application than the particular subject discussed here. For definition and history see Gould 2000 and Krafeld-Daugherty 1994.

6 For references see Aurenche 1981, Krafeld-Daugherty 1994, and Pfälzner 2001.

7 In southern Mesopotamia reeds were also important.

8 Aurenche 1981: 53–9. If the wall is built by hand modeling, it is called *tauf* in Arabic or *chineh* in Persian. The French term *pisé* really refers to mud pressed into a wooden frame with vertical sides, but it can also be used to refer to a *tauf/chineh* wall (Aurenche 1977: 139–9). As Kemp (2000: 80) notes, suitable soils are widespread and villagers who work the land and build their houses from it learn empirically which soils mixed with which tempering materials make the best mud mixture for walls and bricks.

9 *Tauf* walls are still used in various parts of the Middle East for garden walls (Braidwood and Howe 1960: 40; Wulff 1966: 108) and for house walls (Watson 1979a: 119). Perhaps the most spectacular *tauf* buildings are the famous "tower houses" of Yemen (Varanda 1982: 97, 102, 108–9).

10 Or, the mold can be pressed into a layer of the prepared mud. Aurenche 1981: 64–5.

11 A solid with six sides, all of which are parallelograms.

12 Stone was used for the roofs of tombs either as flat slabs (for example, the Early Bronze Age tomb at Tell Banat, Syria, or the megalithic stone cists, or coffins, found in Palestine and Jordan, Wright 1985: 32–3; Stekelis 1977); or as corbelled vaults (Ras Shamra, Saadé 1979: 141). Stone slabs for roofs were also used in the basalt desert regions in Jordan and south Syria (Wright 1985: 459).

13 See Shiloh 1979: 66–8 and table 6 for a discussion of the different grades of quality of Israelite masonry.

14 *Anathyrosis* is a procedure whereby on the sides of the block that would be in contact with other blocks, only a border of some width would be very carefully smoothed, while the area inside this border would be worked to a slightly deeper level (Dinsmoor 1975: 173, 387; Nylander 1970: 35–8).

15 Woolley and Mallowan 1976: 18. In contrast to public buildings, however, the baked bricks were not set in bitumen, but in mud mortar.

16 Woolley and Mallowan 1976: 124–5; Van De Mieroop 1992: 136–7. The street names and numbers of the houses are modern labels Woolley gave them.

17 Originally there had been rooms on the southeast side of the courtyard, but their doorways were later blocked up and they became part of the house to the southeast, Number 7 Church Lane.

18 Woolley and Mallowan 1976: 25–6; Miglus 1999: 75–6; Battini-Villard 1999: 371–85.
19 Woolley and Mallowan 1976: plates 43–5, and figure 40 for illustrations of similar installations in other houses.
20 For different opinions see Miglus 1999: 67–75; Battini-Villard 1999: 185–200; Krafeld-Daugherty 1994: 90–3, 202–3; Keith 1999: 258–62.
21 None of these have their heads, but several are preserved 1.5 to 2 meters high, Assaf 1990: 54–6.
22 The figurative decoration in these last two places was very badly preserved.

FURTHER READING

For the student who wants to study in greater depth two of the most helpful books in English mentioned here are Wright 1985 and Moorey 1994. Wright deals only with Palestine and a few sites in Syria and Jordan, but he gives excellent discussions about building materials and methods, as well as about design. Moorey only examines building materials and techniques, but gives useful references in his bibliography to studies on architecture by other scholars in English, French, or German. Owing to the small amount of space allowed for this chapter, many important works could not be listed in the bibliography. For understanding the particular qualities of mud brick architecture Oates 1990 is excellent. An important example of the use of texts in relation to ancient architecture is Stone 1987. Useful studies of domestic architecture are Aurenche 1981, Krafeld-Daugherty 1994, Pfälzner 2001, and Miglus 1999. Although these are not in English, they contain large bibliographies which include English as well as French and German references. Specialized studies to be highly recommended are Russell 1998, Stronach 1978, Nylander 1970, and Hult 1983. The study of architecture is ultimately based on excavations reports, only a few of which could be listed here (Assaf 1990, Çilingiroglu 2001, Delougaz 1940, Bounni et al. 1979, Frankfort 1934, Kenyon 1981, Lloyd and Mellaart 1965, Mallowan 1966, Meyer 1989, Parrot 1958, Stronach 1978, Woolley and Mallowan 1976). For references to excavation reports about particular sites one can consult *The Oxford Encyclopedia of Archaeology in the Near East* (Meyers 1997).

CHAPTER TWENTY-ONE

Mesopotamian Art

Marian H. Feldman

An article on Ancient Near Eastern art might attempt to describe the vast wealth of artistic production created over many millennia, but such a task proves impossibly large. Instead, the following essay explores several Mesopotamian works of art through a variety of perspectives and interpretations. It concentrates exclusively on Mesopotamia and even then eschews comprehensiveness in order to penetrate more deeply into questions raised by the art objects.

One can divide the modern discipline of the study of Mesopotamian art into three major periods. The first, which followed the archaeological discoveries of the nineteenth and early twentieth centuries, was characterized by basic documentation and sometimes rather speculative conclusions. Starting in the 1930s and culminating in the fifties, sixties, and seventies, a second phase consisted of the publication of lavishly illustrated surveys that sought to chart the full measure of artistic (usually understood as stylistic) development from prehistory to the coming of Alexander the Great. A period of less homogeneous studies emerged in the 1980s, marking the third phase.

Although there are still relatively few art historians specializing in the Ancient Near East, the field has experienced a kind of renaissance during this last phase, especially within American colleges and universities, where scholars have been grappling with conceptual, socio-historical, and methodological questions that push the intellectual purview beyond cataloging and stylistic development. This recent work has broached a host of issues including, for example, aesthetics, the function of art as story telling, relationships between text and image, sexuality, and the nature of representation. Not too surprisingly, the trajectory sketched here parallels that of the discipline of art history as a whole.

An issue that underlies and continues to vex discussions on Mesopotamian art is that of artistic legitimacy. Arguing for a relevance to Western art history often entails viewing Near Eastern art within the value hierarchies of Western art, while conversely, support for its particularity tends to cast the Near East as "other," marginalizing it within the discipline.

The first view tends to see Mesopotamian art as the foundation for Classical Greece. This characterization appears early on, for example in Perrot and Chipiez's two-volume study, *A History of Art in Chaldaea & Assyria* from 1882. They were limited to the first millennium BCE since principally Neo-Assyrian archaeological discoveries in northern Iraq were available. With reference to the depiction of the human body, they write, "[Mesopotamia] created many types that were transmitted to the Mediterranean nations, and soon adopted by them. These types were perfected, but not invented, by the Greeks" (1884: 2: 80). On the other hand, Malraux wrote that Sumerian art was invisible for us, by which he meant it was unimaginable because it lay outside the visual apparatus of Western culture (Malraux 1961: xiii).

The Western versus non-Western tension is evident also in the dichotomy established early in Mesopotamian art scholarship between "conceptual" art and "naturalism" understood as a distinction between non-Greek and Greek arts (Perrot and Chipiez 1884: 2: 82). Working from the normative assumption that the imitation of nature motivates representation, this theory claims that the artists of Mesopotamia strove to depict "what they knew" rather than "what they saw." Such notions persist but are being contested by scholars such as Winter (1995) and Bahrani (2003) who seek to understand Mesopotamian conceptions of art on their own terms. Trends in contemporary art, such as modernism in the early and mid-twentieth century that questioned the basis of art in illusion through movements such as abstraction, have provided an impetus for this reappraisal. For example, both Malraux (1961: xlviii) and Mazenod (1980) consider the modern viewer freed from the constraints of the Classical canon and thus primed fully to appreciate Mesopotamian art.

Concepts of beauty and realism that formerly flowed through much art historical scholarship have faced challenges in the discipline over the past quarter of a century, allowing art historians of the Ancient Near East to position themselves as an independent field that both contributes to and benefits from discussions in the larger discipline of art history. Nevertheless, questions of what constitutes art as distinct from artifact and its relationship to aesthetics and illusionism continue to affect scholarship. For example, Collon in her recent art survey begins with the disclaimer "The objects . . . are not always what we now understand as art. But art is so often a question of personal taste, and what is beautiful to one person or within one culture may not be so to another person or in another context" (1995: 15).

The supposed conflict between art, as the object of disinterested aesthetic contemplation, and artifact, as evidence for ancient history, surfaces in several textbooks. For example, the editor's note to the first edition of Frankfort's *Art and Architecture of the Ancient Orient* hails Frankfort's contributions to art appreciation: "[Frankfort's] greatest love was the work of art for its own sake, and he regarded it as his task – as indeed the present book fully proves – to present oriental art as art, and not as archaeological evidence." But Frankfort himself writes in the introduction, "[Near Eastern arts] remain enigmatic, unless we acquire some insight into the spiritual climate and the geographical and historical conditions in which they were created. In other words, it is the archaeologist who must build the scaffold from which we can view these ancient monuments as works of art" (1954: xxv).

Acknowledging the Euro-centric biases that even the word art carries – namely, the distinction between craft and fine art according to function or lack thereof – Winter has proposed a reconstruction of indigenous terminology and concepts. She suggests as a working definition of art "any work that is imaginatively conceptualized and that affords visual and emotional satisfaction, for which manufacturing skill is required and to which some established standards have been applied" (Winter 1995: 2570). This flexible definition, specific to Mesopotamia rather than universal, has the merit of being derived from the surviving objects and texts rather than imposed from later classically influenced concepts of art.

In the early twentieth century the increasing archaeological finds spurred a desire to construct an unbroken narrative of the history of Mesopotamian art, understanding history as a sequence of causal events and thus art history as stylistic development leading seamlessly from one period to the next. Frankfort begins his seminal book, "Strictly speaking, a history of the art of the ancient Near East has never been written," referring to the new wealth of information at his disposal (1954: xxv). For many scholars tracing an unbroken development of Mesopotamian art formed the primary objective despite the generally acknowledged obstacles of unevenness of evidence and archaeological serendipity (Woolley 1935: 9; Parrot 1961b: 3–4; Garbini 1966: 10; Strommenger and Hirmer 1964: 7; Moortgat 1969: vii; Mazenod 1980; Collon 1995: 40; Harper et al. 1995: 11). Moortgat bemoans the historical and artifactual gaps that make "the writing of a truthful history of the art of Ancient Mesopotamia" extremely difficult (1969: x). A motivating factor in tracing artistic development lies in the belief that artistic products reveal the true nature of a people. Parrot writes, "Looking at the plumed horses [of the Neo-Assyrian period wall paintings from Til Barsip in northern Syria] galloping towards a lion pierced with arrows, we learn something of the mentality of these born fighters ..." (1961a: xviii). More recently, this sentiment has been echoed with respect to carved Neo-Assyrian reliefs: "They... constitute one of the most impressive and eloquent witnesses of ancient Mesopotamian civilization, giving us an extraordinary glimpse into the minds and material culture of [the Assyrians] ..." (Reade 1995: 39).

In recent years, a growing disbelief across disciplines in our ability to discern universal humanistic laws and to construct seamless narratives has prompted more particularized scholarship that focuses on single art works, time periods, or theoretical issues. These specialized studies analyze questions about art's context and relation to society, such as overlapping meanings, audiences, or socio-political impact. As one of many examples, Thomason (in press) explores the role of collecting luxury objects in the formation of Mesopotamian royal identity. Additionally, an interest in the complicated relationship between inscribed text and figural representation has borne intellectual fruit across a range of periods and artifacts (Winter 1989; Russell 1993; Suter 2000; Bahrani 2003; Slanski 2003).

The Warka Vase

The choice of where to begin a narrative of ancient Mesopotamian art remains bound up in the contested definition of art itself as well as in the question of whether to include prehistoric material. However, most scholars include in the canon the carved reliefs and sculptures of the proto-historic Late Uruk period (3500–3000 BCE).

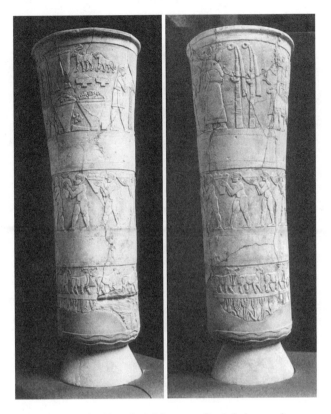

Figure 21.1a and b   The Warka Vase, Iraq Museum, Baghdad, two views.
Source: Staatliche Museen zu Berlin, Preussischer Kulturbesitz, Vorderasiatisches Museum

Foremost among these is the so-called Warka vase, a tall, cylindrically shaped stone vessel carved around its exterior in low relief, and not surprisingly, it appears in all standard treatments of Near Eastern art (see Figures 21.1 and 21.2). At first glance, the vase appears simple: a series of registers, or areas divided by lines, rise from undulating water at the bottom, through paired crops and sheep, nude male offering bearers, to the topmost register depicting a female figure facing a mostly broken person who can be reconstructed as a male authority figure typically known in the scholarship as a "priest-king." The vase was found in a hoard in Level III of the Eanna temple precinct at Uruk. That it was broken and repaired in antiquity, in addition to its style, has suggested to many scholars an earlier date in Uruk IV, which places it more or less contemporary with the first appearance of writing and cylinder seals (about 3300 BCE). A small fragment of an identical second vase preserving part of an attendant from the upper register was bought on the art market, a pairing that was echoed in the self-referential depiction of two such vases on the Warka vase itself.

Since its excavation, the Warka vase has assumed a preeminent place as exemplar of late fourth millennium cultural characteristics from the stylistic to the religious. Frankfort wrote, "By its subject and style it allows us to perceive the spiritual climate

Figure 21.1c The Warka Vase, Iraq Museum, Baghdad, detail. Courtesy of Staatliche Museen zu Berlin, Preussischer Kulturbesitz, Vorderasiatisches Museum

in which the art of this period came into being" (1954: 11). Most scholars have associated the imagery with rituals of the sacred marriage of the goddess Inanna, whose symbol of a curving reed bundle appears twice directly behind the female figure and in whose sacred precinct the vase was discovered (Groenewegen-Frankfort 1951: 151; Frankfort 1954: 10; Parrot 1961b: 71–2; Moortgat 1969: 12–13; Amiet 1980: 70; Hansen 1998: 46; Bahrani 2002; Hansen 2003a: 23–4). The sacred marriage, understood as the event of the upper register, provides the agricultural abundance shown in the lower registers. From a slightly different but complementary point of view, the lower registers have been read as foundational for the event at the top: the water provides life for the crops and herds that in turn supply the offerings to be presented to the goddess.

The Warka vase provokes fundamental questions about narrative, the nature of representation, and the relationship between art and complex society. The compositional structure of the vase, its superimposed registers that encircle the cylindrical body, has been hailed as the earliest representational narrative. Groenewegen-Frankfort writes, "The vase offered an ideal surface for the representation of a cyclic event and the liveliness of the figures is unimpaired by their rhythmic sequence in a broad strip which seems a self-contained spatial world" (1951: 152). Amiet characterizes the depiction as an "unfolding procession" (1980: 70), and Parrot

Figure 21.2 The Warka Vase, line drawing. Source: Ernst Heinrich, *Kleinfunde aus den archaeischen Tempelschriften in Uruk, Berlin 1936*

notes, "the reliefs can be read from top to bottom or vice versa … " (1961b: 70). From a structuralist perspective, the registers order the natural, human, and divine world into a purportedly harmonious and hierarchical whole (Winter 1983). The production of the vase predates known textual narrative by several hundred years since the earliest written narrative is on the Stele of the Vultures from the reign of Eannatum in the twenty-fifth century BCE, but its conception at the same time as the explosion of early record-keeping at Uruk may be linked to an emerging desire to store information in a format that could be retrieved by third parties (Pittmann 1994: 191–2).

Consideration of figurative narrative leads to issues about the nature of representation in Mesopotamia in general, particularly since it was during this period at the end of the fourth millennium that increasingly complex imagery was first produced. The connection with information storage is one possible motivation for this sudden appearance, but it does not fully explain the specific choice of Mesopotamian representational styles.

Discussion of the Warka vase contributes to this issue with the debate surrounding the identification of the female figure, which has occupied most scholarly discussions about the work. For the most part, the debate has revolved around whether she represents the goddess Inanna or her priestess, a question considered pressing because of what Groenewegen-Frankfort describes as the "almost weird concreteness" and "curious actuality" of the scene and the unfortunate ancient breakage of the figure's headdress, the ancient Mesopotamian locus for divine identity from at least the mid-third millennium onward (1951: 151). It is not, in fact, certain whether the conventions for indicating divinity with horns, known from the third millennium, were already in use in the fourth millennium. Moortgat, however, offers a perceptive alternative that obviates the need to choose between one or the other possibility: "we may perhaps come nearest to the truth if we simply avoid this sharp distinction between Myth and Reality" (1969: 13). In a similar vein, Bahrani argues that the ambiguous nature of the representation contributes to a referential loop that ties the imagery to both the ritual enactment by a human priestess and a human king (that is, Moortgat's reality) and the myth of the sacred marriage of gods (2002). The discussions concerning the identity of the female figure recall a much more recent work of art, René Magritte's *La Trahison des Images* (*The Treachery of Images*), the earliest version of which dates to CE 1929. The oil painting consists only of an illusionistically rendered image of a pipe, under which, in elegant script, flows the phrase, "ceci n'est pas une pipe" ("this is not a pipe"). Magritte's painting warns us of the deceit of images, because while they may contain a certain concreteness or actuality, they are always somehow something other than the thing itself. The Warka vase figure, and for that matter all Mesopotamian figurative representation, may occupy a very different relationship with the real from what we are used to considering (Bahrani 2003).

Cylinder Seals

No review of Mesopotamian art can ignore seals, nor should it overlook their relationship to writing and administration. At their most basic level, seals are markers of a self-conscious system of recording and preserving information that worked together with writing and other communication techniques (Winter 2001). During the Late Uruk period (3500–3000 BCE), a peculiarly Mesopotamian form of seal appeared: the cylinder seal, spool shaped and carved in reverse around the circumference of the seal's surface. When rolled across a malleable surface such as clay, it produced a continuous frieze of imagery (see Figure 21.3). The production and use of cylinder seals continued until the end of the first millennium when they were gradually replaced by stamp seals. From the perspective of a comprehensive narrative of art, seals offer the best material for charting development and changes over time and place, since they were produced in fairly large quantities during every major period of Mesopotamian history. Frankfort's treatment of cylinder seals established a chronology of stylistic development, which still stands today albeit with subsequent refinements (Frankfort 1939; Collon 1987). Porada in a summary article at the end

Figure 21.3 Late Uruk seal impression. Source: Staatliche Museen zu Berlin, Preussischer Kulturbesitz, Vorderasiatisches Museum

of her illustrious career calls cylinder seals "remarkably revealing of the people who made and used them . . ." (1993: 563).

The unique characteristics of seals, however, make their fit within normative art historical frameworks somewhat uncomfortable. This includes the nature of their image-making capabilities. The seals themselves, even when made from valuable and probably culturally significant materials such as the blue stone lapis lazuli, served a primary function of creating an image on another surface. These created images could exist in multiples, confounding notions of singular works of art. In addition, ancient sealings on discarded pieces of clay are often broken, preserving only part of the imagery (Collon 1987: 5–7). Their small scale, usually only centimeters in size, has prompted a variety of different justifications for considering these items as art, often referring to them as "miniature masterpieces." A noted exhibition in Paris during the early 1970s hung huge photographic enlargements of modern cylinder seal impressions in a recreation of the European painting gallery (Collon 1987: 7; Winter 2000b: 52). Studies of seals have since branched into an array of different methodologies, the most common being a functional approach to sealing practices (Gibson and Biggs 1977; Hallo and Winter 2001).

Most scholars accept that the appearance of the quintessentially Mesopotamian cylinder seal and the invention of writing during the Late Uruk period were linked to their roles within an emerging complex administrative hierarchy associated with urban temples. What has been less explored are the ways in which this relationship shaped and affected the specific forms that each assumed (Pittmann 1994; Bahrani 2003: 96–120). Pittmann has argued that both writing and seals represent "two facets of a larger system of representation" (1994: 189). She notes that the emphasis on legibility, standardization, and structure characterizes both seals and writing as means of information storage over time and space beyond the single moment of an event (Pittmann 1994: 189–92). Bahrani posits a related argument that archaic writing and visual arts followed similar representational structures, which exerted reciprocal influence on one another (2003: 99, 107). Both arguments stress the need to study the written and the visual realms in concert with one another, seeing both as equal partners in the presentation of abstract or intangible ideas.

Statues

Ancient texts frequently refer to divine statues enshrined in their temples. While no cult statues have survived, numerous stone statues that apparently depict worshipers or dedicators of the statues have been recovered from temples in the Early Dynastic Period (2900–2350 BCE) throughout greater Mesopotamia. Some, such as the hoard from the Square Temple at Tell Asmar in the Diyala River region, were buried as a group within the shrine (see Figure 21.4). Others, for example at Mari and Assur, were found in the ruins of destroyed temples and lay smashed and scattered around the benches on which they probably stood. The largest numbers were excavated at sites in the Diyala River region, Mari, and Nippur, though they have also been found at sites in far southern Mesopotamia, at Assur in the north, and at Tell Khuera in northeastern Syria. Thus, they present a pan-Mesopotamian phenomenon that exhibits a remarkable unity of conception and presumably also of religious belief and ritual practice. Yet within this coherent type, exceptional variation in terms of pose, dress, and gender, combined on occasion with inscriptions citing a named person and title, suggest that these figures represented individuals across a broad spectrum of society. What all share is an emphasis on a frontal view and a focus on the statues' eyes. Particularly in those of the so-called abstract style, the enormous shell, lapis lazuli, and bitumen inlaid eyes stare fixedly upwards with an "eerie sense of absolute and focused attention" (Winter 2000a: 22). The animated nature and active force of these statues, and indeed of all Mesopotamian representation, has been repeatedly remarked upon (Frankfort 1954: 23; Parrot 1961b: 106; Moortgat 1969: 34; Bahrani 2003; Hansen 2003a: 29). Those statues bearing inscriptions verbalize this animation, often exhorting the figure to act on behalf of the dedicator.

Some of the earliest studies attempted to sort the large number of statues into a sequence showing stylistic development over time. Frankfort, who excavated the Diyala examples, proposed a two-fold sequence from Early Dynastic I/II (2900–2600 BCE) to Early Dynastic III (2600–2350 BCE). According to his analysis the earlier style "devotes itself to geometric approximation with passionate intensity. It reduces to abstractions not only the main forms, but even the details like chins, cheeks, and hair" (Frankfort 1954: 26). The subsequent style "is not merely a modification, but . . . the antithesis of the earlier one. Instead of sharply contrasting, clearly articulated masses, we see fluid transitions and infinitely modulated surfaces. Instead of abstract shapes, we see a detailed rendering of the physical peculiarities of the model" (Frankfort 1954: 28). This strictly linear chronological stylistic development has not received confirmation from other archaeological sites, and the

Figure 21.4 Votive statues from Tell Asmar. Courtesy of the Oriental Institute of the University of Chicago

problem remains underexplored.[1] Nevertheless, Frankfort's basic stylistic scheme has remained prominent in discussions about these works.

More recently, study of these statues has shifted to questions of gender and patronage, since they include an unusual diversity of human types, particularly women, who were often absent from ancient Mesopotamian art. Asher-Greve, noting that there were more than two gender categories in Mesopotamia – male, female, castrated, and sexless – reexamines one of the more enigmatic votive statues, that of the singer Ur-Nanshe from Mari (see Figure 21.5) (Asher-Greve 1997a: 438). Seated cross-legged, the beardless figure with long hair wears a short tufted skirt; the bare chest features effeminate breasts. According to understood Mesopotamian gender markers, such as secondary sex features, dress, and name, Ur-Nanshe seems neither wholly female nor male, and a suggestion that the figure represented a castrated person may be supported by the figure's stated profession as singer. Taking the Early Dynastic votive statues together with other such works from later in the third millennium, Bahrani traces women and patronage in Mesopotamia, linking them to archives of elite women who appear to have had a degree of economic autonomy (2001: 97–109).

The nearly twenty or so seated and standing statues of Gudea, ruler of Lagash about 2100 BCE, represent a related form of statuary from a slightly later period.

Figure 21.5   Votive statue of Ur-Nanshe, the singer, from Mari. Source: National Museum, Damascus/Hirmer Fotoarchiv

Typically carved out of gleaming black diorite, they range in size from small to larger than life size (see Figure 21.6). Unlike the Early Dynastic votive statuary, by the end of the third millennium those who might be represented apparently became restricted almost entirely to the ruler. The Gudea statues, while always praised for their technical virtuosity in carving the hard stone, often suffer from the biases of Western art historical values, most acutely that of originality. Winter sums up such views that consider Gudea "the arch-icon of the oriental ruler: relatively narcissistic, else how could there be at least 20 remaining statues of him …; not very imaginative (his statues 'resemble one another so closely' that a small sample 'adequately represent(s) the whole group,' said Frankfort); imbued with traditional values of permanence and piety (his 'immutability' manifest in the cylindrical block, witness to a 'tendency which permeated all the Eastern world,' according to Moortgat)" (Winter 1989: 573–4). Winter's approach differs as she examines "the combined verbal and visual message … with a view toward an understanding of the affective intent of the whole within the specific Mesopotamian context" (Winter 1989: 573). She proposes that Sumerian terminology used to describe Gudea in the texts also underlies stylistic features, such as his muscular right arm, that remain consistent from statue to statue,

Figure 21.6 Gudea of Lagash standing. Source: Louvre, Paris/photo © RMN, Hervé Lewandowski

and she argues that the necessity for these repeated forms lies in their essential role as descriptive of the ideal ruler (Winter 1989, 1998a: 67–70). In addition, Winter situates the statuary within its ancient temple context, arguing for animated and interactive use of the statues in ritual activities (1992).

The Stele of Naram-Sin

Probably the most celebrated of Mesopotamian monuments is the victory stele, or pillar, of Naram-Sin (2250 BCE) (see Figure 21.7). Unlike the Gudea statues, since its discovery in 1898, it has been hailed for its originality, unified composition, carving style, and details (de Morgan 1900: 144; Groenewegen-Frankfort 1951: 163; Frankfort 1954: 43; Parrot 1961b: 174; Moortgat 1969: 51; Amiet 1980: 104; Hansen 2003b: 195). The almost two meter or six and a half feet tall stele, which probably preserves only two-thirds of the original height, showcases the majestic figure of Naram-Sin – the relief carving so deeply undercut that he appears almost sculpted in the round – surmounting a scene of warfare set in the mountains of western Iran.

Figure 21.7 Victory stele of Naram-Sin. Source: Louvre, Paris/photo © RMN, Hervé Lewandowski

Wearing a horned headdress indicating his deification, Naram-Sin dominates the upper part of the stele, while three astral symbols occupy the topmost space, relegating the divine presence to a symbolic level. Standing with one foot placed firmly on the crossed and naked bodies of his enemies, tribal peoples from the mountains, he looks dispassionately at the pleading figures to his right. Below Naram-Sin, the scene divides along a central axis: to the left, the organized ranks of Akkadian soldiers appear relentlessly to ascend the mountain; to the right, the disorganized and uncivilized enemies tumble downward in defeat. A partly preserved text above Naram-Sin identifies him and recounts the victory. A second inscription, added over a thousand years later by an Elamite king, records that he took the stele back to Susa, where it was excavated another 3000 years later.

Much of the scholarship on the Naram-Sin stele has focused on its unique artistic aspects, grappling with the question of continuity and tradition versus discontinuity and innovation. Kantor viewed the depiction of the mountain with its trees as a landscape that was a major innovation of the Akkadian period, breaking from previous Mesopotamian and, in particular, Sumerian tradition (1966). Recently, Winter has contested a reading of Naram-Sin's stele as landscape in the sense of the Western artistic genre. Instead, she argues that the trees and mountain, in their specificity of kind and place, "serve to naturalize, to present as equally 'natural,' the transcendant [sic] stance and status assumed by the ruler" (Winter 1998b: 7).

Comparisons of Naram-Sin's stele with earlier works as well as later pieces have provided material for arguing both for and against the disruptive position of Akkadian art within an overall narrative of Mesopotamian history. There can be little disagreement that the formal qualities of Naram-Sin's stele stand in contrast to those that preceded and followed it, most notably in its apparent disuse of registers as an organizing compositional structure. Actually registers were used, but they were tilted to form diagonal lines that provided dynamic thrust to the composition. What is at issue is the degree to which this was revolutionary rather than developmental, and what it means for a socio-historical understanding of the Akkadian period.

Early scholars saw the break with Sumerian artistic traditions as so radical that they attributed it to the arrival and conquest of a new ethnic group, the Semitic-speaking Akkadians (Groenewegen-Frankfort 1951: 162; Frankfort 1954: 41; Parrot 1961b: 170; Moortgat 1969: 45). Such interpretations are driven by notions of the ethos or spirit of a people, usually defined ethno-linguistically, that manifested itself in cultural production, especially art. Nigro has traced the sequence from the beginning of the Akkadian period, with Sargon's fragmentary stelae, to Naram-Sin, arguing not for an "unspecified 'Akkadian' spirit," but rather for "the specific ideological purpose of celebrating victory as military expansion." He connects an increasing interest in unified narrative to the centralization of a multi-city empire rather than to any ethnic qualities of the Akkadians (Nigro 1998: 292). Nissen offers a related argument, positing that the Akkadian rulers sought to emphasize the material world in order to weaken the influence of local temple institutions that had previously dominated the individual city-states (1988: 165–97).

The Stele of Hammurabi

The stele of Hammurabi (1792–1750 BCE) is perhaps better known for its legal text than its art historical properties (see Figure 21.8). The tall (2.25 m or $7\frac{1}{3}$ feet), irregularly shaped diorite stele was found at Susa in the same area as Naram-Sin's stele. Its inscribed text is indeed monumental, consisting of a prologue, nearly three hundred individual laws, and an epilogue carved into forty-two columns that encircle the boulder. Though not the oldest preserved law code, it is the most complete, and many of the laws contain the Biblical principle of talion ("eye for an eye, tooth for a tooth"), which has ensured it a place in schoolchildren's history books. Only the upper part of the stele's front remains bare of text; there the surface is carved into

Figure 21.8   Code of Hammurabi. Source: Louvre, Paris/photo © RMN, Hervé Lewandowski

high relief, showing Hammurabi standing before the enthroned sun god Šamaš who extends in his right hand a rod and ring, insignia of authority (see Figure 21.9). The manner in which this representational scene was cut away from the original surface of the stone on which the text was inscribed creates the illusion that the text literally forms a platform supporting god and king.

Of the scene itself Frankfort writes, "it conveys, not only a sense of confrontation, but of communication between the lord of justice and the lawgiver" (1954: 59). The composition places Hammurabi at eye level with the god, establishing a reciprocity of visual exchange that can be equated with Babylonian conceptions of the positive regard that emanates from the gods' gaze and that connects this work back to the Early Dynastic votive statues. Winter quotes an Old Babylonian hymn to the goddess Ishtar which gushes, "Prosperity is created by her gaze" (Winter 2000a: 37). Moortgat

Figure 21.9 Code of Hammurabi, detail of upper relief. Source: Louvre, Paris / photo © RMN, Hervé Lewandowski

pointed out that the rendering of the divine horned headdress in true profile occurred for the first time on this stele; this he considers its "unique merit" for blending "three-dimensional reality with a two-dimensional image" (1969: 86). If, however, illusionism simply for the sake of imitating reality did not take precedence in Mesopotamian artistic philosophy, this shift in perspectival rendering instead may be associated with a renewed and monumentalized emphasis on vision as a critical form of divine communication.

Neo-Assyrian Reliefs

The sub-field that has seen probably the greatest amount of study and research is Neo-Assyrian art, particularly in the area of the carved relief orthostats, or dressed stones, that adorned the walls of the great palaces at Nimrud, Khorsabad, and Nineveh from the ninth through the seventh centuries BCE. Groenewegen-Frankfort considers them a "most striking innovation...entirely secular and narrative," and they offer fertile material for her exploration into the depiction of time and space (1951: 170). The notion that Assyrian reliefs presented purely non-religious imagery has recently been disputed by studies of all the reliefs, not just the most commonly published ones, within their architectural setting (Russell 1998). Nonetheless, the historical narrative reliefs, many of which depict detailed representations of battles set in topographically diverse areas, have claimed the greatest attention.

Of particular interest is the apparent linear development of spatial representation from the ninth century down to Assurbanipal, the last important Assyrian king, in the mid-seventh century (Groenewegen-Frankfort 1951: 172–81; Frankfort 1954: 91, 93–9; Parrot 1961a: 42–3; Moortgat 1969: 134, 137, 149, 154, 157; Amiet 1980: 251; Russell 1991: 192–215). The ninth century narratives organize most of the figures on a single ground line so that they stand the full height of a register. An example is the carved orthostats of Assurnasirpal II which are divided into two pictorial registers separated by the so-called Standard Inscription listing his titles and military deeds.

In contrast, a seascape of Sargon II at Khorsabad and almost all of Sennacherib's reliefs from the Southwest Palace at Nineveh used the entire height of the over two meter tall orthostats as a patterned background for numerous small figures (see Figure 21.10). This change has often been interpreted as deriving from a progressive technical ability to depict perspectively accurate space. Assurbanipal's reliefs, how-ever, present a challenge to this developmental account, because they exhibit an inconsistency in using both these as well as other representational modes. It may be highly misleading to evaluate these compositional differences by standards established in Renaissance one-point perspective, an artistic concept that derived from a very different social, political, and religious context. Indeed, the diversity of representa-tional styles used by the Neo-Assyrians for composing figures in space suggests that, rather than striving for a single, all-encompassing illusionistic perspective, they ma-nipulated spatial and perceptual elements in multiple ways to provoke varied mean-ingful responses. Groenewegen-Frankfort's understanding of the spatial presence evoked in Assurbanipal's lion hunts as "dramatic space" and "significant voids" comes close to this idea, although she remains bound to the Euro-centric definition of representational perspective (1951: 181).

Moortgat proposed that the reliefs were created in a program of propaganda for the king. He wrote, "painting and relief are not merely used to decorate vacant wall surfaces as the servant of architecture: on the contrary, sculpture in the round and two-dimensional art combine to create a new organic form of art, *architectural sculpture*: even the words and writing in the ornamental bands of cuneiform combine with the relief friezes to glorify the concepts of king and empire in the great pictorial annals" (1969: 130 emphasis Moortgat's). Winter elaborates upon this concept, arguing that both Assurnasirpal II's ninth-century reliefs and the royal titles carved on every orthostat physically structured a multidimensional definition of Assyrian kingship along the four walls of his Nimrud throne room, which stood as the

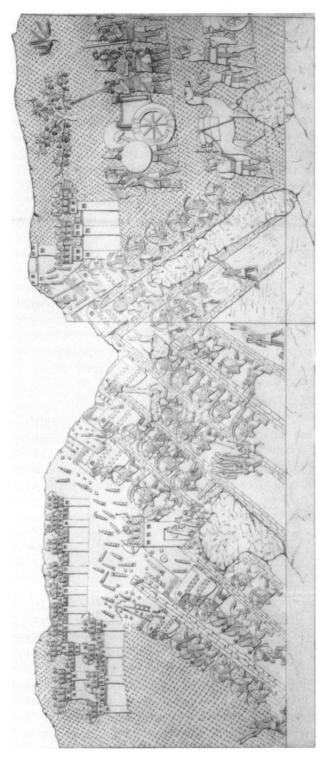

Figure 21.10 The siege of Lachish, Southwest Palace, Nineveh. Source: British Museum, WAA, Or. Dr., 1,59. © British Museum

metaphoric and ideological center of the empire (1981). Further studies of Neo-Assyrian historical narratives have enriched the scope of this scholarship (Marcus 1987; Russell 1987). Several recent studies have extended the inquiry to examine the ways in which the relief imagery itself participated in the construction of imperial ideology (Cifarelli 1998; Thomason 2001).

Specific subjects have also been the focus of research, especially the celebrated lion hunts of Assurbanipal (see Figure 21.11). Scholarly treatment of these has ranged from the almost purely formal to the psychological to a religiously oriented approach.

Our modern response to Assurbanipal's hunts has clearly impacted scholarship. Moortgat wrote, "... when we look at the king's contests with lions, we are moved not so much by a sense of the conquest of evil than by pity for the tragic fate of the beasts" (Moortgat 1969: 157). Groenewegen-Frankfort said, "the artist of the hunting scenes ... showed that he possessed the emotional depth which could convey the tragedy of suffering and defeat, of desperate courage and broken pride ... an artist who revealed the depth of his fear and pity for these doomed creatures and raised his scenes to the stature of tragedy" (Groenewegen-Frankfort 1951: 180–1). It has even been suggested that the artist of such pathos-inducing figures as the so-called Dying Lioness was a captive who identified with the hunted prey and sought to subvert Assyrian imperialism, though this opinion has not received much support (Barnett 1976: 13; Reade 1995: 88). A unique study of the lion hunts by Bersani and Dutoit (1985) makes no attempt to displace our response onto the ancient Assyrians, but rather explores the way in which the formal qualities of their violence tap into our psychological pleasures. Recent studies that draw upon an expanded repertoire of visual and textual sources have sought to situate the reliefs better within the context of Assyrian conceptions and point to the ritual and sacred implications of the imagery in view of scenes that depict the king pouring libations over dead lions and the artificial nature of several of the represented hunts (Weissert 1997; Watanabe 2002). A forthcoming dissertation contends that no one meaning inheres in these reliefs, but rather that the dynamic process of interaction between them and their various audiences produced a spectrum of meanings tied to power relations surrounding the king (Aker forthcoming).

Conclusion

The preceding account of several Mesopotamian artworks reveals the changing lenses through which they have been viewed and interpreted. With such a rich academic tradition, it is little surprise that over the past ten years scholarship has begun to examine the history of European and North American exploration in the Near East and its impact on the field as a discipline. Some have concentrated on the documentation of these activities, charting specific narratives of excavation and scholarship (Larsen 1996; Russell 1997). Others have taken a post-colonial approach, arguing for the Western invention of Mesopotamia and for the multidimensional ways in which archaeology was both affected by and had an effect on the imperialist as well as on the popular identity of the West (Bahrani 2003; Bohrer 2003). As Bohrer states, "... the

Figure 21.11 Detail of Ashurbanipal's lion hunt, North Palace, Nineveh. Source: British Museum, WA 124866 and WA 124887. © British Museum

work of filtering, revising, and reconstructing Assyria was staged not only in nine-teenth-century museums, but throughout its richly varied visual culture . . . Further, the ordering, circulation, and emulation of the Ancient Near East (both within and beyond museums) must be seen in connection with larger complexes of social tensions, suppositions, needs and desires . . . " (2003: 3–4).

NOTE

1   For one example of the lack of exact correlation between the two styles and archaeology, see Hansen 2003: 29.

FURTHER READING

Major illustrated surveys of Near Eastern art include Frankfort 1954, Parrot 1961a, Parrot 1961b, Strommenger and Hirmer 1964, Moortgat 1969, Amiet 1980, and Collon 1995.

CHAPTER TWENTY-TWO

Ancient Mesopotamian Medicine

JoAnn Scurlock

Here we will be treating ancient Mesopotamian medicine as a cumulative tradition with only a brief exploration of its developmental history. First we must look at what we have preserved.

Our evidence for ancient Mesopotamian medicine consists of about half of the original forty tablets of a diagnostic and prognostic handbook, comprising approximately three thousand entries (Heeßel 2000: 58) and over nine hundred tablets or tablet fragments containing instructions for the preparation of treatments. These therapeutic texts include copies of ancient reference works in which treatments were organized into series like IGI.GIG "sore eye." These series progress down the body in the same head to toe order as the diagnostic and prognostic handbook, and they were probably intended as companion pieces to it (Köcher 1978: 20). There are also a few fragments of two series called "The Nature of Plants" and "The Nature of Stones" which gave descriptions and uses of medicinal plants and stones. Most helpful is another text, the pharmacist's companion, a listing of plants in accordance with their medical uses. Also there was the series known to us after its first words URU.AN.NA, which was an ancient plant glossary. We can also add a handful of scattered references in letters, listings of lucky and unlucky days, and other literary texts as sources for Mesopotamian medicine.

Developments in Ancient Mesopotamian Medicine over Time

As with so many other aspects of ancient Mesopotamian high culture, the most complete textual evidence for ancient Mesopotamian medicine comes from the Neo-Assyrian period (934–609 BCE), when ancient Mesopotamian civilization was at its height. A handful of Old Babylonian (1792–1595 BCE) incantations and the largely unpublished therapeutic texts from the Ur III (2112–2004 BCE) and Isin-Larsa (2017–1763 BCE) periods do not yet allow any real attempt to understand the development of this medical tradition over the full course of ancient Mesopotamian history. Adding to the difficulties is the fact that the formatting of medical texts seems to have changed dramatically between the Old Babylonian and Middle Assyrian (1363–1056 BCE) periods. This suggests an innovation in the method of recording medical texts at the very least between the Old Babylonian and Middle Assyrian periods.

This innovation may, in turn, have something to do with the emergence into prominence of one of the two ancient Mesopotamian medical experts, the *āšipu* and of the appearance of the first exemplars of parts of the diagnostic and prognostic handbook. Under the patronage of the Middle Babylonian king Adad-apla-iddina (1068–1047 BCE), the scholar Esagil-kîn-apli from the city of Borsippa made an edition of this handbook, apportioning the available material among forty tablets of varying length by subject matter to allow for future additions and corrections.

The first sub-series (Tablets 1–2) contained all of the ominous occurrences which might take place as the *āšipu* was on his way to the patient's house. The second sub-series (Tablets 3–14) began with headaches and progressed down the body from head to toe. The third sub-series began with two tablets (15–16) containing entries organized in accordance with the number of days the patient had been sick. The remaining tablets of the third sub-series (Tablets 17–25) were devoted for the most part to infectious diseases. Tablets 26–30 constituted the fourth sub-series which collected together entries relating to neurology, an apparent sub-specialty of the *āšipu*'s craft. The fifth sub-series consisted of two surviving tablets: 31 which was devoted to intestinal fever and 33 which gave detailed descriptions of skin lesions. Tablets 36–40 formed the sixth sub-series which contained entries dealing with women and infants.

The fragments of an early pre-Esagil-kîn-apli version of this diagnostic and prognostic handbook from the Hittite capital Hattuša (Wilhelm 1994) as well as late copies and a number of apparently original therapeutic texts from post-Neo-Assyrian Uruk and Sippar give hope that it may someday be possible to trace developments within the corpus between the mid-second and mid-first millennia BCE. In any case, dramatic changes should not be expected within the medical tradition as we have it. We in the twenty-first century are still applying theories derived by a mathematician and alchemist of the seventeenth century, Sir Isaac Newton. Does this mean that we have magic rather than science or are incapable of innovation? Of course not. What it does mean is that since the seventeenth century there has been a more or less continuous development, that we have been able to build on the foundations laid by previous scholarship and that, war and pestilence notwithstanding, we have most fortunately not been reduced to a discontinuous rediscovery of knowledge lost in intervening dark ages.

Subtle changes, then, are what we should be expecting, as when a later version of a treatment varies slightly from its earlier predecessors. There may also be a tendency to record more fully as time proceeds. When, as the Mesopotamians did, you do not record things simply to record them but "in order not to be forgotten," what gets recorded is what cannot easily be remembered. As time goes on and knowledge accumulates, more and more will consequently need to be written down. This factor provides an obvious explanation for why, despite the fact that we have therapeutic texts already in the Ur III period, there are so many recitations and so few treatments from the Old Babylonian period. At that time, there were probably already many treatments, but since ancient Mesopotamian plant mixtures rarely contained more than ten ingredients, there were probably not so many that a practicing doctor could not remember them all. He also knew which recitation to use with which treatment. The exact text of these recitations and in particular the lengthy sections in Sumerian were the only feature of his practice where a written copy might have come in handy. By the Neo-Assyrian period, in contrast, when there could be hundreds of treatments for any given condition, writing everything down in a convenient handbook form became a desideratum.

Neo-Assyrian texts rarely give information about dosages, although physicians clearly recognized the importance of not overdosing a patient and not infrequently gave indications as to the relative proportions of medicinal plants to be employed in a particular treatment. There are, however, several late unpublished texts from the city of Sippar, like British Museum 78963, which appear to give the dosage for an individual patient with the exact quantity of each plant measured in carats. To what do we owe this precious information? Was it perhaps some ancient physician who thought that dosage should be "by the book" rather than left to experience or oral instruction? Or were physicians now using jeweler's scales which made it possible for the first time actually to make up a prescription for an individual treatment, in place of the time-honored method of making up a large batch of medicine and giving the patient an appropriate dose of the resulting mixture?

Asû and āšipu

It has been conventional in Assyriology since the publication of Ritter's classic study on the subject (1965) to divide the medical practices represented by the preserved corpus of texts into two unequal parts. One of these was allegedly presided over by a healing specialist known as the *asû* who attributed diseases to "natural" causes and treated them with exclusively "rational" treatments with medicines. The other healing specialist, by contrast, was a "magician," "charlatan," or even "sorcerer" known as the *āšipu*. He allegedly attributed diseases exclusively to "supernatural" causes, specifically the "hands" of gods, ghosts, or demons and employed exclusively "magical" treatments.

In its inception, this was certainly an attempt, engaged in with the best of intentions, to salvage something in the way of medicine for ancient Mesopotamia. However, it has proved impossible to make this ostensibly unproblematic separation short of roundly ignoring such little direct evidence as we have, like colophons indicating that the person in whose library such and such a treatment was found was an *āšipu*, and without generating a series of guidelines which, as in my childhood initiation into the mysteries of French grammar, seem to have almost as many exceptions to the rules as examples which can be proven to apply.

Not only are there many "irrational" treatments for problems ostensibly attributed to "natural" causes as figurines for fever and conversely "rational" treatments for problems ostensibly attributed to "supernatural" causes like bandages for ghosts, but in the ancient Mesopotamian medical corpus in general, it is precisely those recitations directed against such ostensibly "natural" conditions as headache or low back pain which have the strongest tendency to what we would normally classify as "magic."

Particularly noteworthy in this regard is their use of what is usually termed abracadabra, typically "Subarean," barely comprehensible Sumerian and "nonsense" syllables. They also frequently include lengthy invocations of magical analogies and the histories of the spells, ranging from the boringly formulaic the-god-Ea-gave-it-to-his-son-Marduk type to the wonderfully original toothache-worm cosmology.

What needs questioning is not the presence of essentially correct diagnoses and effective healing practices in ancient Mesopotamia, but the assumption that "magic" is incompatible with medicine in any scientific sense (Scurlock 1999). Thinking of planets as gods did not prevent ancient Mesopotamians from predicting lunar eclipses; why should thinking of diseases as caused by gods have prevented them from having medicine? The *asû* was, in fact, a close equivalent of the European pharmacist. His main job was to know where medicinal plants grew, when to pick them, and how to store them. The diagnostic handbook, which included all of the apparently "natural" causes, was provably meant for the use of the *āšipu* as were many, if not most, of the therapeutic texts containing our "rational" treatments. Also intended for his use was a series of basic texts of pharmacology concerned with the general appearance and uses of plants such as it was customary to give physicians before the advent of the modern pharmaceutical company with its packaged pills.

It is, nevertheless, possible to isolate treatments which could have been (or were even originally intended to be) used by the *asû* within the mass of material which has come down to us despite the fact that most, if not all, of it stems from the archives of *āšipu*s. As we have already noted, the diagnostic and prognostic handbook was undisputedly meant for the *āšipu*. Medical texts with a recitation, label, and "its ritual" format do not particularly recommend themselves as intended for the *asû* either. This leaves two major categories of text which give clear indications as to the purpose for which they were intended, those which a) list symptoms after which the treatment is described and those which b) begin with a list of plants, followed by a label either immediately after the plants or at the end after preparation instructions which indicates that the treatment is to be used for such and such a problem. All are agreed that the *āšipu* was the expert who was versed in the description of symptoms. It follows that if a medical expert using a given treatment was expected to apply it on the basis of observed symptoms, this expert can only have been the *āšipu*, and that those texts (category a) which begin with the description of symptoms were intended for him to use when he chose to treat his patients personally. But what of the others (category b)? The obvious suggestion is they were intended for the use of a medical expert, namely the *asû*, who could not diagnose illnesses by himself but who could be applied to for treatment if the patient knew or had been told what his problem was.

In short, this type of text (category b) was or could have been used as what we call a prescription, a type of text which the physician (*āšipu*) had to be able to generate, and hence would have been found in great numbers in his archive, but which was actually intended for the use of the pharmacist, the *asû*. It is interesting to note that texts of this "prescription" type sometimes use a label which is formulated "it is good for such and such a problem," a phraseology which is typical of a type of text which is also a good candidate for something that the *asû* as well the *āšipu* would have had to master, namely the series that give the descriptions and uses of plants and stones.

Thus, when a person became ill in ancient Mesopotamia, he had many of the same options we have today. He might throw himself on the mercy of the gods, he could repair directly to the pharmacy, or he could first call in a physician to diagnose his problem and then arrive at the pharmacist's shop armed with a doctor's prescription. Unlike his modern counterpart, the *āšipu* made house calls, and, since he was on the staff of a temple, he was in a position to provide his basic service for free, not counting animals for sacrifice, medicines, and such. The *asû* would, obviously, have charged for medicines; we know from the Laws of Hammurapi paragraphs 215–17 (Roth 1997) that he was also allowed to charge for surgical operations, although like Chinese pharmacists and Indian doctors to the present day, that charge was scaled to reflect the patient's ability to pay. Medicine was thus not financially out of the reach of the average ancient Mesopotamian.

Unlike many doctors in the pre-modern era, the *āšipu* was required to maintain a level of personal cleanliness appropriate to a person who had entry to a temple. He would also certainly have washed his hands before examining a patient, since he was required to cast a spell over himself before proceeding to work and could hardly have done so without clean hands. This simple act would have gone a long way toward preventing the accidental spread of disease from one patient to the next.

But if the *āšipu* was not a "filthy sorcerer," and if all of the "rational" treatments of things like headache, and not just all of the spells and rituals directed against things like ghosts, were in some way connected with him, how was it that these, to us opposite, theories of the causation of disease, "natural" versus "supernatural," coexisted as part of the same system? The problem is with us, and not with the *āšipu*.

Diagnosis

The problem presented by the divine language of medical signs and symptoms was to determine which combinations of animal products, minerals, and plants and which recitations were effective for which medical problems. To answer this question, the ancestor of the *āšipu* began by carefully observing his patients and deriving a vocabulary to describe their signs and symptoms so that any treatments which might subsequently be devised could be applied consistently, past successes reproduced, and repetition of past failures avoided. Gradually, it was noted which individual signs and symptoms tended to occur together, and these were grouped into syndromes. Only after the process of gathering information was more or less complete did the ancient Mesopotamian physician attempt to assign syndromes to causal agents. In other words, he did not ask what combinations of signs and symptoms these gods would cause, but which of these gods, if any, would cause this combination of signs and symptoms. This pattern of nomenclature is analogous to the use of syndromes in modern medicine with the exception that the modern physician has the luxury of being better able to correct his classification system by reference to invisible causal agents identified by microscopic analysis.

"Natural" and "Supernatural" Causes

What we are terming a "natural" cause, in our attempt to straitjacket ancient Mesopotamian medicine into Western culture categories, was not considered by the ancient Mesopotamians to be mechanistic dead matter but rather an out of sorts lower order of spirit. These lower-order spirits were rarely if ever given the "god" determinative; they tended to be unindividualized and without character or distinctive personality. That they were spirits is, however, clear from the fact they were expected to hear and understand what was said to them.

Gods were by nature somewhat like foreigners; they lived far, far away and they spoke their own language and were for that reason somewhat dense and difficult to deal with. Lower-order spirits were the same, only more so; that is, they were both more foreign and more dense than upper-order spirits.

As a sort of foreigner, any god was liable to be addressed in what the speaker thought was the god's own language, usually in fact an archaic language or a by-now incomprehensible version of a foreign language (which is what abracadabra actually is), and to have any really important instructions acted out in sign language (which is what magical analogies actually are). The likelihood of a spirit being treated in this "magical" way, however, increased dramatically the further down he ranked on the social scale of spirits. In other words, the great gods of the pantheon were the least likely and the amorphous spiritual essence of, say, a piece of bread the most likely to receive such treatment, with a whole sliding scale of probabilities for the ghosts, demons, and lesser divinities in the middle. It is for this reason, as we noted above, that what appear to us to be the "natural" causes in ancient Mesopotamian medical texts were so often associated with what we would characterize as "magic."

Gods were also entitled to reverence, to sacrifice, and to respectful address in prayer. Lower-order spirits, by contrast, were often mistreated and ordered about, that is, coerced. It has long been obvious that the rigid definition of "magic," with its insistence on "homeopathy" and "contagion," is inappropriate to any "magic" other than that of the self-declared "natural" or "white" magicians of seventeenth-century CE Europe upon whom the definition was based. What readily suggests itself as a replacement is to define as "religion" that part of the *āšipu*'s craft that involved practices typical of the way one dealt with upper-order spirits, for example sacrifices and respectful prayers. "Magic," then, would consist of those practices typical of the way one dealt with lower-order spirits, for example abracadabra, spell histories, and magical analogies but also mistreatment, threats, and forced oaths. No student of magic should have any trouble agreeing with this classification, and it fits ancient Mesopotamian texts quite well as long as it is remembered that this is a tendency rather than a hard and fast rule.

From this perspective, demons including ghosts form a sort of intermediate category. Ghost texts include the odd sacrifice and respectful address to ancestral ghosts being asked for help in the proceedings, and show at least some empathy for the troublesome ghost but also quite frequently include forced oaths and mistreated figurines. Moreover, in non-medical treatments for ghost-induced roaring in the ears, so called "Subarean" and mangled Sumerian recitations actually predominate (Scurlock in press). The presence of this mean between the two extremes is consistent with the fact that upper-order spirits and lower-order spirits were not in opposition but formed a continuum which collectively defined the natural world.

What little evidence we have for ancient Greek spells indicates a similar use of "magic." In the Hellenistic period attitudes changed dramatically. Contrary to popular opinion, however, Hellenistic philosopher-scientists had no quarrel with the notion that the cosmos was animated rather than dead matter as the seventeenth-century CE European mechanists would have it. What they did deny was any continuum between upper-order and lower-order spirits. For them, upper-order spirits (gods and demons) were super natural, that is, they were above and beyond and somewhat apart from the natural world. They drew from this the conclusion that upper-order spirits, the gods, could not be causes for disease (Hippocrates, On the Sacred Disease. 1; Airs, Waters, Places 22 in Hippocrates 1950), and that the use in healing rites of what we are now terming "religion" was inappropriate, even sacrilegious (On the Sacred Disease. 4). Christian theologians embraced the idea of "super natural" spirits as the type definition of transcendent divinity, although parting company on the issue of whether God was capable of causing disease, arguing that God could cause disease. This is why we still use this as our definition of "supernatural" and why Christian theologians can properly be said to attribute diseases to a supernatural cause.

The *āšipu* did not recognize the existence of any such "supernatural" cause. Although ancient Mesopotamians believed in gods, and also that these gods were divine legislators, the fact remained that once rules had been made, even the gods became subject to them. Ancient Mesopotamian gods were, moreover, almost human. They ate, bathed, got dressed, laughed and wept, awoke and slept, fell in and out of love, engaged in sexual intercourse and begat children, fought battles, went on strike, and even got killed. It follows that ancient Mesopotamian gods, like their ancient Greek counterparts before philosophy redefined them, were immanent deities in no significant way beyond or outside of nature. They were thus not "supernatural" causes, and attributing diseases to them did not disqualify the *āšipu* from practicing "medicine" as opposed to "magic."

Conversely, attributing diseases exclusively to "natural" causes by no means removed the "magic" from Hellenistic "medicine." Hellenistic philosopher-scientists may have regarded upper-order spirits as super natural, but this new idea of divinity did not apply to lower-order spirits who still qualified as "natural" causes.

As lower-order spirits, they could theoretically be bossed around and addressed in nonsense syllables, but many Hellenistic philosophers felt that to be undignified. What intrigued them, however, was the sign language which was used to communicate with spirits. The symbolic language used by ancient Mesopotamians to communicate with gods was closely related to the language of omens, for example the so-called astrological omens (Rochberg-Halton 1984: 117), which, it was believed, gods used to communicate with men. For some Hellenistic philosophers, the astrological fatalists, this language of omens was not a language at all but a cosmic conjunction which actually caused the portended event. Other Hellenistic philosophers refused to see the gods as bound by fate; where all could agree, however, was that lower-order spirits were an intrinsic part of nature and hence bound to automatic, unquestioning, obedience to natural laws. It followed logically that the sign language used by ancient Mesopotamians to communicate with these lower-order spirits was not a language but a process which actually caused the desired outcome. In short, spells involving lower-order spirits worked because the practitioner unwittingly tapped into what Hellenistic philosophers called cosmic sympathies.

Hellenistic philosopher-scientists in the know attempted to tap into these sympathies directly to suggest new treatments or preserve already available ones. Since they believed the natural world to be made up of four elements, four principles of cosmic conjunction could minimally be postulated: hot, dry, wet, and cold, corresponding nicely to the four humors. Also theoretically available for use were other intrinsic properties of matter such as color, smell, and texture. Modern Western observers generally recognize this sort of thing as "magic," and Hippocrates only escapes censure because he was a minimalist who largely limited his use of medicines to such things as blistering agents and purgatives which were, obviously, used because they were observed to work.

Testing

As with diagnosis in modern medicine, the object of the exercise for the *āšipu* was less to prove some overarching theory than to make it possible to direct the correct treatments to the correct patients. Ancient Mesopotamian medical remedies were discovered by collecting various plants and other potentially medicinal substances and by trying them out singly or in varying combinations on patients with specific signs or symptoms or "afflicted" with various syndromes to see which treatments produced the best results by simple trial and error or as suggested by previous experience. We know this from a reference to physicians experimenting on themselves (Thompson 1923: 5/2:5) as well as from direct statements that such and such a treatment has been "tested." To describe a remedy as "tested" was obviously the strongest possible recommendation, probably typically used, as with our "tried and true," to refer to treatments which were, in fact, new and unfamiliar to the reader (Leichty 1988b). This testing, if rather tedious and inefficient by modern standards, was still testing in the scientific sense of the word and requires us to assume that herbal medicines were used because they had been observed to work, not because some theory, demonological or otherwise, said they ought to work.

Plants

Information was kept "in order not to be forgotten" in a number of forms, including the ancient plant glossary, URU.AN.NA. At first glance, this series is a great puzzle.

Many of the entries are clearly lexical equivalents, that is, they provide translations of Sumerian and Akkadian plant names into other languages like Kassite, Subarean, and others. However, some of the entries listed together as equivalents are clearly different plants, which has caused modern redactors a great deal of unnecessary grief.

Two medicinal plants could conceivably be equivalent in three different ways. To say that an Akkadian and a Sumerian or Kassite word for the same plant are equivalents is to say that they are translations of one another; you can substitute the Akkadian word for the Sumerian or Kassite word in a sentence without affecting the meaning of the sentence. To say that two different Akkadian words for the same plant are equivalents is to say that they are synonyms so that, once again, you can substitute one for the other without affecting the meaning of your sentence. To say that two different medical plants are equivalent is to say that one could potentially be substituted for the other in a medical prescription or, as we would say, that they have the same action. If, for example, you have a patient with a urinary tract problem and your prescription calls for juniper, but you are all out of juniper, and you find by looking in URU.AN.NA that x and juniper are equivalents, it means that you can put x into your remedy in place of the juniper for which the prescription calls and still cure the urinary tract problem.

Less obvious is why all three types of equivalent are listed together in the same list. However, if you think as Mesopotamians do, the analogy between the last form of substitution and the other two is very close indeed – the lists of plants are not merely propitiatory offerings but also miniature sentences encoding instructions to the spirit or demon which is causing the illness. Witness particularly passages where the Akkadian recitation accompanying a medical procedure actually decodes the messages written into the ingredients. In the case of medicinal plants, one would need to "translate" their messages in medical terms such as "take this and stop giving me a headache and bloodshot eyes" or "take this and stop giving me a tummy ache." Since any given plant usually has more than one intrinsic "meaning," and can be good for tummies and heads, syntax, the method of preparation, the part of the body to which the medicine is applied, other drugs used and so on, is also important to getting your message across to the demon. Such is the theory, and the fact that the prescription is observed to work confirms not only that the demon was correctly identified but that he or she has received the message and accepted the offering. The handbook URU.AN.NA, together with the series on plants and the pharmacological handbooks, unmistakably represent that schema of organization of plants by medical use which the Greek Dioscorides is credited with "inventing" (Riddle 1985: 22–4). The ancient Mesopotamian plant manuals from which he borrowed the idea of organization were probably intended primarily for a pharmacist.

Treatments

The wide variety of different possible treatments for the same condition contained in therapeutic handbooks gave the *āšipu* plenty of leeway in treatment so that patients who did not respond to or who had a severe reaction against or who experienced over time diminished benefits from a particular medicine could be given something else. Some medicines were known to be prone to such difficulties and are quoted with an alternative treatment attached. If the presence of a variety of treatments for simple matters such as headache proved that ancient Mesopotamian treatments did not "really work," then modern twenty-first-century America has no medicine; by this logic if aspirin "really worked," why would there be Tylenol or Advil?

The *āšipu* had at his disposal a wide variety of methods for delivering his medicines. In addition to bandages, enemas, medicinal baths, and potions, he used two procedures whose value is just beginning to be appreciated in modern medicine. One of these is salves or what we call transdermal medication. A surprising number of drugs, including aspirin, work as well or better through the skin as they do when taken orally. The best technique at the *āšipu*'s disposal was, however, fumigation. We tend to think of it as "magic" but the *āšipu* did not use it in that way, and he was right; short of injection, this is the quickest and most efficient way of delivering a drug to the body, which is why nicotine addicts prefer to smoke.

On fumigation one of our rare Middle Assyrian texts describes what is known to us as uterine atony subsequent to delivery:

> (If) a woman gives birth and subsequently she is distended, [her] excrement [. . .], her insides are constipated, and her waters and [her] blood have gone back [inside her] . . . (Lambert 1969: pl. 5:1–3)

What has happened is that the woman's uterus had lost its muscle tone (uterine atony) and was filling with blood. This was one reason why her abdomen was distended, but in addition to this, her intestines seem to have lost their normal contraction which was presumably why she was constipated. The primary cause of this obstetric illness is that part or all of the placenta has been retained in the uterus. The logical treatment, then, is to use a procedure which will encourage the expulsion of this material, and that is precisely what the *āšipu* did. A mixture of medicinal plants was turned into smoke in a bowl over which the woman was made to sit, a treatment which has been used for this purpose till the present day.

The disease *ašû* (not to be confused with the pharmacist *asû* discussed above) was an ancient Mesopotamian syndrome which included diseases like measles and chickenpox as well as allergies. Apart from salves, the *āšipu* had some rather interesting ways of dealing with any accompanying sinus congestion. In the following treatment, he began by clearing the head. The inevitable result of this process was to send mucus down the throat and into the stomach. The treatment thus continued by inducing vomiting to get rid of this mucus before enough was swallowed to upset his stomach. Finally, an inhalant was used to clear the nasal passages:

> If *ašû* afflicts a person, you warm winnowed beerwort and roasted cress seed over a fire. You shave his head (and) bandage (it with it). You have him drink pulverized cress seed (mixed) with beer. You make him vomit with a feather and (if) you put (a resin) into his nostrils, he should recover. (Köcher 1963: 3 i 40–3)

Even more interesting is the following procedure which explains how to make a distillate. Two bowls were required, the top one of which had a hole bored into it. This hole was covered with dough and then the bottom bowl was put onto the fire. When enough drops of distillate had collected in the top bowl, the patient harvested it by means of a straw which was poked through the dough. A slightly more sophisticated version of this apparatus, with a hollow rim to collect the distillate, was found in the Parthian levels of Babylon. The procedure reads as follows:

> If *ašû* [with] falling spells afflicts a person, you crush 5 shekels of (a medicinal plant) (and) 5 shekels of (a spice plant) and you bore a hole in a (kind of) bowl. You cover the face of the bowl with a dough made of emmer flour. You light a fire. You hollow out a reed straw and insert (it) into the bowl. [...] You take the reed straw out (and) he sucks it in his mouth. You boil [fatty meat]. (If) he eats the broth and the fatty meat, he should recover. (Köcher 1963: 494 ii 16–18// 498 iv 2–6)

The specific choice of food or any other medicament by the *āšipu* seems to have had little if anything to do with the normal offering preferences or dislikes of the spirit to whom a medical problem is attributed. The reason that the Mesopotamian doctor ordered the diet high in fat had no theoretical basis, but was quite simply that it had been observed to be useful in controlling seizures, a finding which has now been rediscovered (Sterman 1986).

The Hippocratic procedure for draining the lungs was an almost direct borrowing from ancient Mesopotamia, minus of course the disinfectant wash used by the *āšipu*. Unlike most of its Hippocratic companions, it is medically correct and is still practiced today. But, although the involvement of drainage was sufficient to save it for Hippocratic physicians, the lack of full integration into the humoral system insured that this procedure was one of those Hippocratic treatments which fell out of use in the Roman period and was not revived until the nineteenth century:

> If (a mild headache afflicts a person and) fever persists in his body and also he makes a loud growling noise, that person has a "cleft" [...] and sweat, [to cure him, you] spill ... over him and three ribs ... You make an opening in the fourth rib [with] a flint knife. Water and blood ... You boil x (less than a liter) of (a spice plant's) juice; you filter it ... . You spill it over him and you clear it away. Once again you ... You heat it together and pour it in ... .You make a lead drainage instrument. You thread it on a linen cloth and put it in it ... . You boil the decoction in (the spice plant's) juice. You make it into a dough. (If) you bandage him with it, [he should recover]. (Köcher 1963: 39: 2'–9'// Thompson 1923: 49/4 r. 1–9)

Magic

Where magic came in was at the treatment's end. Remembering that we are talking about spirits with which the "magician" was struggling to communicate and not about impersonal forces, I hasten to add that, for the *āšipu*, this "magic" was never intended as a substitute for "medicine." The presence of completely separate "magical" and "medical" treatments for the same condition, roaring in the ears, warns us that we should never assume that simply because we have only a "magical" treatment in front of us, the actual patient for whom this was designed was not also simultaneously receiving some form of "medicine." A Mesopotamian recitation accompanying a treatment for a disease called *pašittu* reads as follows:

> The she-goat is yellow; her kid is yellow; her shepherd is yellow; her chief herdsman is yellow; she eats yellow grass on the yellow ditch bank; she drinks yellow water from the yellow ditch. He threw a stick at her (but) it did not turn her back; he threw a clod at her (but) it did not raise her head. He threw at her a mixture of thyme and salt (and) the bile began to dissolve like the mist. The recitation is not mine; it is the recitation of E[a and Asal]luhi, the recitation of Damu and Gula. Re[citation f]or *pašittu*. (Köcher 1963: 578 ii 45–50)

In short, the way to cure *pašittu* was not to throw sticks and clods at imaginary goats, but to apply medicine reinforced by an appropriate recitation. We know from the existence of a number of recitation series called names such as "rubbing" and "fumigation" (Finkel 1991) that attempts were made to peg recitations to specific procedures, say, salves or fumigations. This would seem to suggest that which recitation was best used for which treatment was also to some extent the object of experiment. To supplement the effectiveness of herbal medicines, then, the *āšipu* employed a combination of what we might term "religion" and "magic."

Šamaš was the god of the sun and of justice, and hence a soft touch to an appeal couched in terms of the unfairness of being sick when you had done nothing to deserve it. Ea, the Sumerian Enki, was the god of sweet waters, essential for the purificatory rites which were the *āšipu*'s stock in trade. According to a tradition preserved in many histories of spells, Ea transmitted medical knowledge to mankind through the mediation of his son Asalluhi, later identified with Marduk, god of Babylon. He was also supposed to have commissioned the goddess Gula as a patroness of both the *āšipu* and *asû* and thus of ancient Mesopotamian medicine in all its facets (Lambert 1967: 105–32, 143–6, 183).

It was these gods who gave to mankind the formulae for that "bit of magic" which helped the medicine along. This bit varied from the inclusion in the treatment of horse hair or the collection of specific plants growing on graves to the recitation of a simple spell or the preparation of a stone charm to a full-blown ritual complete with prayers and sacrifices. For example, there is a relatively elaborate ritual for ghost roaring in the ears which goes as follows:

> If a ghost afflicts a person (so that) his ears roar, you purify yourself on a favorable day; he (the patient) bathes in well water. You go to the steppe; you sweep the ground with a palm frond. You make a figurine of the sickness out of clay from a potter's pit. You clothe it with a makeshift garment. In groups of seven and seven, you put out a food portion for it. You tie a spindle, carpeting, (and) a pin at its head. You set up a reed altar before Šamaš. You pour out dates (and) fine flour. You set up a censer (burning) juniper. You set up a vessel (with a pointed bottom). You put that figurine before Šamaš. You say as follows:

"Father Enki . . . , father Enki who reveals the spell of Asalluhi, son of Eridu. Asalluhi has seen it. Because of it, the difficulty, because of it, the seizer of heaven and earth, who gives birth to existing things, makes (its) path distant (from) the person."

    You recite this recitation three times over (it). You cut off its hem. You provide it (with) provisions (consisting of) groats, malt, beer bread, (and) dried bread. You take that figurine and bind it to a tamarisk and you make it swear:

    "(By) the lord of gods have I made you swear, (by) Duri (and) Dari, (by) Lahmu (and) Lahamu, (by) Alala (and) Belili, (by) shade, (by) daylight, (by) magic heaps of flour, (by) blazing Girra, (by) pure Nusku, (by) Sîn, lord of the crown, (by) Šamaš, judge of truth, I have made you swear by catch water and wadi; by mountains (and) rivers, are you made to swear. . . .May you be loosed; may you be removed; may you be removed." (Ebeling 1923: 22:1-r. 13//Thompson 1923: 54/2:1-r. 1')

This ritual takes advantage of the fact that attacking demons of the opposite sex were not infrequently described as "choosing" their victims as a marriage partner. Given this situation, the obvious solution to the problem was to "divorce" the ghost figurine from the patient by cutting off its hem and to "marry" it to an obliging tree by the simple expedient of tying the two of them together.

    Rituals of this sort would have been rather expensive, and whether or not to perform them was probably an option left to the discretion of the family. Why go to all this trouble when there were any number of relatively simple and fairly inexpensive treatments for roaring in the ears? Neither would there have been any need to chase away a ghost pestering you in your dreams with prayer and animal sacrifice if a simple amulet consisting of a few knots of cord would do the trick. In fact, bandages, salves, potions, enemas, and amulets, with or without an attached recitation, outnumber the elaborate rituals by a significant margin, well over ten to one.

    There is no reason to suppose from this either that the medicine "did not really work" or that the addition of the "magic" was of no benefit to patients. Recent scientific tests have shown that a significant portion of the effectiveness of modern medicines is due to the placebo effect, that is, psyching up the patient to let his body help the medicine cure him. It is precisely to maximize this placebo effect that Mesopotamian and other medical traditions employed "magic." It is not commonly appreciated that the refusal to acknowledge the effectiveness of "folk" medicine was not based on unbiased scientific experiments but was instead rooted in the unholy seventeenth-century CE alliance between theologians and learned quacks who conspired together to burn cunning folk as witches because their masterful manipulation of psychiatric factors and their keen knowledge of herbal remedies were more effective in curing ills than either the "physic" of physicians or the sermonizing and exorcisms of men of the cloth. Magic works, as we ourselves acknowledge. When we say something works "like magic," we do not mean it was a failure.

The No-Treatment Rule

It is amusing to see how many of those who insist that the *āšipu* practiced only magic and used no rational treatments also insist that in hopeless cases magic was invariably employed (Golz 1974: 11–12). It is well known that the *āšipu* was forbidden by medical ethics to treat hopeless cases, and no treatment meant no treatment, magic or otherwise. What this meant for the patient's family is that they were not subjected to expensive and useless rituals and for the patient that he was given something to relieve specific symptoms such as pain but not deluded with false hopes of survival. This is not "irrational" or even "pre-rational" medicine; this is what, but for our blind attachment to a humoral philosophy which stood in the way of every advance in medicine until it was finally scrapped in the mid-nineteenth century, would be universally acknowledged as the first rational medicine.[1]

NOTE

1   Research for this paper has been supported in part by a grant from the National Endowment for the Humanities, an independent federal agency.

FURTHER READING

On the existence of science in ancient Mesopotamia, see Brown 2000 and Haussperger 1997. For the *asû* "pharmicist" and *āšipu* "physician" see Scurlock 1999. For an edition of all known apotropaic rituals with extensive commentary, see Maul 1994. For magical rituals dealing with ghosts and more on the magic/medicine interface, see Scurlock 2003 in press. For more on ancient diagnostics, see Labat 1951, Heeßel 2000, and Scurlock and Anderson in press. Two fields of medicine have been particularly well studied. On eye diseases, see Fincke 2000. For childbirth and early childhood diseases, see Cadelli 1997, Pangas 2000, Reiner 1982, Scurlock 1991, Scurlock and Anderson in press, Stol 2000, and Volk 1999.

CHAPTER TWENTY-THREE

Mesopotamian Cosmology

Francesca Rochberg

"Wise men," said Socrates, "say that heaven and earth and gods and men are bound together by communion and friendship, orderliness, temperance, and justice and it is for that reason they call this Whole a Cosmos" (Plato 1984: 297 Gorgias 508a). This neat description resembles ancient Mesopotamian thought about the world, but no Sumerian or Akkadian term was equivalent to the Greek word cosmos. Not only was there no word for it, but cosmology, either as an inquiry into the nature of the world, or as a part of astronomical thought about the origins and nature of the universe, was not the focus of any systematic inquiry in ancient Mesopotamia. The absence of a systematic treatment of topics we regard as essential to the conception of the world, however, does not mean that such conceptualization did not exist. In fact the notion of orderliness and justice connects the Mesopotamian with Socrates' definition of cosmos.

Cosmic order and justice in ancient Mesopotamia, however, were altogether different from the Greek tradition. The idea of cosmic concord, which was a central point in Greek cosmologies, was never considered in ancient Mesopotamia as a characteristic of the cosmos itself apart from the gods who were active in it.

Essential parts of a Mesopotamian cosmology can be reconstructed from Sumerian and Akkadian mythology, hymns, celestial divination, and astronomical texts, and can show Mesopotamian views of the creation, structure, and workings of parts of the universe. Here we pose questions to the mostly literary sources in which cosmological subjects appear. Although the questions below were not explicitly formulated by the ancient scribes in texts, what may be viewed as answers were expressed in a variety of textual genres. The purpose of this pastiche method of proceeding is to afford a view into parts of a Mesopotamian cosmology not accessible in any one source alone or at any single period or place in Mesopotamian history.

What is "the world"?

A notion of "world," in the sense of the whole of creation, is expressed as the union of the two principal parts, heaven and earth, and taken as a pair in Sumerian as a n . k i "heaven, earth" and in Akkadian as *šamû u erṣetu* "heaven and earth." The basic meaning of terms meaning "all" points to the notion of "entire (inhabited) world," and by extension "all" or "the universe." Other words such as "all (that exists)," and "totality," similarly could refer to all places or people (or gods), and so in some contexts connoted "the universe." The totality of the world comprised regions beyond the reach of human perception, such as the interior fresh water abyss "which cannot be seen" (Horowitz 1998: 317), but which nonetheless were imagined in relation to the world of human beings.

The world as a whole was referred to in the descriptions of temples that filled the entirety of the cosmos from top to bottom. This motif was repeated often in temple hymns and royal inscriptions that concerned the building of ziggurats and temples, whose tops were so high as to "rival heaven" and whose foundations so deep as to reach into the underworld. The metaphor was traceable to the early third millennium BCE in an archaic hymn: "Great, true temple, reaching the sky, temple, great crown, reaching the sky, temple, rainbow, reaching the sky, temple, whose platform(?) is suspended from the midst of the sky, whose foundation fills the Abzu [the abyss]" (Biggs 1971: 201). It was also a way of expressing great magnitude, as in the description of a mountain encountered by Sargon II (721–705 BCE) on campaign, "whose summit above leans against the heavens, and whose base, below, is firmly rooted in the nether world." The motif was also applied to mythological mountains in the Gilgamesh Epic (George 1999a: 71 IX 38–41) that reached up to the base of heaven and down to the netherworld, as well as in the Erra Epic, to the sacred tree, whose crown touched heaven and whose roots penetrated the Netherworld (Foster 1993a: 779).

How did the world originate?

An essential element in Mesopotamian mythology about the origin of the world was that the world came to be as a result of the separation of heaven and earth. This most basic cosmogonic event accounted for these two fundamental parts of the universe. The motif was preserved in the introduction to the Sumerian myth Gilgamesh, Enkidu, and the netherworld in which the region "heaven" was separated from earth and "carried off" by the god An ("sky") and "earth" became the possession of Enlil ("Lord Wind") (Shaffer 1963: 48–9, 99). The cosmic deities in this myth were, according to divine genealogy, offspring of the goddess Nammu, who represented an eternal watery state. The primeval mother gave birth to the undifferentiated above and below, which then became the two principal elements of all further cosmic evolution. She existed before the differentiated cosmic regions, as seen in her epithet "mother who gave birth to heaven and earth."

A tablet from the Early Dynastic period around 2400 BCE introduced heaven and earth before any gods and before sunlight or moonlight (Sjöberg 2002: 229–39). There An "heaven" and Ki "earth" were personified, and heaven was "a youthful man" (Sjöberg 2002: 231). The cosmic realms of heaven and earth were also personified as father and mother, as in a composition which accounted for the birth of Azag, the demonic opponent of the warrior god Ninurta, by the union of An and Ki (Jacobsen 1976: 95 n. 85). A chief attribute of the divine sky was its generative powers, and the rains from the sky were said to be semen engendering the vegetation on earth (Cagni 1969: 61). But in the theology of the religious capital, Nippur, An was not the creator god. This role was taken by Enlil.

In a list of gods scribes described the descent of the gods. The sky god An descended from Uraš and Ninuraš "Earth and Lady Earth" (Lambert 1975: 51–4). In what seems to echo the descent of the sky god An, the earth god Enlil was derived from Enki (and Ninki) "Lord (and Lady) Earth," not to be confused with Enki Nudimmud, the god of sweet waters. The original unified whole of heaven and earth was separated by the god Enlil, who then introduced into the sky the god Nanna, the moon. The moon god produced children, the sun god Utu and the goddess Inana. With the construction of the genealogies, a generational hierarchy took shape within the pantheon, and An, Enlil, and Enki became a trinity of great gods.

Another strain of cosmogony presented heaven and earth as the divine offspring of ancestor divinities rather than the result of a cosmogonic separation. The Akkadian creation poem saw the origins of the gods in the commingled waters of the male *Apsû* and the female Tiamat, who in time engendered gods within themselves. From these original divine essences came the ancestry of Marduk; from Anšar "the totality of sky" and Kišar "the totality of earth" came An, the sky god, who produced Ea Nudimmud, Marduk's father. The creation poem was a nationalistic Babylonian cosmogony, composed sometime before the reign of Nebuchadnezzar I (1124–1104 BCE) and constructed to explain the elevation of the Babylonian national god Marduk to supremacy among the gods and to attribute order in the universe to his rule (Hunger and Pingree 1999: 62). The principal revision over the older Sumerian cosmogonic tradition was in the identity of the creator, no longer Enlil but Marduk, grandson of Anu and son of Ea.

In the account of Marduk's rise to kingship creation took place following his battle to defend the gods from attack by their evil mother Tiamat. The way had been prepared by Marduk's father Ea, Enki in Sumerian, who slew *Apsû* and established his own dwelling on the "corpse," the realm of sweet waters. Marduk fought Tiamat and her host of monsters and demons, a theme taken over from the mythology of the god Ninurta and his cosmic battle against chaos (Lambert 1985: 55–60). Elements of Sumerian cosmogony persisted, but the supreme rule of Enlil and the divine ordinances of the old mythology were replaced by Marduk's universal kingship and his legitimate possession of the "tablet of destinies."

Marduk fashioned and arranged the physical world. Although the birth of the sky god had taken place generations before, Marduk took the carcass of the slain sea-mother Tiamat and split her body and set up half of her "as a cover," thereby creating the region of heaven. He made use of other parts of her watery body to create the natural world of wind, rainfall, mists, and the rivers Tigris and Euphrates from her eyes. Her tail became "the Great Bond" tying the two halves of the world together (Foster 1993a: 380 V 59).

What is the relation between the gods and the physical world?

Mythological texts and hymns preserved ideas of divine agency. As forces over the basic parts of the physical world, the three great gods Anu, Enlil, and Ea inhabited specific regions of the cosmos. Thus, in the myth of Atra-hasis the divine trinity cast lots, divided the universe, and came to be identified with heaven, earth, and the subterranean waters of *Apsú* (Lambert, Millard, and Civil 1969: 43; Jacobsen 1976: 121). No single relation between the divine and nature can be derived as a general rule. Celestial gods, such as the moon god Nanna, the sun god Utu, and Inana, the planet Venus, were viewed as manifest in the heavenly bodies and as the personified powers in these natural phenomena. The oldest attested Near Eastern storm god, Enlil, brought both the spring winds holding the good rains that made plants flourish as well as the destructive storm cloud with its flood waters. The clouds that produced rains and allowed the crops to grow came through Enlil's agency, but he was also immanent in the storm itself, as a text says, "The mighty one, Enlil...he is the storm" and "his word, a storm cloud lying on the horizon, its heart inscrutable" (Jacobsen 1976: 101–2). His hymns showed his benevolent nature as a fertility god, but lamentation texts revealed him as the destroyer of farmlands, animals, and people (Green 2003: 34–41). Enlil's influence, both positive and negative, was therefore seen as working through the natural forces of the atmosphere that embodied the god but were also transcended by him.

The other gods too were not viewed simply as the personifications of their cosmological regions, but as transcending the limits of the physical world. In the hymn to the sun god he saw into the heavens as one would into a bowl, but the eyesight of the god was greater than the physical limits of both the heavens and the entire earth (Lambert 1960: 134). The scale of the world was dwarfed by the greatness of the deity when a hymn referred to the god Ninurta as wearing "the heavens on his head like a tiara, he is shod with the netherworld as with [san]dals," and in a wisdom composition we hear of "Marduk! The skies cannot sustain the weight of his hand" (Foster 1993a: 497, 310). Marduk's transcendence was also expressed in a prayer recited during the Babylonian New Year's festival: "the expanse of heaven is (but) your insides." If this was the nature of the deity, then natural phenomena, such as storms, the sky, or the moon, were an embodiment of a divine power, and could be a manifestation of an anthropomorphic deity, but were not personified as living beings themselves.

Is there order and justice in the universe?

As forces and agents within natural objects, the gods brought order to the cosmos through authority and law. The cosmos was not seen as a self-governing body, but as ruled by divine law. By virtue of his exalted position, Anu, the supreme divine sovereign, was author of both order and chaos. He engendered the forces of disorder and chaos in the form of seven demons, but in some contexts appeared as protector. The dual role of Anu as creator as well as controller of chaos was paralleled by Enlil, who was at once the bringer of good to humanity as well as the agent of its destruction.

Ninurta was a defender of cosmic order (Vogelsang 1988; Annus 2002). Ninurta's mythic foes represented agents of cosmic disorder. Asag, the child of An and Ki, appeared in magical texts as a demon responsible for disease and death. The winged lion-dragon of iconography may be identified with the Asakku, or Anzû, described in the myth as a lion-bird monster (Black and Green 1992: 107, 121). The association of Ninurta with kingship was seen in the story of his battle with Anzû, who flew off with the tablet of destinies, Enlil's emblem of divine executive power. Ninurta's defeat of chaos resulted in his elevation to the kingship, even over his father Enlil. In view of the image of the human king not only as divinely legitimated but also as an earthly reflection of divine kingship, Ninurta's role as cosmic hero was an essential ingredient in royal ideology (Annus 2002).

The "tablet of destinies" was another representation of the idea of universal order. In the creation poem Tiamat elevated Qingu to supreme status in the divine assembly and gave him the tablet of destinies to ensure the power of his word. Marduk then vanquished Tiamat and her horde and wrested the tablet from the illegitimate possession of Qingu, symbolizing the triumph of order over chaos. Marduk became supreme sovereign over the gods and the universe, which he proceeded to organize. Marduk presented the tablet to Anu, as a restoration of the emblem of supreme divine executive rank to its original place (Foster 1993a: 380 V 70).

The idea that order in the universe came about through divine command is well supported in hymns, mythology, and in the principle of divination. In addition to Anu, Enlil, Ninurta, and Marduk, other gods established order by means of their decrees. The sun god was addressed as the power that kept the entire universe in check, both above and below: "In the lower regions you take charge of the nether-world gods, the demons, the Anunna-gods, in the upper regions you administer all the inhabited world" (Foster 1993a: 537). Ištar too was portrayed as bringing order to the cosmos by issuing decrees. She was praised as one who "ordains destiny foremost with Enlil" and "sets out regulations for the great gods, as Anu does." Also she decreed destinies and "render[ed] final judgement and decision, the command for heaven and netherworld" (Foster 1993a: 505–6, 509–11). Like Marduk she "holds the lead rope of heaven," the symbol of ultimate control; "She alone is to grasp the bridle of heaven and underworld!" (George 1992: 257).

The idea of universal order and justice that characterized Mesopotamian cosmology was tied to divine will. The power to decree all things included evil and misfortune. Given the sometimes incomprehensible mind of the gods, Mesopotamian culture developed divination to gain foreknowledge of what the deities determined would occur, magic to entreat the gods, and incantations to appease them.

By means of what force or agency do things occur in the world?

Divine design, decree, and judgment were conceived as the means by which order and disorder were brought to the world. Because institutions of political power were projected upon the divine realm, the image of the gods as rulers and judges took form. The designations of the gods as determiners of the "nature of things," the "destinies of life," the ones who drew the "cosmic designs" and the "designs of life," evoked the conception of gods as kings who ordered existence. On the divine plane the act that brought forth existence and order was conceived of as "determining destiny." In the temple hymn for the city of Isin sanctity and authority was conveyed in calling the temple the "place where An and Enlil determine destiny" (Sjöberg and Bergmann 1969: 39).

Divination showed that agency was placed in the hands of the gods who both made phenomena appear and determined the meaning of signs for events that would happen on earth. The use of the word "decision" or "verdict" to denote the consequence (we would say "prediction") of an omen points to an interpretation of omens as collections of divine "judgments" (Rochberg 2003: 178). Prophecy texts shared this terminology, like "its decision concerns Elam: Elam will lie waste, its shrines will be destroyed, the regular offerings of the major gods will cease..." (Biggs 1967: 124). Šamaš and the storm god Adad, as gods of divination, sat as kings "on thrones of gold, dining from a tray of lapis" to render judgment in the form of the signs seen on the liver of the sacrificed lamb (Foster 1993a: 149).

Already clear in Sumerian mythology, divine decrees functioned as determiners of what was. The same ideology continued in Babylonian and Assyrian religion, as can be seen in the creation poem where Marduk was made king of all the gods, his status being demonstrated by his ability to decree the things that existed – to create and destroy at will by command: "They set up among them a certain constellation, to Marduk their firstborn said they these words, 'Your destiny O Lord, shall be foremost of the gods. Command destruction or creation, they shall take place. At your word the constellation shall be destroyed, Command again, the constellation shall be intact'" (Foster 1993a: 372 IV 19–24).

The gods of the destinies were the seven Anunnaki (Lambert, Millard, and Civil 1969: 146). Following the establishment of Marduk's new shrine in Babylon in which he sat upon the "dais of destinies," "the seven gods of destinies were confirmed forever for rendering judgment" (Foster 1993a: 386 VI 81). The list of the shrines enumerated the seven seats for Anu, Enlil, Ea, Šamaš, Ninurta, Nabû, and Adad(?) (George 1999b: 74). Ninurta, together with An and Enlil, decreed destinies for humankind in the *Apsû* (Annus 2002: 25).

What is the place of humankind in relation to the whole?

In a world-view where divine power was conceived in terms of rulers, human beings fell into place within the cosmic framework as the ruled, a subject population to support and revere the gods. The motif of the creation of man to toil for the gods went back to the Old Babylonian myth of the hero Atra-hasis, the favorite of Enki/Ea, who survived the great flood sent by Enlil to wipe out all humankind. In this composition Enki and the "Mistress of the gods" formed man from clay mixed with the flesh and blood of a god slaughtered "that god and man may be thoroughly mixed in the clay" (Lambert, Millard, and Civil 1969: 59 I 212–23). The gods not only mixed divine flesh and blood with the clay; the Igigi gods spat on it and Ea trod upon it. The actual creation was carried out in the house of destiny by the birth goddess Mami. In another Sumerian tradition Enlil created humankind in the place where heaven was separated from earth, "where flesh came forth," and he accomplished this by use of the hoe (Black et al. 1998: t.5.5.4, lines 1–7). Marduk not only eased the burden of the gods by the creation of mankind, but he "redeemed" the gods, his enemies, with man's creation and was dubbed "destroyer of the gods of Tiamat, who made men out of their substance" (Foster 1993a: 397 VII 88–90).

The condition of man as forever subject to the determinations of gods was articulated in the myth of Adapa, the wise but all too human sage, who was made wise by the god Ea himself. In a moment of anger, Adapa disabled the south wind which had capsized his boat and in consequence was summoned to heaven to explain why the wind no longer blew. After achieving his ascent to heaven and thereby transcending the mundane world, he nonetheless failed to transcend his nature. Adapa's story was about a god-fearing man who failed to make the right decision, in his case to accept the bread and water of eternal life offered to him by Anu. Neither his purity nor his wisdom helped him and he remained mortal (Foster 1993a: 429-34).

What is the relation of earth to heaven?

A vertical arrangement of cosmic regions or levels comes across in references to the extent of the entire world, placing heaven above earth and earth above the *Apsû* and the netherworld. The basic triple structure of heaven, earth, and netherworld was further divided into the Upper, Middle, and Lower Heavens, and the Upper, Middle, and Lower Earths. Below the heavens, the lower half of the world was comprised first of Upper Earth, where the "souls" of mankind were settled (Horowitz 1998: 3–4). Middle Earth was the residence of Ea, and to the depths of Lower Earth were consigned the 600 Anunnaki gods. These 600 gods were associated with the land of the dead, where the god Nergal ruled. Above the realm of mankind were the three heavens, populated by gods and stars. In accordance with the symmetry of this world picture, the point where the earth of human beings met the heaven of the observable stars became a metaphysical center, the borderline between divine and human.

The whole was bound together as one coherent structure by the mythical "bonds" that held the level of the heavens to the lowest level of the netherworld. A number of ropes served the purpose. The god who held such a cosmic rope exercised control over the universe like the handler who controlled an animal on the other end of a lead-rope. Such an image was found in the divine epithet "who holds the lead-rope of heaven and netherworld" and was implied in the epithet "who holds the totality of the heavens and lands" or "who holds the totality of heaven and netherworld," both of which were used for Marduk (Tallqvist 1974: 242-3). Another image was of a boat's mooring-rope. The name of the temple of Marduk in Babylon was explained in a commentary as the "house of the great mooring rope of heaven."

Akkadian "earth" in a cosmological sense denoted both earth and the nether-world. The term "earth" as "netherworld" can be found in the XIIth Tablet of Gilgamesh (Schaffer 1963). A few sources confirmed the identification of the place where netherworld deities resided as "earth," while others clearly meant the physical earth upon which we stand (Horowitz 1998: 273–4; Lambert, Millard, and Civil 1969: 91: 48). The use of one term to refer both to the earth and the place of the dead was seen as well in the poetic term "great earth."

The question of whether there was a cosmic mountain has been debated, as well as what relation it may have had to another primordial cosmic locality, the "sacred mound." The cosmic "sacred (shining) mound" was the location both of the birth of the gods and the divine assembly. It was the place to which Ninurta repaired following his triumphant presentation of the vanquished gods to Enlil, and where he was called "king of the sacred mound." The sacred mound in heaven, also thought of as "mountain of heaven and earth," with its foundation upon the cosmic *Apsû*, had its earthly parallel in the sacred centers of the world, Nippur, Babylon, or Assur (Wiggermann 1992: 285, 295). In a Neo-Assyrian text that enumerated the cosmic levels, Marduk's "high throne-dais" was located in the Middle Heaven. It was the place where the gods decreed the destinies and became the name of the earthly throne-dais of Enlil in Nippur as well as later that of Marduk in Babylon, the god Assur in the city of Assur, and Anu in Uruk. On the celebration of the New Year, Marduk sat on the Dais of Destinies as "king of the gods in heaven and earth" to decree the destinies. The celebration of the New Year in the seventh month was reflected in the month name "month of the sacred mound." This site therefore held a central place in the cosmos and was paralleled in the earthly center of the temple where the deities decreed destiny.

What is the physical structure of the heavenly regions?

The tradition of three superimposed heavenly realms was known in first millennium texts. The highest heaven belonged to Anu and was populated with 300 Igigi or great gods (Livingstone 1989: 99–102). Middle Heaven belonged to the Igigi, and Marduk had his throne there. Stars and constellations were drawn upon the surface of the Lower Heaven. While invocations to seven heavens and seven earths occurred in Sumerian incantations, the image of a plurality of heavens found there occurred only in incanta-tions. The seven heavens and earths were invoked alongside other groups of seven entities for magic. Being magical rather than cosmological, the seven heavens and earths were not necessarily related to the three heavens and earths found in other texts.

The cosmological picture as presented in the passages concerning the three heavens also entailed poetic speculation about the heavens as made of different stones. These stones varied in color, the heaven of Anu being reddish, speckled with white and black, the middle heaven being blue stone like lapis lazuli, and the lower heaven being translucent jasper, either blue or grey (Horowitz 1998: 9–15). This image was hardly an attempt at empirical description, but presumably the projection of mythological or other associations between stones and gods. Equally poetic was the additional statement that the stars were drawn, or inscribed as "writing," upon the stone surface of the heavens (Livingstone 1989: 100). This metaphor stressed the meaning of the stars as signs "written" by the gods for human beings to observe and from which to forecast the future. The same image of drawing the stars appeared in the series of astronomy tablets.

The heavens contained the waters of Tiamat, which were guarded and held in by a tightly stretched skin, no doubt a reflection in mythological form of the empirical relation between the sky and precipitation (Foster 1993a: 376–7 IV 137–40). In literary texts the celestial realm of the planetary deities was sometimes denoted by the term "base of heaven," but taken to mean "firmament," as in "they installed Sin, Šamaš, and Ištar to keep the firmament in order" (Horowitz 1998: 239) and "through her (Inana as the evening star) the firmament is made beautiful in the evening" (Sjöberg and Bergmann 1969: 36, 115; Horowitz 1998: 240–1). Astronomical terminology did not include this "firmament," but used the word "sky" to refer to the place where celestial phenomena were observable. Because of the difference in character between mythology and astronomy, points of contact in their conceptual landscapes are noteworthy. The beginning of Tablet V of the creation poem, which dealt with the regularity of the appearance of heavenly bodies as the work of Marduk, described features of the heavens also referred to in astronomical texts. Marduk arranged the stars into constellations, the "images" of the gods themselves. By means of the fixed stars he organized the year into twelve months, marked by the risings of three stars in each month in their specified "paths" (Foster 1993a: 378 V 4). He created the zenith, the moon, and the month from the lunar phases.

Celestial divination and astronomical texts required a terminology to specify the positions and times for the occurrences of celestial phenomena. Without the conception of the celestial sphere and its coordinates, a variety of systems denoted celestial positions. The terminology of the "paths" of Anu, Enlil, and Ea was used in early astronomical texts. The Anu path was that which had its gate in the center of the "cattle pen," or eastern horizon; to the south of it lay the path of Ea and to the north the path of Enlil. The stars may have been associated with the gods Anu, Ea, and Enlil even earlier, but were assigned to these paths according to where on the horizon their risings were observed, or in modern astronomical terms, according to their circles of declination, the distance north or south of the celestial equator (Hunger and Pingree 1989: 139). Another system was implied in the device called a "string," which established a relation between stars of similar right ascensions that crossed the meridian at the same time (Hunger and Pingree 1999: 90–7).

The other "path" of importance was that of the moon, whose track was marked by eighteen constellations, recognized at least by the 750s BCE. These constellations were not of equal size, and cannot be used as a standard of reference for the calculation of "distance" along "the path." Later, to mark the passage of the sun with respect to the fixed stars through the months of the year, these constellations were reduced to twelve and formed the basis for the zodiac. As the planets were observed to hug the path of the sun, or the ecliptic, a larger group of ecliptical stars was identified for the purpose of observing the movement of the planets (Sachs and Hunger 1988: 17–19). Although the twelve constellations of the zodiac gave their names to the zodiacal signs, once the signs were defined by longitude rather than constellation, they became a mathematical reference system of twelve 30-degree parts, counted from a defined starting point. In this way, no geometrical dimension was attributed to the heavens in mathematical astronomical texts, whose predictive schemes were strictly arithmetical and linear, and consequently shed no light on the question of the spatial structure of the heavens.

What are the cosmic waters?

The cosmic realm called *Apsû*, whose watery depths lay beneath the earth, appeared in Sumerian and Akkadian mythology. It was the creation, abode, and kingdom of Enki, and was so closely associated with him that Enki's son, Marduk, was known as "first-born son of the *Apsû*." Because of Enki's association with wisdom, magic, and incantations, the *Apsû* was thought of as the fount of wisdom and source of the secret knowledge of incantations. The temple of Enki in the oldest Sumerian city of Eridu was called the E-Abzu "House of the Abyss." Later, the temple of Marduk in Babylon was explained as the replica of *Apsû* (George 1992: 59). As the counterpart to Enki's cosmic abode, Marduk's was also the home of all the gods (George 1999b: 68–70). Enki's shrine in Eridu too was known as the "holy mound" (George 1993: 77; George 1999b). The association of the *Apsû* with the "holy mound" showed the cosmic importance of Ea's domain as a place for the divine assembly and where destiny was decreed.

What is the realm of the dead?

When the entire extent of the world was taken into account, the furthest realm in the direction downward was "the netherworld." In mythological texts the netherworld existed parallel to the land where human beings existed, but as a land of no return, the land beneath the land where demons could be sent or where gods could descend (Horowitz 1998: 272–3). Also belonging to the depiction of the netherworld in literary texts was the idea of this land being dark and distant, inhabited by ghosts, demons, or gods who ruled over the dead or who brought death. In the only text where cosmic regions were placed relative to one another within an overall scheme, the location of the netherworld was specified as being below the *Apsû*, and so became the lowest of all regions (Livingstone 1989: 83). According to another composition the netherworld was the negation of all that was known in the world "above," on earth and in heaven; therefore it was devoid of light, its river carried no water, and its fields produced no grain (Horowitz 1998: 351).

Does the world have a center?

The notion of an axis of the world focused on cities, first Nippur, then Babylon and Assur. Although the centrality of various cities and temples with respect to heaven and earth attests to a Mesopotamian idea of a cosmic center, it was never employed within a system to account for the motions of the celestial bodies within the cosmos and therefore cannot be understood as implying the earth was the center of the universe. Nippur's epithet "bond of heaven and earth/netherworld" reflects the idea of the cosmic regions coming together at the central point of the holy place, the "house of the universe." In his shrine at Nippur, Enlil was the "lord who determines destinies," and the shrine was the place "where destinies are decreed." In an Early Dynastic hymn Nippur was the "city which is grown together with Heaven, embracing Heaven" (Alster 1976: 121). Another epithet of this city touched on the cosmic significance of the place as the "navel of the world," "the city that produced itself," interpreted as an etymology for Nippur's name (George 1992: 146, 441). The idea of the holy city of Nippur influenced later Mesopotamian religious and cosmological thought. In Assur the ziggurat of Assur was seen as the link between heaven and earth in the name "temple, mountain of the entire world" (George 1993: 69). At Isin the same idea was attributed to the temple of Ninisina, called "the axis (between) heaven and earth" (Sjöberg 2002: 245 n. 30). Enlil was said to have suspended the axis of the world as the first act of creation (Black et al. 1998: t.5.5.4:7).

What is the nature of the planetary bodies?

All celestial bodies, stars, constellations, and planets were called stars. The planets were further distinguished by a term meaning a kind of sheep, with the idea that their movements were not fixed in relation to one another as were the fixed stars since they "keep changing their positions" (Hunger and Pingree 1989: 71). The following brief outline highlights only indications about the divine nature of the planets in Mesopotamian cosmological thought (Brown 2000: 54–80).

A word "moon" deriving from the Sumerian divine name could be used to refer to crescent-shaped objects, but when referring to the moon itself, the divine name for the "moon god" was synonymous with "moon." Divination texts favored the symbolic writing 30, referring to the schematic or ideal length of the lunar cycle, but even this name for the moon was frequently written with the divine determinative, showing the lack of a distinction between moon and moon god.

Similarly, the word "sun" was indistinguishable from the name of the sun god Šamaš. In a Sumerian hymn to the temple of the god, the rising and setting of the sun were referred to in anthropomorphic terms: "when he the lord reposes, the people repose (with him). When he arises, the people arise (with him)" (Sjöberg and Bergmann 1969: 45).

Sumerian hymns reveal that already in the third millennium the planet Venus was seen as the astral form of the goddess Inana or Ištar. She was hailed as "the great lady of the horizon and zenith of the heavens" and she was addressed as "the radiant star, Venus, the great light which fills the holy heavens" (Black et al. 1998: t.4.07.2:112, t.2.5.3.1:89). From the third millennium BCE she was already recognized as both the morning and the evening star, as seen in a seal inscription referring to the festival of Inana (Brown 2000: 67). She was associated with Šamaš at sunrise and Ninurta at sunset. In omens Inana could be either male or female: "If Venus rises in the East, she is female, favorable; if she is seen in the West she is male, unfavorable" (Reiner and Pingree 1998: 241).

Jupiter was identified with the god Marduk in its name "Marduk Star." The manifestations of that god in the various appearances of Jupiter took on other names, as when on the eastern horizon he became "Brilliant Youth," and when in the middle of the sky "the Ford." In all these guises, Marduk/Jupiter was "the bearer of signs to the inhabited world" (Livingstone 1989: 6–10).

One of the names of Mercury was "the jumping one," which could have been descriptive of the planet's fast motion and perhaps the fact that it was not often or easily visible. Mercury was associated with the gods Ninurta and Nabû symbolizing the crown prince or son of Marduk (Hunger and Pingree 1989: 71; Gössmann 1950: 113). The association of Mercury with the two gods may relate to the appearances of the planet as a morning and evening star. The planet was also sometimes referred to as an arrow of the heroic warrior god Ninurta (Annus 2002: 134–5).

Mars was associated with Nergal, god of pestilence. The planet's name was interpreted as "the one who reveals deaths," and indeed in the omens the planet portended plague and other evils. But Nergal's manifestation as a heavenly body was nonetheless glorified in prayer: "Nergal star who rises again and again on the horizon, whose glow (stands) high" (Ebeling 1953: 117).

The luminous aspect of the heavenly divine manifestations was their most obvious quality. In Sumerian liturgy the radiance of Venus was frequently mentioned. In one composition the moon god was referred to as "the astral holy bull-calf" who "shines in the heavens like the morning star," and "spreads bright light in the night" (Black et al. 1998: t.1.8.2.1: 202–4). In the creation poem Marduk's ninth name was "bright one," "the shining god who illumines our ways," and his forty-ninth name was "Ford" = Jupiter, "the star which in the skies is brilliant" (Foster 1993a: 390 VI 156, 399 VII 126). In omen texts, descriptions of the appearance of the planets included whether they were bright or dim, or of various colors. Brightness or dimness was interpreted in accordance with the quality of the planet, either beneficial or sinister; accordingly it was favorable if a beneficial body was bright, but unfavorable if a sinister body was bright.

Observation of the heavens for the purpose of celestial divination, the solution of calendrical problems, and eventually, the prediction of the planetary appearances, led to the recognition of their periodic behavior. The study of the relations between planetary periods became the central focus of astronomical work from about 600 BCE. In Babylonian astronomy the interest in heavenly phenomena was focused upon visibilities. Motion, therefore, was approached as the distance traveled between appearances in the cycle, as between first visibilities. The distance referred to is what astronomers now call the synodic arc, described as the number of degrees of longitude traveled by the planet in one synodic cycle, between one phenomenon of conjunction of two celestial objects and the next.

Is there a cosmological significance to the order of the planets?

Late Babylonian astronomical texts enumerated the five planets in the sequence Jupiter, Venus, Mercury, Saturn, and Mars (Rochberg-Halton 1988). This arrangement was at odds with the typically Greek geocentric map of the heavens, which organized the five planetary orbits around the earth in the order Mercury, Venus, Mars, Jupiter, and Saturn, placing the planetary spheres above those of the moon and sun. In the Babylonian sources, however, the order in which the planets were enumerated in texts had nothing to do with geocentric order, but rather with their attributes as gods. Accordingly, Jupiter and Venus were beneficial, but Saturn and Mars were sinister. Mercury held an ambiguous position between the two beneficial and the two sinister stars and was sometimes good and sometimes bad. Old Babylonian references to the planet Mars as a destroyer of the herds suggested an early origin of this doctrine (Rochberg-Halton 1988: 235 n. 2). And in the Neo-Assyrian period Jupiter was a herald of propitious omens for Esarhaddon (Borger 1956: 17).

Was there a conception of circles or spheres? And did the celestial bodies move in them?

The celestial sphere and the spherical earth that were assumed by Western cosmology do not seem to have roots in ancient Mesopotamia. The idea of the cosmos as a sphere was articulated on the basis of metaphysical arguments first in Plato's Timaeus around 400 BCE, that the created world was "a perfect whole and of perfect parts" (Plato 1989: 1164 32 d-33 a). And within that spherical world-view, Greek astronomy from the fourth century BCE to the second century CE constructed geometrical spherical models to describe the motions of the planets. The spherical nature of the earth was also determined by Aristotle as a consequence of the physics of matter.

Instead of the celestial sphere, for the identification of stars and planets the horizon became a reference point in early Babylonian astronomy. Observers named three paths corresponding to roughly defined intervals along the eastern horizon where fixed stars were observed to rise. The interest of Babylonian celestial science in the planetary appearances, as opposed to planetary motion around the celestial sphere, underscores the irrelevancy of the notion of spheres in Babylonian astronomy. The sun was seen as traveling in the zodiac, but this does not necessarily imply that the sun traveled within a sphere (Neugebauer 1955: 194). The discovery of the planetary periods and their relations was not dependent upon a spherical image. The period of a planet, as conceived in Babylonian mathematical astronomy, was defined as the number of synodic arcs the planet had to complete before it returned to a certain position in the sky, reckoned by degrees of the zodiac.

The image of a spherical world, however, may be discerned in metaphor. Reference to the bowl-shape of the heavens and earth appeared in a hymn (Lambert 1960: 134). Another prayer referred to the heaven of Anu as "the incense burner" of the gods, an object at least circular in shape, but differentiated in other texts from bowls (Ebeling

1953: 15). But these passages were not intended as empirical descriptions of the shape of the world.

Outside of the astronomical literature, the heavens were sometimes referred to in the phrase "circle of heaven," and "circle" is a word used for geometric circles and hoops. In these passages the use of "circle" could be read as metaphoric, reflecting a sense of the totality rather than the shape of the celestial region as a whole. Circular diagrams appeared in a number of early Babylonian astronomical texts, presenting a circular image within which the constellations were placed (Horowitz 1998: 206). The early Babylonian reckoning of the length of day given in the texts was underpinned by the concept of the circle of the day measured as 12 "double hours" of 30 degrees each (= 360 degrees). The Path of Enlil was a circle described by 26 stars (Horowitz 1998: 186). Given such evidence, perhaps the reading of "circle of heaven" or "totality of heaven" need not be mutually exclusive.

Finally, despite the apparent lack of a conception of the celestial sphere in Babylonian astronomy, the periodic return of the planets to their synodic appearances with respect to certain points of longitude seems to presuppose the 360-degree circle of the ecliptic, the path of the sun. Whether it was conceived of as such, or as a repeating linear sequence of 360 points, however, is difficult to show. Because the aim of Babylonian mathematical astronomy was to predict the appearances of the planets in their synodic movements, the computational schemes devised to achieve this cannot be taken to reflect any particular conception of the shape or dimensions of the cosmos, nor the nature of the motions of the bodies between their synodic appearances.

FURTHER READING

Horowitz 1998 is the most comprehensive treatment of the cosmological geography of ancient Mesopotomia and sets out all the primary sources for the study of the subject. A good overall reference work on astral sciences with a description of some of the basic texts of early Babylonian astronomy relevant to cosmology is Hunger and Pingree 1999. Lambert 1975 is a still useful summary of Mesopotamian cosmology from mythological and theological sources. For more recent detailed studies see Wiggermann 1992 and Sjöberg 2002. For the cosmological background of Babylonian religion see George 1992.

CHAPTER TWENTY-FOUR

Divine and Non-Divine Kingship

Philip Jones

"Kingship everywhere and at all times has been in some degree a sacred office" (Evans-Pritchard 1962: 210). Some kings, of course, are more sacred than others. In the world of the Ancient Near East, the most prominent examples of this are the kings of Egypt. Throughout the course of ancient Egyptian history, kings were generally accorded some form of divine status (O'Connor and Silverman 1995). In ancient Mesopotamia attributions of divinity to kings were rather more restricted, both in time and space. The phenomenon was limited to certain kings in southern Mesopotamia in the millennium from the twenty-second to the twelfth centuries. Despite this, divine kingship in Mesopotamia generated an impressive amount of source material. We possess inscriptions in which kings claimed divine status, administrative records that registered cultic offerings to their divinity, and literary texts that featured divine kings, both legendary and historical.

But what did the ancient Mesopotamians mean by these honors? Our understanding of the word "god" is conditioned by the monotheistic traditions of Western societies. The term carries connotations of omnipotence and uniformity. As a polytheistic society, however, ancient Mesopotamia knew a multiplicity of divine beings that fulfilled a wide variety of different roles (Lambert 1957–71; Van Dijk 1957–71). Moreover, we must try to explain why in Mesopotamia, unlike ancient Egypt, some kings were considered gods and others were not.

From our perspective, it is not easy to accept that a king's subjects could both be rational and, at the same time, have truly believed him to be a god. Given the level of literacy in ancient Mesopotamia, the texts illustrating any form of kingship were the product of a very small segment of the population. Nor was it a homogenous one. In the third millennium, the very highest administrative officials could be literate (Visicato 2000: 233–9). Most of our Old Babylonian literary tablets are the school exercises of trainee scribes whose ultimate role in society is obscure (Tinney 1998). Most of our first millennium literary and "scientific" tablets are the product of a sophisticated and exclusive scholarly elite (Parpola 1983; Rochberg 1993). The literary nature of much of our evidence renders the concept of divine kingship even more suspicious. Surviving Old Babylonian administrative and commercial letters, contemporary with the bulk of our literary evidence for divine kingship, treated the king as a purely human figure.

But the experience of kingship on any level could not be monolithic. It would be unlikely for a king to experience the institution in exactly the same way as his predecessors, his advisors, or his subjects. We can only analyze those experiences recorded by scribes on tablets recovered. If we wish to posit what those scribes really believed or how the experience of kingship would have been articulated by other, non-literate, members of society, we can only do it through these extant scribal copies.

My focus will be confined to the two periods of Mesopotamian history with the richest intellectual legacies: the Old Babylonian period (2004–1595 BCE) and the first millennium BCE. Not only do they provide much evidence for kingship; they also differed significantly in how they characterized the institution. Kingship was regularly treated as divine in the Old Babylonian corpus and as non-divine in the first millennium one. In considering first the literary portrayals of the cosmic role of kingship and then the possible political contexts, I seek to illuminate rather than solve these problems. Mesopotamian visions of kingship, no matter how fanciful they may seem to us, reveal native understandings of the processes and problems inherent in the constitution of legitimate authority. At the same time, they deepen our comprehension of the sociology of ancient Mesopotamian politics. They give some indication of the political phenomena that stimulated native reflection and the manner in which they did so.

Intellectual experiences of power in ancient Mesopotamia were underlain by fears of royal violence. Contrasting visions of kingship highlight different ways of confronting this problem. Old Babylonian characterizations of the divine king imply that the king had to make a crucial contribution to cosmic order. He had either to restrain his innate tendency to unleash violence on his own people or, more positively, conform to a tightly circumscribed mode of correct behavior. An important way of conveying the behavior required was to characterize the king in terms of more traditional deities. Explicitly he was equated with the god Dumuzi and compared to the sun god. Dumuzi was the spouse of Inana, the fearsome goddess of love and war. His alluring charms provided a means of channeling her potentially destructive power into more constructive uses. The sun god was the divine patron of justice. Just as significant as these positive models, however, was an implicit contrast to the war god Ninurta. Unlike the latter, the king had to avoid using the awesome violence at his disposal against his own homeland.

In contrast, in much of the first millennium material the most that could be expected of the all-too-human king was self-restraint. Any cosmic order had to exist in spite of the king's inherently violent nature. In terms of the varying social experiences of power, we may note significant correlations – without claiming direct lines of causation – between these modes of imagining kingship and specific aspects of the political experience of kingship in the two periods. The Old Babylonian period stood at the beginning of a dual, long-term process of territorial integration and elite differentiation; the first millennium stood at its end. By the later period, literate urban elites tended to conceptualize their political privileges in opposition to the royal administration rather than through it. Therefore, it is perhaps not surprising that visions of a kingship crucial to cosmic order were more common in the Old Babylonian period.

The Intellectual Experiences of Power

Throughout Mesopotamian history, the legitimacy of kings was conceptualized in terms of their closeness to the divine world through divine descent, divine favor, marriage to a goddess, or superhuman stature. All these themes were already alluded to in one of our earliest royal inscriptions, the so-called Stele of the Vultures in honor of Eanatum of Lagash (2450 BCE). His birth and upbringing were described in superhuman terms:

> The god Ningirsu implanted the seed for Eanatum in the womb and . . . rejoiced over him. The goddess Inana accompanied him, proclaimed him "Worthy in the Eana-temple of Inana of the Ibgal-shrine," and set him on the special lap of the goddess Ninhursag. Ninhursag offered him her special breast. Ningirsu rejoiced over Eanatum, the seed implanted in the womb by Ningirsu. Ningirsu laid his span upon him, for (a length of) five forearms he set his forearm upon him: (he measured) five forearms, one span (2.75 meters). Ningirsu, with great joy, gave him the kingship of Lagash. (After Cooper 1986: 34)

Such themes were characteristic of celebrations of the king throughout Mesopotamian history. But the innovation of according the king himself divine status first occurred some time in the middle of the reign of Naram-Sin of Akkad (2254–2218 BCE), and its origin was dramatically described in one of his inscriptions:

> Naram-Sin, the mighty, king of Akkad – when the four quarters together revolted against him, through the love which Ishtar showed him, he was victorious in nine battles in one year, and the king whom they had raised (against him) he captured. In view of the fact that he had protected the foundations of his city from danger, (the citizens of) his city requested from Ištar in Eana, Enlil in Nippur, Dagan in Tuttul, Ninhursag in Kesh, Ea in Eridu, Suen in Ur, Šamaš in Sippar, and Nergal in Kutha, that (Naram-Suen) be (made) the god of their city, and they built within Akkad a temple (dedicated) to him. (Frayne 1993: 113–14)

At the heart of this deification was the writing of the king's name with the determinative for "god." This practice was in regular use down to the end of the Kassite period (Seux 1980–3: 170–1). Other markers of royal divinity were more restricted in time. Akkad, Ur III, and Old Babylonian kings were described in epithets as gods. Ur III and Old Babylonian kings had hymns written in their honor. Ur III kings received religious offerings in their own lifetime (Klein 1981: 29–36; Kraus 1974: 241–50; Römer 1965: 55–7; Sallaberger and Westenholz 1999: 153–4).

For much of this period there is little evidence of any native reflection on divine kingship. Fortunately, the concept suffuses many of the compositions preserved on

Old Babylonian literary tablets. We can contrast this with the non-divine kingship presented in the first millennium corpus. Crucial to each vision of kingship was how the balance of responsibility for cosmic order was distributed between the king and the divine world.

Divine Kingship in the Old Babylonian Period

Old Babylonian literary tablets implied that the divinity of the king reflected the vital role he had to play to ensure an ordered cosmos in the face of divine unpredictability. The texts, however, registered an underlying unease at having to rely on the king's ability to restrain his own destructive tendencies. Looking at how divine government was portrayed, I will focus on four themes: the nature of the divine regime itself, primeval acts of creation that provided a charter for all subsequent cosmic order, individual divine decrees dealing with specific issues, and the way in which human institutions derived their inspiration from the divine world.

As legitimate sovereignty in the material world of ancient Mesopotamia was always envisaged as monarchic, it might be expected that sovereignty in the divine world would be too. But surprisingly in the Old Babylonian literary tablets there was no clear head of the divine pantheon. Supreme cosmic power was held by both the sky god, An, and the patron deity of the city of Nippur, Enlil, with little attempt to harmonize this apparent discrepancy. Cosmic sovereignty was imagined in terms of a number of gods rather than one alone: a dyarchy of An and Enlil together; a triumvirate of An, Enlil, and Enki, the god of wisdom; a tetrarchy of An, Enlil, Enki, and a mother goddess, either Ninmah or Ninhursag; or the totality of all the gods meeting in assembly.

None of these versions of divine government came with strong connotations of stable cosmic order. The sky god An was something of a cipher. Enlil certainly wielded force, but tended to do so in a destructive manner such as unleashing either the flood as in Atra-hasis or barbarian invaders as in Cursing of Agade (Foster 1993a: 158–201; Black et al. 1998–: 2.1.5). Enlil could be characterized more in terms of his absence from human life than his presence. The composition called Enlil and Ninlil imagined ordered human life in the city of Nippur as possible only when Enlil vacated the city (Black et al. 1998–: 1.2.1). As a team, An and Enlil's word was often characterized as unchangeable, but some contexts suggested it was both unfathomable and erratic.

In a similar manner, Old Babylonian depictions of divine actions at the dawn of time did little to suggest a settled cosmos. Neither of the putative heads of the pantheon, An or Enlil, was shown creating ordered space in the manner familiar to us from Yahweh's actions at the beginning of the Biblical book of Genesis. In the Song of the Hoe Enlil was depicted as separating heaven from earth (Black et al. 1998–: 5.5.4). But his only contribution to social and cultural order was to create that most versatile of implements, the hoe. This gave humanity the potential to create its own social and cultural order, but by no means guaranteed it. The efforts of other gods at primeval organization were more far-reaching, but essentially flawed. Both

Enki and his realm, the Abzu, the mythological subterranean ocean of fresh water, were closely associated with the qualities of intelligence and rational thinking. They would therefore obviously have had a role to play in any conception of cosmic order. Indeed, in Enki and the World Order, Enki organized the primeval world and delegated the responsibility for each facet of that organization to a specific deity (Black et al. 1998–: 1.1.3). However, he subverted his own efforts by assigning the wilful goddess Inana the role of negating all that he had achieved. Ninurta, the son of Enlil, imposed order on foreign lands in the poem the Exploits of Ninurta, but achieved no such imposition on the homeland itself (Black et al. 1998–: 1.6.2). Atra-hasis began with junior deities working the land (Foster 1993a: 158–201). Their work, however, was unfinished as they went on strike and their task was left to be completed by human hands.

Generally lacking imagery of either a steady hand on the tiller or primeval organization, Old Babylonian literary texts commonly presented the idea of cosmic order in terms of divine decrees. Their promulgation was usually termed "decreeing a destiny." On rare occasions these decrees were visualized as a finite and predetermined set recorded on the "Tablet of Destinies" possessed by one of the major gods. More regularly, they were presented as a set of ad hoc declarations in response to particular events or prompted by petitions (George 1986; Polonsky 2002: 73–168).

In Old Babylonian thought divine inspiration of human institutions was encapsulated in the concept of the m e, the divine archetypes that underlay all aspects of civilized life. They could originate with An or Enlil, but more fittingly they were generally associated with Enki and the Abzu, the source of divine wisdom. One of the major agents of their transfer from the Abzu to the human realm was the goddess Inana. The process of transfer was celebrated in some detail in the composition Inana and Enki, which described how she brought the m e to her spouse Dumuzi and her city Uruk (Black et al. 1998–:1.3.1). While Inana's explicit associations with the m e were constructive, her reputation for irrational behavior imbued her conveying of the m e with an ominous air. Furthermore, descriptions of the m e in human contexts often stressed the fragility of their integrity (Farber-Flügge 1973: 150–2).

The implications of these divine contributions to cosmic order were not comforting for humanity. The cosmos was characterized as an unpredictable and dangerous place. Humanity's worst fears found expression in both the provoked and unprovoked anger of the gods. While offerings to the gods represented humanity's fulfillment of its cosmic role, pleasing the gods was by no means simple. In Atra-hasis Enlil became hostile to humanity simply because the din of everyday life prevented him from sleeping (Foster 1993a: 158–201). He sent plague, famine, and drought to reduce humanity's numbers. Each time, through the advice of Enki, people were able to target their offerings to the gods best able to alleviate their suffering. When Enlil finally coerced the rest of the gods into unleashing the ultimate divine weapon, the flood, even Enki was rendered powerless to intercede. He was able to arrange for only the survival of a single human family, that of Atra-hasis, the Babylonian Noah.

The unpredictability of unprovoked divine displeasure was well illustrated by the figure of Inana herself. In Enki and the World Order she was characterized as the power that could overturn any cosmic order (Black et al. 1998–: 1.1.3). Furthermore, Inana's involvement also lent a degree of contingency to conceptions of the divine inspiration underlying human institutions.

The two modes of divine anger, provoked and unprovoked, were both found in Cursing of Agade (Black et al. 1998–: 2.1.5). King Naram-Sin attempted to gain a favorable omen to build a temple to Inana in his city of Akkad. Enlil, however, reacted with only silent displeasure. This set in train a course of events that led ultimately to the invasion of the land by the barbarian Gutians. Naram-Sin resolved to destroy Enlil's temple. In retaliation, Enlil sent the barbarian hordes to obliterate the city of Akkad.

The nature of divine government and its implications required other means of countering the vagaries of the cosmos. There were numerous hymns to deities and temples that attempted to prompt a wide variety of gods and goddesses to exert their influence on their fellow divinities on humanity's behalf. More strikingly, they used the figure of the king to evoke cosmic order. This provided the intellectual context for the king's divinity. The nuances of the king's role were conveyed by a subtle set of comparisons both positive and negative with various traditional deities.

The active aspect of his role in preventing the provocation of divine wrath involved a delicate balance. He had to ensure that human actions did not displease the gods and that the temples were provisioned without exercising undue force on his own subjects. This dilemma was reflected in comparisons of the king with two gods. The king was associated with the sun god (Polonsky 2002: 436–9, 471–529). This was expressed by Hammurabi (1792–1750 BCE) in the prologue to his law code:

> At that time, Anu and Enlil, for the enhancement of the well-being of the people, named me by my name, Hammurabi, the pious prince, who venerates the gods, to make justice prevail in the land, to abolish the wicked and the evil, to prevent the strong from oppressing the weak, to rise like the sun god over all humankind, to illuminate the land. (Roth 1997: 76–7)

The sun god was the divine judge. The sun god provided a role model for how the king should positively contribute to human order. Furthermore, the royal hymns often alluded to successful provisioning as a reason for the gods to reward the king with a good fate. It was the sun god who was imagined as presiding over the divine assembly as it met to pronounce its satisfaction or dissatisfaction with human actions through the medium of the innards of a sacrificed sheep (Polonsky 2002: 224–39).

Implicitly, however, a comparison of the king with an even more powerful deity loomed over Old Babylonian royal depictions. The warrior god Ninurta was often acclaimed as "king" in mythological texts. Furthermore, while contemporary royal inscriptions rarely alluded to royal warfare, Ninurta's role of terrorizing or oppressing foreign lands was one for which many royal hymns frequently lauded the king. However, in the composition Ninurta's Return to Nibru, Ninurta's return from victories abroad caused a cosmic crisis as he toyed with challenging his father Enlil for supreme power (Black et al. 1998–:). The exercise of force and violence that was so necessary to deal with enemies abroad would only lead to chaos if turned upon the homeland (Jones in press).

The king's task was to prevent enemies from harming the homeland by either destroying or subduing them. But the fragility of the king's position in the face of external threat was conceptualized through his relationship with Inana. The king incarnated Dumuzi, the divine consort of Inana herself, and married the goddess in the sacred marriage ceremony. Most obviously, the power and capriciousness personified by Inana rendered the position of any spouse, divine or human, precarious (Jones 2003).

Non-Divine Kingship in the First Millennium

The idea that the cosmos was not predetermined and that order required a degree of royal intervention was not absent from first millennium tablets. However, texts extant from this period were dominated by a very different attitude toward cosmic order. Our most commonly attested literary text from this period is the Epic or Poem of Creation (Foster 1993a: 351–402). This commemorated the primeval evolution of the cosmos that culminated in the victory of Marduk, patron deity of Babylon, over the forces of chaos led by Tiamat, the personification of the sea. For this action, the rest of the gods acknowledged the suzerainty of Marduk. This rise of Marduk was widely reflected in other first millennium texts and was paralleled in the north of Mesopotamia by the figure of Assur, the patron god of Assyria. This reflected the increased political importance of the cities these gods personified. However, especially in the case of Marduk, these new gods represented not only new rulers of the cosmos, but also a new type of supreme cosmic authority. According to the Epic of Creation, cosmic order was not a random entity, but rather something determined by Marduk in primeval times. After defeating Tiamat, Marduk created an ordered cosmos by dividing her carcass. In such a cosmos divine decrees and the m e were redundant concepts. Divine decrees were imagined as a completed set of proclamations inscribed on the "Tablet of Destinies" that was seized by the victorious Marduk. The role of the m e was fulfilled by Marduk himself. As the offspring of Ea, it was he who represented divine power in human cultural achievements.

Marduk was not merely a replacement for Enlil at the head of the pantheon. He was a new kind of chief god altogether, one who could impose order on his fellow gods for the benefit of humanity. Moreover, to praise this new kind of leader, the Epic of Creation consciously redeployed motifs prominent in Old Babylonian evocations of order to celebrate the new order.

The motifs of the sun, provisioning, and marriage were reused in the poem to characterize Marduk in a manner reminiscent of the divine king in Old Babylonian compositions. At the first appearance of Marduk in the poem his grandfather, An, the sky god, acclaimed him in solar terms as:

> The son Sun god, the son Sun god,
> The son, the sun, the sunlight of the gods. (Foster 1993a: 357)

Second, the king's old task of provisioning the gods was attributed to the new divine figure:

> When the gods had given kingship over to Marduk
> They said to him expressions of goodwill and obedience,
> "Henceforth, you shall be the provider for our sanctuaries." (Foster 1993a: 382)

The third motif, marriage to a fearsome female figure, was redeployed more elliptic-
ally. Whereas Inana, Ištar in Akkadian, the spouse of the king in Old Babylonian
thought, was the most prominent goddess in first millennium texts, she was never
referred to by name in the Epic of Creation. The only terrifying female figure in the
Epic of Creation was Tiamat. Marduk's cosmic ascension was based on defeating her
in battle, not marrying her. Nevertheless, his relationship to Tiamat had conjugal
undertones. Marduk acknowledged the legitimating qualities of marrying Tiamat. He
merely disagreed with her choice of the obscure figure of Qingu as her spouse and
hinted that this was an honor that should have been his:

> You named Qingu to be spouse for you
> Though he had no right to be, you set him up for chief god. (Foster 1993a: 375)

The sexual undertones of the relationship between Marduk and Tiamat were fully
brought out in a Neo-Assyrian cultic commentary that described Marduk as the one
"who [defeat]ed Tiamat with his penis" (Livingstone 1989: 94).

From this perspective, what needed explaining in history was disorder, not
order. In the poem Erra and Ishum cosmic crises were explained as the result of
Marduk's periodically withdrawing from the world (Foster 1993a: 771–805). Without
his restraining hand, chaos ensued. The poem itself focused on the occasion when
Marduk left the rampaging fire-god Erra in charge. The poem also reinterpreted the
flood as due not to the noise of mankind, but as the result of a previous absence of
Marduk.

The other prominent way of conceptualizing disorder involved the king. Replaced
by Marduk as the regulator of cosmic order, the king was no longer treated as divine.
Outside of royal inscriptions he was often seen as an explicitly problematic figure; his
actions were usually destructive of cosmic order. Historiographic texts could depict
the king as a danger to civilized life. For example, the so-called Weidner Chronicle
presented early Mesopotamian history as a series of royal transgressions against
Marduk and his city:

> By his exalted command, Marduk took away sovereignty from the horde of Gutium and
> gave it to Utuhegal. Utuhegal the "fisherman" laid his evil hand on Marduk's city,
> and his corpse was carried away by the river. Marduk gave sovereignty over all lands
> to Šulgi, the son of Ur-Nammu, and the latter did not carry out Marduk's rites perfectly;
> he profaned the purification rituals, and his sin ... Amar-Suena, his son, altered the
> great bulls and the (sheep) sacrifices of the New Year Festival of Marduk's temple.
> Goring by an ox was foretold for him, and he died from the "bite" of his shoe.
> (Al-Rawi 1990: 10)

A late first millennium text sets out in detail the supposed atrocities of an otherwise
obscure eighth century king, Nabu-šuma-iškun, against Babylon:

Year by year Nabu-šuma-iškun increased the killing, pillaging, murdering and forced labor upon them. In one day he burned alive 16 Kuthians in the Zababa Gate which is in Babylon. He carried off the sons of Babylon to Syria and Elam as gifts. He expelled the sons of Babylon, their wives, their sons, and their slaves and settled them in the countryside. The quarter of the sons of Babylon . . . he heaped into a mound and a ruin and turned it into royal property. (Cole 1994: 235–6)

At a cultic level, both regular rituals, such as the New Year festival, and irregular ones, such as the Substitute King ritual, emphasized the dangers to cosmic order posed by the king. Thus, the New Year Festival, the major state religious ceremony of the first millennium Mesopotamian calendar, culminated in the king's appearing stripped of his insignia of office before the statue of Marduk (Black 1981; Pongratz-Leisten 1999b). The king was seen as fit for renewed office not because of any positive qualities, but rather because he refrained from exhibiting negative ones, as he recited:

I did not sin, lord of the countries. I was not neglectful of your godship. I did not destroy Babylon; I did not command its overthrow. I did not . . . the temple of Esagil, I did not forget its rites. I did not rain blows on the cheek of a subordinate . . . I did not humiliate them. I watched out for Babylon; I did not smash its walls. (Sachs 1969: 334)

The Substitute King ritual was carried out in response to the most ominous of astronomical phenomena, a solar or lunar eclipse. This represented so extreme a sign of divine displeasure at royal misdeeds that only the king's death would assuage the divine anger. To avoid this fate, a substitute would take on the outward trappings of royalty for a few months before being ritually slain (Bottéro 1992b: 138–55; Parpola 1993c).

Characterizations of the king's divinity on Old Babylonian tablets implied a very different cosmic role from his non-divine first millennium counterpart. What correlations to this contrast can we see in contemporary political life?

The Social Experiences of Power

For any complex society the set of social concerns that find articulation in cultural products and the way that they do so are unpredictable. Most of our texts that directly illustrate royal relations with a king's subjects were the internal records of palace or temple administrative hierarchies. But civic institutions provided social experiences of political power that fit with the imaginative experiences identified above even though civic institutions were relatively less well documented (Van De Mieroop 1999b). I will first examine the ways in which the king intervened in the civic life of his subjects. I will then turn to the long-term sociological processes that illuminate the differences between the projections of royal intervention to a cosmic level found on Old Babylonian tablets and those on first millennium ones.

Royal intervention in civic life

Throughout Mesopotamian history the sources regularly highlighted the king's role as the head of extensive palace or temple administrative hierarchies. At the core of royal authority, however, was the king's representation of his community's sense of self. He provided one means of transcending internal jurisdictional and property divisions and mobilizing resources from the whole community. A king's intervention in the lives of his subjects was mainly of two kinds: judicial and fiscal. Judicially the king was the highest court of appeal. Fiscally the king had the right to exact contributions from the citizens, both in kind and in labor. At the same time, a number of those citizens expected such extractions to be canceled. This could be done either retrospectively, through the cancellation of arrears owed, or prospectively, through the grant of exemption from future exactions. In the case of prospective exemptions, the king could have been credited with either acting on his own volition or merely confirming divine will or immemorial custom.

There were significant differences in these civic experiences of royal power between the Old Babylonian period and the first millennium. Old Babylonian cities looked to their kings to cancel their obligations both retrospectively and prospectively. Thus, for retrospective exemptions we possess a number of references in Old Babylonian sources to the king's "establishing justice." From extant texts of the actual decrees, we can see that this action canceled private debts, debt bondage, and arrears of taxes owed to tax farmers. The costs of the tax cancellation were borne by the crown rather than the tax farmer (Charpin 1990). In prospective exemptions we have a number of royal claims to innovative exempting. The kings of Isin, for example, were especially careful of the feelings of the most prestigious cities in their realm. Thus the prologue to the Laws of Lipit-Ishtar boasted of reducing their forced labor burdens:

> At that time, I liberated the sons and daughters of the city of Nippur, the sons and daughters of the city of Ur, the sons and daughters of the city of Isin, the sons and daughters of the lands of Sumer and Akkad, who were subjugated by the yoke(?), and I restored order. (Roth 1997: 25)

In contrast, first millennium retrospective cancellations were rarely attested, while prospective ones were seen as confirmatory rather than innovative on the king's part. Already in the preceding Kassite period we hear of an institution called *kidenūtu*, meaning "protection," whereby cities claimed to be under divine protection and thus free from royal impositions. During the Neo-Assyrian period we know of Nippur, Sippar, Borsippa, and Babylon in the south and Assur and Harran in the north enjoying these privileges (Reviv 1988). The implications of *kidenūtu* were spelled out in the so-called Advice to a Prince:

> If (the king) called up the whole of Sippar, Nippur, and Babylon to impose forced labor on the peoples aforesaid, requiring of them service at the recruiter's cry, Marduk, sage of the gods, deliberative prince, will turn (the king's) land over to his foe so that the forces

of his land will do forced labor for his foe. Anu, Enlil, and Ea, the great gods who dwell in heaven and earth, have confirmed in their assembly the exemption of these (people from such obligations). (Foster 1993a: 761)

The citizens of Babylon, in a letter to their joint Assyrian suzerains Assurbanipal and his brother Šamaš-šum-ukin, loftily claimed that within the limits of their city even a dog shared in these privileges (Pfeiffer 1935: 55–6). Assyrian kings often pandered to the desire of Babylonian cities for tax exemptions, but seem to have garnered little credit for their efforts. Whatever a king's claims, it seems likely that the citizens saw him as simply confirming their traditional privileges. Moreover, these were privileges that were perceived as constantly threatened by a royal potential for intervention that provoked bitter resistance (Brinkman 1984: 22–3; Frame 1992: 35–6).

The term *kidenūtu* itself was not attested after the Neo-Assyrian period. Nevertheless, the basic issue of city autonomy seems to have persisted into later times. Tradition remembered the end of the short-lived Neo-Babylonian dynasty as due to the estrangement between its final king Nabonidus and the citizens of his own capital, conceptualized as royal transgressions against Marduk and his temple (Beaulieu 1989: 149–203; Kuhrt 1990). In contrast to both the Neo-Assyrian and Neo-Babylonian empires, the Achaemenid and Seleucid regimes were far more comfortable with a decentralized structure in which individual cities and regions could enjoy considerable autonomy (Kuhrt and Sherwin-White 1987).

The social relations in the Mesopotamian state

Old Babylonian civic leaders reacted positively, if nervously, to the king's intervention and acquiesced in the projection of it to the cosmic level, but the first millennium leaders evaluated similar interventions less positively. This was probably due to changes in society. Twin long-term developmental processes of territorial integration and elite differentiation provided the context for literate urban elites' increasing feelings of estrangement from royal government.

Before the Old Babylonian period political developments had seen an oscillation between independent city-states and hegemonies such as the Akkad and Ur III "empires." Under these latter regimes a number of Mesopotamian city-states were subsumed into larger polities. However, there was little in the way of direct rule. Authority was delegated to client princes who, whether local or central in origin, were always liable to rebel or defect. Each city-state retained enough sense of its political identity to reemerge when centralized control lapsed. In the early second millennium, after the fall of the Ur III dynasty, however, we begin to see the emergence of integrated regional states larger than the old city-states. This territorial integration was accompanied by elite differentiation. Thus, within southern Mesopotamia, both Rim-Sin of Larsa and Hammurabi of Babylon resisted leaving significant conquests in the hands of subordinate kings. Although Hammurabi's dynasty only controlled the whole of Babylonia for a short time, its decline saw the region split into two sub-regions rather than fragment back into city-states.

Also a number of Old Babylonian dynasties identified themselves in terms not so much of their capitals as with a specific ethnic group, the Amorites. This people had spread over much of the Near East by the early second millennium transcending the boundaries of the individual city-states (Kamp and Yoffee 1980).

Nevertheless, there seems to have been no deep structural division between king and elites. While Old Babylonian kings themselves may have cultivated an air of ethnic distinction from their urban subjects, they were happy enough to employ them in the administration of their realm. Moreover, by the late Old Babylonian period, if not earlier, the kings of Babylon had essentially "privatized" much of their administrative machinery through a form of tax farming (Charpin 1982; Yoffee 1977: 143–51).

Elite involvement in royal administration in the first millennium was rather different. After the Old Babylonian period the process of territorial consolidation had continued. Southern Mesopotamia came to be seen as a single land with Babylon as its natural center. Similarly, in northern Mesopotamia, the former city-state of Assur became the center of the territorial state of Assyria, "the land of Assur."

Particularly in the south, however, this consolidation was accompanied by a degree of social differentiation. Kings of Babylonia often claimed different ethnic status from their subjects as Kassites, Chaldeans, Assyrians, Persians, and finally Macedonians. In the later second millennium, both Assyrian and Kassite rulers periodically moved their capitals from traditional urban centers to new cities. Both Tukulti-Ninurta II of Assyria and Kurigalzu of Babylon founded new capital cities that they named after themselves. First millennium rulers tended to have their seats of government in established centers, although both Assur and Babylon were seldom actual centers of government in the first millennium. The Assyrian capital was moved to Kalhu under Assurnasirpal II (883–859 BCE). Sargon II (721–705) mimicked some of his second millennium predecessors and built the entirely new capital of Dur-Sharukin, "Fortress of Sargon." His son and successor Sennacherib (704–681) abandoned this new site and ruled from the old established city of Nineveh. In the south, Babylonia was effectively under Assyrian domination from the mid-eighth century to the late seventh. The situation was reversed and political power was restored to Babylon with the Neo-Babylonian empire. Not only was this period short-lived, it also included the bizarre episode of the last Neo-Babylonian king, Nabonidus, residing in the North Arabian oasis of Teima for a decade and allegedly ignoring the traditional capital. Subsequently, both Babylonia and Assyria were ruled by foreign dynasties, the Persian Achaemenids, and the Greco-Macedonian Seleucids from a variety of cities outside the traditional circle of Mesopotamian capitals: Susa in south western Iran, Seleucia-on-the-Tigris between Assyria and Babylonia, and Antioch in Syria.

The urban elite of the old established cities probably maintained some connections with royal administrations. But mainly they seem to have found expression for their sense of political identity in the priestly hierarchies of their cities' temples. Tellingly, the walls that protected Old Babylonian cities generally had names that glorified kings. By the first millennium, such names usually glorified gods (George 1996: 368–9).

Conclusions

As portrayed by Old Babylonian and first millennium copyists, divine and non-divine kingship represented contrasting ways of conceptualizing the king's role in the cosmos. Divine kingship implied the need for a king to fulfill a specific role. He had to be both the incarnation of the fertility god Dumuzi and the equal of the judicious sun god, while avoiding the violent excesses associated with the god Ninurta. Non-divine kingship implied that his subjects could not ultimately rely on the king to fulfill this latter condition. They would have to seek other, more reliable, cosmic champions, such as the god Marduk.

Neither of these two visions of kingship dominated either period to the exclusion of the other. However, between the two periods, literate urban elites gradually became estranged from royal administration. This sociological process suggests that each vision expressed something fundamental about the contrasting experience of kingship in the two eras.

FURTHER READING

For a survey of traditional kingships around the world, see Grottanelli et al. 1987. Modern scholarship on the sacred aspects of kingship is magisterially reviewed in Feeley-Harnik 1985. For a comparison of Mesopotamian and Egyptian civilizations, see Baines and Yoffee 1998. For Mesopotamian kingship in general, the only comprehensive monographs, Labat 1939 and Frankfort 1948, are interesting, but dated. More recent short surveys include Edzard 1972–5, Joannès 2001, Lambert 1998, Postgate 1995, Seux 1980–3.

Narrative histories (Kuhrt 1995 and Van De Mieroop 2004) and thematic surveys (Oppenheim 1977, Postgate 1992, and Van De Mieroop 1997a) provide much on the socio-political context of the institution. See also Michalowski 1987. For kingship's ideological context Jacobsen 1946 is idiosyncratic and dated, yet daring. Less ambitious, but more up to date, are Machinist 1976, Zaccagnini 1994, and Liverani 1995.

Much recent scholarship on early Mesopotamian kingship focuses on dichotomies of political versus religious power. See, for example, Heimpel 1992, Steinkeller 1993, 1999b, Selz 1998, along with the classic studies of Jacobsen 1943, 1957. For studies more congruent with the approach adopted in this chapter, compare Michalowski 1983, 1989b, Cooper 1993a, and Liverani 1993b.

Studies of first millennium kingship focus on the relationship of the king to the gods. For Neo-Assyrian kingship, see Liverani 1979 and the controversial studies of Parpola 1993a, 1995. For first millennium Babylonia see Kuhrt 1987 and Pongratz-Leisten 1997.

CHAPTER TWENTY-FIVE

How Religion Was Done

Gary Beckman

I understand "religion" here as the totality of beliefs and practices within a particular society that structure the relationship of men and women to the unseen but ever-present beings and powers with whom they share their world. These para-human elements might include deities, demons, the dead, and impersonal forces such as fate or cosmic harmony.

In regard to the Ancient Near East, the quantity and quality of source material available for the study of religion vary greatly across the different eras and cultures. For most of the third millennium BCE we have little beyond artistic representations of worship on seals (Winter 1986) and stelae, stone slabs, or pillars (Canby 2001), and records of disbursements for cultic purposes extracted from economic archives (Sallaberger 1993: 305–14). In addition, we can draw inferences concerning religious ceremonies from building inscriptions deposited in temples such as the cylinders of Gudea (Edzard 1997) and hymns composed for the gods on behalf of the rulers of the Ur III kingdom (Klein 1989).

In contrast, for the first millennium we can avail ourselves of voluminous instructions for the performance of the state cult in both Assyria (Van Driel 1969: 139–69; Menzel 1981; Pongratz-Leisten 1994) and Babylonia (Thureau-Dangin 1921; Beaulieu 2003b). Furthermore, we have numerous texts describing magical rites (Abusch and Van Der Toorn 1999). This is not to mention the extensive discussion of procedures and requirements for worship presented in the Hebrew Bible, particularly in the book of Leviticus (De Vaux 1961; Miller et al. 1987).

Second millennium sources currently known include a few rituals from the Mesopotamian world (Thureau-Dangin 1939; Westenholz 1994), many texts pertinent to the cult and pantheon of the Middle Euphrates region (Fleming 1992, 2000; Beckman 2002a, in press a), and the tablets discovered at the ancient Syrian port city of Ugarit (Del Olmo Lete 1999; Pardee 2002). But above all we may consult the extensive archives compiled by the Hittite scribes to assist the kings of Hatti, in what is now central Turkey, in fulfilling their obligations toward the gods. Since the topic of Hittite worship is so vast and the cult of Hatti is in many ways representative of that of the Ancient Near East in general, I will limit myself in this chapter to a sketch of how religion was realized in action among the Hittites.

Polytheism

Two points should be borne in mind when we approach the study of the beliefs and cult of any of the civilizations of early western Asia. First there is the difference between traditional polytheistic religious systems like those of Egypt, Mesopotamia, and Hatti, and the "revealed" monotheistic faiths of Judaism, Islam, and Christianity with which most of us are familiar. In contrast to these "religions of the book," which are based on an authoritative text or texts, traditional polytheisms possess no single legitimate (and legitimatizing) written statement of their beliefs, no "scripture." Therefore they are not centered on dogmas whose acceptance is obligatory for all members of the community. Under such conditions heresy is as impossible as orthodoxy.

This leads us directly to the second consideration: the absence of concern with belief brought with it indifference on the part of society to the spiritual life of the individual. In the cuneiform texts of the Ancient Near East we encounter no self-conscious reflections upon religious experience, no theological treatises, spiritual autobiographies, or private devotional materials. The ancients knew what they were about when they "did" religion and saw no need to write theoretical explanations for the benefit of those not already participating in the system. In particular, they did not engage in proselytizing, an activity that would necessarily have called for the composition of religious propaganda and catechisms.

Re-imagining Hittite Religion

Therefore we must reconstruct Hittite religion, for example, from the chance remains of cultic structures and sites, from iconographic representations of deities and worshippers, and above all from the practical documents generated in furtherance of the monarch's cultic responsibilities. To grasp the difficulties inherent in the task, we might imagine an attempt to form a picture of the theology and cultic practice of the contemporary Roman Catholic Church on the basis of the plan of a ruined cathedral, a few pages torn from a hymnal, receipts for the delivery of wine, and several medals depicting the Virgin or Saint Christopher (Oppenheim 1977: 173).

Our problem, then, is to re-imagine the religious conceptions in the service of which the Hittite scribes composed the records that have come down to us. Fortunately there are a great many of these, including regulations for the conduct of temple personnel (McMahon 1997), inventories of temple furnishings (Hazenbos 2003) and of their storerooms (Košak 1982), instructions for the performance of worship (McMahon 1995) and white magic (Ünal 1988; Frantz-Szabó 1995), prayers and vows to the gods (De Roos 1984; Singer 2002), and reports compiled by divinatory experts (Beal 2002). In addition, historical and literary compositions frequently describe the interaction of gods and men.

The Seamless Universe of the Hittites

These sources show clearly that the Hittites conceived of the universe they inhabited as a continuum, with no strict disjunction between the sphere of humans and that of the gods. Rather, the two groups of beings, although vastly different in power, were interdependent, and both ultimately drew their sustenance from the realm of plants and animals alongside of which they lived (Collins 2002). A third category of being was that of the defunct human being, or ancestral spirit. As elsewhere in the ancient world (Schmidt 1996), Hittite ghosts were owed remembrance and periodic gifts of food and drink from their descendants, and could make their continued presence in society manifest in a manner most unpleasant for the living should these obligations be neglected (Archi 1979).

That the gods too relied upon humans for support is clear from a complaint uttered by King Muršili II (1321–1295 BCE) at a time when an epidemic raged in Hatti:

> Listen to me, O gods, my lords. [Send away] the turmoil from my heart. [Let] the plague [be removed] from Hatti. Send [it] to the enemy lands … If you, the gods, my lords, [do not send] the plague [away] from Hatti, the bakers of offering bread and the libation bearers [will die]. And if they die off, [the offering bread] and the libation will be cut off for the gods, [my lords]. Then you will come to me, O gods, [my lords], and hold this to be a sin [on my part] (saying): "Why [don't you give] us offering bread and libations?" (Beckman 1997a: 159)

Here Muršili reminds the deities that it is in their self-interest to halt the plague, since without worship by humans, they themselves would literally go hungry. In return for the honor and support they supplied to the gods, men and women relied upon the divine masters to uphold their side of the bargain by assuring the fertility upon which everything depended. An excerpt from another royal prayer illustrates this expectation:

> To the king, queen, princes, and to [all] of Hatti give life, health, strength, long years, and joy (in) the future! And also give to them future thriving of grain, vines, fruit, cattle, sheep, goats, pigs, mules, asses – together with wild animals – and of human beings! (Singer 2002: 54–6)

Correspondingly, an angry or offended deity could punish an individual, or even all of Hatti, by inflicting such ills as disease like the plague just mentioned, sterility as in the myths of the "Vanishing God" type (Beckman 1997b), or military defeat (Beal 1995).

The Role of the King

Within the human–divine condominium the Hittite monarch occupied a pivotal position. Standing at the point of contact between the realm of men and the realm of the gods, the king both represented the Hittites before their pantheon and directed the activities of the people on behalf of their divine overlords. This function as linchpin of the universe accounts for the three most important roles played by the ruler of Hatti: commander-in-chief of the military, chief judge, and high priest of all the gods (Beckman 1995: 529–33). In the first two positions the monarch protected and controlled his human subordinates; in the last he saw to the fulfillment of his people's obligations toward their immortal superiors. Of course, it was necessary for the king to delegate most of these duties most of the time, but we must never forget that all worship of the state cult was carried out under the authority of the monarch.

The Pampered Life of the Gods

The attention paid to the Hittite gods and goddesses by the royal establishment was undoubtedly similar to that received by the king himself from his servants. The deity's temple was simply his house, as the palace of the ruler was his residence. Both divine and royal employees were subject to strict purity regulations and behavioral regimens (McMahon 1997; Güterbock and Van Den Hout 1991). Among their many chambers, temples and palaces alike included workshops for the production of luxury goods and culinary delicacies as well as magazines for their storage (Güterbock 1975). Kings and gods owned estates in the countryside, and it was largely the produce of these establishments that supported their lavish lifestyles (Klengel 1975).

Indeed, the needs and desires of Hittite deities were thought to be identical to those of high ranking men and women. One text asks, "Are the minds of man and gods somehow different? No! ... (Their) mind is exactly the same" (Ehelolf 1925: 4 i 21'–22'; McMahon 1997: 217). In each sanctuary, the god or goddess was pampered by the priesthood, the cult image was clothed in sumptuous garments, and the altar was piled high with fine food. Musicians and singers praised and serenaded the deity (De Martino 1995), while jesters and athletes entertained him or her with pratfalls and competitions of speed or strength (De Martino 1984; Carter 1988). The ceremonial of the royal court undoubtedly featured similar services and events.

The State Cult

Those activities performed regularly each day are only rarely described in the available texts, but we do know that the more important gods and goddesses of Hatti received daily bread and beverage offerings. Therefore temple employees were required to be at their posts "in the morning at the gods' breakfast." We are better informed about special ceremonies held for various deities, for unusual rites had to be prescribed carefully, lest they be performed incorrectly and thereby forfeit their effectiveness. Labeled with the Sumerian term meaning "festival, party," these acts of worship were carried out according to a regular schedule particular to each god or goddess. Some festivals were held monthly or yearly, while others, such as The Festival of the Sickle or The Festival of Cutting Grapes, took place in connection with events of the agricultural year (Güterbock 1970). A characteristic feature of ceremonies performed in the autumn was the filling of storage vessels, while the opening of these same pots marked the spring rites.

Because he was the high priest of every deity, the periodic presence of the king or a high ranking substitute, the queen, a prince of the immediate royal family, or even just a symbolic leather object (Güterbock 1989) was necessary at the celebration of the most important festivals of the leading deities in cities throughout Hatti. To accommodate this requirement, the festivals were organized into two series, known collectively as The Festival of the Crocus, in the spring (Güterbock 1960), and The Festival of Haste, in the autumn (Nakamura 2002). During the spring tour the monarch was on the road for no fewer than thirty-eight days, and sometimes officiated in one location in the morning and another in the afternoon.

Hittite festival texts make for dull reading, since they often present repetitive ceremonies in excruciating, if necessary, detail. For example:

> The king and queen, seated, toast the War-god. The *halliyari*-men [play] the large INANNA-instruments and sing. The crier cries out. The cup-bearer brings one snack-loaf from outside and gives [it] to the king. The king breaks [it] and takes a bite. The palace-functionaries take the napkins from the king and queen. The crouching (cup-bearer) enters. The king and queen, standing, toast the (deified) Day. The jester speaks; the crier cries out; the *kita*-man cries, "aha!" (Gonnet 1976)

Sacrifice

The focal point of the Hittite state cult was sacrifice (Beckman 2003), which may be defined as the rule-governed, ceremonial transfer of a foodstuff or other physical object from an individual or community of humans into the possession of a deity, demon, ghost, or personified numinous entity. The purpose behind this activity could be the continued sustenance of the para-human being in question or the securing of goodwill and thereby influence over his/her/its actions. Texts from the Hittite archives constitute the single largest body of material available for the study of sacrifice in the Ancient Near East. This corpus, however, is by no means homogeneous; in accordance with the multicultural nature of Hittite religion, sacrificial practice was not a rationalized system, but a continuously evolving composite of conceptions and procedures drawn from the Indo-European, Mesopotamian, Hurrian, and indigenous Hattic strata from which Hittite culture was constituted.

Those given offerings by the Hittites included innumerable gods and goddesses, the "Thousand Gods of Hatti," many known only from their appearance in sacrificial lists (Beckman 2004). Deities conceived anthropomorphically customarily received homage in the form of statues or upright stones. Offerings to deified mountains and springs and gifts to sacred objects and places, such as the throne and various locations in temples, including the four corners, pillars, wall(s), windows, and hearth (Beckman in press b), were generally presented directly to the recipient. Kings, queens, and princes attained the posthumous status of minor deity, as indicated by the employment of the euphemistic expression "to become a god" in reference to their deaths. Their ghosts might be allotted modest offerings in the course of their funerary rites and periodically afterwards (Kassian, Korolev, and Sidel'tsev 2002; Otten 1951). Demonic forces like "the Strangler," could also be appeased with appropriate gifts (Carruba 1966).

Participants and Locations of Sacrifice

The Hittite king was the usual offerant, or presenter of sacrifice, in ceremonies of the state cult, but culinary specialists commonly handled the actual slaughter and butchery of animals. The queen might assist the monarch with an offering, or even preside in her own right, and a prince could be delegated to represent the royal house. Religious professionals and palace personnel also performed offerings in the state cult. Responsibility for the poorly documented routine sacrifices in provincial temples and village shrines fell to local officials under the supervision of the provincial governor (Pecchioli Daddi 2003). Some texts speak of the attendance of a "great congregation" at festivals, but this group was almost certainly composed of notables and not of the populace at large, for the typical Hittite temple was not large enough to accommodate a crowd.

Offerings were most often performed in a place clearly differentiated from the profane sphere. Monumental buildings or parts thereof – temple, chapel, enclosed courtyard, and palace – were frequent locations for sacrifice in the state cult. In such a setting, the divine image, the altar, or an offering-table provided the focus of activity. Sometimes the texts specify the time of day at which an offering should be made; a rite might be prescribed for the predawn twilight, morning, midday, afternoon, evening, or nighttime.

Offering Materials

Foodstuffs were the most frequent offerings. These included raw products like honey, oil, and fruit; processed foods such as flour, ghee, and cheese; and a wide array of baked goods, some of special shape or decoration (Hoffner 1974). Potable liquids (wine, beer, and milk) were employed in the frequent libations. Hittite deities enjoyed a diet far richer than that of the ordinary peasant, as evidenced most strikingly in their prodigious consumption of meat, sometimes in astounding quantities (in one festival 1,000 sheep and 50 oxen). The usual sacrificial animals in Hatti were the same domestic livestock whose meat humans also ate most frequently, sheep, goats, and bovines. Wild animals, such as gazelle, stag, bear, boar, and leopard, were only seldom offered. Dogs, swine, and horses were killed only for special purposes, primarily to appease chthonic or underworld forces or the dead (Collins 1990).

Sacrificial victims were to be "pure," that is, healthy and unblemished. On occasion it was specified that a female animal be virgin, and sometimes the victim had to be of the same gender as the offerant. As a general rule, black animals were appropriate offerings for chthonic gods, white or light-colored ones for all other divinities. Although eagles and falcons already appeared infrequently in early rites, the sacrifice of fowl, usually through incineration, was introduced into Hatti rather late, as part of a Hurro-Luwian cult borrowed from southern Anatolia and Syria. Severe sanctions hung over temple workers who might be tempted to substitute their own inferior animals for prize specimens intended for a deity.

Non-food items, including silver, precious objects, parcels of land, and dependent persons, are mentioned in vows by which an individual promised gifts to the gods in return for divine favor, usually in the form of healing (Otten 1965). When delivered, these pledges presumably became part of the furnishings of temples or of the working capital of their associated economic establishments.

Sacrificial Practice

The bewildering variety of Hittite sacrifices can be reduced to five basic types: (1) attraction offerings, in which converging paths of fruit, sweets, and colored cloth intended to draw in the honored deities were laid out around the ritual site; (2) bloodless offerings consisting primarily of baked goods and libations of beer and wine; (3) animal sacrifice followed by a communal meal; (4) burnt offerings (restricted to ceremonies adopted from Syrian or southeastern Anatolian sources); and (5) "god drinking."

These ideal types do not reflect any native Hittite terminological distinctions. Only in the fourteenth and thirteenth centuries BCE was an elaborate vocabulary borrowed from the Hurrian and Luwian languages to designate varieties of offering. Some of these numerous terms refer to the procedure to be followed (for example, "burnt offering"), others the material employed ("blood"), the purpose of the rite ("purification"), or the problem to be addressed ("sin").

The general principle underlying Hittite offering technique was that the material presented had to be destroyed, in whole or in part, in order to pass over to the intended recipient in the para-human world. Thus liquids were poured out (on the ground, offering table, or altar), breads were broken or crumbled, vessels were smashed, and animals were killed. Bearing in mind that any particular rite might show considerable variation, and that the scribes frequently omitted mention of one or more features, we may summarize Hittite sacrificial procedure as follows (Kühne 1993): the priest or officiant, cultic implements, and the offering itself were ritually purified, after which the offerant washed his or her hands with water. Either of these acts might be intensified through the use of an aromatic substance. If the offering was small, it was handed to the offerant; if it was large, he or she placed a hand upon it, thereby establishing participation in the ceremony. The offering was effected (through breaking, scattering, and libation) either by the officiant or by the offerant personally. In conclusion, the offerant bowed or prostrated him- or herself before the deity.

Bloody Offerings

Animal sacrifice was somewhat more complicated; after the initial ritual cleansing, the victim, perhaps decorated with ribbons or objects of precious metal, was driven into the temple or sacrificial location and dedicated to the recipient. A "sample" of the animal – probably a lock of hair – was conveyed to the deity, after which the beast was led out once more. The victim was then killed and butchered or dismembered, usually at a location somewhat away from the immediate offering site. The animal's death might be accompanied by a joyous shout from the participants (Collins 1995b).

Then there followed the consumption of the slaughtered beast by the god(s) and worshippers (Collins 1995a). The gods preferred the fat and those organs thought to be the seat of life and the emotions – liver and heart above all, but also the gall bladder and kidneys. These entrails were roasted over the flame, chopped, and served to the recipient on bread. The remainder of the carcass was dismembered, cooked as a stew, and shared by the humans present. The skin or hide of the victim became the property of the offerant, the officiant, or the butcher. Nothing was wasted.

Certain rites of the later period attributed particular importance to the victim's blood (Beckman in press c). In these instances the throat of the animal was slit in the presence of the deity and the spurting blood directed from the neck arteries upward or downward toward the divine statue or symbol, or into a bowl or a pit. If purification was the purpose of the ceremony, the person or object to be cleansed might be smeared with the blood.

The later Hurro-Luwian burnt offerings were holocausts, offerings wholly consumed, after the performance of which little or nothing remained for the human participants. The victims – most often birds but sometimes also a sheep or goat – were incinerated in a portable brazier, optionally accompanied by condiments such as bread crumbs, honey, fruit, flour, or salt.

"Drinking a God"

A practice peculiar to the Hittites was "god-drinking," which was performed only by the king or by the royal couple, often serially for a long list of divinities. This act is expressed by a grammatical construction in which the divinity is the direct object ("The king drinks the god X"), which some scholars believe we must understand as denoting a mystical participation by the royal person(s) in the essence of the god or goddess (Güterbock 1998). Others interpret "god-drinking" as a shorthand expression for "drinking to the honor of" or "toasting" a deity (Melchert 1981). I lean toward the latter view.

Ritual and Popular Religion

In addition to the periodic rites of the state cult, other ceremonies, designated by the Sumerian term SISKUR ("ritual"), were executed along with their attendant offerings only as need arose. These occasions included the (re)construction of sacred buildings, the purification of a defeated army (Beal 1995), rites of passage such as birth (Beckman 1983), puberty, and death (Kassian, Korolev, and Sidel'tsev 2002), and personal crises like impotence, insomnia, or family strife. It is these rituals that provide us with a window onto the popular religion of Hatti, in contradistinction to the worship performed in the temples, locations where the common man or woman would but rarely have set foot.

Many of the ritual texts were not composed in the Hittite capital of Hattuša, but were rather collected by royal agents throughout the territories controlled by Hatti. The tablets recording them were then deposited in the central archives so that the information they contained might be available for immediate use should the ruler or a member of the royal court be confronted with a situation they were intended to counter. The diversity of the geographic origin of the ritual texts is apparent because many of them are attributed to a particular "author" from a particular locality, for instance: "Thus says Alli, the woman from Arzawa: If a person is bewitched, then I treat him/her as follows ..." (Jacob-Rost 1972). More than half of these authorities on magic were women (Beckman 1993), and we may confidently recognize the rituals as examples of "folk wisdom." The practitioners of these rites were not the priests and temple employees of the state cult, but were most often called "seer" if male, or "old woman" if female.

Magical ceremonies might take place in a special small building reserved for purifications, in an uncultivated place, or at some other location far removed from habitations and agricultural plots – for instance, on a rock outcropping, on a riverbank, at a spring or well, or simply "in the open air." Some rites directed toward chthonic deities required the digging of an artificial offering pit (Collins 2001).

Pollution and Analogic Magic

Although sacrifice was included in the program of rituals in order to appease the anger of deities or other powers, the central activity in magic was the removal of the impurity held to be responsible for the patient's suffering. This impurity, conceived of as a quasi-substance, might have been laid upon an individual by a hostile or offended god, sent to him or her by a human enemy through the practice of black magic, or even picked up through unwitting physical contact with ritual materials not properly destroyed. It was the task of the practitioner to render pollution harmless, and this was most often done by means of analogic magic, in which the ritual act was almost invariably accompanied by an incantation explicitly setting forth the analogy and its intended effect. For instance, as twigs are burned, an angry deity is addressed:

> (The god) Telipinu is wrathful. His soul and [his] figure were stifled (like) kindling. As they have burned this kindling, let the displeasure, wrath, (perceived) offense, and anger of Telipinu likewise burn. As [malt] is meager (in fertility), and one does not take it to the field to use as seed, nor does one make it into bread, [nor] does one place [it] in the storehouse, so let the displeasure, [wrath], (perceived) offense, and anger of Telipinu likewise become meager (in effect). (Beckman 1997d)

In another rite, the cleansing of a household from evils is accompanied by the following speech:

As a ram mounts an ewe and she becomes pregnant, so let this city and house become a ram, and let it mount the Dark Earth in the steppe! And let the Dark Earth become pregnant with the blood, impurity, and sin! (Otten 1961)

"Scapegoats"

Substitute or "scapegoat" rituals constitute a special class of ceremony. In these rites the moral or literal pollution of a patient was disposed of by transferring it through direct contact to a living carrier, such as a goat or even a human prisoner. The substitute is thereupon driven off into the wilderness or hostile territory, or else simply killed, taking the impurity with him to the underworld. The few attestations of human sacrifice found in Hittite texts are examples of this phenomenon rather than true offerings (Kümmel 1967: 150–68).

Communication

In order for the interdependent universe of the Hittites and their gods to function smoothly, it was necessary that communication be maintained between their two realms. As we have seen, the king addressed deities through prayers, and the latter made their wishes known to men and women by means of omens and oracles. Omens were messages sent directly by the gods to humans, through dreams or portents such as eclipses or violent storms. Of course, the import of a portentous event had to be elucidated by a religious expert, while the content of a dream was usually a clear command or promise to the sleeper by a god or goddess.

A more important line of communication was provided by oracles, that is, established procedures through which humans solicited information from the gods. Innumerable records of augury (observation of the flight of birds within a demarcated area), extispicy (examination of the entrails of butchered animals or birds), a kind of mechanical "lot" oracle, and several other divinatory techniques have been recovered at the Hittite capital. In a complex operation, these various techniques were employed by the Hittites as checks on one another. A short excerpt will convey the flavor of these reports:

> In regard to the fact that you, O deity of (the city of) Arušna, were ascertained to be angry with His Majesty, is this because the queen cursed (the court woman) Ammattalla before the deity of Arušna? Because Ammattalla began to concern herself with the deity, yet did not go back and forth (in service to the deity)? Because the son of Ammattalla has dressed himself in garments entrusted to his mother and was summoned to the palace? If you, O god, are angry about this, let the extispicy be unfavorable. [Here follows a description of features of the entrails. Result:] Unfavorable.
> If you, O god, are angry only about this, let the duck oracle be favorable. Unfavorable. (Beckman 1997c)

The text runs on for a total of more than 150 lines, in which the causes of the divine ill will and possible measures for its amelioration are thoroughly investigated.

Another prayer of Muršili II contains a plea to the gods to avail themselves of one of the means just mentioned in order to make known the cause of their evident displeasure:

> Or if people are dying for some other reason, let me see it in a dream, or let it be established through an oracle, or let a prophet speak it! Or in regard to whatever I communicate (as a possible cause of the epidemic) to all the priests, let them investigate it through incubation! (Beckman 1997a)

Conclusion

Patterns of worship throughout the Ancient Near East, temporally and spatially, were similar to the picture just drawn for Hatti: the state, in the person of the king or of his delegates, transmitted to the divine patrons of human society a symbolic portion of the goods produced, plundered, or otherwise acquired by that society. These deliveries took place every day, and were supplemented with additional gifts on special occasions and in time of trouble. Sacrifice was the core of Ancient Near Eastern religion, at least of that portion we can most readily recover. Hymns, prayers, lofty pronouncements on morality – however beautifully written and edifying to us today – were at best of secondary importance.

And as for the Hittites, the religious beliefs and practices of the common people of Mesopotamia, Syria, and Palestine are far more poorly understood at present than those of the state and the literate elite. To judge from the case of Hatti, the ordinary men and women of these regions too probably paid scant attention to the great deities of their land, and directed their worship primarily to their own ancestors and to secondary deities and forces whose rank within the cosmos was analogous to their own place within human society.

FURTHER READING

Furlani 1936 and Dussaud 1945 are early classic studies on Hittite religion. The standard work is Haas 1994, but this may prove too detailed for many readers. Good summaries in English include Güterbock 1950 and 1964, Gurney 1977, Hoffner 1987 and 1989, Popko 1995, and Beckman 2002b. For the various cultural strands that contributed to the religion of Hatti, see Klinger 1996 on the Hattic population, Trémouille 1999 on the Hurrians, and Hutter 2001 on the Luwians.

Bryce 1998 and 2002 provide accessible introductions to the Hittites and to their civilization, respectively, while Bottéro 2001 describes the religion of Sumer, Babylonia, and Assyria for a general audience.

PART V

Heritage of the Ancient Near East

CHAPTER TWENTY-SIX

The Invention of the Individual

Daniel C. Snell

Did people in the Ancient Near East have outlooks on life and most basically on themselves that differed radically from how we see things? The evidence is mixed and, since this is a philosophical question, it probably cannot be answered definitively to everyone's satisfaction. But it seems good to marshal the evidence for this argument as a caution to avoid too hasty an equation of past attitudes with our own.

Definitions

In biology the individual is rather hard to define because "no organism is at all stable – even the longest-continued adult stage is but a part of a changing life-cycle...The individual thus viewed ceases to be a static *being*; it is rather...a *history*." Instead of an absolute definition of individuality, there are degrees of it, and many animals and plants are so dependent on their group that they show less of it than others (Huxley 1943: 256).

Here we mean by individual someone who exists as a separate entity as contrasted to any group identity. We also mean someone who cannot be seen as composed of lesser parts, for example, of one's emotions viewed as independent things.

The nineteenth-century Swiss historian Jacob Burckhardt said the individual was a new creation in the Renaissance, and it is hard not to see the persons he studied as unusually egotistical. He described the Europe-trotting goldsmith Benvenuto Cellini who wrote an autobiography in the following terms: "He is a man who can do all and dares do all, and who carries his measure in himself" (Burckhardt 1954: 249). Cellini even wrote of his sexual peccadilloes; the group morality did not seem to matter to him, but the acclaim of art-lovers remained of interest. More recent scholars doubt that people really changed in the Renaissance; they draw attention to the continued importance of communal identity and argue that more self-conscious individualism may have come in the Enlightenment or even later, in the nineteenth century (Martin 2002: 219–20).

The Indologist Dumont in his study of the caste system sought to distinguish between two aspects of the individual as the West understands the term. The first is

"*The empirical agent, present in every society...*," that is, the person who is perceived as acting in the world and whom names and other devices clearly differentiate from others. The second is "The rational being and *normative subject* of institutions; this is peculiar to us, as is shown by the values of equality and liberty...only the individual in the full sense of the term must be taken as such, and another word should be used to designate the empirical aspect" (Dumont 1970: 9). He goes on to note that de Toqueville argued, "Individualism is of democratic origins, and it threatens to spread in the same ratio as the equality of condition...[democratic persons] owe nothing to any man; they expect nothing from any man; they acquire the habit of always considering themselves as standing alone,..." (Dumont 1970: 17–18 quoting *Democracy in America* volume 2 part 2 chapter 2). If Dumont is right, it is obvious that there is little chance that a modern democratic self-consciousness could exist in the ancient world. On the other hand, we will see that the question of whether people felt themselves to be even empirical agents has been questioned by scholars. So one of our questions must be whether there is evidence for persons perceiving themselves to be actors in society independent of their group identities.

Corporate Personality

Robinson argued in the 1930s that, though all societies have a tension between the society and the individual, "...in the ancient world they were much more closely and subtly blended than in the more self-conscious modern age..." (1964: 8). When individuals did arise in the Israelite prophets, they should not be seen as in opposition to group consciousness but in addition to it (9). The prophets' messages came to the whole people, "but they asked justice and mercy from the individual Israelite" as a way of getting these for the society as a whole. This ethic of solidarity came directly from "the old nomadic clan spirit, purified and enlightened, and raised to the level of a religious offering to God" (29).

Robinson saw the individual sometimes as an individual and sometimes as one standing for the group (12–15). Robinson looked for example at Psalm 44's transitions from first-person singular to first-person plural and back not as a textual problem but a psychological one; the writer really did see himself moving back and forth. Robinson wrote that the Hebrew Bible writers did not regard the individual as non-existent but were simply more conscious about being a member of the group (21). He examined instances where individuals were depicted primarily as group members. Among them are Joshua 7 where Achan, who pinched some of the spoils of Jericho, was stoned to death along with his family. Robinson also adduces 2 Samuel 21 where seven of Saul's innocent descendants were killed in revenge for his deeds.

Criticism of Robinson's position suggests Robinson's work was "based upon too literal a reading of the text" and missed synecdoche, taking a part for the whole (Johnson 1949:15, n. 2, 82–3 n. 5, 102). For example, Robinson argued that Psalm 44: 5-6's move from "we" to "I" shows that the "I" was actually dissolved in the "we," but critics would say this was a rhetorical device where the leader was identified with the followers. Still, Robinson's position was not an absolute one. He merely noted that clan identity was important and may help explain the variable identity of individual and group especially in some Biblical poems. Robinson saw the prophets as responsible for emphasizing individualism, but even their individualism he saw as much less than ours.

Composite Personality

In contrast to Robinson's emphasis on group identity, Snell argued that ancient persons saw themselves not as members of groups but as composites made up of outside emotions which radically changed their behavior. Snell derived his ideas from the habit of Homer of saying that emotion came upon a character (1960: 1–22). Now modern Classicists tend to view such expressions as modes of speech only, not indications of composite personalities. Jaynes, a psychologist, went further to argue not that emotions came from outside but that the brain had not developed its rational faculties, and persons listening only to their right brains actually heard gods talk and perceived other phenomena that the rational brain has tended to limit (1976).

The problem for both these conceptions is how the more modern mind or concept of the person happened to develop. Also these scholars do not address the rationality we see even in very ancient administrative texts, which would seem to undermine their views and to throw us back on explaining magical or miraculous events as either unique occurrences or as figures of speech (Nissen, Damerow, and Englund 1990: 49–50).

Individual or Corporate Punishment

We can trace an instance of the movement from group to individual responsibility in Mesopotamian culture in the story of the primordial Flood. That story is known at least from the Old Babylonian period around 1800 BCE, but it is set in a mythical earlier time. It appears in a Sumerian story and as part of the Atra-hasis composition and the Gilgamesh Epic, all from roughly the same period. Atra-hasis narrated that the god brought on the flood because of the collective human sins of being too loud; a god said, "The noise of mankind has become too intense for me, with their uproar I am deprived of sleep. Cut off supplies for the peoples, Let there be a scarcity of plant-life to satisfy their hunger" (Lambert, Millard, and Civil 1969: 72–3). The creator goddess Nintu, however, lamented her having gone along with the other gods to impose that punishment (94–5). It is unclear whether individual responsibility was asserted in the Sumerian story, but in the Akkadian Atra-hasis the god was advised to "impose your punishment on the wrongdoer (only)"(100–1). Also in the flood story in Gilgamesh there was an explicit declaration about this, and the god of wisdom advised the high god who had brought on the flood:

> How could you, irrationally, have brought on the flood?
> Punish the wrongdoer for his wrongdoing,
> Punish the transgressor for his transgression,
> But be lenient, lest he be cut off... (Foster 2001: 90 XI lines 186–90)

The high god did as the god of wisdom advised, and he rewarded the flood hero with long life and implicitly agreed not to inflict a world-destroying flood again.

First millennium BCE prayers and incantations sometimes asked gods to disregard the earlier communal sins:

> What is my guilt? . . .
> Dispel, drive off the guilt of my mother and father! (Foster 1993a: 554)

And similarly:

> . . . [lest] I offend,
> [On account of the heed]less deeds of my ancestors and kinfolk,
> who heedlessly neglected [the rites.] (Foster 1993a: 613)

These texts asked gods to free the individual from bad things, diseases or mental afflictions, and they make sense when the person perceived himself to be relatively blameless. If I did nothing wrong, it must be some collective responsibility that leads to my present misfortune.

Within the traditions of law in the Bible, one can see both an emphasis on collective responsibility as well as an emphasis on individual responsibility. The very mentioning of particular incidents that might be subject to court inquiry or to punishment appears to imply that the individual was seen by lawgivers as a separate person who ought to know better than to transgress the promulgated norms. The custom of blood guilt continued to be important when a murder had been committed; the murderer himself would be seen as responsible, but so also was his family, even when no malice or planning was present. The family might have to pay ransom for the life of an accidental murderer to avoid a further extension of a vendetta to other members of the family. These customs are compatible with periods when the state is non-existent or weak, and smaller units like the family had to regulate their members' behavior in ways that would not lead to ongoing bloodshed. If the community could not reestablish harmony, religious and economic cooperation would be difficult. The provisions for cities of refuge in Exodus 21: 13, Numbers 35: 9–15, Deuteronomy 4: 41–43, and 19: 1–13 gave a mechanism for avoiding such conflict over man-slaughter. Here the individual unintentionally committed murder, and lawgivers were trying to recognize the individual case and the actual innocence and protect the slayer from reprisal. The avenger of the blood who pursued him as in Numbers 35: 19 could be seen as a communal representative, but the manslayer was not.

Although the Ten Commandments are imperatives in the masculine singular in Hebrew, implying an individual responsibility to adhere to norms, one of the clauses giving a reason for behavior explicitly invoked corporate punishment. Exodus 20: 5 reads, "Do not bow down to [statues] and do not serve them for I am the Lord your God, a jealous god, visiting the sin of fathers on sons on thirds and fourths of my haters (6) doing kindness to thousands of those who love me and who keep my commands." The thirds and fourths apparently refer to generations. Corporate responsibility was the key assumption, but again the individual was the one who decided to do or not to do the initial evil action. The thousands refer to thousands of generations, so the blessing was also corporate. The dating of legal sections is difficult and controversial, but it seems possible that the Ten Commandments predated the rise of the Israelite state around 1000 BCE. They imply that one cannot rely on state mechanisms for the enforcement of norms, though in later legal material there is not much reference to state and police functions either. A linking of the idea that good deeds are rewarded and bad deeds punished and empirical observation leads to the conclusion that proper retribution does not always show up in an individual's life, so maybe it does in a group over a longer time (J. Assmann 2002: 164).

The issue of individual responsibility was posed acutely in the discussion of the prophet Ezekiel during the exile to Babylon after 593 BCE. Chapter 18 seems to be a unit to itself and rather unlike other statements of the prophet. The context is discussions among upper class persons who had been exiled to Babylonia by the Mesopotamian kings to subvert the tendency to rebellion in the kingdom of Judah. Questions were opened by this exile and the later ones, including especially the role of the land as a blessing from God in reward for doing what He wanted. But the prophet wished to underscore that new conditions obtained, and in those new conditions, corporate responsibility was abrogated.

The section starts with a quotation of a proverbial saying, which we also find in Jeremiah 31: 29: "The fathers have eaten sour grapes, and the children's teeth are set on edge." This saying could be seen merely as an argument for genetics over environment, but Ezekiel applied it, as did Jeremiah, to whether individuals were responsible and were to be punished for the sins of the fathers. The Lord in Ezekiel's view banned the proverb and declared, "Behold, all souls are mine; the soul of the father as well as the soul of the son is mine: the soul that sins shall die." The rest of the chapter spins out the implications of this declaration of individual responsibility while continuing to assert that reward and punishment, as in most of the rest of the Hebrew Bible, would be carried out in this world. A person who "does what is lawful and right . . . he is righteous, he shall surely live . . . " But if his son is bad, the son shall die. Ezekiel also reviewed the case of someone who was bad but turned away from evil; such a person would not die for the sins. Similarly when a good man turned from righteousness, he would die for his recent sins. So deathbed reform was very much encouraged, even though Ezekiel's critics carped at the injustice of this. They said, "The way of the Lord is not just," but the Lord countered, "Is it not your ways that are not just?"

Ezekiel was constructing an ethical system for people who might easily have felt that they could now act without regard to morality since they were already suffering the worst fate imaginable short of death, being landless in a foreign land. His emphasis on the individual, as on the continued relevance of the God of Israel even in exile, contributed to his pleas for right behavior and underscored the importance of the old norms, some of which he carefully listed in a negative confession, reminiscent of the Egyptian Book of the Dead (J. Assmann 1990: 150, chapter 125). Ezekiel 18:

6 reads, "... if he does not eat upon the mountains [= sacrifice to other gods] or lift up his eyes to the idols of the house of Israel, does not defile his neighbor's wife or approach a woman in her time of impurity, (7) does not oppress any one, but restores to the debtor his pledge, commits no robbery, gives his bread to the hungry and covers the naked with a garment, (8) does not lend at interest or take any increase, withholds his hand from iniquity, executes true justice between man and man, (9) walks in my statutes, and is careful to observe my ordinances – he is righteous, he shall surely live, says the Lord God."

Perhaps in simpler times the extended family and the tribe were the units that really counted, but when the religiously minded elite saw that the responsibility was simply too great to be extended to the third and fourth generation, and when such leaders wished to give their fellows hope, they concentrated more on the results of one's own actions.

Corporate references seem to diminish after the advent of the state, and David's reign may be the last one in which much attention is paid to tribal identity. But the tribe that had the least land though perhaps the strongest occupational identity, the Levites, did continue to be mentioned and to function as a source of identity long after late antiquity. The growth of state power after the Assyrian depopulation of Judah's countryside in 701 BCE may have diminished the power of clans and increased the emphasis on the individual (Halpern 1991). Later legal material used both the singular and the plural.

Justice and the Individual

The connection of the individual to right behavior is seen over the greatest sweep of time in Egypt. There it can be argued that the idea of justice, *ma'at*, is a very old one which Old Kingdom rulers believed was to be imposed by them upon their subjects. J. Assmann says that *ma'at* or justice is best seen as a term for traditional religion, which was only effective when the state and king were strong (1990: 18–19). This justice was not automatic but was willed both by king and community, and individual officials could thwart it, though all texts argue that they really should not.

In the New Kingdom, by 1250 BCE, however, a new idea of how the world worked appears to have become current. Though the term *ma'at* still was used, good things came to be seen not as the result of justice proceeding from a well-ordered state with a good ruler but rather as a special grace of the gods. The gods thus became more important and also more arbitrary; not everyone got the deserved rewards, it was now clear, even when the society as a whole was trying to pull together. The human being became less a cooperating part of a larger whole and had to pray individually for the extension of the grace of the gods. This may mean that persons thinking in those terms were more alone, less corporately oriented, less likely to obey old norms just because they were old. In the New Kingdom we know of remarkable scandals involving stealing from the dead and even assassinating the king, but that knowledge may be a function of the larger number of preserved texts we have than earlier (Assmann 1990: 252–60).

The policy of Akhenaton, the so-called heretic pharaoh in the middle of the New Kingdom, has been understood as showing that the king could exercise extensive individual freedom to change old norms, and he established the sun's disk as a different supreme god for all of Egypt. He tried to explain everything by the principle that the sun's light was the source of all power. While this may be physically true for people on earth, Akhenaton was a one-sided proto-fundamentalist and therefore was likely to fail (Hornung 1999: 125–6). His reforms did not last and in most particulars were decisively rejected in later generations, as rulers and the populace ostentatiously returned to the old ways. Akhenaton's excesses of individualism were condemned, and his monuments defaced. And yet something had been changed, at least in art, where there persisted more interest in realism and the depiction of movement (Freed 1999).

The long tradition of wisdom literature in Egypt and in Israel argues for a continuity in the way the individual was supposed to act, however justice might have been conceived. The earliest example, of Ptah-hotep, from after the Old Kingdom, addressed an individual heir to high office and suggested that especially the sin of greed ought to be avoided. The presumed reason is that greed undermined group solidarity and commitment to justice by the society as a whole. If one succumbed to the materialism of the age, one might have fun in the short run, but in the long run, one's own authority as an independent arbiter would be undermined. In later wisdom texts *ma'at* may not have played the same role, and one could always be disappointed by the actions of an arbitrary divinity. But one should behave in ways protective of the downtrodden and not behave in too haughty a manner; the norms appear not to have changed much, even in first millennium texts like the Instructions of Amenemope, part of which was translated into the Biblical Book of Proverbs. The assumption in Proverbs too was that rich young men had the power to make their own decisions, which really ought to conform to old and accepted norms. The language was mostly about individual persons, who were addressed by the second person masculine singular.

The Book of Job and the analogous Mesopotamian texts did not resort to the logic that the person was being punished because of something done wrong by his group or family. In those texts, all of which came from the mid-first millennium or later, it was never assumed that collective responsibility might explain current pain, but the moral responsibility of the individual was asserted. The gods might on occasion actually cause the individual to do evil, but the individual was still responsible for the evil and had to suffer for it (Moran 2002: 195–6).

Identity in Death

Another aspect of ancient expression that might shed light on concepts of the individual is burial inscriptions. In Egypt such inscriptions are very old. In the earliest periods it seems that only the king of Egypt could hope for an afterlife, but an individual bureaucrat might partake of that afterlife as a member of the king's court through royal favor and especially the right to be buried near the grave of the king one had served. Obviously the individual was proud of such distinction, but his eternal role relied entirely on the way he fit into the Egyptian corporate state.

Change took place in this aspect in the First Intermediate Period when the Old Kingdom's apparently permanent power was broken, perhaps because of agricultural failures and political dissolution. What this meant for the afterlife was first that the leaders of individual regions began to write inscriptions that praised their own care for their people; they also built tombs which rivaled those of the kings, if not in size at least in concept. Later wealthy persons bought less grandiose tombs which nonetheless used old texts to assure their continued existence in the West, where the dead lived on. To call this a democratization of death is an exaggeration since there was no indication that everyone could participate, but it is known that relatively humble persons in the New Kingdom could hope for tombs, especially if they were skilled artisans working on the kings' graves.

The themes of such texts are the accomplishments of the person and one's worthiness to be granted an afterlife. In the Middle Kingdom, bureaucrats referred to the motif of the weighing of hearts, where the goddess Justice would help the god of scribes see if the individual's heart, meaning not the emotional center but the moral center of the person, could be judged to be equal to justice. The balance was always shown in favor of the deceased, of course. It has been argued that this sense of sin and consequent forgiveness defines individuals (Wolf 1936: 19).

Among the striking personalities revealed in the epitaphs is the incomparable Ankhtifi, who ruled an upper Egyptian county in the First Intermediate Period, 2150–2000 BCE. On his tomb he wrote of his achievements in difficult times, guiding his local government when others would not take the responsibility:

> I found the Temple of Khuu [= the county of Edfu] inundated like marshland,
> abandoned by him who belonged to it, in the grip of a rebel,
> under the control of a wretch.
> I made a man embrace the slayer of his father, the slayer of his brother, so as to
> reestablish the Horus-Throne county. No power in whom there is a heat of
> [strife] will be accepted, now that all manner of evil, whose doing people
> hate, has been suppressed.
> I was the vanguard of men, the rearguard of men,
> one who finds counsel where needed.
> A leader of the land through active conduct,
> strong in speech, collected in thought,
> on the day the three counties were joined.
> I was the champion who has no peer,
> who spoke out when the nobles were silent,
> on the day fear was cast and Upper Egypt was silent . . .
> I was the vanguard of men, the rearguard of men,
> for my like has not been, will not be,
> my like was not born, will not be born.
> I have surpassed the deeds of my forebears, and my successors
> will not reach me in anything I have done for the next million years.
> (Lichtheim 1988: 25–6)

A million years is by any reckoning a very long time. This effluence of individual vanity may derive from the decay of the royal order of the Old Kingdom; people needed suddenly to exert themselves as individuals and to assert their own powers to avoid famine and military catastrophe (J. Assmann 2002: 94).

These and similar exertions, including inscriptions commissioned by women for their dead husbands, have been termed "an advance in the display of selfhood" (Lichtheim 1988: 37–8.) This advance was underlined recently when it was discovered that Ankhtifi's tomb was itself a pyramid, and so he was exercising the right to a royal burial though he was not himself king (Radford 2002). Ankhtifi's texts and earlier ones presented the Egyptian, at least the elite Egyptian with access to writing, as the creator of his own moral values (Lichtheim 1997: 18). This self-confidence in the face of adversity is also seen in much later Egyptian autobiographical texts (Otto 1954: 121, 124).

The female ruler of Egypt Hatshepsut (1473–1458 BCE) is another figure of distinction in that she was one of few women to rule Egypt and had herself depicted with a beard. But she was usually careful to adhere to the old norms even though, or perhaps because she was a woman (Seipel 1977; Robbins 1993: 45–52). Senenmut, one of her courtiers, however, was not afraid to bend clichés. He had himself depicted as protector of the princess Nefrure, combining a pose of himself as a seated scribe with that of a nursing woman (Waraksa 2002). Senenmut also claimed to be "a great one of the great ones in the whole land" and "a leader of the leaders at the summit of the officials." He seems to have had more power than any non-royal ever, though he did not hold the highest titles and was not a royal scribe. He also stressed his own low birth and consequent rise – an aspect he was apparently the first person in Egyptian history to emphasize (Meyer 1982: 188, 281, 287, 293).

In the latest periods of Ancient Egypt we even see that the individual might boast that he undermined the power of the reigning king with the guidance of the gods and turned instead to support the Persian conqueror: "When you [the god] turned your back on Egypt, you put love of me in the heart of Asia's ruler [the Persian king], His courtiers praised the god for me" (Lichtheim 1980: 42). Here the connection to the king of Egypt appears definitively broken.

By no means so numerous or so culturally important were the funerary inscriptions from Mesopotamia; none of them were really epitaphs summarizing a well-lived life. They appeared first perhaps as early as the 1800s or as late as the 1300s. A set of them implored auditors not to damage the tomb (Bottéro 1982). By the 1100s we find in the West Semitic languages several commemorative inscriptions of petty kings which recounted their deeds and sometimes asked their heirs to continue the homage paid them in life and curse any who might disturb their building works or their tombs. The most extensive memorial inscription like this came from northern Mesopotamia presumably near the grave of the mother of the last independent king of Mesopotamia, Nabonidus, who reigned from 555 to 539 BCE (Oppenheim 1969b: 560–2). The mother, Adad-guppi, boasted of her long and pious life and asked the god to punish her son if he should stray from right. The text runs:

> My eyesight was good (to the end of my life), my hearing excellent, my hands and feet were sound, my words well chosen, food and drink agreed with me, my health was fine,

and my mind happy. I saw my great-great-grandchildren, up to the fourth generation, in good health and (thus) had my fill of old age.

Let me entrust to you, Moon-god, my lord, my son Nabonidus, king of Babylon (since) you have looked upon me with favor and have given me (such) a long life; he should not sin against you as long as he lives. Assign to him the favorable protective spirits whom you have assigned to me and who have made me reach ripe old age. Do not forgive him his trespassing and sins against your great godhead, may he (always) be in awe of your great godhead. (Oppenheim 1969b: 561)

Clearly the son, or his scribes, remembered the mother as an amazing old battleaxe, an individual of unique experience and personality. From the Hittite area too we have a small collection of memorial inscriptions that appear to show that there was concern for the memory of the achievements of the individual (Bonatz 2000).

We conclude that the exceptional people who could afford inscriptions on or near tombs took pains in several periods to distinguish themselves from others. They were proud of their achievements and wanted them remembered, especially if they were not independent rulers of their countries.

The connection of the individual with sin and a close relationship even with the high gods can be traced in the self-conscious names catalogued by A. L. Oppenheim from Mesopotamian sources. The trajectory may be from a sunny self-assurance seen in earlier names like Šu-Sin "He of the Moon-God" to a more conflicted but perhaps more personal dependence on higher powers. Oppenheim found the names first in the Old Babylonian period from Iran on the periphery of Mesopotamia (2004–1595 BCE), but they then became common in the heartland in the Middle Babylonian period (1400s–1155 BCE). Oppenheim felt these names showed what he called an interiority that had not been there earlier, that people felt themselves to have problems that gods could and might solve. Among the names are Usuh-bilti-Marduk "O divine Marduk, remove my burden," Bēl-hīti-ul-īdi "Lord, I do not know my sin," and Nabû-itti-ēdi-ālik "Nabu walks with the alone one" (Oppenheim 1936). This last is particularly striking as testimony that people felt themselves to be in fact alone, although it might also refer to an only child. Personal names were given by parents, and they may say little about the ideas of the people bearing them, and yet these may show a slow transformation in the history of the Mesopotamian individual.

The Axial Age and the Invention of the Individual

At some point there was a new emphasis on the person in the Ancient Near East. Karl Jaspers, the German-American philosopher, proposed soon after World War II that there had been in the first millennium BCE between 800 and 200 an important change in the way some elites viewed themselves and their duties in the world, and this period was one in which, in many civilizations, human thought turned as on an axle in a new direction; he called it the Axial Age. He built on the perception, chronologically indisputable, that a number of seminal thinkers lived at roughly the same time and may have been responding to similar environmental changes or political crises, even though it seems very unlikely that there was direct communication among all their cultures. Jaspers strove for a broad view that did not entirely focus on European or proto-European developments (Jaspers 1968 German 1949).

A. Assmann has stressed the close connection of Jaspers' work to his own times and especially the trauma of Naziism. She sees his work as an incantation against such totalitarian state forms, and Jaspers sought to find "the human being as an autonomous individual" (A. Assmann 1989).

The most revolutionary of Jaspers' suggested thinkers was the Buddha, living in North India as early as 624 BCE or as late as 368 BCE, a young prince who rejected the glories of the world as unreal. He argued that the teaching of eternal rebirth, now ensconced in Hinduism, was wrong, and enlightenment and escape from rebirth was possible for everyone. Instead of seizing on the possibility of liberation for himself, he remained to teach humans the disciplines of liberation. Although Buddhism has since died out in India, it retains enormous influence in southeast Asia and has clearly affected the way millions think about their lives.

The most conservative was Confucius, 551–479 BCE, who refused to speculate about gods which had been earlier revered in China but asserted that the way for a person to become virtuous was to memorize the ancient poetry. One thereby learned filial piety, the only virtue that really counted, and humility which allowed one to serve others. Laotse, the founder of Taoism, living in the 300s BCE, argued that paradoxical folk wisdom could be used to guide one's life and the state.

Zoroaster in the Iranian highlands around 1000 BCE saw the world as a struggle between a good god and a bad god. The duty of the individual was to align oneself with the good god and struggle against the bad. Zoroaster was taking over some elements of earlier religious practice, but he saw his revelation as new.

The 600 years Jaspers selected had many formative thinkers and poets in the Greek-speaking world. The philosophers we call pre-Socratic, because they lived before Socrates, lived between about 600 and 400 BCE. They seem especially to fit the view that old orders were being criticized and new formulations tried.

In the Hebrew-speaking area this was the time of the prophets from whom we have writings from about 750 to about 300 BCE. Their political and religious situations varied, but perhaps their message may be summarized as the idea that individual Israelites ought to concentrate not on the traditional sacrificial cult but on their own ethical action, especially in regard to the poor as in Micah 6: 8.

All of these Axial Age thinkers were of central importance for their respective cultures, and they all argued for the exaltation of the individual. Jaspers defines what he thinks happened in this way: "Consciousness became once more conscious of itself, thinking became its own object." The "Mythical Age" came to an end, and "The Greek, Indian, and Chinese philosophers were unmythical in their decisive insights, as were the prophets in their ideas of God." Religion came to focus less on mythical stories and more on the demands of norms on persons, and consequently "Human beings dared to rely on themselves as individuals" (Jaspers 1968: 2). These statements appear to be reasonable for the Greeks with which Jaspers was most familiar and whom he and his discipline of philosophy saw as precursors. And Confucius was not interested in myth; Zoroaster, in contrast, created what appears to be a new myth of how the world works. It is true nonetheless that each tradition had new or renewed demands to make upon the individual for right action, with the possible exception of the Greek. There an individual philosopher might be trying to get to an idea of right action, but there were apparently no new norms that the philosophers were moving toward. In the Biblical material one might argue that the writing prophets had a new and more individualistic conception of how the person should behave, and, as we saw above, how the person would be judged.

Jaspers was not a historian. He said that he expounded an empirical fact, that these great figures all lived at roughly the same time, but he did not try to understand whether there was a single thread running through their work (A. Assmann 1989). Later historians have looked at aspects of the changes in the first millennium, but they have not tried to test the actuality of Jaspers' suggestion (Schwartz 1975; Eisenstadt 1986). Jaspers himself points out that others had seen the synchronisms of the Axial Age philosophers before him, but they had not seen the significance of the facts (1968: 8–9). He draws a stark distinction between pre-historical unselfconsciousness and historical consciousness, but later concludes that there is no evidence of any transformation since the advent of writing (248). Others have stressed that there is good evidence that people long before the Axial Age perceived the contrast between norm and reality that Jaspers found in the Axial Age thinkers (J. Assmann 1990: 72–3). It could be that the Axial Age thinkers ratified moves toward an emphasis on the individual that had been going on for a long time in their cultures.

Traditional and Confessional Religions

Many societies in the first millennium had traditional religious customs which are usually seen as group activities. An aspect of religion that became much more important in late antiquity is the very idea of belief, something a group might do but also something that unattached individuals might do. The Hebrew Bible does not seem to refer to people believing in something that others did not. There are stories of the conflict of cultures and religion, and in late texts the idea of conversion, of turning one's back on one's own traditional religion and accepting someone else's is present in the Book of Ruth and elsewhere, all in texts firmly from the first millennium BCE. But these converts may not have changed what they believed but rather what they did. At some point belief became important, perhaps for Judaism and its offshoot Christianity after the destruction of the Second Temple in CE 70, since that destruction closed the question of whether you should do most ritual actions but underscored what people thought about what you should do.

This turn from traditional religion to confessional religion seems important and self-evident, but there are many continuities between the two, especially in the two Near Eastern traditions that tended toward the simplicity of monotheism, Zoroastrianism and Judaism. And there is no very clear moment when one can assert that the religion of the individual had definitively overtaken the religion of the group; of course the groups persisted and gave contexts to the individuals. Perhaps only in the time of the Protestant Reformation did anyone imagine that religion was a matter only between an individual and God, though even there the church and its authority continued and continues to be important (Brown 1961: 210–11).

Summary

In the course of ancient history there does seem a trend away from corporate punishment toward individual punishment. This trend paralleled and may have derived from the growth of the power of the state. The emphasis on individuality in death showed no clear trend since there were early and late examples. Because Axial Age formulations have usually obliterated earlier religious manifestations, it is tempting to see in traditions flowing from that time sanction for more concern with individual expression. And yet any ethical system will inevitably ask the one to conform to the norms of the many.

Thus we are left with many hundreds of thousands of named individuals and a smaller number of identified groups in the ancient records who acted in many ways as we still do. Did the people of the past think of themselves as people composed of emotions, histories, and ideas, acting in a world which they could manipulate? Sometimes they did, and in general with ancient texts, one can assume that planned purposes were being fulfilled, rational ideas were being pursued, even in the worship of gods which seem to monotheists to be mostly imaginary. We moderns do not always understand what the purposes were as we cannot share religious practice or faith in exactly the way understood by ancients.

Individualism is a matter of degree, and the degrees of assertion of separateness may in fact be greater in our societies than in ancient ones. A modern observer writes, "Identity, like love, is a story, not an absolute" (Munthe 2003). And stories can change. Though humans in most societies are flexible in their self-definitions, now stressing how like their peers they are, now stressing their differences from others, the ancient range of flexibility appears to be similar to those in later periods where the individual has also been claimed to have been invented.

FURTHER READING

Very little has been directly written on this problem, but one should start with Lichtheim 1988 which presents most striking instances of individualism and the probing study J. Assmann 1990 and his general survey J. Assmann 1983. In the Mesopotamian area there is a lack of studies, and about Israel Robinson 1964 still has some adherents.

CHAPTER TWENTY-SEVEN

Ethnicity

Henri Limet

Ethnicity is difficult to define. If the definition is too short, it does not cover the reality in all its aspects. If you want to be more precise, the definition becomes too long. The concept of ethnicity also is not an easy one to grasp. Any approach to a definition is liable to criticism, and some historians would prefer to ignore the matter. The best thing is to suggest a kind of ideal type.

Let us try a simple definition. An ethnic group is a community of people speaking all one language, practicing the same religion, having an identical way of life, a common history and traditions, and living in a defined place with common institutions and customs. An essential requirement is that this community feel itself aware of being distinct from the other groups and that it also be identified as distinct by others. Gelb saw "nation" as a political term while ethnos was equivalent to "people." Gelb thought the main trait of a people is that it is a community of tradition, customs, religion, culture, language, and geographic position, but he lays stress on language as the prime factor constituting a people (1960: 259). Other historians think that language is not a deciding factor in defining an ethnic group, adducing the case of the Serbs and Croats, both speaking the same language, who come into conflict over religion. A clan or a tribe is a community that might be viewed as an ethnic group, but its members assume a perhaps imaginary blood relation and believe they are descended from a common ancestor (de Planhol, 1997: 15–16).

The Ethnic Players

Some ethnic groups can smoothly share the same territory with others. Such is the case before 2000 BCE for the Sumerians and Akkadians in southern Mesopotamia. The word Sumerians generally means people who spoke the Sumerian language while Akkadians are people who spoke a Semitic language. There was no racial distinction, and there is no evidence of supposed conflict between the groups.

In ancient Mesopotamia the most important division was the opposition between nomadic and sedentary peoples, and that between city dwellers and rural folk. On the other hand, the Mesopotamians did not feel required to respect endogamy, the practice of marrying only within the group. It is also not likely that they referred to racial or biological criteria. In Mesopotamia there is no racial opposition based on physical features: the stature of foreigners, the form of the face, of the eyes, of the nose, or the color of the skin are never described. Also it is not possible to find any solidly based archaeological criteria for identifying physical remains with particular ethnic groups (Cleziou 2000: 151–7).

The Semitic population we call Akkadian dated back to time immemorial and had not posed real problems for many centuries for the Sumerians. Perhaps the Semitic people founded the towns with the Sumerians, or arrived at nearly the same time. The Akkadians settled in the northern part of the country, and the Sumerians were the majority in the south (Heimpel 1974: 171–4).

In the course of time both the Sumerians and the Akkadians adopted the same religious beliefs and rites, the same traditions, and cuneiform writing, so that only with great difficulty can we distinguish how each of them contributed to the development of their culture. Can we say that one of these cultures prevailed against the other? This would mean that the first forced its way of life, its traditions, and even its religion on the second. There was not, I think, an assimilation but an integration of both of them.

Perhaps we should take into account a third ethnic group in the earliest periods that is supposed to be the substratum on which the civilization was developed. Some traces of it are to be observed, for example in the place names, and the words for most craftsmen, like s i m u g "smith," e n g a r "farmer," and a š g a b "leather worker," words which are clearly neither Sumerian nor Akkadian. There is a strong probability that a new ethnic group, the Sumero-Akkadian, was created by ethnogenesis, by superimposition, or by mixing, but how is unclear. Situations of this kind were not unusual in Mesopotamia; for example, the Hurrians who were present among Semitic peoples in northern Mesopotamia, and later, the deported people who were settled in Babylonia and Assyria all assimilated into their new environments.

In the first millennium, in contrast, the Babylonians were anxious to set themselves apart from the Chaldeans dwelling in the southern part of the country, even if both their languages belonged to the Semitic group, and this similarity was not a minor point. In the towns the different ethnic groups tolerated each other more easily than in the countryside.

Prejudices

Sumerian scholars, soldiers, and merchants knew that there were peoples whose way of life was different from their own, but they usually did not express value judgments about these people. They made distinctions between themselves and the others and occasionally were opposed to them. For instance, they felt contempt for the Amorites, a nomadic people living on the western plateau and constituting, along with Elam and Guti, a continuous threat of war. In one text the Guti were called "the fanged serpent of the mountain, who acted with violence against the gods." Later they were called "barbarous people" (Hallo 1957–71: 717a).

Justified or not, the image of the nomadic Amorites in the minds of the inhabitants of Southern Mesopotamia included the following:

1. They dwelled in tents in wind and rain, they did not know what a city or a house was, and they lived in the mountains;
2. They did not cultivate grain, but they dug mushrooms.
3. They ate uncooked meat; they behaved like wild beasts and wolves.
4. They did not bury the dead; they were invaders and plunderers. (Buccellati 1966: 330–1)

Of the Gutians it was said that they "know no inhibitions, with human instincts, but have canine intelligence and monkey's features" (Cooper 1983: lines 154–5). Monkeys perhaps came from the east and were considered evil. In the year name of King Ibbi-Sin's twenty-third year, one hears of "the monkeys coming from the mountains," though the interpretation is questionable.

This is the message the texts express, and these were the ideas usually held by society in those times. Texts show what the rulers and authorities wanted the people to think about the Amorites and the Gutians. Wars against the Amorite tribes were justified by such statements. These Amorites were depicted as a disruptive element in the region.

Amorites coming from the west were aware of belonging to an ethnic group, and they were identified in the documents with tribal names, Sutean, and Benjaminite. In the early centuries of the second millennium the kings of Larsa remembered their own nomadic roots among their titles, although they claimed themselves to be "kings of Sumer and Akkad." Zabaya, for example, claimed he was the sheik of the m a r t u "Amorites" or "westerners." Abi-sare was king of Ur and sheik (a word that elsewhere sometimes means "mayor") of the Martu. Kudur-Mabuk, whose own name seems Elamite like that of his father, was the father of Warad-Sin and of Rim-Sin, claiming also to be the "father of Emutbal," and "father of the land of Martu."

The Greeks showed the same attitude and reaction as the Sumerians did toward strange peoples. Thucydides in the late 400s BCE wrote, "The Aetolians [a backward people in west central Greece]…dwelt in unwalled villages which were widely scattered…they speak a dialect more unintelligible than any of their neighbors, and are believed to eat raw flesh" (1960: 206, III 94). The ancient Greeks had rejected nomadism; that is why Alexander and his successors who knew of it in the Near East reintroduced the institution of the city and founded so many towns. Dionysius of Halicarnassus wrote in the late first century BCE, "I would distinguish Greeks from barbarians, not by their name nor on the basis of their speech, but by their intelligence and their predilection for decent behavior, and particularly by their indulging in no inhuman treatment of one another" (14.6 1950: 267). It was, of course, his personal opinion as a Greek and a totally unjustified assumption, though it was the generally accepted view among the Greeks. He repeated the negative views of the Celts in France: they were like wild beasts in fighting, crazy, and very fond of wine; they ate and drank to excess, and therefore they were indolent (14.8 1950: 269).

Opinions of this kind are seen in the Sumerian and Akkadian vocabulary in the opposition of "his flesh" to "alien offspring" (Landsberger 1937 3 iii 23–7). An Akkadian proverb says, "Flesh is flesh, blood is blood, alien is alien, foreigner is indeed foreigner" (Lambert 1960: 271). The Sumerian word that means foreigner, depending on the context, may also mean "enemy."

City Patriotism versus Nomadism

The Sumerians conceived that a correct and well-organized way of life was possible only in a city, and thus happiness was only conceivable there. According to the myth about the organization of the world the god Enki entrusted to the people "who have no towns nor houses the job of breeding the herds" (Bottéro and Kramer 1989: 171, 348–9).

Nomadism was for the Sumerians horrible, especially since they were suffering from invading nomadic Amorite tribes and other uncontrollable peoples. These invaders lived wild and wandered in unknown places, but the delights of the Mesopotamian plain attracted nomads. As the Instructions of Šuruppak (Alster 1974: proverbs 183–4) put it, "Bread causes the mountaineers to come down; it brings traitors and foreigners along," and in another version (185) "Bread causes men to come down from the mountains," and elsewhere (198–9) "Your slave girl who has been brought from the mountains – she brings pleasure, but she also brings damage." The long-lasting tension between the nomads and the sedentary was later stressed in the second chapter of the *Muqaddimah* of Ibn Khaldun, the North African who settled in Cairo and died in 1406 of our era, who said that the bedouin way of life was to be contrasted with civilization or humanity, which was identical with living in a town (1967).

In the Early Dynastic period in the third millennium before the Akkadian Empire Sumerian cities were in constant hostile contact with each other, even resulting in war. But these wars were not caused by racial or ethnic feelings between nomadic and sedentary peoples (Limet 1994: 27–41).

The citizens of each city took pride in the antiquity of their town and in their temples built and restored through the centuries. The Sumerian city consisted of a main town, with its streets, squares, quarters, and some villages. The town was divided into districts, including residential quarters, industrial areas with workshops, and religious areas, as is obvious in the excavated ruins at Larsa (Huot and Bachelot 1989: 9b). Canals separated the parts of the town and thus divided it into adminis-trative districts, residential quarters, religious quarters, and a harbor (Stone 1995a: 240; Orthmann 1975: 42 figure 4). The town was protected by walls, towers, and gates. All around the cultivated plain stretched orchards of palm groves, swamps, canebrakes, and villages. Along the river or the canal, the town had a harbor, a quay which was also a marketplace. Between the cities, there was the steppe where the shepherds grazed their herds of sheep and goats and beyond the steppe a vast area of uncultivated fields. That was the world of a Sumerian, claiming to be the "son" of his city, and the city was itself considered to be his father or his mother.

The Sumerians and, like them, the Akkadians, accustomed to living in towns, had always mistrusted "the men of the steppe," meaning the plain, the open country between cities, as opposed to the *alum*, the "town," or the "city." In Assyrian times these nomadic peoples were the Aramaeans, Suteans, the Ahlamu, and already some Arab tribes, people living in tents. They could intrude into the towns and throw out the inhabitants. Among the nomads the social system was patriarchal. A foreigner was denoted as the man of the country he was coming from, as in "the man from Marhashi."

It remains to be seen whether the inhabitant of a Sumerian city was a "citizen" in the legal sense. In Athens and in Rome blood ties prevailed; a child became a citizen because his mother and his father were already citizens. Pericles had the Athenians pass a law in 451 BCE by which an Athenian citizen was not allowed to marry a foreign woman. Pericles was the victim of his own law when he wanted to marry Aspasia, who was from Asia Minor. The Hebrews also rejected marriage with foreign women as well as with illegitimate persons (Cassin 1987: 49). Distrust of foreigners was not exceptional. In Mesopotamia in a city or in a vast kingdom the citizen was a free man who was, however, also the subject of the king, using a word elsewhere meaning "slave."

From the end of the fourth millennium BCE there were public buildings in the city, temples, a royal palace, big houses for important persons including priests, scholars, and managers of the official services. Besides these buildings, the city was characterized by a wall and a territory.

One may wonder if a wall was effective in military operations to resist a siege, but it was a symbolic boundary line between outside and inside. The wall enabled the authorities to control foreigners as they came in or went out. Through the centuries of Mesopotamian history, it was the symbol of independence, and its destruction meant the loss of freedom. Victorious kings prided themselves on having destroyed the wall of the enemy town. By restoration of the wall a devastated city was supposed to have recovered its strength and freedom. Building a city wall was customary since the Uruk period. The influence of Sumerian culture was to be seen as far away as Habuba Kabira in Syria, where thirty-two towers and a gate were excavated.

In the Early Dynastic Period when the Sumerian cities were flourishing and independent, their boundaries were defended by surrounding ditches and embankments, and often by a stela, a carved stone slab. Jumping over the ditch or knocking down the stela was a cause for war. Sometimes a sanctuary stood on the embankment whose god protected the border and was there to strike religious fear into any invading army. The city was an enclosed world. Inside the city minority groups might be living; they were a kind of guest workers who were well integrated into the population; they did not threaten the citizens in any way, and the citizens did not, it seems, hate them.

Nomadic Culture

Besides just living in cities, a second criterion by which one could consider a people civilized was that they prepared their food and did not eat it raw. The meals of the

Sumero-Akkadians were cooked; the meat was roasted or boiled, and so were broth and soup; bread and cakes were baked in the oven. Beer, wine, honey, and cheese were not regarded as natural but produced; their preparation was equivalent to cooking. The gods were only given cooked meats, and sacrifices consisted of roasted pieces of beef or mutton. This was considered the civilized diet (Limet 1996: 259–61).

Mesopotamians imagined that the first steps of mankind were "primitive," and they believed that they had gotten beyond this stage of behavior. Long ago men fed on grass like the wild beasts because the gods had not yet given them cereals; they did not wear clothes; flax was unknown.

Some texts recall that in these ancient days there were no domesticated goats or sheep. Therefore there was no wool, no clothes, and no weaving loom. In these remote times men did not eat bread. They drank only water from pools. Enkidu in the Gilgamesh Epic was "constantly feeding on grass with his beasts" (Foster 2001: 14 ii 38). When the harlot led him to Uruk, she dressed him in a piece of her clothing. Enkidu washed his face, anointed himself, drank beer, and "ate bread until he was sated." In this way he became a civilized man. The poets who lost hope after the destruction of their cities complained that beer, wine, and honey were lacking; the oven in which meat was roasted was disused. They alluded to their enemies as "those who are unfamiliar with butter" or with milk and cream (Michalowski 1989a: 311, 335–6).

If some people, in particular the nomads, were deprived of farming and irrigation, that was the reason in the opinion of the Sumerians that the gods were not favorable to them. They were an object of fun and perhaps contempt.

In the way of treating the dead there was a fundamental difference between the sedentary people and the nomads. The dead were to be buried following the usual customs, called "putting into the soil," sometimes inside the house, but at other times in a vault. The dead were not cremated. The ghost of a dead one who had not been properly buried in a grave could appear to his relatives and harass them. A man who drowned in a river or in a well or who was killed or hanged, or a man who fell down from a date palm and died, or whose body was left in the desert, or one who died of hunger or thirst might become a ghost (Bottéro 1987: 342).

The worst humiliation a defeated king might expect was that the bones of his ancestors might be disturbed by a conqueror. A defeated adversary, going into exile, sometimes carried away the bones of one of his generals or the bones of his late parents (Cassin 1987: 248–54). Therefore sedentary peoples felt that it was abominable for nomads to leave the dead of the tribe anywhere the nomads chanced to be on their journeys. Nomads could not insure the continuity of the generations; the connections in a territory where families were living for a long time broke down. Respect for the dead was, for sedentary people, the symbol that they were permanently settled in a definite place.

City and Religion

City territory was considered sacred since the Sumerian believed it was the property of the city god, so that the main deity of Lagash was only called by the name "The Lord of Girsu," Girsu being the quarter where the religious buildings of the city stood. Living there was a happy privilege. The city itself was a sanctuary that went back to primeval time; it follows that even the wars between two cities in the Early Dynastic Period were understood as hostilities between deities; so Nin-Girsu came into conflict with Šara, the god of Umma, as described in the text about the frontier of Šara (Sollberger and Kupper 1971: 91–3).

If the city suffered misfortunes or was invaded, when the inhabitants ran away and religious and economic practices collapsed, it was supposed that the city god caused this situation. According to the conventional wisdom the city was then neglected by its deities. It happened to Akkad: Inanna left her city for unknown reasons and brought about its downfall. Also this is the view of the Lamentation on the destruction of Eridu (Green 1978: section 6). The poet regrets that all the gods were compelled to run away and each of them lamented when he left his city (Michalowski 1989a: 201). A later text says the Guti brought damage and calamity to the people of Mesopotamia, and the chronicler blames them for not being able to honor the gods and not conducting the rituals and sacrifices (Grayson 1975: no. 19).

In order to be characterized as a city, a town had to have the essences, in Sumerian called the m e, from its city god. The word m e refers to an idea close to an essence and cannot be accurately translated into a modern language. The m e is a notion that may be more philosophical than religious, and it is certainly complicated for rational minds. These m e were numerous since they concerned any aspect of social life, public and religious offices, crafts of all kinds, breeding and farming. They could not be destroyed or distorted; trouble with the m e could result from the presence of enemy invaders in the city or from the animosity of the gods. The city could lose its own position and endure many misfortunes. The inhabitants ran away, houses and buildings were wiped out, and religious and economic practices disappeared. But fortunately the m e could be brought back to the city by a king who gained the favor of the gods and drove away the enemies. Such a king could rebuild the city, especially the temples, and the population would return; the city might recover its freedom and prosperity. Ishme-Dagan, for example, is supposed to have rebuilt and restored the city of Uruk (Green 1984: paragraph 112).

Though the Sumerian cities showed a sense of identity, they were already in early times aware of being part of a vast group. Already in the Early Dynastic II/III period, some documents found in Fara, ancient Shuruppak, record lists of workers with their foremen who lived in Shuruppak but came from other cities including Kish, Uruk, Adab, Lagash, and Umma, but never for some reason from Ur or Eridu, the cities farthest south. It is specified in the tablets that these workers lived in Sumer (K e – e n – g i) (Steible and Yildiz 1993). All this goes to show that the land of Sumer was already in very ancient times an area conceived as a separate place.

The kings of Akkad, by raiding into the Sumerian cities and by destroying the walls and making their populations obey, weakened the idea of independence but, paradoxically, consolidated the sense of unity in the country. The religion slowly became unified. Enki, Nanna, Inanna, and other gods were made welcome in all the cities and formed a "pantheon" which Enlil, the god of Nippur, dominated. This pantheon had also welcomed deities such as Sin, Ishtar, and Šamaš, whose Semitic origin is unquestionable. That is why some gods had two names: the sun god was known as Sumerian Utu and Akkadian Šamaš.

When Utu-hegal succeeded in ejecting the Gutian army from Sumer, he announced that the independence of Sumer was restored: "the kingship came back into its hands." Under the reign of his successors, the Ur III kings, religious unity increased and in the same way political unity grew. These kings proclaimed themselves "kings of Ur" as well as "kings of Sumer and Akkad." They subdued the country of Sumer and some northern towns in Akkad. They appointed civil governors and a commanding military officer in each city. Their armies kept threatening and rebellious peoples at a distance in the east as well as the west.

The Ur kings established a very developed bureaucratic administration that is revealed by large numbers of documents, lists of people subject to forced labor, of craftsmen, and of animals; the texts reveal constant close watch over textile workshops and metal workers. We also see a good example of how unified Sumer worked, the system in which each major city had to supply in a monthly rotation animals to the central cattle-pen at Drehem for sacrificial purposes (Hallo 1960: 88).

Later, in the disturbances of the nineteenth century, in wars and sacks of the towns over which the poets lamented in elegies, we notice that the following cities belonged to the country of Sumer: Ur, Eridu, and Umma, and towards the north Nippur and Adab, and much further north Kish and Kazallu. In the collection of temple hymns poems were dedicated to the sanctuaries we think were situated in the traditional territory of Sumer. From the south to the north Eridu, Ur, Uruk, Kesh, Larsa, Lagash, Umma, Nippur, Adab, Isin, Kish, Sippar, and Akkad were commemorated. The kernel of this text is dated to the Sargonic period. This shows that the people were early aware of a Sumero-Akkadian ethnic group's territory, although hymn number 8, mentioning the king of Ur, Shulgi, is obviously an addition inserted later into the text (Sjöberg and Bergmann 1969).

Nationalism

Nationalism is a kind of ethnocentrism expressed in radical ethnic feelings that sometimes slip towards xenophobia and reject other peoples who are held to be of lower rank, edging toward racism. This phenomenon at origin is not old; it was created and developed since the nineteenth century CE with the Romantic Movement. It is more complex than ethnicity. The aim of nationalists is to gather into one nation-state all the parts of homogeneous ethnic groups or to separate their own group from one or some other groups in order to have full independence. At the origin of this secession, there is often a clash of interests.

This nationalism is based above all on common language and religion, so that some areas become unified under the leadership of one of them. So Germany unified under the king of Prussia, and Italy under the king of Piedmont. Besides this centripetal movement, there was, and there still is a possible centrifugal movement; the dismemberment of the Habsburg Empire provides a good example of this.

Nationalism is not a natural sentiment; it is nourished with myths, the so-called foundation myths, legendary stories and rewriting of historical events, making reference to glorious ancestors, for example in France Saint Louis exercising justice under an oak, Joan of Arc, or the anti-Roman Vercingetorix. The nation is now a legal notion, which is completely foreign to the concepts of ancient peoples.

It does not seem that the Mesopotamian people knew this kind of nationalist feeling and above all did not feel racial contempt for the Aramaeans, Hebrews, or others. However, in Babylonia and in Assyria, the ruling class and perhaps the people tried to create a coherent political entity and wanted self-government. The Babylonians had a feeling of superiority over the Assyrians in intellectual activities and made every effort to keep up their own customs and cultural traditions against the Assyrians. Assyrians, on the other hand, glorified their military power and were very proud of exercising their influence on the bordering countries, even in remote regions. It is beyond all doubt that the opposition between these two "nations" certainly resulted from the geopolitical contrast between the northern and the southern parts of Mesopotamia, that is, between Babylonia, an area of irrigated fields with palm groves and flourishing sea-trade through the Persian Gulf, and Assyria, a hilly land with rainfall farming interacting with nearby mountain peoples and Anatolia, modern Turkey.

Ethnicity and Language

The ancient Greeks, who did not themselves ever form a nation, called the foreign peoples "barbarian" because they did not speak Greek, but they spoke unintelligible and not very harmonious languages. Of course, Sumerians and Akkadians had observed that Elamites and Hebrews and other neighbors did not speak the same language as they did. Without xenophobic complexes they had organized services of interpreters to make the sojourn of such foreigners easier. King Šulgi claimed that he actually spoke these languages so well that he was able to correct the translations of his interpreters. He knew, he said, Amorite and Elamite, as well as Sumerian. According to a sentence in his Hymn B, he used and conversed in five languages, but it is difficult to guess which they were, perhaps Sumerian dialects (Civil 1985: 73). In regions where trade is highly developed and where all kinds of people mix, good acquaintance with many languages is usual. The knowledge of languages was often attributed to kings; the famous queen Zenobia obviously spoke Palmyrene, but she was said to know a little Latin since her sons had learned it, and she read Greek too. Cleopatra also knew many languages (Plutarch 1920: Anthony, 27, 196–7).

The usual ancient lack of discussion of linguistic problems can be explained: Sumerians and Akkadians were used to being bilingual and later, at the beginning of the second millennium and perhaps before, students and novice scribes had to study both languages (Sjöberg 1975: 142–3). There is no doubt that there had been changes in the linguistic practices in Mesopotamia; it would be interesting to consider when, why, and how they took place. We should point out that we have to distinguish speaking from writing. Akkadian was possibly spoken by a large part of the people from the Sargonic period on. Sumerian was alive and well and even spoken by scholars; administrative documents were written in Sumerian which still remained a literary and religious language. On the other hand, Akkadian spread more and more. Was it overwhelming? Likely not, but it took advantage of a Semitic population increase, whether it was natural or caused by new Semitic people coming into the country. We do not have an elite that imposed its language as a means of communication or a kind of colonization. On the contrary, educated people continued writing, and perhaps speaking, Sumerian.

We notice in an inscription of Hammurabi that there is an allusion to the fact that there were difficulties presented in speaking some languages used outside Babylonia. But we do not detect contempt here; it is only mentioned that these languages were confused (Gadd 1928: 146 iv 6).

Sumerians and Akkadians were probably familiar with Amorite and other Semitic languages spoken by many immigrants, and consequently they were not put off and had nothing against them, although the Amorite and Chaldean tribes were not very likeable and were not received favorably. Later, by a semantic development in the Persian period, the word meaning "tongue" or "language" came to refer to nationality. The expression "foreign language" has to be translated as "foreign people." In a prophecy, the expression "funny language" referred to a barbarian people that could take command of the city.

Another way of looking at the question is to consider the preeminence of Sumerian in intellectual life, in literature, religion, public office, and law, although there were Semitic peoples well attested in the documents over the entire history of Mesopotamia. Perhaps under the Ur III dynasty Sumerian was the official written business and governmental language, while Akkadian was confined to conversational speech. So scholars had a monopoly on all aspects of writing, and their knowledge of writing, reading, and counting granted them privileges. Even when power went over to the kings of Semitic origin as in the Sargonic and the Old Babylonian dynasties, historical inscriptions were still composed in Sumerian or sometimes with a parallel Akkadian version. In legal documents, ready-made Sumerian phrases were used. By such means Sumerian remained a factor of cultural unity. The language played an important part in maintaining the cohesion of the inhabitants of Babylonia.

Assyrian annals, literary compositions, and diplomatic correspondence used classical or standard Babylonian, a kind of common language. This does not necessarily imply hegemonical intentions, and Babylonian was actually threatened as a spoken language by Aramaic. We cannot know how and to what extent Aramaic spread in the Mesopotamian area. There is no doubt that it became one of the two official languages in the Assyrian empire and also in Babylonia. It constantly gained ground, particularly in the Persian period, but it seems that its spoken and written usage did not threaten Mesopotamian identity.

Art, Religion, and Ethnicity

In the first millennium BCE the Assyrians brought foreign craftsmen into Mesopotamia. Either out of curiosity or in search of the picturesque, the sculptors of bas-reliefs portrayed foreigners distinctly: Negro slaves were very recognizable and Palestinian women with their typical clothes. Later the Persians were concerned about giving accurate images of the prisoners and the bearers of offerings, with the assistance of Greek sculptors, for instance on the Persepolis reliefs. At that time Aramaic became the official language of the empire, and it is well known that the Persian kings tolerated several religions.

In the field of religious beliefs, the god Marduk's exaltation that began at the time of the first dynasty of Babylon reached its peak when the Creation Epic was composed, probably toward the end of the second millennium. This epic was intended to glorify the god Marduk who, following his victorious fight against chaos, obtained the primacy over the other gods and became the national god of Babylon. The Babylonian kings, who wanted to rule over Lower Mesopotamia in its entirety, did not neglect the ancient gods of Sumer, Enlil, Utu, and Inanna. We may conjecture that this pantheon, structured and organized into a hierarchy, is at the root of a form of religious nationalism.

In contrast to Babylonia, from the beginning of the second millennium the Assyrians invoked the god Assur in their historical inscriptions. He was also a national god, but the Assyrians nevertheless kept praying to the old gods, Adad and Šamaš, and they revered the Sumerian god Enlil and above all the war goddess Ishtar. The building and restoring of the temples in honor of these deities did not stop.

Roles of Foreigners

Nationalism often grows from lack of understanding, irritation, and contempt, but not necessarily from hostile feelings toward other ethnic groups. In the edict of king Ammisaduqa (1646–1626 BCE), paragraph 6 about debts specifically mentioned "an Amorite or an Akkadian." In paragraphs 20–1 he included the citizens of Numhia and Emutbal, areas east of the Tigris River, among those who should be released from debts and get their freedom. The king's measures applied to all, regardless of place of origin or ethnicity. Only the slaves were not to benefit from these measures (Kraus 1958).

We have seen that the Sumerians had hard words for invading neighbors; they were affected by them and did not understand their habits or their customs. On the other hand in the Ur III period they appointed some foreigners to the civil service and the army, if we may judge by their foreign names. Dahish-atal, who was of Hurrian origin, was an important official (Sigrist 1992: 31); many Hurrian slave women were working as weavers, and many Amorites were policemen.

Ishbi-Erra, who was a native of Mari in Syria and contributed to the decline of the Ur dynasty, first offered his services to the Sumerian kings and was at the head of their troops. Ibbi-Sin, the rightful king, complained that the god Enlil had this Ishbi-Erra raised to the rank of a "shepherd of Sumer," though he was not a Sumerian by birth (Falkenstein 1950: 59). Many centuries later the Assyrians used very much more unpleasant words about foreigners. The otherwise unknown king Puzur-Sin, who destroyed the palace of his grandfather Šamši-Adad, was called "a foreign plague and not of the flesh of the city of Assur" (Grayson 1987: 1: 78, number 1, 24–5, 112–13). In reaction against Assyrian domination, Nebuchadnezzar of Babylon asserted that he himself was an "excellent offspring of Babylon" (Frame 1995: 22, no. 7, 3); he was of royal descent and a "creation" of Babylon. In a chronicle the Assyrians showed a dislike of Sumer and Akkad whose "treachery is to be announced to the entire world" (Grayson 1975: no. 21). In a document written in Babylonian (Glassner 1993: 235, 51), the Babylonian writer related the disastrous reign of a king named Nabu-šuma-uškun (760–748 BCE) whose wrong actions are enumerated, rightly or wrongly; he was a Chaldean and was suspected of having sided with the Elamites and other enemies of Babylon.

We know that Jerusalem and Tyre put up a fierce resistance against Nebuchadnezzar, who finally besieged them and took them and then deported a part of their population. The Jews also felt attached to their country, but their religion made them quite different; Yahweh was also a national god.

Assyria and Babylonia as National Ideas

Given that modern nationalist feelings were absent from the Ancient Near East, we may ask the question of how foreshadowings of nationalism arose in ancient Mesopotamia and of what the sources and conditions of nationalism were. First, a well-defined territory with a homogenous population was needed, but in this case a population more vast than that of a small city. Agreements defining territorial boundaries are known in all historical periods, for instance around 1300 BCE between the Assyrian Adad-Nirari and the Babylonian Nazi-Maruttash and between the Assyrian Adad-nirari II and the Babylonian Šamaš-mudammiq in 900 BCE.

In addition to an abstractly defined boundary, this line could be made plain on the ground by stelae, stones, and ditches. Nebuchadnezzar built a great wall north of the city of Sippar, the "wall of the Medes" that Xenophon still saw at the time of the Greek expedition of the 10,000 in about 400 BCE (Xenophon 1998: 181 II iv 12). Nebuchadnezzar also built a second wall, farther south between the Tigris and Euphrates. The fortifications remind us of the wall called "pushing away the Amorites" constructed by Šu-Sin, the king of the Ur III dynasty, and also the wall of his predecessor Šulgi. So there was a long history of wall-building to keep invaders out, but the walls may not always have been seen as national boundaries.

The name of the Babylonian territory, after Kassite domination, again became "the land of Akkad" as it was in more ancient times. The sovereigns who previously appeared in the chronicles as "kings of Karduniash" again used the title of "kings of Babylonia." So the chronicles stated that a man "sat on the throne of Babylon" in such and such a year. "The people of Sumer and Akkad" were again mentioned. The connection is obvious with the glorious and splendid city of long ago, and the name of Akkad was in current usage in the Neo-Babylonian chronicles (Grayson 1975), although we now do not know where exactly that great city was.

Similarly, the scholars of those times tried to revive the past traditions and to suggest models of good kings that were more or less mythical. Šulgi and

Ur-Nammu had claimed they belonged to an old and good lineage, that of Lugal-banda and Nin-sun, so that they were brothers of the legendary Gilgamesh (Glassner 1993: 121). Sargon I (1921–1881 BCE) of Assyria took the name of the great king Sargon of Akkad (2334–2279 BCE), and so later did Sargon II (721–705 BCE). We notice that the Assyrian kings were keen on tracing their ancestry. They recalled the names of their ancestors who constructed and restored a temple or a wall. The important thing was to show that the town went back to the earliest antiquity and that the king was connected to a famous dynasty, the members of which had distinguished themselves in defeating enemies or in building city walls and temples. Mesopotamian theologians were insistent upon the antiquity of cities and their temples which were always constructed and restored in the same place. Remembering such historical facts is a foreshadowing of a form of nationalism.

Babylonians against Assyrians

Generally speaking, the grounds on which the Babylonians threw off the yoke of Assyria were geopolitical; the countries were different in regard to economy, language, religion, and customs, and, to a great extent, different in their relations with the bordering peoples. As a rule this is not a matter of xenophobically despising others. The main thing is the desire to maintain the cohesion of the country and the population, eager for autonomy and for freedom of action.

Several elements furthered the integration of the various ethnic groups living in Babylonia and probably in Assyria:

1. Urban life tended over time to destroy the unity of an ethnic group,
2. people dwelling in separate areas could avoid quarrels that went back to their countries of origin,
3. common religious practices, the use of Sumerian in canonical texts, and national gods could create a sense of unity, and
4. continuous and peaceful arrival of foreigners, men and women deported from defeated countries, made the most important distinction how long one had been in town, not where one came from.

For political and economic reasons Assyrians and Babylonians did not agree on several points and this often turned to war, but despite this hostility, there are few traces of nationalism to be found in the texts. Babylonians were true to the traditions and took a great deal of pride in the monuments of the past and in the ancient inscriptions of glorious kings. They restored and built temples. They dared to resist the Assyrian military expeditions for centuries, repelled the Elamites, and contained the Chaldean tribes.They even built a short-lived empire for themselves. Reverence for ancient times, for religious beliefs and cultural traditions of the past are, as noted above, an important element of nationalism, but their leading political figures did not make plans for the future or have a political program; in other words, a political ideology that is characteristic of a national movement in the nineteenth and twentieth centuries CE was absent from Babylonia.

Ethnicity Under the Persians and Later

In Persian times Babylonia and Assyria became provinces of a great empire. During the Hellenistic era, the Greek city system was reintroduced and that is why a kind of regionally based nationalism could not arise. A cosmopolitan population dwelled in the new or recovering towns. Greek colonists, nomads, deported Jews, and later Roman soldiers came from all regions. Following the Arab conquest, the patchwork of languages mostly disappeared. In the Ottoman period the Turkish civil authorities categorized the non-Muslim minority groups, the orthodox Greeks, oriental Christians, and Jews, according to their religions and not according to their language, their origin, or their "race." But some languages are still used for rituals, Aramaic for instance; the case of Hebrew is exceptional. Religious and linguistic communities that survived were often living either in mountainous regions like the Maronites in the mountains of Lebanon or the Alawites on the mountainous coast of Syria and in not very hospitable regions, or in special quarters of towns, as formerly the Jews, the Armenians, and the Christians in Aleppo and Damascus (de Planhol 1997).

In the early 1900s in the Near East artificial countries were created by peace treaties after World War I, Lebanon, Syria, Palestine, Jordan, and Iraq. Their names are neither very old nor did they originally refer to national boundaries: Lebanon is a mountain, Iraq refers only to the southern part of the former Ottoman province of the country, Jordan is the name of a river, and the etymology and ancient extent of Syria are questionable (Lewis 1990). The Near East thus is divided on the European pattern. Each land is awfully centralized, but are they real "nations"? One may well wonder if the people are more aware of national feelings or still of ethnic, tribal and religious ones.

Further Reading

Limet 1972 is a good introduction, but readers of English will prefer Kamp and Yoffee 1980. For Egypt see Baines 1996a: 360–84. Grosby 2002 offers a new interpretation.

CHAPTER TWENTY-EIGHT

Public versus Private
in the Ancient Near East

Steven J. Garfinkle

The study of the Ancient Near East is often viewed as a study of origins. Mesopotamia, the heartland of the Ancient Near East, was home to the first literate societies and provides one of the richest collections of sources for the study of the ancient world. The communities of Mesopotamia, which utilized the cuneiform writing system, produced tens of thousands of clay tablets on which are inscribed the records of three millennia of households, both great and small. Within this tremendous corpus of texts we find evidence for the development of complex and dynamic socio-economic systems, and we can begin to discern the appearance of complex ideas such as the public and the private. Therefore, our main focus in this chapter will be on events in Mesopotamia.

Ordinarily, a strict reliance on definitions has a limiting effect on historical studies. In this case, however, we must establish what we mean by public and private in our own times before we can address what these terms might mean for the Ancient Near East. In our society we assign to the word private the general meaning of that which is withdrawn from public life or public scrutiny. Public, as the opposite of private, means that which pertains to an entire people or society, and in particular to its government. In practice, these terms are often used in discussions of economic questions where the private sector is defined as that part of the economy that is free from direct state control, and the public sector is that part under direct state control.

This chapter is concerned with addressing two questions. Are the terms public and private applicable to the Ancient Near East? And if so, do they coexist in patterns analogous to those of the modern world? The question of the applicability of these terms involves an exploration of whether we can accurately investigate ancient society on the basis of modern ideas and definitions. In order to answer these questions, we will first examine the theoretical issues implied in the title of this chapter and explore avenues for approaching the economy of the Ancient Near East. Following this theoretical discussion, we will apply our findings in a brief chronological survey of developments in Mesopotamia.

Why Is a Discussion of the Ancient Economy Significant?

At the outset we must establish why the question of public versus private in the Ancient Near East is important to us. Our study of the distant past is often a search for our own origins, or at least for the origins of certain aspects of our society. It has become ever clearer that the roots of many of the most prominent institutions and activities of today, with writing and urban society among the best examples, lie in the Ancient Near East. This raises the question of whether we can trace the development of certain ideas from the ancient world to our own. This inquiry, though, may introduce evolutionary or teleological notions that can distort our study of antiquity. The fact that familiar institutions existed in the ancient world does not mean there is a direct genealogical connection between our society and theirs. In particular, the belief that there is a logical pattern of social development that is discernible in history, for example in the movement from a public to a private economy, can substantially prejudice our approach to the ancient world.

In the Ancient Near East we observe the development of public institutions, such as the temple and palace, that have a tremendous impact on the growth of society. We also see the appearance of various forms of ownership that allow property to be held by individuals separately from a group or community. These developments also have an impact on the creation of identity. The appearance of public institutions helps to foster a larger cultural identity that can be shared over great distances, in both space and time. At the same time, the creation of individual property, that is, the discrete ownership of goods that can be sold and inherited, also creates different levels of identity. Obviously, these ideas of public and private are the antecedents of related beliefs in our own world.

And yet, this realization of our connection with the Ancient Near East has perhaps led us to be too quick in asserting parallels between our experiences and those of the ancients. This is a particular danger in the area of economic history where we are inclined to describe activity in familiar terms, and then to ascribe the modern definitions of the terms to the ancient activity. This is more than just a problem of terminology. We cannot escape our own language and vocabulary, but we must be especially cognizant of the impact of language on our discussions of the ancient economy.

Modern versus Ancient

When we speak of public and private, we usually mean something analogous to the public and private sectors of our own society. In our own society, individuals are generally employed in one or the other of these sectors. This does not mean that our public employees do not have private lives and private property, but that their roles as public officials must be kept separate from their private lives. We believe individuals should not play a role in both of these sectors simultaneously. We do not object to a retired general taking up a post with a defense contractor, but we would be rightly suspicious of an active general who was also the vice president of a munitions manufacturer. In contrast, the Ancient Near East was characterized by situations in which individuals filled multiple roles at the same time, and these roles involved what we regard as both public and private functions.

Another difficulty that we encounter is one of scale. In the ancient world the size of the resources in the hands of public institutions appears to dwarf the resources available to individuals. Frequently, this was the result of ideologies that placed the temples or palaces at the center of land tenure systems much different from our own. Nonetheless, there is strong evidence for individual entrepreneurial activity throughout the history of the Ancient Near East.

In the Ancient Near East, the temples and palaces regularly assigned land to individuals or families in exchange for services, most often military service or corvée, or forced, labor. Today, we would consider such services to have a public nature. At the same time, the fact that these properties and obligations could often be sold or inherited poses a problem for our strict categorizations. Additionally, we must be skeptical about making a determination solely on the basis of the ultimate ownership of the land in an environment where land was frequently available, but seed grain, plow teams, and harvesting labor were often scarce (Van Driel 1998: 37–8; Powell 1999: 19).

The desire to apply modern economic understandings to the world of the Ancient Near East is also undermined by many of our own assumptions about ancient society. A hallmark of modern classical economic theory since the end of the eighteenth century CE is the supposition that the private sector is more efficient than the public. In contrast, the study of the Ancient Near East has been characterized by the belief that the public sector is in many ways more efficient. For example, the massive irrigation projects of southern Mesopotamia are assumed to have been impossible without public organization and maintenance.

The ancient economy was an overwhelmingly agrarian economy in a way that is alien to the modern Western world. The inhabitants of the Ancient Near East were employed almost exclusively in agricultural pursuits. Certainly there were craftsmen and entrepreneurs whose work was not agrarian in nature, but they were the exceptions. Indeed, much of the administrative apparatus of ancient society was set up to maintain and record the agricultural production of society. The predominance of agriculture means that the study of the ancient economy requires different patterns of analysis from those used for the modern economy.

What is necessary for the interpretation of the economy of the Ancient Near East is a model that recognizes the alien nature of the ancient economy, and especially the structural differences between the ancient and modern economies, while allowing for the appearance of familiar ideas, such as private ownership. It has become obvious that the ancient entrepreneur operated in an economic system that was not governed by the same mechanisms as the modern economy (Polanyi, Arensberg, and Pearson 1957). At the same time, the entrepreneur of the Ancient Near East was interested in acquiring ever greater wealth, and as a result he sought opportunities to maximize his gain, and to do so on behalf of his own household.

The attempt to describe the society of the Ancient Near East in a way that does not project modern meanings onto ancient practices can begin with the identification of the fundamental economic structures of that society. The most significant of these structures was the household. The household was the chief organizational unit of the ancient economy. Households varied in scale between the individual household of a small family up to the household of one of the chief gods of the pantheon (a temple) or the household of the king (the palace). The ordinary urban household consisted of the immediate family, perhaps some additional dependent relations, and less frequently, a handful of slaves. It was usually a patriarchal household and the head of the family controlled all of the household's material wealth. The family remained a significant locus for economic activity and organization throughout the history of the Ancient Near East, but not in opposition to the state or public sector. Indeed, the families frequently co-opted the structure of the central authority for their own advantage.

Locating Private and Public in the Ancient Near East

Below we will examine the terminology of private versus public, but first we must look at the manner in which we can deduce evidence for public and private in the surviving records. Frequently, the private or public nature of a text is determined based upon the provenance of the tablet. If a tablet is found in a palace, temple, or large administrative complex, we assume that it was a public document. A text found in a residential area is assumed to belong to a private archive. There are numerous difficulties with this method of classification. For example, according to our traditional division of texts into public and private, modern tax returns would certainly be seen as public documents, even though they record transactions that are primarily private in nature. Human history is full of instances when private documents, such as wills, sale documents, and letters, were stored in ostensibly public locations, such as temples, town halls, and government records offices.

Moreover, the people of the Ancient Near East often made no clear distinction between an official's private and public roles. We must stress that any confusion in this regard is our own and probably did not exist among the ancient administrators (Van Driel 1994: 192; Zettler 1991: 261; Michalowski 1991: 46). Observers of the Ancient Near East have been prone to cite this as evidence of the overwhelming public control of the economy. Instead, we must see this as evidence for an absence of the kind of tension between public and private roles that is characteristic of our own world.

Our desire to differentiate public and private in antiquity raises two further problems about our source material. The first difficulty arises because much of the primary documentary evidence has either not survived or has not been unearthed, and this makes quantitative analysis of the Mesopotamian economy extraordinarily difficult. Moreover, the urban bias of the cuneiform record must be reckoned with in any study of Mesopotamia. The majority of the inhabitants of the Ancient Near East, the unnamed individuals who did much of the work for the large institutions about which we are so well informed, are hidden from our view.

The second difficulty stems from the fact that the historian of the Ancient Near East is dealing with societies that were literate in ways that are alien to our society. The conventions surrounding the use of writing and the preservation of texts in antiquity were different from those that operate in modern society. Therefore, we are occasionally just as surprised by the inclusion of some material in the written record as we are puzzled by the absence of so much other documentation. It is precisely the missing tablets, which most likely never existed, that often prevent us from making a qualitative analysis of the Mesopotamian economy. Therefore, we are dealing not only with an ancient and unfamiliar society, but also one that will always remain somewhat inaccessible.

Much of the economic activity that took place in the Ancient Near East may have been undocumented, and further, we have no way of knowing how much of the documented material has survived. Most often we only have one part of the textual equation, as the records may have been recovered or survived from only one area of an ancient city. For example, the Ur III period (2112–2004 BCE) is one of the best documented eras in antiquity, and yet the records that survive are almost exclusively those of the central and provincial administrations. For the succeeding Old Babylonian period, the situation is largely reversed. We only have extensive archival records from both the institutional and non-institutional economies in the second half of the first millennium BCE during the Neo-Babylonian period.

Institutional versus Non-Institutional

At this point we can safely begin to question the value of the terms public and private for our analysis of the Ancient Near East. In developing a critique of this terminology we must also propose a vocabulary to use in its stead. Our survey below will demonstrate that large institutions made an early and forceful appearance in the society of the Ancient Near East. The institutional economy was created by the formation of organizations that superseded, in both size and wealth, the family or village structure of the first agricultural communities. The early institutions served as collection points for resources and as focal points of urban communities. The temples of early Mesopotamia were the clearest examples of these institutions, and we must recognize the extent to which the temples functioned as economic centers (Van De Mieroop 1997a: 24). The institutions were great households, and as their estates expanded, so did their influence. At the same time, the smaller individual households did not disappear, and the heads of these households sought to leverage their positions through participation in institutional hierarchies. Therefore, we will be better served to speak of the institutional versus non-institutional, rather than the public versus private.

In many respects the dichotomy of public versus private is also too simplistic for the Ancient Near East. From the earliest records we have evidence for the significant influence of the temples, the palace, and the family or independent households. Grouping the palaces and the temples together under the rubric of public does not adequately explain their roles in the economy, or in society in general, and together they do not constitute a public sector, as we would define it today. At certain times and places the temples may have fallen under the direct control of the crown, but this was not true at all times and places in the Ancient Near East. Our goal must be to avoid applying terminology to the whole of the historical and geographic entity under consideration that is only accurate for limited parts of that whole.

The large institutional estates dominated the economy of ancient Mesopotamia, but the efficient operation of the economy by the central administration was dependent on the existence of individual entrepreneurs. Such, for example, is the conclusion drawn by Richardson about the royal household of the late Old Babylonian kings and its interactions in the traditional urban environments of Babylonia (2003). The survival of such individual enterprise in the face of the rise of the centralized state in the Ancient Near East is proof of the importance of the individual households. Most of the public officials in antiquity were in a position to take advantage of their status to enrich their own households, and this was probably expected of them. What is striking about this portrait of the economy is that it illustrates the inadequacies of our descriptive categories. The state administrators of the Ancient Near East acted in a manner that was neither private nor public, and which could not be separated from the relationships they maintained with the various households, individual, familial, or institutional, of which they were members.

The states of the Ancient Near East were characterized by patrimonial administration, in which access to institutional accounts was dependent on state connections, but membership in households that had access to such accounts was not determined by the state. Here we should note the continuing importance of familial relationships in the organization of numerous professional groups throughout the early history of the Ancient Near East, and the continued prominence of family firms in the later periods. By patrimonial, we are referring to an organizing, or managing, principle first described by Max Weber, the German sociologist. His ideas have subsequently been applied to Mesopotamia by Michalowski (1991), Zettler (1991), and Schloen (2001). In a patrimonial system, the household of the ruler is regarded as the chief household of the state, but its actions are governed by tradition and a set of existing obligations to subordinate households. Patrimonial administration stands in opposition to bureaucratic administration and is characterized by the importance of personal relationships. One reservation we have in applying the terminology of patrimonial administration to the whole of the Ancient Near East is the way in which the etymology of the term patrimonial presumes that men ruled households. There is strong evidence that women engaged in independent economic activity, and that wives could act as heads of households in the absence of their husbands (Owen 1980).

Patrimonial administration is precisely what we see in the Ancient Near East as evidenced by the operation of households at every level of the economy. Inherently, this is a system of patronage in which what we call public business took place in non-institutional households, and private business took place within the precincts of the great institutions, but in patterns that are not analogous to our own experiences. The interlocking households of the Ancient Near Eastern economy were also arranged hierarchically such that many households were subordinate to others, or subsumed within them.

We are not suggesting that private property in terms of discrete ownership of the means of production by non-institutional households did not exist. Indeed, there was more widespread access to the means of production than has usually been attributed to the Ancient Near East. We are making two proposals. First, the Mesopotamians organized their economic behavior on the basis of the household. Second, a reliance on private versus public ignores the ability of individuals to pursue an advantage for several households simultaneously, and to do so in a manner that institutionalized the kind of conflicts of interest that our system will not tolerate. This means that the individual households, which we might regard as private, and the institutional households, which we might view as public, did not always exist in competition with each other.

A Brief History of the Institutional and Non-Institutional in the Ancient Near East

This survey is organized chronologically, but it does not follow the traditional periodization of Ancient Near Eastern history. The way in which the history of the Ancient Near East has traditionally been divided along political, and particularly dynastic lines, frequently obscures our view of ancient society. The reason for this is that societal change is often assumed to accompany political change. This has been especially true when the political change is also seen as a reflection of a change in the ethnic composition of the ruling elite. Such thinking rarely does justice to the complexity of ancient systems, and it tends to support the notion that ancient economies were highly centralized. One of the characteristics of the economy of the Ancient Near East that will become clear is the long-term significance of regional and local economic power structures.

The chronological scheme that will be employed here is based on the development of integrated political and economic communities of increasing size. This process is a characteristic of the history of the Ancient Near East; however, we must use great caution in the conclusions that we draw from this "fact." First, the absence of integrated political and economic units of great size in the early periods of Mesopotamian history does not mean that the relatively small communities were culturally distinct. Mesopotamia experienced a remarkable degree of cultural homogeneity throughout its history (Yoffee 1988). Second, there is a great tendency to regard the development of the larger states as a natural evolution towards increasingly complex societies. This leads to the corollary assumption that the economy became correspondingly complex. The presumption that economic systems evolve and that such progress leads to growing economic efficiency are assumptions common to modern economic analyses that may have limited value for the ancient world.

Before history

The development of institutional households in the Ancient Near East took place prior to the dawn of the historical era. The beginning of history has traditionally been defined by the presence of the written records on which our histories are based. The earliest appearance of writing took place in the Ancient Near East, and specifically in southern Mesopotamia during the second half of the fourth millennium BCE. A detailed picture of the relationship among the various households only emerges with the advent of writing, since that is when we have the first direct historical evidence for economic transactions that can be assessed on the basis of institutional or non-institutional access to the means of production. We must recognize, however, that transactions involving the institutional and non-institutional sectors of the economy predate our written sources by a considerable length of time.

The origins of the large institutional households in the Ancient Near East lie in prehistory, and they likely emerged during the several millennia prior to writing during which the urban centers of Mesopotamia were forming. There is significant archaeological evidence for the long development of the great households. We need only look to the excavations of the cities of Uruk and Eridu. These excavations have documented long successions of monumental sacred architecture in the hearts of the cities in the fifth and fourth millennia BCE. The scale and wealth of the temples make it clear that much of the resources of these early cities were organized for institutional benefit. Therefore, the development of distinct institutional and non-institutional households took place in "deep prehistory" (Van Driel 2000: 5).

Viewed from a European standpoint, the basis of private property is the ownership of particular and measurable plots of land. In southern Mesopotamia the ownership of individual or small plots of land was rendered impractical by the environment (Liverani 1997; Steinkeller 1999a). Once historical records appear, we can also see that the institutions dominated the ownership of arable land even in other areas of the Ancient Near East where individual families could more easily farm subsistence plots.

Mesopotamia itself was divided between the heavily irrigated south and the dry-farming north, with the margins of these two areas characterized by the steppe, which was home to pastoralists. Already in prehistory, the diversity led to different patterns of economic interaction among both institutional and non-institutional households. For example, in southern Mesopotamia, where the irrigation system required extensive centralized maintenance and control, the temples were involved much more directly in the management of farming.

From villages to cities (3200–2350 BCE)

The development of cities had begun already in the late fifth millennium BCE in southern Mesopotamia, but urban life started to characterize the Mesopotamian experience from the end of the fourth millennium. The written sources are scarce for the beginning of this period, but the archaeological evidence demonstrates that the years between 3200 and 2350 witnessed an explosion in both the number of cities in Mesopotamia as well as in the percentage of the population that likely lived in the cities (Adams 1981: 138). It was at this time, especially in the south, that Mesopotamia began to be dominated by a network of competing city-states, many of which were quite close to each other. The city-states in Mesopotamia were defined by their urban space, enclosed by city walls, and surrounded by the network of fields, canals, and villages that provided the subsistence of the population. The dominant feature of the urban landscape was the main temple that rose in the middle of the city and was dedicated to the city god.

The rise of the city and its institutions also fueled the apparent growth of a communal spirit and identity within the urban communities during the late fourth and early third millennia BCE. The city seals from southern Mesopotamia, which survived from the earliest historical periods bearing the symbols of the various cities, show that the cities acted as distinct socio-political entities, and the use of the seals demonstrates that the cities could also act in concert (Matthews 1993; Steinkeller 2002a). The temples and their gods were standard bearers for their cities and formed the institutional basis for identification that operated in the cities of southern Mesopotamia.

Until recently, our understanding of the development of the political economy in early Mesopotamia was based upon an evolutionary model, and this is still the case in many of the textbook treatments of the Ancient Near East. According to this model, pre-Sargonic Mesopotamia (before 2350 BCE) was characterized by the "Temple-city," the Old Akkadian (Sargonic) and Ur III periods (2350–2000 BCE) witnessed the development of the "statist" economy, and finally, the Old Babylonian period (2000–1595 BCE) saw the rise of the private sector in cooperation with the palace (Falkenstein 1974: 6; Renger 1979: 249–50; Renger 1994: 170–3). This last phase was viewed by many as the inevitable result of a change in the ethnic composition of the political and economic elite from Sumerians to Semitic Amorites.

The "temple-state" theory maintains that all of the arable land in southern Mesopotamia was in the hands of the temples for much of the third millennium BCE. The temples themselves were seen as households of the gods in which the senior temple administrators were perceived as acting on behalf of the gods. The whole of the city and its surroundings were seen as the actual domain of the gods. According to Falkenstein's restatement of the theory, over time the crown instituted secular control over the temple estates, and this trend culminated at the end of the third millennium BCE in the Ur III state (Falkenstein 1974). Numerous studies, however, have shown that the theory rested largely on a limited body of evidence drawn from the archive of one household in the city of Lagash, and that the temples' control of resources was not complete (Gelb 1971; Maekawa 1973–4; Foster 1981).

In spite of the waning of the "temple-state" theory and the repudiation of the idea that ethnicity and culture were inseparable, the evolutionary model for the development of the ancient Mesopotamian economy still exercises a great influence. In part the attractiveness of this model rests on the appeal of modern economic theories regarding economic evolution and efficiency. However, the situation in the Ancient Near East was never so monolithic. There is little proof that the temples of the early period in Mesopotamia existed in the absence of political authority, and our data suggest that the authority of the king grew throughout the third millennium BCE. Moreover, there is evidence in all periods of the presence of non-institutional households.

The expansion of trade and military contacts in the latter part of the Early Dynastic period (about 2600 BCE) has been ascribed to the development of a native, and increasingly secular, elite in southern Mesopotamia (Van De Mieroop 2002: 132). This elite was closely tied to the growing visibility of the royal household. The rise of a political elite, and the accompanying secular institutional households, whether royal or in some cases gubernatorial, was significant for several reasons. First, we must recognize that just as the canal and irrigation network in southern Mesopotamia required some stable central authority for its management, so too were the temples dependent upon the maintenance of political order. This became increasingly important as the size of the state grew, because the temples were always largely local institutions (Van Driel 2000: 6). Second, these secular institutional households competed to some extent with the existing religious institutions, with the royal household eventually establishing itself at the top of a hierarchical arrangement of institutional households. Finally, the crown and its estates fostered the creation of new institutional hierarchies, such as those in the military. In turn, the prominent individuals who served the royal authority also headed their own non-institutional households. Just as the lines were blurred between the official and unofficial roles of individuals within the society of the Ancient Near East, so too were there indistinct borders between the crown and the households of its dependents. A good example of this would be the estates granted to members of the royal family. It is not clear whether these should be considered institutional or non-institutional households.

The invention of writing in the second half of the fourth millennium BCE, and the increase in our written sources throughout this period, highlights the expansion of the institutional economy. Writing developed in order to keep track of the large institutional economy in the growing cities of southern Mesopotamia. The earliest texts are not clearly understood, but they point to the institutional control of vast economic resources (Nissen, Damerow, and Englund 1993). One of the initial concerns with all forms of record-keeping, and particularly with early writing, was the desire to distinguish ownership. This implies that ownership could be defined and that society was anxious to do so. However, a need to make clear distinctions regarding ownership does not imply tension between the institutional and the non-institutional, but simply tension between different owners.

From cities to territorial states (2350–1600 BCE)

The most significant factor in the development of territorial states (which we might also term regional communities) was the increase in the size of the state, and this expresses itself in an increase in the scale of both the institutional and non-institutional economies. There has been a frequent assumption that the increase in the size of the state leads to an increase in the dominance of the institutional sector. As we have seen, with the development of religious and secular authorities there was a transfer of tremendous economic power to these authorities. This transfer was largely complete at the time of the development of the city-state, and certainly by the end of the fourth millennium BCE. Institutional control of resources was well established, and it was simply the size of the institutions themselves that grew along with the size of the states. During this era the growth in the extent of the state resulted in a corresponding growth in the scale and power of the royal household.

In one respect at least, the "temple-state" theory is correct. By the end of the third millennium BCE, the crown had acquired control over many of the institutional estates of the various temples. The administration of these institutional holdings was still dependent throughout this period on the presence of entrepreneurs and craftsmen who were the heads of individual non-institutional households. Zettler (1992: 220–6) illustrates the reliance of the Ur III temple of Inanna at Nippur on the activities of a merchant. There are numerous archives throughout the history of Mesopotamia that document the crown's reliance on entrepreneurs for the management of its estates (Foster 1982: 52–69; Steinkeller and Postgate 1992: 8–10; Van Driel 2000; Steinkeller 2002b: 122–3; Joannès 1995; Stolper 1985).

The non-institutional archives from the Ur III period demonstrate that individuals acting in unofficial capacities played a great role in the state economy. For example, the archive of SI.A-a, a chief shepherd from this era, shows that he also advanced credit to numerous military officials who were part of the royal institutional sector (Garfinkle 2003). Moreover, the royal administration was compelled to acknowledge the local and regional hierarchies that it encountered. This can best be observed during the Ur III period in the relationship between the crown and the households of the provincial governors (Van Driel 1999/2000: 80). The governors retained control over their own considerable households, but their authority was subordinated to that of the king, and they were responsible for administering the provincial institutions for the direct benefit of the crown.

The Old Babylonian period witnessed one of the more significant developments in the interaction of the institutional and non-institutional households. During this era, the crown issued "royal edicts proclaiming the remission of debts, or freedom from dues or service obligations for the inhabitants of entire cities..." (Renger 2002: 139). These edicts attest to the power of the royal authority to intervene in the lives of the people, but they also demonstrate the reliance of the state on the economic activities of non-institutional households. The crown was compelled to intercede on behalf of individuals in order to guarantee the smooth operation of the economy.

From territorial states to empires (1600–323 BCE)

The appearance in the Ancient Near East of imperial communities once again brought about a change in the scale of the chief institutional household of the state, that of the king. The growth in the size of the royal household was accompanied by intensification in its reliance on the activities of non-institutional managers and entrepreneurs, and an increase in the available documentation of this interaction. The rise of empires in the Ancient Near East also fostered an expansion in the institutional role of the military. Surprisingly, the development of imperial authority did not prevent the continued shrinking of the crown's authority over the households in the traditional urban centers of the empire. This trend had likely characterized much of Mesopotamian history, and yet the evidence is most clear during the first millennium BCE, when we see the inhabitants of the cities of Neo-Assyria and Neo-Babylonia exercising enormous rights and privileges.

The international trade and diplomacy of the Late Bronze Age is well known to us from the Amarna Letters of the fourteenth century BCE (Moran 1992). The correspondence found in Egypt at Amarna documents a network of inter-palatial trade and contact. The transactions in the letters provide evidence for state-directed activity, but the opportunities for non-institutional entrepreneurs must have been significant. Kings in the Amarna Letters expressed concern for the safety of caravans, many of which would have been "privately" funded. At the same time, the scale of the trade controlled by the crown demonstrated the significance of the resources under the control of the royal household. In addition, the Amarna Letters make clear the extent to which the various households of the institutional sector had been subsumed by the crown.

The size of the royal household reached its maximum extent, in terms of our ability to observe it in the preserved archaeological record, with the vast palaces of the Neo-Assyrian kings. These palaces provide extensive testimony, in their architecture, artwork, and inscriptional evidence, to the power of the central institutional household. An important illustration of the continuing influence of non-institutional households, even in the face of the rise of imperial kingship, is the apparent reliance of the king on non-institutional sources of credit. A surviving letter details the obligation of a Neo-Assyrian king, Sargon II, to repay an enormous loan that had been advanced to him by a merchant for the completion of his new capital city (Radner 1999: 103–4). The merchants were royal agents empowered by the king to trade on behalf of the state, but they were still the heads of independent non-institutional households. The continuing need for non-institutional households to manage, and often to maintain, the affairs of institutional households is particularly well documented in the Neo-Babylonian and Achaemenid (Persian) periods (Beaulieu 2000a; Stolper 1985).

Conclusions

The history of the Ancient Near East is also the history of the growth of institutions, and the institutions, primarily the temples and the palaces, dominated the economy from the beginnings of urban development in the prehistoric era, down to the conquest of the region by the Greeks, and beyond. These institutions controlled most of the resources of the Ancient Near East, and this included the labor and services of much of the population. The temples and palaces served not only as rallying points for the economy, but also as sources of communal identity. In turn, the institutions provided a basis for the creation and maintenance of social and political hierarchies and a means of social differentiation. At the same time, the Ancient Near East was home to the non-institutional households of individual families. The fact that members of these non-institutional households frequently held positions within the institutional households demonstrates the extent to which these units were integrated. The ability of individuals to maintain membership in more than one household demonstrates the extent to which there was frequently no direct competition between households in the institutional and non-institutional sectors.

The Ancient Near East was characterized by the presence of both institutional and non-institutional households. These households were organized as collectives, in which the resources were marshaled for the benefit of the household and not for any one of its individual constituents. The households existed in a hierarchy, and by the end of the third millennium BCE the king's household had achieved a dominant position in the hierarchy that it would not relinquish for the remainder of Ancient Near Eastern history.

What grew throughout the history of the Ancient Near East was the power of an individual household, that of the king, to dominate and regulate the economy on a greater geographic and demographic scale. At the same time, it is clear that the rights of certain urban communities to exempt themselves from that control also increased. However, whatever tension existed between royal and non-royal households cannot be directly correlated with tension between the public and private sectors. The nature of the economy of ancient Mesopotamia was such that the participants were never in a position to define their roles in the manner expected of actors in the modern economy. Therefore, while the discussion of public versus private may have great relevance to our understanding of the Ancient Near East, it had none to the people who lived at that time.

FURTHER READING

For general surveys of the economy of the Ancient Near East with reference to the issues explored in this chapter see Snell 1997 and Van De Mieroop 1999a. On the institutional and non-institutional sectors in Mesopotamia see Renger 1994 and 1995 and Van Driel 2002. In Renger's view, in contrast to that presented in this chapter, there was a clear progression toward the growth of the private sector in the Ancient Near East.

A number of recent conferences have focused their attention on the society and economy of the Ancient Near East and the interaction of institutional and non-institutional households. See Dercksen 1999, Bongenaar 2000, Hudson and Levine 1996, 1999, Hudson and Van De Mieroop 2002, and Watanabe 1999. Additionally Sasson 1995 has studies of various aspects of the society and economy of the Ancient Near East including Egypt.

For a closer look at the development and interaction of institutional and non-institutional households in the different historical periods of Mesopotamia, see for prehistory Bernbeck 1995; for the Early Dynastic period Van De Mieroop 2002; for the Old Akkadian period Liverani 1993a; for the Ur III period Steinkeller 1991 and 2002b, Van Driel 1994, Maekawa 1996, and Heimpel 1997 (for merchants and the state see Neumann 1999 and Garfinkle 2002); for the Old Assyrian period Dercksen 1996 and 2000; for the Old Babylonian period Yoffee 1977, Renger 1979, 1984, 1994, 1995, and 2002, and Van De Mieroop 1992; for the Neo-Assyrian period Radner 1999; for the Neo-Babylonian Beaulieu 2000a and Bongenaar 2000; and for the Persian period Stolper 1985 and Joannès 1995.

CHAPTER TWENTY-NINE

Democracy and Freedom

Matthew Martin III and Daniel C. Snell

Democracy and a devotion to freedom are hallmarks of modern political thought. These mechanisms of government and associated values have in the past been understood as first appearing in ancient Greece, particularly in the city state of Athens due to reforms begun by Solon in the middle of the sixth century BCE. There is nonetheless older evidence both of institutions that resemble democratic ones and also a devotion to aspects of freedom, some of which we shall examine here.

Here what we mean by democracy and democratic is institutions or actions including broad representation of populations. In Athens the terms democracy and democratic meant "ward-rule" and referred to the divisions in the Athenian male population that constituted electoral constituencies. Athenians restricted participation to adult men from old families and excluded newcomers, who eventually exceeded the number of native Athenians in the population. Rome too had a very restricted population who could participate in its representative institutions (Rhodes 2003).

Similar institutions in the Ancient Near East may or may not have included election of representatives and voting by representatives. In most instances for which we have evidence selection of representatives and their functions were informal. But the informality ought not to blind us to the actual power of the institutions.

Here we shall look at instances of such institutions by region and then in chronological order, even though the stories relaying the events may come from later periods and must be used judiciously when depicting earlier times. The earliest mechanism for democratic rule appears to have been the institution of the assembly in the southern Mesopotamian city-states. It was called the u k k i n in Sumerian, and Akkadians translated this eventually as *puhrum*, a verbal noun from a verb meaning "to collect together." This shadowy institution seems to have been responsible for running the great literate cities of the south, though how it was selected and what the limits to its powers may have been are not depicted in the archival texts that mention it (Postgate 1992: 8–81).

In the tale of Gilgamesh and Agga, which was copied in Old Babylonian schools around 1800 BCE, we hear of Early Dynastic times perhaps as early as 2700 BCE in which two advisory groups seemed to influence the conduct of kings (Jacobsen 1987: 345–55). A group of old men advised against offending an overlord, while the young men were all for it. The assembly of young men is not otherwise attested, and it has been argued that its existence in this text was a literary element not reflecting an early reality. The elders as an assembly was otherwise known, though, and the story here may even underline their importance since in order to oppose them the narrator gave Gilgamesh the support of a god (Katz 1987: 108–11). In the Gilgamesh Epic itself, developing out of this material in Akkadian language, best known from Assurbanipal's library around 700 BCE, one hears also of the two groups who advised for and against the rash action of going on a distant adventure. The old men were against it, of course, and the young encouraged it. But an earlier Old Babylonian version of the story had only the old men (George 1999a: 20–2, 112–13).

There are good indications from literary texts that the kings of the Ur III period (2112–2004 BCE) were dependent on the approval of the assembly, and two men called heads of the assembly are known (Wilcke 1974: 182–3). The assembly might have been a city organization only, or it might be a representative body from the whole area ruled by the state.

These hints and other literary indications of how the gods made decisions, in great meetings by consensus, may reflect early Mesopotamian political practice and have been taken as a sign of "primitive democracy" (Jacobsen 1943). In most periods the judicial system was predominately democratic. And though the details of how assemblies functioned are not so clear, a first millennium proverb assumes that anyone, or perhaps just free males, could stand in the assembly, but it argues that you must be pretty stupid to do so:

> Do not go to stand in the assembly;
> Do not stray in the very place of strife.
> It is precisely in strife that fate may overtake you;
> Besides, you may be made a witness for them
> So that they take you along to testify in a lawsuit not your own.
> (Jacobsen 1943 [1970]: 160)

More recent translations take "assembly" much more generally to mean "a law court" (Lambert 1960: 101, 31) or just "a crowd" (Foster 1993a: 328, 31), both of which are possible.

In spite of the general tendency of Mesopotamian history to increased centralization of political power, assemblies appeared to be the ultimate seats of sovereignty and even to elect monarchs or decide on war and peace in times of crisis. There was a tendency to make the officers of the assembly, including the war leader, permanent, and this tended over time to favor the growth of the power of the king, who may have originated as the war leader (Jacobsen 1957 [1970]: 138, 149–51).

The Old Babylonian Code of Hammurapi, from around 1760 BCE, assumed that the elders of cities would take group responsibility when no one else was available to assume such responsibilities, and other references show that the assembly consisted of judges and witnessed judicial actions (Roth 1995: paragraphs 5, 23, 142, 202, 251).

The record of an Old Babylonian trial for homicide was copied as part of the school curriculum, and it showed who was likely to sit in the assemblies that made judicial decisions. The persons identified by their jobs included various kinds of manual laborers including a bird catcher, a potter, and an orchardman. These men were probably not paid for their work, and it is unclear how they found the time to do this public work as well as their own (Jacobsen 1939a: 134–6; Van De Mieroop 1999b: 146–7). Along with free and presumably prosperous workers, however, there was also a *muškēnum*, a term which probably includes any free lower-class person (Stol 1997). An omen from the same period mentions a woman revealing the business of the assembly; this may mean that women were sometimes in the assembly and that proceedings were secret. But women might learn of business through men, and there is no reason to think all business was secret (Van De Mieroop 1999b: 148).

It has been argued that the way that tribal groups functioned in Old Babylonian Mari was essentially like the democratic forms of rule in Greece. We see this world functioning because the king of Mari claimed also to be a tribal leader and thus had to placate a variety of constituencies, not just the urban leadership to which other Mesopotamian kings looked for support. Elders were important, and so were assemblies. And the strength of democratic traditions appeared to be stronger in older towns (Fleming 2004).

In Assyria there is evidence of communal management in the Old Assyrian period around 1800 BCE where the "harbor" or merchant establishment made decisions, perhaps only if the big men agreed to hear the case (Van De Mieroop 1999b: 149, 151). But even later when there were strong kings there is evidence that the king had to pay attention at least to the great families of Assyria (Tadmor 1986).

In the Hittite Old Kingdom around 1650 BCE there was an assembly which seems to have functioned as a high judicial council judging very high ranking persons accused of some crimes, but always under the king's control. The assembly continued to exist into the Empire period (1400–1200 BCE), but its role was apparently circumscribed. The term for assembly was *panku*, related to the English prefix pan-, and sometimes meaning "all," implying broad representation. But not all citizens sat in it, only some very high officials. Earlier scholarly notions that the assembly might actually have elected the king in the midst of a dynastic crisis seem unlikely; an early edict calls for the assembly's intervention in dynastic crises, but later, when such crises arose, the assembly was not mentioned (Beckman 1982).

From Israel soon before 900 BCE we have the story of the split of the kingdoms which involved three different representative groups (1 Kings 12). Rehoboam, Solomon's son and a southerner himself, went to the northern city of Shechem to assert his right to the kingship, and there he confronted "all of the assembly of Israel," not further defined but representing the northerners in asking for relief in their tax and forced labor burdens. Rehoboam put them off for three days and consulted with two other groups, "the old men who stood before Solomon, his father," and "the boys who grew up with him." The old men suggested leniency, even saying he should be a slave to the northerners, and they would then be slaves to him. But the young men said he should assert his prerogatives and threaten the northerners with an even greater burden. The king, being young himself, chose their advice. The northerners rejected the deal and constituted a separate kingdom. These "old men" and "boys" were loosely constituted bodies connected to the king's court since they had traveled north with the king. And there were obviously democratic representational rights that were being asserted by the "assembly of Israel." This assembly had the power to obey and also to disobey. The two groups of advisors were probably appointed rather than elected, and they constituted here a sort of bicameral senate. Because such stories were told by old men, the wisdom of old men was to be preferred, although later theological reflection declared that God had decided earlier on the split (:15) (Reviv 1989: 99–101; Willis 2001). This bicameralism, like the earlier Sumerian story, may merely be a way of saying that there was broad consultation, and consensus was eventually reached among the courtiers, but not between the northerners and the king.

This story is unique, but there are references throughout the Hebrew Bible to the old men who appeared to be not just informal advisors, but the elders also constituted a steering committee for localities. Their judicial function was foremost (de Vaux 1965 1:137–8, 152–3). The town of Succoth had seventy-seven elders (Judges 8: 14), but there probably could be more or fewer. Perhaps that number may in fact have represented the whole free male population of the village (Wolf 1947: 99). In the judicial cases represented in the Bible it does not seem that there was a huge mass of elders coming to judgment (Ruth 4, Job 29: 7–13). The mentions of the elders were vague throughout the Hebrew Bible and colored by a later historiographic concept that there should have been "pan-national" institutions at an early date (Reviv 1989: 187). Still it seems clear that elders did sometimes take over important functions in the absence of other leadership (39). And when the centralized Israelite states in the north and south fell to outsiders, the elders were the key institution in insuring the continuity of administration at the local level and perhaps even the continuation of national identity where it had been established (190–1). The terms for congregation and assembly appeared mostly in Priestly and Deuteronomic writings, the later strands of the first five books of the Bible. These terms may have designated "the responsible elements of the nation, the full citizens who have the rights and duties of looking after the affairs of the nation" (Pope 1962: 669), but how such bodies functioned was not described. These institutions may have been most important after the Babylonian exile ending around 520 BCE when there was no Israelite king, and appointed governors might or might not be responsive to local needs (Liverani 2003: 371–2).

Herodotus conveyed a story, perhaps more relevant to Greek thought than to Persian, but still perhaps of interest in his eastern Mediterranean milieu, in which Persian nobles debated the varieties of types of governments they might choose. They naturally accepted the later king Darius' argument that monarchy was better than oligarchy or democracy, but they clearly assumed that everyone would want to minimize tyrannical government (Liverani 1993c: 29; Snell 2001: 18; n. 17 to Herodotus 1987 III, 80–2).

In Egypt, though from earliest times the role of the king was paramount, there is clear evidence of the functioning of the assembly, called *qnbt* in Egyptian, that may have been responsible for administering towns or even whole nomes, or counties.

Initially in the Old Kingdom this assembly may have been made up of high administrators appointed by the king. The assembly fulfilled judicial functions as early as the Eleventh Dynasty, 1975–1940 BCE. There seem to have been separate assemblies in temples and in regions. In the New Kingdom there were "assemblies of notables" but also a grand assembly under the vizier himself associated with the king, perhaps one assembly each for Thebes and Heliopolis (Edgerton 1947: 155–6). Certainly in times of weakness of the central authority assemblies of worthies met and made decisions about local issues. We do not know how one became a member of such an assembly or how it worked, but the focus was on administrative and judicial matters (Helck 1980; Trigger et al. 1983: 214). But when we seek what law might have been enforced, we find there was no written collection of the legal norms, perhaps because they could change from king to king (Edgerton 1947: 154). Or it may be that judges in their assemblies had great personal power to make what they regarded as just decisions, and this may explain the lack of a code in Egyptian law (Jin 2003: 273).

In later Egypt the town councils had apparently been abolished under the Ptolemies, 305–30 BCE, but there was a council of elders, perhaps consisting of former magistrates, that persisted. The city of Alexandria petitioned the Roman emperor Augustus (30 BCE–14 CE) for a council, and the other big cities also lacked councils; the emperor apparently refused. It was not until Septimus Severus in 200 CE that new grants of councils were made to Alexandria and the other large cities (Bowman and Rathbone 1992: 114–15, 118, 124, 127). Once one had been a member of the council, one apparently remained known as a "councilor" for life, so clearly this was an honor (Lewis 1983: 50.)

Very obscure but suggestive is a letter from the last important Assyrian king to the otherwise unknown "elders of Elam," meaning the Iranian part of the Mesopotamian basin. The elders had complained of ill-treatment and implied that they were in charge of their area's political fate (Waters 2002).

Phoenician cities on what is now the Lebanese and Syrian coast were in contact with Greece, and so they are of particular interest in their democratic processes, but the early evidence for them is not good. They were ruled by kings who left royal burial inscriptions, but one Egyptian text may indicate that around 1000 BCE there was an assembly which a king consulted (Wilson 1945). The text is the Report of Wen-Amun, which traced the many disappointments that faced an official of a weakened Egypt as he tried to buy wood on the Phoenician coast (Lichtheim 1973–80: 2, 229).

The Phoenicians preceded the Greeks in sending out colonies around the Mediterranean. This diffusion of persons may have diffused royal authority and also opened the way to more democratic decision-making among the immigrants. The situation is unclear, but immigrants still saw themselves as belonging to the communities of the mother cities back on the Lebanese coast. In the Persian period and later (539 BCE–) there were assemblies with councilors in Phoenician cities and a mixture of democracy and oligarchy in the best known of the colonies, the north African city of Carthage. At Carthage officials were elected by broad-based assemblies, but the highest offices could be held only by rich men on the grounds that they would have the leisure to perform the official functions (Sommer 1999: 248, 251; Aristotle 1990 II, viii, 1273a).

The influence of decentralized Phoenician rule with democratic elements on the later Greek democracies is disputed now. Some would still say that the Greeks invented the essence of democracy, while others would say that, along with the alphabetic writing system, city government was a borrowing from the Orient. Obviously there were local variations on a theme seen earlier in the Ancient Near East, and one cannot say that institutions are ever completely taken over without modification. This political culture of combining the rule of the rich with the representation at least of influential groups continued to be a mark of European society, some might say even down to the present day (Sommer 1999: 271, 284–5).

The evidence for voting in the Ancient Near Eastern assemblies is slight, and that may have been a Greek innovation (Wolf 1947: 102 n. 27), previous assemblies having relied on consensus. But there is some evidence of voting by groups in Old Assyrian times around 1800 BCE (Evans 1958: 7). The passage in a fragmentary decree reads, "the clerk shall divide them into [three] and they shall settle [the affair]. Where they do not settle [the affair], on assembling both small and great [they shall settle the affair] of their neighbors [at the mouth] of the majority, and … [at the mouth of] the majority they shall settle the affair" (Driver and Miles 1975: 377). In Greek the Homeric poems clearly assumed that there would not be voting. As late as Thucydides (460?–404 BCE) (1963: 65, I, 87, 2) the Spartans shouted instead of voting. But the reforms of Solon at Athens presupposed voting in the sixth century, and the existence of potsherds inscribed with names apparently in preparation for ostracism argues that in the course of the fifth century at Athens voting became common (Larsen 1949: 164, 168, 170–3). The secret ballot, however, was first mentioned at Rome in the second century BCE (Larsen 1949: 180–1).

The advantages of tending toward democracy are universal since such systems promote the feeling among the governed that they participate in the making of decisions and therefore have a stake in the success of policies. Liverani expressed it well: "Democracy is an effective multiplier of energies, which transforms a quantitative scantiness of resources into a qualitative preeminence, while despotism condemns the oriental empire to an under use of potentialities still present in its immense resources" (1993c: 8).[1] Any sensible leader can see that that is true, and many sacrificed efficiency for, as we now crassly say, buy-in over the course of history ancient and modern.

Residual Control by the Community

In general we can say that there was a continuing undercurrent of community home-rule at least among property-owning men in the Ancient Near East (Liverani 1993c). We do not see this as a progressive trend but a recurring mode that seems to have emerged, or at least to have become more perceptible, especially when other organizations did not function well. When kings were strong, these democratic institutions disappeared from the record, though probably not from reality, and when kings were weak, these were the institutions that persisted (Van De Mieroop 1999b: 161).

We will leave to others the question of how different Greek institutions may have become from the institutions outlined here. But I would suggest that the difference is less in actual procedure and more in the self-consciousness that literate observers brought to the question of how polities worked. Subjecting social conventions to analysis did not originate with the Greeks, but they pursued it more actively than others had done, at least in texts that have been preserved. This aspect of the so-called Greek miracle seems to constitute a difference in expositional style, in what was seen as worth recording and analyzing. In itself it does not seem a startling breakthrough, but it does bring a difference in cultural style. Perhaps the Old Oligarch in his Constitution of the Athenians made lists just as the Mesopotamians had before him, but he heavily annotated them, as Mesopotamians were not inclined to do (Hornblower 1996).

The Value of Freedom

Let us now turn to another aspect of culture that is harder to trace than the existence of democratic institutions, the question of whether people valued freedom. Recent study has identified three kinds of freedom that might be valued: personal, sovereignal, and civic (Patterson 1991: 1–5). Personal freedom may be summarized as the freedom of movement; most modern definitions of freedom focus on that aspect, and the Akkadian word sometimes translated as "freedom," *andurārum*, derives from a verb meaning "to move freely, to run off." This meaning also appears to apply to the Egyptian word for "freedom," *wstn*, which at base meant "to move freely." Indeed the Greek term most usually used for "freedom," *eleutheria*, may be related to a form of the verb *erkhomai*, meaning "to come or go" (Snell 2001: 21–9). By sovereignal freedom one means the freedom to make decisions about one's life without the interference of others; rulers in the ancient world were the persons most clearly endowed with this power, of course, but some interpreters see this as a central characteristic of men in democratic Greek states. Civic freedom is the power to participate in governmental deliberations and decisions. In most polities in the ancient world this freedom was more assumed than asserted, though there was considerable variety in different times and places about how widely this freedom was shared.

While believers in the Greek miracle may stress how cunningly the aspects of freedom combined at Athens, they will readily admit that Greek city-states were societies dominated by slavery, and the leisure the free had was provided by the labor of others who had legally no freedom at all. A key question is whether in pre-Greek times elites from whom we have written evidence valued freedom as an important element in their understanding of what it meant to be human. It has been argued that Greeks' valuing of freedom derived from their observation of the treatment of women captured by Greeks and led away into slavery. The empathy that arose for the women in such situations may have developed into a broader appreciation of the qualities of freedom at least for free men (Patterson 1991: 47–132). It is clear that the empathy with enslaved women was an important aspect of Greek drama at least of the playwright Euripides (480–406 BCE), and perhaps of Greek thought after him. From the Ancient Near East, nonetheless, one can see that even in archival records of the flight of unfree laborers there is a demonstration that the common people resisted the dictates of the elites by flight and so valued their freedom. But the elites did not obviously empathize with them in their plight, and the record of the flight was for accounting purposes only (Snell 2001: 46–62).

There is nonetheless clear evidence that elites did value freedom in some senses as seen in royal edicts especially from the Old Babylonian period (2004–1595 BCE). In that time we have many references to kings' "setting freedom" for various groups, but we have only two actual decrees that may be the records of such acts. These edicts may be an extension of Early Dynastic references to kings' canceling obligations for groups of citizens (Snell 2001: 64). The edicts themselves appear to have tried to state moral precepts of a general nature but also to abrogate specific kinds of loans and taxes, presumably for a limited period and probably for a limited population. They were the reflection of kings' economic policies and were decreed when conditions became noticeably difficult for the poor. Their implementation and effect are not well understood, but there were references to them in archival texts, indicating that scribes were concerned with how and when they would be imposed (Charpin 1990). In the more extensive of the edicts the king made clear that he wanted to free persons who had been enslaved as guarantees for loans, but he did not intend that other slaves should be free (Finkelstein 1969: 528 paragraphs 20–1).

Somewhat later in the Hittite Kingdom in what is now Turkey a king declared that he freed the citizens of a part of Syria he had conquered from their previous obligations to bring taxes and to do forced labor (Neu 1996: 11–12). Also from North Syria there is a literary text that shows that the gods had been unhappy because the rich people of the city of Ebla had not seen fit to make a debt release (Snell 2001: 68–9).

In almost every period of Ancient Near Eastern history there are references to royal decrees and releases from debt, indicating that such efforts at an economic policy were carried out with varying success and also that the elites were aware of them and their possible implications. Such decrees were anti-reformist in that they did not address causes of economic hardship or try to change basic institutions. They merely set the clock back on the taxes and loans owed by the poor (Charpin 1990).

Did the Mesopotamians value freedom in the same ways that Greeks appear to have valued their understanding of freedom? Of this we cannot be sure since Mesopotamians did not in general write discursive essays about anything, but I believe we can say that the kings were not operating in a vacuum of public opinion and in fact were appealing to it.

In the legal collections from the Ancient Near East also we see kings boasting, like Ur-Nammu (2050 BCE), "I freed the Akkadians and foreigners (?) in the lands of Sumer and Akkad" (Roth 1995: 15–16). Slaves themselves, however, were treated fairly harshly within the codes, though it is interesting that slaves actually escaping were to be punished only in the Hittite Laws from around 1200 BCE, while the harborers who facilitated the runaways' progress were more consistently condemned (Snell 2001: 85).

In literary texts the reaction to freedom and to flight may have been more sympathetic. In a Neo-Assyrian incantation collection from around 700 BCE, a passage indicates that freedom was cherished as a value by the people who composed the text:

Who estranged companion from companion,
who did not free a captive, did not release a man in bonds,
who did not let the prisoner see the light,
who said to the captive: "Leave him captive!" to the man in bonds: "Bind him tighter!"
He does not know what is a crime against god, he does not know what is a sin against the goddess. (Reiner 1958: 13)

The god could be any great god, and lording one's freedom over another and not releasing the prisoner was seen here as a grave crime. But it was the sort of crime that courts would have difficulty proving, and so it remained in the realm of moral instruction.

There is one society of the Ancient Near East where the valuing of freedom seems even more palpable, at least in the literary form in which we can study it, and that is Ancient Israel. The emphasis of the Biblical texts on getting out from Egypt "from the house of bondage" and the relative slavery that that entailed is clear in many periods. It has been argued that the liberation from slavery was not liberation in the later Greek sense but a liberation for service to God. This seems to be a misreading of texts similar to Exodus 10: 26, which commands people to go forth in order to serve God. But the service of God was not to be like the service of men; it involved freedom of movement in that the people were expected to leave the land of Egypt (Snell 2001: 119–20).

It is also clear that within the history of Israel there was a continuing strain of distrust for human authority figures, especially kings. This may derive from the fact that almost all the sources for the Biblical texts were not closely associated with kings, unlike much of the literature in the rest of the Ancient Near East. We thus hear the voice probably not of the common person but of a literate elite very protective of its prerogatives as critics of the regime. The Book of Judges in particular, though clearly crafted long after the events that established a separate monarchy in Israel, seethes with ambivalence about kingship, and the most pious judge refused to be king because in his view God should continue to be king (Judges 8: 22–3). Practically this meant that the judge favored the older, less intrusive ways of governing.

It is in the legal material in Deuteronomy where one hears most persistently of the importance of remembering that we were "slaves in Egypt," and therefore must consistently treat the downtrodden and poor and foreign in our midst with kindness and sympathy (Deuteronomy 16: 12, 24: 18). Such admonitions appear as motive clauses to various kinds of stipulations, and motive clauses were not the oldest part of the legal tradition and appeared to proliferate over time (Sonsino 1980: 221).

The culmination of this line of thinking was Deuteronomy 23: 15–16 (Hebrew 16–17), which may be a reaction to the Ancient Near Eastern treaties which called for the return of fugitives. Such treaties might be taken as evidence that some elites did not value freedom. Deuteronomy itself has been recognized in modern scholarship as having the outline of an Ancient Near Eastern treaty, and so the inclusion of the opposite of what was expected in such treaties may be an indication of the condemnation by some Israelite intellectuals for the customs of other Ancient Near Eastern cultures (Weinfeld 1992: 169–70). The Deuteronomy passage may have come from north Israelite intellectuals who escaped to the southern kingdom of Judah after the fall of their state in 722 BCE. But obviously it must have found some support in the south too, or it would not have been copied into and passed down along with the other early writings. It reads:

> Do not give up a slave to his masters who saves himself from his masters to you. With you he shall live in your midst in the place which he shall choose in one of your gates in a place that seems good to him; do not oppress him.

This passage was understood in traditional Jewish interpretation as referring to an Israelite slave who had escaped from a foreign master back to the land of Israel. The Israelite was to take him in and allow him to live where he wished in the community of Israel. This understanding undermines the revolutionary nature of the statement and tames it for future slave-holding ages. But that is not what the passage says, and Biblical literalists have seen it as a sanction for any slave wishing to escape any kind of slave-holding (Snell 2001: 129–30).

The Deuteronomy passage is probably the most radical assertion of the value of freedom in the Hebrew Bible, but there are others that indicate a similar feeling. Exodus 21: 16 says, "Whoever steals a man, whether he sells him or is found in possession of him, shall be put to death." This stipulation would not outlaw enslavement for debt, but it would ban child-snatching. Leviticus 25: 39–41 further mandated a limited slavery at least for Israelite slaves that ended with the jubilee year of remission of debts and restoration of land. The slavery of a limited seven-year term for Israelites enslaved by Israelites was also preached in Exodus 21: 2–6 and the parallel Deuteronomy 15: 12–14.

In addition to the legal passages there is a story that indicates that the religious people thought such restrictions on slave-owning and such freeing of slaves ought to have been a regular thing in Israel. Jeremiah 34: 8–17 argues that the liberation was supposed to be periodic but in fact had never been carried out until the state of Judah was threatened with destruction by the Babylonians in 597 BCE. The slave-owners consented to a freeing of the slaves apparently to placate religious opinion, but they then recaptured their freed slaves, and the prophet saw this as rebellion against God's will. After the return from exile the Jewish governor Nehemiah in the fourth century BCE tried to stop the debt slavery that had become rampant among Israelites (Nehemiah 5: 1–13). The persistence of slavery in such circumstances as in most later societies was to be expected, but any reader can see that there were strong and persistent strands within the Biblical tradition that valued what can be clearly categorized as personal freedom.

The Continuing Valuing of Freedom

Ancient Near Eastern ideas about freedom have come down to us in various traditions, some more direct and clear than others, but all continuing to hint that a core understanding of the human being was as a free actor, free to go where one pleased and to do as one pleased, and frequently free to participate in important decisions taken by the community. The later reception of these ideas has been checkered, and as the thinkers of the Western tradition came increasingly to be separated from the actual rulers and alienated from them, the ideas became associated with similar Greek values, but they became an ideal rather than a realizable reality.

Since the Enlightenment revolutions that relativized all institutions and pushed forward the value of individual freedom, most Western societies have rediscovered the ancient intellectual legacy. And non-Western societies too have found that their own traditions frequently harbor at least small-scale democratic institutions and values of individual freedom. Although in both the West and the non-West the predominate institutions even in the modern age have tended to be hierarchical, recent study has found that "There are universal ideas of freedom to be found in diverse intellectual and political traditions of the globe" (Taylor 2002: 1). The future of such ideas is unclear, but they embody such an old and basic desire of human beings that it seems unlikely they will ever grow less important than they are now.

NOTE

1   "La democrazia è un moltiplicatore efficace di energie, che trasforma un'esiguità quantitiva in una preminenza qualitative, mentre il despotismo condanna l'impero orientale ad un sotto-impiego delle potentialità pur presenti nelle sue immense risorse."

FURTHER READING

Van De Mieroop 1999b offers a good survey of representative institutions in the cities of Mesopotamia. Jacobsen 1943 is still basic, and Liverani 1993c is full of insights. For the history of freedom see Snell 2001.

CHAPTER THIRTY

Monotheism and Ancient Israelite Religion

S. David Sperling

The peoples of the Ancient Near East remain a source of fascination to moderns. No one can fail to be impressed by the pyramids, the ziggurats, and the artistic monuments of ancient Egypt and western Asia. But the interest in these great ancient civilizations is antiquarian. In contrast, ancient Israel, which was never the home of a great ruling power or of monumental architecture, is the ultimate birthplace of the monotheistic religions, Judaism, Christianity, and Islam. For good and ill the stories of Abraham and not those of Gilgamesh remain sources of inspiration and guidance for moderns. As such, the recovery of ancient Israelite religion is relevant within the academy and without, and therein lies a problem.

Scholars with personal religious attachments to the Bible must always exert themselves to avoid the kinds of apologetics that they would never offer in other fields. They must resist the temptation to explain away elements in Israelite religion, child sacrifice for example, if they find them abhorrent. Contrariwise, scholars with the opposite bent must resist emphasizing the Bible's nefarious support of ideologies and institutions of which they disapprove, if such disapproval impairs understanding of what the texts meant in their time of composition and early reception.

A second problem is the paucity of primary data, a situation in stark contrast to Mesopotamia, Egypt, Ugarit, Anatolia (Turkey), and Greece, which, in addition to their literary productions, have left us temples and temple offering lists telling us which gods were worshiped and what attention they received. These same "extrabiblical" cultures have provided a wealth of pictorial representations of their divinities enabling us to visualize their gods the way they did. Different size temples to different gods in the same geographic area are another indication of relative importance, and these too are lacking in ancient Israel. Ancient Israel has thus far provided no undisputed pictorial representations of the Hebrew god Yahweh. Our only offering list from the biblical period comes from the fifth century Jewish temple at Elephantine in Egypt, a structure destroyed by hostile Egyptians in antiquity. The list indicates that offerings were made to YHW/YHH (forms of Yahweh) along with the goddesses (?) Anat-Yahu and Anat-Bethel (Van Der Toorn 1992: 80–1). Although we have ancient Hebrew letters, inscriptions, and artifacts, most of our information about

Israelite religion comes from the Hebrew Bible, a selective anthology containing material written over a period of some eight hundred years but completed late in the first pre-Christian millennium. As such, the Bible's religion is not necessarily ancient Israelite religion but a later understanding. In contrast to the situation of other Ancient Near Eastern texts, we have no originals of the Bible, only copies far removed chronologically from their original authors or scribes.

The greatest problem in studying Israelite religion is the figure of the Hebrew god, the hero of the Bible absent only from the books of Esther and Song of Songs. Within the Bible the Hebrew god is depicted as creator, law-giver, provider, and director of all the events of what would later be called "nature" and "history," Biblical Hebrew having no word for either concept. At some point this Hebrew divinity came to be viewed by followers as the sole god in existence. His proper name is Yahweh, usually translated "Lord," or "Eternal," god of "Israel," a small politically insignificant people in western Asia first attested in the late second millennium BCE. Yahweh has thus far not been found in any pre-Israelite pantheons (Van Der Toorn 1999b). Yahweh was known by various names and epithets, among them Adonay, El, Eloah, Elohim, Shadday, and Elyon, some of which were originally the names of other gods absorbed into the figure of Yahweh. He came in the course of time to be simply the only "God" of Christianity, Islam, and Judaism (Van Der Toorn 1999a, b; Spronk 1999; Cross 1973: 44; Miller 2000: 2–3; Herrmann 1999; Knauf 1999; Elnes and Miller 1999; Pardee 1999). The figure of El is the best documented of those folded into the god of Israel. In a complicated process, El, once head of a North Syrian pantheon, became so thoroughly identified with Yahweh that his separate existence was virtually unacknowledged by the Hebrew writers (Cross 1973: 44; Miller 2000: 2–3; Herrmann 1999).

The name Yahweh is a scholarly reconstruction of the consonant cluster YHWH attested more than 6,600 times in the Hebrew Bible, and in the Moabite Stone of the ninth century BCE. The Hebrew writing system employed to compose what were to become the books of the Hebrew Bible is primarily consonantal. The vowel points were added during the first millennium of our era because Jews had come to avoid the pronunciation of the ancient divine name, and the original vowels of YHWH are not included in the Hebrew Bible. Instead readers are directed to pronounce YHWH as though it were another less sacred name, "Adonay," meaning "Lord."

The authors of the Bible consistently portrayed Yahweh as a unique divinity, but differed about the extent of that uniqueness. At one pole we have full-blown Yahwistic monotheism, that is, the claim that there is only one god in existence, and that his name is Yahweh. The prophet known as "Isaiah of the Exile" or Deutero-Isaiah declared Yahweh to be the sole god in existence (Isaiah 43: 10–11, 45: 5–7, 14, 18, 21–2, 46: 9; Wildberger 1977). For this prophet the claim that Yahweh alone is god entails the cultic corollary of Yahweh's demand for exclusive worship. Other gods must cease to exist (Versnel 2000: 83). Accordingly, Yahweh demands the worship of all humanity, not just that of Israelites or Jews (Isaiah 44: 6, 66: 23). At the opposite pole, we find Yahweh jealous of other gods (Exodus 20: 5, 34: 15; Deuteronomy 5: 9; Joshua 24: 19), defeating other gods (Exodus 12: 12; Numbers 33: 4), acting as king of gods (Psalm 95: 3) or god of gods (Psalm 136: 2), and accepting the homage

of other gods (Psalm 29: 1–2, 96: 4). These passages all take for granted the
existence, if inferiority, of other divinities. Deuteronomy chapter 4, despite its rhetorical monotheizing flourishes (4: 35, 39), avers that Yahweh himself had allotted
the depersonalized sun, moon, and stars to the gentiles as legitimate objects of
worship (4: 19). The gentiles could not worship Yahweh himself. For the author
of Deuteronomy 4 the exclusive worship of Yahweh was both an Israelite obligation
and an Israelite privilege.

Because the Bible is the work of many authors and not a systematic treatise, there
are numerous disagreements about matters that are of fundamental importance to
students of ancient Israelite religion. According to Genesis 4 the name of Yahweh was
known to the earliest humans. In contrast, Exodus 6: 3 claims that Yahweh first
revealed his proper name to Moses, but not to the earlier patriarchs Abraham, Isaac,
and Jacob, who knew him only as El Shadday. Individual contributors to the biblical
anthology differed on the question of whether other gods existed, or whether
gentiles were to worship Yahweh. All agreed, though, that Yahweh was the sole
legitimate object of Israelite worship. Israelites who worshiped other gods than
Yahweh, or in addition to Yahweh, were both sinful and stupid (Jeremiah 5: 19–23;
7: 8–11). Despite biblical rhetoric accusing Israelites of abandoning Yahweh for other
gods, it appears that it was more often the case that polytheistic Israelites viewed
Yahweh as the head of an Israelite pantheon, supplementing his worship with that of
others.

It is precisely that supplementary worship which is condemned in I Kings 18: 21
and Jeremiah 7: 9–10. Nowhere in the Hebrew Bible do we find any of the "good
guys" supporting Israelite worship of Yahweh's rivals. Whenever the biblical writers
describe Israelite worship of other gods, male and female, which they do with
considerable frequency (Exodus 32: 7–8; Numbers 25: 1–5; Judges 2: 10–13; 1
Kings 11: 33; 2 Kings 17: 16; Jeremiah 3: 6–10, 44: 2–10; Ezekiel 8: 5–17, 20:
7–8, 27–31; Psalm 106: 34–9), they characterize such worship as "backsliding," or as
deviation from the worship of Yahweh alone as demanded by the "ten words"
(Exodus 34: 28; Deuteronomy 4: 13, 10: 4) or decalogue, as spoken by Yahweh to
Moses (Exodus 20: 3–5; Deuteronomy 5: 7–9; compare Hosea 13: 4). Often,
Israelite deviation is attributed to the potential and actual influence of the local and
neighboring gentiles, and to Israelite sexual contact and intermarriage with them
(Exodus 23: 32–3, 34: 11–16; Numbers 25: 1–9, 31: 14–18; Deuteronomy 12: 2–3,
29–31). The view of the Old Testament that the worship of Yahweh alone was
normative in Israel from the earliest days of the nation was canonized in the New
Testament (Acts 7: 35–43) and held sway until challenged during the rise of modern
biblical criticism in the nineteenth century.

The best known of the early modern Bible critics, the German scholar Julius
Wellhausen (1844–1918), employed analytical literary criticism, called source criticism, to distinguish earlier from later writings within the Hebrew Bible. Based on his
system of dating biblical texts, Wellhausen reconstructed Israelite religious development, and concluded that monotheism had evolved gradually out of polytheism,
passing through a stage of monolatry, the worship of a single god at the same time
that other gods are believed to exist. No humanist of the time could escape the

ramifications of Darwin's theory of evolution. Whether Wellhausen was also influenced by Hegel is another matter (Perlitt 1965). According to Wellhausen, in the earlier biblical period Yahweh was a national god, much like Chemosh in Moab and Assur in Assyria. The fact that as a national god Yahweh claimed the allegiance of every Israelite did not entail the rejection of other gods any more than allegiance to Assur entailed the neglect of the cults of Šamaš or Ishtar.

Wellhausen's thesis presented a problem. If Yahweh had at the outset been a god no different qualitatively from the Moabite Chemosh and the Assyrian Assur, why did monotheism never arise in Moab or Assyria? We do not have enough Moabite material to deny categorically that other gods in addition to Chemosh were worshiped in Moab. The Moabite Stone of the ninth century BCE mentions an Ashtar-Chemosh along with Chemosh. Does this indicate the merger of Chemosh with the god Ashtar, known as a defunct deity in the Ugaritic texts of the thirteenth century (Müller 1999)? With Assur, the Assyriologist Simo Parpola has argued that underneath the apparent polytheism of Assyrian religion was a unifying monotheistic notion (Parpola 2000). But even Parpola does not deny that Assyrian religion was polytheistic for all but the most sophisticated thinkers.

For Wellhausen the new direction was to be sought in the teaching of the eighth century Hebrew prophets. Only after Hosea and Amos began to interpret the political upheavals of the eighth century BCE as Yahweh's means of enforcing his demands upon Israel, demands that were primarily ethical and moral rather than cultic, did monotheism begin to emerge. As interpreted by Wellhausen, Hosea, Amos, and Isaiah shortly thereafter, taught that Yahweh could move all the peoples of the earth either to punish or reward his people Israel. If so, he must be much more than a national god; he must have no rivals at all. "Ethical monotheism," though taught by succeeding prophets, took two centuries to take root among most of the populace. In Wellhausen's view, only during the Babylonian exile of the sixth century BCE did the masses of Jews, prodded by a guilty conscience, begin to realize that the prophets had been right (Zechariah 1: 1–6). Both the northern and southern kingdoms of Israel had fallen because of their failure to serve Yahweh exclusively. It was at that point that the demand that Yahweh alone was to be worshiped was retrojected into the laws and narratives set in earlier centuries.

Wellhausen's view was largely accepted until the 1940s when it began to be attacked by the American archaeologist William Foxwell Albright (1891–1971) and his followers, and the Israeli Yehezkel Kaufmann (1889–1963) and his mostly Jewish followers.[1] Wellhausen had reached his conclusions solely on the internal evidence of the Bible. Albright, in contrast, insisted that the biblical texts could be understood and dated only in the light of the Near Eastern world in which ancient Israel had emerged.

In Albright's view there was archaeological evidence that many biblical texts written centuries later than the events they portrayed had faithfully preserved ancient traditions. That being the case, the biblical claims about the roots of monotheism in the age of Moses ought to be historically credible. In his 1940 classic *From the Stone Age to Christianity: Monotheism and the Historical Process*,[2] Albright broke with the evolutionary explanations of monotheistic origins in favor of a monotheistic revolution led by Moses. For him Mosaic monotheism was "functional," rather than systematic. Nonetheless, Moses was the first Hebrew to teach

> the existence of one God, the creator of everything, the source of justice, who is equally powerful in the desert, and in Palestine, who has no sexuality and no mythology, who is human in form but cannot be seen by human eye and cannot be represented in any form. (Albright 1957: 272)

Thus, monotheism was not an evolutionary development within Israel, though the groundwork had been laid for it in the high gods of other cultures and especially in the exaltation of the solar disk, called the Aten, and the ban on all competing cults by King Akhenaten of Egypt in the fourteenth century BCE. According to Albright, "the Aten cult was...a true monotheism" (1957: 221). The Egyptologist Donald Redford observes, "The Roman world might have called Akhenaten an 'atheist,' for what was left to Egypt was not a 'god' at all, but a disc in the heavens" (1984: 170; J. Foster 1995 especially 1760; Propp 1999 and the bibliography, 537, n. 1).

Albright thought that the Mosaic revolution proved to be a great success with the masses of the Israelite population. Of course there were always "ignorant" or "moronic" Israelites who were attracted to polytheism (Albright 1957: 288). There was also the corrupting influence of the monarchy, sometimes tempted to adopt or promote gentile practices (1 Kings 11: 4–8, 16: 30–33; 2 Kings 16: 10–11, 21: 1–7). At the opposite pole stood zealots who felt the need to make Mosaic monotheism consistent by standardizing worship and eliminating vestiges of polytheistic practice and mythic language. But these zealots were reformers rather than innovators. Essentially, Albright held that Moses was a historical figure who brought a functional, if not systematic, monotheism to Israel in the thirteenth century BCE.

As noted by Mark Smith (2001:150), Albright's definition of monotheism is a composite drawn from various biblical sources of varying dates. In addition, these features do not have equal weight in regard to the question of the sole existence of Yahweh: 1) In some cultures creation is a specialized function of lower rather than higher gods. 2) In Mesopotamian sources the deities Kittu (truth) and Mesharu (justice) are gods responsible for justice. The Egyptian goddess Ma'at and a whole host of other gods are sources of justice without being unique. In Zoroastrianism, Ahura Mazda is the source of justice, but the existence of opposition by the thoroughly evil and very powerful Angra Mainyu does not permit us to call Zoroastrianism "monotheism." 3) As for the ban on images, its date is unclear. From the perspective of art history Schroer argues that the anti-image tradition arose late in Israel (1987); Mettinger believes that early absence of images is itself not determinative because we must distinguish between *de facto* absence of images, a phenomenon attested widely in West Semitic polytheistic cults, and programmatic avoidance of images, the explicit prohibition of images, which did not appear in biblical sources composed before the exilic period. Indeed, several scholars have argued that the second commandment, which prohibits images (Exodus 20: 4 = Deuteronomy 5: 8), is an interpolation that interrupts the natural flow between "You shall have no gods in my presence" and "You shall not bow down to them in worship" (Mettinger 1995, 1997; Hendel 1997).

Yehezkel Kaufmann went further than Albright. Kaufmann wrote his magnum opus in eight volumes between 1938 and 1956, a period in which few gentile scholars could read Modern Hebrew. An abridgment of the first seven volumes, *The Religion of Israel* (Chicago: Chicago University Press), translated into English by Moshe Greenberg, appeared in 1960 and extended Kaufmann's influence somewhat, but mostly among those Jews whose Hebrew was not fluent. The complete eighth volume was translated by Efroymson (1997). The German scholar Krapf has brought renewed attention to Kaufmann's work (Krapf 1992); Krapf had earlier treated Kaufmann's intellectual history (1990).

In Kaufmann's view the Mosaic revolution had thoroughly eradicated paganism from Israel in one fell swoop. Whereas the tales of the biblical patriarchs Abraham, Isaac, and Jacob reflect a polytheistic background (1938–56 II/1: 25–32), Moses had successfully taught Israel that no other gods existed but Yahweh. Any biblical references to other gods in Israel subsequent to the Mosaic revolution should be understood as literary conceits, or petrified language emptied of mythic significance. Albright had attributed infidelity to Yahweh to morons, and other scholars had distinguished between "official" religion faithful to Yahweh alone and "popular" religion which was polytheistic and syncretistic. But Kaufmann attempted to demonstrate that the number of morons as well as the differences between the "official" and the "popular" had been greatly exaggerated.[3] Kaufmann conceded that the royal courts sometimes imported foreign cults. The wives of Solomon had private chapels for their own use (1 Kings 11). King Ahab had permitted Queen Jezebel to bring the gods Baal and Asherah and their prophets into the northern capital Samaria (1 Kings 16: 31–3, 18: 19). But these were aberrations and no more.

Problematic for Kaufmann's thesis were the many denunciations of Israelite idolatry and polytheism in the prophetic books as well as in the editorial comments in the biblical narratives that give the impression that wholehearted fidelity to Yahweh was in short supply among the masses. Kaufmann's ingenious response was that biblical writers were not denouncing the real worship of other gods, which was not to be found in Israel, but the occasional superstitious resort to stick and stone fetishes. Indeed, by the eighth century BCE, Israelites had become so far removed from the worship of gods other than Yahweh that they projected their own vestigial fetishism on the gentiles, assuming the gods of the nations to be fetishes, rather than divinities with real personalities whose loves and wars were celebrated in myth and cult. In sum, Israelites could never worship the gods of the gentiles because they did not know how. According to Kaufmann, the Hebrew prophets denounced these minor lapses into superstition out of puritanical zeal for monotheism. We might compare the prophetic zeal with that of an Orthodox rabbi who equates a Jewish child's visit to a department store Santa Claus or that child's participation in an Easter egg hunt with his conversion to Christianity.

The prophets also needed to vindicate divine justice, an activity that theologians call "theodicy." Israel held the land conditionally, so biblical theology taught, through a covenant with Yahweh. The primary condition of that covenant was that Israel was to serve Yahweh exclusively. Failure to do so was a breach of that covenant punishable by destruction by foreigners and expulsion of the population from the land. Since both Israelite kingdoms came to be destroyed by foreigners and both populations suffered expulsion, Kaufmann argued that the biblical writers were required to exaggerate Israelite infidelity to Yahweh, or even to invent it, in order to show that Israel had violated the covenant, and that Yahweh had justly punished them.

The "theodicy" element and the attention paid to prophetic rhetoric surely have merit, but otherwise Kaufmann's ingenious thesis is seriously flawed. First, he claims that Israel differed so fundamentally from its neighbors that Israelites told no myths about Yahweh and assumed naively that gentiles told no myths about their gods, who were therefore no more than fetishes. But Kaufmann's claim is unsustainable. Comparative study of the Bible and Near Eastern myths shows keen Israelite awareness of gentile myth as well as the use, adaptation, and transformation of mythic motifs by Hebrew writers (Cross 1973: 143–4). Kaufmann's further claims about Israelite ignorance of the religions of the gentiles are likewise flawed, while the supposed qualitative differences between Israel and its neighbors are greatly exaggerated (Smith 1952).

Indeed, newer discussions of ancient Israelite religion stimulated by inscriptions and drawings discovered at Kuntillet Ajrud in the Sinai and at Khirbet el-Qôm on the west bank of the Jordan demonstrate that Israelite worship of gods in addition to Yahweh was not completely fabricated by the authors of the Bible. These texts from the ninth to eighth centuries BCE apparently mention the goddess Asherah in close connection to Yahweh (Becking 2001; Dever 1999; Miller 2000: 29–43; Wyatt 1999). The Kuntillet Ajrud text was found on a jar, and the inscription follows the epistolary genre and is probably a school exercise text (Renz and Röllig 1995–2003: I 61). More than one reading and interpretation are possible:

a) "I bless you by/ commend you to/ Yahweh of Samaria and his Asherah."

On this interpretation "Asherah" is a proper name referring to the goddess Asherah known from the Hebrew Bible, from the Ugaritic writings of Northern Syria dating from the late second millennium BCE and, apparently, from the recent excavations at Ekron (Tell Miqne), a Philistine site of the earlier first millennium BCE (Müller, 1992: 15–51; Wyatt 1999).[4]

Some scholars maintain that the name of the goddess has been reduced to a common noun meaning "consort," and that the phrase is to be rendered (Hillers 1998 especially 44–8):

b) "I bless you by/commend you to/Yahweh of Samaria and his consort."

Other scholars translate:

c) "I bless you by/commend you to/Yahweh of Samaria and its *asherah*."

As do the first two renderings, this translation understands the last word as a noun with a possessive feminine suffix, but takes the antecedent to be the city of Samaria.

In addition, *asherah* is not taken as the goddess but as the illicit cultic object *asherah*, said to have stood in Samaria according to 2 Kings 13: 6, and appearing in Deuteronomy 16: 21 and Judges 6: 25–6, 28, 30. The connection between the goddess and the cultic object of the same name remains a matter of dispute (Emerton 1999).

Some scholars have opted to explain the final letter in the last word not as the feminine possessive suffix, but as an element of the name of the goddess:

d) "I bless you by/commend you to/Yahweh of Samaria and to Asheratah/ Ashirtah."
(Zevitt 1984; Angerstorfer 1982)

This last interpretation seems the most likely for a number of reasons. First, it is unusual in the Semitic languages to attach a possessive suffix to a proper name. Second, the alternative form "Ashirta" is attested in the proper name Abdi-Ashirtah of the Amarna letters of the fourteenth century BCE. Third, it is common in greeting formulae of the Ancient Near East to bless an individual by one or more gods. Indeed a very similar formula was discovered in the Jewish colony of Elephantine in Egypt from the fifth century BCE:

"I bless you by/commend you to YHH and to Khnub"(Porten 2003).

Khnub was an Egyptian god. According to Porten the name of the sender may indicate his non-Jewish origin. Even if Porten is correct, the formal structure is the same. The sender of the Kuntillet Ajrud letter cited here was named Amariah, indicating that his origins were from a family of worshipers of Yahweh; the *-iah* suffix is a form of Yahweh. This same interpretation that the goddess was known in Israelite venues as Ashirtah/Asheratah best suits the grave inscription from Khirbet el-Qôm on the west bank of the Jordan in what was the kingdom of Judah in the eighth century BCE. The main portion of that text reads:

> Uriyahu the rich. His inscription:
> Uriyahu paid homage to[5] Yahweh,
> and out of his straits, to Asheratah.
> Save him! (Renz and Röllig 1995–2003: I 207–11)

It especially noteworthy that in all of the proper names in the inscriptions from Kuntillet Ajrud and Khirbet el-Qôm that contain a god's name, that name is written *-Yhw*, a short form of YHWH, an indication that all of these individuals not only worshiped Yahweh themselves but belonged to families who worshiped Yahweh over generations (Heide 2002: 114–17). As a statistical sample of worship in ancient Israel the data are insignificant. As snapshots, however, they tend to support the view best articulated by Morton Smith in his *Palestinian Parties and Politics that Shaped the Old Testament* (1971). In that book, by now a classic, Smith takes seriously the biblical portrayal of Israelite vacillation between periods of "following other gods" and periods of consistent fidelity to Yahweh. Behind that vacillation, argues Smith, is a struggle between two parties: the first, the "Yahweh-alone" party, insisted that

Yahweh was the only god to be worshiped by Israelites. On the other side stood what we might call the "Yahweh-plus" party, which acknowledged the divinity of Yahweh within a larger grouping of gods.[6] For example, Smith observed that even Ahab and Jezebel, notorious in the Bible for their support of Baal's cult, gave their children names with Yahweh as the divine element. The different parties struggled for power over centuries. Ultimate victory came to the "Yahweh-alone" party during the Persian period, 539–331 BCE. The grand narrative of the Old Testament was shaped by the victors who divided the kings of Israel and Judah into the "just" and the "unjust" depending on their degree of adherence to the principles of the "Yahweh-alone" party.

In contrast to Albright and Kaufmann, Smith by examining the Yahweh-alone theology from a political standpoint avoids any appeal to Israelite uniqueness. His thesis has the additional advantage of not having to explain the demand that Yahweh be worshiped by Israelites to the exclusion of all other gods as a retrojection. The task remains, however, to account in the first place for the monolatrous demand made in the name of Yahweh.

The demand that one god is to be worshiped even though the existence of others is not necessarily denied was not unique to the Yahweh-alone party in the ancient world. Reference has already been made to the reform of King Akhenaten, which forbade the worship of all gods but the sun-disk. Albright and Redford refer to Aten's worship as monotheistic. Others have withheld that characterization because under the reform the king and the royal family continued to receive the divine honors that had been accorded the earlier pharaohs. But the phenomenon is close enough to the demands for Yahweh's exclusive worship to warrant serious comparison. Mesopotamian mythology refers to the worship of a single god in times of emergency. The prayer literature of the Ancient Near East regularly employed the language of monolatry. A worshiper might approach different gods in succession, declaring that each, in turn, was the only divinity worthy of human worship. At other times worshipers would declare to the god whom they were supplicating that all the other gods were aspects or limbs of the god addressed (Sperling 1998: 148 n. 35–7).

The cause of the monolatrous demand in Israel is to be sought in the particular historical circumstances in which Israel arose. It is clear from the archaeological researches of the past decades, especially in the wake of the 1967 Arab–Israeli war, that the Bible's central traditions of enslavement in Egypt, exodus from Egypt, and armed conquest of the promised land are not historical. While no full positive consensus on the origin of Israel has emerged, there is general agreement that:

a)   There is no archaeological evidence in Egyptian sources that any elements of later Israel were ever in Egypt. Likewise, the early Israelite settlements do not contain Egyptian elements in their material culture, which an Egyptian sojourn would have produced (Dever 1992: 546). As such we cannot speak of a historical exodus from Egypt.
b)   The related tradition of Israel's journey of forty years through the desert is likewise unsupported archaeologically. Extensive exploration of the Sinai has found no evidence of occupation during the appropriate period.

c) Israel did not arise out of a group that had escaped from Egyptian servitude. Instead, the nucleus of Israel was "derived from the local Late Bronze culture through relatively normal social processes" (Dever 1992: 553).

d) Israel was not a single unified ethnic group. Instead, "Israelite ethnic identity came about through the process whereby the indigenous population began to understand and identify itself as Israelite" (Thompson 1987: 37).

e) Whatever movement of population occurred to produce an Israelite culture was internal, probably from the lowlands eastward and northward into the highlands (Bloch-Smith and Nakhai 1999: 103).

The biblical traditions about enslavement, exodus, and conquest must be understood as ideologically motivated accounts usually composed centuries later than the events, real or imagined, that they report. Behind these traditions it is often possible to recover historical information, usually more relevant to the account's time of composition than to its setting. Nonetheless, when judiciously combined with the data provided by archaeology and other historical sources a reasonable synthesis of early Israelite history and religion is possible.[7]

One biblical text refers to 430 years of servitude in Egypt (Exodus 12: 40); Genesis 15: 13 has 400. Attempts to explain the figures schematically have proved unpersuasive (Propp 1998: 415–16). In contrast, the figure fits remarkably well with the chronology of the rise and decline of imperial Egyptian power in Asia (Sperling 1986: 8–12, 1998: 53–60). The Egyptian Empire was part of the international system of the Bronze Age in the second millennium BCE during which the great powers extended their dominion well beyond their borders. Among the powers, which included the Hittites, Mitanni, Assyria, and the Minoan–Mycenean civilization in the Aegean, the Egyptian New Kingdom (about 1550–1069 BCE) was the greatest. Egypt's power extended from northern Sudan in the south and into Syria and Lebanon in the north (Kuhrt 1995: I 185–224). The New Kingdom began after King Ahmose of Egypt overthrew the Hyksos invaders in the mid-sixteenth century BCE and Egypt began to campaign extensively in western Asia. At the battle of Megiddo Thutmose III won a decisive victory after which the local Asiatic rulers became vassals of Egypt. Though rival superpowers, first Mitanni and then the Hittite Kingdom, challenged Egyptian expansion in Asia, the Syria-Palestine coastline and the interior of Palestine remained solidly in Egyptian control. Egyptian correspondence of the fourteenth century BCE shows the heavy economic burdens of taxation and compulsory labor to which the population of Syria-Palestine was subjected (Moran 1992). Local rulers subject to the Pharaoh would round up work gangs to cultivate royal lands. Naturally, this was greatly resented by the locals who could themselves be rallied to attempt to throw off their domination by Egypt and the local Canaanite rulers who cooperated with Egypt (Moran 1992: EA 74, EA 365; Kuhrt 1995: I 324–7.).

About 1200 BCE the international system collapsed in what is termed "the catastrophe." Throughout the eastern Mediterranean, "the twelfth century BCE ushered in a dark age" in which forty-seven major sites were destroyed in Greece, Crete, Anatolia, Cyprus and Syria-Palestine (Drews 1993: 9). In Turkey the Hittite Empire collapsed. Mass movements of population, notably the Sea Peoples, among them the Philistines, transformed the face of the Middle East. Indeed, comparison between the social and political terminology of the Bible and the Bronze Age shows an almost complete discontinuity (Rainey 1987: 542). Against the turbulent international background we see populations caught in the middle of fighting among rival city-states, traders who functioned poorly in the unstable conditions, debtors and dislocated peasants, and the ever-present pastoralists who were always potentially disruptive. In Syria-Palestine we witness "the destruction of the Canaanite urban culture and the withdrawal of Egypt from Canaan" (Finkelstein and Na'aman 1994: 12). By the death of Rameses III about 1153 Egypt no longer dominated Canaan, though some sites continued a bit longer under Egyptian control (Bloch-Smith and Nakhai 1999: 83).

Gradually new groups emerged out of the disorder, among them a group called "Israel." Made up of locals seeking a place in the new social order, these new groups denied their connections to Canaan and gave themselves a new "national" counter-identity (Machinist 1991, 1994; Sperling 1998: 41–60). They began to depict themselves as an invading group from outside the land, much like the Philistines. The Bible's ideological claim to Israel's religious, social, and moral distinctiveness is framed in terms of geography. The Canaanite heritage is denied by the Torah in its claims that all of Israel's laws and institutions were given by Yahweh through Moses to the people when they wandered in the desert. Nothing good in terms of law, morality, or religion came from the land. In line with this ideological geography, the historical traditions about the subjugation of the people who became "Israel" to Egyptians ruling the land of Canaan were transformed into traditions of subjugation in Egypt proper. The withdrawal of Egypt from Canaan became the escape from the land of Egypt itself. Given that the name of the new polity was "Israel," a name which has El as the divine element, the god El must have been the group's patron. At an early date, however, Yahweh completely absorbed the figure of El, and it was Yahweh who became Israel's god. Because of the circumstances of its formation, as a political coalition rather than as an ethnic group, Israel constructed its mythic consciousness out of figures that we would call "political."

The notion that Israel is linked to Yahweh by a "covenant" is central to the Torah. Mendenhall was the first biblical scholar to draw attention to the fact that the biblical notion of covenant was based on treaty formulae employed already in the second millennium BCE. In the treaties a great king bound subordinate kings to exclusive loyalty. Characteristically, divinities were called upon to bear witness to the treaty. Faithful adherence to the treaty was to be greatly rewarded while disloyalty would be punished with the severest forms of destruction (Mendenhall 1954). While subsequent scholarship has shown that several elements in Mendenhall's description require correction, there can be little doubt that his main observation was correct, namely, that the demand that Israel serve Yahweh exclusively was based on the treaty form. Ironically, Mendenhall himself saw the treaty formula as a model for monotheism: one god = one overlord. In fact, the covenant is a perfect metaphor of the religious notion of monolatry. Political treaties demanded exclusive service because there was always another great king who might be served. A Hittite king bound a minor Syrian king precisely because the minor king might serve the king of Egypt. Yahweh binds Israel because Israel might serve another god. What is of particular interest is that in biblical books of the exilic and post-exilic periods, when true monotheism emerges, the conditional covenant becomes a dead letter (Sperling 1989).

The theological construct of covenant with Yahweh mirrored the mundane fact of political union. Yahweh became, in essence, "the flag" that every Israelite saluted. Because Yahweh himself had no known prior connections to Canaanite cult and myth, exclusive loyalty to him served to strengthen the solidarity of the newly formed group. Initially an advantage, the absence of Yahweh from the local mythic traditions meant that the religious necessities served by gods of weather, agriculture, fertility, and the heavenly bodies would be unmet. In a monotheistic environment, monolatry is perfectly sensible; you worship one god because it is the only one. In contrast, restricting worship to one god when others are acknowledged to exist is difficult to uphold. In fact, ignoring powers that one knew to be potent could be dangerous, and relatively few Israelites in the early first millennium BCE took the risk. But if Morton Smith is right, there was always a minority who did.

Because the monolatrous demand as expressed in the primitive[8] notion of covenant was central to the formation of the Israelite polity, the call to serve Yahweh alone could resonate in times of crisis and serve as a general rallying point to encourage group solidarity (Exodus 32: 25–9; I Samuel 7: 1–14; I Kings 18; 2 Kings 9–10, 22–3). The crisis occasioned by the fall of the last Israelite state in 586 BCE proved decisive. Once Yahweh had proved his power by scattering his people "in a diaspora from one end of the known world to the other, what was left for him but monotheism?" (Smith 1952: 147).

NOTES

1   The discussion of Albright is based on Gnuse 1997: 64–6. See there, 62–128 for an extensive summary of recent scholarship on monotheism. Important recent works are: Edelman 1996, Porter 2000, Van Der Toorn 1997, Propp 1999, and Smith 1990, 2002. For general critiques of Kaufmann's work see Hayes 1999 2:16–17, Greenberg 1995, Levenson 1982, and Sperling 1986, especially 16–21.

2   All citations herein are from the reprint by Doubleday Anchor (1957) of the second Johns Hopkins edition of 1946.

3   The terms "popular" and "official" have not been rigorously employed by students of Israelite religion (Berlinerblau 1996: 1–45, 1999).

4   For a photograph of a Philistine inscription that reads "To Asherat," see *Biblical Archaeologist* 53/4 (1990): 232.

5   This is how the verb *brk* with indirect object is used in Biblical Hebrew. See Psalm 95: 6.

6   This is an oversimplification. In the ancient world one would not be an abstract monotheist or polytheist. Whereas the "Yahweh-alone party" would tend to be an identifiable group, the "Yahweh-plus" party would be more diverse.

7   In their summary of Iron Age I, Bloch-Smith and Nakhai 1999: 118 write: "Given the
    rather late and tendentious nature of the biblical text, it is somewhat unexpected to discover
    that archaeological evidence presents a similar, though not identical, picture of the events of
    the period." See also Dever 1998.
8   I owe the apt characterization of covenant as "primitive" to Redford 1992: 275.

FURTHER READING

Gnuse 1997 is a good place to begin, supplemented by Edelman 1996, Porter 2000, Van Der
    Toorn 1997, Propp 1999, and Smith 1990, 2002.

CHAPTER THIRTY-ONE

The Decipherment of the Ancient Near East

Peter T. Daniels

The decipherment of the Ancient Near East began long before Champollion in 1822 compared the Rosetta Stone's *Ptolemy* with an obelisk in England's *Cleopatra*, or Grotefend in 1802 compared recurrent sequences of wedges with the patterns of royal names in Sassanian inscriptions, or even before Jean-Jacques Barthélemy in 1754 compared names in plain Greek with stretches of text in Palmyrene.[a]

In ancient Mesopotamia itself, the past was wondered at and even collected. The Assyriologist R. D. Biggs described:[1]

> the "palace museum" in Babylon, built in the time of Nebuchadnezzar. It contained some remarkable antiquities such as the famous lion of Babylon, a statue of Puzur-Ishtar, an Ur III official in Mari, Assyrian stelas and reliefs, as well as inscriptions from various areas of the city of Babylon [and from] Sippar, also a relief with a Hittite hieroglyphic inscription. Some of these items were likely taken as booty on various Babylonian raids. Interestingly, they were not presented to the gods as votive offerings, but were installed in the museum. This museum was obviously kept up since the collection was added to after the time of Nebuchadnezzar and in fact included an inscription of Nabonidus and even a stele of Darius. The collection also included some cuneiform tablets, one of which has a colophon identifying it as the property of Nebuchadnezzar. It seems likely that this museum was not only a royal cabinet of antiquities, but was also open for citizens to view.

The continual recopying and reinterpreting of ancient texts – whether the literary tradition represented by the great epics, or the scholarly tradition recorded in the great lists that were begun almost when writing itself began – is a kind of decipherment. And decipherment in a narrower sense was known as well. Examples exist of the ordinary lists of cuneiform signs (from which schoolboys learned to be scribes) with archaic forms included; to some of them a parallel column of pictorial shapes is added. Although it turns out that these pictures supposed by the ancient scribes were guesses as to the pictograms that might have underlain the signs they used (that is, they don't match the shapes excavated from two millennia earlier), their very existence shows that at least some people were interested in – and aware of – the history of their writing system.[b]

Unfortunately, even by the time of Xenophon, Mesopotamian civilization had all but disappeared. Neither he, nor Herodotus before him, or Alexander's chroniclers after him, took any steps to inform their Greek readers about the writing or texts of the lands they were traversing. (Of course, considering the fantasies that *were* reported about Egyptian writing, this might have been for the best.[c]) What little the worlds of Europe and Islam knew of Mesopotamia was gleaned from the Bible and the Classics. For a later age, the quality that could be achieved from such sources shines from every page of Gibbon's *Decline and Fall of the Roman Empire* (1776–88); for the end of the age that has been our concern in this volume, a comparable work crowned the career of the abbé Barthélemy (1716–1795), that same scholar who was the first ever to decipher any ancient script.[2] He labored at this immense book for more than thirty years, and in 1788 there appeared the first edition (of three in his lifetime – quickly expanded to seven octavo volumes plus a large volume of plates) of *The Voyage of Young Anacharsis in Greece*, a picaresque novel, a *Bildungsroman*, detailing in four quarto volumes extending upwards of 2,500 pages the travels of a fictional Scythian youth around the Greek world of the mid fourth century BCE. An English translation came out in 1791 and kept being reprinted until 1825 (the only American edition was printed in Philadelphia in 1804, its four volumes matching those of the original French), while the French kept being brought out for more than a century. Every page bristles with footnotes referring the reader to the Greek or Latin source for every factual statement. The hero learns politics and logic straight from Aristotle. But does Anacharsis visit Mesopotamia? He must have done so, to cross into Iran, but the only passage set outside the Greek world (including Ionia on the Asia Minor coast) is a mere six pages devoted to the Persian empire (1788: 3.272–77, chap. lxi). Barthélemy mines the same Classical sources Pierre Briant was to use nearly a quarter millennium later,[3] yet from them he constructs not a political history, but rather a description of the splendors of Persepolis and of the *paradisoi* of Persian aristocrats. Anacharsis stays at that belonging to Arsames, a satrap in the west who figures in many a historical anecdote (Briant 2002 index s.v.), but Barthélemy makes of him a sort of *ancien régime* nobleman retired to his estate and surrounded by *philosophes*. It was not the first, and far from the last, time that a writer remade the ancient world in his own image.

Barthélemy cites some of the early modern travelers' descriptions of sites in Persia, but he seems not to have known the books (1772–78) by the Dane Carsten Niebuhr, who brought back the first drawings of inscriptions from Persepolis (in three similar but distinct scripts) that were accurate enough to be fodder for decipherment; perhaps, in his old age, he would have made progress on them himself. His long life came to an end shortly before the discovery of the Rosetta Stone held out the promise of unparalleled insight into a deceased culture, for Napoleon had invaded Egypt with an army of scholars as well as an army of soldiers (Parkinson 1999). The value of the Rosetta Stone, with inscriptions, presumably versions of the same text, in Greek and two varieties of Egyptian, was recognized immediately as the potential key to the ancient language, but it would be two decades before results were achieved. But besides the antiquities that came back to Paris, the scholars also brought reams of careful, exquisite drawings depicting the glories of the structures on the banks of the

Nile.[4] (The soldiers did not fare so well as the scholars: the Stone itself was taken as booty within three years and has been a centerpiece of the British Museum's wonders since 1802.) Upon publication, they stimulated the imagination of a generation of artists, designers, and craftsmen, and the first quarter of the nineteenth century was awash in a style that came to be called Egyptomania.[d] (Its mark on architecture came somewhat later, and erections like The Tombs prison and the 42nd Street Reservoir in New York City and the Washington Monument were some of its later achievements.) Champollion's decipherment of Egyptian hieroglyphs, announced in 1822, was nearly anti-climactic, and he died young, little acclaimed, his contribution recognized by scholars but not appreciated by the public.[5]

Meanwhile, the relics from western Asia were not being neglected. A high school teacher in Göttingen, Georg Friedrich Grotefend (1775–1853), had been scrutinizing the texts published by Niebuhr. Building on Sylvestre de Sacy's decipherment of royal inscriptions of the Sassanian era (some centuries subsequent to the Achaemenid), he searched the records for patterns of characters that might be read as containing the pattern "Xerxes, great king, son of Darius, great king, son of Hystaspes" (who was not a king) – the names he knew from Herodotus. He found these patterns, but was not familiar with ancient or modern Persian languages; specialists built on his insight over the next decades, and the finishing touches were put on the Old Persian decipherment by Edward Hincks (1792–1866), a Church of Ireland clergyman (son of a Belfast professor), who simultaneously forwarded the interpretation of the other two scripts and, after several years' intensive labor, successfully read the most complicated one, which proved to record the Semitic language that would come to be called Akkadian. (His findings were regularly reported to H. C. Rawlinson in Baghdad, who incorporated them into his own publications on the great inscription at Behistun: his copying of that text was a remarkable achievement but made no contribution to the decipherment.)[6] There was, though, not much "Assyriomania" to parallel the earlier Egyptomania, even with the spectacular recovery of countless wall reliefs from excavations by Layard and Botha at Nineveh (Larsen 1996) that came to London, Paris, New York, and many other places and drew respectful crowds (Russell 1997).

Only later in the century – though it was Hincks who became the first to recognize a biblical name, that of Omri, king of Israel, in any ancient text (Daniels 1994: 43) – did Mesopotamia capture the public imagination. Owing to the centrality of the Bible in Western culture, anything that might be seen as illuminating the Bible text seized the public's attention; for the cuneiform civilizations, the decisive discovery was half a large cuneiform tablet bearing part of what was immediately seen to be an epic description of a universal flood – or Flood. An enterprising newspaper reporter declared that he would return to the spot and dig up the other half of that tablet. Astoundingly, he did exactly that! (Frustratingly, this incredible achievement is said to have happened on the very first day of the expedition, and all else was anti-climactic.[e]) An episode in biblical interpretation that came to be known as *Babel und Bibel*, Babylon and Bible, or "pan-Babylonianism," ensued, where everything pertaining to biblical matters was refracted through a Mesopotamian prism.[f] The effect was only heightened with the discovery of the "Code" of Hammurapi in 1902, with its startling, nearly word-for-word parallels with Pentateuchal injunctions.[g] Mesopotamian hegemony was briefly interrupted by a second bout of Egyptomania, when the tomb of the boy king Tutankhamen was discovered in 1922 – uniquely, its treasures were intact, not looted in antiquity – and rumors of a "curse" seized the imagination of a credulous public and film industry.

In the middle half of the twentieth century, a quartet of archaeological discoveries promised revolutions in biblical studies, though only one captured the public imagination. First was the accidental finding of the site of Ras Shamra, ancient Ugarit, on the Syrian coast in 1929. Excavation began almost immediately, and clay tablets were found bearing texts in what had to be an alphabet like the Hebrew (though the letters comprised wedge-shaped impressions as in Mesopotamia); decipherment proceeded along three or four lines simultaneously with several scholars producing nearly identical results in a year or so.[7] The local language proved to be closely related to an ancestor of Hebrew. Most of the documents were of the quotidian sort so valuable in reconstructing a culture's lifeways, but among them were copies of epics and other poetic texts that were far more similar to biblical compositions than there was any right to expect. Comprehension of the Hebrew Scriptures' prosody, grammar, and mythological background were immeasurably improved.[h]

The second and third discoveries were nearly simultaneous, but only one became a household word. In 1947, in war-torn Palestine, bedouin explorers came across at least one cave in cliffs alongside the Dead Sea (near the site of Qumran), and in this cave scrolls had been hidden in jars nearly two thousand years before. Through wars of politics and religion, scholars studied, archaeologists prospected, and eventually thousands of fragments – from nearly intact scrolls to tiny scraps with a letter or two – were recovered; they proved to hold both biblical texts (the earliest yet discovered, all but identical to the readings that were standardized some eight centuries later) and sectarian writings whose interpretation continues to be hotly argued to this day. At least some explanation for the renown of the Dead Sea Scrolls may be found in the fact that Edmund Wilson's account first appeared in the *New Yorker* in 1955 and soon became a best-selling book.[i] The discovery of Gnostic codices at Nag Hammadi in Egypt (in the Coptic language) in 1945 could not boast a popular and eloquent narrator, on the other hand; yet these volumes are as illuminative of the development of Christianity – they represent the writings of a theology that lost out to what proved to be Orthodoxy – as the Scrolls are of the origins of both Christianity and rabbinic Judaism.[j]

Here is where there ought to be a mention of "biblical archaeology," an approach that in effect sought to "prove" the truth of the Bible by exploring the physical remains of ancient civilizations in the "Holy Land" and related regions.[k] The dean of biblical archaeologists was W. F. Albright, as a writer nearly as prolific and popular as Edmund Wilson but also a combination of excavator and philologist. While archaeology is no longer carried out with such explicitly sectarian motives, with his colleagues G. Ernest Wright and Nelson Glueck and his phalanx of brilliant students he shaped the twentieth century's view of the Ancient Near East.[l] His longest-lasting monument is the Anchor Bible series of commentaries, commenced in 1964; many of the originally announced cohort of contributors, adherents to the biblical archaeology approach, did not eventually write their volumes, but many of those that did produced some of the most readable and illuminating treatments of the biblical texts.[8] (In later years, under the editorship of David Noel Freedman, a much wider range of approaches was welcomed into the series, and as of 2006 almost the entire Bible had been covered, and some of the earlier, directly Albright-influenced volumes were in course of replacement.) Perhaps the apotheosis of "pan-Ugariti-cism" can be seen in the Psalms volumes by Mitchell J. Dahood and in Marvin Pope's Job and Song of Songs. One reviewer remarked that if even a quarter of Dahood's proposals for emending the text in light of Ugaritic were accepted, biblical philology would be revolutionized; but a wag queried at an international meeting commemor-ating the fiftieth anniversary of Ugarit's discovery, "Ah, but which twenty-five percent?" (Young 1981: 190 [edited for politeness]).

The fourth of the twentieth century's archaeological discoveries that unexpectedly illuminated biblical study was of a tablet archive at Ebla (Tell Mardikh), in Syria in 1975. Some hasty readings and some clever publicity fostered the idea that texts had been found from 2500 BCE in a direct ancestor of Hebrew – M. J. Dahood made the rounds of the cultural institutions giving public lectures during which he would let the first volume of published Ebla texts fall open purportedly at random, pick a line (the language is written in fairly standard cuneiform), and relate it to a Bible passage that had previously been difficult to interpret. After a few years, and the commend-ably quick publication of the tablets, sobriety set in and it was recognized that the language of Ebla is not so close to Hebrew, but is rather a variety of Akkadian that happened to be used far to the west of where it was expected to be found at the date that proved to be not quite so old as first supposed.[m]

But Oriental studies were not to be left in peace, either to interpret the Bible or more objectively to investigate the origins of Western civilization. With the decolo-nialization of much of the world proceeding in the wake of World War II and largely accomplished by the 1970s, "Third World" voices that had previously been sub-sumed or co-opted within Euro-American scholarship began to assert themselves and be heard. No longer were the treasures and minutiae of archaeological excavations carted off wholesale to the home institutions of the scholars leading the expeditions; at most the finds were shared, and more likely they remained carefully housed in the institutions of the countries that were home to the antiquities, where visiting scholars could study them and whence they could from time to time be loaned for exhibition abroad. (Egyptomania broke out for the third time when the "Treasures of King Tut's Tomb" were displayed world-wide. This event had the further consequence of introducing the concept of the "blockbuster" museum show. Art history would never be the same.)

A less benign manifestation of the new intellectual freedom of the former client peoples was resentment of past generations of European intellectuals' attitude toward "native" peoples. One objection was to the name of the field whose scope is the civilizations of Asia: "Oriental studies," defining its object (yes, objectified) as "east" of some "objective" "standard," i.e., "the West." (Happily, the field has remained largely free of postmodern modes of scholarship, in which such punning is welcome and perhaps passes for analysis.) An early casualty was the name of the then century-old International Congress of Orientalists, which from 1986 has been the International Congress of Asian and North African Studies;[9] the Oriental Division of the century-old New York Public Library has just (2002) been renamed; the century-and-a-half-old American Oriental Society has not. The flood of criticism crested in 1978 with the publication of *Orientalism* by Edward Said, a Columbia University professor of literature, claiming Palestinian Arab heritage, with no discernible qualifications to speak on the topic (he evidently did not even read German, the language of a large majority of Orientalist scholarship). His more outrageous accusations received prompt refutation by the eminent English Islamist Bernard Lewis of Princeton University, at a plenary session of the American Oriental Society in 1980 and in the *New York Review of Books* (Lewis 1982).[n] From his scattershot attacks, though, one caution can be salvaged. We do observe that Theodor Nöldeke, writing before the turn of the twentieth century, or even Berthold Spuler, writing at mid-century, devalued Islam.[10] But, aware, we can compensate for bias. It will not stain contemporary scholarship.

More pernicious is unrecognized bias, which figures doubly or triply in another well-publicized affray. Martin Bernal, a scholar of contemporary Chinese politics with a Classical education, tried to explain why Greeks beginning with Herodotus attributed many of the basics of their lifeways to borrowing or inspiration from Egypt, whereas modern Classicists did not. He traced the difference to the late eighteenth century invention of "race" and the infection of antisemitism in the intellectual establishment, such that the scholars who established the paradigms for the study of history were unable to conceive of African or Semitic underpinnings to Western Civilization (Bernal 1986). Had he stopped with these historiographic demonstrations, he would have made a real contribution to understanding the development of the discipline; but he opted instead to demonstrate the validity of the ancient view of Greek history, focusing moreover almost entirely on Egypt. Unequipped with the requisite philological tools, he has not persuaded (Bernal 1987–91). (Meanwhile, the search for connections to the East, more than to the South, is proceeding successfully, led by e.g. Burkert 1992.) However, in no small measure owing to the provocative title *Black Athena* insisted on (he says) by his publisher, he has attracted the enthusiasm of "Afrocentric" scholars, who like Said for Asia seek to redress the neglect and scorn that have been the lot of the civilizations of Africa, by embracing the most discredited aspects of eighteenth century "race" theory and insisting that ancient Egyptians were "black," so that all good things came "out of Africa." The result was a right-wing backlash that tries to deny any validity at all to cross-cultural fertilization.[o]

Another misunderstanding of the Ancient Near East by Classicists is associated with Eric Havelock, formerly of the "Toronto School" that formed around Marshall McLuhan. It was Havelock's claim that true "literacy" was not possible with a non-alphabetic script; neither biblical nor Mesopotamian "literature" deserves the label. But Havelock knew the Semitic texts only in (archaizing) translation.[p]

A last, more recent fallacy in deciphering difficult data impinges indirectly on the Ancient Near East but may stand for many a problem of hasty judgment as well as showing how archaeological evidence can sometimes inform a philological problem.

In the remote now-deserts of the Tarim Basin, in what once was called Chinese Turkestan and now comprises part of the semi-autonomous region of Xinjiang (Sinkiang), desiccated corpses (which have come to be called the "mummies of Ürümchi," though they were not embalmed and Ürümchi is merely the location of the museum where they are housed) of a strikingly European appearance have been found. The first Western investigator to view them and some associated cave paintings leaped to the conclusion that they must represent the ancestors of people who spoke Tokharian (an Indo-European language discovered early in the twentieth century in manuscript hoards). Only when a specialist in ancient textiles was able to study the grave goods associated with the bodies did it emerge that there were three widely separate finds: the earliest group was buried with sprigs of ephedra, the source of a psychoactive agent now believed to be the key component of the Indic/Iranian mystic beverage *soma/haoma*; the second group in time had textiles remarkably similar to those associated with Celtic burials in Europe; and the latest group's textiles showed clear affinity with the earliest group's. It may thus be tentatively suggested that the earliest of the three communities spoke an undifferentiated Indo-Iranian language (earlier even than the few tantalizing traces of Indic names in the Mitanni cuneiform materials); only the second community spoke an early form of Tokharian; and the latest group represented an Iranian-speaking community.[q]

In this quick survey of modern attitudes toward the Ancient Near East, certain themes recur: the interpretation of ancient relics in contemporary terms; the jumping to hasty conclusions; and the importance of attention to minute detail. Decipherment is the very first task of the philologist, but it does not stop with the interpretation of a script. Every thing that comes to us from the past must be deciphered, and the philologist's main occupation is making sense of texts after they have been deciphered.

NOTES

1   In his unpublished Presidential Address to the Middle West Branch of the American Oriental Society, Madison, 1979; I am grateful to him for providing me with this paragraph from the manuscript.

2   Barthélemy's pioneering achievement exhibits many of the characteristics of a typical decipherment. (0) The fundamental prerequisite is accurate reproductions of the enigmatic materials. Depictions of Palmyrene texts had been available for a century and a half, but, as it turned out, they bore little resemblance to the actual inscriptions and were uninterpretable. But, literally overnight, as soon as responsible engravings of paired Palmyrene and Greek inscriptions were published in London and Paris, Barthélemy was able to interpret them. (1) The least problematic sort of decipherment involves bilingual texts, like these from Palmyra, or indeed like the Rosetta Stone – but bilinguals are not all that common among the world's inscriptions. (2) The Greek inscriptions were seen to contain a number of proper names, and proper names can usually be expected to read fairly similarly in the unknown language as well. (3) The Palmyrene language was known from Classical sources to be similar to a familiar language, namely, Syriac (the Christian literary Aramaic language

of many Near Eastern churches). (4) After Barthélemy had identified the readings of many of the twenty-two Palmyrene letters, their similarity in shape to the corresponding Hebrew and Syriac letters became clear.

3 Xenophon, Diodorus Siculus, Quintus Curtius – see Briant 2002, passim.

4 All the plates have been reproduced, much reduced, in a single compact volume (Néret 1994), not to be confused with Néret's selection of about one-fifth of these illustrations for Taschen's "Icons" series, published in 2001 under the same title.

5 Contrary to popular belief, the Rosetta Stone was not by itself the key to Egyptian hieroglyphics. It was easy enough to identify proper names in the text – "cartouches" (ovals surrounding groups of hieroglyphs) occurred in positions corresponding to the appearance of the name of the pharaoh Ptolemy in the Greek text, and Barthélemy had suggested years before that the cartouches in Egyptian inscriptions marked royal names – but no name *other than* Ptolemy appeared. It was thus impossible to determine which characters corresponded to which sounds in the name. The name of Cleopatra, however, was found on an obelisk that had been taken to England, and (it is believed) Thomas Young, a brilliant but intellectually undisciplined polymath, sent this identification to Champollion (1790–1832). There is sufficient overlap in the names that Champollion was able to make tentative assignments of sounds to letters. With these few starting-points, he was able to begin to apply his key insight: that the Coptic language, of contemporary Egptian Christians, is a direct descendant of ancient Egyptian, so that Coptic words could provide the key to Egyptian words. The first, and conclusive, result involved another royal name. A cartouche contained what appeared to be a depiction of the sun; the letter *m*, known from *Ptolemy*, and an unidentified sign, twice. The Coptic word for "sun" is *re*. Champollion guessed at the reading of the final pair of signs, and identified the well-known pharaoh Ramses. This was immensely significant, because it showed that native Egyptian names like *Ramses*, not just Greek names like *Ptolemy* and *Cleopatra*, were written phonetically. The hieroglyphs were thus not some sort of mystical ideography, but a true writing system that recorded the sounds of the language it represented. The conceptual barrier was broken, and Champollion could use Coptic to interpret much Egyptian vocabulary. He had made considerable progress on the grammar of the language by his untimely death at the age of 41.

6 Bermant and Weitzman (1979: 85–108) seem to have been the first authors in nearly a century to recognize Hincks's contribution to the decipherment of cuneiform in a popular work, but they remain under the spell of Rawlinson and his publicists (his brother was the ancient historian George Rawlinson, and his successor as Keeper of Western Asiatic Antiquities at the British Museum was E. A. Wallis Budge). They dismiss as "insinuation" (100) Hincks's demonstration that Rawlinson adopted some of his results without acknowledgment (Daniels 1994: 51) – with access to Rawlinson's unpublished working manuscripts in the British Museum, they could have discovered whether his "all manner of lists" (ibid.) included recopyings of Hincks's publications (Hincks's manuscripts seem to have been discarded by his descendants in the late nineteenth century). And they overlook Hincks's most important – and most accessible – publication, in the *Journal of the Royal Asiatic Society* for 1848: "It most clearly lays out the reasoning behind the assignment of values to cuneiform signs, and it shows great astuteness in working out the grammar of the unknown language we call Urartian" (Daniels 1994: 38f.).

7 The decipherment is well described by Corré (1966) and Day (2002). In the case of Ugaritic, there were at first no bilingual texts. The location and date (14th c. BCE) of the finds, and the small number of different letters in the inscriptions, made reasonable the

guess that the language was similar, perhaps ancestral, to Hebrew. One approach sought letters that might correspond to the single-letter prefixes and suffixes found in Hebrew and, by either contextual or statistical analysis, led to plausible identifications. Another approach took advantage of the happy accident that one of the first tablets discovered appeared to be an accounting document, and a word appeared with three signs, one repeated: *XYX*. It is very unusual in a Semitic language to find the same letter in first and third position within a word, but one of the exceptions is the word for "three." The two letters involved, *sh* and *l*, happen to be fairly frequent, so this proved a very useful entrée into the interpretation of the script.

8   Until recently, every Anchor Bible volume's dust jacket included a list of all prospective authors, and the list was regularly updated. Since dust jackets are highly ephemeral, it will be useful to append the original list of Old Testament contributors (from a 1965 printing of Jeremiah, the second volume to be published; Apocrypha volumes were not yet contemplated; students of Albright's are marked with an asterisk, and italics indicate those who actually completed all or part of their original assignment): 1, Gen., *E. A. Speiser*; 4, Num., G. E. Mendenhall*; 5, Deut., William L. Moran, S.J.*; 6, Josh.-Judg., *G. Ernest Wright* [Josh.]*; 7, Ruth-Esther-Song of Sol.-Lam., *E. F. Campbell, Jr.* [Ruth]*; 8–9, Sam., F. M. Cross, Jr.*; 12–14, Chron.-Ezra-Neh., *J. M. Myers*; 15, Job, *Marvin H. Pope*; 16–17, Pss., *Mitchell Dahood, S.J.*; 18, Prov.-Eccles., *R. B. Y. Scott*; 19, Isa. I, H. L. Ginsberg; 20, Isa. II, *J. L. McKenzie*; 21, Jer., *John Bright*; 22, Ezek., *Moshe Greenberg*; 23, Dan., *Louis F. Hartman*; 24, Hos.-Joel-Amos-Obad.-Jon.-Mic.-Nah.-Hab., B. W. Anderson; 25, Zeph.-Hag.-Zech.-Mal., Walter Harrelson. (I thank M. O'Connor for assistance with this note.)

9   Actually the 30th (Mexico City, 1976) and 31st (Tokyo–Kyoto, 1984) congresses were the International Congress of Human Sciences in Asia and North Africa; the slightly shorter title has been used since the 32nd (Hamburg, 1986).

10   The Koran "has been truly described as the most widely read book in existence. This circumstance alone is sufficient to give it an urgent claim on our attention, whether it suit our taste and fall in with our religious and philosophical views or not. . . . It must be owned that the first perusal leaves on a European an impression of chaotic confusion" (Nöldeke 1883: 597). For Spuler's attitude, see the closing pages of the Introduction by Jane Hathaway to Spuler 1995.

FURTHER READING

[a] A few of the decipherments of Ancient Near Eastern scripts are sketched within the text; for fuller accounts, the best available descriptions of most of them are found in Pope 1999. For the decipherments of Palmyrene and Mesopotamian cuneiform, however, reference must be made to Daniels 1988 and 1994 respectively. Summaries will be found in Daniels 1995, 1996b; the latter includes what is meant to be a full bibliography of the original publications of decipherments of ancient scripts.

[b] The so-called "paleographic tablets" are discussed in Daniels 1992.

[c] The classic treatment of premodern understandings of Egyptian hieroglyphics is Iversen 1961. A dense but informative summary may be found in Pope 1999: 11–59.

[d] The ever-growing literature on the reception of "the Orient" throughout the nineteenth century, particularly in European fine and decorative arts and belles lettres, cannot be gone into here.

[e] The story about recovering the flood tablets is told with vim by Ceram 1951: 274–78. This book, once immensely popular, is rich with romantic anecdote but less than careful about factual detail; in particular its accounts of decipherments are more fanciful than anything else.

[f] A useful summary of the "Babel and Bible controversy" is Larsen 1995. It continues to be studied, especially in German-language literature, e.g. Johanning 1988, Lehmann 1994; a late echo, controversial in its time and still valuable for its illumination of the relation between Western and Mesopotamian conceptions of the divine, is J. J. Finkelstein 1958.

[g] The Laws of Hammurapi should not be considered a "law code" in anything like the modern sense (Roth n.d.). For a brilliant exposition of the relevance of ancient law to subsequent Western legal practice, we again turn to J. J. Finkelstein (his 1981, published posthumously, is the first two parts of his study; his 1973, the third).

[h] Concise and extensive overviews of Ugaritology are available in Young 1981 and Watson and Wyatt 1999, respectively.

[i] Wilson (1969) revised his Dead Sea Scrolls book several times; its popularity was rivalled by the work of a scholar rather than a journalist, Millar Burrows, whose two volumes have been reprinted as Burrows 1978. The Scrolls returned to the news decades later, as protests over the languid rate of publication grew, but all of them are now available to scholars in photographs, and nearly all in scholarly editions. Complete translations, and complete texts and translations, of the non-biblical texts are available in García Martínez 1996 and García Martínez and Tigchelaar 2000 respectively; more readily available and more popularly presented are the many editions of what was originally published as Vermes 1962.

[j] The principal introductions to the Nag Hammadi codices for the general public have been by a scholar whose dissertation dealt with one of the first published texts, beginning with Pagels 1979. The complete collection became available in English in Robinson 1977.

[k] Two recent books offer complementary histories of biblical archaeology. Dever (2003), formerly an arch-secularist, now places his archaeology at the service of the biblical text; I. Finkelstein and Silberman (2002) remain staunchly scientific. (I thank Jack M. Sasson for advice on this note.)

[l] An astonishing achievement, all but unknown to the scholarly world, is Albright's magisterial three-page overview of Near Eastern civilizations, from prehistory down to the Islamic Conquest, published in the *Encyclopædia Britannica* (1974); in the 1985 revision, it was orphaned as "The example of the Middle East" (the sole example) under the division "Civilizations" in the article "Prehistoric Peoples and Cultures" (vol. 26).

[m] The initial rather sensationalized presentations of the Ebla discoveries were quickly-translated competing accounts by the excavator, Paolo Matthiae (1981), and the epigrapher, Giovanni Pettinato (1981), of the Italian mission at Tell Mardikh. They had been anticipated in English by an overview produced by Bermant and Weitzman (1979). Typically, the scientific reconsiderations have not received the publicity of the original biblically oriented news headlines. The evidence that Eblaite is an outlying form of Akkadian (rather than a close relative of Hebrew) is presented by Krebernik (1996), in a volume honoring the centennial of W. F. Albright's birth that is overall not inaccessible to the general reader

[n] The literature on "Orientalism" is extensive, partisan, and polemical. The key documents are gathered by Macfie (2000). From his introductions, and from his own monograph (2002), the impression is received that he wants to embrace Said's point of view, but that the details make this impossible; Sardar (2003) is more accepting.

[o] Lefkowitz 1996 is ostensibly a rebuttal of Afrocentric claims, but devolves into an attack on Bernal. Lefkowitz and Rogers (1996) collected attacks (some new, some reprinted) on Bernal and his work and refused to include Bernal's responses (some published, some to

be prepared; Bernal 2001: 13), and they have now been collected in Bernal 2001. Daniels 1999 is a linguistic critique of aspects of Afrocentrism (unfortunately all accented letters are missing from the webpage).

[p] Havelock's position on ancient literacy is most clearly stated in his brief, posthumous volume (1986). Echoes of his notion can still be found in discussions of the foundations of Western civilization; a sketch of an exposure of its perniciousness is attempted in Daniels 1996a: 27–28.

[q] The principal source for discussion of the problems raised by the Ürümchi materials is Mair 1998. Unfortunately, Barber 1999 was not yet available, and the significance of Barber's contribution to the 1996 conference underlying Mair's publication was not recognized at the time. Daniels (2000) reviews the question, particularly from the linguistic point of view.

CHAPTER THIRTY-TWO

Legacies of the Ancient Near East

Daniel C. Snell

What, of all this, comes down to later ages and comes down to us? In surveying this span of history and cultural achievement, we can see that the Ancient Near East has bequeathed to later ages a myriad of ideas, institutions, and techniques which have been important and in many cases centrally important to later developments in Western civilization. It is obvious to readers of the essays here that scholars are still struggling to understand how and when the transitions of these elements to later ages took place. Sometimes we have the clear evidence of transmission and other times we are left to guess at the mechanisms. And some elements became so basic to how people lived that we do not have to speak of transmission but only of continuity.

The elements that come to mind include the following, not necessarily in order of importance. And other scholars might highlight other aspects of the Ancient Near Eastern legacy:

- Cities. There were cities elsewhere, but it was in the Near East that the biggest ones were formed first, and the norms of living in cities seem to have come down almost unbroken to later ages. People came to Uruk, even though it might have been unhealthy, because it was the biggest and most exciting market where all the best things could be seen, and the government would attempt to guarantee your safety to see them.
- Writing. Writing was devised first in or near Mesopotamia, and though various systems were devised, the cuneiform system and the hieroglyphic system and their offshoots, among which is the alphabetic system in which we now write, came to dominate how people recorded things for later times. Humans developed writing elsewhere probably independently, but it is the Near Eastern-originated system that has come to spread most widely.
- Royal or governmental authority. Again this appeared elsewhere independently, but the role of the king in protecting the weak and securing the safety of the others first found formulation among the rulers of the Near East, and their rhetoric echoes with us now as we face very different challenges.

- Representative local government. The localities were governed through time by consensus generated among well-off men, and though outsiders might hope to swerve their deliberations and could sometimes force them to do things they did not want to do, when those coercers retreated, as they always did, the kind of ward government that became the norm in much later ages reemerged to manage how things actually got done.

- Bureaucracy and the passion for record-keeping. When it was too detailed but potentially important and difficult to remember, they wrote it down. But the obsessiveness and meticulousness with which they worried about records has fanned out through the writing world. Perhaps even the categories of bureaucracy practiced in the Early Modern Near East had something to do with the ancients' approach, and if one feels that bureaucracy died with the Ottomans, perhaps one should arrange to visit any Middle Eastern country today.

- The spirit of laws. The texts that look legal to us may not have been laws intended to be enforced, and yet they embodied the values of the community as conceived by the kings and scribes who put such texts together. And if one looks at the codes as a programmed course of instruction by example of what justice is, one can see that already in very early times the assumptions were there about what the norms of justice ought to be. These might be summarized in the idea that the rich should not oppress the weak, as Hammurapi explicitly said, and that access to the means of redress for the powerless should not be restricted by officials. Also there is an assumption that a king, a government, ought to have a policy that assured some kind of social equity. If they did not, they might be accused of impiety. These ideals about how states ought to function and how society ought to operate have enjoyed extraordinary continuity in the Western tradition, even though we must admit that kings and states have frequently fallen short of them. Our politicians may not want to be called "king of justice" as Hammurapi did, but they all have to show that they care about the little guy and will be ready to right wrongs brought to their attention by the eloquent peasants of our day.

- An idea of freedom. The kings boasted of their establishing the right to move without restrictions for their populations, and though this boast frequently was hollow and unfounded, people from all walks of life found it a worthy goal. It accords with other, more obviously religious, ideas that attribute to individuals the responsibility for their own conduct and lives. Although kings strived ironically also to assert their powers and restrict their subjects' decisions, the freedom of persons and of corporate entities like cities was a thing to be struggled over, negotiated, and asserted. It was not an absolute, but it was an ideal widely held. The Muslims later said explicitly that the basic assumption in cases of lack of clarity of status was freedom; earlier Near Easterners would have agreed.

- Some forms of poetry. Through the influence of the Hebrew Bible the devices of repetition with changes has become part of our rhetoric. And the so-called Gilgamesh Epic along with a few other compositions may have bequeathed to later ages the idea of writing on a vast canvas, geographically at least, and exploring the basic questions about human existence, life, and death. More sadly, the lament has had a long legacy from its Mesopotamian origins, but so have other genres like the apologetic autobiography of the sort first found on Egyptian tombs. Literary tastes and genres change with time, and it is not possible to prove descent for many genres. And yet, perhaps because of the assumptions about life that remain the same, some of these ancient expressions retain for us the vitality they probably had for their first hearers.

- The religious idea that you only live once. This is so basic to the Western view of human beings that it is important to remind ourselves that much of the world does not share it. But these dead ancients did. And if they did not themselves invent the notion, for it is likely to have been millennia-old when writing was devised, they saw it as self-evident, as most of us still do. And they were not afraid to explain the corollary of this being our only time to make an impression on the world and its sense of the right. They were willing to look at why the righteous suffered, and why the good all too often died young. These questions are unanswerable, and the angry and young will find that unacceptable in every age.
- Monotheism. A late innovation in the first millennium's age of crises, this way of seeing the forces in the world simplified the position of human beings. It exacerbated the problem of evil if the evil had also to come from the one true god, but it gave comfort and assurance to many. Its spread transformed the way people thought about the cosmos and themselves and, as the nineteenth century French Orientalist Ernest Renan once remarked, monotheism dulls the taste for all other forms of religion, so that even organized polytheisms of our day have reconceived themselves as confessions of faith. There is no way to minimize the originality and the power of this Ancient Near Eastern idea.
- The individual. The integrity of the individual human being is rooted in biology, but in fact it has been flexible over time, and in ancient times, as in our own days, on occasion persons stressed their uniqueness, and sometimes they emphasized their group solidarity. The range of assertions the ancients made does not appear different from what we find in our own time. Again, the way they thought about themselves probably did not change with the invention of writing, but for the first time we know of it.
- The week, the calendar. The units of seven days came down from the Near East, along with ways of resolving the fact that counting lunar months gets the months out of season with the solar year.
- Encyclopedism. The idea that the way to understand the world is to make a list of the elements relevant to an area of inquiry definitely started with the Mesopotamians. Sometimes we call it "list science" since they tried to collect names for trees, appearances of planets, instances of just rulings, almost anything lexical, the instances of the Pythagorean theorem, and of course the omens that might reveal to the careful student what the gods had written in nature to tell us how to behave and what to do. This cultural style was one that avoided generalization as a needlessly simple-minded exercise. Because the Greeks liked generalization, we do too, but there is still the tendency to collect examples and hope that generalizations will emerge from them.
- Data and the practice of astronomy. Out of the practical and wondrous sky-watching that all human societies do, came the efforts precisely to measure and

then to record the movement of planets and other bodies. These efforts were meticulously preserved and passed down to Greek-speakers, and Ptolemy said he had records going back to 747 BCE. Although the West has now moved beyond Ptolemy, the Mesopotamian data obviously was of central importance to his view.

- Medicine. The practical medicine of the Mesopotamian practitioners obliquely filtered down to Greek and Roman physicians, but it did not always accord with their theoretical assumptions and so did not always survive.

- The idea of education. Samuel Kramer's assertion that in Sumer we see the first school days is perhaps a bit exaggerated; surely before in other cultures children were educated at least in oral lore. But it is true that among the Ancient Near Eastern scribes one sees for the first time a school tradition that lasted over millennia. We who have followed the ancient scribes in getting our wedges straight and our hieroglyphs in order feel a special kinship to that kind of learning, even though it may not be in fashion today.

- The wheel. The origins of this basic device lurk in prehistory, but its importance was great for ease of transport, and it rolled forth from the Ancient Near East. Here it seems likely that the device was only invented once in human endeavor, and the New World civilizations that lacked it paid a price in relatively restricted ability to distribute their surpluses.

- Domesticated plants and animals. Humans poked around their favorite plants and animals and manipulated them in many times and places, but it is the things domesticated in the Near East that went on to become the staple crops of much of the world, the grains, the foods, even the pets that sustain life in many places to this day.

- Pottery. A practical and lowly technique, perhaps, and again one that was reinvented elsewhere, but it was in the Near East that the uses of pots for cooking and storing were first devised.

These things seem a hodge-podge, not necessarily making a coherent whole, and they were not introduced at the same times in the same places, but they cluster together out of the Ancient Near East and drift down through later ages, plumes of smoke above their scrap of history, but still breathed in and used by us and by millions quite unaware that the anonymous originators lived so very long ago in the Ancient Near East.

FURTHER READING

Kramer 1981 is a good overview, and more recently Hallo 1996 and Dalley 1998a have brought together insights.

References

Abusch, T. and K. Van Der Toorn (eds) 1999: *Mesopotamian Magic. Textual, Historical, and Interpretative Perspectives.* Groningen: Styx.

Adams, R. 1966: *The Evolution of Urban Society.* Chicago, IL: University of Chicago Press.

Adams, R. 1974: Anthropological Perspectives on Ancient Trade. *Current Anthropology*, 15, 239–58.

Adams, R. 1978: Strategies of Maximization, Stability, and Resilience in Mesopotamian Society, Settlement, and Agriculture. *Proceedings of the American Philosophical Society*, 122, 329–35.

Adams, R. 1981: *Heartland of Cities: Surveys of Ancient Settlement and Land Use on the Central Floodplain of the Euphrates.* Chicago, IL: University of Chicago Press.

Adams, R. and H. Nissen 1972: *The Uruk Countryside: The Natural Setting of Urban Societies.* Chicago, IL: University of Chicago Press.

Adiego, J. Ignacio. 2006: *The Carian Language.* Leiden: Brill.

Adkins, L. and R. Adkins 2000: *The Keys of Egypt. The Obsession to Decipher Egyptian Hieroglyphs.* New York: HarperCollins.

Adler, H.-P. 1976: *Das Akkadische des Königs Tušratta von Mitanni.* Neukirchen-Vluyn: Neukirchener Verlag.

Aerts, E. and H. Klengel (eds) 1990: *The Town as Regional Economic Centre in the Ancient Near East.* Leuven: Leuven University Press.

Aitken, K. T. 1990: *The Aqhat Narrative: A Study in the Narrative Structure and Composition of an Ugaritic Tale.* JSSM 13. Manchester: Journal of Semitic Studies.

Aker, J. forthcoming: Rhetoric of Transgression: Ashurbanipal's Babylonian Policy and Transformations in the Visual Domain. Ph.D. dissertation, Harvard University.

Albright, W. 1957: *From the Stone Age to Christianity.* Garden City: Doubleday Anchor.

Albright, William Foxwell. 1974: "Near East, Ancient." *Encyclopædia Britannica*, 15th edn, *Macropædia*, vol. 12.

Al-Dbiyat, M. 1980: *Salamieh et sa Région.* Tours: Université François Rabelais.

Algaze, G. 1989: The Uruk Expansion: Cross-cultural Exchange in the Early Mesopotamian Civilization. *Current Anthropology*, 30, 571–608.

Algaze, G. 1993: *The Uruk World System: The Dynamics of Expansion of Early Mesopotamian Civilization.* Chicago, IL: University of Chicago Press.

Algaze, G. 2001a: Initial Social Complexity in Southwestern Asia, The Mesopotamian Advantage. *Current Anthropology*, 42, 199–233.

Algaze, G. 2001b: The Prehistory of Imperialism: The Case of Uruk Period Mesopotamia. In Rothman 2001, 27–83.

Algaze, G., T. Matney, D. Schlee, and J. Kelly 1996: Late EBA Urban Structure at Titriş Höyük, Southeastern Turkey. The 1995 season. *Anatolica*, 22, 129–43.

Allen, J. P. 1984: *The Inflection of the Verb in the Pyramid Texts*. Malibu: Undena.

Allen, J. P. 2000: *Middle Egyptian: An Introduction to the Language and Culture of Hieroglyphs*. Cambridge: Cambridge University Press.

Allen, J. P. 1988: *Genesis in Egypt: the Philosophy of Ancient Egyptian Creation Accounts*. New Haven: Yale University Peabody Museum.

Al-Rawi, F. 1990: Tablets from the Sippar Library, I. The "Weidner Chronicle": A Suppositious Royal Letter concerning a Vision. *Iraq*, 52, 1–13.

Alster, B. 1974: *The Instructions of Suruppak*. Copenhagen: Akademisk.

Alster, B. 1976: On the Earliest Sumerian Literary Tradition. *Journal of Cuneiform Studies*, 28, 109–26.

Alster, B. 1990: Sumerian Literary Dialogues and Debates and their Place in the Ancient Near Eastern Literature. In E. Keck et al., *Living Waters (Fs. Løkkegaard)*, Copenhagen: Museum Tusculanum, 1–16.

Alster, Bendt. 1995: "Epic Tales from Ancient Sumer: Enmerkar, Lugalbanda, and Other Cunning Heroes." in *Civilizations of the Ancient Near East*, vol. 3, edited by Jack M. Sasson, 2315–26. New York: Scribner.

Alster, Bendt. 1997: *Proverbs of Ancient Sumer: The World's Earliest Proverb Collections*, 2 vols. Bethesda, Maryland: CDL Press.

Alster, Bendt. 2005: *Wisdom of Ancient Sumer*. Bethesda, Maryland: CDL Press.

Altenmüller, H. 2001: Trade and Markets. In Redford 2001, 3, 445–50.

Amiet, P. 1980: *Art of the Ancient Near East*. New York: Abrams. French 1977.

Anbar, M. 1985: La distribution géographique des Bini-Yamina, d'après les archives royales de Mari. In Durand and Kupper 1985, 17–24.

Andrae, W. 1925: *Colored Ceramics from Ashur*. London: Kegan, Paul, Trench, Trubner.

Angerstorfer, A. 1982: Asherah als "Consort of Yahweh" oder Ashirtah? *Biblische Notizen*, 17, 7–16.

Annus, A. 2002: *The God Ninurta in the Mythology and Royal Ideology of Ancient Mesopotamia*. Helsinki: Neo-Assyrian Text Corpus Project.

Archi, A. 1979: Il dio Zawalli: sul culto dei morti presso gli Ittiti. *Altorientalische Forschungen*, 6, 81–94.

Archi, A. 1990: The City of Ebla and the Organization of the Rural Territory. In Aerts and Klengel 1990, 15–19.

Archi, A. 2002: Women in the Society of Ebla. In Parpola and Whiting 2002, 1–9.

Aristotle 1990: *Politics*. H. Rackham, translator. Cambridge, London: Harvard University Press.

Arnaud, D. 1986: *Recherches au pays d'Aštata: Emar* VI, 3. Paris: Editions Recherche sur les Civilisations.

Artzi, P. 1987: The Influence of Political Marriages on the International Relations of the Amarna-Age. In Durand 1987, 23–6.

Artzi, P. and A. Malamat 1971: The Correspondence of Shibtu, Queen of Mari in ARM X. *Orientalia*, 40, 75–89.

Artzy, M. and D. Hillel 1988: A Defense of the Theory of Progressive Soil Salinization in Ancient Southern Mesopotamia. *Geoarchaeology: An International Journal*, 3, 235–8.

Arutiunian Арутюнян [Harouthiounyan]), N. V. 2001: Корпус урартских клинообразных надписей Erevan: Gitutiun (Institut Vostokovedeniya).

Arutiunian, N. 2001: *Korpus urartskikh klinoobraznykh nadpisey.* Erevan: Gitutiun.

Aruz, J. (ed.) 2003: *Art of the First Cities.* New Haven and London: Yale University Press.

Asher-Greve, J. 1985: *Frauen in altsumerischer Zeit.* Malibu: Undena.

Asher-Greve, J. 1987: The Oldest Female Oneiromancer. In Durand 1987, 27–32.

Asher-Greve, J. 1997a: The Essential Body: Mesopotamian Conceptions of the Gendered Body. *Gender and History*, 9, 432–61.

Asher-Greve, J. 1997b: Feminist Research and Ancient Mesopotamia: Problems and Prospects. In A. Brenner and C. Fontaine (eds), *A Feminist Companion to Reading the Bible*, Sheffield: Sheffield Academic, 218–37.

Assaf, A. Abou 1990: *Der Tempel von 'Ain Dara.* Mainz: Zabern.

Assaf, A. Abou 1994: Zwei neue Stelenfragmente aus 'Ain Dara. In P. Calmeyer, K. Hecker, L. Jacob-Rost, and C. B. F. Walker (eds), *Beiträge zur Altorientalischen Archäologie und Alterumskunde: Festschrift für Barthel Hrouda zum 65. Geburtstag*, Wiesbaden: Harrassowitz, 1–7.

Assmann, A. 1989: Jaspers Achsenzeit, oder: Schwierigkeiten mit der Zentralperspective in der Geschichte. In D. Harth (ed.), *Karl Jaspers. Denken zwischen Wissenschaft, Politik und Philosophie*, Stuttgart: Metzler, 187–205.

Assmann, J. 1975: *Ägyptische Hymnen und Gebete.* Zürich: Artemis.

Assmann, J. 1983: Persönlichkeitsbegriff und -bewußtsein. In W. Helck (ed.), *Lexikon der Ägyptologie*, Wiesbaden: Harrassowitz, 4: 963–78.

Assmann, J. 1990: *Ma'at. Gerechtigkeit und Unsterblichkeit im Alten Ägypten.* Munich: Beck.

Assmann, J. 2002: *The Mind of Egypt.* New York: Holt. German 1996.

Astour, M. C. 1987: Semites and Hurrians in Northern Syria. In *Studies on the Civilization and Culture of Nuzi and the Hurrians, 2*, Winona Lake, Ind.: Eisenbrauns, 3–68.

Attinger, P. 1993: *Eléments de linguistique sumérienne: La construction de du₁₁/e/di «dire».* Fribourg/Göttingen: Editions Universitaires/Vandenhoeck&Ruprecht.

Attridge, Harold W. and Robert A. Oden, Jr. 1981: *Philo of Byblos: The Phoenician History.* CBQMS, vol. 9. Washington, D.C.: The Catholic Biblical Association of America.

Aurenche, O. (ed.) 1984: *Nomades et Sédentaires. Perspectives ethnoarchéologiques.* Paris: Editions Recherche sur les Civilisations.

Aurenche, O. 1977: *Dictionnaire illustré multilingue de l'architecture du Proche Orient ancien.* Paris: Boccard.

Aurenche, O. 1981: *La Maison Oriental: L'architecture du Proche Orient ancien des origines au milieu du quatrième millénaire.* Paris: Geuthner.

Aurenche, O. 1993: L'Origine de la brique dans le Proche Orient Ancien. In M. Frangipane and A. Palmieri (eds), *Between the Rivers and Over the Mountains*, Rome: Università di Roma "La Sapienza," 75–85.

Avalos, H. 1995: Legal and Social Institutions in Canaan and Ancient Israel. In Sasson 1995, 615–31.

Averbeck, R. 2003: Daily Life and Culture in "Enki and the World Order" and other Sumerian Literary Compositions. In Averbeck, Chavalas, and Weisberg 2003, 23–61.

Averbeck, R., M. Chavalas, and D. Weisberg (eds) 2003: *Life and Culture in the Ancient Near East.* Bethesda, MD: CDL.

Azarpay, G. 1990: A Canon of Proportions in the Art of the Ancient Near East. In A. Gunter (ed.), *Investigating Artistic Environments in the Ancient Near East*, Washington, DC: Smithsonian Institution, 93–103.

Bagnall, R. 1995: *Reading Papyri, Writing Ancient History.* London, New York: Routledge.

Bahrani, Z. 2001: *Women of Babylon: Gender and Representation in Mesopotamia.* London: Routledge.

Bahrani, Z. 2002: Performativity and the Image: Narrative, Representation, and the Uruk Vase. In E. Ehrenberg (ed.), *Leaving No Stones Unturned: Essays on the Ancient Near East and Egypt in Honor of Donald P. Hansen*, Winona Lake, IN: Eisenbrauns, 15–22.

Bahrani, Z. 2003: *The Graven Image: Representation in Babylonia and Assyria.* Philadelphia, PA: University of Pennsylvania Press.

Baines, J. 1996a: Contextualizing Egyptian Representations of Society and Ethnicity. In J. Cooper and G. Schwartz (eds), *The Study of the Ancient Near East in the Twenty-First Century*, Winona Lake, IN: Eisenbrauns, 339–84.

Baines, J. 1996b: Myth and Literature. In Loprieno 1996b, 361–77.

Baines, J. and J. Malek 2000: *Cultural Atlas of Ancient Egypt.* New York: Facts on File.

Baines, J. and N. Yoffee 1998: Order, Legitimacy and Wealth in Ancient Egypt and Mesopotamia. In G. Feinman and J. Markus (eds), *Archaic States*, Santa Fe, NM: School of American Research, 199–260.

Baines, John. 1996: "Myth and Literature." in *Ancient Egyptian Literature: History and Forms*, edited by Antonio Loprieno, 361–77. Leiden: Brill.

Balkan, K. 1954: *Kassitenstudien, 1: Die Sprache der Kassiten.* New Haven: American Oriental Society.

Baqir, T. 1946: Tell Harmal: a Preliminary Report. *Sumer*, 2, 22–30.

Baqir, T. 1959: *Tell Harmal.* Baghdad: Directorate General of Antiquities.

Barakat, H. 1993: *The Arab World: Society, Culture, and State.* Berkeley, CA: University of California Press.

Barber, Elizabeth Wayland. 1999: *The Mummies of Ürümchi.* New York: Norton.

Bardet, G. 1984: *Archives administratives de Mari* 1. Paris: Recherche sur les Civilisations.

Barker, G. 2000: Farmers, Herders and Miners in the Wadi Faynan, Southern Jordan: a 10,000-year Landscape Archaeology. In G. Barker and D. Gilbertson (eds), *The Archaeology of Arid Lands*, London: Routledge, 63–85.

Bar-Matthews, M., A. Ayalon, A. Kaufman, and G. Wasserburg. 1999: The Eastern Mediterranean Paleoclimate as a Reflection of Regional Events: Soreq Cave, Israel. *Earth and Planetary Science Letters*, 166, 85–95.

Barnett, R. 1976: *Sculptures from the North Palace of Ashurbanipal at Nineveh (668–627 BC).* London: British Museum.

Barthélemy, Jean-Jacques. 1788: *Voyage du jeune Anacharsis en Grèce, dans le milieu du quatrième siècle avant l'ère vulgaire.* 4 vols. Paris: De Bure.

Baruch, U. 1990: Palynological Evidence of Human Impact on the Vegetation as Recorded in Late Holocene Lake Sediments in Israel. In Bottema, Entjes-Nieborg, and Van Zeist 1990, 283–93.

Barucq, André and François Daumas. 1980: *Hymnes et Prières ee l'Égypte Ancienne.* Paris: Cerf.

Bar-Yosef and R. Kra (eds) 1994: *Chronology and Paleoclimates of the Eastern Mediterranean.* Tucson, AZ: Radiocarbon, University of Arizona.

Bar-Yosef, O. 1986: The Walls of Jericho. *Current Anthropology*, 27, 157–62.

Bar-Yosef, O. 1996: The Impact of Late Pleistocene–Early Holocene Climatic Changes on Humans in Southwest Asia. In L. Straus, B. Eriksen, J. Erlandsen, and D. Yesner (eds), *Humans at the End of the Ice Age*, New York: Plenum, 61–78.

Bar-Yosef, O. 2002: The Upper Paleolithic Revolution. *Annual Review of Anthropology*, 31, 363–93.

Bar-Yosef, O. and A. Belfer-Cohen 1989: The Origins of Sedentism and Farming Communities in the Levant. *Journal of World Prehistory*, 3, 447–98.

Bar-Yosef, O. and A. Belfer-Cohen 1992: From Foraging to Farming in the Mediterranean Levant. In A. Gebauer and T. Price (eds), *Transition to Agriculture in Prehistory*, Madison, WI: Prehistory, 21–48.

Bar-Yosef, O. and R. Meadow 1995: The Origins of Agriculture in the Near East. In T. Price and A. Gebauer (eds), *Last Hunters, First Farmers*, Santa Fe, NM: School of American Research, 39–94.

Barzun, J. and H. Graff 1985: *The Modern Researcher*. Fort Worth, TX: Harcourt Brace Jovanovich.

Bass, G. 1995: Sea and River Craft in the Ancient Near East. In Sasson 1995, 1421–31.

Battini-Villard, L. 1999: *L'espace doméstique en Mésopotamie de la IIIe dynastie d'Ur à l'époque paléo-babylonienne*. Oxford: British Archaeological Reports.

Batto, B. 1974: *Studies on Women at Mari*. Baltimore, MD: Johns Hopkins University Press.

Beal, R. 1992: *The Organisation of the Hittite Military*. Heidelberg: Winter.

Beal, R. 1995: Hittite Military Rituals. In M. Meyer and P. Mirecki (eds), *Ancient Magic and Ritual Power*, Leiden: Brill, 63–76.

Beal, R. 2002: Hittite Oracles. In L. Ciraolo and J. Seidel (eds), *Magic and Divination in the Ancient World*, Leiden: Brill-Styx, 57–81.

Beale, T. 1978: Beveled Rim Bowls and their Implications for Change and Economic Organization in the Later Fourth Millennium BC. *Journal of Near Eastern Studies*, 37, 289–313.

Beaulieu, P.-A. 1989: *The Reign of Nabonidus King of Babylon 556–539 BC*. New Haven, CT: Yale University Press.

Beaulieu, P.-A. 2000a: A Finger in Every Pie: The Institutional Connections of a Family of Entrepreneurs in Neo-Babylonian Larsa. In Bongenaar 2000, 43–71.

Beaulieu, P.-A. 2000b: Neo-Babylonian Royal Inscriptions. In Hallo and Younger 2000: 306–14.

Beaulieu, P.-A. 2003: Nabopolassar and the Antiquity of Babylon. *Eretz-Israel*, 27, 1*–9*.

Beaulieu, P.-A. 2003: *The Pantheon of Uruk during the Neo-Babylonian Period*. Leiden: Styx-Brill.

Beaumont, P. 1971: Qanat Systems in Iran. *Bulletin of the International Association of Scientific Hydrology*, 16, 39–50.

Becking B. 2001: *Only One God? Monotheism in Israel and the Veneration of the Goddess Asherah*. London: Sheffield.

Beckman, G. 1982: The Hittite Assembly. *Journal of the American Oriental Society*, 102, 435–42.

Beckman, G. 1983: *Hittite Birth Rituals*. Wiesbaden: Harrassowitz.

Beckman, G. 1993: From Cradle to Grave: Women's Role in Hittite Medicine and Magic. *Journal of Ancient Civilizations*, 8, 25–39.

Beckman, G. 1995: Royal Ideology and State Administration in Hittite Anatolia. In Sasson 1995, 529–43.

Beckman, G. 1997a: Plague Prayers of Muršili II. In Hallo and Younger 1997, 156–60.

Beckman, G. 1997b: Instructions to Priests and Temple Officials. In Hallo and Younger 1997, 151–3.

Beckman, G. 1997c: Excerpt from an Oracle Report. In Hallo and Younger 1997, 204–6.

Beckman, G. 1997d: The Wrath of Telipinu. In Hallo and Younger 1997, 151–3.

Beckman, G. 2002a: The Pantheon of Emar. In P. Taracha (ed.), *Silva Anatolia: Festschrift M. Popko*, Warsaw: Agade, 39–54.

Beckman, G. 2002b: The Religion of the Hittites. In D. Hopkins (ed.), *Across the Anatolian Plateau: Readings in the Archaeology of Ancient Turkey*, Boston, MA: ASOR, 133–43.

Beckman, G. 2003: Opfer, nach schriftlichen Quellen, Anatolien. In Ebeling et al. 1928–, 10, 106–11.

Beckman, G. 2004: Pantheon. Bei den Hethitern. In Ebeling et al. 1928–, 10.

Beckman, G. In press a: La religion d'Émar. In D. Del Olmo Lete (ed.), *Mitología y Religión del Oriente Antiguo*, Barcelona: AUSA.

Beckman, G. In press b: Sacred Times and Spaces: Anatolia. In S. Johnston (ed.), *Religions of the Ancient World: A Guide*, Cambridge, MA: Harvard University Press.

Beckman, G. In press c: Blood in Hittite Ritual. In *Gedenkschrift für Erich Neu*.

Beeston, A. F. L. 1981: Languages of pre-Islamic Arabia. *Arabica*, 28, 181–6.

Beeston, A. F. L., M. A. Ghul, W. W. Müller, and J. Ryckmans. 1982: *Sabaic Dictionary.* Louvain: Peeters.

Behcet, L. 1994: Phytosociological Investigation on the Macrophytic Vegetation of Lake Van. *Turkish Journal of Botany*, 18, 229–43. Turkish.

Ben-Barak, Z. 1987: The Queen Consort and the Struggle for the Throne. In Durand 1987, 34–40.

Ben-Barak, Z. 1996: Mutual Influences in the Ancient Near East: Inheritance as a Case in Point. In M. Malul (ed.), *Mutual Influences of Peoples and Cultures in the Ancient Near East*, Haifa: University of Haifa, 1–15.

Bender, B. 1975: *Farming in Prehistory.* London: Baker.

Bergsträsser, G. 1983: *Introduction to the Semitic Languages.* Translated and annotated by Peter T. Daniels. Winona Lake, Ind.: Eisenbrauns [original German edn., Munich: Hueber, 1928].

Berlev, O. 1967a: Some Remarks on the Social Terms of Ancient Egypt (the *hrdw*). In *Ancient Egypt and Ancient Africa. Collection of Studies Dedicated to the Memory of the Academician V. V. Struve*, Moscow: Nauka, 11–14. Russian.

Berlev, O. 1967b: The Egyptian Navy in the Middle Kingdom. *Palestinskij Sbornik*, 80, 6–20. Russian.

Berlev, O. 1971: Les prétendus 'citadins' au Moyen Empire. *Revue d'Égyptologie*, 23, 31–7.

Berlev, O. 1972: *The Workforce of Egypt in the Epoch of the Middle Kingdom.* Moscow: Nauka Russian.

Berlev, O. 1987: A Social Experiment in Nubia during the Years 9–17 of Sesostris I. In M. Powell (ed.), *Labor in the Ancient Near East*, New Haven, CT: American Oriental Society, 143–57.

Berlinerblau, J. 1996: *The Vow and the "Popular Religious Groups" of Ancient Israel: A Philological and Sociological Inquiry.* Sheffield: Sheffield Academic.

Berman, H. 1983: *Law and Revolution.* Cambridge, MA: Harvard University Press.

Bermant, Chaim, and Michael Weitzman. 1979: *Ebla: A Revelation in Archaeology.* London: Weidenfeld and Nicholson; New York: Times Books.

Bernal, Martin. 1986: "Black Athena Denied: The Tyranny of Germany over Greece and the Rejection of the Afroasiatic Roots of Europe: 1780–1980." *Comparative Criticism* 8: 3–69.

Bernal, Martin. 1987–91: *Black Athena: The Afroasiatic Roots of Classical Civilization*, vol. 1: *The Fabrication of Ancient Greece 1785–1985*; vol. 2: *The Archaeological and Documentary Evidence*. New Brunswick, N.J.: Rutgers University Press.

Bernal, Martin. 2001: *Black Athena Writes Back: Martin Bernal Responds to His Critics*, ed. David Chioni Moore. Durham, N.C.: Duke University Press.

Bernbeck, R. 1995: Lasting Alliances and Emerging Competition: Economic Developments in Early Mesopotamia. *Journal of Anthropological Archaeology*, 14, 1–25.

Bersani, L. and U. Dutoit 1985: *The Forms of Violence: Narrative in Assyrian Art and Modern Culture*. New York: Schocken.

Besenval, R. 1984: *Technologie de la voûte dans l'Orient Ancien*. Paris: Editions Recherche sur les Civilisations.

Betancourt, P. 1977: *The Aeolic Style in Architecture*. Princeton, NJ: Princeton University Press.

Beyer, K. 1986: *The Aramaic Language*. Göttingen: Vandenhoeck & Ruprecht.

Biella, J. C. 1982: *Dictionary of Old South Arabic (Sabaean Dialect)*. Chico, Ca.: Scholar Press.

Bietak, M. 1996: *Avaris: the Capital of the Hyksos*. London: British Museum.

Biga, M. 1987: Femmes de la famille royale d'Ebla. In Durand 1987, 41–8.

Biggs, R. 1967: More Babylonian Prophecies. *Iraq*, 29, 117–32.

Biggs, R. 1971: An Archaic Sumerian Version of the Kesh Temple Hymn. *Zeitschrift für Assyriologie*, 61, 193–207.

Biggs, R. 1979: Unpublished Presidential Address to the Middle West Branch of the American Oriental Society, Madison, Wisconsin.

Binford, L. 1968: Post-pleistocene adaptations. In S. Binford and L. Binford (eds), *New Perspectives in Archaeology*, Chicago, IL: Aldine, 313–41.

Birot, M. 1980: Un rituel de Mari relatif au *kispum*. In B. Alster (ed.), *Death in Mesopotamia*, Copenhagen: Akademisk, 139–50.

Birot, M. 1993: *Correspondance des gouverneurs de Qattunan*. Paris: Editions Recherche sur les Civilisations.

Björkman, G. 1964: Egyptology and Historical Method. *Orientalia Suecana*, 13, 9–33.

Black, J., G. Cunningham, J. Ebeling, E. Fluckiger-Hawker, E. Robson, J. Taylor, and G. Zólyomi 1998–: The Electronic Text Corpus of Sumerian Literature, Oxford, at *http://www-etcsl.orient.ox.ac.uk*.

Black, J. A. 1984: *Sumerian Grammar in Babylonian Theory*. Rome: Biblical Institute Press.

Black, J. A. et al. 2000: *A Concise Dictionary of Akkadian*. 2nd edn. Wiesbaden: Harrassowitz.

Black, J. 1981: The New Year Ceremonies in Ancient Babylon: "Taking Bel by the Hand" and a Cultic Picnic. *Religion*, 11, 39–59.

Black, J. 2002: *A Concise Dictionary of Akkadian*. Wiesbaden: Harrassowitz.

Black, J. and A. Green 1992: *Gods, Demons and Symbols of Ancient Mesopotamia*. Austin: University of Texas Press.

Black, Jeremy. 1998: *Reading Sumerian Poetry*. Ithaca, New York: Cornell University Press.

Black, Jeremy, et al. 1998–: *The Electronic Text Corpus of Sumerian Literature*. http://www-etcsl.orient.ox.ac.uk/. Oxford.

Black, Jeremy, et al. 2004: *The Literature of Ancient Sumer*. Oxford: Oxford University Press.

Blanchet, G., P. Sanlaville, and M. Traboulsi 1998: Le Moyen-Orient de 20,000 ans BP à 6,000 ans BP essai de reconstitution paléoclimatique. *Paléorient*, 32, 187–96.

Blau, J. 1982: *On polyphony in Biblical Hebrew.* Jerusalem: Israel Academy of Sciences and Humanities.

Bleiberg, E. 1995: The Economy of Ancient Egypt. In Sasson 1995, 1373–85.

Bloch, M. 1953: *The Historian's Craft.* New York: Random House.

Bloch-Smith, E., and B. Nakhai 1999: A Landscape Comes to Life. *Near Eastern Archaeology,* 62, 62–92, 101–28.

Boardman, J., et al. (eds) 1991: *The Assyrian and Babylonian Empires and Other States of the Near East, from the Eighth to the Sixth Centuries BC.* Cambridge, New York: Cambridge University Press.

Bocco, R. 2000: International Organizations and the Settlement of Nomadism in the Arab Middle East, 1950–1990. In Mundy and Musallam 2000, 197–217.

Boehmer, R. 1991: Gebel-el-Arak und Gebel-et-Tarif-Griff: keine Fälschungen. *Mitteilungen des Deutschen Archäologischen Instituts, Abteilung Kairo,* 47, 51–60.

Bohrer, F. 2003: *Orientalism and Visual Culture: Imaging Mesopotamia in Nineteenth Century Europe.* Cambridge: Cambridge University Press.

Bonatz, D. 2000: *Das Syro-hethitische Grabdenkmal.* Mainz: Zabern.

Bongenaar, A. (ed.) 2000: *Interdependency of Institutions and Private Entrepreneurs.* Leiden: Nederlands Historisch-Archaeologisch Instituut te Istanbul.

Bongenaar, A. and M. Jursa 1993: Ein babylonischer Mäusefänger. *Wiener Zeitschrift für die Kunde des Morgenlandes,* 83, 837–47.

Borger, R. 1956: *Die Inschriften Asarhaddons, Königs von Assyrien.* Graz: Archiv für Orientforschung.

Borger, R. 1967–75: *Handbuch der Keilschriftliteratur.* Berlin: de Gruyter.

Boserup, E. 1965: *The Conditions of Agricultural Growth.* Chicago, IL: Aldine.

Bottema, S. 1995: The Younger Dryas in the Eastern Mediterranean. *Quaternary Science Reviews,* 14, 883–91.

Bottema, S. and H. Woldring 1990: Anthropogenic Indicators in the Pollen Record of the Eastern Mediterranean. In Bottema, Entjes-Nieborg, and Van Zeist 1990, 231–64.

Bottema, S., G. Entjes-Nieborg, and W. Van Zeist (eds) 1990: *Man's Role in the Shaping of the Eastern Mediterranean Landscape.* Rotterdam: Balkema.

Bottema, S., H. Woldring, and B. Aytug 1993: Late Quaternary Vegetation History of Northern Turkey. *Palaeohistoria,* 35/36, 13–72.

Bottéro, J. 1965: La Femme dans la Mésopotamie Ancienne. In P. Grimal et al. (eds), *Histoire mondiale de la Femme: Préhistoire et Antiquité,* Paris: Nouvelle Librairie de France, 155–214.

Bottéro, J. 1974: Symptômes, signes, écritures en Mésopotamie ancienne. In J. Vernant (ed.), *Divination et rationalité,* Paris: Seuil, 70–197.

Bottéro, J. 1982: Les inscriptions cunéiformes funéraires. In G. Gnoli and J.-P. Vernant (eds), *La mort, les morts dans les sociétés anciennes,* Cambridge, Paris: Cambridge University Press, Sciences humaines, 373–406.

Bottéro, J. 1987: *Mésopotamie. L'Ecriture, la raison, les dieux.* Paris: Gallimard.

Bottéro, J. 1992a: The "Code" of Hammurabi. In 1992b, 156–84.

Bottéro, J. 1992b: *Mesopotamia: Writing, Reason and the Gods.* Chicago, IL: University of Chicago Press.

Bottéro, J. 1995: *Textes culinaires mésopotamiens.* Winona Lake, IN: Eisenbrauns.

Bottéro, J. 2001: *Religion in Ancient Mesopotamia.* Chicago, IL: University of Chicago Press.

Bottéro, J. and S. Kramer 1989: *Lorsque les dieux faisaient l'homme.* Paris: Gallimard.

Bounni, A., J. and E. Lagarce, N. Saliby, and L. Badre 1979: Rapport préliminaire sur la troisième campagne de fouilles (1977) à Ibn Hani (Syrie). *Syria,* 56, 217–91.

Bourriau, J. 2000: The Second Intermediate Period (c. 1650–1550 BC). In Shaw 2000, 185–217.

Bowman, A. and D. Rathbone 1992: Cities and Administration in Roman Egypt. *Journal of Roman Studies*, 82, 107–27.

Bowman, R. A. 1970: *Aramaic Ritual Texts from Persepolis*. Chicago: Oriental Institute.

Boyer, G. 1958: *Textes juridiques*. Paris: Geuthner.

Braidwood, R. 1960: The Agricultural Revolution. *Scientific American*, 203, 130–48.

Braidwood, R. and B. Howe 1960: *Prehistoric Investigations in Iraqi Kurdistan*. Chicago, IL: University of Chicago Press.

Braidwood, R., L. Braidwood, B. Howe, C. Reed, and P.-J. Watson 1983: *Prehistoric Archaeology along the Zagros Flanks*. Chicago, IL: University of Chicago Press.

Braudel, F. 1972: *The Mediterranean and the Mediterranean World in the Age of Philip II*. Second edition. New York: Harper and Row.

Braudel, F. 1984: *The Perspective of the World*. New York: Harper and Row. French 1979.

Bresciani, E. 1969, 1990, 1999: *Letteratura e Poesia Dell' Antico Egitto*. Turin: Einaudi.

Bresciani, E. 2001: *Testi Religiosi Dell'antico Egitto*. Milano: Mondadori.

Bretschneider, J. 1991: *Architekturmodelle in Vorderasien und der östlichen Ägais vom Neolithikum bis in das 1. Jahrtausend*. Neukirchen: Butzon and Bercker Kevelaer.

Brewer, D. and E. Teeter 1999: *Egypt and the Egyptians*. Cambridge: Cambridge University Press.

Briant, P. 1987: Pouvoir central et polycentrisme culturel dans l'empire achéménide. In H. Sancisi-Weerdenburg (ed.), *Achaemenid History* 1, Leiden: Nederlands Instituut voor het Nabije Oosten, 1–31.

Briant, P. 1993: L'histoire politique de l'empire achéménide: problèmes et méthodes. *Revue des études anciennes*, 95, 399–423.

Briant, Pierre. 2002: *From Cyrus to Alexander: A History of the Persian Empire*, trans. Peter T. Daniels. Winona Lake, Ind.: Eisenbrauns.

Brinkman, J. A. 1984: *Prelude to Empire. Babylonian Society and Politics, 747–626 BC*. Philadelphia, PA: University Museum.

Brookes, I. 1990: Anthropogenic irrigation sediments, Dakhla Oasis, Egypt. In Bottema, Entjes-Nieborg, and Van Zeist 1990, 113–25.

Brookes, I., L. Levine, and R. Dennell 1982: Alluvial Sequence in Central West Iran and Implications for Archaeological Survey. *Journal of Field Archaeology*, 9, 285–99.

Brosius, M. 1996: *Women in Ancient Persia (559–331 BC)*. Oxford: Oxford University Press.

Brothwell, D. 1972: The Question of Pollution in Earlier and Less Developed Societies. In P. Cox and J. Peel (eds), *Population and Pollution*, London: Academic, 15–27.

Brown, D. 2000: *Mesopotamian Planetary Astronomy-Astrology*. Groningen: Styx.

Brown, J. 1981: The Role of Women and the Treaty in the Ancient World. *Biblische Zeitschrift*, 25, 1–28.

Brown, R. 1961: *The Spirit of Protestantism*. New York: Oxford University Press.

Brumfiel, E. and T. Earle 1987: Specialization, Exchange, and Complex Societies: An Introduction. In E. Brumfiel and T. Earle (eds), *Specialization, Exchange, and Complex Societies*, Cambridge: Cambridge University Press, 1–9.

Brunner, Helmut. 1988: *Altäyptische Weisheit: Lehren für das Leben*. München: Artemis.

Brunner-Traut, Emma. 1989: *Altägyptische Märchen*, 8th edn. München: Eugen Diederichs.

Bryce, G. 1979: *A Legacy of Wisdom*. Lewisburg: Bucknell University Press.

Bryce, T. R. 1998: *The Kingdom of the Hittites*. Oxford: Clarendon.

Bryce, T. R. 2003: *Life and Society in the Hittite World*. Oxford: Oxford University Press.

Buccellati, G. 1966: *The Amorites of the Ur III Period*. Naples: Seminario di Semitistica.

Buccellati, G. 1967: *Cities and Nations of Ancient Syria*. Rome: Istituto di Studi del Vicino Oriente.

Buccellati, G. 1990: Salt at the Dawn of History: The Case of the Beveled-Rim Bowls. In P. Matthiae, M. Van Loon, and H. Weiss (eds), *Resurrecting the Past: A Joint Tribute to Adnan Bounni*, Leiden: Nederlands Instituut voor het Nabije Oosten, 17–40.

Buccellati, G. 1996: *A Structural Grammar of Babylonian*. Wiesbaden: Harrassowitz.

Buccellati, G., and M. Kelly-Buccellati. 1995–6: The royal storehouse of Urkesh. *Archiv für Orientforschung*, 42–3, 1–32.

Bulliet, R. 1990: *The Camel and the Wheel*. New York: Columbia University Press.

Burckhardt, J. 1954: *The Civilization of the Renaissance in Italy*. New York: Modern Library. German 1860.

Burkert, Walter. 1992: *The Orientalizing Revolution: Near Eastern Influences on Greek Culture in the Early Archaic Age*, trans. M. E. Pindert and W. Burkert. Cambridge: Harvard University Press. German original, 1984.

Burrows, Millar. 1978: *Burrows on the Dead Sea Scrolls*. Grand Rapids, Mich.: Baker Book House. Repr. of *The Dead Sea Scrolls* (New York: Viking, 1955) and *More Light on the Dead Sea Scrolls* (New York: Viking, 1958).

Butzer, K. 1976: *Early Hydraulic Civilization in Egypt*. Chicago, IL: Chicago University Press.

Butzer, K. 1995: Environmental Change in the Near East and Human Impact on the Land. In Sasson 1995, 123–51.

Butzer, K. 1997: Sociopolitical Discontinuity in the Near East c. 2200 BCE: Scenarios from Palestine and Egypt. In Dalfes, Kukla, and Weiss 1997, 245–96.

Byrd, B. 1989: The Natufian: Settlement Variability and Economic Adaptations in the Levant at the End of the Pleistocene. *Journal of World Prehistory*, 3, 159–97.

Byrd, B. 1994: Public and Private, Domestic and Corporate: The Emergence of the Southwest Asian Village. *American Antiquity*, 59, 639–66.

Cadelli, D. 1997: Lorsque l'enfant paraît malade. In B. Lion, C. Michel, P. Villard (eds), *Enfance et éducation dans le Proche-Orient ancien, Ktema*, 22, 11–33.

Cagni, L. 1969: *L'Epopea di Erra*. Rome: Istituto di Studi del Vicino Oriente.

Cagni, L. (ed.) 1981: *La lingua di Ebla*. Naples: Istituto Universitario Orientale.

Cagni, L. (ed.) 1984: *Il bilinguismo a Ebla*. Naples: Istituto Universitario Orientale.

Cagni, L. (ed.) 1987: *Ebla 1975–1985*. Naples: Istituto Universitario Orientale.

Callender, G. 2000: The Middle Kingdom Renaissance. In Shaw 2000, 148–83.

Caminos, R. 1954: *Late-Egyptian Miscellanies*. Oxford: Oxford University Press.

Canby, J. 2001: *The "Ur-Nammu" Stela*. Philadelphia, PA: University Museum.

Capel, A. and G. Markoe 1996: *Mistress of the House, Mistress of Heaven: Women in Ancient Egypt*. New York: Hudson Hills.

Carruba, O. 1966: *Das Beschwörungsritual für die Göttin Wišurianza*. Wiesbaden: Harrassowitz.

Carter, C. 1988: Athletic Contests in Hittite Religious Festivals. *Journal of Near Eastern Studies*, 47, 185–7.

Casanova, M. In press: *Le Lapis Lazuli: La pierre précieuse de l'Orient ancien*.

Cassin, E. 1987: *Le semblable et le différent*. Paris: la Découverte.

Castellino, G. 1972: *Two Sulgi Hymns (BC)*. Rome: Istituto di Studi del Vicino Oriente.

Castle, E. 1992: Shipping and Trade in Ramesside Egypt. *Journal of the Economic and Social History of the Orient*, 35, 239–77.

Catsanicos, J. 1996: L'apport de la bilingue de Ḫattuša à la lexicographie hourrite. *Amurru*, 1, 197–296.

Cauvin, J. 2000: *The Birth of the Gods and the Origins of Agriculture*. Cambridge: Cambridge University Press. French 1994.

Cavigneaux, A. 1980–3: Lexikalische Listen. *Reallexikon der Assyriologie*, 6, 609–641.

Cavigneaux, A. 1987: Aux sources du Midrash: l'herméneutique babylonienne. *Aula Orientalis*, 5, 243–55.

Ceram, C. W. 1951: *Gods, Graves, and Scholars: The Story of Archæology*, trans. E. B. Garside. New York: Knopf (numerous reprints). German original, 1949.

Černý, J. 1976: *Coptic Etymological Dictionary*. London: Cambridge University Press.

Černý, J. 1993: *A Late Egyptian Grammar*. 4th edn. Adapted by Sarah Israelit Groll and Cristopher Eyre. Rome: Pontificio Istituto Biblico.

Charpin, D. 1982: Marchands du palais et marchands du temple à la fin de la Ire Dynastie de Babylone. *Journal Asiatique*, 270, 25–65.

Charpin, D. 1986: *Le Clergé d'Ur au siècle d'Hammurapi (xixe–xviiie siècles av. J.-C.)*. Geneva, Paris: Droz.

Charpin, D. 1987: Le Rôle économique du palais en Babylonie sous Hammurabi et ses successeurs. In E. Lévy (ed.), *Le système palatial en orient, en Grèce et à Rome*, Strasbourg: Université des sciences humaines de Strasbourg, 111–26.

Charpin, D. 1990: Les édits de 'Restauration' des Rois babyloniens et leur application. In C. Nicolet (ed.), *Du Pouvoir dans l'Antiquité*, Geneva: Droz, 13–24.

Charpin, D. 1994: Le sumérien, langue morte parlée. *Nouvelles assyriologiques brèves et utilitaires: N.A.B.U.* no. 6.

Charpin, D. 1998: L'évocation du passé dans les lettres de Mari. In Prosecký 1998, 91–110.

Charpin, D. 2001: Prophètes et rois dans le Proche-Orient amorrite. In A. Lemaire (ed.), *Prophètes et rois, Bible et Proche-Orient*, Paris: Cerf, 22–53.

Charpin, D. and J.-M. Durand 1985: La prise du pouvoir par Zimri-lim. *M.A.R.I.*, 4, 293–343.

Charvat, P. 1978: The Growth of Lugalzagesi's Empire. In B. Hruška and G. Komoróczy (eds), *Festschrift Lubor Matouš*, Budapest: Eötvös Loránd Tudományegyetem, 43–9.

Chase-Dunn, C. and T. Hall 1997: *Rise and Demise*. Boulder, CO: Westview.

Chazan, M. and M. Lehner 1990: An Ancient Analogy: Pot Baked Bread in Ancient Egypt and Mesopotamia. *Paléorient*, 16, 21–35.

Chiera, E. 1934: *Joint Expedition with the Iraq Museum at Nuzi IV: Proceedings in Court*. Philadelphia, PA: University of Pennsylvania Press.

Childe, V. G. 1928: *The Most Ancient East*. London: Kegan Paul.

Cifarelli, M. 1998: Gesture and Alterity in the Art of Ashurnasirpal II of Assyria. *Art Bulletin*, 80, 210–28.

Çilingiroglu, A. 2001: Military Architecture. In A. Çilingiroglu and M. Salvini (eds), *Ayanis I: Ten Years' Excavations at Rusahinili Eiduru-kai 1989–1998*, Rome: Istituto per gli Studi Micenei ed Egeo-Anatolici, 25–36.

Civil, M. 1985: Sur les "livres d'écolier" à l'époque paléo-babylonienne. In Durand and Kupper 1985, 67–78.

Civil, M. 1995: Ancient Mesopotamian Lexicography. In J. M. Sasson (ed.), *Civilizations of the Ancient Near East*, New York: Scribner, vol. IV, 2305–2314.

Civil, M. 2002: The Forerunners of *marú* and *ḫamṭu* in Old Babylonian. In T. Abusch (ed.), *Riches Hidden in Secret Places: Ancient Near Eastern Studies in Memory of Thorkild Jacobsen*, Winona Lake, Ind.: Eisenbrauns, 63–71.

Civil, M., and G. Rubio. 1999: An Ebla Incantation against Insomnia and the Semiticization of Sumerian. *Orientalia* n.s., 68, 254–266.

Clark, C. and M. Haswell 1967: *The Economics of Subsistence Agriculture*. New York: St. Martins.

Cleziou, S. 2000: Quel peut être l'apport du concept d'ethnicité au modèle de la colonisation urukéenne? *Paléorient*, 215, 151–7.

Cohen, D. et al. 1970–99: *Dictionnaire des racines sémitiques ou attestées dans les langues sémitiques, 1–8*. Facicles 1 (1970) and 2 (1976), The Hague: Mouton. Facicles 3 (1993), 4 (1993), 5 (1995), 6 (1996), 7 (1997), 8 (1999). Leuven: Peeters.

Cohen, M., D. Snell, and D. Weisberg (eds) 1993. *The Tablet and the Scroll, Near Eastern Studies in Honor of William W. Hallo*. Bethesda, MD: CDL.

Cohen, Mark E. 1981: *Sumerian Hymnology: The Eršemma*. HUCA Supplements, No. 2. Cincinnati: Hebrew Union College-Jewish Institute of Religion.

Cohen, Mark E. 1988: *The Canonical Lamentations of Ancient Mesopotamia*, vol. 1. Potomac, Md: Capital Decisions Limited.

Cohen, S. 1973: Enmerkar and the Lord of Aratta. Ph.D. dissertation, University of Pennsylvania.

Cole, S. 1994: The Crimes and Sacrileges of Nabû-šuma-iškun. *Zeitschrift für Assyriologie*, 84, 220–52.

Cole, S. and P. Machinist 1998: *Letters from Priests to the Kings Esarhaddon and Assurbanipal*. Helsinki: Helsinki University Press.

Collins, B. J. 1990: The Puppy in Hittite Ritual. *Journal of Cuneiform Studies*, 42, 211–26.

Collins, B. J. 1995b: Greek ὀλολύζω and Hittite *palwai-*: Exultation in the Ritual Slaughter of Animals. *Greek, Roman and Byzantine Studies*, 26, 319–25.

Collins, B. J. 2001: Necromancy, Fertility and the Dark Earth: The Use of Ritual Pits in Hittite Cult. In M. Meyer and P. Mirecki (eds), *Ritual Magic in the Ancient World*, Leiden, Brill, 224–41.

Collins, B. J. 2002: Animals in the Religions of Ancient Anatolia. In B. J. Collins (ed.), *A History of the Animal World in the Ancient Near East*, Leiden: Brill, 309–34.

Collins. B. J. 1995a: Ritual Meals in the Hittite Cult. In M. Meyer and P. Mirecki (eds), *Ancient Magic and Ritual Power*, Leiden: Brill, 77–92.

Collombert, P. and L. Coulon 2000: Les dieux contre la mer. Le début du "papyrus d'Astarté" (pBN 202). *Bulletin de l'Institut Français d'Archéologie Orientale*, 100, 193–242.

Collon, D. 1987: *First Impressions: Cylinder Seals in the Ancient Near East*. Chicago, IL: University of Chicago Press.

Collon, D. 1995: *Ancient Near Eastern Art*. Berkeley, CA: University of California Press.

Condon, V. 1984: Two Account Papyri of the Late Eighteenth Dynasty. *Revue d'Égyptologie*, 35. 57–82.

Conti, G. 1990: *Il sillabario della quarta fonte della lista lessicale bilingue eblaita*. Florence: Università di Firenze.

Contini, R. and C. Grottanelli. 2005: *Il Saggio Ahiqar: Fortuna E Trasformazioni Di Uno Scritto Sapienziale. Il Testo Più Antico E Le Sue Versioni*. Studi Biblici 148. Brescia: Paideia Editrice.

Coogan, Michael David. (ed.) 1978: *Stories from Ancient Canaan*. Philadelphia: Westminster.

Coon, C. 1951: *Caravan: The Story of the Middle East*. New York: Holt.

Cooper, J. 1986: *Sumerian and Akkadian Royal Inscriptions, I: Presargonic Inscriptions.* New Haven, CT: American Oriental Society.

Cooper, J. 1993a: Paradigm and Propaganda. The Dynasty of Akkade in the 21st Century BC. In Liverani 1993, 11–23.

Cooper, Jerrold S. 1971: "New Cuneiform Parallels to the Song of Songs." *JBL* 90: 157–62.

Cooper, J. S. 1973: Sumerian and Akkadian in Sumer and Akkad. *Orientalia* n.s., 42, 239–246.

Cooper, Jerrold S. 1975: "Structure, Humor, and Satire in the Poor Man of Nippur," *JCS* 27: 163–74.

Cooper, Jerrold S. 1983: *The Curse of Agade.* Baltimore: Johns Hopkins University Press.

Cooper, Jerrold S. 1993: "Sacred Marriage and Popular Cult in Early Mesopotamia." in *Official Cult and Popular Religion in the Ancient Near East*, edited by Eiko Matsushima, 81–96. Heidelberg: Universitätsverlag C. Winter.

Cordova, C. 1999: Landscape Transformation in the Mediterranean-Steppe Transition Zone of Jordan: A Geoarchaeological Approach. *The Arab World Geographer*, 2, 188–201.

Cordova, C. 2000: Geomorphological Evidence of Intense Prehistoric Soil Erosion in the Highlands of Central Jordan. *Physical Geography*, 21, 538–67.

Corré, Alan D. 1966: "Anatomy of a Decipherment." *Proceedings of the Wisconsin Academy of Sciences, Arts and Letters* 55: 11–20.

Costin, C. 1991: Craft Specialization: Issues in Defining, Documenting, and Explaining the Organization of Production. *Archaeological Method and Theory*, 3, 1–56.

Crawford, M. 1996: *Roman Statutes.* Two vols. London: University of London.

Cross, F. 1973: *Canaanite Myth and Hebrew Epic. Essays in the History of the Religion of Israel.* Cambridge, MA: Harvard University Press.

Crum, W. E. 1939: *A Coptic Dictionary, Compiled with the Help of Many Scholars.* Oxford: Clarendon Press.

Curtin, P. 1984: *Cross-cultural Trade in World History.* Cambridge: Cambridge University Press.

D'Agostino, Franco. 2000: *Testi Umoristici Babilonesi e Assiri.* Brescia: Paideia.

Dalfes, H., G. Kukla, and H. Weiss (eds) 1997: *Third Millennium BC Climate Change and Old World Collapse.* Berlin: Springer.

Dalley, S, 1998b: Yabâ, Atalya and the Foreign Policy of Late Assyrian Kings. *State Archives of Assyria Bulletin*, 12, 83–98.

Dalley, S. (ed.) 1998a: *The Legacy of Mesopotamia.* Oxford: Oxford University Press.

Dalley, Stephanie. 1989: *Myths from Mesopotamia: Creation, the Flood, Gilgamesh, and Others.* Oxford: Oxford University Press.

D'Altroy, T. and T. Earle 1985: Staple Finance, Wealth Finance, and Storage in the Inka Political Economy. *Current Anthropology*, 26, 187–206.

Dandamaev, M. 1984: *Slavery in Babylonia.* DeKalb, IL: Northern Illinois University Press.

Daniels, Peter T. 1988: "'Shewing of Hard Sentences and Dissolving of Doubts': The First Decipherment," *JAOS* 108: 419–36.

Daniels, Peter T. 1992: "What Can the Paleographic Tablets Tell Us of Mesopotamian Scholars' Understanding of the History of Their Script?" *Mar Shipri Newsletter of the Mesopotamian Studies Group, ASOR* 4/2.

Daniels, Peter T. 1994: "Edward Hincks's Decipherment of Mesopotamian Cuneiform," in *The Edward Hincks Bicentenary Lectures*, ed. Kevin Cathcart, 30–57. (Dublin: Dept. of Near Eastern Languages, University College Dublin).

Daniels, Peter T. 1995: "The Decipherment of Ancient Near Eastern Scripts." In *Civilizations of the Ancient Near East*, ed. Jack M. Sasson et al., 81–93. New York: Scribners. Repr. (4 vols. in 2) Peabody, Mass.: Hendrickson, 2000.

Daniels, Peter T. 1996a: "The First Civilizations." In *The World's Writing Systems*, ed. Peter T. Daniels and William Bright, 21–32. New York: Oxford University Press.

Daniels, Peter T. 1996b: "Methods of Decipherment." In *The World's Writing Systems*, ed. Peter T. Daniels and William Bright, 141–57. New York: Oxford University Press.

Daniels, Peter T. 1999: H-Net Africana review of *Ethiopic: An African Writing System, Its History and Principles*, by Ayele Bekerie. http://www3.aa.tufs.ac.jp/P_aflang/TEXTS/review/Daniels.html

Daniels, Peter T. 2000: Review of Mair 1998. *Sino-Platonic Papers* 98: 4–47.

Darnell, J. 1991: Supposed Depictions of Hittites in the Amarna Period. *Studien zur altägyptische Kultur*, 18, 113–39.

Day, Peggy. 2002: *"Dies Diem Docet*: The Decipherment of Ugaritic " *Studi Epigrafici e Linguistici sul Vicino Oriente antico* 19: 37–57.

De Genouillac, H., ed. 1936a: *Fouilles de Telloh* I. Paris: Geuthner.

De Genouillac, H., ed. 1936b: *Fouilles de Telloh* II. Paris: Geuthner.

De Martino, S. 1984: Il LÚ.ALAN.ZÚ come 'mimo' e come 'attore' nei testi ittiti. *Studi micenei ed egeo-anatolici*, 24, 131–48.

De Martino, S. 1995: Music, Dance, and Processions in Hittite Anatolia. In Sasson 1995, 2661–9.

de Meyer, L. 1962: *L'accadien des contrats de Suse*. Leiden: Brill.

De Moor, Johannes C. 1987: *An Anthology of Religious Texts from Ugarit*. Leiden: Brill.

De Morgan, J. 1900: *Mémoires de la Délégation en Perse I. Recherches archéologiques* 1. Paris: Lebroux.

De Odorico, M. 1995: *The Use of Numbers and Quantifications in the Assyrian Royal Inscriptions*. Helsinki: Neo-Assyrian Text Corpus Project.

De Planhol, X. 1997: *Minorités en Islam*, Paris: Flammarion.

De Roos, J. 1984: Hettitische Geloften. Ph.D. dissertation, University of Amsterdam.

De Roos, Johan. 1995: "Hittite Prayers." in *Civilizations of the Ancient Near East*, vol. 3, edited by Jack M. Sasson, 1997–2005. New York: Scribner.

De Vaux, R. 1965: *Ancient Israel*. New York: McGraw-Hill.

Degen, R. 1969: *Altaramäische Grammatik der Inschriften des 10.–8. jh.v. Chr*. Wiesbaden: F. Steiner.

del Olmo Lete, G. 1981: *Mitos Y Leyendas De Canaan: Según La Tradición De Ugarit*. Madrid: Ediciones Cristianidad; Valencia: Institución San Jerónimo.

Del Olmo Lete, G. 1999: *Canaanite Religion according to the Liturgical Texts of Ugarit*. Bethesda, MD: CDL.

Del Olmo Lete, G. and J. Montero Fenollós 1998: Du temple à l'entrepôt: un exemple de transformation de l'espace urbain à tell Qara Qûzâq en Syrie du Nord. In Fortin and Aurenche 1998, 295–304.

del Olmo Lete, G., and J. Sanmartín. 2003: *A Dictionary of the Ugaritic Language in the Alphabetic Tradition, I–II*. Leiden Brill.

Delaunay, J. A. 1974: À propos des *Aramaic rituals from Persepolis*, de R. A. Bowman. In *Commémoration Cyrus: Hommage universel, II*, Leiden: Brill, 193–217.

Delougaz, P. 1940: *The Temple Oval at Khafajah*. Chicago, IL: University of Chicago Press.

Delougaz, P. 1952: *Pottery from the Diyala Region*. Chicago, IL: University of Chicago Press.

Delougaz, P., H. Hill, and S. Lloyd 1967: *Private Houses and Graves in the Diyala Region.* Chicago, IL: University of Chicago Press.

Depauw, Mark. 1997: *A Companion to Demotic Studies.* Papyrologica Bruxellensia 28. Bruxelles: Fondation Égyptologique Reine Élisabeth.

Depuydt, L. 1993: *Conjunction, Contiguity, Contingency: On Relationships Between Events in the Egyptian and Coptic Verbal Systems.* Oxford: Oxford University Press.

Depuydt, L. 1999: *Fundamentals of Egyptian Grammar, 1: Elements.* Norton, Mass.: Frog.

Derchain, Philippe. 1996: "Auteur Et Société." in *Ancient Egyptian Literature: History and Forms*, edited by Antonio Loprieno, 83–94. Leiden: Brill.

Dercksen, J. (ed.) 1999: *Money and Finance in Ancient Mesopotamia.* Leiden: Nederlands Historisch-Archaeologisch Instituut.

Dercksen, J. 1996: *The Old Assyrian Copper Trade in Anatolia.* Istanbul: Nederlands Historisch-Archeologisch Instituut.

Dercksen, J. 2000: Institutional and Private in the Old Assyrian Period. In Bongenaar 2000, 135–52.

Desroches-Noblecourt, C. 1953: Concubines du Mort. *Bulletin de l'Institut Français d'Archéologie Orientale*, 53, 7–47.

Dever, W. 1992: Archaeology and the Israelite "Conquest." In Freedman 1992, 3, 545–58.

Dever, W. 1998: Archaeology, Ideology, and the Quest for an "Ancient" or "Biblical" Israel. *Near Eastern Archaeology*, 61, 39–52.

Dever, W. 1999: Archaeology and the Ancient Israelite Cult: How the Kh. El-Qôm and Kuntillet Ajrûd "Asherah" Texts Have Changed the Picture. *Eretz Israel*, 26, *9–15*.

Dever, William G. 2003: *Who Were the Early Israelites and Where Did They Come From?* Grand Rapids, Mich.: Eerdmans.

D'Hont, O. 1991: Sédentarisation et passage récent au nomadisme en Mésopotamie syrienne. In *Mutations rurales au Moyen Orient*, Amman, Beirut: CERMOC, 197–208.

Diakonoff, I. 1979: "Nesemitskie". In *Yazyki drevney peredney Azii.* Moscow: Nauka, 5–86.

Diakonoff, I. 1982: The Structure of Near Eastern Society Before the Middle of the 2nd Millennium BC. *Oikumene*, 3, 7–100.

Diakonoff, I. 1995: Old Babylonian Ur. *Journal of the Economic and Social History of the Orient*, 38, 91–4.

Diakonoff, I. M. 1967: Языкн древней Передней Азии. Moscow: Nauka.

Diakonoff, I. M. 1970: The Origin of the 'Old Persian' Writing System and the Ancient Oriental Epigraphic and Annalistic Traditions. In *W. B. Henning Memorial Volume*, London: Lund Humphries, 98–124.

Diakonoff, I. M. 1971: *Hurrisch und Urartäisch.* Munich: Kitzinger.

Diakonoff, I. M. 1972: Die Arier im Vorderen Orient: Ende eines Mythos. *Orientalia* n.s., 41, 91–120.

Diakonoff, I. M. 1975: Ancient Writing and Ancient Written Language. In *Sumerological Studies in Honor of Th. Jacobsen*, Chicago: University of Chicago Press, 99–121.

Diakonoff, I. M. 1979: Несемитские. In Языкн древней передней Азии, Moscow: Nauka, 5–96.

Diakonoff, I. M. 1985: Hurro-Urartian Borrowings in Old Armenian. *Journal of the American Oriental Society*, 105, 597–603.

Diakonoff, I. M. 1988: *Afrasian Languages.* Moscow: Nauka.

Diakonoff, I. M. 1991–92: Proto-Afrasian and Old Akkadian: A Study in Historical Phonetics. *Journal of Afroasiatic Languages*, 4.1/2.

Diakonoff, I. M. 1993: On Some Supposed Indo-Iranian Glosses in Cuneiform Languages. *Bulletin of the Asia Institute*, 7, 47–9.

Diakonoff, I. M. [И. М. Дьяконов]. 1965: *Semito-Hamitic Languages*. Moscow: Nauka.

Diakonoff, I. M., and S. A. Starostin. 1986: *Hurro-Urartian as an Eastern Caucasian language*. Munich: Kitzinger.

Dietrich, M., O. Loretz, and J. Sanmartín. 1995: *The Cuneiform Alphabetic Texts from Ugarit, Ras Ibn Hani and Other Places*. ALASP 8, Münster: Ugarit-Verlag.

Dijkstra, Meindert. 1999: "Ugaritic Prose." in *Handbook of Ugaritic Studies*, edited by Wilfred G. E. Watson and Nicolas Wyatt, 140–64. Handbuch der Orientalistik: Abt. 1, Der Nahe und Mittlere Osten: Bd. 39. Leiden: Brill.

Dinsmoor, W. 1975: *The Architecture of Ancient Greece*. New York: Norton.

Dion, P. E. 1974: *La langue de Yaʔudi*. Waterloo, Ont.: Editions SR.

Dionysius of Halicarnassus 1950: *The Roman Antiquities*. Vol. vii. E. Cary, translator. Cambridge, MA, London: Harvard University Press, Heinemann.

Dombradi, E. 1996: *Die Darstellung des Rechtsaustrags in den altbabylonischen Prozessurkunden*. Two vols. Stuttgart: Steiner.

Doret, É. 1986: *The Narrative Verbal System of Old and Middle Egyptian*. Geneva: Patrick Cramer.

Dossin, G. 1964: A Propos de la tablette administrative de A.R.M.T., XIII, No. 1. *Syria*, 41, 21–4.

Dothan, T. and M. Dothan 1992: *People of the Sea*. New York, Toronto: Macmillan.

Douglas, M. and B. Isherwood 1979: *The World of Goods*. New York: Basic.

Doyle, M. 1986: *Empires*. Ithaca, NY: Cornell University Press.

Drews, R. 1993: *The End of the Bronze Age. Changes in Warfare and the Catastrophe ca. 1200 BC*. Princeton: Princeton University Press.

Dreyer, G. 1998: *Umm el-Qaab I: Das prädynastische Königsgrab U-j und seine frühen Schriftzeugnisse*. Mainz: Zabern.

Driver, G. R. 1956: *Canaanite Myths and Legends*. Edinburgh: T. & T. Clark.

Driver, S. and J. Miles 1975: *The Assyrian Laws*. Darmstadt: Scientia. First 1935.

Dumont, L. 1970: *Homo Hierarchicus. An Essay on the Caste System*. Chicago, IL: University of Chicago Press. French 1966.

Dunand, M. 1954: *Fouilles de Byblos* II. Paris: Maisonneuve.

Dunand, M. 1966: La défense du front mediterranéen de l'émpire achéménide. In W. Ward (ed.), *The Role of the Phoenicians in the Interaction of Mediterranean Civilizations*, Beirut: American University of Beirut, 43–51.

Dunand, M. 1968: *Byblos*. Paris: Maisonneuve.

Dunham, S. 1980: A Study of Ancient Mesopotamian Foundations. Ph.D. dissertation, Columbia University.

Durand, J.-M. (ed.) 1987: *La Femme dans le Proche-Orient antique*. Paris: Editions Recherche sur les Civilisations.

Durand, J.-M. 1992: Unité et diversités au Proche Orient à l'époque Amorrite. In D. Charpin and F. Joannès (eds), *La circulation des biens, des personnes et des idées dans le Proche-Orient ancien*, Paris: Recherche sur les Civilisations, 97–128.

Durand, J.-M. 1997, 1998, 2000: *Documents épistolaires du Palais de Mari*. Three vols. Paris: Cerf.

Durand, J.-M. and J.-R. Kupper (eds) 1985: *Miscellanea Babylonica: mélanges offerts à Maurice Birot*. Paris: Recherche sur les Civilisations.

Dussaud, R. 1945: *Les religions des hittites et des hourrites, des phéniciens et des syriens*. Paris: Presses Universitaires de France.

Dyson, R. 1989: The Iron Age Architecture at Hasanlu: an Essay. *Expedition*, 31, 107–27.

Earle, T. 1987: Chiefdoms in Archaeological and Ethnohistorical Perspective. *Annual Review of Anthropology*, 16, 279–308.

Earle, T. 1991: Property Rights and the Evolution of Chiefdoms. In T. Earle (ed.), *Chiefdoms: Power, Economy and Ideology*, Cambridge: Cambridge University Press, 71–99.

Eastwood, W., N. Roberts, H. Lamb, and J. Tibby 1999: Holocene Environmental Change in Southwest Turkey: A Palaeoecological Record of Lake and Catchment-Related Changes. *Quaternary Science Reviews*, 18, 671–95.

Ebeling, E. 1923: *Keilschrifttexte aus Assur religiösen Inhalts* II. Leipzig: self-published.

Ebeling, E. 1953: *Die akkadische Gebetsserie "Handerhebung."* Berlin: Akademie.

Ebeling, E., B. Meissner, E. Weidner, W. Von Soden, and D. Edzard (eds.) 1928–: *Reallexikon der Assyriologie und vorderasiatischen Archäologie*. Berlin: de Gruyter.

Edel, E. 1955–64: *Altägyptische Grammatik*. Rome: Pontificium Institutum Biblicum.

Edelman, D. 1996: *The Triumph of Elohim. From Yahwisms to Judaisms*. Grand Rapids, MI: Eerdmanns.

Edens, C. 1992: Dynamics of Trade in the Ancient Mesopotamian "World System." *American Anthropologist*, 94, 118–39.

Edgerton, W. 1947: The Government and the Governed in the Egyptian Empire. *Journal of Near Eastern Studies*, 6, 152–60.

Edwards, I. E. S., C. J. Gadd, and N. G. L. Hammond (eds) 1971–92: *The Cambridge Ancient History*. vols I.2 (1971), II.1 (1973), II.2 (1975), III.1 (1982), III.2 (1992). Cambridge: Cambridge University Press.

Edzard, D. 1972–75: Herrscher. A. Philologisch. In Ebeling et al. 1928–, 6, 335–42.

Edzard, D. 1981: Mesopotamian Nomads in the Third Millennium BC. In Silva 1981, 37–46.

Edzard, D. 1997: *Gudea and His Dynasty*. Toronto: University of Toronto Press.

Edzard, D. O. 1995: The Sumerian Language. In J. M. Sasson (ed.), *Civilizations of the Ancient Near East*, New York: Scribner, vol. IV, pp. 2107–2116.

Edzard, D. O. 2003: *Sumerian Grammar*. Leiden: Brill.

Edzard, Dietz Otto. 1994: "Sumerian Epic: Epic or Fairy Tale?" *BCMS* 27: 7–14.

Efroymson, C. 1997: *Yehezkel Kaufmann: The History of the Religion of Israel from the Babylonian Exile to the End of Prophecy* Vol. 4. New York: Ktav.

Ehelolf, H. 1925: *Hethitische Texte: Instruktionen, Keilschrifturkunden aus Boghazköy* 13. Berlin: Vorderasiatische Abteilung der Staatlichen Museen.

Eichler, E. 1993: *Untersuchungen zum Expeditionswesen des ägyptischen Alten Reiches*. Wiesbaden: Harrassowitz.

Eickelman, D. 2002: *The Middle East and Central Asia: an Anthropological Approach*. Upper Saddle River, NJ: Prentice Hall.

Eidem, J. 1992: *The Shemshāra Archives 2: The Administrative Texts*. Copenhagen: Royal Danish Academy of Sciences and Letters.

Eisenstadt, S. (ed.) 1986: *Axial Age Civilizations*. Albany, NY: State University of New York Press.

Eisenstadt, S. 1963: *The Political Systems of Empires*. New York: Free Press.

Elnes, E. and P. Miller 1999: Elyon. In Van Der Toorn, Becking, and Van Der Horst 1999, 293–9.

Emerton, J. 1999: "Yahweh and his Asherah": The Goddess or her Symbol? *Vetus Testamentum*, 49, 315–37.

Empson, William. 1930: *Seven Types of Ambiguity*. London: Chatto and Windus.

Englund, G. 1988: *Middle Egyptian: An Introduction*. Uppsala: Uppsala University.

Englund, R. 1991: Hard Work – Where Will It Get You? *Journal of Near Eastern Studies*, 50, 255–80.

Englund, R. K. 1998: Texts from the Late Uruk Period. In *Mesopotamien, 1: Späturuk-Zeit und Frühdynastische Zeit*, Göttingen: Vandenhoeck & Ruprecht, 13–223.

Englund, R. K. 2004: The State of Decipherment of Proto-Elamite. In S. D. Houston (ed.), *The First Writing*, Cambridge: Cambridge University Press, 100–149.

Ephal, I. 1982: *The Ancient Arabs*. Jerusalem: Magnes, Hebrew University Press.

Erichsen, W. 1954: *Demotisches Glossar*. Kopenhagen: E. Munksgaard.

Erman, A. 1923: *Die Literatur de Aegypter: Gedichte, Erzählung und Lehrbücher aus den 3. und 2. Jahrtausend V. Chr.* Leipzig: Hinrichs. English translation by A. M. Blackman (London: Methuen, 1927).

Erman, A., and H. Grapow. 1926–1963: *Wörterbuch der ägyptischen Sprache, I–XII*. Berlin: Akademie Verlag.

Ertem, E., G. Summers, and Ş. Demirci 1998: An Archaeometric Study on Plain Wares from Hittite Period Kizilirmak Basin. In S. Alp and A. Süel (eds), *III. Uluslararasi Hititoloji Kongresi Bildirileri*, Ankara: Uyum Ajans, 197–215.

Evans, G. 1958: Ancient Mesopotamian Assemblies. *Journal of the American Oriental Society*, 78, 1–11.

Evans-Pritchard, E. 1962: *Social Anthropology and Other Essays*. Glencoe: Free Press.

Evenari, M., L. Shanan, and N. Tadmor 1982: *The Negev: The Challenge of a Desert*. Cambridge, MA: Harvard University Press.

Evers, H.-D. and H. Schrader (eds) 1994: *The Moral Economy of Trade*. New York: Routledge.

Fabietti, U. 2000: State Policies and Bedouin Adaptations in Saudi Arabia, 1900–1980. In Mundy and Musallam 2000, 82–9.

Fales, F. 2001: *L'Impero Assiro*. Rome: Laterza.

Fales, F. M. 1986: *Aramaic Epigraphs on Clay Tablets of the Neo-Assyrian Period*. Rome: La Sapienza.

Fales, F. M. 2000: The Use and Function of the Aramaic Tablets. In G. Bunnens (ed.), *Essays on Syria in the Iron Age*, Louvain: Peeters, 89–124.

Fales, Mario 1989: Pastorizia e politica: nuovi dati sugli Arabi nelle fonti di età Neo-Assira. In A. Avanzini (ed.), *Problemi di onomastica semitica meridionale*, Pisa: Giardini, 119–34.

Falkenstein, A. 1950: Ibbisîn-Išbi'erra. *Zeitschrift für Assyriologie*, 49, 59ff.

Falkenstein, A. 1956–1957: *Die neusumerischen Gerichtsurkunden*. Three vols. Munich: Bayerische Akademie der Wissenschaften.

Falkenstein, A. 1974: *The Sumerian Temple City*. Malibu: Undena.

Farber, H. 1978: A Price and Wage Study for Northern Babylonian During the Old Babylonian Period. *Journal of the Economic and Social History of the Orient*, 21, 1–51.

Farber-Flügge, G. 1973: *Der Mythos "Inanna und Enki" unter besonderer Berücksichtigung der Liste der m e*. Rome: Pontificial Biblical Institute.

Faulkner, R. O. 1962: *A Concise Dictionary of Middle Egyptian*. Oxford: Griffith Institute.

Feeley-Harnik, G. 1985: Issues in Divine Kingship. *Annual Review of Anthropology*, 14, 273–313.

Fernea, R. 1970: *Shaykh and Effendi: Changing Patterns of Authority among the El Shabana of Southern Iraq*. Cambridge, MA: Harvard University Press.

Fincke, J. 2000: *Augenleiden nach keilschriftlichen Quellen*. Würzburg: Königshausen & Neumann.

Finet, A. 1956: *L'accadien des lettres de Mari*. Bruxelles: Palais des Académies.

Finkbeiner, U. 1991: *Uruk: Kampagne 35–37, 1982–1984*. Mainz: Zabern.

Finkel, I. 1991: Muššu'u, Qutāru and the Scribe Tanittu-Bēl. *Aula Orientalis*, 9, 91–104.

Finkelstein, I. and N. Na'aman 1994: *From Nomadism to Monarchy: Archaeological and Historical Aspects of Early Israel*. Washington, DC: Biblical Archaeology Society.

Finkelstein, Israel, and Neil Silberman. 2002: *The Bible Unearthed: Archaeology's New Vision of Ancient Israel and the Origin of Its Sacred Texts*. New York: Free Press.

Finkelstein, J. 1969: The Edict of Ammisaduqa. In Pritchard 1969, 526–8.

Finkelstein, J. 1981: *The Ox That Gored*. Philadelphia, PA: American Philosophical Society.

Finkelstein, Jacob J. 1958: "Bible and Babel: A Comparative Study of the Hebrew and Babylonian Religious Spirit." *Commentary* 26 (November): 431–44.

Finkelstein, Jacob J. 1973: "The Goring Ox: Some Historical Perspectives on Deodands, Forfeitures, Wrongful Death and the Western Notion of Sovereignty." *Temple Law Quarterly* 46: 169–290.

Finkelstein, Jacob J. 1981: *The Ox That Gored*, ed. Maria deJ. Ellis. *Transactions of the American Philosophical Society* 71/2.

Fischer, H. 1960: The Nubian Mercenaries of Gebelein during the First Intermediate Period. *Kush*, 9, 44–80.

Fischer, H. 2000: *Egyptian Women of the Old Kingdom and of the Heracleopolitan Period*. Second edition. New York: Metropolitan Museum of Art.

Fisher, M. 2001: *The Sons of Ramesses II*. Wiesbaden: Harrassowitz.

Fitzpatrick-McKinley, A. 1999: *The Transformation of Torah from Scribal Advice to Law*. Sheffield: Sheffield Academic.

Flannery, K. 1973: The Origins of Agriculture. *Annual Review of Anthropology*, 2, 271–310.

Fleming, D. 1992: *The Installation of Baal's High Priestess at Emar*. Atlanta, GA: Scholars.

Fleming, D. 2000: *Time at Emar. The Cultic Calendar and the Rituals from the Diviner's Archive*. Winona Lake, IN: Eisenbrauns.

Fleming, D. 2004: *Democracy's Ancient Ancestors: Mari and Early Collective Governance*. Cambridge: Cambridge University Press.

Folmer, M. L. 1995: *The Aramaic Language in the Achaemenid Period: A Study in Linguistic Variation*. Leuven: Peeters.

Forest, J.-D. 1987: Les Bevelled Rim Bowls, Nouvelle tentative d'interpretation. *Akkadica*, 53, 1–24.

Forsberg, S. 1995: *Near Eastern Destruction Datings as Sources for Greek and Near Eastern Iron Age Chronology*. Uppsala: Academia Ubsaliensis.

Fortin, M. 1998: L'habitat de la station commerciale de tell 'Atij, sur le moyen Khabour, au IIIème millénaire av. J.-C. In Fortin and Aurenche 1998, 229–42.

Fortin, M. and O. Aurenche (eds) 1998: *Espace naturel, espace habité en Syrie du Nord (10e–2e millénaires av. J-C.)*. Québec, Lyon: de Boccard.

Foster, B. 1981: A New Look at the Sumerian Temple State. *Journal of the Economic and Social History of the Orient*, 24, 225–41.

Foster, B. 1982: *Administration and Use of Institutional Land in Sargonic Sumer*. Copenhagen: Akademisk.

Foster, B. 1987a: Gilgamesh: Sex, Love, and the Ascent of Knowledge. In J. Marks and R. Good (eds), *Love & Death in the Ancient Near East, Essays in Honor of Marvin H. Pope*, Guilford, CT: Four Quarters, 21–42.

Foster, B. 1987b: Notes on Women in Sargonic Society. In Durand 1987, 53–61.

Foster, B. 1993b: International Trade at Sargonic Susa (Susa in the Sargonic Period III). *Altorientalische Forschungen*, 20, 59–68.

Foster, B. 1993c: Letters and Literature: A Ghost's Entreaty. In Cohen, Snell, and Weisberg 1993, 98–102.

Foster, B. 1995: *From Distant Days: Myths, Tales, and Poetry of Ancient Mesopotamia.* Bethesda, MD: CDL.

Foster, B. 2002: Yale and the Study of Near Eastern Languages in America. In A. Amanat and M. Bernhardsson (eds), *The United States and the Middle East*, New Haven, CT: Yale Center for International and Area Studies, 1–56.

Foster, Benjamin. 1974: "Humor and Cuneiform Literature." *JANES* 6: 69–85.

Foster, Benjamin. 1991: "On Authorship in Akkadian Literature." *Annali, Istituto Universitario Orientale, Napoli* 51: 17–32.

Foster, Benjamin. 1993, 1996, 2005: *Before the Muses: An Anthology of Akkadian Literature, I–II.* 2nd edn. Potomac, Maryland: CDL Press.

Foster, Benjamin. 1995: *From Distant Days: Myths, Tales, and Poetry of Ancient Mesopotamia.* Bethesda, Maryland: CDL Press.

Foster, Benjamin. 2001: *The Epic of Gilgamesh: A New Translation, Analogues, Criticism.* New York: Norton.

Foster, J. 1995: The Hymn to Aten: Akhenaten Worships the Sole God. In Sasson 1995, 1751–61.

Foster, John L. 1974: *The Love Songs of the New Kingdom.* New York : Scribner.

Foster, John L. 1992: *Echoes of Egyptian Voices: An Anthology of Ancient Egyptian Poetry.* Transl. Norman: University of Oklahoma Press.

Fowler, A. 1982: *Kinds of Literature: An Introduction to the Theory of Genres and Modes.* Cambridge, Mass.: Harvard University Press.

Fox, Michael V. 1985: *The Song of Songs and the Ancient Egyptian Love Songs.* Madison: University of Wisconsin Press.

Frame, G. 1992: *Babylonia 689–627 BC: a Political History.* Leiden: Nederlands Historisch-Archaeologisch Instituut.

Frame, G. 1995: *Rulers of Babylonia. From the Second Dynasty of Isin to the End of Assyrian Domination, 1157–612 BC.* Toronto: University of Toronto Press.

Frangiapani, M. and A. Palmieri 1987: Urbanization in Peri-Mesopotamian Areas: The Case of Eastern Anatolia. In L. Manzanilla (ed.), *Studies in the Neolithic and Urban Revolutions*, Oxford: BAR, 295–318.

Franke, D. 1990: Erste und Zweite Zwischenzeit – Ein Vergleich. *Zeitschrift für ägyptische Sprache*, 117, 119–29.

Franke, D. 1991: The Career of Khnumhotep III of Beni Hasan and the So-called "Decline of the Nomarchs." In S. Quirke and J. Bourriau (eds), *Middle Kingdom Studies*, New Malden, Surrey: SIA, 51–67.

Franke, D. 1997: "Schöpfer, Schützer, Guter Hirte": Zum Königsbild des Mittleren Reiches. In R. Gundlach and Christine Raedler (eds), *Selbsverständnis und Realität*, Wiesbaden: Harrassowitz, 175–209.

Frankfort, H. 1934: *The Iraq Excavations of the Oriental Institute 1932/33.* Chicago, IL: University of Chicago Press.

Frankfort, H. 1939: *Cylinder Seals.* London: Macmillan.

Frankfort, H. 1948: *Kingship and the Gods.* Chicago, IL: University of Chicago Press.

Frankfort, H. 1954: *The Art and Architecture of the Ancient Orient.* Harmondsworth, Middlesex and Baltimore, MD: Penguin Books.

Frankfort, H., S. Lloyd, and T. Jacobsen 1940: *The Gimilsin Temple and the Palace of the Rulers at Tell Asmar*. Chicago, IL: University of Chicago Press.

Frantz-Szabó, G. 1995: Hittite Witchcraft, Magic, and Divination. In Sasson 1995, 2007–19.

Frayne, D. 1993: *Sargonic and Gutian Periods (2334–2113 BC)*. Toronto: University of Toronto Press.

Freed, R. 1999: Akenaten's Artistic Legacy. In R. Freed, Y. Markowitz., S. D'Auria (eds), *Pharaohs of the Sun*, Boston, MA, New York, London: Museum of Fine Arts, 187–97.

Freedman, D. (ed.) 1992: *Anchor Bible Dictionary*. New York: Doubleday.

Freedman, S. 1998: *If a City Is Set on a Height, The Akkadian Omen Series Šumma Ālu ina Mēlê šakin*. Philadelphia, PA: University Museum.

Fried, L. 2001: "You Shall Appoint Judges": Ezra's Mission and the Rescript of Artaxerxes. In J. Watts (ed.), *Persia and Torah: The Theory of Imperial Authorization of the Pentateuch*, Atlanta, GA: Scholars, 63–89.

Friedrich, J. 1960–67: *Hethitisches Elementarbuch*. 2nd edn. Heidelberg: Winter.

Friedrich, J., and W. Röllig. 1999: *Phönizisch-Punische Grammatik*. 3rd edn. by M. G. Amadasi Guzzo. Rome: Pontificio Istituto Biblico.

Fronzaroli, P. (ed.). 1984: *Studies on the Language of Ebla*. Florence: Università di Firenze.

Fronzaroli, P. (ed.). 1988: *Miscellanea eblaitica, 1*. Florence: Università di Firenze.

Fronzaroli, P. (ed.). 1989: *Miscellanea eblaitica, 2*. Florence: Università di Firenze.

Fronzaroli, P. (ed.). 1992: *Literature and Literary Language at Ebla*. Florence: Università di Firenze.

Fronzaroli, P. (ed.). 1997: *Miscellanea eblaitica, 4*. Florence: Università di Firenze.

Fronzaroli, P. 2003: *Testi di cancelleria: I rapporti con le città*. Archivi Reali di Ebla, Testi, XIII. Rome: La Sapienza.

Frye, R. 1992: Assyria and Syria: Synonyms. *Journal of Near Eastern Studies*, 51, 281–5.

Frymer-Kensky, T. 1981: Suprarational Legal Procedures in Elam and Nuzi. In M. Morrison and D. Owen (eds), *Studies on the Civilization and Culture of Nuzi and the Hurrians in Honor of Ernest R. Lacheman*, Winona Lake, IN: Eisenbrauns, 115–31.

Furlani, G. 1936: *La religione degli hittiti*. Bologna: Zanichelli.

Gaballa, G. 1975: *Narrative in Egyptian Art*. Mainz: Zabern.

Gadd, C. J. 1928: *Ur Excavations Texts* I. London: The British Museum.

Galter, H. (ed.) 1993: *Die Rolle der Astronomie in den Kulturen Mesopotamiens*. Graz: GrazKult.

Galvin, M. 1984: The Hereditary Status of the Titles of the Cult of Hathor. *Journal of Egyptian Archaeology*, 70, 42–9.

Gammie, J. and L. Perdue (eds) 1990: *The Sage in Israel and the Ancient Near East*. Winona Lake, IN: Eisenbrauns.

Garbini, G. 1966: *The Ancient World*. New York: McGraw-Hill.

García Berrio, A. 1992: *Teoría de la Literatura* (Madrid: Cátedra, 1989); Translated as *A Theory of the Literary Text*, Berlin: De Gruyter.

García Martínez, Florentino. 1996: *The Dead Sea Scrolls Translated: The Qumran Texts in English*, 2nd edn, trans. Wilfred G. E. Watson. Leiden: Brill; Grand Rapids, Mich.: Eerdmans. Spanish original, 1992.

García Martínez, Florentino, and Eibert J. C. Tigchelaar. 2000: *The Dead Sea Scrolls: Study Edition*, 2 vols., corrected pbk. edn Leiden: Brill; Grand Rapids, Mich.: Eerdmans. Original edn Leiden: Brill, 1997–98.

García Trabazo, José Virgilio. 2002: *Textos Religiosos Hititas: Mitos, Plegarias y Rituales*. Madrid: Editorial Trotta.

Gardiner, A. 1916: The Defeat of the Hyksos by Kamose: The Carnarvon Tablet, No. 1. *Journal of Egyptian Archaeology*, 3, 95–110.

Gardiner, A. 1937: *Late-Egyptian Miscellanies*. Brussels: Fondation égyptologique Reine Elisabeth.

Gardiner, A. 1957: *Egyptian Grammar*. 3rd edn. Oxford: Griffith Institute.

Gardiner, A. 1961: *Egypt of the Pharaohs*. Oxford: Oxford University Press.

Garelli, P. 1982: Importance et rôle des araméens dans l'administration de l'empire assyrien. In H. Nissen and J. Renger (eds), *Mesopotamien und seine Nachbarn*, Berlin: Reimer, 437–47.

Garfinkle, S. 2002: Turam-ili and the Community of Merchants in the Ur III Period. *Journal of Cuneiform Studies*, 54, 29–48.

Garfinkle, S. 2003: SI.A-a and His Family: the Archive of a 21st Century (BC) Entrepreneur. *Zeitschrift für Assyriologie*, 93, 161–98.

Gasche, H., J. Armstrong, S. Cole, and V. Gurzadyan 1998: *Dating the Fall of Babylon*. Ghent, Chicago, IL: University of Ghent, Oriental Institute.

Gates, M.-H. 2001: Potmarks at Kinet Höyük and the Hittite ceramic industry. In E. Jean, A. Dinçol, and S. Durugönül (eds), *La Cilicie: espaces et pouvoirs locaux*, Istanbul, Paris: de Boccard, 137–57.

Gay, P. 1974: *Style in History*. New York: Basic Books.

Gelb, I. J. 1960: Sumerians and Akkadians in their Ethno-Linguistic Relationship. *Genava*, 8, 258–271.

Gelb, I. J. 1961: *Old Akkadian Writing and Grammar*. 2nd edn. Chicago: University of Chicago Press.

Gelb, I. J. 1967: Approaches to the Study of Ancient Society. *Journal of the American Oriental Society*, 87, 1–8.

Gelb, I. J. 1971: On the Alleged Temple and State Economies in Ancient Mesopotamia. *Studi in Onore di Edoardo Volterra*, 6, 137–54.

Gelb, I. J. 1981: Ebla and the Kish Civilization. In L. Cagni (ed.), *La Lingua di Ebla*, Naples: Istituto Universitario Orientale, 10–73.

Gelb, I. J. 1992: Mari and the Kish Civilization. In G. D. Young, *Mari in Retrospect*, Winona Lake: Eisenbrauns, 121–202.

Gelb, I. J., A. L. Oppenheim, E. Reiner, M. Civil *et al.* 1956–: *Chicago Assyrian Dictionary*. Chicago: Oriental Institute.

Geller, M. J. 1997: The Last Wedge. *Zeitschrift für Assyriologie*, 87, 43–95.

George, A. 1986: Sennacherib and the Tablet of Destinies. *Iraq*, 48, 133–46.

George, A. 1990: Royal Tombs at Nimrud. *Minerva*, 29, 29–31.

George, A. 1992: *Babylonian Topographical Texts*. Leuven: Peeters.

George, A. 1993: *House Most High. The Temples of Ancient Mesopotamia*. Winona Lake, IN: Eisenbrauns.

George, A. 1996: Studies in Cultic Topography and Ideology. *Bibliotheca Orientalis*, 53, 363–95.

George, A. 1999a: *The Epic of Gilgamesh*. Harmondsworth, Middlesex: Allen Lane, Penguin.

George, A. 1999b: E-sangil and E-temen-anki, The Archetypal Cult-Centre. In J. Renger (ed.), *Babylon*, Saarbrücken: Saarbrücker, 67–86.

George, Andrew. 1999: *The Epic of Gilgamesh: A New Translation*. New York: Penguin.

George, Andrew. 2003: *The Babylonian Gilgamesh Epic: Introduction, Critical Edition and Cuneiform Texts*, 2 vols. Oxford: Oxford University Press.

Gershevitch, I. 1979: The Alloglottography of Old Persian. *Transactions of the Philological Society*, 114–190.

Gesenius, W., and E. Kautzsch. 1910: *Gesenius' Hebrew Grammar as Edited and Enlarged by E. Kautzsch*. 2nd edn. by A. E. Cowley. Oxford: Clarendon Press.

Gibbon, Edward. 1776–88: *The History of the Decline and Fall of the Roman Empire*. 6 vols. Edited, with an introduction and appendices, by David Womersley. 3 vols. London: Allen Lane The Penguin Press, 1994.

Gibson, John C. L. 1978: *Canaanite Myths & Legends*. 2nd edn. Edinburgh: T. & T. Clark.

Gibson, John C. L. 1999: "The Mythological Texts." in *Handbook of Ugaritic Studies*, edited by Wilfred G. E. Watson and Nicolas Wyatt, 193–202. Handbuch der Orientalistik: Abt. 1, Der Nahe und Mittlere Osten: Bd. 39. Leiden: Brill.

Gibson, M. 1992: Patterns of Occupation at Nippur. In M. Ellis (ed.), *Nippur at the Centennial*, Philadelphia, PA: University Museum, 33–54.

Gibson, M. and R. Biggs (eds) 1977: *Seals and Sealing*. Malibu, CA: Undena.

Gibson, M. and R. Biggs (eds) 1987, 1991: *The Organization of Power: Aspects of Bureaucracy in the Ancient Near East*. Chicago, IL: University of Chicago Press.

Gibson, S. and G. Edelstein 1985: Investigating Jerusalem's Rural Landscape. *Levant*, 17, 139–55.

Gilbert, A. 1995: The Flora and Fauna of the Ancient Near East. In Sasson 1995, 153–74.

Gilbertson, D., C. Hunt, N. Fieller, and G. Barker 1994: The Environmental Consequences and Context of Ancient Floodwater Farming in the Tripolitanian Pre-Desert. In A. Millington and K. Pye (eds), *Environmental Change in Drylands: Biogeographical and Geomorphological Perspectives*, Chichester: Wiley, 220–51.

Giogieri, M. 2000: Schizzo grammaticale della lingua hurrita. In *La civiltà dei hurriti*, La parola del passato, vol. 310–315, Naples: Maccchiaroli, 171–277.

Girbal, C. 1986: *Beiträge zur Grammatik des Hattischen*. Frankfurt am Main: P. Lang.

Gitin, S. 1997: The Neo-Assyrian Empire and its Western Periphery: the Levant, with a Focus on Philistine Ekron. In Parpola and Whiting 1997, 77–103.

Giumlía-Mair, A. and S. Quirke 1997: Black Copper in Bronze Age Egypt. *Revue d'Égyptologie*, 48, 95–108.

Glassner, J.-J. 1993: *Chroniques mésopotamiennes*. Paris: Les Belles-Lettres.

Glassner, J.-J. 1995: Progress, Science, and the Use of Knowledge in Ancient Mesopotamia. In Sasson 1995, 1815–23.

Glassner, J.-J. 1999: Oralité et écriture en Asie. *Critique*, 629, 837–47.

Glassner, J.-J. 2003: *Writing in Sumer*. Baltimore, MD: Johns Hopkins University Press.

Gnirs, A. 1999: Ancient Egypt. In K. Raaflaub and N. Rosenstein (eds), *War and Society in the Ancient and Medieval Worlds*, Cambridge, MA: Harvard University Press.

Gnirs, Andrea M. 1996: "Die Ägyptische Autobiographie." in *Ancient Egyptian Literature: History and Forms*, edited by Antonio Loprieno, 191–241. Leiden: Brill.

Gnuse, R. 1997: *No Other Gods: Emergent Monotheism in Israel*. Sheffield: Sheffield Academic.

Goedicke, H. (ed.) 1985: *Perspectives on the Battle of Kadesh*. Baltimore, MD: Halgo.

Goedicke, H. 1967: *Königliche Dokumente aus dem Alten Reiches*.Wiesbaden: Harrassowitz.

Gogel, S. L. 1998: *A Grammar of Epigraphic Hebrew*. Atlanta, Ga.: Scholars Press.

Golz, D. 1974: *Studien zur altorientalischen und griechischen Heilkunde*. Wiesbaden: Steiner.

Gonnet, H. 1976: Rituel des fêtes d'automne et de printemps du dieu de l'orage de Zippalanda. *Anadolou*, 19, 123–62.

Goodfriend, G. 1999: Terrestrial stable isotope records of Late Quaternary paleoclimates in the eastern Mediterranean region. *Quaternary Science Reviews*, 18, 501–13.

Goodnick Westenholz, Joan. 1995: "Love Lyrics from the Ancient Near East." in *Civilizations of the Ancient Near East*, vol. 3, edited by Jack M. Sasson, 2471–84. New York: Scribner.

Goodnick Westenholz, Joan. 1997: *Legends of the Kings of Akkade.* Winona Lake: Eisenbrauns.

Gould, R. 2000: Ethnoarchaeology. In L. Ellis (ed.), *Archaeological Method and Theory, an Encyclopedia*, New York: Garland, 181–7.

Gragg, G. B. 1995: Less-Understood Languages of Ancient Western Asia. In J. M. Sasson (ed.), *Civilizations of the Ancient Near East*, New York: Scribner, vol. IV, 2161–2179.

Grandet, P. 1994: *Le Papyrus Harris I (BM 9999).* Cairo: Institut Français d'Archéologie Orientale.

Grayson, A. K. 1975: *Assyrian and Babylonian Chronicles.* Locust Valley, NY: Augustin.

Grayson, A. K. 1976: *Assyrian Royal Inscriptions, Part 2: From Tiglath-pileser I to Ashur-nasir-apli II.* Wiesbaden: Harrassowitz.

Grayson, A. K. 1987: *Assyrian Rulers of the Third and Second Millennia BC.* Toronto: University of Toronto Press.

Grayson, A. K. 1995: Assyrian Rule of Conquered Territory. In Sasson 1995, 959–68.

Green, A. 2003: *The Storm-God in the Ancient Near East.* Winona Lake, IN: Eisenbrauns.

Green, M. 1978: The Eridu Lament. *Journal of Cuneiform Studies*, 30, 127–67.

Green, M. 1984: The Uruk Lament. *Journal of the American Oriental Society*, 104, 253–79.

Green, M. 1986: Urum and Uqair. *Acta Sumerologica*, 8, 77–83.

Greenberg, M. 1995: Kaufmann on the Bible: An Appreciation. In M. Greenberg (ed.), *Studies in the Bible and Jewish Thought*, Philadelphia, PA: Jewish Publication Society, 175–88.

Greengus, S. 1969: The Old Babylonian Marriage Contract. *Journal of the American Oriental Society*, 89, 505–632.

Greengus, S. 1995: Legal and Social Institutions of Ancient Mesopotamia. In Sasson 1995, 469–84.

Greenstein, Edward L. 1995: "Autobiographies in Ancient Western Asia." in *Civilizations of the Ancient Near East*, vol. 3, edited by Jack M. Sasson, 2421–32. New York: Scribner.

Greppin, J. A., and I. M. Diakonoff. 1991: Some Effects of the Hurro-Urartian People and their Languages upon the Earliest Armenians. *Journal of the American Oriental Society*, 11, 720–730.

Griffiths, John G. 1960: *The Conflict of Horus and Seth, from Egyptian and Classical Sources: A Study in Ancient Mythology.* Liverpool: Liverpool University Press.

Griffiths, John G. 1970: *Plutarch's "De Iside et Osiride."* Cardiff: University of Wales Press.

Grillot-Susini, F. 1987: *Eléments de grammaire élamite.* Paris: ÉRC.

Groenewegen-Frankfort, H. 1951: *Arrest and Movement: Space and Time in the Art of the Ancient Near East.* Chicago, IL: University of Chicago Press.

Groneberg, B. 1987: *Syntax, Morphologie und Stil der jungbabylonischen "hymnischen" Literatur, I–II.* Stuttgart: F. Steiner.

Gronenberg, Brigitte. 1996: "Towards a Definition of Literariness as Applied to Akkadian Literature." in *Mesopotamian Poetic Language: Sumerian and Akkadian. Proceedings of the Groningen Group for the Study of Mesopotamian Literature, vol. 2*, edited by M. E. Vogelzang and H. L. J. Vanstiphout, 59–84. CM 6. Groningen: Styx.

Grosby, S. 2002: *Biblical Ideas of Nationality. Ancient and Modern.* Winona Lake, IN: Eisenbrauns.

Grottanelli, C., W. MacGaffey, D. Carrasco, M. Waida, and M. Aung-Thwin 1987: Kingship. In M. Eliade (ed.), *The Encyclopedia of Religion*, New York: Macmillan, 8, 312–36.

Grunert, S., and I. Hafemann. 1999: *Textcorpus und Wörterbuch: Aspekte zur ägyptischen Lexikographie.* Leiden: Brill.

Gössmann, P. 1950: *Planetarium Babylonicum.* Rome: Pontifical Biblical Institute.

Guglielmi, Waltraud. 1996: "Die Ägyptische Liebespoesie." in *Ancient Egyptian Literature: History and Forms*, edited by Antonio Loprieno, 335–47. Leiden: Brill.

Güterbock, H. 1950: Hittite Religion. In V. Ferm (ed.), *Ancient Religions*, New York: Philosophical Library, 83–109.

Güterbock, H. 1960: An Outline of the Hittite AN.TAH.ŠUM Festival. *Journal of Near Eastern Studies*, 19, 80–89.

Güterbock, H. 1964: Religion und Kultus der Hethiter. In G. Walser (ed.), *Neuere Hethiterforschung*, Wiesbaden: Steiner, 54–73.

Güterbock, H. 1970: Some Aspects of Hittite Festivals. In A. Finet (ed.), *Actes de la XVIIe Rencontre Assyriologique Internationale* (1969), Brussels: Comité Belge de Recherches en Mésopotamie, 175–80.

Güterbock, H. 1975: The Hittite Temple according to Written Sources. In E. Van Donzel (ed.), *Le temple et le cult*, Istanbul: Nederlands Historisch-archaeologisch Instituut, 125–32.

Güterbock, H. 1982: *Les hiéroglyphes de Yazilikaya (à propos d'un travail récent)*. Paris: Institut français d'études anatoliennes.

Güterbock, H. 1989: Hittite *kursa* 'Hunting Bag.' In A. Leonard and B. Williams (eds), *Essays in Ancient Civilization Presented to Helene J. Kantor*, Chicago, IL: Oriental Institute, 113–19.

Güterbock, H. 1998: To Drink a God. In H. Erkanal, V. Donbaz, and A. Uğuroğlu (eds), *XXXIVème Rencontre Assyriologique Internationale*, Ankara: Türk Tarih Kurumu, 121–9.

Güterbock, H., and T. P. J. Van Den Hout 1991: *The Hittite Instruction for the Royal Bodyguard*. Chicago, IL: Oriental Institute.

Gurney, O. 1977: *Some Aspects of Hittite Religion*. Oxford: Oxford University Press.

Haas, V. 1994: *Geschichte der hethitischen Religion*. Leiden: Brill.

Haas, V. 2006: *Die Hethitische Literatur: Texte, Stilistik, Motive*. Berlin: De Gruyter.

Habachi, L. 1972: *The Second Stela of Kamose, and his Struggle against the Hyksos Ruler and his Capital*. Glückstadt: Augustin.

Hall, H. R. and C. L. Woolley 1927: *Ur Excavations I: Al 'Ubaid*. London, Philadelphia, PA: British Museum, University Museum.

Hallo, W. 1957: *Early Mesopotamian Royal Titles*. New Haven, CT: American Oriental Society.

Hallo, W. 1957–1971. Gutium. In Ebeling et al. 1928–, 3: 708–21.

Hallo, W. 1960: A Sumerian Amphictyony. *Journal of Cuneiform Studies*, 14, 88–114.

Hallo, W. 1978: Women of Sumer. In D. Schmandt-Besserat (ed.), *The Legacy of Sumer*, Malibu, CA: Undena, 23–40.

Hallo, W. 1996: *Origins: the Ancient Near Eastern Background of Some Modern Western Institutions*. Leiden: Brill.

Hallo, W. and I. Winter (eds) 2001: *Seals and Seal Impressions*. Bethesda, MD: CDL.

Hallo, W. and J. Van Dijk 1968: *The Exaltation of Innana*. New Haven, CT: Yale University Press.

Hallo, W. and W. K. Simpson 1971: *The Ancient Near East. A History*. New York: Harcourt Brace Jovanovich.

Hallo, William W. 1995: "Lamentations and Prayers in Sumer and Akkad." in *Civilizations of the Ancient Near East*, vol. 3, edited by Jack M. Sasson, 1871–81. New York: Scribner.

Hallo, William W. and K. Lawson Younger. (eds) 1997, 2000, 2002: *The Context of Scripture: Canonical Compositions, Monumental Inscriptions, and Archival Documents from the Biblical World*, 3 vols. Leiden: Brill.

Halpern, B. 1991: Jerusalem and the Lineages in the Seventh Century BCE: Kinship and the Rise of Individual Moral Liability. In B. Halpern and D. Hobson (eds), *Law and Ideology in Monarchic Israel*, Sheffield: JSOT, 11–107.

Hamdan, G. 1961: Evolution of Irrigation Agriculture in Egypt. *Arid Zone Research*, 17, 119–42.

Hämeen-Anttila, J., and R. Rollinger. 2001: Herodot und die arabische Göttin 'Alilat.' *Journal of Near Eastern Religions*, 1, 84–99.

Hämeen-Anttila, J. 2000: *A Sketch of Neo-Assyrian Grammar*. Helsinki: The Neo-Assyrian Text Corpus Project.

Hannig, R. 1995: *Großes Handwörterbuch Ägyptisch-Deutsch (2800–950 v. Chr.): Die Sprache der Pharaonen*. Mainz: von Zabern.

Hannig, R. 2000: *Großes Handwörterbuch Deutsch-Ägyptisch (2800–950 v. Chr.): Die Sprache der Pharaonen*. Mainz: von Zabern.

Hannig, R. 2003: *Ägyptisches Worterbuch I: Altes Reich und Erste Zwischenzeit*. Mainz: von Zabern.

Hansen, D. 1998: Art of the Royal Tombs of Ur: A Brief Interpretation. In R. Zettler and L. Horne (eds), *Treasures from the Royal Tombs of Ur*, Philadelphia, PA: University of Pennsylvania Museum, 43–72.

Hansen, D. 2003a: Art of the Early City-States. In Aruz 2003, 21–37.

Hansen, D. 2003b: Art of the Akkadian Dynasty. In Aruz 2003, 189–98.

Harak, A. 1990: The Royal Tombs of Nimrud and Their Jewelry. *Canadian Society for Mesopotamian Studies Bulletin*, 20, 5–14.

Harlan, J. and D. Zohary 1966: Distribution of Wild Wheats and Barley. *Science*, 153, 1074–80.

Harper, P., E. Klengel-Brandt, J. Aruz, and K. Benzel 1995: *Assyrian Origins: Discoveries at Ashur on the Tigris*. New York: Metropolitan Museum.

Harper, P., J. Aruz, and F. Tallon (eds) 1992: *The Royal City of Susa*. New York: Metropolitan Museum of Art.

Harris, R. 1992: Women. In Freedman 1992, 6, 947–51.

Harris, R. 2000: The Female "Sage" in Mesopotamian Literature. In *Gender and Aging in Mesopotamia*, Norman, OK: University of Oklahoma Press, 147–57.

Hartman, L. and A. Di Lella 1978: *The Book of Daniel*. Garden City, New York: Doubleday.

Hassan, F. and S. Robinson 1987: High-Precision Radiocarbon Chronometry of Ancient Egypt, and Comparisons with Nubia, Palestine and Mesopotamia. *Antiquity*, 61, 119–35.

Hasselbach, R. 2005: *Sargonic Akkadian: A Historical and Comparative Study of the Syllabic Texts*. Wiesbaden: Harrassowitz.

Hauptmann, A. 1992: Feinan/Wadi Feinan. *American Journal of Archaeology*, 96, 510–12.

Hauptmann, H. 1993: Ein Kultgebäude in Nevali Çori. In M. Frangipane and A. Palmieri (eds), *Between the Rivers and over the Mountains*, Rome: Università "La Sapienza," 37–69.

Haussperger, M. 1997: Die mesopotamische Medizin und ihre Ärtze aus heutiger Sicht. *Zeitschrift für Assyriologie*, 87, 196–218.

Havelock, Eric A. 1986: *The Muse Learns to Write: Reflections on Orality and Literacy from Antiquity to the Present*. New Haven: Yale University Press.

Hawass, Z. 2000: *Silent Images: Women in Pharaonic Egypt*. New York: Abrams.

Hawkins, J. D., and H. Çambel. 1999–2000: *Corpus of Hieroglyphic Luwian Inscriptions, 1–4*. Berlin: De Gruyter.

Hawkins, J. (ed.) 1977: *Trade in the Ancient Near East. = Iraq 39*.

Hayes, J. 1999: Kaufmann, Yehezkel. In J. Hayes (ed.), *Dictionary of Biblical Interpretation*, Nashville, TN: Abingdon, 2,16–7.

Hayes, W. 1972: *A Papyrus of the Late Middle Kingdom*. New York: Brooklyn Museum.

Hazenbos, J. 2003: *The Organization of the Anatolian Local Cults during the Thirteenth Century BC*. Leiden: Brill/Styx.

Hecker, K. 1968: *Grammatik der Kültepe-Texte*. Rome: Pontificium Institutum Biblicum.

Heeßel, N. 2000: *Babylonisch-assyrische Diagnostik*. Münster: Ugarit.

Heide, M. 2002: Die theophoren Personennamen der Kuntillet Agrud-Inschriften. *Welt des Orients*, 32, 110–20.

Heimpel, W. 1974: Sumerische und Akkadische Personnennamen in Sumer und Akkad. *Archiv für Orientforschung*, 25, 171–4.

Heimpel, W. 1992: Herrentum und Königtum im vor- und frühgeschichtlichen Alten Orient. *Zeitschrift für Assyriologie*, 82, 4–21.

Heimpel, W. 1997: Disposition of Households of Officials in Ur III and Mari. *Acta Sumerologica*, 19, 63–82.

Heimpel, W. 2003: *Letters to the King of Mari*. Winona Lake, IN: Eisenbrauns.

Heinrich, E. 1934: *Schilf und Lehm*. Berlin: Kunstwissenschaft.

Heinrich, E. 1957: *Bauwerke in der altsumerischen Bildkunst*. Wiesbaden: Harrassowitz.

Heinz, S. 2001: *Die Feldzugsdarstellungen des Neuen Reiches*. Vienna: Akademie der Wissenschaften.

Helck, W. 1980: Kenbet. *Reallexikon der Ägyptologie*. Wiesbaden: Harrassowitz, 3, 386–7.

Heltzer, M. 1978: *Goods, Prices and the Organization of Trade in Ugarit*. Wiesbaden: Harrassowitz.

Heltzer, M. 1982: *The Internal Organization of the Kingdom of Ugarit*. Wiesbaden: Reichert.

Heltzer, M. and S. Arbeli-Raveh 1981: *The Suteans*. Naples: Istituto Universitario Orientale.

Hendel, R. 1997: Aniconism and Anthropomorphism in Ancient Israel. In Van Der Toorn 1997, 205–8.

Hendrickson, E. 1981: Non-religious Residential Settlement Patterning in the Early Dynastic of the Diyala Region. *Mesopotamia*, 16, 43–140.

Hendrickson, E. 1982: Functional Analysis of Elite Residences in the Late Early Dynastic of the Diyala Region. *Mesopotamia*, 17, 5–34.

Henry, D. 1989: *From Foraging to Agriculture*. Philadelphia, PA: University of Pennsylvania Press.

Hermann, Alfred. 1959: *Altägyptische Liebesdichtung*. Wiesbaden: Harrassowitz.

Herodotus 1987: *The History*. D. Grene, translator. Chicago, IL: University of Chicago Press.

Herold, A. 1999: *Streitwagentechnologie in der Ramses-Stadt*. Mainz: Zabern.

Herrmann, W. 1999: El. In Van Der Toorn, Becking, and Van Der Horst 1999, 274–80.

Hetzron, R. (ed). 1997: *The Semitic Languages*. London: Routledge.

Heun, M., R. Schäfer-Pregl, D. Klawan, R. Castagna, M. Accerbi, B. Borghi, and F. Salamini 1997: Site of Einkorn Wheat Domestication Identified by DNA Fingerprinting. *Science*, 278, 1312–14.

Hilgert, M. 2002: *Akkadisch in der Ur III-Zeit*. Münster: Rhema.

Hillers, D. 1998: Palmyrene Inscriptions and the Bible. *Zeitschrift für Althebraistik*, 11, 32–49.

Hillman, G. and M. Davies 1990: Measured Domestication Rates in Wild Wheats and Barley under Primitive Cultivation, and Their Archaeological Implications. *Journal of World Prehistory*, 4, 157–222.

Hinz, W. 1969: *Altiranische Funde und Forschungen*. Berlin: De Gruyter.

Hinz, W., and H. Koch. 1987: *Elamisches Wörterbuch, I–II*. Berlin: D. Reimer.

Hippocrates 1950: *The Medical Works of Hippocrates*. J. Chadwick and W. Mann, translators. Oxford: Blackwell.

Hoch, J. E. 1994: *Semitic Words in Egyptian Texts of the New Kingdom and the Third Intermediate Period*. Princeton: Princeton University Press.

Hoch, J. E. 1997: *Middle Egyptian Grammar*. Mississauga: Benben Publications.

Hoff, C. 2002: The Mass Marriage at Susa in 324 BC and the Achaemenid Tradition. In Parpola and Whiting 2002, 239–44.

Hoffner, H. 1974: *Alimenta Hethaeorum*. New Haven, CT: American Oriental Society.

Hoffner, H. 1987: Hittite Religion. In M. Eliade (ed.), *The Encyclopedia of Religion*, New York: Macmillan, 6, 408–14.

Hoffner, H. 1989: The Religion of the Hittites. In R. Seltzer (ed.), *Religions of Antiquity*, New York: Macmillan, 69–79.

Hoffner, H. 1995: Legal and social institutions of Hittite Anatolia. In Sasson 1995, 555–69.

Hoffner, H. A., and H. C. Melchert. 2007: *A Grammar of the Hittite Language, I–II*. Winona Lake, Ind.: Eisenbrauns.

Hoffner, Harry A. Jr. 1998: *Hittite Myths*, 2nd edn. edited by Gary Beckman. SBL Writings from the Ancient World Series No. 2. Atlanta: Scholars Press.

Hoftijzer, J., and G. van der Kooij (eds.). 1991: *The Balaam Text from Deir ʿAlla Re-evaluated*. Leiden: Brill.

Hoftijzer, J., K. Jongeling *et al.* 1995: *Dictionary of the North-west Semitic Inscriptions, I–II*. Leiden: Brill.

Hole, F. 1984: A Reassessment of the Neolithic Revolution. *Paléorient*, 10, 49–60.

Hole, F. 1994: Environmental Instabilities and Urban Origins. In G. Stein and M. Rothman (eds), *Chiefdoms and Early States in the Near East*, Madison, WI: Prehistory, 121–51.

Hole, F. 1997: Paleoenvironment and Human Society in the Jezireh of Northern Mesopotamia 20,000–6000 BP. *Paléorient*, 23, 39–49.

Hornblower, S. 1996: Old Oligarch. In S. Hornblower and A. Spawforth (eds), *The Oxford Classical Dictionary*, Oxford, New York: Oxford University Press, 1063–4.

Hornung, E. 1982a: *Der ägyptische Mythos von der Himmelskuh*. Freiburg, Göttingen: Universitätsverlag, Vandenhoeck & Ruprecht.

Hornung, E. 1982b: *The Conception of God in Ancient Egypt: The One and the Many*. Ithaca, NY: Cornell University Press.

Hornung, E. 1990: *Einführung in die Ägyptologie*. Darmstadt: Wissenschaftliche Buchgesellschaft.

Hornung, E. 1999: *Akhenaton and the Religion of Light*. Ithaca, NY: Cornell University Press.

Hornung, E. 2001: *The Secret Lore of Egypt: Its Impact on the West*. Ithaca, NY: Cornell University Press. German 1999.

Hornung, Erik. 1991: *Der Ägyptische Mythos von der Himmelskuh: Eine Ätiologie des Unvollkommen* 1972; 2nd edn.

Horowitz, W. 1998: *Mesopotamian Cosmic Geography*. Winona Lake, IN: Eisenbrauns.

Hudson, M. and B. Levine (eds) 1996: *Privatization in the Ancient Near East and Classical World*. Cambridge, MA: Peabody Museum.

Hudson, M. and B. Levine (eds) 1999: *Urbanization and Land Ownership in the Ancient Near East*. Cambridge, MA: Peabody Museum.

Hudson, M. and M. Van De Mieroop (eds) 2002: *Debt and Economic Renewal in the Ancient Near East*. Bethesda, MD: CDL.

Huehnergard, J. 1987: *Ugaritic Vocabulary in Syllabic Transcription*. Atlanta, Ga.: Scholars Press.

Huehnergard, J. 1989: *The Akkadian of Ugarit*. Atlanta, Ga.: Scholars Press.

Huehnergard, J. 1995: Semitic Languages. In J. M. Sasson (ed.), *Civilizations of the Ancient Near East*, New York: Scribner, vol. IV, pp. 2117–2134.

Huehnergard, J. 1995a: What is Aramaic? *ARAM*, 7, 261–282.

Huehnergard, J. 2005: *A Grammar of Akkadian*. 2nd edn. Winona Lake, Ind.: Eisenbrauns.

Huehnergard, J. 2005a: *Key to a Grammar of Akkadian*. 2nd edn. Winona Lake, Ind.: Eisenbrauns.

Huehnergard, J. et al. 1992: Languages. In D. N. Freedman (ed.), *The Anchor Bible Dictionary*, New York: Doubleday, vol. 4, 155–229.

Huehnergard, J. 2000a: *A Grammar of Akkadian*. Winona Lake, IN: Eisenbrauns.

Huehnergard, J. 2000b: *Key to a Grammar of Akkadian*. Winona Lake, IN: Eisenbrauns.

Hug, V. 1993: *Altaramäische Grammatik der Texte des 7. und 6. Jh.s v.Chr.* Heidelberg: Heidelberger Orientverlag.

Hult, G. 1983: *Bronze Age Ashlar Masonry in the Eastern Mediterranean*. Göteborg: Aström.

Hunger, H. 1968: *Babylonische und assyrische Kolophone*. Kevelaer, Neukirchen-Vluyn: Butzon and Becker, Neukirchener.

Hunger, H. and D. Pingree 1989: *MUL.APIN: An Astronomical Compendium in Cuneiform*. Horn: Berger.

Hunger, H. and D. Pingree 1999: *Astral Sciences in Mesopotamia*. Leiden: Brill.

Huntington, E. 1911: *Palestine and its transformation*. Boston, MA and New York: Houghton Mifflin and Cambridge University Press.

Huot, J.-L. 1996: *Oueili, Travaux de 1987 et 1989*. Paris: Recherche sur les Civilisations.

Huot, J.-L. and L. Bachelot 1989: *Larsa. Travaux de 1985*. Paris: Edition Recherche sur les Civilisations.

Huot, J.-L., A. Rougeulle and J. Suire 1989: La structure urbaine de Larsa. Une approche provisoire. In J-L. Huot (ed.), *Larsa: Travaux de 1985*, Paris: Recherche sur les Civilisations, 19–52.

Hutter, M. 2001: Luwische Religion in den Traditionen aus Arzawa. In G. Wilhelm (ed.), *Akten des IV. Internationalen Kongresses für Hethitologie*, Wiesbaden: Harrassowitz, 224–34.

Huxley, J. 1943: Individuality. In *Encyclopaedia Britannica*, Chicago, IL, Toronto, London: Britannica, 12, 256–7.

Ibn Khaldun, 1967, 1969: *Muqaddimah*. Princeton, NJ: Princeton University Press.

Inomata, T. 2001: The Power and Ideology of Artistic Creation, Elite Craft Specialists in Classic Maya Society. *Current Anthropology*, 42, 321–49.

Iversen, E. 1961: *The Myth of Egypt and Its Hieroglyphs in European Tradition*. Copenhagen: Gad.

Iversen, Erik. 1961: *The Myth of Egypt and Its Hieroglyphs in European Tradition*. Repr. Princeton: Princeton University Press, 1993.

Izre'el, Sh. 1991: *Amurru Akkadian: A Linguistic Study, I–II*. Atlanta, Ga.: Scholars Press.

Izre'el, Sh. (ed.). 2002. *Semitic Linguistics: The State of the Art at the Turn of the Twenty-First Century*. Israel Oriental Studies, 20. Winona Lake, Ind.: Eisenbrauns.

Izre'el, Shlomo. 2001: *Adapa and the South Wind: Language has the Power of Life and Death*. Mesopotamian Civilizations; 10. Winona Lake, Ind.: Eisenbrauns.

Jackson, B. 1973: Reflections on Biblical Criminal Law. *Journal of Jewish Studies*, 24, 8–38.

Jacobsen, T. 1939a [1970]: An Ancient Mesopotamian Trial for Homicide. *Analecta Biblica et Orientalia*, 12, 130–50 = Jacobsen 1970: 139–214.

Jacobsen, T. 1939b: *The Sumerian King List*. Chicago, IL: University of Chicago Press.

Jacobsen, T. 1943 [1970]: Primitive Democracy in Ancient Mesopotamia. *Journal of Near Eastern Studies*, 2, 159–72 = Jacobsen 1970: 157–70.

Jacobsen, T. 1946: Mesopotamia. In H. Frankfort, J. Wilson, T. Jacobsen, and W. Irwin, *The Intellectual Adventure of Ancient Man*, Chicago, IL: University of Chicago Press, 125–219.

Jacobsen, T. 1953a [1970]: The Reign of Ibbi-Sin. *Journal of Cuneiform Studies*, 7, 36–47. = Jacobsen 1970: 173–86.

Jacobsen, T. 1953b: Review of L. Legrain, *Ur Excavation Texts* III. *American Journal of Archaeology*, 57, 125–8.

Jacobsen, T. 1957 [1970]: Early Political Developments in Mesopotamia. *Zeitschrift für Assyriologie*, 52, 91–140 = Jacobsen 1970: 132–6.

Jacobsen, T. 1970: *Toward the Image of Tammuz*. Cambridge, MA: Harvard University Press.

Jacobsen, T. 1976: *The Treasures of Darkness: A History of Mesopotamian Religion*. New Haven, CT, London: Yale University Press.

Jacobsen, T. and R. Adams 1958: Salt and silt in ancient Mesopotamian agriculture. *Science*, 128, 1251–8.

Jacobsen, Th. 1988: Sumerian Grammar Today. *Journal of the American Oriental Society*, 108, 123–133.

Jacobsen, Thorkild. 1987: *The Harps that Once . . . : Sumerian Poetry in Translation*. New Haven: Yale University Press.

Jakob-Rost, L. 1972: *Das Ritual der Malli aus Arzawa gegen Behexung*. Heidelberg: Winter.

James, T. G. H. 1984: *Pharaoh's People*. London: Tauris Parke.

Jansen-Winkeln, K. 1987: Zum militarischen Befehlsbereich der Hohenpriester des Amun. *Göttinger Miszellen*, 99, 19–22.

Jansen-Winkeln, K. 1992: Das Ende des Neuen Reiches. *Zeitschrift für ägyptische Sprache*, 119, 22–37.

Jansen-Winkeln, K. 1994: Der Begin der libyschen Herrschaft in Ägypten. *Biblische Notizen*, 71, 78–97.

Janssen, J. 1975: *Commodity Prices from the Ramesside Period*. Leiden: Brill.

Janssen, J. 1980: Absence from Work by the Necropolis Workmen of Thebes. *Studien zur Altägyptischen Kultur*, 8, 127–52.

Janssen, J. 1994: Debts and Credit in the New Kingdom. *Journal of Egyptian Archaeology*, 80, 129–36.

Jasanoff, J. H. 2003: *Hittite and the Indo-European Verb*. Oxford: Oxford University Press.

Jaspers, K. 1968: *The End and Goal of History*. New Haven, CT: Yale University Press. German 1949.

Jaynes, D. 1976: *The Origins of Consciousness in the Breakdown of the Bicameral Mind*. Boston, MA: Houghton Mifflin.

Jeyes, U. 1980: The Art of Extispicy in Ancient Mesopotamia, an Outline. *Assyriological Miscellanies*, 1, 13–32.

Jin, S. 2003: Der Furchtsame und der Unschuldige: Über zwei soziojuristische Begriffe aus dem alten Ägypten. *Journal of Near Eastern Studies*, 62, 267–73.

Joannès, F. (ed.) 2000: *Rendre la justice en Mésopotamie: Archives judiciaires du Proche-Orient ancien (IIIe–Ier millénaires avant J.-C.)*. Saint-Denis: Presses Universitaires de Vincennes.

Joannès, F. 1982: La localisation de urru à l'époque néo-babylonienne. *Semitica*, 32, 35–43.

Joannès, F. 1995: Private Commerce and Banking in Achaemenid Babylon. In Sasson 1995, 1475–85.

Joannès, F. 2001: Roi. In F. Joannès (ed.), *Dictionnaire de la Civilisation Mésopotamienne*, Paris: Laffont, 729–33.

Johanning, Klaus. 1988: *Der Bibel-Babel-Streit: Eine forschungsgeschichtliche Studie*. Frankfurt am Main: Peter Lang.

Johnson, A. 1949: *The Vitality of the Individual in the Thought in Ancient Israel*. Cardiff: University of Wales.

Johnson, J. H. 1976: *The Demotic Verbal System*. Chicago: Oriental Institute of the University of Chicago.

Johnson, J. H. 1986: *Thus Wrote 'Onchsheshonqy: An Introductory Grammar of Demotic*. Chicago: Oriental Institute of the University of Chicago.

Jones, P. 2003: Embracing Inana: Legitimation and Mediation in the Ancient Mesopotamian Sacred Marriage Hymn Iddin-Dagan A. *Journal of the American Oriental Society*, 123, 291–302.

Jones, P. In press: Kingship and the Anuna-Gods in the Old Babylonian Sumerian Literary Corpus.

Jordanova, L. 2000: *History in Practice*. London, New York: Arnold, Oxford.

Junge, F. 2001: *Late Egyptian Grammar: An introduction*. Oxford: Griffith Institute.

Kahl, J. 2002–: *Frühägyptisches Wörterbuch 1–*. Wiesbaden: Harrassowitz.

Kaiser, Otto, Rykle Borger, et al. 1983–: *Texte aus der Umwelt des Alten Testaments*. Gütersloh: G. Mohn.

Kaltner, J., and S. L. McKenzie (eds.). 2002: *Beyond Babel: A handbook for Biblical Hebrew and Related Languages*. Atlanta: Society for Biblical Literature.

Kammerzell, F. 1993: *Studien zu Sprache und Geshichte der Karer in Ägypten*. Wiesbaden: Harrassowitz.

Kamp, K. and N. Yoffee 1980: Ethnicity in Ancient Western Asia: Archaeological Assessments and Ethnoarchaeological Perspectives. *Bulletin of the American Schools of Oriental Research*, 237, 88–104.

Kang, S. 1971: The Role of Women at Drehem. In C. Keiser (ed.), *Neo-Sumerian Account Texts from Drehem*, New Haven, CT: Yale University Press, 2–7.

Kantor, H. 1966: Landscape in Akkadian Art. *Journal of Near Eastern Studies*, 25, 145–52.

Kaplony, P. 1977: "Die Definition der Schönen Literatur im Alten Ägypten." in *Fragen an die Altägyptische Literatur. Studien Zum Geenken an Eberhard Otto*, edited by J. Assmann Et Al, 289–314. Wiesbaden: Harrassowitz.

Karahashi, F. 2000 (2005): The Locative-Terminative Verbal Infix in Sumerian. *Acta Sumerologica*, 22, 113–133.

Kassian, A., A. Korolev, and A. Sidel'tsev 2002: *Hittite Funerary Ritual*. Münster: Ugarit-Verlag.

Kaster, J. 1968: *Wings of the Falcon: Life and Thought of Ancient Egypt*. New York: Holt, Rinehard and Winston.

Katary S. L. D. 1983: Cultivator, Scribe, Stablemaster, Soldier: The Late Egyptian Miscellanies in Light of P. *Wilbour. The Ancient World*, 6, 71–93.

Katz, D. 1987: Gilgamesh and Akka: Was Uruk Ruled by Two Assemblies? *Revue d'Assyriologie*, 81, 105–14.

Kaufmann, Y. 1938–1956: *The History of the Israelite Faith*. 8 vols. Tel-Aviv: Devir. Hebrew.

Köcher, F. 1963: *Die babylonisch-assyrische Medizin in Texten und Untersuchungen*. Berlin: Gruyter.

Köcher, F. 1978: Spätbabylonische medizinische Texte aus Uruk. In C. Habrich, F. Marguth, and J. Wolf (eds), *Medizinische Diagnostik in Geschichte und Gegenwart*, Munich: Fritsch, 17–34.

Kedar, B. 1985: The Arab Conquests and Agriculture: A Seventh Century Apocalypse, Satellite Imagery, and Palynology. *Asian and African Studies*, 19, 1–15.

Keith, K. 1999: Cities, Neighborhoods and Houses: Urban Spatial Organization in Old Babylonian Mesopotamia. Ph.D. dissertation, University of Michigan.

Kemp, B. 1978: Imperialism and Empire in New Kingdom Egypt (c. 1575–1087 BC). In P. Garnsey and C. Whittaker (eds), *Imperialism in the Ancient World*, Cambridge, New York: Cambridge University Press, 7–57.

Kemp, B. 1983: Old Kingdom, Middle Kingdom and Second Intermediate Period. In Trigger et al. 1983, 71–182.

Kemp, B. 1986: Large Middle Kingdom Granary Buildings. *Zeitschrift für ägyptische Sprache*, 113, 120–36.

Kemp, B. 1989: *Ancient Egypt, Anatomy of a Civilization*. London, New York: Routledge.

Kemp, B. 2000: Soil (including mud-brick architecture). In P. Nicholson and I. Shaw (eds), *Ancient Egyptian Materials and Technology*, New York: Cambridge University Press, 78–103.

Kent, R. G. 1953: *Old Persian: Grammar, Texts, Lexicon*. 2nd edn. New Haven, Conn.: American Oriental Society.

Kenyon, K. 1981: *Excavations at Jericho 3. The Architecture and Stratigraphy of the Tell*. London: British School of Archaeology in Jerusalem.

Kepinski-Lecomte, C. 1992: *Haradum I: Une ville nouvelle sur le Moyen-Euphrate*. Paris: Recherche sur les Civilisations.

Kepinski-Lecomte, C. 1996: Spatial Occupation of a New Town: Haradum. In Veenhof 1996, 191–6.

Khačikjan, M. L. 1985: Хурритский и урартский языки. Erevan: Izdatel'stvo Akademija Nauk Armjanskoj SSR.

Khačikjan, M. L. 1998: *The Elamite Language*. Rome: C.N.R.

Kühne, C. 1993: Zum Vor-opfer im alten Anatolien. In B. Janowski, K. Koch and G. Wilhelm (eds), *Religionsgeschichtliche Beziehungen zwischen Kleinasien, Nordsyrien und dem Alten Testament*, Freiburg: Universitätsverlag, 225–83.

Kühne, H. 1997: Sheikh Hamad, Tell (Dur Katlimmu). In Meyers 1997, 5, 25–6.

Kienast, B. 2001: *Historische Semitische Sprachwissenschaft*. Wiesbaden: Harrassowitz.

Kimball, S. E. 1999: *Hittite Historical Phonology*. Innsbruck: Universität Innsbruck.

Kinnier-Wilson, J. 1972: *The Nimrud Wine Lists*. London: British School of Archaeology in Iraq.

Kirk, G. S. 1970: *Myth: Its Meaning and Functions in Ancient and Other Cultures*. Berkeley: University of California Press.

Kitchen, K. 1969: Interrelations of Egypt and Syria. In M. Liverani (ed.), *La Siria nel Tardo Bronzo*, Rome: Centro per le antichità e la storia dell'arte del Vicino Oriente, 77–95.

Kitchen, K. 1990: The Arrival of the Libyans in Late New Kingdom Egypt. In A. Leahy (ed.), *Libya and Egypt c 1300–750 BC*, London: School of Oriental and African Studies, 15–27.

Kitchen, K. A. 1999: *Poetry of Ancient Egypt*. Jonsered: Aströms.

Klein, J. 1981: *Three Šulgi Hymns*. Ramat-Gan: Bar-Ilan University Press.

Klein, J. 1989: Building and Dedication Hymns in Sumerian Literature. *Acta Sumerologica*, 11, 27–67.

Klejn, L. 1993: To Separate a Centaur: on the Relationship of Archaeology and History in Soviet Tradition. *Antiquity*, 67, 339–48.

Klengel, H. 1975: Zur ökonomischen Funktion der hethitischen Tempel. *Studi micenei ed egeo-anatolici*, 16, 181–200.

Klengel, H. 1987–1990: Lullu(bum). *Reallexikon der Assyriologie*, 7, 164–8.

Klinger, J. 1996: *Untersuchungen zur Rekonstruktion der hattischen Kultschicht*. Wiesbaden: Harrassowitz.

Kümmel, H. 1967: *Ersatzrituale für den hethitischen König*. Wiesbaden: Harrassowitz.

Knapp, A. B. (ed.) 1992: *Archaeology, Annales and Ethnohistory*. Cambridge: Cambridge University Press.

Knauf, E. 1999: Shadday. In Van Der Toorn, Becking, and Van Der Horst 1999, 749–53.

Košak, S. 1982: *Hittite Inventory Texts*. Heidelberg: Winter.

Koch, H. 1993: Elamisches Gilgameš-Epos oder doch Verwaltungstäfelchen? *Zeitschrift für Assyriologie*, 83, 219–236.

Koehler, L., W. Baumgartner et al. 2001: *The Hebrew and Aramaic Lexicon of the Old Testament: I–II (Study edition)*. Leiden: Brill.

Kogan, L. E., and A. V. Korotayev. 1997: Sayhadic (Epigraphic South Arabian). In Hetzron 1997, 220–41.

Korpel, M. C. A. 1998: "Exegesis in the Work of Ilimilku of Ugarit." *OTS* 40: 86–111.

Kottsieper, I. 1990: *Die Sprache der Aḥīqarsprüche*. Berlin: De Gruyter.

Krafeld-Daugherty, M. 1994: *Wohnen im Alten Orient*. Münster: Ugarit.

Krahmalkov, C. R. 2000: *Phoenician-Punic Dictionary*. Leuven: Peeters.

Krahmalkov, C. R. 2001: *A Phoenician-Punic Grammar*. Leiden: Brill.

Kramer, C. (ed.) 1979: *Ethnoarchaeology. Implications of Ethnography for Archaeology*. New York: Columbia University Press.

Kramer, C. 1982: *Village Ethnoarchaeology: Rural Iran in Archaeological Perspective*. New York: Academic.

Kramer, S. 1981: *History Begins at Sumer*. Philadelphia, PA: University of Pennsylvania Press.

Kramer, S. N. 1971: u₅-a a-ù-a: A Sumerian Lullaby. In *Studi in onore di Edoardo Volterra, VI*, Milan: Giuffrè, 191–205.

Krapf, T. 1990: *Yehezkel Kaufmann: Ein Lebens- und Erkenntnisweg zur Theologie der hebräischen Bibel*. Berlin: Institut Kirche und Judentum.

Krapf, T. 1992: *Die Priesterschaft und die vorexilische Zeit: Yehezkel Kaufmanns vernachlässigte Beitrag zur Geschichte der biblischen Religion*. Göttingen: Vandenhoeck & Ruprecht.

Kraus, F. 1958: *Ein Edikt des Königs Ammisaduqa*. Leiden: Brill.

Kraus, F. 1960: Ein zentrales Problem des altmesopotamischen Rechtes: Was ist der Codex Hammurabi? *Genava*, 8, 283–96.

Kraus, F. 1963: Altbabylonische Quellensammlungen zur altmesopotamischen Geschichte. *Archiv für Orientforschung*, 20, 153–5.

Kraus, F. 1974: Das Altbabylonische Königtum. In P. Garelli (ed.), *Le Palais et la Royauté: Archéologie et Civilisation*, Paris: Geuthner, 235–61.

Kraus, F. 1984: *Königliche Verfügungen in altbabylonischer Zeit*. Leiden: Brill.

Kraus, F. R. 1970: *Sumerer und Akkader, ein Problem der altmesopotamischen Geschichte*. Amsterdam: Koninklijke Nederlandse Akademie van Wetenschappen.

Krebernik, M. 1994: Review of M. W. Green and H. J. Nissen, *Zeichenliste der archaischen Texte aus Uruk* (ATU 2. Berlin, 1987). *Orientalische Literaturzeitung*, 89, 380–5.

Krebernik, Manfred. 1996: "The Linguistic Classification of Eblaite: Methods, Problems, and Results." In *The Study of the Ancient Near East in the 21st Century: The William Foxwell Albright Centennial Conference*, ed. Jerrold S. Cooper and Glenn M. Schwarz, 233–49. Winona Lake, Ind.: Eisenbrauns.

Krispijn, Th. J. H. 1991–92: The Early Mesopotamian Lexical Lists and the Dawn of Linguistics. *Jaarbericht van het Voor-Aziatisch-Egyptisch-Gezelschap: Ex Oriente Lux*, 32, 12–22.

Kuhrt, A. 1987: Usurpation, Conquest, and Ceremonial: from Babylon to Persia. In D. Cannadine and S. Price (eds), *Rituals of Royalty*, Cambridge: Cambridge University Press, 20–55.

Kuhrt, A. 1990: Nabonidus and the Babylonian Priesthood. In M. Beard and J. North (eds), *Pagan Priests*, Ithaca, NY: Cornell University Press, 117–55.

Kuhrt, A. 1995: *The Ancient Near East c. 3000–330 BC* I–II. London, New York: Routledge.

Kuhrt, A. and S. Sherwin-White (eds) 1987: *Hellenism in the East*. Berkeley and Los Angeles, CA: University of California Press.

Kuniholm, P. 1996: The Prehistoric Aegean: Dendrochronological Progress as of 1995. *Acta Archaeologica*, 67, 327–35.

Kuniholm, P. 2001: Dendrochronology and Other Applications of Tree-Ring Studies in Archaeology. In D. Brothwell and A. Pollard (eds), *Handbook of Archaeological Sciences*, London: Wiley, 35–46.

Kupper, J.-R. 1957: *Les nomades en Mésopotamie au temps des rois de Mari*. Paris: Belles Lettres.

Kupper, J.-R. 1959: Le Rôle des nomades dans l'histoire de la Mésopotamie ancienne. *Journal of the Economic and Social History of the Orient*, 2, 113–27.

Kutscher, R. 1975: *O Angry Sea*. New Haven, CT: Yale University Press.

Labat, R. 1939: *Le caractère religieux de la royauté assyro-babylonienne*. Paris: Librairie d'Amérique et d'Orient.

Labat, R. 1951: *Traité akkadien de diagnostics et pronostics médicaux*. Paris: Académie Internationale d'Histoire des Sciences.

Lacheman, E. 1976: Tablets from Arraphe and Nuzi in the Iraq Museum. *Sumer*, 32, 113–48.

Lafont, B. 1987: Les Filles du Roi de Mari. In Durand 1987, 113–21.

Lafont, S. 1997: La procédure par serment au Proche-Orient ancien. In S. Lafont (ed.), *Jurer et maudire: Pratiques politiques et usages juridiques du serment dans le Proche-Orient ancien*, Paris: L'Harmattan, 185–98.

Lafont, S. 2000: Codification et subsidiarité dans les droits du Proche-Orient ancien. In Lévy 2000, 49–64.

Lambert, W. 1957–1971: Gott. B. Nach akkadischen Texten. In Ebeling et al. 1928–, 3: 543–6.

Lambert, W. 1959: Ancestors, Authors, and Canonicity. *Journal of Cuneiform Studies*, 11, 1–14, 112.

Lambert, W. 1967: The Gula Hymn of Bullutsa-rabi. *Orientalia*, 36, 105–32.

Lambert, W. 1969: A Middle Assyrian Medical Text. *Iraq*, 31, 28–39.

Lambert, W. 1975: The Cosmology of Sumer and Babylon. In C. Blacker and M. Loewe (eds), *Ancient Cosmologies*, London: Allen and Unwin, 42–62.

Lambert, W. 1985: Ninurta Mythology in the Babylonian Epic of Creation. In K. Hecker and W. Sommerfeld (eds), *Keilschriftliche Literaturen*, Berlin: Reimer, 55–60.

Lambert, W. 1998: Kingship in Ancient Mesopotamia. In J. Day (ed.), *King and Messiah in Israel and the Ancient Near East*, Sheffield: Sheffield Academic, 54–70.

Lambert, W., A. Millard, and M. Civil 1969: *Atra-ḫasīs: The Babylonian Story of the Flood*. Oxford: Clarendon.

Lambert, W. G. 1960: *Babylonian Wisdom Literature*. Oxford: Clarendon Press.

Lambert, W. G. and A. R. Millard. 1969: *Atra-ḫasīs: The Babylonian Story of the Flood*; with *The Sumerian Flood Story* By M. Civil. Oxford: Clarendon Press.

Landsberger, B. 1937: *Die Serie ana ittišu. Materials for the Sumerian Lexicon* 1. Rome: Pontifical Biblical Institute.

Landsberger, B. 1974: *Three Essays on the Sumerians*. Transl. of the 1944 German origininal by Maria DeJ. Ellis. Los Angeles: Undena.

Landsberger, B. 1976: *The Conceptual Autonomy of the Babylonian World*. Malibu: Undena. German 1926.

Landy, F. 1981: *The Tale of AQHAT*. London: Menard.

Langdon, S. and J. K. Fotheringham 1928: *The Venus Tablets of Ammizaduqa*. Oxford, London: Oxford University Press, Milford.

Lapidus, I. 1984: *Muslim Cities in the later Middle Ages*. Cambridge: Cambridge University Press.

Laroche, E. 1980: *Glossaire de la langue hourrite*. Paris: Klincksieck.

Larsen, J. 1949: The Origin and Significance of the Counting of Votes. *Classical Philology*, 44: 164–81.

Larsen, M. T. 1979: The Tradition of Empire in Mesopotamia. In M. T. Larsen (ed.), *Power and Propaganda: A Symposium on Ancient Empires*, Copenhagen: Akademisk, 75–103.

Larsen, M. T. 1987a: The Babylonian Lukewarm Mind: Reflections on Science, Divination and Literacy. In F. Rochberg-Halton 1987, 203–25.

Larsen, M. T. 1987b: Commercial Networks in the Ancient Near East. In M. Rowlands and M. T. Larsen (eds), *Centre and Periphery in the Ancient World*, Cambridge: Cambridge University Press, 47–56.

Larsen, Mogens Trolle. 1995: "The Babel–Bibel Controversy." In *Civilizations of the Ancient Near East*, ed. Jack M. Sasson et al., 95–106. New York: Scribners. Repr. (4 vols. in 2) Peabody, Mass.: Hendrickson, 2000.

Larsen, Mogens Trolle. 1996: *The Conquest of Assyria: Excavations in an Antique Land 1840–1860*. London: Routledge.

Layton, B. 2004: *A Coptic Grammar with Chrestomathy and Glossary (Sahidic Dialect)*. 2nd edn. Wiesbaden: Harrassowitz.

Lecoq, P. 1997: *Les inscriptions de la Perse achéménide*. Paris: Gallimard.

Leemans, W. 1960: *Foreign Trade in the Old Babylonian Period*. Leiden: Brill.

Lefebvre, G. 1949: *Romans et Contes Égyptiens de l'époque Pharaonique*. Paris: Maisonneuve.

Lefkowitz, Mary. 1996: *Not Out of Africa: How Afrocentrism Became an Excuse to Treat Myth as History*. New York: Basic Books.

Lefkowitz, Mary, and Guy MacLean Rogers. (eds) 1996: *Black Athena Revisited*. Chapel Hill: University of North Carolina Press.

Lehmann, Reinhard G. 1994: *Friedrich Delitzsch und der Babel-Bibel-Streit*. Freiburg: Universitätsverlag; Göttingen: Vandenhoeck & Ruprecht.

Lehner, M. 1997: *The Complete Pyramids*. London: Thames & Hudson.

Leichty, E. 1988a: Ashurbanipal's Library at Nineveh. *Bulletin of the Canadian Society for Mesopotamian Studies* 15: 13–18.

Leichty, E. 1988b: Guaranteed to Cure. In E. Leichty and M. Ellis (eds), *A Scientific Humanist: Studies in Memory of Abraham Sachs*, Philadelphia, PA: University Museum, 261–4.

Lemche, N. 1992: *Habiru, hapiru*. In Freedman 1992, 3, 6–10.

Lemche, N. 1995: The History of Ancient Syria and Palestine. In Sasson 1995, 1195–218.

Lerner, G. 1986: *The Creation of Patriarchy*. Oxford: Oxford University Press.

Lesko, B. (ed.) 1989: *Women's Earliest Records from Ancient Egypt and Western Asia*. Atlanta, GA: Scholars.

Lesko, L. 1994: *Pharaoh's Workers: the Villagers of Deir el Medina.* Ithaca, NY: Cornell University Press.

Lesko, L. H., and B. S. Lesko. 2000–2004: *A Dictionary of Late Egyptian, I–II.* 2nd edn. Providence, R.I.: B.C. Scribe Publications.

Levenson, J. 1982: Yehezkel Kaufmann and Mythology. *Conservative Judaism,* 36, 36–43.

Levinson, B. (ed.) 1994: *Theory and Method in Biblical and Cuneiform Law: Revision, Interpolation and Development.* Sheffield: Sheffield Academic.

Levy, T., R. Adams, and R. Shafiq 1999: The Jebel Hamrat Fidan Project. Excavations at the Wadi Fidan 40 cemetery, Jordan (1997). *Levant,* 31, 299–315.

Lev-Yadun, S., A. Gopher and S. Abbo 2000: The Cradle of Agriculture. *Science,* 288, 1602–3.

Lewis, B. 1990: Europe, Islam et société civile. *Le Débat,* 62, 11–31.

Lewis, Bernard. 1982: "The Question of Orientalism." *New York Review of Books* (June 24): 49–56; "extensively revised and recast" in Lewis 1993. 99–118, 192–4, this version repr. in Macfie 2000: 249–70.

Lewis, Bernard. 1993: *Islam and the West.* New York: Oxford University Press.

Lewis, Brian. 1980: *The Sargon Legend: A Study of the Akkadian Text and the Tale of the Hero who was Exposed at Birth.* ASOR Dissertation Series, No. 4. ASOR.

Lewis, D. M. 1994: The Persepolis Tablets: Speech, Seal and Script. In A. K. Bowman and G. Woolf (eds.), *Literacy and Power in the Ancient World,* Cambridge: Cambridge University Press, 12–32.

Lewis, N. 1983: *Life in Egypt under Roman Rule.* Oxford: Clarendon.

Lichtheim, M. 1997: *Moral Values in Ancient Egypt.* Fribourg, Göttingen: Vandenhoeck & Ruprecht.

Lichtheim, Miriam. 1973, 1976, 1980: *Ancient Egyptian Literature, I–III.* Berkeley: University of California Press.

Lichtheim, Miriam. 1983: *Late Egyptian Wisdom Literature in the International Context: A Study of Demotic Instructions.* OBO 52. Freiburg, Schweiz: Universitätsverlag/Göttingen: Vandenhoeck and Ruprecht.

Lichtheim, Miriam. 1988: *Ancient Egyptian Autobiographies Chiefly of the Middle Kingdom: A Study and an Anthology.* OBO 84. Freiburg, Schweiz: Universtätsverlag/Göttingen: Vandenhoeck und Ruprecht.

Lichtheim, Miriam. 1996: "Didactic Literature." in *Ancient Egyptian Literature: History and Forms,* edited by Antonio Loprieno, 243–62. Leiden: Brill.

Lieberman, S. J. 1977: *The Sumerian Loanwords in Old-Babylonian Akkadian.* Missoula, Mont.: Scholar Press.

Liebesny, H. 1941: Evidence in Nuzi Legal Procedure. *Journal of the American Oriental Society,* 61, 130–42.

Limet, H. 1972: L'étranger dans la société sumérienne. In D. Edzard (ed.), *Gesellschaftsklassen im Alten Orient,* Munich: Bayerische Akademie, 123–38.

Limet, H. 1986: *Textes administratifs relatifs aux métaux.* Paris: Editions Recherche sur les Civilisations.

Limet, H. 1994: Les guerres à l'époque sumérienne. *Acta Orientalia Belgica,* 9, 27–41.

Limet, H. 1996: Le sacrifice sanglant. *Wiener Zeitschrift für die Kunde des Morgenlandes,* 86, 251–62.

Lindenberger, J. M. 1983: *The Aramaic Proverbs of Ahiqar.* Baltimore: the Johns Hopkins University Press.

Lindenberger, J. M. 1985: "Ahiqar." in *The Old Testament Pseudepigrapha*, vol. 2, edited by James H. Charlesworth, 479–507. Garden City, N.Y.: Doubleday.

Lipiński, E. 2000: *The Aramaeans*. Leuven, Sterling, Va.: Peeters.

Lipiński, E. 2000: The Linguistic Geography of Syria in Iron Age II (c. 1000–600 B.C.). In G. Bunnens (ed.), *Essays on Syria in the Iron Age*, Louvain: Peeters, 125–142.

Lipiński, E. 2001: *Semitic Languages: Outline of Comparative Grammar*. 2nd edn. Leuven: Peeters.

Lipiński, E. 2002: New Aramaic Clay Tablets. *Bibliotheca Orientalis*, 59, 245–259.f

Liverani, M. (ed.) 1993a: *Akkad, the First World Empire*. Padua: Sargon.

Liverani, M. 1979: The Ideology of the Assyrian Empire. In M. Larsen (ed.), *Power and Propaganda*, Copenhagen: Akademisk, 297–317.

Liverani, M. 1988a, 1991: *Antico Oriente: Storia, società, economia*. Rome: Laterza.

Liverani, M. 1988b: The Growth of the Assyrian Empire in the Habur/Middle Euphrates area: a New Paradigm. *State Archives of Assyria Bulletin*, 2, 81–98.

Liverani, M. 1990: *Prestige and Interest: International Relations in the Near East, ca. 1600–1100* B.C. Padua: Sargon.

Liverani, M. 1993b: Model and Actualization. The Kings of Akkad in the Historical Tradition. In Liverani 1993, 41–67.

Liverani, M. 1993c: Nelle Pieghe del Despotismo. Organismi rappresentative nell'Antico Oriente. *Studi Storici*, 34, 7–33.

Liverani, M. 1995: The Deeds of Ancient Mesopotamian Kings. In Sasson 1995, 2353–66.

Liverani, M. 1997: Lower Mesopotamian Fields: South vs. North. In B. Pongratz-Leisten, H. Kuhne, and P. Xella (eds), *Ana šadî Labnāni lūallik: Beiträge zu altorientalischen und mittelmeerischen Kulturen. Festschrift für Wolfgang Röllig*, Neukirchen-Vluyn: Neukirchener, 219–27.

Liverani, M. 2003: *Oltre la Bibbia*. Rome, Bari: Laterza.

Livingstone, A. 1986: *Mystical and Mythological Explanatory Works of Babylonian Scholars*. Oxford: Clarendon.

Livingstone, A. 1989: *Court Poetry and Literary Miscellanea*. Helsinki: Helsinki University Press.

Livingstone, A. 1997: An Early Attestation of the Arabic Definite Article. *Journal of Semitic Studies*, 42, 259–261.

Lloyd, S. 1980: *Foundations in the Dust*. Revised edition. London, New York: Thames and Hudson.

Lloyd, S. 1984: *The Archaeology of Mesopotamia from the Old Stone Age to the Persian Conquest*. Revised edition. London, New York: Thames and Hudson.

Lloyd, S. and J. Mellaart 1965: *Beycesultan Volume II: Middle Bronze Age Architecture and Pottery*. London: British Institute of Archaeology at Ankara.

Long, J. and C. Cordova 2003: Archaeological Expedition to Khirbet Iskander and its Environs. In S. Richard and J. Long (eds), *Final Report on the Early Bronze IV Area C Gateway*, Boston, MA: American Schools of Oriental Research.

Longman, Tremper, III. 1991: *Fictional Akkadian Autobiography: A Generic and Comparative Study*. Winona Lake: Eisenbrauns.

Loprieno, A. (ed.) 1996b: *Ancient Egyptian Literature: History and Forms*. Leiden: Brill.

Loprieno, A. 1986: *Das Verbalsystem im Ägyptischen und im Semitischen: Zur Grundlegung einer Aspekttheorie*. Wiesbaden: Harrassowitz.

Loprieno, A. 1995: *Ancient Egyptian: A Linguistic Introduction*. Cambridge: Cambridge University Press.

Loprieno, A. 1995a: Ancient Egyptian and other Afroasiatic Languages. In J. M. Sasson (ed.), *Civilizations of the Ancient Near East*, New York: Scribner, vol. IV, 2135–2150.

Loprieno, Antonio. 1996: "Defining Egyptian Literature: Ancient Texts and Modern Theories." in *Ancient Egyptian Literature: History and Forms*, edited by Antonio Loprieno, 39–58. Leiden: Brill.

Lorton, D. 1995: Legal and Social Institutions of Pharaonic Egypt. In Sasson 1995, 345–62.

Lowdermilk, W. 1944: *Palestine: Land of Promise*. New York: Harper.

Lowenthal, D. 2000: *George Perkins Marsh: Prophet of Conservation*. Seattle: University of Washington Press.

Luby, E. 1990: Social Variation in Ancient Mesopotamia: an Architectural and Mortuary Analysis of Ur in the Early Second Millennium BC. Ph.D. dissertation, State University of New York at Stony Brook.

Luckenbill, D. 1989 [1926]: *Ancient Records of Assyria and Babylonia*, 1. London: Histories and Mysteries of Man.

Luke, J. 1965: Pastoralism and Politics in the Mari Period. Ph.D. dissertation, University of Michigan.

Lundh, P. 2002: *Actor and Event. Military Activity in Ancient Egyptian Narrative Texts from Thutmosis II to Merenptah*. Uppsala: Akademitryck.

Lustig, J. 1997: Kingship, Gender and Age in Middle Kingdom Tomb Scenes and Texts. In J. Lustig (ed.), *Anthropology and Egyptology*, Sheffield: Sheffield Academic, 43–65.

Luukko, M. 2004: *Grammatical Variation in Neo-Assyrian*. Helsinki: The Neo-Assyrian Text Corpus Project.

Lévy, E. (ed.) 2000: *La codification des lois dans l'antiquité*. Paris: Boccard.

Mabry, J. 1992: Alluvial Cycles and Early Agricultural Settlement Phases in the Jordan Valley. Ph.D. dissertation. Tucson, AZ: University of Arizona.

MacDonald, M. C. A. 2000: Reflections on the Linguistic Map of pre-Islamic Arabia. *Arabian Archaeology and Epigraphy*, 11, 28–79.

Macfie, Alexander Lyon. (ed.) 2000: *Orientalism: A Reader*. New York: NYU Press.

Macfie, Alexander Lyon. 2002: *Orientalism*. London: Longman.

Machinist, P. 1976: Literature as Politics: the Tukulti-Ninurta Epic and the Bible. *Catholic Biblical Quarterly*, 38, 455–82.

Machinist, P. 1984/85: The Assyrians and their Babylonian Problem: Some Reflections. *Jahrbuch (Wissenschaftskolleg zu Berlin)* 353–64.

Machinist, P. 1991: Distinctiveness in Ancient Israel. *Scripta Hierosolymitana*, 33, 196–212.

Machinist, P. 1994: Outsiders or Insiders: The Biblical View of Emergent Israel in its Contexts. In R. Cohn and H. Silberstein (eds), *The Other in Jewish Thought and History: Constructions of Jewish Culture and Identity*, New York: New York University Press, 41–60.

Machinist, P. and H. Tadmor 1993: Heavenly Wisdom. In Cohen, Snell, and Weisberg 1993, 146–50.

Maeda, T. 1981: King of Kish in Pre-Sargonic Sumer. *Orient*, 17, 1–17.

Maekawa, K. 1973–74: The Development of the É-MÍ in Lagash during the Early Dynastic III. *Mesopotamia*, 8–9, 77–144.

Maekawa, K. 1996: Confiscation of Private Properties in the Ur III Period. *Acta Sumerologica*, 18, 103–68.

Maidman, M. 1995: Nuzi: Portrait of an Ancient Mesopotamian Provincial Town. In Sasson 1995, 931–48.

Mair, Victor H. (ed.) 1998: *The Bronze Age and Early Iron Age Peoples of Eastern Central Asia.* 2 vols. *Journal of Indo-European Studies* Monograph 26. Washington, D.C.: Institute for the Study of Man; Philadelphia: University of Pennsylvania Museum Publications.

Malaise, M., and J. Winand. 1999: *Grammaire raisonnée de l'égyptien classique.* Liège: Université de Liège.

Malbran-Labat, F. 1981: Le nomadisme à l'époque Néo-Assyrienne. In Silva 1981, 57–76.

Malbran-Labat, F.1982: *L'armée et l'organisation militaire de l'Assyrie.* Geneva: Droz.

Mallowan, M. 1933: The Prehistoric Sondage at Nineveh 1931–1932. *Liverpool Annals of Archaeology and Anthropology,* 20, 127–77.

Mallowan, M. 1966: *Nimrud and its Remains.* New York: Dodd, Mead.

Mallowan, M. 1970: The Development of Cities from Al-'Ubaid to Uruk V. In Edwards, Gadd, and Hammond 1970, I, 1, 327–462.

Mallowan, M. 1971: The Early Dynastic Period in Mesopotamia. In Edwards, Gadd, and Hammond 1971, I, 2, 238–314.

Mallowan, M. 1978: Samaria and Calah-Nimrud: Conjunctions in History and Archaeology. In P. R. S. Moorey and P. Parr (eds), *Archaeology in the Levant: Essays for Kathleen Kenyon,* Warminster: Aris and Phillips, 155–63.

Malraux, A. 1961: Preface. In Parrot 1961b, xiii–xlviii. French 1960.

Manassa, C. 2003: *The Great Karnak Inscription of Merenptah: Grand Strategy in the 13th Century BC.* Yale Egyptological Seminar, New Haven, CT.

Manniche, L. 1987: *Sexual Life in Ancient Egypt.* London: KPI.

Manning, S. 1999: *A Test of Time. The Volcano of Thera and the Chronology and History of the Aegean and East Mediterranean in the Mid Second Millennium BC.* Oxford, Oakville: Oxbow.

Manning, S., B. Kromer, P. Kuniholm, and M. Newton 2001: Anatolian Tree Rings and a New Chronology for the East Mediterranean Bronze–Iron Ages. *Science,* 294, 2532–5.

Marcus, M. 1987: Geography as an Organizing Principle in the Imperial Art of Shalmaneser III. *Iraq,* 49, 77–90.

Margalit, Baruch. 1989: *The Ugaritic Poem of Aqhat.* BZAW 182. Berlin: De Gruyter.

Margueron, J.-C. 1982: *Recherches sur les palais mésopotamiens de l'âge du Bronze.* Paris: Geuthner.

Martin, J. 2002: The Myth of Renaissance Individualism. In G. Ruggiero (ed.), *A Companion to the Worlds of the Renaissance,* Oxford: Blackwell, 208–24.

Martínez Borobio, E. 2003: *Arameo antiguo: Gramática y textos comentados.* Barcelona: Universitat de Barcelona.

Maspero, G. 1915: *Popular Stories of Ancient Egypt.* New York: G. P. Putnam's Sons. Reprint. 1967.

Mathieu, Bernard. 1996: *La Poésie Amoureuse de l'Égypte Ancienne: Rescherches sur un Genre Littéraire au Nouvel Empire.* Cairo: Institut Français D'archéologie Orientale.

Matney, T. and G. Algaze 1995: Urban Development at mid–late Early Bronze Age Titriş Höyük in southeastern Anatolia. *Bulletin of the American Schools of Oriental Research,* 299/300, 33–52.

Matthews, R. 1993: *Cities, Seals and Writing: Archaic Seal Impressions from Jemdet Nasr and Ur.* Berlin: Mann.

Matthews, R. 2003: *The Archaeology of Mesopotamia.* London: Routledge.

Matthews, V. 1978: *Pastoral Nomadism in the Mari Kingdom.* Cambridge, MA: American Schools of Oriental Research.

Matthiae, P. 1985: *I tesori di Ebla.* Roma, Bari: Laterza.

Matthiae, Paolo. 1981: *Ebla: An Empire Rediscovered*, trans. Christopher Holme. Garden City, N.Y.: Doubleday. Italian original, 1977.

Matthiae, P., F. Pinnock, and G. Scandone-Matthiae 1995: *Ebla alle origini della civiltà urbana: trent'anni di scavi in Siria dell'Università Roma "La Sapienza"*. Milan: Electa.

Maul, S. 1994: *Zukunftsbewältigung: Eine Untersuchung altorientalischen Denkens anhand der babylonisch-assyrischen Löserituale (Namburbi)*. Mainz: Zabern.

Maul, Stefan M. 1988: *"Herzberuhigungsklagen:' Die Sumerisch-Akkadischen Eršahunga-Gebete*. Wiesbaden: Harrassowitz.

Mayer, W. 1970: *Untersuchungen zur Grammatik des Mittelassyrischen*. Neukirchen-Vluyn: Neukirchener.

Mayer, W. 1995: *Politik und Kriegskunst der Assyrer*. Munster: Ugarit.

Mazenod, L. 1980: Foreword. In Amiet 1980. French 1977.

Mazzoni, S. 1986–87: A Sculptures Quarry at Sikizlar. *Annales Archéologiques Arabes Syriennes*, 36–37, 268–75.

McAlpin, D. W. 1981: *Proto-Elamo-Dravidian: The Evidence and its Implications*. Philadelphia: American Philosophical Society.

McCorriston, J. and F. Hole 1991: The Ecology of Seasonal Stress and the Origin of Agriculture in the Near East. *American Anthropologist*, 93, 46–69.

McCown, D. and R. Haines 1967: *Nippur I: Temple of Enlil, Scribal Quarter, and Soundings*. Chicago, IL: University of Chicago Press.

McDowell, A. 1999: *Village Life in Ancient Egypt: Laundry Lists and Love Songs*. Oxford: Oxford University Press.

McEwan, G. 1981: *Priest and Temple in Hellenistic Babylonia*. Wiesbaden: Steiner.

McMahon, G. 1995: Theology, Priests, and Worship in Hittite Anatolia. In Sasson 1995, 1981–95.

McMahon, G. 1997: Instructions to Priests and Temple Officials. In Hallo and Younger 1997, 217–21.

Meeks, D. 2002: Aspects de la lexicographie égyptienne. *Bibliotheca Orientalis*, 59, 5–18.

Meier, S. 2000: Diplomacy and International Marriages. In R. Cohen and R. Westbrook, (eds), *Amarna Diplomacy*, Baltimore, MD: Johns Hopkins University Press, 165–73.

Meissner, B. 1893: *Beiträge zum altbabylonischen Privatrecht*. Leipzig: Hinrichs.

Melchert, H. C. 1981: "God-Drinking": A Syntactic Transformation in Hittite. *Journal of Indoeuropean Studies*, 9, 245–54.

Melchert, H. C. 1994: *Anatolian Historical Phonology*. Amsterdam: Rodopi.

Melchert, H. C. 1995: Indo-European languages of Anatolia. In J. M. Sasson (ed.), *Civilizations of the Ancient Near East*, New York: Scribner, vol. IV, 2151–2159.

Melchert, H. C. 2003: Language. In C. H. Melchert (ed.), *The Luwians*, Leiden: Brill, 170–210.

Melikišvili, G. A. 1971: *Die urartäische Sprache*. Rome: Pontificium Institutum Biblicum.

Melville, S. 1999: *The Role of Naqia/Zakutu in Sargonid Politics*. Helsinki: Helsinki University Press.

Melville, S. In press: Neo Assyrian Royal Women and Male Identity: Status as a Social Tool. *Journal of the American Oriental Society.*

Mendenhall, G. 1954: Covenant Forms in Israelite Tradition. *Biblical Archaeologist*, 17, 52–76.

Menzel, B. 1981: *Assyrische Tempel*. Rome: Pontifical Biblical Institute.

Mettinger, T. 1995: *No Graven Images?* Stockholm: Almqvist & Wiksell.

Mettinger, T. 1997: Israelite Aniconism: Developments and Origins. In Van Der Toorn 1997, 173–204.

Meyer, C. 1982: *Senenmut*. Hamburg: Borg.

Meyer, J.-W. 1989: Die Grabungen im Planquadrat Q. In W. Orthmann (ed.), *Halawa 1980–1986*, Bonn: Habelt, 19–56.

Meyers, C. 2003: Everyday Life in Biblical Israel: Women's Social Networks. In Averbeck, Chavalas, and Weisberg 2003, 185–204.

Meyers, E. (ed.) 1997: *The Oxford Encyclopedia of Archaeology in the Near East*. New York: Oxford University Press.

Michalowski, P. 1980: Adapa and the Ritual Process. *Rocznik Orientalistyczny*, 41, 77–82.

Michalowski, P. 1983: History as Charter: Some Observations on the Sumerian King List. *Journal of the American Oriental Society*, 103, 237–48.

Michalowski, P. 1986: Mental Maps and Ideology: Reflections on Subartu. In H. Weiss (ed.), *The Origins of Cities in Dry-Farming Syria and Mesopotamia in the Third Millennium B.C.*, Guilford, Conn: Four Quarters, 129–156.

Michalowski, P. 1987: Charisma and Control: On Continuity and Change in Early Mesopotamian Bureaucratic Systems. In Biggs, and Gibson 1987, 55–68.

Michalowski, P. 1989: *The Lamentation over the Destruction of Sumer and Ur*. Winona Lake: Eisenbrauns.

Michalowski, P. 1989b: Thoughts about Ibrium. In W. Waetzoldt and H. Hauptmann (eds), *Wirtschaft und Gesellschaft von Ebla*, Heidelberg: Heidelberger Orientverlag, 267–77.

Michalowski, P. 1990: Early Mesopotamian Communicative Systems: Art, Literature, and Writing. In A. Gunter (ed.), *Investigating Artistic Environments in the Ancient Near East*, Washington DC: Smithsonian, 53–69.

Michalowski, P. 1991: Charisma and Control: On Continuity and Change in Early Mesopotamian Bureaucratic Systems. In Gibson and Biggs 1991, 45–57.

Michalowski, P. 1993a: Memory and Deed: The Historiography of the Political Expansion of the Akkad State. In Liverani 1993, 69–90.

Michalowski, P. 1993b: Tokenism. *American Anthropologist*, 95, 996–9.

Michalowski, P. 1995: "Sumerian Literature: An Overview." in *Civilizations of the Ancient Near East*, vol. 3, edited by Jack M. Sasson, 2279–91. New York: Scribner.

Michalowski, P. 1999: Sumer Dreams of Subartu: Politics and the Geographical Imagination. In K. van Lerberghe and G. Voet (eds.), *Languages and Cultures in Contact* (CRRAI 42), Leuven: Peeters, 305–315.

Michalowski, P. 1999a: "Commemoration, Writing, and Genre in Ancient Mesopotamia." in *The Limits of Historiography: Genre and Narrative in Ancient Historical Texts*, edited by Christina Shuttleworth Kraus, 69–90. Mnemosyne; Bibliotheca Classica Batava 191; Leiden: Brill.

Michalowski, P. 2004: Sumerian. In R. D. Woodard (ed.), *The Cambridge Encylopedia of Ancient Languages*, Cambridge: Cambridge University Press, 19–59.

Miglus, P. 1999: *Städtische Wohnarchitektur in Babylonien und Assyrien*. Mainz: Zabern.

Militarev, A., and L. Kogan. 2000: *Semitic Etymological Dictionary, 1: Anatomy of Man and Animals*. Münster: Ugarit-Verlag, 2000.

Militarev, A., and L. Kogan. 2005: *Semitic Etymological Dictionary, 2: Animal Names*. Münster: Ugarit-Verlag, 2005.

Millard, A. 1988: The Beveled-Rim Bowls: Their Purpose and Significance. *Iraq*, 50, 49–57.

Miller, P. 2000: *The Religion of Ancient Israel*. Louisville: Westminster.

Miller, P., P. Hanson, and S. D. McBride (eds) 1987: *Ancient Israelite Religion. Essays in Honor of Frank Moore Cross*. Philadelphia, PA: Fortress.

Müller, H.-P. 1992: Kolloquial Sprache und Volksreligion in den Schriften von Kuntillet Agrud und Khirbet el Qôm. *Zeitschrift für Althebraistik*, 5, 15–51.

Müller, H.-P. 1999: Chemosh. In Van Der Toorn, Becking, and Van Der Horst 1999, 186–9.

Müller-Karpe, A. 2002a: Kuşakli Sarissa: a Hittite town in the "Upper Land." In A. Yener and H. Hoffner (eds), *Recent Developments in Hittite Archaeology and History*, Winona Lake, IN: Eisenbrauns, 145–55.

Müller-Karpe, A. 2002b: Kuşakli Sarissa. Kultort im Oberen Land. In T. Özgüç (ed.), *Die Hethiter und ihr Reich*, Stuttgart: Theiss, 176–89.

Müller-Wollermann, R. 1985: Warenaustausch im Ägypten des Alten Reiches. *Journal of the Economic and Social History of the Orient*, 28, 121–68.

Molleson, T. 2000: The Human Remains. In A. Moore, G. Hillman, and A. Legge (eds), *Village on the Euphrates*, Oxford: Oxford University Press, 533–44.

Monson, J. 2000: The New 'Ain Dara Temple, Closest Solomonic Parallel. *Biblical Archaeology Review*, 26, 20–35, 67.

Montserrat, D. 1996: *Sex and Society in Graeco-Roman Egypt*. London: KPI.

Moore, A. and G. Hillman 1992: The Pleistocene to Holocene Transition and Human Economy in Southwest Asia: the Impact of the Younger Dryas. *American Antiquity*, 57, 482–94.

Moorey, P. R. S. 1982: *Ur 'of the Chaldees': A Revised and Updated Edition of Sir Leonard Woolley's Excavations at Ur*. Ithaca, NY: Cornell University Press.

Moorey, P. R. S. 1994: *Ancient Mesopotamian Materials and Industries, the Archaeological Evidence*. Oxford: Oxford University Press.

Moorey, P. R. S. and J. N. Postgate 1992: Some Wood Identifications from Mesopotamian Sites. In. P. R. S. Moorey and J. N. Postgate (eds), *Trees and Timber in Mesopotamia*, Cambridge: Sumerian Agriculture Group, 197–9.

Moortgat, A. 1969: *The Art of Ancient Mesopotamia*. New York: Phaidon. German 1967.

Moran, W. 1992: *The Amarna Letters*. Baltimore, MD: Johns Hopkins University Press.

Moran, W. 2002: The Babylonian Job. In R. Hendel (ed.), *The Most Magic Word*, Washington, DC: Catholic Biblical Quarterly, 182–200.

Moran, W. L. 2003: *Amarna Studies: Collected Writings*. Winona Lake, Ind.: Eisenbrauns.

Moran, William. 1991: "The Epic of Gilgamesh: A Document of Ancient Humanism," *Bulletin, Canadian Society for Mesopotamian Studies* 22: 15–22. Toronto.

Moran, William. 1995: "The Gilgamesh Epic: A Masterpiece from Ancient Mesopotamia." in *Civilizations of the Ancient Near East*, vol. 3, edited by Jack M. Sasson, 2327–36. New York: Scribner.

Morrison, M. 1992: Nuzi. In Freedman 1992, 3, 1156–62.

Moscati, S. et al. 1964: *An Introduction to the Comparative Grammar of the Semitic Languages (Phonolgy and Morphology)*. Wiesbaden: Harrassowitz.

Métral, F. 2000: Managing Risk: Sheep-Rearing and Agriculture in the Syrian Steppe. In Mundy and Musallam 2000, 123–44.

Muchiki, Y. 1999: *Egyptian Proper Names and Loanwords in North-west Semitic*. Atlanta, Ga.: Society of Biblical Literature.

Mundy, M. and B. Musallam (eds) 2000: *The Transformation of the Nomadic Society in the Arab East*. Cambridge: University of Cambridge Oriental Publications.

Munthe, T. 2003: Summon the Nations. *Times Literary Supplement*, August 1: 9.

Muraoka, T., and B. Porten. 1998: *A Grammar of Egyptian Aramaic*. Leiden: Brill.

Murnane, W. 1995: The Kingship of the Nineteenth Dynasty: A Study in the Resilience of an Institution. In D. O'Connor and D. Silverman (eds), *Ancient Egyptian Kingship*, Leiden: Brill, 199–202.

Murphy, S. 2002: The Practice of Power in the Ancient Near East: Sorceresses and Serpents in Hittite Myths. In Parpola and Whiting 2002, 433–42.

Nakamura, M. 2002: *Das Hethitische nuntarriyasha-Fest*. Istanbul: Nederlands Historisch-archaeologisch Instituut.

Naumann, R. 1971: *Die Architektur Kleinasiens*. Tübingen: Wasmuth.

Naveh, J., and Sh. Shaked. 1973: Ritual Texts or Treasury Documents? *Orientalia* n.s., 42, 445–57.

Nemet-Nejat, K. 1999: Women in Ancient Mesopotamia. In B. Vivante (ed.), *Women's Roles in Ancient Civilizations*, Westport, CT: Greenwood, 85–114.

Néret, Gilles. 1994: *Description de l'Egypte: Publiée par les ordres de Napoléon Bonaparte*. Cologne: Benedikt Taschen.

Nesbitt, M. and D. Samuel 1998: Letter to the Editor. *Science*, 279, 1433.

Neu, E. 1988: *Das Hurritische: Eine altorientalische Sprache in neuem Licht*. Stuttgart: F. Steiner.

Neu, E. 1988a: Zum hurritischen 'Essiv' in der hurritisch-hethitischen Bilingue aus Ḫattuša. *Hethitica*, 9, 157–170.

Neu, E. 1996: *Das Hurritische Epos der Freilassung I*. Studien Zu Den Boğazköy-Texten 32. Wiesbaden: Otto Harrassowitz.

Neugebauer, O. 1929: Zur Frage der astronomischen Fixierung der babylonischen Chronologie. *Orientalische Literaturzeitung*, 32, 913–21.

Neugebauer, O. 1955: *Astronomical Cuneiform Texts*. London: Lund Humphries.

Neumann, H. 1999: Ur-Dumuzida and Ur-Dun: Reflections on the Relationship between State-Initiated Foreign Trade and Private Economic Activity in Mesopotamia towards the End of the Third Millennium BC. In Dercksen 1999, 45–53.

Newberry, P. 1893: *Beni Hasan II*. London: Egypt Exploration Society.

Niebuhr, Carsten. 1772–78: *(Reise)beschreibung von Arabien*. 3 vols. Copenhagen.

Nigro, L. 1998: Visual Role and Ideological Meaning of the Enemies in the Royal Akkadian Relief. In Prosecký 1998, 283–97.

Nissen, H. 1970: Grabung in den Quadraten K/L XII in Uruk-Warka. *Baghdader Mitteilungen*, 5, 101–91.

Nissen, H. 1988: *The Early History of the Ancient Near East, 9000–2000 BC*. Chicago, IL: University of Chicago Press. German 1983.

Nissen, H. 2002: Uruk: Key Site of the Period and Key Site of the Problem. In J. N. Postgate (ed.), *Artefacts of Complexity, Tracking the Uruk in the Near East*, London: British School of Archaeology in Iraq, 1–16.

Nissen, H., P. Damerow, and R. Englund 1993: *Archaic Bookkeeping*. Chicago, IL: University of Chicago Press. German 1990.

Nöldeke, Theodor. 1883: "Mohammedanism, 3. The Koran." *Encyclopædia Britannica*, 9th edn, 16: 597–606. Repr. unchanged as "Koran," *Encyclopædia Britannica*, 11th edn, 15: 898–906, 1911.

Novick, P. 1988: *That Noble Dream. The "Objectivity Question" and the American Historical Profession*. Cambridge: Cambridge University Press.

Nur el-Din, A. 1995: *The Role of Women in the Ancient Egyptian Society*. Cairo: SCA.

Nylander, C. 1970: *Ionians in Pasargadae*. Uppsala: University of Uppsala.

Oates, D. 1990: Innovations in Mud-Brick: Decorative and Structural Techniques in Ancient Mesopotamia. *World Archaeology*, 21, 388–406.

Oates, J. 1993: Trade and Power in the Fifth and Fourth Millennia BC: New Evidence from Northern Mesopotamia. *World Archaeology*, 24, 403–22.

Ockinga, B. G. 1998: *A Concise Grammar of Middle Egyptian*. Mainz: von Zabern.

O'Connor, D. 1972: The Geography of Settlement in Ancient Egypt. In P. Ucko, R. Tringham, and G. Dimbleby (eds), *Man, Settlement and Urbanism*, London: Duckworth, 681–98.

O'Connor, D. 1990: The Nature of Tjemhu (Libyan) Society in the Late New Kingdom. In A. Leahy (ed.), *Libya and Egypt c 1300–750 BC*, London: School of Oriental and African Studies, 29–113.

O'Connor, D. 1991: Early States along the Nubian Nile. In W. Davies (ed.), *Egypt and Africa*, London: British Museum, 145–65.

O'Connor, D. 1993: *Ancient Nubia: Egypt's Rival in Africa*. Philadelphia, PA: University of Pennsylvania Press.

O'Connor, D. 1995: The Social and Economic Organization of Ancient Egyptian Temples. In Sasson 1995, 319–29.

O'Connor, D. and D. Silverman (eds) 1995: *Ancient Egyptian Kingship*. Leiden: Brill.

O'Connor, M. 1997: *Hebrew Verse Structure*. Winona Lake: Eisenbrauns.

Oded, B. 1979: *Mass Deportations and Deportees in the Neo-Assyrian Empire*. Wiesbaden: Harrassowitz.

Oelsner, J. 1997: Erwägungen zu Aufbau, Charakter und Datierung des sog. "Neubabylonischen Gesetzesfragments." *Altorientalische Forschungen*, 24, 219–25.

Oppenheim, A. L. 1936: Die akkadischen Personennamen der 'Kassitenzeit'. *Anthropos*, 31, 470–88.

Oppenheim, A. L. 1954: The Seafaring Merchants of Ur. *Journal of the American Oriental Society*, 74, 6–17.

Oppenheim, A. L. 1960: The City of Assur in 714 BC. *Journal of Near Eastern Studies*, 19, 133–47.

Oppenheim, A. L. 1966: Mantic Dreams in the Ancient Near East. In G. Von Grunebaum and R. Caillois (eds). *The Dream and Human Society*, Berkeley, CA: University of California Press, 341–50.

Oppenheim, A. L. 1969a: Mesopotamia – Land of Many Cities. In I. Lapidus (ed.), *Middle Eastern Cities*, Berkeley, CA: University of California Press, 3–18.

Oppenheim, A. L. 1969b: The Mother of Nabonidus. In Pritchard 1969, 560–2.

Oppenheim, A. L. 1975: The Position of the Intellectual in Mesopotamian Society. *Daedalus*, 104, 37–46.

Oppenheim, A. L. 1977: *Ancient Mesopotamia*. Revised edition. Chicago, IL: University of Chicago Press.

Oppenheim, A. L. and R. Brill, D. Barag, and A. Von Salder (eds) 1970: *Glass and Glassmaking in Ancient Mesopotamia*. Corning: Corning Museum of Glass.

Oren, E. D. (ed.) 2000: The Sea Peoples and their World. A Reassessment. Philadelphia: University Museum.

Ornan, T. 2002: The Queen in Public: Royal Women in Neo-Assyrian Art. In Parpola and Whiting 2002, 461–78.

Orthmann, W. 1971: *Untersuchungen zur Spräthethitischen Kunst*. Bonn: Habelt.

Orthmann, W. 1975: *Der alte Orient*. Berlin: Propyläen.

Otten, H. 1951: Die hethitischen 'Königslisten' und die altorientalische Chronologie. *Mitteilungen der Deutschen Orient-Gesellschaft*, 83, 47–71.

Otten, H. 1961: Eine Beschwörung der Unterirdischen aus Boğazköy. *Zeitschrift für Assyriologie*, 54, 114–57.

Otten, H. 1964: Die Religionen des alten Kleinasien. In B. Spuler (ed.), *Religionsgeschichte des Alten Orients*, Leiden: Brill, 92–121.

Otten, H. 1965: *Das Gelübde der Königin Puduhepa an die Göttin Lelwani*. Wiesbaden: Harrassowitz.

Otten, H. 1975: *Puduhepa. Eine hethitische Königin in ihren Textzeugnissen*. Mainz: Steiner.

Otto, E. 1954: *Die Biographischen Inschriften der ägyptischen Spätzeit*. Leiden: Brill.

Otto, E. 2000: Kodifizierung und Kanonisierung von Rechtssätzen in keilschriftlichen und biblischen Rechtssammlungen. In Lévy 2000, 77–124.

Owen, D. 1980: Widow's Rights in Ur III Sumer. *Zeitschrift für Assyriologie*, 70, 170–84.

Özdogan, A. 1999: "Çayönü 1999." In Özdogan and Basgelen 1999, 35–63.

Özdogan, M. and N. Basgelen (eds) 1999: *Neolithic in Turkey*. Istanbul: Arkeoloji ve Sanat Yayinlari.

Özgüç, N. 1980: Seal Impressions from the Palaces at Acemhöyük. In E. Porada (ed.), *Ancient Art in Seals*, Princeton, NJ: Princeton University Press, 61–99.

Özkan, H., A. Brandolini, R. Schäfer-Pregl, and F. Salamini 2002: AFLP Analysis of a Collection of Tetraploid Wheats Indicates the Origin of Emmer and Hard Wheat Domestication in Southeast Turkey. *Molecular Biology and Evolution*, 19, 1797–801.

Pagels, Elaine. 1979: *The Gnostic Gospels*. New York: Random House.

Pangas, J. 2000: Birth Malformations in Babylon and Assyria. *American Journal of Medical Genetics*, 91, 318–21.

Pardee, D. 1999: Eloah. In Van Der Toorn, Becking, and Van Der Horst 1999, 285–8.

Pardee, Dennis. 2002: *Ritual and Cult at Ugarit*. Writings from the Ancient World Society of Biblical Literature 10. Atlanta: Scholars Press.

Parker, B. 2001: *The Mechanics of Empire*. Helsinki: Neo-Assyrian Text Corpus Project.

Parker, Simon B. 1997: *Ugaritic Narrative Poetry*. SBL Writings from the Ancient World Series; No. 9. Atlanta: Scholars Press.

Parkinson, R. 1991: *Voices from Ancient Egypt*. Norman: University of Oklahoma Press.

Parkinson, R. B. 1997: *The Tale of Sinuhe and Other Ancient Egyptian Poems, 1940–1640 BC*. Oxford: Oxford University Press.

Parkinson, Richard. 1999: *Cracking Codes: The Rosetta Stone and Decipherment*. London: British Museum Press; Berkeley and Los Angeles: University of California Press.

Parpola, S. 1983: Assyrian Library Records. *Journal of Near Eastern Studies*, 42, 1–29.

Parpola, S. 1987a: Climatic Change and the Eleventh–Tenth-Century Eclipse of Assyria and Babylonia. *Journal of Near Eastern Studies*, 46, 161–82.

Parpola, S. 1987b: The Forlorn Scholar. In F. Rochberg-Halton 1987, 257–78.

Parpola, S. 1993a: The Assyrian Tree of Life: Tracing the Origins of Jewish Monotheism and Greek Philosophy. *Journal of Near Eastern Studies*, 52, 161–208.

Parpola, S. 1993b: *Letters from Assyrian Scholars*. Helsinki: The Neo-Assyrian Text Corpus Project.

Parpola, S. 1993c: Mesopotamian Astrology and Astronomy as Domains of the Mesopotamian "Wisdom." In Galter 1993, 47–59.

Parpola, S. 1995: The Assyrian Cabinet. In M. Dietrich and O. Loretz (eds), *Vom Alten Orient zum Alten Testament: Festschrift für Wolfram Freiherr Von Soden*, Neukirchen-Vluyn: Neukirchener, 379–401.

Parpola, S. 2000: Monotheism in Ancient Assyria. In Porter 2000, 165–209.

Parpola, S. and R. Whiting (eds) 1997: *Assyria 1995*. Helsinki: Neo-Assyrian Texts Corpus Project.

Parpola, S. and R. Whiting (eds) 2002: *Sex and Gender in the Ancient Near East.* Helsinki: Neo-Assyrian Text Corpus.

Parrot, A. 1953: *Archéologie mésopotamienne 2, Technique et problèmes.* Paris: Albin Michel.

Parrot, A. 1958: *Mission archéologique de Mari 2, Le Palais, 1: Architecture.* Paris: Geuthner.

Parrot, A. 1959: *Mission archéologique de Mari 2, Le palais: Documents et Monuments.* Paris: Geuthner.

Parrot, A. 1961a: *Nineveh and Babylon.* London: Thames and Hudson. French 1961.

Parrot, A. 1961b: *Sumer: The Dawn of Art.* New York: Golden Press. French 1958.

Parrot, A. 1974: *Mari, capitale fabuleuse.* Paris: Payot.

Partridge, R. 2002: *Fighting Pharaohs, Weapons and Warfare in Ancient Egypt.* Manchester: Peartree.

Patrick, D. 1985: *Old Testament Law.* Atlanta, GA: Knox.

Patterson, O. 1991: *Freedom. I Freedom in the Making of Western Culture.* New York: Basic Books.

Payne, A. 2004: *Hieroglyphic Luwian.* Wiesbaden: Harrassowitz.

Pearce, L. 1993: Statements of Purpose: Why the Scribes Wrote. In Cohen, Snell, and Weisberg, 1993, 185–93.

Pearce, L. 1998: Babylonian Commentaries and Intellectual Innovation. In Prosecký 1998, 331–38.

Pecchioli Daddi, F. 2003: *Il vincolo per i governatori di provincia.* Pavia: Italian University Press.

Pecchioli Daddi, F. and A. M. Polvani. 1990: *La Mitologia Ittita.* Testi Del Vicino Oriente Antico 4.1. Brescia: Paideia Editrice.

Perdu, Olivier. 1995: "Ancient Egyptian Autobiographies." in *Civilizations of the Ancient Near East,* vol. 3, edited by Jack M. Sasson, 2243–54. New York: Scribner.

Perlitt, L. 1965: *Vatke und Wellhausen: geschichtsphilosophische Voraussetzungen und historiographische Motive für die Darstellung der Religion und Geschichte Israels durch Wilhelm Vatke und Julius Wellhausen.* Berlin: Töpelmann.

Perrot, G. and C. Chipiez 1884: *A History of Art in Chaldaea & Assyria.* London: Chapman and Hall. French 1882.

Petschow, H. 1984: Die §§ 45 and 46 des Codex Hammurapi – Ein Beitrag zum altbabylonischen Bodenpachtrecht und zum Problem: Was ist der Codex Hammurapi. *Zeitschrift für Assyriologie,* 74, 181–212.

Pettinato, Giovanni. 1981: *The Archives of Ebla.* Garden City, N.Y.: Doubleday. Italian original, 1979.

Peust, C. 1999: *Egyptian Phonology.* Göttingen: Peust & Gutschmidt Verlag.

Pfeiffer, R.1935: *State Letters of Assyria.* New Haven, CT: American Oriental Society.

Pfälzner, P. 2001: *Haus und Haushalt: Wohnformen des dritten Jahrtausends vor Christus in Nordmesopotamien.* Mainz: Zabern.

Piacentini, P. 2001: Scribes. In Redford 2001, 3, 187–92.

Pinch, G. 1983: Childbirth and Female Figurines at Deir el-Medina and el-Amarna. *Orientalia,* 52, 405–14.

Pinch, G. 1995: Private Life in Ancient Egypt. In Sasson 1995, 363–81.

Pittmann, H. 1994: Towards an Understanding of the Role of Glyptic Imagery in the Administrative Systems of Proto-literate Greater Mesopotamia. In P. Ferioli (ed.), *Archives before Writing,* Turin: Scriptorum, 177–205.

Pittmann, H. 1996: Constructing Context: The Gebel el-Arak Knife – Greater Mesopotamian and Egyptian Interaction in the Late Fourth Millennium BCE. In J. Cooper and G. Schwartz (eds), *The Study of the Ancient Near East in the 21st Century*, Winona Lake, IN: Eisenbrauns, 9–32.

Plank, F. (ed.). 1995: *Double case: Agreement by Suffixaufnahme*. Oxford: Oxford University Press.

Plato 1984: *The Dialogues of Plato*. R. Allen, translator. New Haven, CT, London: Yale University Press.

Plato 1989: Timaeus. B. Jowett, translator. In E. Hamilton and H. Cairns (eds), *The Collected Dialogues of Plato*, Princeton, NJ: Princeton University Press.

Plutarch 1920: *Life of Anthony*. B. Perrin, translator. *Plutarch's Lives* ix. London, New York: Heinemann, Putnam.

Plutarch 1970: *Plutarch's "De Iside et Osiride."* J. Griffiths, translator. Cardiff: University of Wales Press.

Polanyi, K. 1957: Marketless Trading in Hammurabi's Time. In Polanyi, Arensberg, and Pearson 1957, 12–26.

Polanyi, K., C. Arensberg, and H. Pearson (eds) 1957: *Trade and Market in the Early Empires*. Chicago, IL: Regnery.

Pollock, S. 1991: Women in a Men's World: Images of Sumerian Women. In J. Gero and M. Conkley (eds), *Engendering Archaeology: Women and Prehistory*, Oxford, Cambridge, Mass.: Blackwell, 366–87.

Pollock, S. 1992: Bureaucrats and Managers, Peasants and Pastoralists, Imperialists and Traders: Research on the Uruk and Jemdet Nasr Periods in Mesopotamia. *Journal of World Prehistory*, 6, 297–336.

Pollock, S., M. Pope, and C. Coursey 1996: Household Production at the Uruk Mound, Abu Salabikh, Iraq. *American Journal of Archaeology*, 100, 683–98.

Polonsky, J. 2002: The Rise of the Sun God and the Determination of Destiny in Ancient Mesopotamia. Ph.D. dissertation, University of Pennsylvania.

Polotsky, H. J. 1971: *Collected Papers*. Jerusalem: Magnes Press.

Polotsky, H. J. 1987–1990: *Grundlagen des koptischen Satzbaus, I–II*. Decatur, Ga.: Scholars Press.

Pomeroy, S. 1990: *Women in Hellenistic Egypt: From Alexander to Cleopatra*. Detroit, IL: Wayne State University Press.

Pongratz-Leisten, B. 1994: *Ina šulmi Īrub. Die kulttopographische und ideologische Programmatik der akitu-Prozession in Babylonien und Assyrien im 1. Jahrtausend V. Chr*. Mainz: Zabern.

Pongratz-Leisten, B. 1997: Das "negative Sündenbekenntnis" des Königs anlässlich des babylonischen Neujahrfestes und die *kidinnūtu* von Babylon. In J. Assmann and T. Sundermeier (eds), *Schuld, Gewissen, und Person*, Gütersloh: Gütersloher, 83–101.

Pongratz-Leisten, B. 1999a: *Herrschaftswissen in Mesopotamien*. Helsinki: The Neo-Assyrian Text Corpus Project.

Pongratz-Leisten, B. 1999b: Neujahr(sfest). B. nach akkadischen Quellen. In Ebeling et al. 1928–, 9, 294–8.

Pope, M. 1962: Congregation, Assembly. In G. Buttrick (ed.), *The Interpreter's Dictionary of the Bible*, Nashville, New York: Abingdon, 1, 669–70.

Pope, Maurice. 1999: *The Story of Decipherment: From Egyptian Hieroglyphs to Maya Script*, 2nd edn New York: Thames & Hudson.

Popko, M. 1995: *Religions of Asia Minor*. Warsaw: Academic Publications Dialog.

Porada, E. 1967: Battlements in the Military Architecture and in the Symbolism of the Ancient Near East. In D. Fraser, H. Hibbard, and M. Lewine (eds), *Essays in the History of Architecture Presented to Rudolf Wittkower*, New York: Phaidon, 1–10.

Porada, E. 1993: Why Cylinder Seals? Engraved Cylindrical Seal Stones of the Ancient Near East, Fourth to First Millennium BC. *Art Bulletin*, 75, 563–82.

Porada, E., D. Hansen, S. Dunham, S. Babcock 1992: The Chronology of Mesopotamia ca. 7000–1600 BC. In R. Ehrich (ed.), *Chronologies in Old World Archaeology*, Chicago, IL: University of Chicago Press, third edition, 77–121.

Porten, B. 2003: Offer to Sew a Garment. In Hallo and Younger 2002, 3, 210–11.

Porten, Bezalel and Ada Yardeni. 1986–99. *Textbook of Aramaic Documents from Ancient Egypt, I–IV or A-D* (Jerusalem: Hebrew University.

Porter, B. (ed.) 2000: *One God or Many? Concepts of Divinity in the Ancient World*. Chebeague, Maine: Casco Bay Assyriological Institute.

Posener-Kriéger, P. 1992: Les tablettes en terre crue de Balat. In E. Lalou (ed.), *Les tablettes à écrire à l'Antiquité à l'époque moderne*, Turnhout, Belgium: Brepols, 41–52.

Postgate, J. N. 1981: Nomads and Sedentaries in the Middle Assyrian Sources. In Silva 1981, 47–56.

Postgate, J. N. 1983: *The West Mound Surface Clearance*. London: British School of Archaeology in Iraq.

Postgate, J. N. 1991–1992: The Land of Assur and the Yoke of Assur. *World Archaeology*, 23, 247–63.

Postgate, J. N. 1992, 1994: *Early Mesopotamia*. London, New York: Routledge.

Postgate, J. N. 1995: Royal Ideology and State Administration in Sumer and Akkad. In Sasson 1995, 395–411.

Potts, D. 1997: *Mesopotamian Civilization. The Material Foundations*. Ithaca, NY: Cornell University Press.

Potts, D. 2000: Before Alexandria: Libraries in the Ancient Near East. In R. MacLeod (ed.), *The Library of Alexandria*, London, New York: Tauris, 19–33.

Powell, M. (ed.) 1987: *Labor in the Ancient Near East*. New Haven, CT: American Oriental Society.

Powell, M. 1978: Götter, Könige, und "Kapitalisten" im Mesopotamien des 3. Jahrtausends v. u. Z. *Okumene*, 2, 127–44.

Powell, M. 1990a: Identification and Interpretation of Long Term Price Fluctuations in Babylonia: More on the History of Money in Mesopotamia. *Altorientalische Forschungen*, 17, 76–99.

Powell, M. 1990b: Urban–Rural Interface: Movement of Goods and Services in a Third Millennium City-State. In Aerts and Klengel 1990, 7–14.

Powell, M. 1996. Money in Mesopotamia. *Journal of the Economic and Social History of the Orient*, 39, 224–42.

Powell, M. 1999: Wir müssen unsere Nische nutzen: Monies, Motives, and Methods in Babylonian Economics. In Dercksen 1999, 5–24.

Poyck, A. 1962: *Farm studies in Iraq*. Wageningen: Veeman.

Pritchard, J. (ed.) 1975: *The Ancient Near East. An Anthology of Texts and Pictures*. Princeton, NJ: Princeton University Press.

Pritchard, James B. (ed.) 1969: *Ancient Near Eastern Texts Relating to the Old Testament*. 3rd edn. Princeton: Princeton University Press.

Propp, W. 1998: *Exodus 1–18*. New York: Doubleday.

Propp, W. 1999: Monotheism and "Moses." The Problem of Early Israelite Religion. *Ugaritforschungen*, 31, 537–75.

Prosecký, J. (ed.) 1998: *Intellectual Life of the Ancient Near East*. Prague: Academy of Sciences of the Czech Republic, Oriental Literature.

Puech, É. 1986: Origine de l'alphabet. *Revue biblique*, 93, 161–213.

Puhvel, J. 1984–2004: *Hittite Etymological Dictionary, I–VI*. Berlin: Mouton.

Pulak, C. 1997: The Uluburun Shipwreck. In S. Swiny and R. Hohlfelder (eds), *Res Maritimae*, Atlanta, GA: Scholars, 233–62.

Quaegebeur, J. 1982: De la préhistoire de l'écriture copte. *Orientalia Lovaniensia Periodica*, 13, 125–136.

Quirke, S. 1990: *The Administration of Egypt in the Middle Kingdom: The Hieratic Documents*. New Malden, Surrey: SIA.

Radford, T. 2002: Study of Humble Grave Unearths Pyramid Tomb. *The Guardian*, September 24.

Radner, K. 1999: Traders in the Neo-Assyrian Period. In Dercksen 1999, 101–26.

Rainey, A. 1987: Review of O. Loretz, *Habiru-Hebräer*. *Journal of the American Oriental Society*, 107, 539–41.

Rainey, A. F. 1996: *Canaanite in the Amarna Tablets: A linguistic Analysis of the Mixed Dialect used by Scribes from Canaan, I–IV*. Leiden: Brill.

Rainey, A. F. 1998: Egyptian Evidence for Semitic Linguistics. *Israel Oriental studies*, 18, 431–453.

Reade, J. 1995: Reliefs and Sculptures. In J. Curtis and J. Reade (eds), *Art and Empire: Treasures from Assyria in the British Museum*, New York: Metropolitan Museum, 39–91.

Reade, J. 2001: Assyrian King-Lists, the Royal Tombs of Ur, and Indus Origins. *Journal of Near Eastern Studies*, 60, 1–29.

Redford, D. (ed.) 2001: *The Oxford Encyclopedia of Ancient Egypt*. Oxford: Oxford University Press.

Redford, D. 1984: *Akhenaten the Heretic King*. Princeton, NJ: Princeton University Press.

Redford, D. 1992: *Egypt, Canaan, and Israel in Ancient Times*. Princeton, NJ: Princeton University Press.

Redford, D. 2003: The Wars in Syria and Palestine of Thutmose III. Leiden: Brill.

Redford, Donald B. (ed.) 1995: "Ancient Egyptian Literature: An Overview." in *Civilizations of the Ancient Near East*, vol. 3, edited by Jack M. Sasson, 2223–2241. New York: Scribner.

Redman, C. 1978: *The Rise of Civilization*. San Francisco: Freeman.

Reich, R. 1992: Building Materials and Architectural Elements in Ancient Israel. In A. Kempinski and R. Reich (eds), *The Architecture of Ancient Israel from the Prehistoric to the Persian Periods*, Jerusalem: Israel Exploration Society, 1–16.

Reichel, C. 2001: Seals and Sealings at Tell Asmar. In Hallo and Winter 2001, 101–31.

Reifenberg, A. 1955: *The Struggle between the Desert and the Sown: Rise and Fall of Agriculture in the Levant*. Jerusalem: Government Press.

Reiner, E. 1958: *Šurpu*. Graz: Archiv für Orientforschung.

Reiner, E. 1966: *A Linguistic Analysis of Akkadian*. The Hague: Mouton.

Reiner, E. 1969: The Elamite Language. In B. Spuler (ed.), *Altkleinasiatische Sprachen*, Brill: Leiden, 54–118.

Reiner, E. 1982: Babylonian Birth Prognoses. *Zeitschrift für Assyriologie*, 72, 124–38.

Reiner, E. and D. Pingree 1975: *The Venus Tablets of Ammizaduqa*. Malibu: Undena.

Reiner, E. and D. Pingree 1998: *Babylonian Planetary Omens* 3. Groningen: Styx.

Reiner, Erica. 1985: *Your Thwarts in Pieces, Your Mooring Rope Cut: Poetry from Babylonia and Assyria.* Ann Arbor, Michigan: University of Michigan.

Renfrew, C. 1980: The Great Tradition versus the Great Divide: Archaeology as Anthropology? *American Journal of Archaeology,* 84, 287–98.

Renger, J. 1977: Wrongdoing and Its Sanctions: On "Criminal" and "Civil" Law in the Old Babylonian Period. In J. Sasson (ed.), *The Treatment of Criminals in the Ancient Near East,* Leiden: Brill, 65–77.

Renger, J. 1979: Interaction of Temple, Palace, and "Private Enterprise" in the Old Babylonian Economy. In E. Lipiński (ed.), *State and Temple Economy in the Ancient Near East* I, Leuven: Departement Oriëntalistiek, 249–56.

Renger, J. 1984: Patterns of Non-Institutional Trade and Non-Commercial Exchange in Ancient Mesopotamia at the Beginning of the Second Millennium BC. In A. Archi (ed.), *Circulation of Goods in Non-Palatial Context in the Ancient Near East,* Rome: Dell'Ateneo, 31–123.

Renger, J. 1994: On Economic Structures in Ancient Mesopotamia. *Orientalia,* 63, 157–208.

Renger, J. 1995: Institutional, Communal, and Individual Ownership or Possession of Arable Land in Ancient Mesopotamia from the End of the Fourth to the End of the First Millennium BC. *Chicago Kent Law Review,* 71, 269–319.

Renger, J. 2002: Royal Edicts of the Old Babylonian Period – Structural Background. In Hudson and Van De Mieroop 2002, 139–62.

Renz, J., and W. Röllig. 1995: *Handbuch der althebräischen Epigraphik, I–III.* Darmstadt: Wissenschaftliche Buchgesellschaft.

Reviv, H. 1988: *Kidinnu:* Observations on Privileges of Mesopotamian Cities. *Journal of the Economic and Social History of the Orient,* 31, 286–98.

Reviv, H. 1989: *The Elders in Ancient Israel.* Jerusalem: Magness.

Rhodes, P. 2003: *Ancient Democracy and Modern Ideology.* London: Duckworth.

Richardson, S. 2003: Trouble in the Countryside, *ana tarṣi* Samsuditana: Militarism, Kassites, and the Fall of Babylon I. In W. Van Soldt (ed.), *Ethnicity in Ancient Mesopotamia,* Leiden: Nederlands Historisch-Archaeologisch Instituut.

Riddle, J. 1985: *Dioscorides on Pharmacy and Medicine.* Austin, TX: University of Texas Press.

Ries, G. 1984: Ein neubabylonischer Mitgiftprozess (559 v. Chr.): Gleichzeitig ein Eintrag zur Frage der Geltung keilschriftlicher Gesetze. In D. Nörr and D. Simon (eds), *Gedächtnisschrift für Wolfgang Kunkel,* Frankfurt: Klostermann, 345–63.

Ritter, E. 1965: Magical-expert (= *āšipu*) and Physician (= *Asû*): Notes on Two Complementary Professions in Babylonian Medicine. In *Studies in Honor of Benno Landsberger on his Seventy-Fifth Birthday,* Chicago, IL: University of Chicago Press, 299–321.

Ritter, H. 1986: *Dictionary of Concepts in History.* Westport, CT: Greenwood.

Röllig, W. (ed.) 1977–: *Tübinger Atlas des Vorderen Orients.* Wiesbaden: Reichert.

Röllig, W. 1974: Politische Heiraten im Alten Orient. *Saeculum,* 25, 11–23.

Römer, W. 1965: *Sumerische 'Königshymnen' der Isin-Zeit.* Leiden: Brill.

Roaf, M. 1990: *Cultural Atlas of Mesopotamia and the Ancient Near East.* New York, Oxford: Equinox, Facts on File.

Roberts, N. and H. Wright 1993: The Near East and Southwest Asia. In H. Wright, J. Kutzbach, T. Webb, W. Ruddiman, F. Street-Perrott, and P. Bartlein (eds), *Global Climatic Changes since the Last Glacial Maximum,* Minneapolis, MN: University of Minnesota Press, 194–220.

Robins, G. 1989: Some Images of Women in New Kingdom Art and Literature. In Lesko 1989, 105–16.

Robins, G. 1993: *Women in Ancient Egypt*. Cambridge, MA: Harvard University Press.

Robinson, H. W. 1964: *Corporate Personality in Ancient Israel*. Philadelphia, PA: Fortress. First 1935–1937.

Robinson, James M. (ed.) 1977: *The Nag Hammadi Library in English*. Leiden: Brill. Repr. San Francisco: Harper and Row, 1981.

Rochberg, F. 1993: The Cultural Locus of Astronomy in Late Babylonia. In Galter 1993, 31–45.

Rochberg, F. 2003: Heaven and Earth: Divine–Human Relations in Mesopotamian Celestial Divination. In S. Noegel, J. Walker, and B. Wheeler (eds.), *Prayer, Magic, and the Stars in the Ancient and Late Antique World*, University Park, PA: Pennsylvania State University Press, 169–85.

Rochberg-Halton, F. (ed.) 1987: *Language, Literature, and History: Philological and Historical Studies Presented to Erica Reiner*. New Haven, CT: American Oriental Society.

Rochberg-Halton, F. 1984: New Evidence for the History of Astrology. *Journal of Near Eastern Studies*, 43, 115–40.

Rochberg-Halton, F. 1988: *Aspects of Babylonian Celestial Divination*. Horn: Berger.

Rommelaere, C. 1991: *Les chevaux du Nouvel Empire égyptien: origines, races, harnachement*. Brussels: Connaissance de l'Égypte ancienne.

Rosen, A. 1997a: Environmental Change and Human Adaptational Failure at the End of the Early Bronze Age in the Southern Levant. In Dalfes, Kukla, and Weiss 1997, 25–38.

Rosen, A. 1997b: The Geoarchaeology of Holocene Environments and Land Use at Kazane Höyük, S.E. Turkey. *Geoarchaeology: An International Journal*, 12, 395–416.

Rosenberg, M. 1999: Hallan Çemi 1999. In Özdogan and Basgelen 1999, 25–33.

Rosenthal, F. 1995: *A Grammar of Biblical Aramaic*. 6th edn. Wiesbaden: Harrassowitz.

Rossignol-Strick, M. 1999: The Holocene Climate Optimum and Pollen Records of Sapropel 1 in the Eastern Mediterranean, 9000–6000 BP. *Quaternary Science Reviews*, 18, 515–30.

Roth, A. 2000: Mother Earth, Father Sky. In A. Rautmann (ed.), *Reading the Body: Representations and Remains in the Archaeological Record*, Philadelphia, PA: University of Pennsylvania Press, 187–201.

Roth, A. 2002: The Usurpation of Hem-Reʿ: An Old Kingdom "Sex-Change Operation." In M. El-Damaty and M. Trad (eds), *Egyptian Museum Collections around the World*, Cairo: American University Press, 2, 1011–23.

Roth, M. 1987: Age at Marriage and the Household: A Study of Neo-Babylonian and Neo-Assyrian Forms. *Comparative Studies in Society and History*, 29, 715–47.

Roth, M. 1989: *Babylonian Marriage Agreements, 7th–3rd Centuries BC*. Kevelaer: Butzon & Bercker.

Roth, M. 2000: The Law Collection of King Hammurabi: Toward an Understanding of Codification and Text. In Lévy 2000, 9–31.

Roth, Martha T. n.d: *Law Collections from Mesopotamia and Asia Minor* (SBL Writings from the Ancient World, 6), 2nd edn Atlanta: Scholars Press.

Rothman, M. (ed.) 2001: *Uruk Mesopotamia and its Neighbors: Cross-Cultural Interactions in the Era of State Formation*. Santa Fe, NM: School of American Research.

Rouault, O. 1977: *Mukanniśum: L'Administration et l'économie palatiales à Mari*. Paris: Geuthner.

Rouault, O. 1998: Villes, villages, campagnes et steppe dans la région de Terqa: données nouvelles. In Fortin and Aurenche 1998, 191–8.

Rowton, M. 1965a: The Physical Environment and the Problem of the Nomads. In J.-R. Kupper (ed.), *La Civilisation de Mari*, Paris: Belles Lettres, 109–21.

Rowton, M. 1965b: The Topological Factor in the Hapiru Problem. *Assyriological Studies,* 16, 375–87.

Rowton, M. 1967: The Woodlands of Ancient Western Asia. *Journal of Near Eastern Studies,* 26, 261–77.

Rowton, M. 1973a: Autonomy and Nomadism in Western Asia. *Orientalia,* 42, 247–58.

Rowton, M. 1973b: Urban Autonomy in a Nomadic Environment. *Journal of Near Eastern Studies,* 33, 201–15.

Rowton, M. 1974: Enclosed Nomadism. *Journal of the Economic and Social History of the Orient,* 17, 1–30

Rowton, M. 1976a: Dimorphic Structure and the Problem of the ʿApirû ʿibrím. *Journal of Near Eastern Studies,* 35, 13–20.

Rowton, M. 1976b: Dimorphic Structure and Tribal Elite. *Studia Instituti Anthropos* 28: 219–57.

Rowton, M. 1976c: Dimorphic Structure and Typology. *Oriens Antiquus* 15: 17–31.

Rowton, M. 1977: Dimorphic Structure and the Parasocial Element. *Journal of Near Eastern Studies,* 36, 181–98.

Rowton, M. 1980: Pastoralism and the Periphery in Evolutionary Perspective. In M.-T. Barrelet (ed.), *L'Archéologie de l'Iraq,* Paris: CNRS, 291–301.

Rowton, M. 1981: Economic and Political Factors in Ancient Nomadism. In Silva 1981, 25–36.

Rubio, G. 1999: On the Alleged pre-Sumerian Substratum. *Journal of Cuneiform Studies,* 51, 1–16.

Rubio, G. 2001: Inanna and Dumuzi: A Sumerian Love Story. *Journal of the American Oriental Society,* 121, 268–274.

Rubio, G. 2002: On a Recent Volume of Mari Letters. *Aula Orientalis,* 20, 239–244.

Rubio, G. 2003: Falling Trees and Forking Tongues: The Place of Akkadian and Eblaite within Semitic. In L. Kogan (ed.), *Studia Semitica* (Fs. A. Militarev), Moscow: Russian State University for the Humanities, 152–189.

Rubio, G. 2003a: Review of W. Sommerfeld, *Die Texte der Akkade-Zeit, 1. Das Dijala-Gebiet: Tutub* (Münster, 1999). *Orientalische Literaturzeitung,* 98, 362–9.

Rubio, G. 2004: "Early Sumerian Literature: Enumerating the Whole." in *De la Tablilla a la Inteligencia Artificial: Homenaje al Prof. J. L. Cunchillos en su 65 Aniversario,* edited by J.-P. Vita and A. González Blanco, 131–42. Madrid: C.S.I.C.

Rubio, G. 2004b: Sumerian. In P. Strazny (ed.), *The Routledge Encyclopedia of Linguistics,* London: Routledge.

Rubio, G. 2005: Sumerian. In P. Strazny (ed.), *Encyclopedia of Linguistics,* New York: Fitzroy Dearborn, vol. 2, 1045–1051.

Rubio, G. 2005a: The Linguistic Landscape of Early Mesopotamia. In W. H. van Soldt (ed.), *Ethnicity in Ancient Mesopotamia* (CRRAI 47), Leiden: Institute historique-archéologique néerlandais de Stamboul, 316–332.

Rubio, G. 2005b: Chasing the Semitic Root: The Skeleton in the Closet. *Aula Orientalis,* 23, 37–55.

Rubio, G. 2006: Writing in Another Tongue: Alloglottography in the Ancient Near East. In S. L. Sanders (ed.), *Margins of Writing, Origins of Cultures,* Chicago: University of Chicago Press, 31–64.

Rubio, G. 2006a: Eblaite, Akkadian, and East Semitic. In N. C. Kouwenberg and G. Deutscher (eds.), *The Akkadian Language in its Semitic Context,* Leiden: Institute historique-archéologique néerlandais de Stamboul, 110–139.

Russell, J. 1987: Bulls for the Palace and Order in the Empire: The Sculptural Program of Sennacherib's Court VI at Nineveh. *Art Bulletin*, 69, 520–39.

Russell, J. 1991: *Sennacherib's Palace without Rival at Nineveh*. Chicago, IL: University of Chicago Press.

Russell, J. 1993: Sennacherib's Lachish Narratives. In P. Holliday (ed.), *Narrative and Event in Ancient Art*, Cambridge: Cambridge University Press, 55–79.

Russell, J. 1998: The Program of the Palace of Assurnasirpal II at Nimrud: Issues in the Research and Presentation of Assyrian Art. *American Journal of Archaeology*, 102, 655–715.

Russell, John Malcolm. 1997: *From Nineveh to New York: The Strange Story of the Assyrian Reliefs in the Metropolitan Museum and the Hidden Masterpiece at Canford School*. New Haven: Yale University Press.

Saadé, G. 1979: *Ougarit métropole Cananéenne*. Beirut: Imprimerie Catholique.

Sachs, A. 1969: Temple Program for the New Year's Festival at Babylon. In Pritchard 1969, 331–4.

Sachs, A. and H. Hunger 1988–2001: *Astronomical Diaries and Related Texts from Babylonia*. Vienna: Österreichische Akademie der Wissenschaften.

Sader, H. 1987: *Les états araméens de Syrie depuis leur fondation jusqu'à leur transformation en provinces assyriennes*. Wiesbaden: Steiner.

Sáenz-Badillos, Á. 1996: *A History of the Hebrew Language*. Cambridge: Cambridge University Press.

Safar, F., M. Mustafa, and S. Lloyd 1981: *Eridu*. Baghdad: State Organization of Antiquities and Heritage.

Saggs, H. 1984: *The Might That Was Assyria*. London: Sidgwick and Jackson.

Said, Edward W. 1978: *Orientalism*. New York: Pantheon.

Sallaberger, W. 1993: *Der kultische Kalender der Ur III-Zeit*. Teil 1. Berlin: de Gruyter.

Sallaberger, W. and A. Westenholz 1999: *Mesopotamien: Akkade-Zeit und Ur III-Zeit*. Freiburg, Göttingen: Universitätsverlag and Vandenhoeck & Ruprecht.

Sanlaville, P. 1989: Considérations sur l'evolution de la Basse Mésopotamie au cours des dernières millénaires. *Paléorient*, 15, 5–26.

Sanlaville, P. 2000: Environment and Development. In Mundy and Musallam 2000, 6–16.

Sardar, Z. 2003. *Orientalism*. London: Open Universities.

Sasson, J. 1969: *The Military Establishments at Mari*. Rome: Pontifical Biblical Institute.

Sasson, J. 1973: Biographical Notices on Some Royal Ladies from Mari. *Journal of Cuneiform Studies*, 25, 59–78.

Sasson, J. 1981: On Choosing Models for Recreating Israelite Pre-Monarchic History. *Journal for the Study of the Old Testament*, 21, 3–24.

Sasson, Jack M. (ed.) 1995: *Civilizations of the Ancient Near East*, 3 vols. New York: Scribner.

Sasson, Jack M. 1987: "A Major Contribution to Song of Songs Scholarship." *JAOS* 107: 733–9.

Satzinger, H. 1984: Die altkoptischen Texte als Zeugnisse der Beziehungen zwischen Ägyptern und Griechen. In P. Nagel (ed.), *Graeco-coptica: Griechen und Kopten im byzantinischen Ägypten*, Halle (Saale): Martin-Luther-Universität, 137–146.

Satzinger, H. 1997: Egyptian in the Afroasiatic Frame. In A. Bausi and M. Tosco (eds.), *Afroasiatica neapolitana*, Naples: Istituto Universitario Orientale, 27–48.

Sauneron, S. 1954: La manufacture d'armes de Memphis. *Bulletin de l'Institut français d'Archéologie orientale*, 54, 7–12.

Sauvage, M. 1998: *La Brique et sa mise en oeuvre en Mésopotamie: Des origines à l'époque achéménide*. Paris: Editions Recherche sur les Civilisations.

Sauvaget, J. 1934: Esquisse d'une histoire de la ville de Damas. *Révue des études islamiques*, 8, 425–80.

Schenkel, W. 1997: *Tübinger Einführung in die klassisch-ägyptische Sprache und Schrift*. Tübingen: Wolfgang Schenkel.

Schenkel, W. 2001: Unterrichtsbehelfe und linguistische Theoriebildung in der Vermittlung der klassisch-ägyptischen Grammatik. *Bibliotheca Orientalis*, 58, 5–41.

Schiffer, M. 1976: *Behavioral Archeology*. New York: Academic.

Schloen, J. 2001: *The House of the Father as Fact and Symbol: Patrimonialism in Ugarit and the Ancient Near East*. Cambridge, MA: Harvard Semitic Museum.

Schmandt-Besserat, D.1992: *Before Writing*. Austin, TX: University of Texas Press.

Schmidt, B. 1996: *Israel's Beneficent Dead. Ancestor Cult and Necromancy in Ancient Israelite Religion and Tradition*. Winona Lake, IN: Eisenbrauns.

Schmidt, Brian B. 1995: "Flood Narratives of Ancient Western Asia." in *Civilizations of the Ancient Near East*, vol. 3, edited by Jack M. Sasson, 2337–51. New York: Scribner.

Schmidt, K. 2000: Zuerst kam der Tempel, dann die Stadt. Vorläufiger Bericht zu den Grabungen am Göbekli Tepe und am Gürcütepe 1995–1999. *Istanbuler Mitteilungen*, 50, 5–40.

Schmitt, R. 1989: Bísotūn, I: Introduction. *Encyclopaedia Iranica*, 4/3, 289–290.

Schmitz, B. 1976: *Untersuchungen zum Title S3-njswt "Königssohn"*. Bonn: Habelt.

Schott, S. 1990: *Bücher und Bibliotheken im Alten Ägypten. Verzeichnis der Buch- und Spruchtitel und der Termini Technici*. Wiesbaden: Harrassowitz.

Schretter, M. K. 1990: *Emesal-Studien*. Innsbrucker Beiträge zur Kulturwissenschaft 69. Innsbruck: Universität Innsbruck.

Schroer, S. 1987: *In Israel gab es Bilder: Nachrichten von darstellender Kunst im Alten Testament*. Fribourg: Universitätsverlag.

Schüle, A. 2000: *Die Syntax der althebräischen Inschriften*. Münster: Ugarit-Verlag.

Schulman, A. 1964: *Military Rank, Title and Organization in the Egyptian New Kingdom*. Berlin: Hessling.

Schulman, A. 1979: Diplomatic Marriages in the Egyptian New Kingdom. *Journal of Near Eastern Studies*, 38, 177–93.

Schwartz, B. (ed.) 1975: *Wisdom, Revelation, and Doubt: Perspectives on the First Millennium* BC. = *Daedalus* 104.

Schwartz, G. 1994: Before Ebla: Models of Pre-State Political Organization in Syria and Northern Mesopotamia. In G. Stein and M. Rothman (eds), *Chiefdoms and Early States in the Near East*, Madison, WI: Prehistory, 153–74.

Schwartz, G. 1995: Pastoral Nomadism in Ancient Western Asia. In Sasson 1995, 249–58.

Schwartz, G. and E. Klucas 1998: Spatial Analysis and Social Structure at Tell al-Raqa'i. In Fortin and Aurenche 1998, 199–207.

Scurlock, J. 1991: Baby-Snatching Demons, Restless Souls and the Dangers of Childbirth: Medico-Magical Means of Dealing with Some of the Perils of Motherhood in Ancient Mesopotamia. *Incognita*, 2, 137–85.

Scurlock, J. 1999: Physician, Conjurer, Magician: A Tale of Two Healing Professionals. In T. Abusch and K. Van Der Toorn (eds), *Mesopotamian Magic: Textual, Historical and Interpretive Perspectives*, Groningen: Styx, 69–79.

Scurlock, J. and B. Anderson in press: *Assyrian and Babylonian Medicine: Diagnostics*. Chicago, IL: University of Illinois Press.

Scurlock, J. in press: *Magico-Medical Means of Treating Ghost-Induced Illnesses in Ancient Mesopotamia*. Groningen: Styx.

ïati, Yitschak. 1998: *Love Songs in Sumerian Literature*. Ramat Gan: Bar-Ilan University Press.

Segert, S. 1975: *Altaramäische Grammatik*. Leipzig: VEB Verlag Enzyklopädie.

Segert, S. 1976: *A Grammar of Phoenician and Punic*. Munich: Beck.

Segert, S. 1985: *A Basic Grammar of the Ugaritic Language*. Berkeley: University of California Press.

Seidlmeyer, S. 2000: The First Intermediate Period (c. 2160–2025 BC). In Shaw 2000, 118–47.

Seipel, W. 1977: Hatschepsut I. In W. Helck and E. Otto (eds), *Lexikon der Ägyptologie*, Weisbaden: Harrassowitz, 2, 1045–51.

Selz, G. 1998: Über Mesopotamische Herrschaftskonzepte: Zu den Ursprüngen mesopotamischer Herrscherideologie im 3. Jahrtausend. In M. Dietrich and O. Loretz (eds), *Dub-Sar An-ta-Me-En: Studien zur Altorientalistik: Festschrift für Willem H. Ph. Römer*, Münster: Ugarit, 281–344.

Seminara, S. 1998: *L'accadico di Emar*. Rome: La Sapienza.

Seminara, S. 2001: *La Versione accadica del Lugal-e, La tecnica babilonese della traduzione dal sumerico e le sue 'regole.'* Rome: Università degli Studi di Roma "La Sapienza," Dipartimento di Studi Orientali.

Service, E. 1975: *The Origins of the State and Civilization*. New York: Norton.

Seux, M-J. 1980–1983: Königtum. B. II. und I. Jahrtausend. In Ebeling et al. 1928–, 6, 140–73.

Shaffer, A. 1963: Sumerian Sources of Tablet XII of the Epic of Gilgameš. Ph.D. dissertation, University of Pennsylvania.

Shanks, H. (ed.) 1992: *Understanding the Dead Sea Scrolls*. New York: Random House.

Shaw, I. (ed.) 2000: *The Oxford History of Ancient Egypt*. Oxford: Oxford University Press.

Shaw, I. 1991: *Egyptian Warfare and Weapons*. Princes Risborough: Shire.

Shaw, I. 1996: Battle in Ancient Egypt: The Triumph of Horus or the Cutting Edge of the Temple Economy. In A. Lloyd (ed.), *Battle in Antiquity*, London, 239–69.

Sherratt, A. 1980: Water, soil and seasonality in early cereal cultivation. *World Archaeology*, 11, 313–30.

Sherratt, A. 1997: Climatic Cycles and Behavioural Revolutions. *Antiquity*, 71, 271–87.

Shiloh, Y. 1979: *The Proto-Aeolic Capital and Israelite Ashlar Masonry*. Jerusalem: Institute of Archaeology, Hebrew University.

Shiloh, Y. and A. Horowitz 1975: Ashlar Quarries of the Iron Age in the Hill Country of Israel. *Bulletin of the American Schools of Oriental Research*, 217, 37–48.

Shisha-Halevy, A. 1986: *Coptic Grammatical Categories: Structural Studies in the Syntax of Shenoutean Sahidic*. Rome: Pontificium Institutum Biblicum.

Shisha-Halevy, A. 2000: Stability in Clausal/Phrasal Pattern Constituent Sequencing: 4000 years of Egyptian. In R. Sornicola et al. (eds), *Stability, Variation and Change of Word-Order Patterns Over Time*, Amsterdam: Benjamins, 71–100.

Sievertsen, U. 1999: Early Buttress-Recess Architecture in Mesopotamia and Syria. *Baghdader Mitteilungen*, 30, 7–20.

Sigrist, M. 1992: *Drehem*. Bethesda, MD: CDL.

Silva Castillo, J. (ed.) 1981: *Nomads and Sedentary Peoples*. Mexico City: El Colegio de México.

Sima, A. 2000: *Tiere, Pflanzen, Steine und Metalle in den altsüdarabischen Inschriften*. Wiesbaden: Harrassowitz.

Simon, W. 1973: Positivism in Europe to 1900. In P. Wiener (ed.), *Dictionary of the History of Ideas*, New York: Scribner's, 3, 532–9.

Simpson, R. E. 1996: *Demotic Grammar in the Ptolemaic Sacerdotal Decrees*. Oxford: Griffith Institute.

Simpson, W. K. 1977: Amor dei: *Ntr mrr rmt m t3 w3* (Sh. Sai. 147–148) and the Embrace. In J. Assmann, E. Feucht, and R. Grieshammer (eds), *Fragen an die altägyptische Literatur: Studien zum Gedenken an Eberhard Otto*, Wiesbaden: Harrassowitz, 493–8.

Simpson, William Kelly. (ed.) 2003: *The Literature of Ancient Egypt: An Anthology of Stories, Instructions, Stelae, Autobiographies, and Poetry*, 3rd edn. New Haven: Yale University Press.

Singer, I. 2002: *Hittite Prayers*. Atlanta, GA: Society of Biblical Literature.

Singer, Itamar. 1999: "A Political History of Ugarit." in *Handbook of Ugaritic Studies*, edited by W. G. E. Watson and Nicolas Wyatt, 603–733. Handbuch der Orientalistik: Abt. 1, Der Nahe und Mittlere Osten: Bd. 39. Leiden: Brill.

Sinopoli, C. 1994: The Archaeology of Empire. *Annual Review of Anthropology*, 23, 159–80.

Sinopoli, C. 1995: The Archaeology of Empires: The View from South Asia. *Bulletin of the American Schools of Oriental Research*, 299/300, 3–11.

Sjöberg, Å. 1975: Der Examentext A. *Zeitschrift für Assyriologie*, 64, 137–76.

Sjöberg, Å. 1976: The Old Babylonian Eduba. *Assyriological Studies*, 20, 159–79.

Sjöberg, Å. 2002: In the Beginning. In T. Abusch (ed.), *Riches Hidden in Secret Places: Ancient Near Eastern Studies in Memory of Thorkild Jacobsen*, Winona Lake, IN: Eisenbrauns, 229–47.

Sjöberg, Å. and E. Bergmann 1969: *The Collection of the Sumerian Temple Hymns*. Locust Valley, NY: Augustin.

Slanski, K. 2003: *The Babylonian Entitlement narûs (kudurrus)*. Boston, MA: American Schools of Oriental Research.

Smith, H. and A. Smith 1976: A Reconsideration of the Kamose Texts. *Zeitschrift für ägyptische Sprache*, 103, 48–76.

Smith, M. 1952: The Common Theology of the Ancient Near East. *Journal of Biblical Literature*, 71, 135–47.

Smith, M. 1971: *Palestinian Parties and Politics that Shaped the Old Testament*. New York: Columbia University Press.

Smith, M. 1990, 2002: *The Early History of God*. San Francisco, CA, Grand Rapids, MI: Harper & Row, Eerdmans.

Smith, M. 1992: Braudel's Temporal Rhythms and Chronology Theory in Archaeology. In Knapp 1992, 23–34.

Smith, Mark, S. 1994-: *The Ugaritic Baal Cycle*, vol. 1-. Vtsup 55-. Leiden: Brill.

Smith, Mark, S. 1995: "Myth and Mythmaking in Canaan and Ancient Israel." in *Civilizations of the Ancient Near East*, vol. 3, edited by Jack M. Sasson, 2031–41. New York: Scribner.

Smith, Mark, S. 2001: *The Origins of Biblical Monotheism: Israel's Polytheistic Background and the Ugaritic Texts*. Oxford: Oxford University Press.

Smith, P. and T. C. Young 1972: The Evolution of Early Agriculture and Culture in Greater Mesopotamia: A Trial Model. In B. Spooner (ed.), *Population Growth: Anthropological Implications*, Cambridge, MA: MIT Press.

Smith, P., O. Bar-Yosef, and A. Sillen 1984: Archaeological and Skeletal Evidence for Dietary Change during the Late Pleistocene / Early Holocene in the Levant. In M. Cohen and G. Armelagos (eds), *Palaeopathology at the Origins of Agriculture*, London: Academic, 101–36.

Smith, S. 1951: Comments. *Compte rendu de la seconde Rencontre Assyriologique Internationale*. Paris: Imprimerie nationale, 67.

ell, B. 1960: *The Discovery of the Mind*. New York: Harper. German 1939, 1948.

Snell, D. 1982: *Ledgers and Prices*. New Haven, CT, London: Yale University Press.

Snell, D. 1986: The Rams of Lagash. *Acta Sumerologica*, 8, 133–217.

Snell, D. 1995: Methods of Exchange and Coinage in Ancient Western Asia. In Sasson 1995, 1487–97.

Snell, D. 1997: *Life in the Ancient Near East, 3100–332 BC*. New Haven, CT: Yale University Press.

Snell, D. 1998: Intellectual Freedom in the Ancient Near East? In Prosecký 1998, 359–63.

Snell, D. 2000: The Structure of Politics in the Age of David. In S. Graziani (ed.), *Studi sul Vicino Oriente Antico dedicati alla memoria di Luigi Cagni*, Naples: Istituto universitario orientale, 2131–42.

Snell, D. 2001: *Flight and Freedom in the Ancient Near East*. Leiden: Brill.

Snell, D. 2003: The Ordinarity of the Peculiar Institution. In Averbeck, Chavalas, and Weisberg 2003, 3–22.

Sollberger, E. 1967: Ladies of the Ur III Empire. *Revue d'Assyriologie*, 61, 69–70.

Sollberger, E., and J. Kupper, 1971: *Inscriptions 'royales' sumériennes et akkadiennes*. Paris: Cerf.

Sommer, M. 1999: *Europas Ahnen. Ursprünge des Politischen bei den Phönikern*. Darmstadt: Wissenschaftliche Buchgesellschaft.

Sonsino, R. 1980: *Motive Clauses in Hebrew Law*. Chico, CA: Scholars.

Soysal, O. 2004: *Hattischer Wortschatz in hethitischer Textüberlieferung*. Leiden: Brill.

Spalinger, A. 1982: *Aspects of the Military Documents of the Ancient Egyptians*. New Haven, CT: Yale University Press.

Spalinger, A. 2002a: Review of Heinz 2001. *Journal of the American Oriental Society*, 122, 125–7.

Spalinger, A. 2002b: *The Transformation of an Ancient Egyptian Narrative: P. Sallie III and the Battle of Kadesh*. Wiesbaden: Harrassowitz.

Spalinger, A. 2004: *War in Ancient Egypt*. Oxford: Blackwell.

Spalinger, A. In press: The Paradise of Scribes and the Tartarus of Soldiers. To appear in a volume edited by A. Loprieno.

Sperling, S. D. 1986: Israel's Religion in the Ancient Near East. In A. Green (ed.), *Jewish Spirituality: From the Bible to the Middle Ages*, New York: Crossroad, 5–31.

Sperling, S. D. 1989: Rethinking Covenant in Late Biblical Books. *Biblica*, 70, 50–72.

Sperling, S. D. 1998: *The Original Torah: The Political Intent of the Bible's Writers*. New York: New York University Press.

Spiegelberg, W. 1925: *Demotische Grammatik*. Heidelberg: Carl Winter.

Spronk, K. 1999: Lord. In Van Der Toorn, Becking, and Van Der Horst 1999, 531–3.

Spuler, Bertold. 1995: *The Age of the Caliphs* (History of the Muslim World, 1), trans. F. R. C. Bagley. Leiden: Brill, 1969. Repr. Princeton, N.J.: Markus Wiener, with introduction by Jane Hathaway, ix–xxx. German original, 1952.

Sürenhagen, D. 1986a: Archaische Keramik aus Uruk I. *Baghdader Mitteilungen*, 17, 7–95.

Sürenhagen, D. 1986b: The Dry Farming Belt: The Uruk Period and Subsequent Developments. In H. Weiss (ed.), *The Origins of Cities in Dry-Farming Syria and Mesopotamia in the Third Millennium BC*, Guilford, CT: Four Quarters, 7–43.

Sürenhagen, D. 1987: Archaische Keramik aus Uruk II. *Baghdader Mitteilungen*, 18, 1–92.

Stager, L. 1996: Ashkelon and the Archaeology of Destruction: Kislev 604 BCE. *Eretz Israel*, 25, 61*–74*.

Stanley, D. and A. Warne 1993: Nile Delta: Recent Geological Evolution and Human Impact. *Science*, 260, 628–34.

Steible, H., and F. Yildiz 1993: Ki'engi aus der Sicht von Šuruppak. *Istanbuler Mitteilungen*, 43, 17–26.

Stein, G. 1994: Economy, Ritual and Power in 'Ubaid Mesopotamia. In G. Stein and M. Rothman (eds), *Chiefdoms and Early States in the Near East*, Madison, WI: Prehistory, 35–46.

Stein, G. 1996: Producers, Patrons, and Prestige: Craft Specialists and Emergent Elites in Mesopotamia from 5500–3100 BC. In B. Wailes (ed.), *Craft Specialization and Social Evolution*, Philadelphia, PA: University of Pennsylvania Museum, 25–38.

Stein, G. 1999: *Rethinking World Systems: Diasporas, Colonies, and Interaction in Uruk Mesopotamia*. Tucson, AZ: The University of Arizona Press.

Stein, G. 2001: Indigenous Social Complexity at Hacinebi (Turkey) and the Organization of Uruk Colonial Contact. In Rothman 2001, 265–305.

Stein, P. 2000. *Die mittel- und neubabylonischen Königsinschriften bis zum Ende der Assyrerherrschaft: Grammatische Untersuchungen*. Wiesbaden: Harrassowitz.

Steiner, R. 1997: The Aramaic Text in Demotic script. In Hallo and Lawson 1997, 309–27.

Steiner, R. C. 1992: Northwest Semitic Incantations in an Egyptian Medical Papyrus of the Fourteenth Century B.C.E. *Journal of Near Eastern Studies*, 51, 191–200.

Steiner, R. C. 1995: Papyrus Amherst 63: A New Source for the Language, Literature, Religion, and History of the Arameans. In M. J. Geller (ed.), *Studia Aramaica: New Sources and New Approaches*, Oxford: Oxford University Press, 199–207.

Steiner, R. C. 2005: On the Dating of Hebrew Sound Changes ($^{*}H{>}H$ and $^{*}\dot{G}{>}^{c}$) and Greek Translations (2 Esdras and Judith). *Journal of Biblical Literature*, 124, 229–67.

Steiner, R. C., and C. F. Nims. 1983: A Paganized Version of Psalm 20:2–6 from the Aramaic Text in Demotic Script. *Journal of the American Oriental Society*, 103, 261–274.

Steiner, R. C., and C. F. Nims. 1984: You Can't Offer Your Sacrifice and Eat it Too: A Polemical Poem from the Aramaic Text in Demotic Script. *Journal of Near Eastern Studies*, 43, 87–115.

Steiner, R. C., and C. F. Nims. 1985: Assurbanipal and Shamash-shumukin: A Tale of Two Brothers from the Aramaic Text in the Demotic Script. *Revue Biblique*, 92, 60–81.

Steiner, Richard C. 1997–2002. "The Aramaic Text in Demotic Script." in *The Context of Scripture: Canonical Compositions, Monumental Inscriptions, and Archival Documents from the Biblical World*, 3 vols., edited by William W. Hallo, 309–27. Leiden: Brill.

Steinkeller, P. 1981: More on Ur III Royal Wives. *Acta Sumerologica*, 3, 77–92.

Steinkeller, P. 1987a: The Administrative and Economic Organization of the Ur III State: The Core and Periphery. In Gibson and Biggs 1987, 19–41.

Steinkeller, P. 1987b: The Foresters of Umma: Toward a Definition of Ur III Labor. In Powell 1987, 73–115.

Steinkeller, P. 1991: The Administration and Economic Organization of the Ur III State: The Core and the Periphery. In Gibson and Biggs 1991, 15–33.

Steinkeller, P. 1993: Early Political Development in Mesopotamia and the Origins of the Sargonic Empire. In Liverani 1993, 107–29.

Steinkeller, P. 1995: Review of M. W. Green and H. J. Nissen, *Zeichenliste der archaischen Texte aus Uruk* (ATU 2. Berlin, 1987). *Bibliotheca Orientalis*, 52, 689–713.

Steinkeller, P. 1999a: Land-Tenure Conditions in Third Millennium Babylonia: The Problem of Regional Variation (With Glenn R. Magid). In Hudson and Levine 1999, 289–329.

Steinkeller, P. 1999b: On Rulers, Priests and Sacred Marriage: Tracing the Evolution of Early Mesopotamian Kingship. In Watanabe 1999, 103–37.

Steinkeller, P. 2002a: Archaic City Seals and the Question of Early Babylonian Unity. In T. Abusch (ed.), *Riches Hidden in Secret Places: Ancient Near Eastern Studies in Memory of Thorkild Jacobsen*, Winona Lake, IN: Eisenbrauns, 249–57.

Steinkeller, P. 2002b: Money-Lending Practices in Ur III Babylonia: The Issue of Economic Motivation. In Hudson and Van De Mieroop 2002, 109–37.

Steinkeller, P. and J. N. Postgate 1992: *Third-Millennium Legal and Administrative Texts in the Iraq Museum, Baghdad*. Winona Lake, IN: Eisenbrauns.

Steinkeller, P. n.d.: City and Countryside in Third Millennium Southern Babylonia. In E. Stone (ed.), *Settlement and Society: Ecology, Urbanism, Trade and Technology in Mesopotamia and Beyond*, Los Angeles, CA: Costen.

Stekelis, M. 1977: "Megalithic Monuments." In Michael Avi-Yonah and Ephraim Stern, eds. Encyclopedia of Archaeological Excavations in the Holy Land. New York: Oxford University Press, 3: 827–30.

Sterman, M. 1986: Nutritional Factors in the Mechanisms and Treatment of Epilepsy. In J. Bland (ed.), *1986: A Year of Nutritional Medicine*, New Canaan, CT: Keats.

Stol, M. 1982: State and Private Business in the Land of Larsa. *Journal of Cuneiform Studies*, 34, 127–230.

Stol, M. 1995: Women in Mesopotamia. *Journal of the Ancient Near Eastern Society*, 38, 123–44.

Stol, M. 1997: *Muškēnum*. In Ebeling et al. 1928–, 7/8, 492–3.

Stol, M. 2000: *Birth in Babylonia and the Bible: Its Mediterranean Setting*. Groningen: Styx.

Stolper, M. 1985: *Entrepreneurs and Empire*. Leiden: Nederlands Historisch-Archaeologisch Instituut.

Stolper, M. 1989: The Governor of Babylon and Across-the-River in 486 BC. *Journal of Cuneiform Studies*, 48, 283–305.

Stolper, M. W. 2001: Review of Khačikjan 1998. *Journal of Near Eastern Studies*, 60, 275–280.

Stone, E. 1981: Texts, Architecture and Ethnographic Analogy: Patterns of Residence in Old Babylonian Nippur. *Iraq*, 43, 19–34.

Stone, E. 1987: *Nippur neighborhoods*. Chicago, IL: Oriental Institute.

Stone, E. 1995a: The Development of Cities in Ancient Mesopotamia. In Sasson 1995, 235–48.

Stone, E. 1995b: The Tapestry of Power in a Mesopotamian City: The Mashkan-shapir Project. *Scientific American*, 272/4, 92–7.

Stone, E. 1996: Houses, Households and Neighborhoods in the Old Babylonian Period: The Role of Extended Families. In Veenhof 1996, 229–35.

Stone, E. 1997: City States and their Centers: The Mesopotamian Example. In D. Nichols and T. Charleton (eds), *The Archaeology of City States*, Washington, DC: Smithsonian Institution, 15–26.

Stone, E. and D. Owen 1992: *Adoption in Old Babylonian Nippur*. Winona Lake, IN: Eisenbrauns.

Stone, E. and P. Zimansky 1992: Mashkan-Shapir and the Anatomy of an Old Babylonian City. *Biblical Archaeologist*, 55, 212–18.

Stone, E. In press: *The Anatomy of a Mesopotamian City: Survey and Soundings at Mashkan-shapir*. Winona Lake, IN: Eisenbrauns.

Stone, L. 1971: Prosopography. *Historical Studies Today* = *Daedalus*, Winter, 46–79.

Streck, M. P. (ed.). 2006: *Sprachen des Alten Orients.* 2nd edn. Darmstadt: Wissenschaftliche Buchgesellschaft.

Streck, M. P. 2000: *Das amurritische Onomastikon der altbabylonischen Zeit, I.* Münster: Ugarit-Verlag.

Strommenger, E. and M. Hirmer 1964: *5000 Years of the Art of Mesopotamia.* New York: Abrams. German 1962.

Stronach, D. 1978: *Pasargadae.* New York: Oxford University Press.

Summers, G. 2000: The Median Empire Reconsidered: a View from Kerkenes Dağ. *Anatolian Studies,* 50, 55–73.

Suter, C. 2000: *Gudea's Temple Building.* Groningen: Styx.

Säve-Söderbergh, T. 1946: *The Navy of the Eighteenth Egyptian Dynasty.* Uppsala, Leipzig: Lundequistska, Harrassowitz.

Sweeney, D. 1992: Women's Correspondence from Deir el-Medineh. In J. Leclant (ed.), *Atti Sesto Congresso Internazionale di Egittologia,* Turin: International Association of Egyptologists, 2: 523–9.

Tadmor, H. 1981: History and Ideology in the Assyrian Royal Inscriptions. In F. Fales (ed.), *Assyrian Royal Inscriptions,* Rome: Istituto per l'Oriente, 13–33.

Tadmor, H. 1982: The Aramaization of Assyria: Aspects of Western Impact. In H. Nissen and J. Renger (eds), *Mesopotamien und seine Nachbarn,* Berlin: Reimer, 449–70.

Tadmor, H. 1986: Monarchy and the Elite in Assyria and Babylonia: The Question of Royal Accountability. In Eisenstadt 1986, 203–24.

Tadmor, H. 1997: Propaganda, Literature, Historiography: Cracking the Code of the Assyrian Royal Inscriptions. In Parpola and Whiting 1997, 325–38.

Tadmor, H. 1999: World Dominion: The Expanding Horizon of the Assyrian Empire. In L. Milano (ed.), *Landscapes, Territories, Frontiers and Horizons in the Ancient Near East,* Padua: Sargon, 55–62.

Takács, G. 1999–2001: *Etymological Dictionary of Egyptian, I–II.* Leiden: Brill.

Tallqvist, K. 1974: *Akkadische Götterepitheta.* Hildesheim, New York: Olms.

Talon, P. 1985: Quelques réflexions sur les clans Hanéens. In Durand and Kupper 1985, 277–84.

Talon, P. 1993: Le rituel comme moyen de légitimation politique au 1er millénaire en Mésopotamie. In J. Quaegebeur (ed.), *Ritual and Sacrifice in the Ancient Near East,* Leuven: Peeters, 421–33.

Tanret, M. (ed.) 2000: *Just in Time. Proceedings of the International Colloquium on Ancient Near Eastern Chronology (2nd Millennium BC)* [= *Akkadica* 119–120].

Taylor, R. (ed.) 2002: *The Idea of Freedom in Asia and Africa.* Stanford, CA: Stanford University Press.

Tchalenko, G. 1953: *Villages Antiques de la Syrie du Nord. Le Massif du Bélus à l'Epoque Romaine.* Three vols. Paris: Paul Geuthner.

Thomason, A. 2001: Representations of the North Syrian Landscape in Neo-Assyrian Art. *Bulletin of the American Schools of Oriental Research,* 323, 63–96.

Thomason, A. in press: *Luxury and Legitimation: Royal Collecting in Ancient Mesopotamia.* Aldershot, UK: Ashgate.

Thompson, R. C. 1923: *Assyrian Medical Texts.* London: Bale and Danielson.

Thompson, T. 1987: *The Origin Tradition of Ancient Israel,* 1: *The Literary Formation of Genesis and Exodus 1–23.* Sheffield: JSOT.

Thomsen, M.-L. 1984: *The Sumerian Language.* Copenhagen: Academic Press 1984 [reprinted with no changes but with additional bibliography in 2001].

Thucydides 1960, 1963: *The Peloponnesian War.* B. Jowett, translator. New York: Bantam.

Thureau-Dangin, F. 1921: *Rituels accadiens*. Paris: Leroux.

Thureau-Dangin, F. 1939: Tablettes Hurrites provenant de Mâri. *Revue d'Assyriologie*, 36, 1–28.

Tigay, Jeffrey H. 1982: *The Evolution of the Gilgamesh Epic*. Philadelphia: University of Pennsylvania Press.

Tinney, S. 1998: Texts, Tablets, and Teaching: Scribal Education in Nippur and Ur. *Expedition*, 40, 40–50.

Tinney, Steve. 1996: *The Nippur Lament: Royal Rhetoric and Divine Legitimation in the Reign of Išme-Dagan of Isin (1953-1935 B.C.)*. Occasional Publications of the Samuel Noah Kramer Fund, 16. Philadelphia: University of Pennsylvania Museum.

Tischler, J. 1977–2004: *Hethitisches etymologisches Glossar, 1–13*. Innsbruck: Universität Innsbruck.

Tischler, J. 1977–2001: *Hethitisches etymologisches Glossar, 1–12*. Innsbruck: Universität Innsbruck.

Tosh, J. 2000: *The Pursuit of History*. London, New York: Longman.

Trigger, B. 1976: *Nubia under the Pharaohs*. London: Thames and Hudson.

Trigger, B. 1989: *A History of Archaeological Thought*. Cambridge: Cambridge University Press.

Trigger, B. 1990: Monumental Architecture: A Thermodynamic Explanation of Symbolic Behavior. *World Archaeology*, 22, 119–32.

Trigger, B., B. Kemp, D. O'Connor, and A. Lloyd 1983: *Ancient Egypt. A Social History*. Cambridge: Cambridge University Press.

Trémouille, M.-C. 1999: La religion des Hourrites: état actuel de nos connaissances. *Studies on the Civilization and Culture of Nuzi and the Hurrians*, 10, 277–91.

Tropper, J. 1993: *Die Inschriften von Zinçirli*. Münster: Ugarit-Verlag.

Tropper, J. 1999: Ugaritic Grammar. In W. G. E. Watson and N. Wyatt (eds.), *Handbook of Ugaritic Studies*, Leiden: Brill, 1999, 91–121.

Tropper, J. 2000: *Ugaritische Grammatik*. Münster: Ugarit-Verlag.

Trouillot, M.-R. 2001: The Anthropology of the State in the Age of Globalization, Close Encounters of the Deceptive Kind. *Current Anthropology*, 42, 125–38.

Troy, L. 1986: *Patterns of Queenship in Ancient Egyptian Myth and History*. Stockholm: Almquist & Wiksell.

Tunça, Ö. 1984: *L'architecture religieuse protodynastique en Mésopotamie*. Leuven: Peeters.

Tyldesley, J. 1994: *Daughters of Isis: Women of Ancient Egypt*. London: Penguin.

Uerpman, H. 1987: *The Ancient Distribution of Ungulate Mammals in the Middle East.* Wiesbaden: Reichert.

Ünal, A. 1988: The Role of Magic in the Ancient Anatolian Religions according to the Cuneiform Texts from Boğazköy-Hattuša. In T. Mikasa (ed.), *Essays on Anatolian Studies in the Second Millennium BC*, Wiesbaden: Harrassowitz, 52–85.

Valbelle, D. 1985: *«Les Ouvriers de la Tombe» Deir el-Médineh à l'époque Ramesside*. Cairo: Institut français d'archéologie orientale.

Vallat, F. 1986: The Most Ancient Scripts of Iran: The Current Situation. *World Archaeology*, 17, 335–47.

Vallat, F. 1995: Epopée de Gilgamesh ou tablette économique de Persépolis? Ni l'un, ni l'autre! *Nouvelles assyriologiques brèves et utilitaires: N.A.B.U.* no. 39.

Van Andel, T., E. Zangger, and A. Demitrack 1990: Land Use and Soil Erosion in Prehistoric and Historical Greece. *Journal of Field Archaeology*, 17, 379–96.

Van De Mieroop, M. 1989: Women in the Economy of Sumer. In Lesko 1989, 53–66.

Van De Mieroop, M. 1992: *Society and Enterprise in Old Babylonian Ur*. Berlin: Reimer.

Van De Mieroop, M. 1997a: *The Ancient Mesopotamian City.* Oxford: Clarendon.

Van De Mieroop, M. 1997b: On Writing a History of the Ancient Near East. *Bibliotheca Orientalis*, 54, 285–305.

Van De Mieroop, M. 1999a: *Cuneiform Texts and the Writing of History.* London, New York: Routledge.

Van De Mieroop, M. 1999b: The Government of an Ancient Mesopotamian City: What We Know and Why We Know So Little. In Watanabe 1999, 139–61.

Van De Mieroop, M. 2002: Foreign Contacts and the Rise of an Elite in Early Dynastic Babylonia. In E. Ehrenberg (ed.), *Leaving No Stones Unturned, Essays on the Ancient Near East and Egypt in Honor of Donald P. Hansen,* Winona Lake, IN: Eisenbrauns, 125–37.

Van De Mieroop, M. 2004: *A History of the Ancient Near East ca. 3000–323 BC.* Oxford: Blackwell.

Van Den Boorn, G. 1988: *The Duties of the Vizier: Civil Administration in the Early New Kingdom.* London, New York: Kegan Paul.

van der Molen, R. 2000: *A Hieroglyphic Dictionary of Egyptian Coffin Texts.* Leiden: Brill.

Van Der Toorn, K. (ed.) 1997: *The Image and the Book: Iconic Cults, Aniconism, and the Rise of Book Religion in Israel and the Ancient Near East.* Leuven: Peeters.

Van Der Toorn, K. 1992: Anat-yahu, Some Other Deities, and the Jews of Elephantine. *Numen*, 39, 80–101.

Van Der Toorn, K. 1999a: God. In Van Der Toorn, Becking, and Van Der Horst 1999, 352–65.

Van Der Toorn, K. 1999b: Yahweh. In Van Der Toorn, Becking, and Van Der Horst 1999, 910–19.

Van Der Toorn, K., B. Becking, and P. Van Der Horst (eds) 1999: *Dictionary of Deities and Demons in the Bible.* Leiden: Brill.

Van Dijk, J. 1957–1971: Gott. A. Nach sumerischen Texten. In Ebeling et al. 1928–, 3: 532–43.

Van Dijk, Jacobus. 1995: "Myth and Mythmaking in Ancient Egypt." in *Civilizations of the Ancient Near East*, vol. 3, edited by Jack M. Sasson, 1697–709. New York: Scribner.

Van Driel, G. 1969: *The Cult of Aššur.* Assen: Van Gorcum.

Van Driel, G. 1994: Private or Not-So-Private: Nippur Ur III Files. In H. Gasche, M. Tanret, C. Janssen, and A. Degraeve (eds), *Cinquante-deux réflexions sur le Proche-Orient Ancien, offertes en hommage à Léon De Meyer,* Leuven: Peeters, 181–92.

Van Driel, G. 1998: Land in Ancient Mesopotamia: "That what remains undocumented does not exist." In R. Haring and R. de Maaijer (eds), *Landless and Hungry? Access to Land in Early and Traditional Societies,* Leiden: School of Asian, African, and Amerindian Studies, 19–49.

Van Driel, G. 1999/2000: The Size of Institutional Umma. *Archiv für Orientforschung*, 46/47, 80–91.

Van Driel, G. 2000: Institutional and Non-institutional Economy in Ancient Mesopotamia. In Bongenaar 2000, 5–24.

van Soldt, W. H. 1991: *Studies in the Akkadian of Ugarit: Dating and Grammar.* Neukirchen-Vluyn: Neukirchener.

Van Zeist, W. and S. Bottema, 1991: *Late Quaternary Vegetation of the Near East.* Wiesbaden: Reichert.

Vandersleyen, C. 1971: *Les guerres d'Amosis, fondateur de la XVIIIe dynastie.* Brussels: Fondation égyptologique Reine Élisabeth.

Vanstiphout, H. 1979: How Did They Learn Sumerian? *Journal of Cuneiform Studies*, 31, 118–26.

Vanstiphout, H. L. J. 1985: On the Verbal Prefix /i/ in Standard Sumerian. *Revue d'Assyriologie*, 79, 1–15.

Vanstiphout, Herman. 2003: *Epics of Sumerian Kings: the Matter of Aratta*. Atlanta: Society of Biblical Literature.

Varanda, F. 1982: *The Art of Building in Yemen*. Cambridge, MA: M.I.T. Press.

Veenhof, K. (ed.) 1996: *Houses and Households in Ancient Mesopotamia*. Leiden: Nederlands Historisch-Archaeologisch Instituut.

Veenhof, K. 1972: *Aspects of Old Assyrian Trade and its Terminology*. Leiden: Brill.

Veenhof, K. 1977: Some Social Effects of Old Assyrian Trade. *Iraq*, 39, 109–18.

Veenhof, K. 1982: The Old Assyrian Merchants and their Relations with the Native Populations of Anatolia. In H. Nissen and J. Renger (eds), *Mesopotamien und seine Nachbarn*, Berlin: Reimer, 147–60.

Veenhof, K. 1995: Kanesh: an Assyrian Colony in Anatolia. In Sasson 1995, 859–71.

Veenhof, K. 1997: "Modern" Features in Old Assyrian Trade. *Journal of the Economic and Social History of the Orient*, 40, 336–66.

Veenhof, K. 1997–2000: The Relation between Royal Decrees and "Law Codes" of the Old Babylonian Period. *Jaarbericht Ex Oriente Lux*, 35/36, 49–83.

Veldhuis, N. 1997: *Elementary Education at Nippur: The Lists of Trees and Wooden Objects*. Ph.D. diss. Rijksuniversiteit Groningen.

Veldhuis, N. 2001: A Multiple Month Account from the Gu'abba Rest House. *Zeitschrift für Assyriologie*, 91, 85–109.

Veldhuis, Niek. 2004: *Religion, Literature, and Scholarship: the Sumerian Composition of Nanše and the Birds, with a Catalogue of Sumerian Bird Names*. CM 22. Leiden: Brill/Styx.

Vercoutter, J. 1959: The Gold of Kusch. *Kush*, 7, 120–53.

Vermes, G. 1962: *The Dead Sea Scrolls in English*. Harmondsworth: Penguin.

Versnel, H. 2000: Three Greek Experiments in Oneness. In Porter 2000, 79–163.

Versteeg, R. 2002: *Law in the Ancient World*. Durham, NC: Carolina Academic.

Visicato, G. 2000: *The Power and the Writing*. Bethesda, MD: CDL.

Visicato, G., and A. Westenholz 2000: Some Unpublished Sale Contracts from Fara. In S. Graziani (ed.), *Studi sul Vicino Oriente antico dedicati alla memoria di Luigi Cagni*, Naples: Istituto Universitario Orientale, 1107–33.

Vogelsang, M. 1988: *Bin šar dadmē. Edition and Analysis of the Akkadian Anzu Poem*. Groningen: Styx.

Vogelzang, Marianna, E. and Herman L. J. Vanstiphout. (eds) 1992: *Mesopotamian Epic Literature: Oral or Aural?* Lewiston: Edwin Mellen.

Vogelzang, Marianna, E. and Herman L. J. Vanstiphout. (eds) 1996: *Mesopotamian Poetic Language: Sumerian and Akkadian. Proceedings of the Groningen Group for the Study of Mesopotamian Literature*, vol. 2. CM 6. Groningen: Styx.

Voigt, R. 1987: The Classification of Central Semitic. *Journal of Semitic Studies*, 32, 1–21.

Volk, K. 1999: Kinderkrankheiten nach der Darstellung babylonisch-assyrischer Keilschrifttexte. *Orientalia*, 68, 1–30.

Von Beckerath, J. 1984: *Handbuch der ägyptischen Königsnamen*. Munich: Kunstverlag.

von Dassow, E. 2003: What the Canaanite Cuneiformists Wrote. *Israel Exploration Journal*, 53, 196–217.

Von Den Driesch, A. and J. Peters 2001: Frühe Pferde- und Maultierskelette aus Auaris (Tell el-Dab'a), östlisches Nildelta. *Ägypten und Levante*, 11, 301–11.

Von Der Way, T. 1984: *Die Textüberlieferung Ramses' II zur Qadeß-Schlacht. Analyse und Struktur.* Hildesheim: Gerstenberg.

von Soden, W. 1965–1981: *Akkadisches Handwörterbuch.* Wiesbaden: Harrassowitz [= *AHw*].

von Soden, W. 1995: *Grundriß der akkadischen Grammatik.* 3rd edn. by W. R. Mayer *et al.* Rome: Pontificium Institutum Biblicum.

Vycichl, W. 1983: *Dictionnaire étymologique de la langue copte.* Leuven: Peeters.

Vycichl, W. 1990: *La vocalisation de la langue égyptienne, 1: La phonétique.* Caire: Institut français d'archéologie orientale du Caire.

Wachsmann, S. 1998: *Seagoing Ships & Seamanship in the Bronze Age Levant.* College Station, TX, London: Texas A. & M. University Press, Chatham.

Waetzoldt, H. 1987: Compensation of Craft Workers and Officials in the Ur III Period. In Powell 1987, 117–41.

Wagstaff, J. 1985: *The Evolution of Middle Eastern Landscapes An Outline to A.D. 1840.* London: Croom Helm.

Wagstaff, M. 1992: Agricultural Terraces: The Vasylikos Valley, Cyprus. In M. Bell and J. Boardman (eds), *Past and Present Soil Erosion*, Oxford: Oxbow Books, 155–61.

Wallerstein, I. 1974/80: *The Modern World System* Two vols. New York: Academic.

Wallerstein, I. 1990: World Systems Analysis: The Second Phase. *Review*, 13, 287–93.

Waltke, B. K., and M. O'Connor. 1990: *An Introduction to Biblical Hebrew Syntax.* Winona Lake, Ind.: Eisenbrauns.

Waraksa, E. 2002: Statue of Senenmut and Nefrure. In B. Bryan and E. Hornung (eds), *The Quest for Immortality*, Munich, London, New York: National Gallery of Art, United Exhibits, Prestell, 90.

Warburton, D. 1997: *State and Economy in Ancient Egypt: Fiscal Vocabulary of the New Kingdom.* Freiburg, Göttingen: Universitätsverlag, Vandenhoeck & Ruprecht.

Warburton, D. 2000: Before the IMF: The Economic Implications of Unintentional Structural Adjustment in Ancient Egypt. *Journal of the Economic and Social History of the Orient*, 43, 65–131.

Warburton, D. 2003. *Macroeconomics from the Beginning.* Neuchâtel-Paris: Recherche et Publications.

Ward, W. 1986: *Essays on Feminine Titles of the Middle Kingdom and Related Subjects.* Beirut: American University of Beirut.

Ward, W. 1989: Non-Royal Women and their Occupations in the Middle Kingdom. In Lesko 1989, 33–43.

Watanabe, C. E. 2002: *Animal Symbolism in Mesopotamia.* Vienna: Institut für Orientalistik.

Watanabe, K. (ed.) 1999: *Priests and Officials in the Ancient Near East.* Heidelberg: Winter.

Waters, M. 2002: A Letter from Assurbanipal to the Elders of Elam. *Journal of Cuneiform Studies*, 54, 79–86.

Watkins, T. 1992: The Beginning of the Neolithic: Searching for Meaning in Material Culture Change. *Paléorient*, 18, 63–75.

Watson, A. 2001: *The Evolution of Western Private Law.* Baltimore, MD: The Johns Hopkins University Press.

Watson, P.-J. 1979a: *Archaeological Ethnography in Western Iran.* Tucson, AZ: University of Arizona Press.

Watson, P.-J. 1979b: The Idea of Ethnoarchaeology: Notes and Comments. In C. Kramer (ed.), *Ethnoarchaeology. Implications of Ethnography for Archaeology*, New York: Columbia University Press, 277–87.

Watson, W. G. E., and N. Wyatt. (eds) 1999: *Handbook of Ugaritic Studies* (Handbuch der Orientalistik, division 1, vol. 39). Leiden: Brill.

Watson, Wilfred G. E. 1999: "Ugaritic Poetry." in *Handbook of Ugaritic Studies*, edited by Wilfred G. E. Watson and Nicolas Wyatt, 165–92. Handbuch der Orientalistik: Abt. 1, Der Nahe und Mittlere Osten: Bd. 39. Leiden: Brill.

Watson, Wilfred G. E. and Nicolas Wyatt. (eds) 1999: *Handbook of Ugaritic Studies*. Handbuch der Orientalistik: Abt. 1, Der Nahe und Mittlere Osten: Bd. 39. Leiden: Brill.

Watterson, B. 1992: *Women in Ancient Egypt*. New York: St. Martin's.

Wegner, I. 2000: *Einführung in die hurritische Sprache*. Wiesbaden: Harrassowitz.

Weidemann, K. 1983: *Könige aus dem Yemen*. Mainz: Römisch-Germanisch Zentralmuseum.

Weidner, E. 1939: Jojachin, König von Juda, in babylonischen Keilschrifttexten. In *Mélanges syriens offerts à Monsieur René Dussaud*, Geuthner: Paris, 923–35.

Weinfeld, M. 1992: Deuteronomy, Book of. In Freedman 1992, 2, 168–83.

Weisberg, D. 1974: Royal Women of the Neo-Babylonian Period. In P. Garelli (ed.), *Le Palais et la Royauté*, Paris: Geuthner, 447–54.

Weiss, H. 1985: Tell Leilan on the Habur Plains of Syria. *Biblical Archaeologist*, 41, 5–34.

Weiss, H. 2000: Beyond the Younger Dryas: Collapse as Adaptation to Abrupt Climate Change in Ancient West Asia and the Eastern Mediterranean. In G. Bawden and R. Reycraft (eds), *Confronting Natural Disaster: Engaging the Past to Understand the Future*, Albuquerque, NM: University of New Mexico Press, 75–98.

Weiss, H. and R. Bradley 2001: What Drives Societal Collapse? *Science*, 291, 609–10.

Weissert, E. 1997: Royal Hunt and Royal Triumph in a Prism Fragment of Ashurbanipal. In Parpola and Whiting 1997, 339–58.

Wente, E. 1984: Some Graffiti from the Age of Hatshepsut. *Journal of Near Eastern Studies*, 43, 47–54.

Wente, E. 1990: *Letters from Ancient Egypt*. Atlanta, GA: Scholars.

Werner, P. 1994: *Die Entwicklung der Sakralarchitektur in Nordsyrien und Südostkleinasien*. Munich: Profil.

Werner, R. 1991: *Kleine Einführung ins Hieroglyphen-Luwische*. Göttingen: Vandenhoeck & Ruprecht.

Westbrook, R. (ed.) 2003: *A History of Ancient Near Eastern Law*. Leiden: Brill.

Westbrook, R. 1985: Biblical and Cuneiform Law Codes. *Revue Biblique*, 92, 247–64.

Westbrook, R. 1989: Cuneiform Law Codes and the Origins of Legislation. *Zeitschrift für Assyriologie*, 79, 201–22.

Westbrook, R. 1992: Punishments and Crimes. In Freedman 1992, 5, 546–56.

Westbrook, R. 1995: The Development of Law in the Ancient Near East: Slave and Master in Ancient Near Eastern Law. *Chicago-Kent Law Review*, 70, 1631–76.

Westbrook, R. 1998: The Female Slave. In V. Matthews, B. Levinson, and T. Frymer-Kensky (eds), *Gender and Law in the Hebrew Bible and the Ancient Near East*, Sheffield: Sheffield Academic, 214–38.

Westbrook, R. 2000: Codification and Canonization. In Lévy 2000, 33–47.

Westbrook, R. and R. Jasnow (eds) 2001: *Security for Debt in Ancient Near Eastern Law*. Leiden: Brill.

Westendorf, W. 1965–1977: *Koptisches Handwörterbuch bearbeitet auf Grund des Koptischen Handwörterbuchs von Wilhelm Spiegelberg*. Heidelberg: Carl Winter.

Westendorf, W. 1967: Bemerkung zur "Kammer der Wiedergeburt" im Tutanchamungrab. *Zeitschrift für ägyptische Sprache*, 94, 139–50.

Westenholz, J. 1990: Towards a New Conceptualization of the Female Role in Mesopotamian Society. *Journal of the American Oriental Society*, 110, 510–21.

Westenholz, J. 1994: *Eight Days in the Temples of Larsa*. Jerusalem: Sirkis.

Westenholz, J. 1998: Thoughts on Esoteric Knowledge and Secret Lore. In Prosecky 1998, 451–562.

White, H. 1973: *Metahistory*. Baltimore, MD, London: Johns Hopkins University Press.

Whiting, R. 1987: *Old Babylonian Letters from Tell Asmar*. Chicago, IL: Oriental Institute.

Widmer, W. 1976: Zur Darstellung der Seevölker am Großen Tempel von Medinet Habu. *Zeitschrift für ägyptische Sprache*, 102, 67–78.

Wiesehöfer, J. 1996: *Ancient Persia*. London, New York: Tauris.

Wiggermann, F. 1992: Mythological Foundations of Nature. In D. Meijer (ed.), *Natural Phenomena: Their Meaning, Depiction and Description in the Ancient Near East*, Amsterdam: Nederlandse Akademie van Wetenschappen, Letterkunde 152, 279–306.

Wilcke, C. 1974: Zum Königtum in der Ur III-Zeit. In P. Garelli (ed.), *Le Palais et la Royauté*, Paris: Geuthner, 177–232.

Wilcke, Claus. 1976: "Formale Gesichtspunkte in der Sumerischen Literatur." *AS* 20: 205–316.

Wildberger, H. 1977: Der Monotheismus Deuterojesajas. In H. Donner, R. Hanhart, and R. Smend (eds), *Beiträge zur alttestamentlischen Theologie. Festschrift für Walther Zimmerli zum 70. Geburtstag*, Göttingen:Vandenhoeck & Ruprecht, 506–30.

Wilfong, T. 1992: *Women in the Ancient Near East: A Bibliographic Survey of Recent Literature in the Oriental Institute Research Archives*. Chicago, IL: Oriental Institute.

Wilfong, T. 1997: *Women and Gender in Egypt: From Prehistory to Late Antiquity*. Ann Arbor: Kelsey Museum.

Wilfong, T. 2002: *The Women of Jéme: Lives in a Coptic Town in Late Antique Egypt*. Ann Arbor, MI: University of Michigan Press.

Wilhelm, G. 1970: *Untersuchungen zum Hurro-Akkadischen von Nuzi*. Neukirchen-Vluyn: Neukirchener Verlag.

Wilhelm, G. 1992: Hurritische Lexicographie und Grammatik: Die hurritisch-hethitische Bilingue ais Boğazköy. *Orientalia* n.s., 61, 122–141.

Wilhelm, G. 1993: Zum Grammatik und zum Lexikon des Hurritischen. *Zeitschrift für Assyriologie*, 83, 99–118.

Wilhelm, G. 1994: *Medizinische Omina aus Hattuša in akkadischer Sprache*. Wiesbaden: Harrassowitz.

Wilkinson, T. 1997a: Environmental Fluctuations, Agricultural Production and Collapse: A View from Bronze Age Upper Mesopotamia. In Dalfes, Kukla, and Weiss 1997, 67–106.

Wilkinson, T. 1997b: Holocene Environments of the High Plateau, Yemen. Recent Geoarchaeological Investigations. *Geoarchaeology: An International Journal*, 12, 833–64.

Wilkinson, T. 1999: Holocene Valley fills of Southern Turkey and Northwestern Syria: Recent Geoarchaeological Contributions. *Quaternary Science Reviews*, 18, 555–71.

Willcox, G. 1999: Agrarian Change and the Beginnings of Cultivation in the Near East: Evidence from Wild Progenitors, Experimental Cultivation and Archaeobotanical Data. In C. Gosden and J. Hather (eds), *The Prehistory of Food*, London: Routledge, 478–500.

Willetts, R. 1967: *The Law Code of Gortyn*. Berlin: de Gruyter.

Willis, T. 2001: *The Elders of the City*. Atlanta, GA: Society of Biblical Literature.

Wilson, Edmund. 1969: *The Dead Sea Scrolls 1947–1969*. New York: Oxford University Press. Rev. and expanded edn of *The Scrolls from the Dead Sea*, 1955.

Wilson, J. 1945: The Assembly of a Phoenician City. *Journal of Near Eastern Studies*, 4, 245.

Wilson, J. 1964: *Signs and Wonders upon Pharaoh. A History of American Egyptology.* Chicago, IL: University of Chicago Press.

Wilson, P. 1997: *A Ptolemaic Lexikon: A Lexicographical Study of the Texts in the Temple of Edfu.* Leuven: Peeters.

Winlock, H. 1945: *The Slain Soldiers of Neb-hep-et-Re' Mentu-hotpe.* New York: Metropolitan Museum of Art.

Winter, I. 1981: Royal Rhetoric and the Development of Historical Narrative in Neo-Assyrian Reliefs. *Studies in Visual Communication*, 7, 2–38.

Winter, I. 1983: The Warka Vase: Structure of Art and Structure of Society in Early Urban Mesopotamia. Unpublished paper, American Oriental Society, Baltimore.

Winter, I. 1986: The King and the Cup: Iconography of the Royal Presentation Scene on Ur III Seals. In M. Kelly-Buccellati (ed.), *Insight through Images. Studies in Honor of Edith Porada*, Malibu: Undena, 253–68.

Winter, I. 1987: Women in Public: the Disk of Enheduanna, the Beginning of the Office of EN-Priestess and the Weight of Visual Evidence. In Durand 1987, 189–202.

Winter, I. 1989: The Body of the Able Ruler: Toward an Understanding of the Statues of Gudea. In H. Behrens, D. Loding, and M. Roth (eds), *DUMU-E$_2$.DUB.BA.A: Studies in Honor of Åke W. Sjöberg*, Philadelphia, PA: University Museum, 573–83.

Winter, I. 1992: Idols of the King: Royal Images as Recipients of Ritual Action in Ancient Mesopotamia. *Journal of Ritual Studies*, 6: 13–42.

Winter, I. 1995: Aesthetics in Ancient Mesopotamian Art. In Sasson 1995, 2569–82.

Winter, I. 1998a: The Affective Properties of Styles: an Inquiry into Analytical Process and the Inscription of Meaning in Art History. In C. Jones and P. Galison (eds), *Picturing Science Producing Art*, New York and London: Routledge, 55–77.

Winter, I. 1998b: Tree(s) on the Mountain: Landscape and Territory on the Victory Stele of Naram-Sin of Agade. In S. De Martino, F. Fales, G. Lanfranchi, and L. Milano (eds.), *Landscapes: Territories, Frontiers and Horizons in the Ancient Near East*, Padua: Sargon, 1–10.

Winter, I. 2000a: The Eyes Have It: Votive Statuary, Gilgamesh's Axe, and Cathected Viewing in the Ancient Near East. In R. Nelson (ed.), *Visuality Before and Beyond the Renaissance*, Cambridge: Cambridge University Press, 22–44.

Winter, I. 2000b: Le Palais imaginaire: Scale and Meaning in the Iconography of Neo-Assyrian Cylinder Seals. In C. Uehlinger (ed.), *Images as Media: Sources for the Cultural History of the Near East and the Eastern Mediterranean (1st Millennium BCE)*, Fribourg and Göttingen: Universitätsverlag and Vandenhoeck & Ruprecht, 51–87.

Winter, I. 2001: Introduction: Glyptic, History, and Historiography. In Hallo and Winter 2001, 1–13.

Wittfogel, K. 1957: *Oriental Despotism.* New Haven, CT: Yale University Press.

Wolf, C. U. 1947: Traces of Primitive Democracy in Ancient Israel. *Journal of Near Eastern Studies*, 6, 98–108.

Wolf, W. 1936: *Individuum und Gemeinschaft in der ägyptischen Kultur.* Glückstadt: Augustin.

Wolff, H. 1951: *Roman Law: An Historical Introduction.* Norman, OK: University of Oklahoma Press.

Woodington, N. R. 1982: *A Grammar of the Neo-Babylonian Letters of the Kuyunjik Collection.* Ph.D. diss. Yale University.

Woolley, C. L. 1930: *Ur of the Chaldees.* New York: Scribner's.

Woolley, C. L. 1935: *The Development of Sumerian Art.* London: Faber and Faber.

Woolley, L. and M. Mallowan 1976: *Ur Excavations VII: The Old Babylonian Period*. London: British Museum.

Wright, G. 1971: Origins of Food Production in Southwest Asia: A Survey of Ideas. *Current Anthropology*, 12, 447–70.

Wright, G. 1985: *Ancient Building in South Syria and Palestine*. Leiden: Brill.

Wright, H. 1977: Recent Research on the Origin of the State. *Annual Review of Anthropology*, 6, 379–97.

Wright, H. 1984: Pre-State Political Formations. In T. Earle (ed.) *On the Evolution of Complex Societies*, Malibu, CA: Undena, 41–78.

Wright, H. 1993: Environmental Determinism in Near Eastern Prehistory. *Current Anthropology*, 34, 458–69.

Wright, H. and E. Rupley 2001: Calibrated Radiocarbon Age Determinations of Uruk-related Assemblages. In M. Rothman 2001, 85–122.

Wright, H. and G. Johnson 1975: Population, Exchange, and Early State Development in Southwestern Iran. *American Anthropologist*, 77, 267–89.

Wulff, H. 1966: *The Traditional Crafts of Persia*. Cambridge, MA: M.I.T. Press.

Wyatt, N. 1999: Asherah. In Van Der Toorn, Becking, and Van Der Horst 1999, 99–105.

Wyatt, Nicolas. 1999: "The Story of Aqhat (KTU 1.17-19)." in *Handbook of Ugaritic Studies*, edited by Wilfred G. E. Watson and Nicolas Wyatt, 234–58. Leiden: Brill.

Wyatt, Nicolas. 1997: "Ilimilku's Ideological Programme: Ugaritic Royal Propaganda, and a Biblical Postscript." *UF* 29:778–96.

Xenophon 1998: *Anabasis*. C. Browson, translator. Cambridge, MA, London: Harvard University Press.

Yadin, Y. 1963: *The Art of Warfare in Biblical Lands*. New York, Toronto, London: McGraw-Hill.

Yaron, R. 2000: The Nature of the Early Mesopotamian Collections of Laws: Another Approach. In Lévy 2000, 65–76.

Yasuda, Y., H. Kitagawa, and T. Nakagawa 2000: The Earliest Record of Major Anthropogenic Deforestation in the Ghab Valley, Northwest Syria: a Palynological Study. *Quaternary International*, 73/74, 127–36.

Yitzhaki, M. 1986: Citation Patterns of the Research Literature of Ancient Near Eastern Studies. *Journal of Cuneiform Studies*, 38, 81–93.

Yitzhaki, M. 1987: The Relationship between Biblical Studies and Ancient Near Eastern Studies: A Bibliometric Approach. *Zeitschrift für die alttestamentliche Wissenschaft*, 99, 232–48.

Yoffee, N. 1977: *The Economic Role of the Crown in the Old Babylonian Period*. Malibu, CA: Undena.

Yoffee, N. 1980: *Explaining Trade in Ancient Western Asia*. Malibu: Undena.

Yoffee, N. 1988: The Collapse of Ancient Mesopotamian States and Civilization. In N. Yoffee and G. Cowgill (eds), *The Collapse of Ancient States and Civilizations*, Tucson, AZ: University of Arizona Press, 44–68.

Yoffee, N. 1993a: The Late Great Tradition in Ancient Mesopotamia. In M. Cohen, D. Snell, and D. Weisberg (eds), *The Tablet and the Scroll: Near Eastern Studies in Honor of William W. Hallo*, Bethesda, MD: CDL, 300–8.

Yoffee, N. 1993b: Too Many Chiefs (or Safe Texts for the 90's). In N. Yoffee and A. Sherratt (eds), *Archaeological Theory: Who Sets the Agenda?*, Cambridge: Cambridge University Press, 60–78.

Yoffee, N. 1995: Political Economy in Early Mesopotamian States. *Annual Review of Anthropology*, 24, 281–311.

Yon, M. 1997: Ugarit. In Meyers 1997, 5, 255–62.

Yoshikawa, M. 1993: *Studies in the Sumerian Verbal System*. Hiroshima: The Middle Eastern Culture Center in Japan.

Young, Gordon D. 1981: *Ugarit in Retrospect: 50 Years of Ugarit and Ugaritic*. Winona Lake, Ind.: Eisenbrauns.

Younger, K. L. 2003: "Give us our daily bread." Everyday life for the Israelite deportees. In Averbeck, Chavalas, and Weisberg 2003, 269–88.

Yoyotte, J. and J. López 1969: L'organisation de l'armée au Nouvel Empire égyptien. *Bibliotheca Orientalis*, 26, 3–19.

Yurko, F. 1986: Merenptah's Canaanite Campaign. *Journal of the American Research Center in Egypt*, 23, 189–215.

Yurko, F. 1997: Merenptah's Canaanite Campaign and Israel's Origins. In E. Frerichs and L. Lesko (eds), *Exodus: The Egyptian Evidence*, Winona Lake, IN: Eisenbrauns, 27–55.

Zaccagnini, C. 1983a: On Gift Exchange in the Old Babylonian Period. In O. Carruba, M. Liverani, and C. Zaccagnini (eds), *Studi orientalistici in ricordo di Franco Pintore*, Pavia: CJES, 189–253.

Zaccagnini, C. 1983b: Patterns of Mobility Among Ancient Near Eastern Craftsmen. *Journal of Near Eastern Studies*, 42, 245–64.

Zaccagnini, C. 1994: Sacred and Human Components in Ancient Near Eastern Law. *History of Religions*, 33, 265–86.

Zaccagnini, C. 1997: Price and Price Formation in the Ancient Near East: A Methodological Approach. In J. Andreau, P. Briant and R. Descat (eds), *Économie Antique: Prix et formation des prix dans les économies antiques*, Saint-Bernard-de-Comminges: Musée archéologique, 361–84.

Zagarell, A. 1986: Trade, Women, Class, and Society in Ancient Western Asia. *Current Anthropology*, 27, 415–30.

Zeder, M. 1994: After the Revolution: Post-Neolithic Subsistence in Northern Mesopotamia. *American Anthropologist*, 96, 97–126.

Zeder, M. and B. Hesse 2000: The Initial Domestication of Goats (*Capra hircus*) in the Zagros Mountains 10,000 Years Ago. *Science*, 287, 2254–57.

Zettler, R. 1991: Nippur under the Third Dynasty of Ur: Area TB. *Aula Orientalis*, 9, 251–81.

Zettler, R. 1992: *The Ur III temple of Inanna at Nippur*. Berlin: Reimer.

Zettler, R. 1996: Written Documents as Excavated Artifacts and the Holistic Interpretation of the Mesopotamian Archaeological Record. In J. Cooper and G. Schwartz (eds), *The Study of the Ancient Near East in the 21st Century*, Winona Lake, IN: Eisenbrauns, 81–101.

Zettler, R. 2003: Reconstructing the World of Ancient Mesopotamia: Divided Beginnings and Holistic History. *Journal of the Economic and Social History of the Orient*, 46, 3–45.

Zevitt, Z. 1984: The Khirbet el-Qôm Inscription Mentioning a Goddess. *Bulletin of the American Schools of Oriental Research*, 255, 39–47.

Ziegler, C. 1993: *Le Mastaba d'Akhethetep*. Paris: Réunion des Musées Nationaux.

Ziermann, M. 1993: *Elephantine, 16. Befestigungsanlagen in der Frühzeit und im frühen Alten Reich*. Mainz: Zabern.

Zimansky, P. E. 1998: *Ancient Ararat: A Handbook of Urartian Studies*, Delman, N.Y.: Caravan Books.

Zimmern, H. 1917: *Akkadische Fremdwörter als Beweis für babylonische Kultureinfluss*. Leipzig: Hinrichs.

Zohary, M. 1973: *Geobotanical Foundations of the Middle East*. Two vols. Stuttgart: Fischer.

Zurro, E. 1987: *Procedimientos Iterativos en la Poesía Ugarítica y Hebrea*. Rome: Biblical Institute Press.

Index